BLACKS IN SCIENCE AND MEDICINE

BLACKS IN SCIENCE AND MEDICINE

Vivian Ovelton Sammons

⬤HEMISPHERE PUBLISHING CORPORATION
A member of the Taylor & Francis Group
New York   Washington   Philadelphia   London

BLACKS IN SCIENCE AND MEDICINE

2 3 4 5 6 7 8 9 BRBR 8 9 8 7 6 5 4 3 2 1 0

Acknowledgment. Selected entries reprinted by permission of Howard University Press from *Black Engineers in the United States, A Directory* by James K. K. Ho. Copyright © 1974 Howard University Press.

On the Jacket. George Washington Carver, photograph by P. H. Polk from the Washington Collection, Hollis Burke Frissell Library, Tuskegee University, Tuskegee, Alabama. Used by permission.

This book was set in century by Hemisphere Publishing Corporation. The editors were Amy Lyles Wilson, W. Ralph Eubanks, and Sandra Tamburrino; the production supervisor was Peggy M. Rote; and the typesetters were Phoebe Carter and Laurie Agee. Cover design by Debra Eubanks Riffe.
Braun-Brumfield, Inc., was printer and binder.

Library of Congress Cataloging-in-Publication Data

Blacks in science and medicine / Vivian Ovelton Sammons.
    p.   cm.
    Bibliography: p.
    Includes index.
    1. Afro-American scientists—Biography. I. Sammons, Vivian O.
  Q141.B58 1989
509'.2—dc20
[B]   89-32934
ISBN 0-89116-665-3   CIP

To my father, Rexford Flood Ovelton, Sr. (1893–1970), a teacher of elementary science in the District of Columbia (1925–1958), who taught me to love books, history, and science—in that order.

PREFACE

Vivian Ovelton Sammons

About five years ago, several students walked into the Science Reading Room of the Library of Congress and requested the names of 75 black scientists. I replied that I could give them 10 names off the top of my head but that 75 was another matter. After several days of digging, my colleagues and I had identified about that many. The difficulty we encountered made me realize that if it took science librarians this long, untrained individuals would face many more obstacles in pursuing a search of this kind.

The experience led me to collect references to published sources of information. This compilation eventually became the *Library of Congress Tracer Bullet, TB 85-5, Blacks in Science and Related Disciplines*, published in 1985 and available at no cost from the Library's Science and Technology Division.

As this publication became increasingly sought after, I decided to expand my references. My nights and weekends became devoted to the beginnings of this publication. I searched through many sources, some cover to cover, for names of individuals who had advanced degrees in the sciences, who were working in and making contributions to science, or who had obtained patents for their inventions. The publications that were searched from cover to cover are listed here.

JOURNALS

Crisis
Ebony
Jet
National Medical Association *Journal*

BOOKS

Black Engineers in the United States
Even the Rat was White
Holders of Doctorates Among American Negroes
In Black and White
The Negro in Science
Who's Who of the Colored Race 1915
Who's Who in Colored America 1927–1944

Among those books searched selectively are:
Beacon Lights of the Race
A Century of Black Surgeons
Contributions of Black Women to America, Vol. II
History of the Negro in Medicine
Men of Mark
The Path We Tread
Who's Who Among Black Americas 1977–1985

Full citations to all of these works can be found in the bibliography.

All scientists included in this volume are listed in the published literature. I conducted no interviews, and no suggestions were accepted solely on the basis of hearsay. There is no intent to be all inclusive. The selections are strictly mine, with as many pre-World War II scientists included as possible. Some scientists by nature of their popularity and the availability of biographical information had many references in the literature and were thus included over less-referenced individuals. Unfortunately, many important contributors have been omitted, especially those of recent years, because a limit had to be set.

Several facts must be noted concerning this biographical directory. In 1943, the date *Holders of Doctorates Among American Negroes* was compiled, there were 381 black Ph.D.s, nearly all of whom are listed in that volume. Ninety-three of the doctorates were in the sciences (physical and biological). All of these have been included in this listing.

Since the end of World War II, the number of black scientists has steadily increased, mostly due to the acceptance of blacks in accredited, prestigious, graduate schools. This volume contains entries for 475 holders of Ph.D.s in science and related disciplines. Of these, 65 are female. Where available, titles of dissertations are included. Of the 586 physicians listed, 82 are female, 198 are surgeons, 32 are psychiatrists, and 22 are pathologists, 2 of whom are women.

There are a great number of physicians included, not only because medicine was the first scientific endeavor of the black man, but also because a physician uses an enormous amount of scientific information in the treatment of patients and in the research leading to the cure of disease.

Several military personnel are listed, including 19 generals, beginning with Benjamin O. Davis, Sr., the first black general in the U.S. Army (1940).

Computer scientists are not included mainly because computer science is a relatively new field. However, there are a few scientists listed whose primary field, although not computers, is in a related area, such as mathematics.

Individuals are listed in alphabetical order. Birth and death dates, major specialties, educational background, significant employment, and organizational affiliations are given where available. Some people are known only for their accomplishments without available biographical information. Only scientific and Greek letter affiliations are given. The symbol [p] indicates a photograph. Consult the references for further information.

The Index indicates the first blacks in a given field, the first black scientist in an area of the country, as well as any research area of significance. Inventions are listed by patentee as well as by invention.

In the case of individuals whose date of death is unknown, they are assumed to be deceased if they were born prior to 1900. Those born after 1900 are assumed to be alive if they are listed in the 1985 *Who's Who Among Black Americans.* For those individuals whose date of probable death is not known, 19?? has been entered. For scientists who do not have a verifiable date of birth or death, the century in which they were professionally active has been indicated.

Although I used other libraries in researching this compilation, I was told by other librarians that the book would be very valuable to them and to black studies professors. Two examples of its value follow. In reading another publication recently, I noticed that Ida Gray was the first black female dentist. In checking my alphabetical list, I found that her name was not included. I then checked the index under first black female dentist. I found that she was there but listed under her married name, Nelson. On another occasion a friend asked about a psychiatrist with whom she had a job interview. I checked his name and gave her four references for information on him. Therefore, the compilation has proven useful even before publication.

Suggestions for the next expanded edition of this work are requested from black studies professors, librarians, and other academians as well as the general public. The individuals suggested for listing must be people who have made quality contributions in the sciences and are verifiable in reference books or journal articles. Suggestions may be sent to me in care of Hemisphere Publishing Corporation, 1101 Vermont Avenue, N.W., Suite 200, Washington, D.C. 20005.

Over 1500 individuals are included in this volume. Although by no means a complete list, it is hoped that this directory of scientists' lives and accomplishments will assist the researcher in black studies, the librarian, and the student looking for role models.

ACKNOWLEDGMENTS

Thanks to my friend and coworker Kay Rodgers, who entered the entire book into the computer, incorporating changes and updates, and to my friend Camilla Ann Scott, who made the computer and its software perform superbly to produce the index.

Thanks to the staff of the National Library of Medicine, who granted me stack passes to search the entire run of the *Journal* of the National Medical Association and to the individuals in the stacks who assisted and encouraged me.

Thanks to the staff of the Carter G. Woodson Branch of the Chicago Public Library for their assistance in using the Vivian Marsh all-black collection in June and August of 1988.

Thanks to the staff of the Science and Technology Division of the Library of Congress, my former coworkers, who not only encouraged me but also supplied me with numerous books, journal articles, pictures, newspaper clippings, and other information on black scientists.

Thanks to Verna Reynolds and Valerie Stockton, who assisted greatly in the final stages of manuscript preparation, to Ruth Freitag for her evaluation of the Introduction, and to Denise Dempsey and Leroy Davis, who assisted in proofreading.

INTRODUCTION

Thousands of books, as well as articles in newspapers and journals, have been written that praise the accomplishments of black athletes, entertainers, politicians, and authors. However, the scientific ingenuity of the black man until recently has been overlooked and therefore omitted from the scientific histories of the world. It is as if the scientific community did not want to admit that blacks have always had intelligent and inquiring minds along with their other talents. On the contrary, blacks have invented, experimented, discovered, and passed on to others their expertise in the areas of science, technology, invention, and medicine for centuries.

After much research, it has been determined that man, as we know him, began in Africa. Although William Leo Hansberry, a black professor at Howard University, proposed this theory in 1929, it was only when Dr. Louis B. Leakey, the white archeologist, suggested this theory that it was accepted by the world. However, Dr. Leakey's son, Richard, gives much of the credit for their latest discoveries to a Kenyan, Kamoya Kimue, whom the Leakeys trained and worked with for over 25 years. The National Geographic Society has honored Mr. Kimue for his discoveries.[1]

Because modern man began in Africa, it stands to reason that the progress of civilization also began there. According to Herodotus and Homer, there was much advancement in ancient Ethiopia and Egypt. For over 5,000 years these two countries coexisted and exchanged ideas, which helped to greatly elevate their cultures.[2]

Imhotep (3000 B.C.), an Egyptian, was the first individual considered to be a scientist and physician. Physicians today are progenies of Imhotep, through Hippocrates and Asclepios, the Greeks who followed the work of Imhotep 1,500 years later.[3]

Although scientists of European descent are slow to agree, it has been established recently that accomplishments in Ethiopia, Egypt, and other black African countries, such as Ghana, Mali, Songhay, and Tanzania, were the source of much knowledge contributed by the Greeks and Romans. This knowledge passed from these African countries to Europeans and was improved upon to make great contributions to society.[4]

Examples of this can be seen throughout history. Africans were smelting iron by a process passed down from generation to generation by word of mouth. The Haya people of Tanzania can be credited with this accomplishment.[5] In 1978 Peter Schmidt, Professor of Engineering, and Donald Avery, both of Brown University, announced that approximately 1,500 to 2,000 years ago Africans on the western shore of Lake Victoria produced carbon steel.[6] Three hundred years before Christ, the people of Kenya built an astronomical observatory in a place called Namoratunga—an African Stonehenge. The stones were lined up where the stars would have risen in 300 B.C. The Dogon people of Mali knew for centuries about the rings of Saturn, the moons of Jupiter, and the spiral structure of the Milky Way. Only 200 miles from there, at the University of Timbuktu, they were surgically removing cataracts from eyes in the thirteenth to fifteenth centuries.[7] Africans had voluntarily traveled from the west coast of Africa to South America and contributed greatly to this culture, according to Van Sertima's *They Came Before Columbus* and Lerone Bennet's *Before the Mayflower*, based on a series of his articles in *Ebony*. This early black influence is still being discovered in South America today.

The early accomplishments of black men and women were slowed considerably with the advent of the slave trade. However, the slaves brought with them their knowledge of the medical value of herbs. These slaves performed as "nurses" and "doctors" not only to the slave population but also, in some cases, to the master's family. As was customary, however, the white owners often took credit for their slaves' knowledge.

Cotton Mather asked his newly acquired slave, Onesimus, if he had ever had smallpox. The slave answered that he had and he had not. Onesimus explained that, although his arm had been scratched and infected with the virus in Africa, he had a very mild case and the disease would not recur. Cotton Mather told his friend Dr. Boylston about Onesimus. Dr. Boylston experimented with his son and two of his slaves, finding the theory sound. For "his" discovery, Dr. Boylston was called to London and made a fellow of the Royal Society.

The introduction of the patent process in America did not protect the inventions of blacks. Since slaves were not considered people, they could not acquire patents for their work, nor could their masters acquire patents for them. It has been said that in order to make their lives easier, certain slaves were working on the production of a cotton gin. Eli Whitney discovered this, improved upon the invention, and patented it in his name. However, not all early white Americans took credit for their slaves' accomplishments. Cyrus McCormick's grandson reported that he had seen their slave, Jo Anderson, working with

---

[1] *Washington Post*, October 23, 1985, p. A6.

[2] Golden Age of Africa. *Ebony Pictorial History of Black Americans*, vol. 1, p. 11.

[3] Finch, C. S., African Background of Medical Science. *Blacks in Science; Ancient and Modern*, p. 140.

[4] Newsome, F., Black Contributions to the History of Western Medicine. *Blacks in Science: Ancient and Modern*, p. 34.

[5] Van Sertima, I., The Last Sciences of Africa: An Overview. *Blacks in Science: Ancient and Modern*, p. 9.

[6] Shore, D., Steel Making in Ancient Africa. *Blacks in Science: Ancient and Modern*, p. 157.

[7] Van Sertima I., The Last Sciences of Africa: An Overview. *Blacks in Science: Ancient and Modern*, p. 10.

his grandfather and offering suggestions for the reaper. For this reason, International Harvester, a McCormick company, has always had a nondiscriminatory practice of hiring, even in the South.

Eventually, in the 1800s, blacks were permitted to obtain patents. In 1900 Henry Baker, an employee of the Patent Office in Washington D.C., compiled a list of black patentees and their inventions for the International Exposition in Paris. According to this list, Henry Blair received the first patent in 1834 for his seed planter. However, Patricia Ives stated in her *Creativity and Inventions* that a patent was granted to a black man in 1821. In searching Baker's list, one must carefully check the patent since invention titles can be misleading, as in the case of the child's carriage by W. H. Richardson. In checking this patent, I found the invention was actually a leveling device that prevented the carriage from tipping over and was not the carriage itself. When investigating a patent, one will find that the patentee always states exactly what has been invented, rather than broadly classifying the invention, as has been done in patent lists.

An invention, of course, is the direct result of a need. Blacks throughout history have responded to these needs accordingly. Frederick Jones heard a friend say that a truckload of his chickens had spoiled because he was on the road too long. Jones responded to this need by inventing the refrigeration system still used today in the cross-country transport of perishable goods. Every school child knows the story about George Washington Carver and the peanut and the sweet potato. Although he did not patent most of his inventions, Carver did obtain patents for three of them dealing with a dye process. "The real McCoy" refers to an invention by Elijah McCoy. He invented the drip cup for overall lubrication still used in industry today. Jan Matzeliger's shoe-lasting machine revolutionized the shoe industry. Benjamin Banneker not only helped lay out the city of Washington, D.C., but also wrote an almanac and created the first striking clock in the United States. Garrett Augustus Morgan invented the gas mask. However, his invention was not bought when it was discovered that the inventor was black. Eventually an explosion in a tunnel under Lake Erie forced rescuers to summon Morgan and his gas mask, saving the lives of several people. Morgan's gas mask also saved many lives in World War I and is still used by firemen today. One of the more recent inventions by a black scientist to answer a need is that of Dr. George Carruthers, who invented the ultraviolet camera spectrograph, a special gold-plated camera that is on the surface of the moon.[8]

[8]Spady, James G. Blackspace. *Blacks in Science: Ancient and Modern*, p. 261.

These and other inventions are discussed at length in *Black Inventors of America* (McKinley, Burt) and *Creativity and Inventions* (Ives, Patricia). The latter is an excellent publication on black and female inventors.

Education of the black man throughout United States history has been slow in coming. Since it was forbidden for a slave to learn to read and write, it was at great risk that some masters and other whites taught them to read, write, and calculate. With this knowledge some slaves wrote passes to freedom for themselves. Thomas Fuller, known as the "Virginia calculator," could calculate the number of seconds in a year according to whether it was a leap year faster than a man could work out the problem on paper.

The most significant advances for blacks during and immediately after slavery were in medicine. As far back as the eighteenth century, the medical practitioner Papan was so successful in the treatment of skin and venereal diseases that he was freed and began to practice medicine. Cesar, another slave, devised a formula to cure rattlesnake bites and was also freed to practice medicine. His discovery was published in the *South Carolina Gazette* in 1751.

In fields other than medicine, progress was much slower. In 1876 Edward Bouchet received a doctorate in physics. Although he was a graduate of Yale University and the first black Phi Beta Kappa, the only job he could find was teaching high school.

Eventually, several of the larger white universities began quietly accepting black candidates for advanced degrees. In many instances, however, these students were isolated. Some were even forced to sit in hallways during lectures because the other students or the professor did not want them in the classroom. The early black Ph.D.s did indeed lead a lonely existence. But in spite of many obstacles, they achieved. However, since industry and laboratories were not willing to hire them, most became professors, usually in black colleges. While some were accepted during and just after World War II to work in laboratories, government and government-contracted institutions hired only a small number, indicating their value in white society at the time.

Today, as times continue to change, there are many more black achievers. We have astronauts with Ph.D.s in aerospace engineering (Guian Bluford) and physics (Robert McNair, killed in 1986); a female Ph.D. in physics from MIT; cancer specialists like Lasalle Lefall at Howard University Hospital; pediatric neurosurgeons like Benjamin Carson at Johns Hopkins; and electronic engineers and researchers in medicine, chemistry, and biology in institutions all over the country. Although the war is not over, clearly many battles have been won. This directory serves as proof of our victories.

*   *   *   *   *

Each person mentioned in this introduction is included in the biographical section.

BLACKS IN SCIENCE AND MEDICINE

A

Abbott, Anderson Ruffin   (1837–1913, M)

Physician. Surgeon. Born in Toronto, Ontario, Canada, April 7, 1837. Oberlin College Preparatory Department, 1856–58; B.M., Trinity College, University of Toronto, 1863; M.D., University of Toronto. Acting Assistant Surgeon, U.S. Army Medical Corps, 1863–66; Private practice, 1866–90s, Ontario, Canada. One of eight black physicians in the U.S. Army Medical Corps during the Civil War. Assigned to establish a contraband hospital out of which Freedmen's Hospital in Washington, DC, grew. Director, Abbott Hospital, Freedmen's Village, VA, 1864–66. Surgeon-in-Chief, Provident Hospital, Chicago, 1894–97.

Ref: Robinson, Henry S. Anderson Ruffin Abbott, M.D., 1837–1913. National Medical Association, *Journal*, v. 72, July, 1980, p. 713–716
Dictionary of American Medical Biography, v. 1, p. 3.

Abraham, Guy Emmanuel   (1936– ——, M)

Physician. Born in Haiti, April 12, 1936. B.A., Mont-Saint-Louis College, 1955; M.D., Montreal University, 1961. Chief Resident Physician, Deaconess Hospital, Buffalo, 1964–65; Staff Physician, Medical Department, Worcester State Hospital, 1968–69; Chief, Division of Reproductive Biology, Department of Obstetrics and Gynecology, Harbor General Hospital, University of California School of Medicine, Torrence, 1971–; Associate Professor, 1971–; Consultant, WHO, Contraceptive Review Branch, National Institutes of Health, 1972.

Memberships and awards: Fellow, Steroid Training Program, Worcester Foundation for Experimental Biology, Shrewsbury, 1965–67; Research fellow, Endocrinology Research Unit, Harbor General Hospital, Torrence, 1969–71.

Pub: *Handbook of Radioimmunoassay*, edited by Guy E. Abraham. New York, M. Dekkar, 1977. 822 p.
Radioassay Systems in Clinical Endocrinology, edited by Guy E. Abraham. New York, M. Dekkar, 1981. 669 p.
Abraham, Guy E., *Premenstrual Tension*. Chicago, Ill., Year Book Medical Publishers, 1981. 39 p.

Ref: *Who's Who Among Black Americans*, 1980–81, p. 2.
Who's Who Among Black Americans, 1985, p. 2.

Abrahams, Andrew Wordsworth   (1936– ——, M)

Physician. Born in Jamaica, B.W.I., Oct. 8, 1936. B.S., Columbia University, 1961; M.D., New York Medical College, 1966. Founder-Director, Bedford Stuyvesant Alcoholism Treatment Center, 1972; Medical Director of the Bureau of Alcoholism of New York City, 1970–72; Medical Consultant for Community Health Facilities Board.

Memberships and awards: New York City Affiliate of the National Counsel on Alcoholism, 1972; Certificate of Appreciation, Bedford Stuyvesant Alcoholism Treatment Center, New York State Association of Alcoholism Counsel.

Ref: *Who's Who Among Black Americans*, 1980–81, p. 2.
Who's Who Among Black Americans, 1985, p. 2.

Abram, James Baker, Jr.   (1937– ——, M)

Biologist. Zoologist. Parasitologist. Born in Tulsa, OK, Dec. 5, 1937. B.S., Langston University, OK, 1959; M.S., Oklahoma State University, 1963; Ph.D. (zoology), 1968. Professor of Biology, Hampton Institute, 1970–82; Assistant Dean, School of Mathematics and Science, Central State University, Edman, OK, 1982–83; Professor and Chairman of the Biology Department, Norfolk State University, 1983–.

Memberships and awards: American Society of Parasitologists; Helminthological Society of Washington; Sigma Xi; Kappa Alpha Psi from which he received achievement awards in 1970 and 1974; Outstanding Teacher of the Year, University of Maryland, Eastern Shore, 1969; Outstanding Educators of America, 1970.

Dissertation title: Ecological Factors Influencing Gastrointestinal Helminths of the Maryland Muskrat *Ondatra zibethicus Linnaeus*.

Ref: *American Men and Women of Science*, 16th ed., p. 12.
National Faculty Directory, 1986, p. 7.
Who's Who Among Black Americans, 1980–81, p. 2.
Who's Who Among Black Americans, 1985, p. 2.

Abrams, W. B.   (1800s, M)

Inventor. Invented the HAME Attachment.

Ref: *Afro-American Encyclopedia*, v. 1, p. 16.
Baker, Inventions By Blacks, 1871–1900 *Negro Almanac*, p. 1069.

Abron-Robinson, Lillia Ann   (1945– ——, F)

Chemist. Engineer (sanitary). Born in Memphis, TN, Mar. 8, 1945. B.S., LeMoyne College, 1966; M.S. (sanitary engineering), Washington University, 1968; Ph.D. (chemical engineering), University of Iowa, 1972. Research Chemist, Chicago Metropolitan Sanitary Department, 1968; Chemist, Kansas City, 1967–68. Assistant Professor, Civil Engineering, Tennessee State University.

Memberships and awards: In 1978, she became President of Peer Consultants, Inc., American Water Works Association; Water Pollution Control Federation; Sigma Xi.

Dissertation title: A Transport Mechanism in Hollow Nylon Fiber Reverse Osmosis Membranes for The Removal of DDT and Aldrin from Water.

Ref: *Black Engineers in the United States*, p. 3.
Black Women Achievements Against All Odds, Smithsonian publication, p. 39.

Acker, Daniel R. (1910- ——, M)

Chemist. Born in Radford, VA, Feb. 28, 1910. B.S., West Virginia State College; M.A., University of Michigan, 1942. Analytical Research Chemist, Group Supervisor, Sandusky, 1942–44; Research Chemist, Group Leader, Mass Spectroscopy Laboratory, Union Carbide Corporation, 1944–.

Memberships and awards: American Chemical Society; Kappa Alpha Psi; Northern Province Achievement Award; Community Service Award, Minority Student Organization, 1974.

Ref: *Who's Who Among Black Americans*, 1980–81, p. 2.
Who's Who Among Black Americans, 1985, p. 2.

Adair, Robert A. (1943- ——, M)

Physician. Born in New York, NY, June 27, 1943. B.A., University of Pennsylvania, 1965; M.D., Howard University Medical College, 1969; M.P.H., Columbia University, 1972. Acting District Health Officer for Central Harlem, 1970–71; WNBC-TV Medical Consultant and Co-producer of four TV films 1971–72; taught special health courses, Manhattansville College, 1972.

Memberships and awards: Fellow, American Public Health Association, 1969. New York County Medical Society; New York State Medical Society; National Medical Society; Black American Medical and Dental Association of Students; Black Caucus of Health Workers; American Medical Association; Medical Advisory Board, Foundation for Research and Education in Sickle Cell Disease; Board President of the Medical Board of Sydenham Hospital. Chairman of Preventive Medicine Section of 1973 National Medical Convention.

Ref: *Who's Who Among Black Americans*, 1980–81, p. 2.
Who's Who Among Black Americans, 1985, p. 2.

Adair, Roman T. (1884–1961, M)

Physician. Surgeon. Born in Hardaway, AL, 1884, B.S., Alabama State Normal School, 1905; M.D., American Medical Missionary College, MI, 1910. One of Montgomery, Alabama's first black Physicians. Only Medical Director of the Alabama State College.

Ref: *Jet*, Jan. 28, 1961
National Medical Association, *Journal*, v. 53, Nov. 1961, p. 657, obit.

Adams, Billie Morris Wright (19??- ——, F)

Physician. Pediatrician. Hematologist. Born in Bluefield, WV. B.S., Fisk University, 1950; M.A., Indiana University, 1951; M.D., Howard University Medical College, 1960. Research Associate, Hematology Department Hekutoen Institute, 1965–67; Pediatrician, Martin Luther King Center, 1967–68; Pediatric Hematologist, Director of Pediatric Hematology Clinic, Mercy Hospital; Associate with Pediatric Association of South Carolina.

Memberships and awards: Hematology fellowship 1963–65; American Academy of Pediatrics; National Medical Association; Cook County Physicians Association, Treasurer, 1974–; American Society of Hematology, Advisor to the Committee on Planned Parenthood, 1972–75; Medical Advisory Committee, Chicago Board of Health's Child & Maternal Committee; American Medical Association; Chicago Institute of Medicine; Operational Consultant, Sickle Cell Comprehensive Center, University of Illinois College of Medicine; Chicago Medical Society; PUSH-Woman of the Year, 1975; appointed Chairperson, State of Illinois Commission for Sickle Cell Anemia; Diplomate American Board of Pediatrics, 1964.

Ref: *Who's Who Among Black Americans*, 1980–81, p. 3.
Who's Who Among Black Americans, 1985, p. 3.
ABMS Compendium of Certified Medical Specialists, v. 4, p. 640.

Adams, George Williams (1894–1969, M)

Physician. Pathologist. Born in Washington, DC, Mar. 9, 1894. B.S., Dartmouth College, 1915; M.D., Howard University Medical College, 1918. Assistant Professor of Physiology and Physiologic Chemistry, Howard University, 1921–23; Pathologist, Freedmen's Hospital, 1923–.

Memberships and awards: Rosenwald fellow, Harvard University, 1920; President, Medico-Chirurgical Society, Washington, DC; Kappa Alpha Psi.

Ref: *Who's Who in Colored America*, 1928–29, p. 2.
Who's Who in Colored America, 1933–37, p. 16.
Who's Who in Colored America, 1938–40, p. 16.
Who's Who in Colored America, 1941–44, p. 16.
National Medical Association, *Journal*, v. 61, Mar. 1969, p. 203, obit.

Adams, Numa Pompilius Garfield (1885–1940, M)

Physician. Born in Delaplane, Fauquier County, VA, Feb. 26, 1885. B.A., Howard University (summa cum laude), 1911; M.A., Columbia University, 1912; M.D., Rush Medical School of the University of Chicago, 1924. Interned at St. Louis City Hospital no. 2 (Homer G. Phillips) in 1924. Practiced medicine in Chicago from 1925 to 1929. Instructor in Chemistry, Howard University, 1912–14; Assistant Professor, 1914–19; Associate Professor, 1919–; Assistant Medical Director, Victory Life Insurance Company, 1927–29; first black Dean of Howard University Medical College, June 4, 1929; Professor of Medicine, 1930–.

Memberships and awards: National Medical Association; Board of Directors, Tuberculosis Association of DC; Advisory Health Council of Washington Council on Social

Agencies; fellow, AAAS; National Medical Association; Cook County (IL) Physicians Association; Alpha Omega Alpha.

Pub: Contributed to medical journals.

Ref: *American Men of Science*, 6th ed., p. 7.
  Crisis, Apr. 1924, p. 266. [p]
  Dictionary of American Medical Biography, p. 7–8.
  Dictionary of American Negro Biography, p. 5.
  Encyclopedia of Black America, 1981, p. 3.
  History of the Negro in Medicine, p. 90–93. [p]
  National Medical Association, *Journal*, v. 64, Nov. 1972, p. 539–554.
  Who Was Who in American History—Science & Technology, p. 5.
  National Medical Association, *Journal*, v. 32, Nov. 1940, p. 257–258, obit and biography.
  Cobb, W. Montague, M.D., Numa P. G. Adams, M.D., 1885–1940. National Medical Association, *Journal*, v. 43, Jan. 1951, p. 42–54. [p]
  National Medical Association, *Journal*, v. 47, Sept. 1955. [p] on cover.

Adams, Walter Anderson   (1900–1959, M)

Physician. Psychiatrist. Born in Sabin Co., TX, Mar. 13, 1900. M.D., Howard University, 1926; Residency, Boston Psychopathic Hospital, Chicago, 1931–32; Post-Graduate training, Chicago Institute for Psychoanalysis; Licensed, DC, IL; First Black Psychiatrist, Chief of Provident Hospital Medical Counsel Clinic for Narcotic Addicts; Chief, Division of Psychiatry, Consulting Psychiatrist, Chicago Welfare Department, 1948–55. Died after surgery to remove blood clot from the brain at Michael Reese Hospital Chicago.

Pub: *Color and Human Nature*. Westport, CN, Negro Universities Press, 1970. 301 p. Co-authored by Lloyd Warner and Buford Junker.

Ref: *Jet*, Mar. 19, 1959, p. 29. [p]
  American Psychiatric Association, *Directory*, 1958, p. 3.

Adams-Ender, Clara I.   (1939– ——, F)

Nurse. Military (Army). Colonel. Born in Wake County, NC, July 11, 1939. Nursing, North Carolina A & T State University, 1961; M.S. (medical-surgical nursing), University of Minnesota, 1969; M.S. (first woman in the army to earn Master of Military Art and Science), U.S. Army Command and General Staff College, 1976. Chief Army Nurse Corps Division, U.S. Army Recruiting Command, Fort Sheridan, IL, 1981–84; First Black Chief, Department of Nursing, Walter Reed Army Medical Center, Washington, DC, 1984–.

Memberships and awards: American Nurses Association; National League for Nursing; Foundation of Thanatology; Sigma Theta Tau.

Pub: Publications in medical bulletins.

Ref: *Who's Who in American Nursing*, 1986–87, p. 3.
  The Path We Tread, p. 175. [p]

Adamson, Garland Norman   (1896–1967, M)

Physician. Surgeon. Born in Benson, AL, Sept. 17, 1896. B.A., Talladega College, AL, 1918; M.D., Meharry Medical College, 1922. President, Alabama State University.

Memberships and awards: President, Birmingham District Medical, Dental and Pharmaceutical Association; National Medical Association; Alpha Phi Alpha; John A. Andrew Clinical Society; Alabama Medical, Dental and Pharmaceutical Association.

Pub: Contributor to "For Health's Sake" column in Birmingham Reporter.

Ref: *Jet*, Feb. 23, 1967, p. 18. Death notice. [p]
  Who's Who in Colored America, 1928–29, p. 2.
  Who's Who in Colored America, 1930–32, p. 5.
  Who's Who in Colored America, 1933–37, p. 19.
  Who's Who in Colored America, 1938–40, p. 16, 18.
  Who's Who in Colored America, 1941–44, p. 19.

Adom, Edwin   (1940– ——, M)

Physician. Psychiatrist. Born in Accra, Ghana, Jan. 12, 1940. B.A., University of Pennsylvania, 1963; M.D., Meharry Medical College, 1968; Post-Graduate training in Psychiatry, Thomas Jefferson University, PA, 1969–70; Resident, 1970–72. Attending Psychiatrist, Friends Hospital, W. Park Hospital & St. Joseph Hospital; Office of Visually Handicapped; State of Pennsylvania Disability Determination Consultant; Clinical Associate, University of Pennsylvania School of Medicine; Psychiatrist for West Philadelphia Mental Health; Private Psychiatric practice, 1972–.

Memberships and awards: Royal Society of Health Engineering; fellow, Royal Society of Health of England; first black blind Physician and Psychiatrist in the United States; American Medical Association Physician Recognition Award, 1976.

Ref: *Who's Who Among Black Americans*, 1980–81, p. 5.
  Who's Who Among Black Americans, 1985, p. 6.
  ABMS Compendium of Certified Medical Specialists, v. 5, p. 306.
  American Psychiatric Association, *Directory*, 1983, p. 11.

Agbanobi, Raymond Omavuobe   (1938– ——, M)

Engineer (civil). Engineer (water resources). Born in Ovrode, Nigeria, Nov. 3, 1938. B.S., Blackburn College of Technology, Britain; M.S. (civil engineering), University of Missouri; Ph.D. (water resources), North Carolina State University, 1972. Design Engineer, Wooten & Co., 1972; Projects Engineer Design, Addison Engineering Service, 1969; Assistant Professor, Shaw University, Raleigh, NC, 1972–.

Dissertation title: Project Appraisal in a Developing Economy: A Master Plan Project for the Metropolitan Area of Lagos.

Ref: *Black Engineers in the United States*, p. 3.

Agee, Robert Edward   (1935- ——, M)

Physician. Urologist. Born in Jenks, OK, July 11, 1935. B.S., Central State College, OH, 1957; M.D., Meharry Medical College, 1961. Chief of Urology Services at several military hospitals.

Memberships and awards: American Board of Urology Diplomate, 1975; fellow, American College of Surgeons, 1975; Consultant to Surgeon General of the United States Army, 1985–; Association of Military Surgeons of the United States; National Medical Association; American Medical Association; Association of Government Service Urologists; American Urological Association; American Medical Association Physician Recognition Award, 1973–76, 1976–79.

Pub: Acute urinary retention in women: brief discussion and unusual case report, *Journal of Urology*, 1973.
Malignant fibrous histocytoma of the spermatic cord, 1982.

Ref: *Who's Who Among Black Americans*, 1980–81, p. 5.
Who's Who Among Black Americans, 1985, p. 6.
ABMS Compendium of Certified Medical Specialists, v. 6, p. 964.

Aheart, Andrew Norwood   (1921- ——, M)

Mathematician. Born in Wildwood, VA, April 13, 1921. B.S., Virginia Union University, 1942; M.A., Harvard University, 1948. Teacher, South Carolina Abrams High School, Palmyra, VA, 1946–47; Instructor in Mathematics, West Virginia State College, 1948–50; Assistant Professor in Mathematics, West Virginia State College 1950–.

Memberships and awards: American Mathematical Society; Mathematical Association of America; AAAS; West Virginia Academy of Sciences; American Association of University Professors; Rosenwald Scholar, Harvard University, 1942–43; Association of Higher Education of West Virginia.

Ref: *American Men and Women of Science*, 12th ed., p. 41.
National Faculty Directory, 1986, p. 25.
The Negro in Science, p. 187.

Albert, A. P.   (1800s, M)

Inventor. Lawyer. Born in Louisana. Law degree, Howard University Law School. Invented a cotton picking machine and won his case to get it patented by preparing a brief and appearing before a Board for Examiners-in-Chief composed of legal and technical experts. He won by his painstaking presentation of the technical points involved.

Ref: *Negro in Our History*, 5th ed., p. 462.
Baker, Henry, Negro in the Field of Invention, *Journal of Negro History*, Jan. 1917, p. 33.

Aldrich, James Thomas   (1892–1968, M)

Physician. Born in Dudley, SC, May 14, 1892. B.S., Shaw University, 1916; M.D., Meharry Medical College, 1920.

Memberships and awards: President of National Medical Association, 1960–61; Chairman of the Board of Trustees, 1956–58, and Speaker of its House of Delegates, 1949–52; President, Mound City Medical Forum, 1929; St. Louis Medical Society; American Medical Association; Phi Beta Sigma.

Ref: *Encyclopedia of Black America*, 1961, p. 86.
National Medical Association, *Journal*, v. 49, Jan. 1957, p. 66. [p]
National Medical Association, *Journal*, v. 51, Nov. 1959, p. 473. [p]
National Medical Association, *Journal*, v. 60, Mar. 1968, obit. [p]

Alexander, Archie Alphonso   (1888–1958, M)

Engineer (architectural). Born in Ottumwa, IA, May 14, 1888. B.S. (civil engineering), University of Iowa, 1912. Took courses in bridge design at the University of London, 1921. Builder of tunnels, bridges and hydraulic plants. Designer for Marsh Engineering Company in 1914, he built the Tidal Basin Bridge in Washington, DC and the K Street Freeway, among other notable viaducts and bridges. He and George Higbee formed a general contracting business, Alexander and Higbee, specializing in the design and construction of concrete and steel bridges. After the accidental death of Higbee while supervising the construction of a bridge, Alexander kept the business going alone. First Republican Governor to the Virgin islands, 1954–55. Died at his home in Des Moines, Iowa.

Memberships and awards: The University of Iowa conferred honorary Civil Engineering Degree upon him. A member and founder of Omega Chapter of Kappa Alpha Psi Fraternity and awarded the "Laural Wreath" given to the member who had accomplished the most outstanding thing during the year, 1926. Spingarn Medal, 1928, given annually by the NAACP for the "highest achievement of a black man." Named "one of the first 100 citizens of merit" among University of Iowa's 30,000 alumni. A trustee of Tuskegee Institute; Honorary Dr. of Civil Engineering, Howard University, 1946.

Ref: *Afro-American Encyclopedia*, v. 1, p. 107.
Blacks in Science: Astrophysicist to Zoologist, p. 20.
Current Biography, 1955, p. 9–11. [p]
Biographical History of Blacks in America Since 1528, p. 246–247.
Black Contributors to Science & Energy Technology, p. 6.

Ebony, Mar. 1967, p. 124–129.
Ebony, Sept. 1949, p. 59–60.
Ebony, June 1961, p. 70.
Encyclopedia of Black America, p. 97.
Jet, Jan. 16, 1958, p. 28.
Negro Builders and Heroes, p. 254.
In Spite of Handicaps, p. 79–84. [p] (Reprint in 1968 of 1927 edition.)
Historical Afro-American Biographies, p. 154–155.
Crisis, June 1926, p. 79–80. [p]

Alexander, Benjamin Harold   (1921- ——, M)

Chemist (organic). Born in Roberta, GA, Oct. 18, 1921. B.A., University of Cincinnati, 1943; M.S., Bradley University, 1950; Ph.D., Georgetown University, 1957. Technician, Cincinnati Chemical Works, 1944–45; Chemist; Agricultural Research Service, USDA, IL, 1945–54; Research Chemist, Maryland, 1954–62; Chemist, Walter Reed Army Institute of Research, 1962–67; Health Scientist Administrator, NIH, 1967–68; Special Assistant to Director for Disadvantaged, National Center for Health Services Research & Development, Health Service & Mental Health Administration, USPHS, 1968–69; Administrator of new health career projects and Deputy Equal Employment Officer, 1969–70; Program Officer, Health Care Organization and Resources Division, 1970–74; President, Chicago State University, 1974–83; Consultant, National Center for Health Services Research & National Science Foundation, 1977. Research in the synthesis of organophosphorus compounds for medicinal purposes, synthesis of pesticide chemicals and preparation of useful compounds from agricultural wastes.

Memberships and awards: Certificate of Achievement from American Chemical Society of which he is a member.

Dissertation title: The Phosphate Enzyme Activity of DDT Resistant and Normal House Flies, and Chlordane Resistant and Normal Cockroaches.

Ref: *American Men and Women of Science*, 16th ed., p. 66.
Ebony, Mar. 1967, p. 124–126, 128. [p]
Encyclopedia of Black America, p. 744.
Historical Negro Biographies, p. 154.
In Black and White, p. 12.
Who's Who Among Black Americans, 1980–81, p. 7.
Who's Who in America, 1986–87, p.34.

Alexander, Ernest R.   (1892–1960, M)

Physician. Dermatologist. Born in Nashville, TN, 1892. B.A., Fisk University, 1914; two years medical work, University of Minnesota; B.S., University of Minnesota; M.D., University of Vermont, 1919. Only Black in medical class and took all honors in medicine offered by the university. Physician-in-charge of Dermatology & Syphilology at Harlem Hospital.

Memberships and awards: "Honor Man in Medicine"; first prize for "Special Merit in Medicine"; Wood-

bury prize for "Clinical Proficiency in Medicine"; National Medical Association.

Pub: Bismuth Compounds in the Treatment of Active Syphilis, Clinical and Laboratory Study of 286 cases of Cutaneous Syphilis. *Archives of Dermatology and Syphilology*, Sept. 1933, p. 320–352. With others.
Superficial Pustular Folliculitis of New Born. *Archives of Dermatology and Syphilology*, Aug. 1934, p. 257–259.

Ref: *Who's Who in Colored America*, 1928–29, p. 2.
Who's Who in Colored America, 1930–32, p. 5–6.
Who's Who in Colored America, 1938–40, p. 19.
National Medical Association, *Journal*, v. 27, Nov. 1935, p. 146.
National Medical Association, *Journal*, v.52, 1960, p. 455, obit.
Crisis, June 1926, p. 78–79. [p]
Crisis, Feb. 1947, p. 49. [p]

Alexander, Joseph Lee   (1929- ——, M)

Physician. Surgeon. Born in Oneonta, AL, Oct. 29, 1929. B.A., Fisk University, 1951; M.D., University of Louisville, 1955; M.P.H., UCLA, School of Public Health. Chairman, Department of Surgery, King-Drew Medical Center, 1971-.

Memberships and awards: Research fellow in Surgery, Harvard University, 1967–69.

Pub: Alexander, Joseph L. King-Drew Trauma Center Notes, National Medical Association, *Journal*, v. 68, Sept. 1976, p. 384–386.

Ref: *ABMS Compendium of Medical Specialists*, v. 6, p. 28.
A Century of Black Surgeons, p. 383–385, 395–408 [p] p. 384.

Alexander, Leslie Luther   (1917- ——, M)

Physician. Radiologist. Born in Kingston, Jamaica, Oct. 10, 1917. B.A., New York University, 1947; M.A., 1948; M.D., Howard University, 1952. Radiology Professor of Health Services, State University of New York at Stonybrook and Director of Radiology, Long Island Jewish Hillside Medical Center, affiliate of Owens Hospital Center, 1977-; Consultant, Brooklyn Veterinary Hospital, 1962–71; Consultant, Bureau of Medical Devices, Food & Drug Administration, HEW, 1975-; Research in radiology, including radiation therapy, nuclear medicine, radiobiology and cancer.

Memberships and awards: Board of Chancellors, American College of Radiology, Chicago, 1980-; American Medical Association; Association of University Radiologists; American Society of Therapeutic Radiologists; fellow of New York Academy of Medicine; Diplomate, American Board of Radiology; National Medical Association; Distinguished Service Award, National Medical Association, 1974.

Pub: Cancer of the penis: radiation therapy or surgery. National Medical Association, *Journal,* v. 64, Nov. 1972, p. 533–536.

Burkitt's tumor. National Medical Association, *Journal,* v. 65, Sept. 1973, p. 386–390.

Hospitals of West Africa: Liberia, Ghana and Nigeria. National Medical Association, *Journal,* v. 65, Sept. 1973, p. 373–375.

Position of minority radiologists in the United States. National Medical Association, *Journal,* v. 66, Mar. 1974, p. 171–173.

Cobb, W. Montague. Alexander distinguished service medalist for 1974. National Medical Association, *Journal,* v. 66, Nov. 1974, p. 516–518.

Ref: ABMS Directory of Certified Radiologists, v. 5, p. 894.
American Men and Women of Science, 16th ed., p. 68.
Encyclopedia of Black America, p. 97.
In Black and White, p. 13.
National Medical Association, *Journal,* v. 57, Sept. 1965, p. 426. [p]

Alexander, Lloyd Ephraim   (1902- ——, M)

Biologist. Embryologist. Born in Salem, VA, Aug. 17, 1902. B.A., University of Michigan, 1927; M.A., 1928; Ph.D. (embryology), University of Rochester, 1936. From Instructor to Professor and Head of the Department of Biology, Fisk University, 1930–72; Research in experimental embryology, grafting and transplanting tissues in vertebrates.

Memberships and awards: Sigma Xi; Phi Sigma; American Society of Zoology.

Dissertation title: An Experimental Study of the Role of the Optic Cup and Overlying Ectoderm in Lens Formation in the Chick Embryo.

Ref: American Men and Women of Science, 16th ed., p. 68.
Holders of Doctorates Among American Negroes, p. 184–185.
The Negro in Science, p. 175.

Alexander, Walter Gilbert   (1880–1953, M)

Physician. Surgeon. Born in Lynchburg, VA, Dec. 3, 1880. B.A., Lincoln University, PA, 1899; M.D., College of Physicians and Surgeons, Boston, 1903. First Honor Man from Lincoln University, Salutatorian.

Memberships and awards: First prize College of Surgeons for his thesis "Cerebral localizations"; second prize for thesis on tuberculosis. State University President; National Medical Association, 1902–12; General Secretary, President, National Medical Association, 1925–26; Negro Advisory Committee of the New Jersey Anti-Tuberculosis Association; first Black doctor elected to New Jersey Senate; while in New Jersey State Senate, he was the principal defender of the Medical License bill, which governed the practice of medicine in New Jersey; he was the proposer of the Marriage License Bill, which required a medical examination of applicants for marriage; Distinguished Service Medal of the National Medical Association, 1944.

Ref: Encyclopedia of Black America, 1981, p. 98.
Jet, Dec. 9, 1965, p. 11.
Who's Who of the Colored Race, 1915, p. 3.
Who's Who in Colored America, 1927, p. 2–3.
Who's Who in Colored America, 1928–29, p. 5.
Who's Who in Colored America, 1930–32, p. 6. [p] p. 7.
Who's Who in Colored America, 1938–40, p. 20. [p] p. 21.
Who's Who in Colored America, 1941–44, p. 20. [p] p. 21.
National Medical Association, *Journal,* v. 17, Oct.–Dec., 1925, p. 186. [p]
Dictionary of American Medical Biography, p. 11–12.
Cobb, W. Montague. Walter Gilbert Alexander, M.D., 1880–1953, National Medical Association, *Journal,* v. 45, 1953, p. 281–82.

Alexander, Walter Gilbert, II   (1922- ——, M)

Dentist. Engineer (mechanical). Born in Petersburg, VA, July 6, 1922. B.S. (mechanical engineering), Rutgers University, 1943; D.D.S., Howard University, 1952. Designer, Douglas Aircraft Co., L.A., 1943; Private practice Dentist, 1952; Post Graduate Dental Faculty, New Jersey College of Medicine and Dentistry, 1967; Clinical Assistant Professor, 1969–.

Memberships and awards: New Jersey State Board of Dentistry, 1972–76, President, 1976; American Association of Dental Examiners; Tau Beta Pi; Northeast Regional Board of Dental Examiners; Omicron Kappa Upsilon.

Ref: Who's Who Among Black Americans, 1985, p. 10.

Alexander, Winser Edward   (1942- ——, M)

Engineer (electrical). Inventor. Born in Columbia, NC, Aug. 19, 1942. B.S., North Carolina A & T State University, 1964; M.S (electrical engineering), University of New Mexico, 1966; Ph.D., 1974. Member of the Technical Staff, Sandia Laboratories, 1964–70; Patent #3541333 for a System for Enhancing Fine Detail in Thermal Photographs.

Memberships and awards: IEEE; Office of Aerospace Research Award, 1968.

Dissertation title: Stability and Synthesis of Two-Dimensional Digital Recursive Filters.

Ref: Black Engineers in the United States, p. 4–5.
Who's Who Among Black Americans, 1977–78, p. 10.

Alexis, Carlton Peter   (1929- ——, M)

Physician. Endocrinologist. Internist. Born in Trinidad, June 19, 1929. B.A., New York University, 1953; M.D., Howard University Medical College, 1957; D.H.C., Haiti, 1972; D.Sc., Georgetown University, 1980. Instructor and Professor of Medicine, Howard University, 1964–.

Memberships and awards: Fellow in Endocrinology, Georgetown University Hospital, 1963–64; President, Med-Dent Staff, Freedmen's Hospital, 1968–69; National Medical Association; American Medical Association; fellow, American College of Physicians; American Society of Internal Medicine; Medical Society of DC; Medical Chirurgical Society of DC; Chairman of the Governing Board of DC General Hospital; Mayor's Task Force on Reorganizing the Department of Human Resources of DC; Mayor's Commission on Drug Abuse; Outstanding Teacher, Howard University College of Medicine, 1966; Diplomate, American Board of Internal Medicine, 1964; Alpha Omega Alpha.

Ref:　*Who's Who Among Black Americans,* 1980–81, p. 9.
　　Who's Who Among Black Americans, 1985, p. 10.
　　ABMS Compendium of Medical Specialists, v. 2, p. 40.
　　National Medical Association, *Journal,* v. 62, Jan. 1970, p. 70. [p] Biog.

Alfred, Carolyn Cannon-Alfred　(1934– ——, F)

Pharmacologist. Born in Tyler, TX, Aug. 16, 1934. B.S., University of Toledo, 1954; M.S., Howard University, 1957; Ph.D. (pharmacology), Georgetown University, 1961. Assistant Pharmacologist, Howard University, 1957–59; Instructor, 1961; Senior Pharmacologist, Riker Laboratories, 1961–62; Research Associate, California, Riverside, 1962–64; Assistant Professor, Pharmacology, School of Medicine, Southern California University, 1964–.

Memberships and awards: National Heart Institute Grant, 1964–66.

Pub:　Co-Author of *Medical Handbook for the Layman,* written with her physician husband. Los Angeles, 1969. 202 p.

Ref:　*American Men and Women of Science,* 11th ed., Suppl 1, p. 8.

Alfred, Dewitt Clinton, Jr.　(1937– ——, M)

Physician. Psychiatrist. Born in Chattanooga, TN, Oct. 12, 1937. B.S., Morehouse College (cum laude), 1956; M.D., Howard University Medical School, 1960. Assistant Resident in Psychiatry, Washington University, St. Louis, 1961–62; Psychiatrist, Walter Reed Hospital, DC, 1964–67. Medical Officer in the Neuro-Psychiatry Clinic, 1967–68; Diplomate, American Board of Psychiatry and Neurology, 1970; Staff Psychiatrist, Emory University, 1971–; Grady Memorial Hospital, 1973–.

Memberships and awards: Fellow of American Psychiatric Association, 1977; National Medical Association; American Academy of Psychiatry and Law; Society of USAF Psychiatrists; Black Psychiatrists of America; American Medical Association.

Ref:　*Who's Who Among Black Americans,* 1980–81, p. 10.
　　Who's Who Among Black Americans, 1985, p. 11.
　　ABMS Compendium of Medical Specialists, v. 5, p. 309.

Allen, Aris T.　(1910– ——, M)

Physician. Born in Beeville, TX, Dec. 27, 1910. M.D. Howard University Medical School, 1944; B.S.W., 1985. Private practice, 1945–81; Maryland State Legislature, 1966–74; State Senator, 1978–81; Medical Affairs Advisor, Health Care Financial Administration, U.S. Department of Health and Human Services, 1981–85.

Memberships and awards: Honorary member, Anne Arundel County General Hospital Staff; Anne Arundel County Medical Society; Monumental Medical Society; American Medical Association; Vice-President, Medical Chirurgical Faculty of the State of Maryland; American Academy of Family Physicians; Johnson Publication Award, 1980; Wisdom Award of Honor; Howard University Alumni Achievement Award, 1981; Recognition from the Maryland State Legislature for unusual service to Annapolis, 1971; fellow, American Board of Family Practice.

Ref:　*Afro-American Encyclopedia,* v. 1, p. 114. [p]
　　Who's Who Among Black Americans, 1980–81, p. 10.
　　Who's Who Among Black Americans, 1985, p. 11–12.
　　Ebony Success Library, v. 1, p. 8. [p]
　　National Medical Association, *Journal,* v. 62, Jan. 1970, p. 89. [p]
　　National Medical Association, *Journal,* v. 67, Sept. 1975, p. 409–410. [p]
　　Maryland State Medical Journal, June 1977, (article about him).
　　National Medical Association, *Journal,* v. 69, Nov. 1977, p. 833.

Allen, Browning E., Jr.　(1925– ——, M)

Physician. Surgeon. Urologist. Born in Ratou, NM, Mar. 24, 1925. B.S., University of Oregon, 1947; M.D., Meharry Medical College, 1949. Residency in Urology, 1951–56; Instructor, Department of Urology, University of Southern California Medical School, 1957–69; Chief, Department of Surgery, Kaiser Hospital, Sacramento, 1966–67; Assistant Director, Department of Urology, 1969–70; Private Practice, 1970–.

Memberships and awards: American Medical Association; National Medical Association; Western Section, American Urological Association, Inc.; Society for Pediatric Urology; President, Los Angeles Urological Society, 1981; Aesclepiads Premedical Honorary Fraternity, University of Oregon, 1944; Alpha Phi Alpha, 1945–; Kappa Pi Honorary Fraternity, Meharry Medical College, 1948.

Ref:　*Who's Who Among Black Americans,* 1980–81, p. 11.
　　Who's Who Among Black Americans, 1985, p. 12.

Allen, C. W.　(1800s, M)

Inventor. Invented a self-leveling table, Nov. 1, 1898. Patent #613 436.

Ref: *Afro-American Encyclopedia,* v. 1, p. 114.
The Negro Almanac, p. 1069.
Baker, Inventions By Blacks, 1871–1900.

Allen, Elbert E.   (1921– , M)

Dentist. Born in Shreveport, LA, Sept. 19, 1921. B.S., Wiley College, TX, 1942; D.D.S., Meharry Medical College, 1945. Academy of General Dentistry fellow, 1969. Private practice.

Memberships and awards: First black to receive a Society of Dental Surgeons fellowship; Founding member, Chicago Dental Society; Louisiana State Dental Association; American Dental Association; First Black elected to public office in Shreveport, LA (Caddo Parish School Board); Honorary Citizen of New Orleans, 1959; Notable American Award.

Ref: *Who's Who Among Black Americans,* 1985, p. 12.
Ebony Success Library, v. 1, p. 9. [p]

Allen, Farrow Robert   (1898– , M)

Physician. Surgeon. Born in Chatanooga, TN, Feb. 24, 1898. Fisk University, 1913–17; B.A., Harvard University, 1923; M.D., Harvard University, School of Medicine, 1926. Attending Surgeon, Sydenham Hospital, 1953–68; Assistant Director of Surgery, 1963–68; Consulting Surgeon, 1968–. Assisted in the removal of the knife from the chest of Dr. Martin Luther King, Jr., in 1958 at Harlem Hospital.

Memberships and awards: American College of Surgeons, 1947–; New York Academy of Medicine, 1945–76; American Medical Association; New York State and County Medical Societies, 1930–; Harvard Medical Society, 1930–; National Medical Society Board of Managers; Alpha Phi Alpha; Sigma Pi Phi; 50 year Club of American Medical Association, 1976; Citation from the Medical Society of New York for Fifty years of Service to the Public in the practice of medicine.

Ref: *Who's Who Among Black Americans,* 1980–81, p. 11.
Who's Who Among Black Americans, 1985, p. 13.

Allen, Gloria Marie   (192?– , F)

Physician. Pediatrician. Born in Washington, DC. B.S., Howard University, 1947; M.D., Howard University Medical School, 1951. Chief, Pediatrics, Carter Community Health Center, 1974–.

Memberships and awards: Medical Society of the County of Queens, 1964–; Secretary, Empire State Medical Association, 1975–; Treasurer and Charter Member, Susan S. McKinney Smith Medical Society, 1976–.

Ref: *Who's Who Among Black Americans,* 1980–81, p. 11.
Who's Who Among Black Americans, 1985, p. 13.

Allen, J. B.   (1800s, M)

Inventor. Patent #551,105, Dec. 10, 1895, for a clothes line support.

Ref: *Afro-American Encyclopedia,* v. 1, p. 116.
The Negro Almanac, p. 1069.

Allen, John Henry, Jr.   (1938– , M)

Engineer (electrical). Inventor. Born in Youngstown, OH, Jan. 16, 1938. B.S., California State University, Los Angeles, 1964; M.S.E.E., 1969. Systems Technician, Packard Bell Electronics, 1959–61; Research Engineer, Lockheed Aircraft, 1961–64; Dynamics Engineer, General Dynamics, 1964–66; MTS, Teledyne Systems, Co., 1965–66; Assistant Manager, Systems Integration and Support Centers, 1966–70; Assistant Professor, California State College, 1969–78. He has a Patent for a Doppler Operation Test Set (DOTS) and a Dissimilar Metal Anti-Corrosion Ground Stub (DMAGS).

Memberships and awards: IEEE; EIT.

Ref: *Ebony Success Library,* v. III, p. 6–7. [p]
Who's Who Among Black Americans, 1980–81, p. 12.
Who's Who Among Black Americans, 1985, p. 13.

Allen, Raleigh H.   (1900s, M)

Veterinarian. Born in Tampa, FL. First black to pass 3-day test and be licensed as a Veterinarian in Alabama.

Ref: *Jet,* Nov. 9, 1961, p. 18.

Allen, William Edward, Jr.   (1903–1982, M)

Physician. Radiotherapist. Born in Pensacola, FL, Aug. 14, 1903. B.S., Howard University, 1927; M.D., Howard University Medical College, 1930; D.A.B.R., 1935; F.A.C.R., 1945. Medical Director of Radiology, Homer G. Phillips Hospital, 1945–73; Instructor to Clinical Professor, 1967–78; Radiotherapist, School of Medicine, St. Louis University, 1970–; Clinical Professor Radiation Oncology, 1979–; Research in nuclear medicine; radiation therapy-carcinoma of prostate; simplified radiation dosimetry—carcinoma of the cervix.

Memberships and awards: Emeritus Professor of Clinical Radiology, School of Medicine, Washington University; National Medical Association Distinguished Service Award, 1967; American College of Radiologists Gold Medal, 1974; AAAS; National Medical Association, Vice-President, 1962–63; fellow American College of Radiologists; American Society of Therapeutic Radiologists; Radiological Society of North America; First Black to be certified as a Diplomate, American Board of Radiologists; annual lectures set up in his honor, 1978.

Pub: Supervoltage Isocentric Arc Therapy in Carcinoma of the Bladder, National Medical Association, *Journal,* v. 65, Nov. 1973, p. 465–470.

Ref: *American Men and Women of Science*, 15th ed., p. 82.
  Who's Who Among Black Americans, 1980–81, p. 13.
  Who's Who Among Black Americans, 1985, p. 14.
  Jet, Feb. 15, 1982, p. 13.
  National Medical Association, *Journal*, v. 53, Nov. 1961, p. 554. [p] p. 553.
  National Medical Association, *Journal*, v. 60, Jan. 1968, p. 47–49. [p] Biog.
  National Medical Association, *Journal*, v. 65, Nov. 1973, p. 558. [p]
  National Medical Association, *Journal*, v. 71, Mar. 1979, p. 394–395. [p]

Allinsworth, Allen   (1842–1914, M)

Military (Army). Lt. Colonel. Born in 1842. Joined the Union forces during the Civil War; rejoined as a chaplain in 1886. He retired 20 years later as a Lieutenant Colonel, the highest ranking Black Officer of his time.

Memberships and awards: The Colonel Allensworth State Historic Park in California is named for him at a location that was a town begun by him in 1909. The town had a library, with Ethel Hall Norton as librarian.

Ref: *American Libraries*, v. 18, Feb. 1987: p. 140–141. [p]

Allison, James M., Jr.   (1926– ——, M)

Physician. Surgeon. Born in Chicago, IL, June 10, 1926. B.A., Fisk University, 1949; M.D., Meharry Medical College, 1953. Resident in General Surgery for four years; Associate in Surgery, Northwestern University, 1974; Attending Surgeon, Provident Hospital, Columbus Hospital, and Illinois Masonic Hospital.

Memberships and awards: Diplomate, American Board of Surgery; fellow, American College of Surgeons; President, Cook County Physicians Association; Chicago Medical Society; Illinois State Medical Society; American Medical Association.

Ref: *Who's Who Among Black Americans*, 1980–81, p. 13.
  Who's Who Among Black Americans, 1985, p. 13.

Allman, Marian Isabel   (1946– ——, F)

Physician. Ophthalmologist. Born in Birmingham, AL, Feb. 18, 1946. B.A., Fisk University, 1966; M.D., Meharry Medical College, 1970. Homer G. Phillips Hospital, 1971–74; Ophthalmology staff, V.A. Hospital, 1976–77; Chief Ophthalmology Section, 1977.

Memberships and awards: Association for Research and Vision in Ophthalmology; Association of V.A. Ophthalmologists; American Academy of Ophthalmology and Otolaryngology; National Medical Association; Medical Association of the State of Alabama; Macon County Medical Society; Alpha Kappa Alpha; fellow, University of Pennsylvania, 1974–76; Board of Advisors, Habitat for Humanity; Outstanding Young Women of America, 1976; Physicians Recognition Award.

Pub: Several articles in *Archives of Ophthalmology*, 1976.

Ref: *Who's Who Among Black Americans*, 1980–81, p. 13.
  Who's Who Among Black Americans, 1985, p. 13.

Alston, John Henry   (1868–1926, M)

Physician. Born in Charleston, SC, Jan. 27, 1868. Attended local schools in Summerville, preparatory training, Cookman Baptist School of Jacksonville, FL; M.D., Leonard Medical College at Shaw University, NC, 1893. Founded Alston Graded School in 1910 and Arthur B. Lee Hospital in 1912. Pioneer Black Physician in Dorchester County.

Memberships and awards: Received a medal from the American Red Cross Society for his heroic work during the influenza epidemic of 1918.

Ref: National Medical Association *Journal*, v. 18, April–June, 1926, p. 109.

Alsup, Frederick Werthly   (1914– ——, M)

Physician. Zoologist. Born in Nashville, TN, Aug. 5, 1914. B.A., Fisk University, 1934; M.A., 1936; M.A., Michigan University, 1938; Rosenwald Fellow, Pennsylvania, 1938–41; Ph.D. (zoology), University of Pennsylvania, 1941; M.D., Howard University Medical College, 1947. Graduate Assistant at Fisk University, 1934–36; Professor of Science, Morristown Normal & Industrial College, TN, 1936–38; Instructor in Zoology, Howard University, 1941–42; Associate Professor, 1946; Medical Investigator, District of Columbia Public Health Department, 1947–; Director of Student Health, Florida A & M University, 1948–.

Memberships and awards: Philadelphia Physiological Society; Sigma Xi.

Dissertation title: The Effects of Light Alone and Photodynamic Action on the Relative Viscosity of Amoeba Protoplasm.

Ref: *American Men of Science*, 8th ed., p. 40.
  Holders of Doctorates Among American Negroes, p. 185.

Altemus, Leonard A.   (1900s, M)

Dentist. Orthodontist. Associate Professor of Orthodontics, Howard University. Awarded $92,509 to study head and face of the American Negro Child by the U.S. Public Health Service.

Ref: *Jet*, Feb. 15, 1962, p. 22.

Ames, James Webb   (1864–19??, M)

Physician. Born in New Orleans, LA, Oct. 12, 1864. B.S., Straight University, 1888; M.D., Howard University Medical College, 1894. Practiced medicine in Detroit, 1894–; was physician to U.S. prisoners, 1899–1900; Diagnostician of Contagious Diseases for Detroit Board of Health,

1901; first black to hold such municipal positions; Medical Director, Dunbar Memorial Hospital; Member of Michigan House of Representatives, 1901–02.

Memberships and awards: Michigan State Medical Society; Wayne County Medical Society; Associate Member Alumni Association of Detroit College of Medicine.

Ref: *Who's Who in Colored America,* 1928–29, p. 9.
Who's Who in Colored America, 1930–31, p. 13.
Who's Who of the Colored Race, 1915, p. 6.
Who's Who in Colored America, 1938–40, p. 27.
Who's Who in Colored America, 1941–44, p. 25.

Amory, Reginald L.   (1936– —— , M)

Engineer (civil). Born in Peekskill, NJ, July 17, 1936. B.C.E., New York University, 1960; M.D.E., Clarkson College, 1963; Ph.D., Rensselaer Polytechnic Institute, 1967. Engineer, Throap and Feiden, 1960–61; Engineer, Abbott, Jerkt and Co., 1961–63; Technical Assistant, Rensselaer Polytechnic Institute, 1963–64; Instructor, 1965–66; Assistant Professor, Northeastern University, 1966–68; Dean, North Carolina A & T University, 1968–74; Professor, Northeastern University, 1974–87. Consultant to G.E. Co., National Science Foundation, U.S. Department of Energy, Educational Development Corporation, National Academy of Engineering, Tennessee State University, and Mobil Oil Co.

Memberships and awards: American Society of Engineering Education (Executive Board); American Society of Civil Engineers; International Association of Bridge and Structural Engineers; National Society of Professional Engineers; AAAS; Advisory Panel of the Engineering Mechanical Section of the National Science Foundation; Chairman of the Commission of Education for the Engineering Profession; Board of Trustees, St. Augustine's College; Sigma Psi Phi; Excellence award, North Carolina A & T State University, 1972; Engineer of Distinction, Engineering Joint Council, 1973; National Science Honor Society.

Dissertation title: Creep of the Polysulfide Rubber Under Nonsteady Atmospheric Temperatures and Loads.

Ref: *Who's Who Among Black Americans,* 1985, p. 16.

Amos, Harold   (1919– —— , M)

Bacteriologist. Born in Pennsauken, NJ, Sept. 7, 1919. B.S., Springfield College, 1941; M.A., Harvard University, 1947; Ph.D. (bacteriology), Harvard University, 1952. Instructor in Bacteriology, Springfield College, 1948–49; Assistant Professor, 1954–59; from Assistant to Associate Professor, 1959–70; Maude and Lillian Presley Professor of Microbiology and Molecular Genetics, Harvard Medical School, 1975–; Chairman, Department of Microbiology, 1979–.

Memberships and awards: National Institute of Allergy & Infectious Diseases; National Academy of Sciences; AAAS; Candidate for Board of Directors for 1987; Fulbright research fellow, Pasteur Institute, France 1951–52; Research fellow, Harvard Medical School, 1952–54; U.S.P.H.S. fellow, 1952–54; Senior Research fellow, 1958; research in hexose metabolism in mammalian cells; surface changes and hormonal influences; National Cancer Advisory Board; American Society of Microbiology; American Society of Biological Chemists; Tissue Culture Association.

Dissertation title: Study of the Factors Contributing to the loss of Infectivity of Herpes Simplex Virus.

Ref: *American Men and Women of Science,* 16th ed., p. 109.
Encyclopedia of Black America, p. 744.
1987 AAAS Elections, 1987–88, p. 3. [p]
Scientists in the Black Perspective.

Anderson, Albert Douglas   (1928– —— , M)

Physician. Physical and Rehabilitation Medicine. Born in New York, NY, Jan. 11, 1928. B.A., Columbia University, 1948; M.D., Harvard Medical School, 1952. Director of Rehabilitation Medicine, Harlem Hospital; Assistant Attending Physician, Medical Division, Montefiore Hospital, 1957–59; Adjutant Attendant of Rehabilitation Medicine, 1960–65; Coordinator, Amputee Service, 1963–65; Professor of Clinical Rehabilitation Medicine and Director of Rehabilitation Medicine, Harlem Hospital; affiliate Columbia University, 1966–; United Cerebral Palsy Consultant, Suffolk Rehabilitation Center, 1962–65; Consultant Hebrew Home for Aged, 1962–70.

Memberships and awards: American Rheumatism Association; American Academy of Physical Medicine and Rehabilitation. Research in physiology of the elderly, disabled and chronically ill; disability in the poor, the black, the ghetto dweller.

Pub: About different view of the black disabled. *Encore,* v. 6, Sept. 12, 1977, p. 20.

Ref: *American Men and Women of Science,* 15th ed., p. 111.
In Black and White, p. 25.

Anderson, Arnett Artis   (1931– —— , M)

Dentist. Orthodontist. Born in Georgia, April 1, 1931. B.S., Howard University, 1953; Graduate School, Howard University, 1955–57; D.D.S., 1962; M.S., University of Michigan 1965. Institute of Health, Endocrinology research, 1956–58; Cardiovascular research, part-time, 1960–62; Director of Children's Orthodontic Clinic Livonia, MI; D.C. Board of Dental Examiners.

Memberships and awards: American Association of Orthodontists; Middle Atlantic Society of Orthodontists; American College of Dentists, American Association of Dental Examiners, National Dental Association; International Association of Dental Research, American Society of Dentistry for Children; Robert T. Freeman Dental Society; Alpha Phi Alpha; Best Thesis Award, University of

Michigan School of Orthodontics; C. Edward Martin Award, 1965; First Place International Competition in Dental Research; Edward H. Hitton Award, 1966; Outstanding Young Men of America; Omicron Kappa Upsilon National Honorary Dental Society; Sigma Xi; Beta Kappa Chi; Alpha Kappa Mu.

Ref: *Who's Who Among Black Americans*, 1980-81, p. 15.
Who's Who Among Black Americans, 1985, p. 17.

Anderson, Carey Laine   (1950– ——, M)

Architect. Born in Louisville, KY, Jan. 12, 1950. B.Arch., University of Kentucky, 1973. Architectural Draftsman, Arrowsmith, Judd Rapp & Associates, Architects, 1973-77; First black Architect licensed in Kentucky in 1977; Associate Project Architect and Project Architect, Robert F. Crump Architects, 1977-78; City Architect, City of Louisville Public Works Department, 1978-79.

Ref: *Who's Who Among Black Americans*, 1980-81, p. 15.
Who's Who Among Black Americans, 1985, p. 17.

Anderson, Carolyn Virginia Still   (1848-1919, F)

Physician. Born in Philadelphia, PA, 1848. B.A., Oberlin College, 1868; M.D., Women's Medical College of Philadelphia, 1878. She was the daughter of William Still, the abolitionist and the niece of James Still, the physician. She conducted a dispensary in connection with the work of the Berean Presbyterian Church in Philadelphia where her husband was the pastor.

Ref: *Historical Afro-American Biographies*, p. 45-46.
Profiles of Negro Womanhood, p. 217.
Send Us a Lady Physician, p. 110-111. [p]
Afro-American Encyclopedia, v. 1, p. 141.

Anderson, Charles A.   (1900s, M)

Pilot. First black to hold a Commercial Pilot's License. Helped train the pilots at Tuskegee during World War II.

Ref: *Strength for the Fight*, p. 143-144.

Anderson, Charles Edward   (1919– ——, M)

Meteorologist. Born in St. Louis, MO, Aug. 13, 1919. B.S., Lincoln University, MO, 1941; Certified in Meteorology, University of Chicago, 1943; M.S., Polytechnic Institute of Brooklyn, 1948; Ph.D. (meteorology), Massachusetts Institute of Technology, 1960. First known black Ph.D. in Meteorology; Chief Cloud Physics Branch, Air Force Cambridge Research Center, MA, 1948-61; Atmospheric Science Branch, Douglas Aircraft Co., CA, 1961-65; Director, Office of Federal Coordination in Meteorology, Environmental Science Service Administration, U.S. Department of Commerce, 1965-66; Professor of Space Science and Engineering, 1967-69; Professor of Meteorology and Chairman of Contemporary Trends

Course, University of Wisconsin, Madison, 1966–; Professor of Afro-American Studies and Chairman of the Department, 1970; Associate Dean, 1978–; Research in Cloud and Aerosal Physics and Meteorology of other Planets.

Memberships and awards: Chairman, Aviation Advisory Panel, National Center for Atmospheric Research, Colorado, 1963–; AAAS; Sigma Xi.

Dissertation title: Study of the Pulsating Growth of Cumulus Clouds.

Ref: *American Men and Women of Science*, 15th ed., p. 113.
Negroes in Science: Natural Science Doctorates, 1876-1969, p. 53.

Anderson, Edgar L., Jr.   (1931– ——, M)

Respiratory Therapist. Nurse. Born in New York, NY, Sept. 24, 1931. A.A.S., B.S., B.S.N., M.S. in Health Care Administration. St. Vincent's Medical Center, Chief Nurse Anesthetist, Respiratory Care Coordinator, 1967-70. State University of New York at Stonybrook, Director of Respiratory Education, 1970–; Associate Professor and Chairman of the Division of Cardiorespiratory School, School of Allied Health Professions Program, State University of New York.

Memberships and awards: Board of Directors of the American Association of Respiratory Therapies, 1973-76; Chairman, Board of Directors of the Federal Interagency Commission for AART; American Lung Association, Nassau/Suffolk County, NY, 1973–; Education Committee of the American Society of Allied Health Professionals, 1974–; American Registered Respiratory Therapist, 1970; Registered Professional Nurse, 1957; Certified Registered Nurse Anesthetist, 1959; Certified Hypno-Therapist; Society for Critical Care Medicine, 1974; Task Force Planning Committee of the University Hospital, Stonybrook; Consultant, Northport V.A. Hospital in Respiratory Care and Anesthesia; National Consultant for CardioRespiratory Therapy Education; Consultant in Hypnotherapy, Stress Center, Huntington, NY, 1980; Outstanding Educators of America—1972 nomination; Certificate of Appreciation, Cover Day; Bronze Plate from Stonybrook Emergency Medical Technicians.

Ref: *Who's Who Among Black Americans*, 1980-81, p. 18.
Who's Who Among Black Americans, 1985, p. 18.

Anderson, Everett   (1928– ——, M)

Cytologist. Born in Houston, TX, Aug. 12, 1928. B.A., Fisk University, 1949; M.A., 1951; Ph.D., University of Iowa, 1955. Assistant, Fisk University, 1947-51; Assistant Professor of Zoology, Texas Southern University, 1952; Assistant, University of Iowa, 1953; Research Associate, Colorado Medical Center, 1956-57; Instructor, Anatomy, Howard University Medical School, 1957-58; Research and Assistant Professor of Zoology, University of Iowa, 1958–61; Professor, University of Massachusetts, Amherst, 1961–. Research in the uses of the electron microscope on cell sections.

Memberships and awards: AAAS; American Society of Zoologists; Electron Microscopy Society of America; American Association of Anatomists; $82,000 U.S. Public Health Service Grant, 1962.

Dissertation title: The Electron Microscopy of *Trichomonas muris.*

Pub: The Meiotic Process: Pairing, Recombination, and Chromosome Movements: Papers. New York, MSS Information Corp., 1972. 2 v.
The Anatomy of Bovine & Ovine Pineals; Light & Electron Microscopic Studies. New York, Academic Press, 1965.

Ref: *American Men and Women of Science*, 12th ed., p. 114.
In Black and White, p. 26.
Ebony, Nov. 1962, p. 7. [p]

Anderson, Giovonnae   (1900s, F)

Engineer (electrical). B.S. (physics); M.S. (electrical engineering); Ph.D., University of California, Davis, 1979. Project Engineer Hewlett-Packard, Santa Rosa, CA.

Dissertation title: The Effect of Nonuniform Channel Doping on High Frequency JFET and MESFET.

Ref: *Black Collegian*, Aug./Sept. 1981, p. 187. [p]

Anderson, Gloria Long   (1938– ——, F)

Chemist (organic). Born in Altheimer, AZ, Nov. 5, 1938. B.S., A & M, Normal College, AR, 1958. M.S., Atlanta University, 1961; Ph.D. (organic chemistry), University of Chicago, 1968. Instructor in Chemistry, South Carolina State College, 1961–62; Morehouse College, 1962–64; Teaching and Research Assistant, University of Chicago, 1964–68; Professor in Summer School, South Carolina State College, 1967; Calloway Associate Professor and Chairman of the Chemistry Department, Morris Brown College, 1968–73; Professor and Chairman of the Chemistry Department, 1973–84; Chairman of the Natural Science Division and Dean of Academic Affairs, Morris Brown College, 1984–; Research in synthetic organic fluorine chemistry; fluorine-19 nuclear magnetic resonance spectroscopy.

Memberships and awards: AAAS; American Chemical Society; National Science Teachers Association; National Institute of Science; Georgia Academy of Science; New York Academy of Science; American Association of University Professors; Delta Sigma Theta; Atlanta University Science Research Institute; Alpha Kappa Mu, National Honor Society; Beta Kappa Chi Scientific Honor Society; Rockefeller Scholarship, 1956–58.

Dissertation title: Fluorine-19 Substituent Chemical Shifts of Bicyclic and Aromatic Molecules.

Ref: *American Men and Women of Science*, 15th ed., p. 117.
Dictionary of International Biography, 1986, p. 29.
In Black and White, p. 27.
Who's Who Among Black Americans, 1980–81, p. 16.
Who's Who Among Black Americans, 1985, p. 18.
Contributions of Black Women to America, v. 2, p. 438–439.

Anderson, James, Jr.   (1900s, M)

Military (Marine). Medal of Honor, 1968; first black Marine, Vietnam; 47th black serviceman. Pfc. Milton Olive was the first in Vietnam, 1965, Oct. 22.

Ref: *Jet*, Sept. 5, 1968, p. 49. [p]
Black Americans in Defense of Our Nation, p. 67. [p]

Anderson, Jo.   (1800s, M)

Inventor. Slave. A slave in the McCormick family who, according to McCormick's grandson, Cyrus, deserves honor as working beside McCormick in the building of the reaper. Because a black man assisted in the invention of the reaper, International Harvester has always had a non-discriminatory practice in hiring even in the south.

Ref: *The Negro Impact on Western Civilization*, p. 55.
Afro-American Encyclopedia, v. 5, p. 1275.
Ebony, Oct. 1964, p. 80. [p] of display in Chicago Museum of Science and Industry.

Anderson, John Alexander   (1937– ——, M)

Physician. Radiologist. Born in Gary, WV, Mar. 9, 1937. B.S., University of Chicago, 1958; M.D., Howard University College of Medicine, 1962. Interned Wright-Patterson Air Force Base Hospital, 1962–63; Residency in Radiology, 1965–68; Chief of Radiology, Davis-Monthau USAF Hospital, Tucson, AZ, 1963–65. Diplomate, American Board of Radiology, 1968; Radiologist and Director of Education, David Grant USAF Medical Center, Department of Radiology, Travis AF Base, 1968–71; Radiologist, Boulevard General Hospital, Sumby Hospital, and S.W. Detroit Hospital, 1971–; Radiologist and Chief of Radiology, Highland Park General Hospital, 1974–.

Memberships and awards: President and Founder of Southwest Medical Association, Inc., 1973–74; USAF Medical Corps, Major, 1961–71; Air Force Commendation Medal, 1968.

Pub: Anderson, J., and John Cornyn. Radiologic and pathologic diagnosis of tumors of the jaws. National Medical Association, *Journal*, v. 67, July 1975, p. 277–281.

Ref: *Who's Who Among Black Americans*, 1980–81, p. 17.
Who's Who Among Black Americans, 1985, p. 19.
ABMS Directory of Certified Radiologists, p. 11.

Anderson, John Thomas   (1892–19??, M)

Physician. Surgeon. Born in Charlotte, NC, July 29, 1892. B.A., Lincoln University, PA, 1913; M.D., University of Pennsylvania, 1917. Assistant Surgeon, Park Sanitarium, Guthrie, OK, 1918–19; Resident Surgeon, City Hospital, St. Louis, MO, 1919–20; Chief Surgeon, U.S. Veterans' Hospital, no. 91, Tuskegee, 1925–.

Memberships and awards: Alpha Phi Alpha.

Pub: Pre and post operative treatment, surgical. National Medical Association, *Journal.*

Ref: *Who's Who in Colored America,* 1927, p. 5.
     Who's Who in Colored America, 1928–29, p. 13.
     Who's Who in Colored America, 1930–32, p. 15.
     Who's Who in Colored America, 1938–80, p. 31.
     Who's Who in Colored America, 1941–44, p. 29.

Anderson, John Wesley   (1861–1947, M)

Physician. Born in Lexington, MO, May 30, 1861. B.A., University of Kansas, 1881; M.D., Meharry Medical College, 1885; Post-Graduate Course, University of Michigan, 1886; D.D.S., Meharry Dental School, 1887; D.N.T. (Doctor of Natural Therapeutics), Chicago University, 1889; Studied Phrenology, New York, NY, 1900. Taught and was Principal, Wyandotte High School from which he graduated, 1881–83; Lecturer in Anatomy and Chemistry while a dental student, 1885–87. Practiced general medicine among blacks, Hispanics and poor whites of Dallas for 60 years.

Memberships and awards: Gave large sums of money to Meharry for the construction of an anatomical hall named for him in 1917.

Ref: *Dictionary of American Medical Biography,* v. 1, p. 13.
     Cobb, W. Montague. Dr. John Wesley Anderson. National Medical Association, *Journal,* v. 45, Nov. 1953, p. 442–444. [p] on cover

Anderson, Peyton Fortine   (1890–1945, M)

Physician. Born in King William County, WV, Nov. 5, 1890. M.D., New York Medical College and Flower Hospital, 1913. Post-Graduate, University of Vienna, Austria, 1913–14. Licensed 1913 by examination in Connecticut and New York. Was among top 10 in a class of 65 finishing medical school, where he had been admitted without examination.

Memberships and awards: President, Cosmopolitan Medical Club; Medical Committee, Harlem Health Center; Chairman, Harlem Tuberculosis Committee; Tuberculosis Committee, City and Health Association; Manhatten Medical Society; Alpha Phi Alpha.

Ref: *Who's Who of the Colored Race,* 1915, p. 9–10.
     Who's Who in Colored America, 1927, p. 5.
     Who's Who in Colored America, 1930–32, p. 16.
     Who's Who in Colored America, 1938–40, p. 31–32.
     Who's Who in Colored America, 1941–44, p. 29.

Anderson, Robert Spencer   (1922– ——, M)

Physician. Internist. Born in Wilmington, DE, June 7, 1922. B.A., Lincoln University, 1946; M.D., Meharry Medical College, 1946; Health Association added a physician to its Board of Directors, 1964; Chairman, Department of Internal Medicine, Meharry Medical College; from Instructor to Associate Professor of Internal Medicine, George W. Hubbard Hospital, Nashville, TN, 1950–60; Chairman of the Department, 1960–69; Chairman, Administration Committee, 1966–68; Director of Comprehensive Health Service Program, 1969–72; Vice President, Health Service, 1972–75; Professor of Internal Medicine, Meharry Medical College, 1960–; fellow in Cardiology, George W. Hubbard Hospital, Nashville, TN, 1950–51; research fellow in Internal Medicine, College of Physicians and Surgeons, Colorado University, 1952–53; Instructor of Internal Medicine, George W. Hubbard, 1950–51; Acting Medical Director, 1958–60; Director, Fisk-Meharry Student Health Center, 1967–; Research in heart disease drug therapy and diabetes mellitus.

Memberships and awards: Diplomate American Board of Internal Medicine, 1954; Board of Crestview Convalescent Center and various other committees; American Medical Association; fellow American College of Physicians; American Diabetes Association; American Heart Association; National Medical Association.

Ref: *American Men and Women of Science,* 16th ed. p. 132–133.
     National Medical Association, *Journal,* v. 65, July 1973, p. 288. [p] (article by him)

Anderson, Russell Lloyd   (1907– ——, M)

Physician. Biologist. Morphologist. Born in Pittsburgh, PA, Jan. 12, 1907. B.S., University of Pittsburgh, 1928; M.S., 1930; Ph.D. (experimental morphology), 1934; M.D., Howard University Medical College, 1946. Professor of Biology, J. C. Smith University, 1930–43; Professor of Biology, Florida A & M University, 1946–50; Anderson-Brickler Medical Clinic, Tallahassee, FL, 1956–; Director of Student Health Services, Florida A & M, 1956–67.

Memberships and awards: National Medical Association; American Medical Association; AAAS; Sigma Xi.

Dissertation title: Skin Graft Reactions in Relations to Taxonomy in Urodeles of the Genus triturus. Published 1933.

Ref: *Holders of Doctorates Among American Negroes,* p. 185.
     Who's Who Among Black Americans, 1985, p. 20.
     American Men and Women of Science, 12th ed., p. 128.

Anderson, Subbeal Stewart   (1896–1961, M)

Dentist. Born in Richmond, VA, Mar. 23, 1896. B.A., Virginia Union University, 1919; D.D.S., Howard University, 1923; Post graduate work in Oral Surgery, New York University, 1924. Harlem Dentist for nearly 40 years; died Elmhurst Hospital in Queens.

Memberships and awards: Phi Beta Sigma (Vice President, 1927–29); North Harlem Dental Association.

Ref: *Who's Who in Colored America,* 1928–29, p. 13.
Who's Who in Colored America, 1930–32, p. 16.
Jet, (obit). Mar. 9. 1961, p. 12.
Who's Who in Colored America, 1933–37, p. 32. [p] p. 25.
Who's Who in Colored America, 1938–40, p. 32. [p] p. 25.
Who's Who in Colored America, 1941–44, p. 29–30. [p] p. 27.

Andrews, Bert   (1929- ——, M)

Photographer. Broadway Shows. Born in Chicago, IL, Mar. 21, 1929. Photographer for Charles Stewart Photography, 1953–57; Owner of Bert Andrews Photography, 1957–. Photographer for Equity Library Theatre, Actors Equity, Negro Ensemble Co., for many off-Broadway and Broadway plays, including "Bubbling Brown Sugar."

Ref: *Dawn Magazine,* April 1983, p. 17–18.
Who's Who Among Black Americans, 1985, p. 21.

Andrews, Ludie A.   (18??–19??, F)

Nurse. Nurse Training Course, Spelman College, 1906. Superintendent, Lula Grove Hospital and Training School for Colored Nurses and Patients for seven years; Superintendent of Students Infirmary, Morehouse College, 1920–28; Superintendent of Nurses, McVicker Hospital on the Spelman Campus. She secured registration for black nurses in the state of Georgia in 1920; Superintendent of black nurses Grady Hospital, Atlanta, Ga., where she organized the Municipal Training School for Colored Nurses, 1914–20. The nurses who graduated from her school have been able to pass state examinations in Alabama, North Carolina, South Carolina, Illinois, Pennsylvania, Connecticut, and New York.

Memberships and awards: NACGN Mary Mahoney Award, 1943; Grady Nurses Conclave presents a "Ludie Andrews Distinguished Service Award."

Ref: *Pathfinders,* p. 144–147, [p], after p. 96.
The Path We Tread, p. 156–157, [p], p. 156.

Anthony, Benjamin William   (1902- ——, M)

Physician. Radiologist. Born in Columbus, MS, 1902. B.A., Talladega College, 1922; B.S., University of Chicago, 1923; M.D., Rush Medical College, University of Chicago, 1927. Specialist in Department of Roentgenology, Billings Hospital, University of Chicago. Fellow of the Rockefeller Foundation for three years. He was Head of the Department of Roentgenology, Greater Provident Hospital, Chicago, IL. He and Dr. Paul C. Hedges gave a demonstration on "Estimation of Cardiac Area in Children" before the American Medical Association which met in Milwaukee, WI.

Memberships and awards: American College of Radiology; American Medical Association; National Medical Association.

Ref: *Who's Who in Colored America,* 1933–37, p. 32.
Who's Who in Colored America, 1938–1940, p. 32.
ABMS Directory of Certified Medical Specialists, v. 5, p. 899.

Antoine, Albert Cornelius   (1925- ——, M)

Chemist (organic). Born in New York, NY, Jan. 14, 1925. B.S., City College of New York, 1946; Ph.D. (chemistry), Ohio State University, 1953. Control Chemist, Penetone Company, NJ, 1947–48; Associate Professor, Chemistry, Clark College, 1953–54; Aircraft Engine Research Laboratory (now NASA Lewis Research Center), 1954–; research in photochemistry.

Memberships and awards: American Chemical Society.

Ref: *American Men of Science,* 11th ed., p. 123.
Blacks in Science: Astrophysicist to Zoologist, p. 37–38. [p] after p. 48.
Profiles in Excellence, p. 5 [p]

Apea, Joseph Bennet Kyeremateny   (1932- ——, M)

Engineer (civil). Born in Aburi, Ghana, Aug. 19, 1932. B.C.E., Illinois Institute of Technology, 1968; Architecture, University of Illinois. Civil Engineer, Westenhoff & Novic, Inc., Chicago, 1961–64; Kaiser Engineers, Chicago, Structural Engineer, 1964–65; Structural Engineer, Sargent & Lundy Engineers, Chicago, 1965–72; President, Samuels, Apea & Associates, Inc. 1972–80.

Memberships and awards: National Society of Professional Engineers; American Society of Civil Engineers; Illinois Association of Structural Engineers.

Ref: *Black Engineers in the United States,* p. 7.
Who's Who Among Black Americans, 1980–81, p. 20.
Who's Who Among Black Americans, 1985, p.22.

Arbulu, Augustin   (1928- ——, M)

Physician. Surgeon (thoracic). Born in Lima, Peru, Sept. 15, 1928. U.S. Citizen. B.M., San Marcos University, Lima, 1954; M.D., 1955. Assistant Chief Surgeon, Wichita V.A. Hospital, KS, 1961–62; Instructor to Associate Professor, 1962–72; Professor of Surgery, School of Medicine, Wayne State University, MI, 1972–. Removed tricuspid valve from drug addict and he lived.

Memberships and awards: American College of Surgeons; Cecile Lehman Mayer Research Award; American College of Chest Physicians Regent's Award, 1972; American Thoracic Society; Society of Thoracic Surgeons; President, Peruvian American Medical Society, 1973–74.

Ref: *Jet,* Dec. 16, 71, p. 27. [p]
        American Men and Women of Science, 14th ed., p. 124.

Archer, Juanita Almetta   (1934- ——, F)

Physician. Internist. Endocrinologist. Born in Washington, DC, Nov. 3, 1934. B.S., Howard University, 1956; M.S., 1958; M.D., 1965. NIH, 1970-73; Instructor in Department of Medicine, 1973-75; Associate Professor, Medicine and Director of Endocrine/Metabolic Laboratory, Howard University Hospital, 1977-; Josiah Macy faculty fellow, Department of Internal Medicine, Howard University, 1974-. Research in physiological significance of insulin receptors in man with studies to determine whether insulin receptors can be altered so as to effect better diabetic therapy.

Memberships and awards: Fellow in Endocrinology, 1969-70; Endocrine Society; American Federation of Clinical Research; Sigma Xi; Beta Kappa Chi; DC Medical Society; New York Academy of Science; Delta Sigma Theta; General Clinical Research Commission; Physician's Recognition Award, 1983-86.

Pub: Archer, J. A., R. Knopp, J. Olefsky, and C. R. Shuman. *Clinical Diabetes Update 11.* Upjohn Monograph. Jan. 1980.
        Archer, J. A., P. Gorden and J. Roth. Defect in insulin binding to receptors. *Clinical Investigations,* v. 55, 1975, p. 166-175.

Ref: *American Men and Women of Science,* 16th ed., p. 161.
        Who's Who Among Black Americans, 1985, p. 23.

Armstrong, Prince Winston   (1938- ——, F)

Mathematician. Born in Montgomery, AL, April 25, 1938. B.S., Alabama State University, 1958; M.S. (mathematics), Atlanta University; D.Ed., University of Oklahoma, 1972. Instructor Spelman College, 1959-60; Assistant Professor of Mathematics, Albany State College, 1960-61; Instructor of Mathematics, Southern University, 1965-67; Visiting Instructor in Mathematics, Atlanta University, summers 1961-62; Associate Professor of Mathematics, Southern University (Baton Rouge), 1972-.

Memberships and awards: Alpha Kappa Mu; Beta Kappa Chi; Pi Mu Epsilon; fellow, Atlanta University, 1959.

Dissertation title: The Ability of Fifth and Sixth Graders to Learn Selected Topics in Probability.

Ref: *Black Mathematicians and Their Works,* p. 277. [p]
        National Faculty Directory, 1986, p. 97.
        Who's Who in American Education, 1967-68, p. 33.

Armstrong, Wiley T.   (1909- ——, M)

Physician. Born in Rocky Mount, NC, Feb. 11, 1909. B.S., Shaw University, 1929; Graduate work in Physical Education, Harvard University; attended Columbia University; M.D., Meharry Medical College, 1944.

Memberships and awards: President, National Medical Association, 1970-71; Secretary-Treasurer, Old North State Medical Society, 1954-; Chairman, Board of Trustees, National Medical Association; Chairman, Board of Trustees, North Carolina Central University, 1973-; Omega Psi Phi; Doctor of the Year, Old North State Medical Society, 1954; Achievement Award, National Medical Association, 1972; Alumni Award, Meharry Medical College, 1972.

Ref: National Medical Association, *Journal,* v. 57, Mar. 1965, p. 1983. [p]
        National Medical Association, *Journal,* v. 62, Jan. 1970, p. 62-63. [p] Biog.
        Who's Who Among Black Americans, 1985, p. 24.

Arrington, Richard, Jr.   (1934- ——, M)

Zoologist (invertebrate). Born in Livingston, AL, Oct. 19, 1934. B.A., Miles College, 1955; M.S., University of Detroit, 1957; Ph.D. (zoology), University of Oklahoma, 1966. Assistant Professor, 1957-61; Professor of Biology, Miles College, 1966-; Dean, 1965-; Research in insect morphology; Executive Director, Alabama Center for Higher Education, 1970-79; Mayor of Birmingham, Ala. 1979-.

Memberships and awards: American Institute of Biological Sciences; Oklahoma Academy of Sciences; AAAS; American Society of Zoologists; Phi Sigma National Biological Society; Sigma Xi; Alpha Phi Alpha; Ortenburger Award for Outstanding Work in Biology, University of Oklahoma, 1966; Alpha Phi Alpha Man of the Year, 1969; Charles A. Billups Community Service Award, 1972; Public Service Award, Birmingham Chapter of Delta Sigma Theta, 1974.

Dissertation title: Comparative Morphology of Some Dryopoid Beetles.

Ref: *American Men and Women of Science,* 15th ed., p. 175.
        Who's Who Among Black Americans, 1985, p. 26.
        Who's Who in America, 1986-87, p. 92.

Arrington-Idowu, Elayne   (1940- ——, F)

Mathematician. Born in Pittsburgh, PA, Feb. 3, 1940. B.S., University of Pittsburgh, 1961; M.S., University of Dayton, 1968; Ph.D. (mathematics), University of Cincinnati, 1974. Aerospace Engineer, Wright-Patterson AFB, 1962-66; Instructor, University of Cincinnati, 1973-74; Faculty member, University of Pittsburgh, 1974-.

Memberships and awards: American Mathematical Society; Mathematical Association of America.

Dissertation title: The p-Frattini Subgroup of a Finite Group.

Pub: p-Saturated Formations, *Israel Journal of Mathematics,* Nov. 1978.

Ref: Kenschaft, Patricia C. "Black Women in Mathematics in the United States," *American Mathematical Monthly*, v. 88, Oct. 1981, p. 600–601.
American Men and Women of Science, 16th ed., p. 936 (under Idowu).

Ashley, Harry E.   (1896–19??, M)

Pharmacist. Manufacturer (pharmaceuticals). Born in Philadelphia, PA, July 19, 1896. Philadelphia School of Industrial Arts; Temple University Preparatory School, Philadelphia; Ph.G., Temple University School of Pharmacy, 1921. Proprietor of ACO Chemical Laboratories; manufacturer of pharmaceutical preparations.

Memberships and awards: State Medical Association; Academy of Medicine and Allied Sciences; National Medical Association; Kappa Alpha Psi.

Ref: *Who's Who in Colored America*, 1930–32, p. 20.

Ashley, William Ford   (1920– ——, M)

Chemist. Born in Pittsburgh, PA, Mar. 14, 1920. B.S., Duquesne University, 1948. Research Chemist, Frankford Arsenal, 1948. Research in the kinetics of gaseous reactions; Theoretical interpretation of pilot plant processes.

Memberships and awards: American Chemical Society; Research Society of America.

Ref: *The Negro in Science*, p. 181.

Atkins, Cyril Fitzgerald   (1899–19??, M)

Chemist. Educator. Inventor. Born in Barbados, B.W.I., July 15, 1899. B.S. (chemistry), Tufts College, Boston, MA, 1924; M.S., University of Iowa, 1925; Ph.D., 1936. Professor of Chemistry, A & T College, Greensboro, NC, 1926–29; Professor of Chemistry, Wiley College, Marshall, TX, 1929–31; Professor of Chemistry, Johnson C. Smith University, 1931–47; Morgan State College, 1947–; with Office of Production Research and Development, 1944; with Ulysses Simpson Brooks he discovered a new paper producing process for the manufacture of corrugated shipping containers from cotton stems usually left standing in fields after the cotton is picked.

Memberships and awards: AAAS; American Chemical Society; Omega Psi Phi.

Dissertation title: Formyl Derivatives of Orthoaminophenols and Their Relations to Molecular Rearrangement.

Pub: Preparation of Phynyl Mustard Oils of Selenium.
The Relative Activity of the Alcoholic and Phenolic Hydroxides in Certain Types of Chemical Change.

Ref: *American Men and Women of Science*, 11th ed., p. 160.
Holders of Doctorates Among American Negroes, p. 142.
Who's Who in Colored America, 1930–32, p. 20.
Who's Who in Colored America, 1938–40, p. 34.
Who's Who in Colored America, 1941–44, p. 33.
The Negro in Science, p. 181.

Negro Yearbook, 1947, p. 30.
Crisis, Jan. 1936, p. 21.

Atkins, Leland L.   (1917– ——, M)

Physician. Surgeon. Born in Oberlin, OH, June 23, 1917. B.S., West Virginia State College; M.D., Meharry Medical College. Staff of Terrell Memorial Hospital and Collins Chapel.

Memberships and awards: C. V. Mosby Awards for Surgery, Pediatrics, Obstetrics and Gynecology as a resident, Cleveland City Hospital; Alpha Delta Sigma Scholastic Society; Kappa Pi Honorary Medical Society.

Ref: *The National Register*, 1952, p. 548–549.
Jet, June 19, 1958, p. 29.

Atkinson, Whittier Cinclair   (1893–19??, M)

Physician. Born in Brunswick, GA, April 23, 1893. B.S., Howard University, 1922; M.D., 1925. Founder of Clement Atkinson Memorial Hospital, a 30-bed interracial hospital. For years he was the only doctor in Coatsville, PA.

Memberships and awards: General Practitioner of the Year, 1960, by the Pennsylvania Medical Society, first Black; President, National Medical Association, 1952–53; President, Philadelphia Academy of Medicine and Allied Sciences; Chester County Medical Society; Pennsylvania State Medical Association; American Medical Association; American Academy of General Practice; General Alumni Council of Howard University.

Ref: *Who's Who Among Black Americans*, 1985, p. 29.
Jet, Aug. 11, 1960, p. 48. [p]
National Medical Association, *Journal*, v. 43, 1951, p. 405. [p]
National Medical Association, *Journal*, v. 48, 1956, p. 206. [p]
National Medical Association, *Journal*, v. 50, July 1958, p. 294. [p]
National Medical Association, *Journal*, v. 53, Jan. 1961, p. 85. [p]

Atwood, Rufus Ballard   (1897–19??, M)

Agriculturist. College President. Born in Hickman, KY, Mar. 15, 1897. B.S., Fisk University, 1920; B.S. (agricultural education), Iowa State College, 1923. Director of Agriculture, Prairie View College, TX, 1923–29. Trying to bring more advanced ideas of scientific farming to 500,000 black farmers. President of Kentucky State Industrial College, Frankford, KY, 1929–.

Memberships and awards: Secretary of the Conference of Presidents of Negro Land Grant Colleges; Alpha Phi Alpha; Board of Directors, Association of Negro Colleges; Chairman of the Executive Committee, Fisk University Alumni.

Ref: *Who's Who in Colored America,* 1928–29, p. 17.
        Who's Who in Colored America, 1930–32, p. 20.
        Who's Who in Colored America, 1938–40, p. 34.
        Who's Who in Colored America, 1941–44, p. 34.

Augusta, Alexander Thomas   (1825–1890, M)

Physician. Surgeon. Born in Norfolk, VA, Mar. 8, 1825. M.D., Trinity Medical College of Toronto, 1856. He was later in charge of Toronto City Hospital. First Black doctor to head Freedmen's Hospital, Washington, DC. He was the only Black on the original five member faculty of Howard University Medical School and the first Black on the faculty of any medical school. One of the few Blacks to become a Surgeon in the U.S. Army, appointed April 14, 1863, with the rank of Major; first Black to hold a medical commission.

Memberships and awards: He was presented, along with Dr. C. B. Purvis, as a trial for membership to the white Medical Society of the District of Columbia in 1869 but was refused admission and again rejected in 1870.

Ref: *Afro-American Encyclopedia,* v. 1, p. 174.
        Cobb, W. M. "Alexander Thomas Augusta," National Medical Association, *Journal,* v. 44, July 1952. p. 327–329. [p] on cover.
        Dictionary of American Medical Biography, p. 23. [p] p. 37.
        Dictionary of American Negro Biography, p. 19–20.
        Encyclopedia of Black America, p. 144.
        History of the Negro in Medicine, p. 37, 52–57. [p]
        Howard University Medical Department: Historical, Biographical & Statistical Souvenir, p. 110–111. [p]
        Journal of Negro History, v. 32, Jan. 1947, p. 10–80.
        Journal of Negro History, v. 1, April 1969, p. 99–109.
        Jet, April 14, 1960, p. 9.
        Send Us a Lady Physician, p. 109.

B

Bacon-Berey, June   (1934– ——, F)

Meterologist. Born in June 1934. In 1979 became Chief Administrator of TV activities for NOAA.

Ref: *Black Women Achievements Against Odds,* p. 39.

Badger, Robert   (1829–????, M)

Dentist. Born in DeKalb County, GA, in 1829. His father was a white dentist and his mother was a black woman. He and his brother, Roderick, learned dentistry from their father. Although there was a petition presented in 1859 to the Atlanta City Council, he and his brother continued to practice in Atlanta and became leading citizens.

Ref: *Nine Black American Doctors,* p. 12.

Badger, Roderick   (1834–????, M)

Dentist. Born in DeKalb County, GA, in 1834. His father was a white dentist and his mother a black woman. He and his brother, Robert, learned dentistry from their father. Although there was a petition presented in 1859 to the Atlanta City Council, he and his brother continued to practice and became leading citizens in Atlanta.

Ref: *Nine Black American Doctors,* p. 12.

Bailes, William   (1800s, M)

Inventor. Patent #218,154, Aug. 5, 1879, for a ladder scaffold-support.

Ref: *Afro-American Encyclopedia,* v. 1, p. 178.
        Negro Almanac, 4th ed., p. 1069.

Bailey, L. C.   (1800s, M)

Inventor. Folding bed used in upper berth in a Pullman compartment for riding trains long distances, patent #629,286 in 1899; invented a combined truss and bandage, Sept. 25, 1983, patent #485,545.

Ref: *At Last Recognition in America,* v. 1, p. 43.

Bailey, Margaret E.   (19??– ——, F)

Military (Army). Colonel. Nurse (psychiatric). Born in Selma, AL. R.N., Fraternal Hospital School of Nursing, Montgomery, AL; Certificate in Psychiatric Nursing, Brooke Army Medical Center; B.A., San Francisco State College, 1959. First black nurse to attain rank of Colonel, 1970; Head Nurse on a psychiatric nursing service.

Ref: *The Path We Tread,* p. 171–172. [p] p. 172.
        Encyclopedia of Black America, v. 1, p. 178–179.
        Ebony, Sept. 1966, p. 50, 52, 52. [p]

Bailey, Walter Thomas   (1884–19??, M)

Architect. Born in Kewanee, IL, Jan. 11, 1884. B.S., University of Illinois, 1904; M.A. (architecture), 1910. Draftsman for Henry Eckland, Kewanee and for Spencer & Temple, Champaign, IL, 1905; Head, Architectural Department, Tuskegee Institute, 1905–1914. Architect in Memphis beginning in 1914.

Ref: *Who's Who of the Colored Race,* 1915, p. 16.
        Who's Who in Colored America, 1928–29, p. 18–19.
        Who's Who in Colored America, 1930–32, p. 22.
        Who's Who in Colored America, 1933–37, p. 38.
        Who's Who in Colored America, 1938–40, p. 38.
        Who's Who in Colored America, 1941–44, p. 38.

Bailliff, C. O.   (1800s, F)

Inventor. Patent #612,008, Oct. 11, 1898, for a shampoo headrest.

Ref: *Afro-American Encyclopedia,* v. 1, p. 181. [p] of head-
        rest.
        The Negro Almanac, p. 1069.

Baker, David   (1881–19??, M)

Inventor. Born in Louisville, KY, April 2, 1881. Took a
course from Media Night School in New Orleans and
from National Correspondence School, Washington, DC.
In charge of the elevator service of the Board of Trade
Building, New Orleans, for 10 years. Invented scales for
use in elevators to prevent overloading. Also invented a
sanitary cuspidor with Professor T. V. Baquet of New Orleans. Also invented street car transom opener, railway
signal apparatus to be adjacent to railway bridges over
streams.

Ref: *Who's Who of the Colored Race,* 1915, p. 16.

Baker, Percy Hayes   (1906– ——, M)

Zoologist. Born in Williamsburg, VA, April 17, 1906. B.S.,
University of Pittsburgh; M.S., 1930; Ph.D. (zoology, genetics), 1944. Instructor in Biology, North Carolina College for Negroes, 1930–34; from instructor to Professor,
Virginia State College, 1934–49; Professor, Morgan State
College, 1949–50; Program Director, American Friends
Service Committee, 1950–58; Professor of Biology;
1958–69; Chairman, Division of Natural Science,
1963–66; Department of Biology, 1966–69; Dean of the
College, 1969–72; Professor Biology, Morgan State University, 1969–.

Memberships and awards: AAAS; Society for Experimental Biology and Medicine; Genetics Society of America.

Dissertation title: The Influence of Environmental Factors on
        the Expression of the Pufdi Gene in Drosophila Me-
        lanogaster.

Ref: *American Men and Women of Science,* 14th ed., p. 200.

Baker, Thomas Nelson, Jr.   (1906– ——, M)

Chemist (organic). Born in Pittsfield, MA, July 6, 1906.
B.A., Oberlin College, 1929; M.S., 1930; Ph.D. (organic
chemistry), Ohio State University, 1941. Instructor in
Chemistry, Tougaloo College, 1930–31; Acting Assistant
Professor, Talladega College, 1931–32; Associate Profes-
sor, Virginia State College, 1932–44; Professor, 1944–.

Memberships and awards: Chemical Society; General
Education Board fellow, Ohio State, 1937–38.

Dissertation title: The Molecular Size of Glycogen and of Man-
        nan A by the Mercaptalation Method.

Ref: *American Men and Women of Science,* 11th ed., p. 211.
        National Register, 1952, p. 252.
        Holders of Doctorates Among American Negroes, p.
        142–143. .

Ballard, William Henry   (1862–19??, M)

Pharmacist. Born in Franklin Co., KY, Oct. 31, 1862.
Took special course at Roger William University, Nashville, TN; graduate in Pharmacy, Northwestern University, Chicago, IL, 1892. Opened Ballard's Pharmacy, Lexington, KY, 1893. First Black to open a drug store in
Kentucky.

Ref: *Who's Who of the Colored Race,* 1915, p. 17.

Ballow, W. J.   (1800s, M)

Inventor. Patent #601,422, Mar. 29, 1898, for a combined
hatrack and table.

Ref: *Afro-American Encyclopedia,* v. 1, p. 190. [sketch of ha-
        track]
        The Negro Almanac, p. 1069.

Baltimore, Jeremiah Daniel   (1852–19??, M)

Engineer. Machinist. Inventor. Born in Washington, DC,
April 15, 1852. Graduated from Franklin Institute, 1873.
Went to Navy Yard as an apprentice, transferred to Philadelphia Navy Yard. In spite of the fact that his coworkers refused to show him or help him, he completed
his apprenticeship. Worked for Sellers & Bros., U.S.
Coast Survey and Freedmen's Hospital as an engineer. He
made an engine which was placed on exhibition in the
public school and carried to the Patent Office. Invented
the pyrometer.

Memberships and awards: He was the second black
admitted to the Franklin Institute of Philadelphia; Royal
Society for the Encouragement of Art, Manufacturers
and Commerce of London.

Ref: *Men of Mark,* p. 166–170. 1970 ed. [p]
        Afro-American Enclyclopedia, v. 1, p. 191.
        Crisis, Feb. 1924, p. 181. [p]

Banks, Floyd Regan, Jr.   (1913– ——, M)

Physicist. Born in Philadelphia, PA, Mar. 14, 1913. B.A.,
Temple University, 1934; M.A., University of Pennsylvania, 1935; Ph.D., 1939. Instructure in Physics and Chemistry, Morgan State College, 1939–40; Assistant Professor
of Physical Science, 1942–50; Staff Member of the Radiation Laboratory, Massachusetts Institute of Technology,
1942–45; Member of the Staff of Haskins Laboratories,
1945–.

Memberships and awards: Physical Society; Frazier
fellow.

Dissertation title: The Measurement of Self-Diffusion by
        Means of Radioactive Isotopes.

Ref: *American Men of Science,* 9th ed., p. 83.
        Holders of Doctorates Among American Negros, p. 143.
        The Negro in Science, p. 189.

Negro Year Book, 1947, p. 44 (List of publications up to 1946)

Banks, Harvey Washington (1923–198?, M)

Astronomer. Astrophysicist. Born in Atlantic City, NJ, Feb. 7, 1923. B.S., Howard University, 1946; M.S., 1948; Ph.D. (astronomy), Georgetown University, 1961. Research Assistant in Physics, Howard University, 1948–50; Engineer, National Electronics, Inc., 1952–54; Teacher, Public Schools of DC, 1954–56; Research Assistant in Astronomy, Georgetown College Observatory, 1956–61; Lecturer and Research Associate, 1963–67; fellow, Georgetown University, 1961–62; Professor of Astronomy and Mathematics and Director of the Observatory, Delaware State College Observatory, 1967–69; Associate Professor of Astronomy, 1969–71; Associate Professor of Physics, Howard University, 1971–; Coordinator of Astronomy and Associate Director of Comprehensive Science, 1970–.

Memberships and awards: American Astronomical Society.

Dissertation title: The First Spectrum of Titanium from 6000 to 3000 Angstroms.

Ref: *American Men and Women of Science,* 14th ed., p. 220.
Negroes in Science Natural Science Doctorates, 1876–1969, p. 53.

Banks, Jerry L. (1943– ——, M)

Medical artist. Born in Sikeston, MO, Nov. 3, 1943. Worsham School of Mortuary Science, 1967; B.S., Lincoln University, 1969; Medical Art Degree, University of Illinois School of Medical Illustrations, 1972. Pathology Assistant, Hektoen Institue, 1967–68; Teacher, Chicago, IL, 1970–71; Research Assistant, Medical Opportunity Program, University of Illinois, 1971–72; Director of Anatomy Museum, University of Illinois Medical School, 1972–.

Memberships and awards: Alpha Phi Alpha; Afam Art Gallery; National Conference of Artists.

Pub: *Functional Human Anatomy; The Regional Approach.* Black Artist Guild, 1965.

Ref: *Who's Who Among Black Americans,* 1980–81, p. 34.
Ebony, Feb. 1973, p. 6. [p]

Banneker, Benjamin (1731–1806, M)

Inventor. Surveyor. Almanac Maker. Astronomer. Mathematician. Born in Ellicott's Mills, MD, Nov. 9, 1731. He attended Quaker School near Joppa, MD. He helped plan the city of Washington, DC, with L'Enfant in 1790. When L'Enfant left America and took his plans with him, Banneker reproduced them from memory in two days. Banneker published an almanac in 1792; wrote a dissertation on bees and did a study of locust plaque cycles; he wrote a famous letter to Thomas Jefferson on segregationist trends in America. His earliest invention was a wooden striking clock, 1761—it was the first clock of its kind built in the United States; accurately predicted an eclipse of April 14, 1789 from his own calculations. He died in Baltimore, MD, 1806.

Ref: *National Cyclopedia of American Biography,* v. 5, p. 36.
The Hidden Contributors.
Biographical Dictionary of American Science, p. 23.
Walton, Norman W. "The Price of Birth: Benjamin Franklin vs. Benjamin Banneker." *Negro History Bulletin,* Jan. 1955, p. 79.
Black Pioneers of Science & Invention, p. 1–12.
Your Most Humble Servant, Shirley Graham, New York, 1949.
American Negro Reference Book.
Black Mathematicians and Their Works, p. 277.
Dictionary of American Negro Biography, p. 22–25.
Encyclopedia of Black America, p. 158.
Great Negroes Past and Present, p. 18.
Life of Benjamin Banneker, Silvio Belini, New York, Scribner, 1971.
Men of Mark, 1970 ed., p. 224–228.
Who Was Who in American History: Science & Technology, p. 34.
Historical Afro-American Biographies, p. 9. [p]
The Role of the American Negro in the Fields of Science, p. 9–11.
Afro-American Encyclopedia, v. 1, p. 194–198. [p]
Significant American Blacks.
Seven Black American Scientists.
Scientists in the Black Perspective.
Webster's American Biographies, p. 62.
Ebony, Mar. 1964, p. 48–50, 52–54, 56–58. [p]
Zimmerman, Jesse. A Secretary of Peace. *Crisis,* April 1950, p. 214–218.
Journal of Negro History, v. 3, 19.

Barabin, Joseph Hercules (1874–19??, M)

Physician. Born in Jeannerette on the Le Tache Bayou, Iberia, LA, Mar. 19, 1874. B.A., Fisk University, 1900; M.D., Illinois Medical College, 1905. Practiced in Marianna, AR, having passed medical exam with second best exam in the state of Arkansas.

Memberships and awards: Received special diploma for excellence in scholarship in medical school, given to only 13 previous students; Resident on Board of Directors, President Hospital and Nurse Training School of Arkansas; President, Arkansas Association of Negro Physicians, Surgeons, Dentists and Pharmacists.

Ref: *Beacon Lights of the Race,* p. 325–332. Biog. & [p]
Who's Who of the Colored Race, 1915, p. 18.

Barber, Jesse Belmary, Jr. (1924– ——, M)

Physician. Surgeon. Neurosurgeon. Born in Chattanooga, TN, June 22, 1924. Attended Swift Memorial Junior College, Hampton Institute and Yale University; B.A., Lincoln University; M.D., Howard University Medical College, 1948. Instructor in Surgery and Pathology, 1956–58; McGill University Neurological Institute, Resident 1958–61; Professor of Surgery, Howard University College of Medicine, Chief Division of Neurosurgery, 1961–; Founder and Director, Howard University Medical Stroke Project, 1968–70.

Memberships and awards: President, National Medical Association, 1977–78; President, Washington Academy of Neurosurgery, 1973–74; Neuro-Psychiatric Section, National Medical Association, 1974–76; National Capital Medical Foundation, 1974–75; House of Delegates, National Medical Association, 1973–74; National Advisory Committee, Epilepsy Foundation of America; Executive Committee for Strokes, American Heart Association; Kappa Pi; Alpha Omega Alpha; fellow, American College of Surgeons, 1963; Student Council Award for Outstanding Professor, Howard University, 1966; William Alonzo Warfield Award, 1974; Distinguished Surgeon Award, National Medical Association, 1984; American Board of Neurosurgery, certified 1963.

Ref: *Who's Who Among Black Americans*, 1985, p. 40.
National Medical Association, *Journal*, v. 71, Jan. 1979, p. 87. [p] Inaugural Address.
National Medical Association, *Journal*, v. 71, June 1979. [p] cover
A Century of Black Surgeons, p. 27.

Barker, Prince Patanilla (1897–19??, M)

Physician. Neurologist. Psychiatrist. Born in Barbados, B.W.I., Dec. 15, 1897. B.A., City College of New York, 1918; M.D., Howard University Medical College, 1923; Columbia University, 1939. Neuropsychiatrist, Veterans Administration Hospital, 1924–47; Specialist in Neuropsychiatry, 1927–36; Chief, Acute Service, 1936–46; Neuropsychiatric Services, 1946–56; Director of Professional Services, 1956–58; Hospital Manager, 1958–59; Private practice in Psychiatry, New York, NY, 1959–; Consultant, John A. Andrew Memorial Hospital. Tuskegee Institute and Director of the Mental Hygiene Clinic, 1951; Attending Staff of Neuropsychiatry, Harlem Hospital, 1959–.

Memberships and awards: AAAS; National Association of Mental Health; fellow, American Medical Association; fellow, Psychiatric Association; Association of Military Surgeons; National Medical Association; fellow, College of Physicians; fellow, New York Academy of Medicine.

Pub: Results and Observations on Insulin Shock Therapy in Negro Ex-Service men, paper accepted for presentation at the May 1941 meeting of the American Psychiatric Association in Richmond, VA.

Ref: *American Men of Science*, 11th ed., p. 242.
National Medical Association, *Journal*, v. 33, Mar. 1941, p. 91.

National Medical Association, *Journal*, v. 27, Nov. 1935, p. 147. Has list of publications.
National Medical Association, *Journal*, v. 51, Nov. 1959, p. 479. [p]

Barnes, G. A. E. (1800s, M)

Inventor. Patent #29,193, Aug. 19, 1889, for a design for a sign.

Ref: *Afro-American Encyclopedia*, v. 1, p. 202.
Negro Almanac, p. 1069.

Barnes, Julia O. (1937- ——, F)

Military (Navy). Captain. Nurse. Born in Henderson, NC, 1937. Nursing diploma from Hahnemann Hospital School for Nursing; Entered the Navy in 1958. Executive Officer, Naval Hospital, Camp Lejeune, NC; Director, Nursing Service, U.S. Naval Hospital, Portsmouth, VA; Commander, Naval Hospital, Great Lakes, IL, one of the Navy's largest medical complexes.

Memberships and awards: National Naval Officers Association.

Ref: *Jet*, Sept. 1, 1986.
The Path We Tread, p. 177–178. [p] p. 178.
Ebony, Dec. 1981, p. 6. [p]

Barnes, Robert Percy (1898–19??, M)

Chemist (organic). Born in Washington, DC, Feb. 26, 1898. B.A., Amherst College, 1921; M.A., Harvard, 1930; Ph.D. (chemistry), 1933. Research Assistant in Chemistry at Amherst College, 1921–22; from Instructor to Professor, Howard University, 1922–45.

Memberships and awards: General Education Board fellow, Harvard, 1928–31; National Science Foundation Board, 1950–58; Phi Beta Kappa.

Dissertation title: The Reaction and Keto-Enol Equilibria of an Alpha Diketone.

Pub: The Second Order Beckmann Rearrangement.
Steric Hindrance in Alpha Diketones.
Contribution in scientific journals.

Ref: *American Men and Women of Science*, 12th ed., p. 296.
Holders of Doctorates Among American Negroes, p. 143.
The Negro in Science, p. 181.
Negro Yearbook, 1947. (List of publications up to 1946)
The Role of the American Negro in the Fields of Science, p. 48.
Scientists in the Black Perspective.
Crisis, Oct. 1933, p. 233. [p] only

Barnes, William Harry (1887–1945, M)

Physician. Otolaryngologist. Inventor. Surgeon. Born in Philadelphia, PA, April 4, 1887. B.S., M.D., University of Pennsylvania, 1908–12. Ear, Nose and Throat, 1920–21; University of Paris, 1924; O.R.L., University of Bordeaux, 1924. Consultant Otolaryngologist, Mercy Hospital, 1924. Lecturer on Bronchoscopy, Howard University, 1931; Inventor of an instrument to facilitate the approach of the pituitary gland; Chief of Otolaryngology, Jefferson Medical College Hospital.

Memberships and awards: American Medical Association; Alpha Phi Alpha; President, National Medical Association, 1935–36; Philadelphia Academy of Medicine; American Board of Otolaryngology, 1927–; Scholarship to Medical School, University of Pennsylvania. For years he was the only certified black specialist; Society for the Promotion of Negro Specialists in Medicine.

Pub: Numerous monographs, articles in medical journals.

Ref: Cobb, W. Montague. "William Harry Barnes, 1887–1945," National Medical Association, *Journal,* v. 47, Jan. 1955, p. 64–66. [p] cover
Dictionary of American Medical Biography, p. 37–38.
History of the Negro in Medicine, p. 105–106. [p]
National Medical Association, *Journal,* v. 27, Nov. 1935, p. 1. [p]
Who's Who in Colored America, 1927, p. 10.
Who's Who in Colored America, 1928–29, p. 422.
Who's Who in Colored America, 1930–32, p. 26–27.
Who's Who in Colored America, 1933–37, p. 43. [p] p. 41.
National Medical Association, *Journal,* v. 62, Nov. 1970, p. 435. [p]

Barnett, Constantine Clinton   (1869–1935, M)

Physician. Born in New Canton, VA, Nov. 30, 1869. B.S., University of Michigan, 1896; M.D., Howard University, 1899. Founded Barnett Hospital and Nurse Training School in Huntington, WV and helped establish a mental hospital for blacks in WV in 1926. The Barnett Hospital and Nurse Training School became the largest and best-equipped private hospital of its kind and was later taken over by the city of Huntington as a hospital for both white and black.

Memberships and awards: National Medical Association; Central Tri-State Medical Association; First Mental Hygiene Association; American Hospital Association; State Medical Association.

Ref: *Crisis,* Sept. 1931, p. 311–312. [p]
Encyclopedia of Black America, p. 167.
Who's Who in Colored America, 1930–32, p. 27. [p] p. 29.
Who's Who in Colored America, 1933–37, p. 43.
Who's Who in Colored America, 1938–40, p. 43.
Who's Who in Colored America, 1941–44, p. 40, 43.

Barringer, Elizabeth Tyler   (18??–19??, F)

Nurse. Freedman's Hospital School of Nursing Graduate. In 1906 became the first black nurse appointed to the staff of Henry Street Visiting Nurse Service which later became the visiting Nurse Service of New York. She later worked with the Henry Phipps Institute for Tuberculosis in Philadelphia, the State and Welfare Commission of

Delaware, and the Essex County Tuberculosis Association in New Jersey.

Ref: *The Path We Tread,* p. 148–149. [p] p. 148.
Pathfinders, p. 98. [p] opp. p. 96.

Basri, Gibor Broitman   (1951– ——, M)

Astrophysicist. Born in New York, NY, May 3, 1951. B.S. (physics), Stanford University, 1933; Ph.D. (astrophysics), University of Colorado, Boulder, 1979. Research Assistant, University of Colorado, 1974–79; Assistant Professor, University of California, 1982–.

Memberships and awards: Postdoctoral fellow, University of California, 1979–82; American Astronomical Society; International Astronomical Union, 1984; Astronomical Society of the Pacific, 1984; Chancellors fellow, University of California, 1979–81.

Dissertation title: Supergiant Chromospheres.

Pub: Several articles in the *Astronomical Journal.*

Ref: *Ebony,* Aug. 1985, p. 7. [p]
Who's Who Among Black Americans, 1985, p. 45.

Bassett, Emmett   (1921– ——, M)

Agriculturist. Dairy Technologist. Born in Martinsville, VA, Jan. 23, 1921. B.S., Tuskegee Institute, 1942; M.S., University of Massachusetts, 1950; Ph.D. (dairy technology), Ohio State University, 1956. First black to earn a Ph.D. in Dairy Technology. Research Associate in Microbiology, College of Physicians & Surgeons, Columbia University, 1955–59; Assistant Professor, 1959–67; Senior Scientist, Ortho Research Foundation, NJ, 1967–69; Assistant Professor, 1969–73; Associate Professor of Microbiology, College of Medicine & Dentistry, NJ, 1973–.

Memberships and awards: American Society of Biological Chemists.

Dissertation title: Isolation and Identification of Acidic and Neural Carbonyl Compounds in Various Cheese Varieties.

Ref: *Negroes in Science: Natural Science Doctorates, 1876–1969,* p. 56.
American Men and Women of Science, 16th ed., p. 340.

Bate, Langston Fairchild   (1900– ——, M)

Chemist. Born in Danville, KY, 1900. B.A., Illinois State Normal, 1920; M.A., University of Chicago, 1923; Ph.D. (chemistry), 1926. Science Teacher, Kentucky Normal Industrial Institute, 1920–22; Assistant Department of Chemistry, University of Chicago, 1925; Head, Department of Chemistry, Lincoln University, MO, 1926–29. West Virginia State College, 1929–31; Science Teacher, Miner Teachers' College, DC, 1931–57; Professor and Chairman of the Science Division, DC Teachers College (same as Miner), 1957–64; Professor of Chemistry, Huston-Tillotson College, 1964–. Research in fatty acids.

Memberships and awards: Sigma Xi; Kappa Alpha Psi; American Chemical Society; University of Missouri Chemical Society; AAAS; Scholarship Winner, University of Chicago; National Science Teacher's Association.

Dissertation title: Some Pseudo-Thiohydantoins and Alpha Mercapto Acids from Higher Fatty Acids.

Ref: *American Men and Women of Science,* 12th ed., p. 328.
    Crisis, Jan. 1927, p. 147, 149. [p]
    In Black and White, p. 64.
    Holders of Doctorates Among American Negroes, p. 143–144.
    Who's Who in Colored America, 1938–40, p.
    Who's Who in Colored America, 1941–44, p. 43.

Bateman, Mildred Mitchell   (1922– ——, F)

Physician. Psychiatrist. Born in Cordele, GA, 1922. B.S., Johnson C. Smith University, 1941; M.D., Women's Medical College of Pennsylvania, 1946, first black to do so; Three-year Psychiatrist Residency. Director of West Virginia Department of Mental Health, 1962–.

Memberships and awards: fellow, Menninger School of Psychiatry, 1957; Diplomate of American Board of Psychiatry; Honorary Sci.D., from Johnson C. Smith University,

Ref: *Afro-American Encyclopedia,* v. 1, p. 211.
    American Men and Women of Science, 15th ed., p. 328.
    Encyclopedia of Black America, p. 168.
    In Black and White, p. 64; supplement, p. 28.
    Negro Almanac, 1976, p. 1011.
    Ebony Success Library, v. 1, p. 224. [p]
    Ebony, May 1964, p. 74. [p]
    Ebony, Jan. 1964, p. 63–68. [p]

Bates, Clayton Wilson, Jr.   (1932– ——, M)

Engineer (electrical). Physicist. Born in New York, NY, Sept. 5, 1932. B.S. (electrical engineering), Manhattan College, 1954; M.E.E., Polytech Institute, Brooklyn, 1956; M.E., Harvard, 1960; Ph.D. (physics), Washington University, 1966. Electrical Engineer, RCA, 1955; Ford Instrument Co., 1955; Physicist, Sylvania, 1955–57; Physicist, AVCO, 1960; Senior Research Engineer, Varian Associates, 1966–72; Associate Professor, Stanford University, 1972–77; Professor, Stanford University, 1977–; research in electrical and optical properties of crystalline and amorphous solids and surfaces, photoelectric emission.

Memberships and awards: Fellow, American Physical Society; Optical Society of America; IEEE; AAAS; American Society of University Professors; Society of Photo-Optical Instrument Engineers; Sigma Xi; Eta Kappa Nu; Sigma Pi Sigma; American Ceramic Society; Faculty Advisor for the Society of Black Scientists and Engineers, Stanford University; National Academy of

Sciences Evaluation Panel; Visiting Professor, University of London, 1968.

Dissertation title: Nonlinear Resonance Effects in Multilevel Systems.

Pub: Over 50 articles in science journals.

Ref: *American Men and Women of Science,* 15th ed., p. 329.
    Encyclopedia of Black America, p. 744.
    Who's Who Among Black Americans, 1985, p. 46.

Battle, Joseph   (1930– ——, M)

Mathematician. Born in Rocky Mount, NC, Feb. 22, 1930. B.S. (mathematics and physics), North Carolina Central University, 1953; M.S., University of Michigan, 1955; Ph.D. (mathematics), 1963. Mathematics Instructor, Rocky Mount Public Schools, 1955–56; Assistant Professor, Associate Professor, Professor, Mathematics, Morgan State College, 1956–58; Professor, Mathematics, North Carolina Central University, 1962–64; Mathematics Specialist in Nigeria for the University of California at Los Angeles; Chairman, Department of Mathematics, College of Education, University of Lagos, 1946–68; Director of Operations Analysis and Institutional Research/ Professor, Mathematics, Shaw University, 1968–70; Consultant to Registrar, Duke University; Visiting Scholar, North Carolina Central University, 1969–70; Associate Professor, Graduate School of Business Administration, Duke University, 1970–.

Memberships and awards: Alpha Kappa Mu; Beta Kappa Chi.

Dissertation title: Imbedding of Graphs in Orientable 2-Manifolds.

Pub: Every Planar Graph with Nine Points Has a Nonplanar Compliment. American Mathematic Society, *Bulletin,* v. 68, Nov. 1962.
    On the Genus of a Graph. American Mathematic Society, *Bulletin,* v. 68, Nov. 1962.

Ref: *Black Mathematicians and Their Works,* p. 277. [p]

Baulknight, Charles Wesley, Jr.   (1911–1981, M)

Chemist. Born in Concord, NC, Nov. 15, 1911. B.S., Johnson C. Smith University, 1935. Chemical Assistant, University of Pennsylvania, 1938–40; Junior Chemist, Chemical Warfare Service, Edgewood Arsenal, MD, 1941–43; Research Chemist, National Defense Research Committee, University of Pennsylvania, 1944–45; Research Associate, Mellon Institute, 1945–46; Physical Chemist, Pitman-Dunn Laboratories, Frankford Arsenal, Philadelphia, 1946–56; Valley Forge Research Center, General Electric Co., 1956–63; Research Scientist, Grumman Aerospace Camp., 1963–76; Chairman and President, Institute of Scientific Inquiry, Inc., Consultants, Bethpage, NY, 1976–. Research in high temperature fluid properties of gases including transport phenomena and chemical kinetics.

Memberships and awards: Board of Trustees and Executive Committee, Johnson C. Smith University, 1965–; Board of Trustees, Dowling College; Board of Trustees, Friends of Nassau County Museum; AAAS; fellow, American Physical Society; fellow, American Institute of Chemists; American Chemical Society; Sigma Xi.

Ref: *American Men and Women of Science*, 14th ed., p. 276.
    Ebony, Sept. 1970, p. 36. [p]

Bayton, James Arthur (1912– ——, M)

Psychologist. Born in Whitestone, VA, April 5, 1912. B.S., Howard University, 1935; M.S., 1936; Ph.D. (psychology), University of Pennsylvania, 1943. Assistant Professor of Psychology, Virginia State College, 1939–43; Social Science Analyst, USDA, 1943–45; Professor of Psychology, Southern University, 1945–46; Morgan State College, 1946–47; Professor of Psychology, Howard University, 1947–.

Memberships and awards: Senior fellow, Brookings Institute, 1967–68; Senior Psychologist, Chilton Research Services, 1968; Superior Service Award, USDA, 1954; American Market Association Award, 1958; fellow, American Psychological Association; American Marketing Association; Beta Kappa Chi; Sigma Xi; George Lieb Harrison Scholar; Vice-President, National Analysts, 1953–62, 1966–67; Vice-President, Universal Marketing Research, 1962–66; Phi Beta Kappa.

Dissertation title: Interrelation between Levels of Aspiration, Performance, and Estimates of Past Performance.

Ref: *American Men and Women of Science*, 13th ed., p. 74.
    Holders of Doctorates Among American Negroes, p. 203.
    Even the Rat Was White, p. 161–163. [p]
    Living Black American Authors, p. 11.

Beal, Robert S. (1900s, M)

Chemist. B.S., West Virginia State College; M.S., University of Pennsylvania; Ph.D. Pennsylvania State College, 1942. Professor of Chemistry, Delaware State College, 1949.

Dissertation title: I. The Permanganate Titration of Thallous Salts, II. The Determination of Bismuth by Caffeine Tetraiodobismuthate.

Ref: *Holders of Doctorates Among American Negroes*, p. 144.
    National Register, 1952, p. 253.

Beamon, Reginald Emmett (1890–??, M)

Dentist. Born in Newport News, VA, Oct. 13, 1890. B.A., Howard University, 1913; D.D.S., 1916;

Memberships and awards: Founder and President, Cincinnati Medical Association 1933–. National Medical Association; Interstate Dental Society; Alpha Phi Alpha;

President, Howard Alumni Association of Cincinnati, 1923–.

Ref: *Who's Who in Colored America*, 1933–37, p. 46.
    Who's Who in Colored America, 1938–40, p. 45.
    Who's Who in Colored America, 1941–44, p. 45.

Beard, Andrew Jackson (1850–1921, M)

Inventor. Born in Eastlake, AL, 1850. Inventor of the "Jenny Coupler" for railroad cars, Patent #594,059, 1897, an automatic car coupling device. Sold to a New York company for $50,000. He also invented a rotary engine, Patent #478,271 (1892). The "Jenny Coupler" saved the lives of thousands of trainmen.

Ref: *Afro-American Encyclopedia*, v. 1, p. 216. Sketch of rotary engine
    At Last Recognition in America, v. 1, p. 26.
    Black Inventors of America, p. 17–23.
    Significant American Blacks, p. 16. [p]

Beck, James (1800s, M)

Military (Army). Lt. Colonel. He was a Lt. Colonel in the 23rd Kansas Volunteer Infantry Regiment, Spanish-American War in 1898.

Ref: *Afro-American Encyclopedia*, v. 1, p. 221. [p]

Beck, James T. (1905– ——, M)

Chemist. Born in Savannah, GA, May 17, 1905. B.A., Lincoln University (PA), 1926; M.A., Kansas University, 1935; University of Wisconsin, 1946. Teacher of Science, Albion Academy, 1926–28; Instructor in Chemistry & Biology, Lane College, 1928–35; Professor of Chemistry 1935–; Chairman of the Science Department. Research on the effect of x-rays on living tissue.

Ref: *American Men of Science*, 9th ed., p. 116.

Becket, G. E. (1800s, M)

Inventor. Patent #483,525, Oct. 4, 1892, for a letter box.

Ref: *Afro-American Encyclopedia*, v. 1, p. 221. sketch, p. 223.

Beckford, Samuel McDonald (1886–19??, M)

Physician. Surgeon. Born in Jamaica, B.W.I., Sept. 12, 1886. B.S., Howard University, 1911; M.D., Boston University, 1917. Professor of Anatomy and Assistant in Physiology, Shaw University, 1917–18; Surgeon-in-Chief, Jubilee Hospital, Henderson, NC, 1922–.

Ref: *Who's Who in Colored America*, 1930–32, p. 32. [p] p. 30.
    Who's Who in Colored America, 1933–37, p. 49. [p] p. 48.
    Who's Who in Colored America, 1941–44, p. 46. [p] p. 47.

Beckham, Ruth Winifred Howard   (1900- ——, F)

Psychologist. Born in Washington, DC, 1900. B.A., Simmons College, 1921; M.S., 1927; Ph.D. (psychology), University of Minnesota, 1934. Co-director of the Center for Psychological Services with her Psychologist husband, 1940–64; Psychologist, Chicago's Provident Hospital School of Nursing, 1940–64; Psychologist for McKinley Center for Retarded Children, 1964–66; Psychologist for Chicago Board of Health, Mental Health Division, 1968–72.

Memberships and awards: Chicago Psychology Club; Illinois Psychological Association; American Psychological Association; AAAS; International Reading Association.

Dissertation title: A Study of the Development of Triplets.

Pub: Developmental History of a Group of Triplets.
Fantasy and the Play Interview.

Ref: *Holders of Doctorates Among American Negroes,* p. 203.
Even the Rat was White, p. 138–140. [p] p. 139.
Women Scientists in America, p. 362, no. 23.

Beckwourth, James Pierson   (1798–1867, M)

Explorer. Born in Virginia, April 6, 1798. He accompanied General William Ashley on a fur trading expedition to the Rocky Mountains in 1824–25. He went to live with the Crow Indians and discovered Beckwourth Pass in California.

Pub: Several Books on his Life.

Ref: Felton, Harold. *Jim Beckwourth Negro Mountain Man.*
New York, Dodd, Mead & Co., 1966, 173 p.
Jet, April 7, 1986, p. 18. [p]
Life & Adventures of James P. Beckwourth, Mountaineer, Scout & Pioneer & Chief of the Crow Nation of Indians. Minneapolis, Rose & Haines, 1965, 547 p.
Historical Afro-American Biographies, p. 49–50. [p]
Afro-American Encyclopedia, v. 1, p. 222–225. [p]

Becton, Julius Wesley, Jr.   (1926- ——, M)

Military (Army). Lieutenant General. Born in Bryn Mawr, PA, June 29, 1926. B.S., (mathematics), Prairie View A & M College, 1960; M.S., (economics), University of Maryland, 1966; Nadunac War College, 1970; D.Laws, Houston-Tillohon, 1982. Commanding General, 1st Cavalry Division, 1975–76; Commanding General, U.S. Army Operations Test and Evaluation Agency, 1976–78; VII U.S. Corps, 1978–81; Army Inspector of Training, 1981–83; Office of Foreign Disaster, Assistant Director; Brigadier Commander, 2nd Brigade, 2nd Armoured Division, Fort Hood. Retired.

Memberships and awards: Silver Star with Oak Leaf Cluster; Bronze Star with two Oak Leaf Clusters; Republic of South Vietnam Cross of Gallantry; Retired Officers' Association.

Ref: *Afro-American Encyclopedia,* v. 1, p. 226. [p]
Ebony, July 1979, p. 44–46, 48, 50. [p]
Who's Who Among Black Americans, 1985, p. 52.
Black Americans in Defense of Our Nation, p. 121. [p]

Beekman, Walter Nathaniel   (1878–1962, M)

Dentist. Born in Charleston, SC, 1878. Avery Normal Institute, 1897 (two years of Pharmacy); D.D.S., New York Dental School (now Columbia University School of Dentistry), 1902. Brooklyn Dentist, first black graduated from a school of dentistry in New York state.

Memberships and awards: Columbia University Citation for 50 years of Dentistry; National Dental Association; American Dental Association; Sigma Pi Phi Fraternity.

Ref: *Jet,* Aug. 16, 1962.
National Medical Association, *Journal,* v. 53, July 1961, p. 408–409. [p]

Bell, Alexander F.   (1904–1986, M)

Pharmacist. Born in Casanova, VA, Nov. 27, 1904. B.A., Howard University, 19??; Dr. Pharm., Howard University, 19??. For 50 years a pharmacist at Ethical Pharmacy on Florida Ave., N.W., Washington, DC. Taught for 10 years at Howard University. Research on the biochemistry of diuretics and presented papers to the Pan American Congress of Pharmacy and Biochemistry.

Ref: *Washington Post,* May 15, 1986, p. B6, col. 1. obit.
Who's Who Among Black Americans, 1985, p. 53.

Bell, Carl Compton   (1947- ——, M)

Physician. Psychiatrist. Born in Chicago, IL, Oct. 28, 1947. B.S., University of Illinois, 1967; M.D., Meharry Medical College, 1971; Psychiatric Residency, Illinois State Psychiatric Institute, 1974. Director, Jackson Park Hospital Psychiatric Emergency Services Program, 1976–77; Staff Psychiatrist, Chatham Avalon Mental Health Center, 1977–79; Associate Professor of Clinical Psychiatry, University of Illinois School of Medicine, 1983-.

Memberships and awards: American Psychiatric Association; Alpha Omega Alpha; Falk fellowship of the American Psychiatric Association.

Ref: *Who's Who Among Black Americans,* 1985, p. 53.
Biographical Directory of the American Psychiatric Association, 1983, p. 78.

Bell, James Milton   (1921- ——, M)

Physician. Psychiatrist. Born in Portsmouth, VA, Nov. 5, 1921. B.S., North Carolina College, Durham, 1943; M.D., Meharry Medical College, 1947; From Assistant Physician to Clinical Director, Lakin State Hospital, WV, 1948–51; Assistant Section Chief, Children's Unit, Topeka State Hospital, KS, 1956–58; Clinical Assistant Professor to Clinical Professor, Albany Medical College, 1959–80.

Memberships and awards: Fellow in Psychiatry, Menninger School of Psychiatry, 1953–56; American Board of Psychiatry and Neurology; Medical Advisory Board, New York State Division for Youth, 1967–76; American Academy of Child Psychiatry; American Psychiatric Association; President's Award, Meharry Medical College, 1972; fellow, American Psychopathic Association; American College of Psychiatry.

Ref: *American Men and Women of Science*, 14th ed., p. 410.
    Leaders in American Science, 5th ed., 1962–63, p. 52. [p]
    Who's Who Among Black Americans, 1985, p. 54.
    Biographical Directory of the American Psychological Association, 1983, p. 79.

Bell, L.   (1800s, M)

Inventor. Locomotive smoke stack, patent #115,153, 1871, a cone-shaped device preventing embers from flying from the locomotive to the passenger compartments the result of which in some cases started fires.

Ref: *At Last Recognition in America*, v. 1, p. 30.

Bellamy, Verdelle B.   (19?? ——, F)

Nurse. Diploma, Grady Hospital School of Nursing, GA, 19??; B.S., Tuskegee Institute School of Nursing, AL, 19??; M.S.N., Emory University, GA, 1963.

Memberships and awards: Appointed by President Carter in 1974 to the Georgia Board of Nursing Education; American Nursing Association Mary Mahoney Award, 1984; Ludie Andrews Distinguished Service Award, 1977; in 1976, she was reappointed to the Georgia Board of Nursing Education for three more years and in 1978 became its President.

Ref: *The Path We Tread*, p. 84–85, 157. [p] p. 85.

Belsaw, E. T.   (1800s, M)

Dentist. Born in Madison, GA,. Attended Dickerson Institute, Pittsburgh, PA, and had private instruction from Professor G. E. Masterson of Morris Brown College, Atlanta, GA. Taught school, 1879 and 1898. An excellent business man, he went to Meharry Medical College in 1904. While there he was assistant demonstrator of operative dentistry and won prizes for metallurgy and general proficiency for all-around dental work. Passed dental exams in 1908 with best theoretical exam by any previous persons in the history of the board. Practiced in Mobile, AL with largest dental practice in the south.

Memberships and awards: President, Mobile Medical, Dental and Pharmaceutical Association; President,

Mobile Emancipation Association; Director, YMCA; Secretary, Executive Board, National Medical Association.

Ref: *Beacon Lights of the Race*, p. 226–231. [p]
    Who's Who in Colored America, 1915, p. 24. [p] & biog

Belton, William Edward   (1904–1960, M)

Chemist. Born in Rock Hill, SC, Nov. 23, 1904. B.S., Johnson C. Smith University, 1928; M.S., University of Iowa, 1930; Ph.D. (chemistry), Iowa State College, 1942. Instructor in Chemistry, New Orleans University, 1930–35; Dillard University, 1935–42; Professor, Tuskegee Institute, 1943–; Head, Chemistry Department, Tuskegee Institute.

Memberships and awards: American Chemical Society; Institute of Biochemistry; AAAS; Sigma Xi; Beta Kappa Chi.

Dissertation title: Studies on the Salvate Formation of Certain Tetrahalides of the IV Group in Liquid Dioxide.

Ref: *American Men of Science*, 10th ed., p. 264.
    National Register, p. 253.
    The Negro in Science, p. 181.
    Holders of Doctorates Among American Negroes, p. 144.

Bembry, Thomas Henry   (1907–19??, M)

Chemist (organic). Born in Hawkinsville, GA, Dec. 19, 1907. B.S., Howard University, 1929; M.A., Columbia University, 1932; Ph.D., 1941. Head, Department of Chemistry, Livingstone College, 1932–39; Instructor in Chemistry, City College of New York, 1940–50; Assistant Professor, 1950–61; Associate Professor, 1961–; Research Chemist, Office of Scientific Research and Development Contract, Columbia University, 1943–46.

Memberships and awards: Rosenwald fellow, 1940–41; Smith Kline & French fellow, Columbia University, 1941–42; Eli Lilly fellow, 1946–48; AAAS; Chemical Society.

Dissertation title: Compounds of the Cannabinol Type.

Ref: *American Men of Science*, 11th ed., p. 341.
    Holders of Doctorates Among American Negroes, p. 144–145.
    National Register, 1952, p. 252.

Benjamin, L. W.   (1800s, M)

Inventor. Patent #497,747, May 16, 1893, for broom moisteners and bridles.

Ref: *Afro-American Encyclopedia*, v. 1, p. 242. Sketch of broom moistener

Benjamin, Miriam E.   (1800s, F)

Inventor. Patent #386,286, July 17, 1888, for a gong and signal chair whose principle was adapted by the U.S.

House of Representatives for the Congressmen to call the pages to run errands for them.

Ref: *Afro-American Encyclopedia,* v. 1, p. 242.
    Haber, Louis. *The Role of the American Negro in the Fields of Science, p. 33.*

Bennett, John Henry   (1935- ——, M)

Mathematician. Born in Cincinnati, OH, July 21, 1935. B.A., Harvard University, 1957; M.S., 1958; Ph.D. (applied mathematics), 1962. Former Senior Mathematician, Bettis Atomic Power Laboratory, 1962–64; Directory of Data Processing, United Technologies Camp., 1973–. Research in numerical solution of the neutron transport equation and the Navier-Stokes equation.

Ref: *American Men and Women of Science,* 14th ed., p. 337.
    Ebony, Aug. 1964, p. 7. [p]

Benoit, Edith B.   (1918- ——, F)

Nurse. Born in New York, NY, Mar. 7, 1918. B.A., Hunter College, 1938; R.N., Harlem Hospital School of Nursing, 1942; M.A., Teachers College, Columbia University, 1945; Professional Diploma, 1959. Assistant Supervisor of Nursing, Harlem Hospital, 1942–51; Supervisor and Assistant Chief of Nursing Research and Coordination, V.A. Hospital, Brooklyn, NY, 1951–64; Associate Chief of Nursing Service, V.A. Hospital, East Orange, NJ, 1964–65; Assistant Professor, Columbia University, 1967; Board of Directors, National League for Nursing.

    Memberships and awards: American Nurses Association; National League for Nursing.

Ref: *Who's Who Among Black Americans,* 1985, p. 59–60.

Bently, Charles E.   (1859–1929, M)

Dentist. Born in Cincinnati, OH, 1859. D.D.S., Chicago College of Dental Surgery, 1887, only black in a class of 60. In 1889 he was elected Clinician in Chicago College of Dental Surgery. First to suggest dental examinations in public schools which after his suggestion to the Odontographic Society, led to the nationwide practice of examining school children's teeth.

    Memberships and awards: President, Chicago Dental Association; Chicago Dental Club; Founder and President, Odontographic Association; Secretary, President Hospital.

Ref: *The College Life,* Northrop, p. 137. [p]
    Crisis, Sept. 1915, p. 238–239. [p]
    Crisis, May 1911, p. 10–11. [p]
    Crisis, June 1921, p. 72–73, 87. [p]
    Crisis, Dec. 1929, p. 423. [p] obit
    National Medical Association, *Journal,* v. 75, Dec. 1983, p. 1235–1236. (article about him)

Benton, J. W.   (1800s, M)

Inventor. Born in Kentucky. Invented a derrick for hoisting heavy weights. Walked from Kentucky to Washington to obtain his patent Oct. 2, 1900.

Ref: *Negro Makers of History,* 5th ed., p. 464.
    Afro-American Encyclopedia, v. 1, p. 244.

Berry, Jesse Frank   (1932- ——, M)

Engineer. Born in 1932. B.S., University of Southern California, 1962; M.S., California State University, 1969. Worked on research projects at North American Aviation in Los Angeles. Systems Engineer, Hughes Aircraft Company, Fullerton, California. Principal Engineer, Honeywell-Marine Systems, 1971–.

Ref: *Encyclopedia of Black America,* p. 172.

Berry, Joseph A.   (1895–19??, M)

Physician. Surgeon. Born in Charleston, SC, Aug. 4, 1895. B.A., Fisk University, 1919; B.S., University of Chicago, 1921; M.D., Rush Medical College, 1924. Began his practice as an Associate of Dr. U. G. Dailey of Chicago. Has been Assistant Surgeon in Chief of Dailey Hospital and on Roentgenological Staff of that hospital.

    Memberships and awards: Omega Psi Phi; Chicago Medical Society; Illinois State Society; American Medical Association; Physicians Association of Cook County.

Pub: Current Medical Thought. National Medical Association, *Quarterly.*

Ref: *Who's Who in Colored America,* 1930–32, p. 34.
    Who's Who in Colored America, 1933–37, p. 53. [p] p. 51.
    Who's Who in Colored America, 1938–40, p. 50.
    Who's Who in Colored America, 1941–44, p. 50.

Berry, Leonidas Harris   (1902- ——, M)

Physician. Gastroenterologist. Internist. Pathologist. Born in Woodsdale, NC, July 20, 1902; B.S., Wilberforce University, OH, 1924; B.S. ,University of Chicago, 1925; M.D., Rush Medical College, 1929; M.S., (pathology), University of Illinois, 1933. Senior Attending Physician and Gastroenterologist, Cook County Hospital, Chicago, 1946–74; Emeritus, 1975–; world expert on endoscopy.

    Memberships and awards: President, National Medical Association, 1965; Honorary L.L.D. from Lincoln University, PA, 1983; Diplomate, American Board of Internal Medicine and Gastroenterology; National Board of Medical Examiners; American Medical Association; American Gastroscopic Society; American College of Gastroenterology; Medical Society of Gastrointestinal Endoscopy; National Society of Gastroenterology; Japan Endoscopy Society; Association for the Study of Afro-American Life and History; fellow, New York Academy of Medicine; Honorary Sc.D., Wilberforce University, OH, 1945; Distinguished Service Award, National Medical Association, 1958; Schindler Award, American Society for Gastrointestinal Endoscopy, 1977; Alpha Omega Alpha Medical Honor Society, Rush Medical College; Organizer for Flying Black Medics; Sigma Xi; Alpha Phi Alpha.

Pub: *Gastrointestinal Pan-Endoscopy.* Springfield, IL, Charles C. Thomas, 1974. (co-author) 632 p.

I Wouldn't Take Nothing for My Journey: Two Centuries of an Afro-American Minister's Family. Chicago, IL, Johnson Pub. Co., 1981. 459 p.

Ref: *American Men and Women of Science,* 16th ed., p. 478.
Blacks in Science: Astrophysicist to Zoologist, p. 30.
Ebony, June 1975, p. 75–76, 78, 80, 82. [p]
Ebony Success Library, v. 1, p. 26 [p]
National Medical Association, *Journal,* v. 73, Dec. 1981, p. 1238.
National Medical Association, *Journal,* v. 56, Nov. 1964, p. 538–539. [p]
Who's Who Among Black Americans, 1985, p. 61–62.
Who's Who in America, 1986–87, p. 227

Berthoud, Kenneth H., Jr.   (1928– ——, M)

Military (Marines). Colonel. Born in New York, NY, Dec. 28, 1928. B.A., Long Island University, 1952; M.S., George Washington University, 1972. Deputy Director, Headquarters, Marine Corps, 1975–77; Department Manager, CACI, 1978–80; Deputy Division General Manager, Advanced Technology, Inc., 1980–; Chairman, Job Placement, Society of Logistics Engineering, 1984–85; One of two first black Majors in the Marine Corps; U.S. Marine Corps Colonel for 31 years.

Memberships and awards: Korean and Vietnam campaign medals.

Ref: *Who's Who Among Black Americans,* 1985, p. 62.

Beshears, Rufas P.   (????–1961, M)

Dentist. B.A.; D.D.S., University of Iowa Dental School. First black to enter University of Iowa Dental School.

Ref: *Jet,* Nov. 2, 1961, p. 43.

Bessent, Hattie   (1926– ——, F)

Nurse. Born in Jacksonville, FL, Dec. 26, 1926. B.S., Florida A & M University School of Nursing, 1959; M.S., Indiana University, 1962; Ed.D., University of Florida, Gainesville, 1970; Certificate, Institute for Educational Management, Harvard University. Administrative Interne, American Council on Education, Visiting Professor in Research and Family Dynamics, Vanderbilt University. Director of American Nursing Association Minority Fellowship Program; Assistant Professor Psychiatric Nursing, Florida A & M University, 1962–67.

Memberships and awards: American Nurses Association; American Educational Research Association; Delta Sigma Theta; Florida Nurses Association National League

for Nursing; Sigma Theta Tau; Phi Lambda Theta; Phi Delta Kappa.

Ref: *The Path We Tread,* p. 60. [p] p. 60.
Who's Who Among Black Americans, 1985, p. 62.

Beverly, Clara E.   (1900s, F)

Nurse. Military. Captain. Graduated in Nursing, Freedmen's Hospital, 1947. Helped draft the nurse's code in Liberia for 30 years, in DC, Tuskegee and Liberia. Served as Nursing Arts Instructor in the School of Nursing sponsored by the Liberian Government; Freedmen's Hospital, 1949; Director of Nursing Education, Liberia, 1952; Navajo Medical Center, Fort Defiance, AZ, 1952.

Memberships and awards: Honored in March 1959 by Freedmen's Hospital nurses.

Ref: *Jet,* April 2, 1959, p.
The Path We Tread, p. 206.

Bharucha-Reid, Albert Turner   (1927– ——, M)

Mathematician. Born in Hampton, VA, Nov. 13, 1927. B.S., Iowa State University, 1949; Mathematics and Biology, 1950; Mathematical Biology, Mathematics, Probability and Statistics, University of Chicago, 1950–53; Probability and Statistics, Columbia University, 1953–54. Research Assistant, Mathematical Biology, University of Chicago, 1950–53; Research Associate, Mathematical Statistics, Columbia University, 1953–55; Assistant Research Statistician, University of California at Berkeley, 1955–56; Instructor, Mathematics, University of Oregon, 1956–58; fellow, Mathematical Institute, Polish Academy of Sciences, Wrocaw, Poland, 1958–59; Assistant Professor, Mathematics, University of Oregon, 1959–61; Associate Professor, Mathematics, Wayne State University, 1961–65; Visiting Professor, Applied Mathematics, Institute of Mathematical Sciences, Madras, India, 1963–64; Professor, Mathematics and Graduate Dean of Arts and Sciences, Wayne State University, 1965; Director, Center for Research in Probability, 1967–81; Visiting Professor, Mathematics Research Center, University of Wisconsin, Madison, 1966–67; Professor, Mathematics, Georgia Institute of Technology, 1981–.

Memberships and awards: American Mathematical Society; Indian Statistical Institute; Indian Mathematical Society; Polish Mathematical Society; Society for Industrial and Applied Mathematics; AAAS; New York Academy of Science; fellow, Iowa Academy of Sciences; Sigma Xi.

Pub: Many articles in various journals.

Ref: *American Men and Women of Science,* 14th ed., p. 386.
Black Mathematicians and Their Works, p. 277–279, [p] p. 6.

Bianchi, La Bonnie   (1938- ——, F)

Engineer (electrical). Born in Winston Salem, NC, 1938.
B.A. (electrical engineering), Howard University; M.S.
(scientific writing), Rensselaer Polytechnic Institute.

Memberships and awards: First woman graduate of
Howard University Electrical Engineering Department.

Ref: *Ebony,* Dec. 1961, p. 87–92. [p]

Bias, John Henry   (1879–19??, M)

Science educator. Born in Palmyra, MO, June 11, 1879.
B.A., Lincoln University, (Jefferson City, MO), 1901; special work in Mathematics and Science, University of Chicago, 1902–04; special work in Administration and Supervision, Columbia University, 1924. Instructor, Science
and Mathematics, Lincoln University, Jefferson City, MO;
Instructor, Science and Mathematics, State Normal
School, NC; Instructor, Biology and Chemistry, Shaw University, 1908–18; Head, Chemistry Department, Leonard
Medical School; Collected and mounted numerous insects and reptiles, made reports on trees near Raleigh to
U.S. Department of Agriculture; Experimented with
plant Bionaea, commonly called "Venus Fly Trap"; Vice-
principal, State Normal School, Elizabeth City, NC,
1922-.

Ref: *Who's Who in Colored America,* 1915, p. 26.
Who's Who in Colored America, 1927, p. 14 [p] opp. p.
14.
Who's Who in Colored America, 1930–32, p. 37.
Who's Who in Colored America, 1938–40, p. 54 [p] p. 57.

Billups, Rufus   (19??- ——, M)

Military (Air Force). Major General.

Ref: *Ebony,* May 1978, p. 46. [p] only
Jet, May 8, 1980, p. 32. [p]
Black Americans in Defense of Our Nation, p. 129. [p]

Binga, M. W.   (1800s, M)

Inventor, Patent #217,843, July 22, 1879, for a street
sprinkling apparatus.

Ref: *Afro-American Encyclopedia,* v. 1, p. 264. sketch
Negro Almanac, p. 1069.

Birnie, James Hope   (1909–1974, M)

Physiologist. Biologist. Endocrinologist. Born in Augusta,
GA, Oct. 11, 1909. B.A., Morehouse College, 1930; M.A.,
Brown University, 1932; Ph.D., Syracuse University,
1948. Instructor, Morehouse College, 1935–36; Assistant
Professor, South Carolina State College, 1936–45; Associ-
ate Professor, Syracuse University, 1947–50; Department
Chairman, Morehouse College, 1950–52, Atomic Energy
Commission Study, Atlanta University, 1950s; Section
Head, Endocrinology Department, Smith, Kline &

French Laboratories, 1962–69; Assistant Director, Scientific Liaison Research and Development Division, 1969–;
Research on adrenal cortex and water metabolism.

Memberships and awards: AAAS; Endocrine Society; American Physiological Society; American Diabetes
Association; fellow, New York Academy of Sciences.

Ref: *American Men and Women of Science,* 12th ed., p. 500.
Ebony, Dec. 1954, p. 88. [p]
Ebony, May 1961, p. 27. [p]
Jet, Jan. 2, 1975, p. 17.
The Negro in Science, p. 175.

Bishop, Alfred A.   (1924- ——, M)

Engineer (chemical). Engineer (mechanical). Inventor.
Born in Philadelphia, PA, May 10, 1924. B.S., University
of Pennsylvania, 1950; M.S. (chemical engineering), University of Pittsburgh, 1965; Ph.D. (mechanical engineering, Carnegie-Mellon University, 1974. Chemical Engineer, Philadelphia Naval Experimental Station, 1950–51;
Chemical Engineer, Fischer & Porter Co., Hatharo, PA,
1953–56; Engineer, Westinghouse, 1956–65; Manager Hydraulic Divices, Westinghouse Atomic Power Division,
1963–65; Manager, Thermofluids, Westinghouse Reactors
Division, 1965–69; Associate Professor of Chemical Engineering, University of Pittsburgh; has patent for flow
distributor for nuclear reactor core; work in thermodynamics; reaction rates.

Memberships and awards: Instrument Society;
American Society of Chemical Engineers; American Society of Mechanical Engineers; National Science Foundation Award, 1975.

Dissertation title: Chrystallite Induction Time for Calcium Sul-
fate on a Heated Surface During Single-Phase and
Subcooled Nucleate Boiling Flows.

Ref: *Black Engineers in the U.S.,* p. 18.
The Negro in Science, p. 181.
National Faculty Directory, 1987, p. 305.
Who's Who Among Black Americans, 1985, p. 65.

Blache, Julian Owen   (1900–1964, M)

Physician. Obstetrician. Gynecologist. Pathologist. Born
in Port of Spain, Trinidad, Oct. 18, 1900. B.A., New York
University, 1928; M.D., Howard University, 1952. Head,
Department of Pathology, Homer G. Phillips Hospital,
1941–; Acting Medical Director, Homer G. Phillips Hospital.

Memberships and awards: Diplomate, American
Board of Pathology; fellow, American College of Pathology.

Ref: *Encyclopedia of Black America,* p. 181.
National Medical Association, Journal, v. 56, May 1964,
p. 297. [p]

Blackburn, A. B.   (1800s, M)

Inventor. Patent #376,362, 1888, railroad signal, used to alert engineer in trains to danger along the route; Patent #380,420, a spring seat for chairs, April 3, 1888.

Ref: *At Last Recognition in America*, v. 1, p. 39.
　　　The Negro Almanac, p. 1069.

Blackburn, Laura   (1900s, F)

Midwife. Nurse. Born in Allendate, SC.

Ref: *Contributions of Black Women to America*, v. 2, 360.

Blackman, Edson Ervin   (1890–1961, M)

Physician. Surgeon. Born in Barbados, B.W.I., Nov., 1890. St. Augustine College, NC, 1913; M.D., Meharry Medical College, Nashville, TN, 1917. Medical Examiner for North Carolina Mutual Insurance Company, 1920–; Attending Surgeon and Staff Secretary, Good Samaritan Hospital, Charlotte, NC, 1929–.

Memberships and awards: Phi Beta Sigma; National Medical Association; John A. Andrews Clinical Society; President, Old North State Medical, Dental and Pharmaceutical Association, 1929–32.

Ref: *Who's Who in Colored America*, p. 38.
　　　Who's Who in Colored America, 1933–37, p. 56.
　　　Who's Who in Colored America, 1938–40, p. 56.
　　　Who's Who in Colored America, 1941–44, p. 57.
　　　National Medical Association, *Journal*, v. 54, Nov. 1962,
　　　　p. 724. obit

Blackwell, David Harold   (1919– ——, M)

Mathematician. Statistician. Born in Centralia, IL, April 24, 1919. B.A., University of Illinois, 1938; M.A., 1939; Ph.D. (mathematics), 1941; D.Sci, 1966. Professor, Howard University, 1944–54; Professor, Statistics and Mathematics and Director of Study Center, University of California, UK, and Ireland, 1973–; Research in Markoff chains and sequential analysis.

Memberships and awards: First Black Mathematician of the National Academy of Sciences, 1965; Pi Mu Epsilon; Sigma Xi; Honorary D.Sci., 1965; Von Neumann theory prize ORSA-TIMS, 1979; fellow, Institute of Mathematical Statistics; President, American Statistical Association; Rosenwald fellow, Institute of Advanced Study, Princeton, 1941–42; American Mathematical Society.

Dissertation title: Some Properties of Markoff Chains.

Pub: (Co-author) *Theory of Games and Statistical Decisions.*
　　　New York, Dover Publications, 1979. c1954. 355 p.
　　　Basic Statistics. New York, McGraw-Hill, 1969. 143 p.
　　　Published over 40 research article.

Ref: *Holders of Doctorates Among American Negroes*, p. 145.
　　　American Men and Women of Science, 14th ed., p. 163.

Encyclopedia of Black America, p. 183. [p]
In Black and White, p. 85.
Who's Who Among Black Americans, 1980–81, p. 63.
The Negro in Science, p. 187–188.
Black Mathematicians and Their Works, p. 279–280. [p]
　　p. 32.
Negro Year Book, 1947, p. 40.
Who's Who in America, 1986–87, p. 255.
Living Black American Authors, p. 14.

Blair, Henry   (1804–1860, M)

Inventor. Born in Glenross, MD, 1804. Corn planting machine. First black man to receive a U.S. Patent, Oct. 14, 1834. Aug. 31, 1836, patent for a cotton planter.

Ref: *Negro Almanac*, p. 635, 1st ed., p. 1055, 4th ed.
　　　At Last Recognition in America, v. 1, p. 2.
　　　Afro-American Encyclopedia, v. 2, p. 343.
　　　Afro-American Encyclopedia, v. 5, p. 1275.

Blair, Joseph N.   (1904–19??, M)

Inventor. Born in Augusta, GA, 1904. A talented speed boat inventor (1942); an aerial torpedo for long range bombing (1944), 5mm aircraft gun. He offered his inventions to the government several times but was turned down each time until 1958.

Ref: *Jet*, Mar. 20, 1958, p. 22–28. [p]

Blakney, Eustis Joel   (1944– ——, M)

Engineer (electrical). Born in Atlanta, GA, Oct. 18, 1944. B.S. (electrical engineering), Tuskegee Institute, 1968. Electrical Engineering, University of Florida and the University of Kentucky. Electrical Engineer, IBM Office Products Division, 1968–69; Test Engineer, U.S. Air Force, Eglin AF Base, 1969–70; Design Engineer, U.S. Air Force, Eglin AF Base, 1970–71; Project Engineer, U.S. Air Force, Vandenberg, AF Base, California.

Memberships and awards: IEEE; AAU; B. Z. Jarkowski Award in Material Science; M. Erdey Award in Electrical Engineering; Eta Kappa Nu; Alpha Phi Omega; Outstanding Unit Award, U.S. Air Force.

Ref: *Black Engineers in the United States*, p. 19.

Blakney, Simmie Samuel   (1928– ——, M)

Mathematician. Born in Shubuta, MS, 1928. B.A. (mathematics), Tougaloo College; M.S. (mathematics), University of Illinois, 1955; Ph.D. (analysis, algebra, education administration), University of Illinois, 1963. Instructor, Utica Junior College, 1954–55; Assistant Professor and Chairman, Department of Mathematics, Grambling College, 1955–56; Professor and Chairman, Mathematics Department, University of Toledo, 1956–.

Dissertation title: Lusin's Theorem in Metric Theory.

Pub: (With Thomas Gibney) "Guidelines for Operation of a Summer Conference," 1969.

Lusin's Theorem in Abstract Space. *Matematich—fyzikving Casopis,* Czechoslovakia, 1969.

(With Thomas Gibney) Improving Elementary Instruction in Mathematics.

American Mathematical Monthly, v. 76, 1969, p. 1057–1060.

Ref: *National Faculty Directory,* 1987, p. 318.
Black Mathematicians and Their Works, p. 280, 40–43.
[p] p. 40

Blanchet, Waldo Willie Emerson   (1910– ——, M)

Science Educator. Born in New Orleans, LA, Aug. 6, 1910. B.A., Talladega College, AL, 1931; M.S., University of Michigan, 1936; Ph.D. (science education), 1947. Science Teacher, Fort Valley N & I School, 1932–35; Academic Director and Head of the Science Department, 1936–38; Administrative Dean and Professor of Physical Science, Fort Valley State College, 1939–66; President, 1966–73; President Emeritus, 1973–.

Memberships and awards: Fellow, Atlanta University, 1931–32; fellow, General Education Board, University of Michigan, 1935–36, 1938–39; AAAS; National Institute of Science; National Association for Research in Science Teaching; Phi Delta Kappa.

Dissertation title: A Basis for the Selection of Course Content for Survey Courses in the Natural Sciences.

Ref: *American Men and Women of Science,* 16th p. 549.
The Negro in Science, p. 175.
Who's Who Among Black Americans, 1985, p. 70.

Blanton, John W.   (1922– ——, M)

Engineer (mechanical). Born in Louisville, KY, Jan. 25, 1922. B.S. (mechanical engineering), Purdue University, 1943. Research Engineer in Thermodynamics and Power Plants, Buffalo, NY; helped design and build the first jet-propelled plane in America, the P-59, Air Comet Fighter; Chief Thermodynamics Engineer, Frederick Flader, Inc., Buffalo, NY, 1945–50.

Memberships and awards: Governor, Ohio's Coordinating Council on Drug Abuse.

Ref: *Ebony,* May 1958, p. 22. [p]
Blacks in Science; Astrophysicists to Zoologist, p. 38.
Black Engineers in the United States, p. 19.

Bliss, Norman Randolph   (1937– ——, M)

Engineer (mechanical). Engineer (civil). Born in Cleveland, OH, Nov. 10, 1937. B.S. (mechanical engineering), Case Institute of Technology, 1959; M.B.A., Western Reserve University, 1968. Cleveland Electrical Illuminating

Company, 1959–69; President, Polytech, Inc., Cleveland, OH, 1969–.

Memberships and awards: Society of Automotive Engineers; American Society of Mechanical Engineers; National Society of Professional Engineers.

Ref: *Black Engineers in the United States,* p. 19–20.

Blue, L.   (1800s, M)

Inventor. Patent #298,937, May 20, 1884, for a hand corn shelling device.

Ref: *Afro-American Encyclopedia,* v. 2, p. 348. sketch of device
Negro Almanac, p. 1069.

Bluford, Guion Stewart, Jr   (1942– ——, M)

Astronaut. Military (Air Force). Lt. Colonel. Born in Philadelphia, PA, Nov. 22, 1942. B.S. (aeronautical engineering), Pennsylvania State, 1964; M.S. (aerospace engineering), AF Institute of Technology, 1974; Ph.D., 1978. One hundred forty-four combat missions over Vietnam. First Black American in space, launched Aug. 30, 1983.

Memberships and awards: Honorary D.Sci., Florida A & M University, 1983; Meritorious Service Award, Commendation Medal; Air Medal with nine Oak Leaf Clusters; Cross of Gallantry with Palm Vietnam; Leadership Award, Phi Delta Kappa, 1962; Tau Beta Pi; American Institute of Aeronautics and Astronautics; Outstanding Flight Safety Award, Air Force Institute of Technology, 1974; distinguished National Scientist Award, National Society of Black Engineers.

Dissertation title: A Numerical Solution of Supersonic and Hypersonic Viscous Flow Fields Around Thin Planar Delta Wings.

Ref: *Who's Who Among Black Americans,* 1980–81, p. 67.
Space Challenger: The Story of Guion Bluford, p. 22–23.
Black Engineers in the United States, p. 20.
Who's Who in America, 1986–87, p. 269.
Ebony, Mar. 1979, p. 54–56, 58, 60, 62. [p]

Bluford, John Henry   (1876–19??, M)

Chemist. Born in Gloucester Co., VA, May 16, 1876. B.S., Howard University, 1900; M.A., 1904. Graduate student in Agriculture and Chemistry, Cornell University, 1900–01. Certificate from Jefferson Laboratory of Physics, Harvard University, 1903. Chemistry Professor, North Carolina A & T, Greensboro, NC, 1903–; City Chemist, Greensboro, NC, 1904–.

Memberships and awards: "University Scholar," in Chemistry, Graduate School, University of Pennsylvania, 1900; President, Farmers' Educational Co-operative Union of America; Secretary, Negro Section, American

Association Agricultural Colleges and Experiment Stations; American Association Farmers' Institute Workers; NC Forestry Association.

Pub: Outline on Qualitative Chemical Analysis; contributed to *Southern Workmen and Cyclopedia of American Agriculture.*

Ref: *Who's Who of the Colored Race,* 1915, p. 28–29.

Boddie, William Fisher (1884–1940, M)

Physician. Born in Prospect Circuit AME Church parsonage, 10 miles from Columbus, GA., Dec. 25, 1884. B.S., Morris Brown College; M.D., Meharry Medical College, 1906. Practiced medicine in Forsyth, GA. Very active in National Medical Association affairs. Post Graduate study and observations, Grady Hospital, Atlanta, GA; University of Georgia School of Medicine; Charity Hospital in New Orleans; Mayo Clinic.

Memberships and awards: National Medical Association, Executive Board, President's Advisory Council, Committee on special Legislation, Budget Committee and Chairman, Committee on the Revision of the Constitution and By-Laws.

Ref: National Medical Association, *Journal,* v. 33, Jan. 1941, p. 47. obit & biog

Bolden, Charles F. (1946– ——, M)

Astronaut. Born in Columbia, S.C., in 1946. B.S. (electrical science), U.S. Naval Academy, 1968; M.S. (systems management), U.S.C., 1978. U.S. Naval Test Pilot School, 1979; selected as an astronaut, 1980. Flew Shuttle Columbia in 1986.

Memberships and awards: Received outstanding alumni award from University of Southern California.

Ref: *Jet,* May 10, 1982, p. 15. [p]
       Negro Almanac, 4th ed., p. 1055.

Bolden, Theodore Edward (1920– ——, M)

Pathologist (dental). Dentist. Born in Middleburg, VA, April 19, 1920. B.A., Lincoln University, 1941; D.D.S., Meharry Medical College, 1947; M.S., University of Illinois, 1951; Ph.D. (pathology), 1958. Chairman, Oral Pathology, School of Dentistry, Meharry Medical College, 1962–77; Professor of Pathology, College of Medicine and Dentistry, New Jersey Dental School, 1977; Dean of the College, 1977–78; Acting Chairman, General & Oral Pathology, 1979–80; Trustee Advisor, American Fund for Dental Health, 1978–82, 1982–85; research in histology, peridontal disease, salivary gland pathology.

Memberships and awards: National Institutes of Health Advisory Committee; John Hay Whitney Foundation opportunity fellow, 1951; USPHS fellow, 1958; Diplomate, American Board of Oral Pathology; National Dental Association; Pan Tennessee Dental Association;

Capital City Dental Society; International Association of Dental Research; Sigma Xi; Omicron Kappa Upsilon; Kappa Sigma Pi.

Dissertation title: Changes in the Submaxillary Gland of the Rat Induced by Ligation of the Excretory Duct.

Pub: *Outline of Pathology,* 1960.
       Dental Hygiene Examination Review Book, 4th ed., 1982. (with E. Mobley and E. Chandler)

Ref: *American Men and Women of Science,* 15th ed., p. 574.
       Encyclopedia of Black America, p. 744.
       Who's Who in America, 1986–87, p. 281.
       Who's Who Among Black Americans, 1985, p. 74.

Booker, L. F. (1800s, M)

Inventor. Patent #30,404, Mar. 28, 1899, for a design rubber scraping knife.

Ref: *Afro-American Encyclopedia,* v. 2, p. 357.
       Negro Almanac, p. 1069.

Booker, Walter Monroe (1907–1988, M)

Biologist. Physiologist. Pharmacologist. Born in Little Rock, AR, Nov. 4, 1907. B.A., Morehouse College, 1928; M.S., University of Iowa, 1932; Ph.D., University of Chicago, 1943. Instructor, Biology and Chemistry, Leland College, 1928–29; Instructor, Prairie View College, 1929–31; Head, Department of Biology, 1932–43. From Instructor to Associate Professor, 1943–53; Acting Chairman of the Department, 1953–54; Professor, Pharmacology and Chairman, Department of Pharmacology of the College of Medicine, Howard University, 1954–73; Professor, 1973–. Retired. Area B Mental Health Center; worked on liver drainage in trauma, effects of anesthesia and gastrointestinal physiology.

Memberships and awards: Fellow, American College of Cardiology, 1973–; University of Chicago Club of Washington, Alumnus Award, 1975; Senior Fulbright Scholar 1957 & 1958; Board Director, Washington Heart Association, 1969–; American Society for Pharmacology and Experimental Therapeutics of the National Research Council.

Dissertation title: Acute Effects Resulting from Downward Traction of the Liver.

Pub: Over one hundred scientific papers.

Ref: Drew, C. R. Negro scholars in scientific research. *Journal of Negro History,* v. 35, 1950, p. 145.
       Holders of Doctorates Among American Negroes, p. 186.
       American Men and Women of Science, 14th ed., p. 478.
       Who's Who Among Black Americans, 1985, p. 77.
       Washington Post, C6, Sept. 1, 1988. obit.

Bookert, Charles C.   (1918- ——, M)

Physician. Born in Cottonwood, AL, Aug. 8, 1918. B.S., Morris Brown College; M.D., Meharry Medical College, 1945. Private Practice.

Memberships and awards: Chairman, Board of Trustees, National Medical Association, 1974-75; President, National Medical Association, 1977-78; Distinguished Service Medal, National Medical Association, 1981; American Academy of Family Practice; President, Gateway Medical Group; McKeesport Academy of Medicine; Keystone State Medical Society; Board of Directors, Allegheny County Comprehensive Health Care Commission; Allegheny Regional Health Commission, Allegheny City Medical Society; Medical Society of Pennsylvania; Chi Delta Med.; Phi Beta Sigma; Outstanding Alumnus, Morris Brown College, 1971; Black Achiever, OES, 1974; Contemporary Black Leaders, Yale University Press, 1974.

Ref: Who's Who Among Black Americans, 1985, p. 77.
        National Medical Association, Journal, v. 67, Mar. 1975,
          p. 182. [p]
        National Medical Association, Journal, v. 74, May 1982,
          p. 492. [p]

Bookhardt, A. L.   (1900s, M)

Physician. Discovered chloroseptic throat mouthwash with J. W. Giles.

Ref: Jet, Jan. 15, 1961, p. 15.

Boone, Sarah   (1800s, F)

Inventor. Devised a narrow wooden board with a padded covering with collapsible leg support and called an ironing board. Prior to her invention tables and boards across chairs were used. Patent #473,653 in 1892.

Ref: At Last Recognition in America, v. 1, p. 10.
        Afro-American Encyclopedia, v. 1, p. 358. sketch of iron-
          ing board

Boswell, Paul P.   (1905-1982, M)

Physician. Dermatologist. Born in Pittsburgh, PA, June 12, 1905. B.A., Lincoln University, 1930; B.S., M.B., University of Minnesota; M.D., 1940. Dermatology Consultant, Chicago Board of Health; Lecturer, Michael Reese Nursing School; Lecturer, Provident Hospital Nursing School.

Memberships and awards: National Medical Association; Chicago Dermatology Society; American Academy of Dermatology; Pan American Medical Association; International Society of Tropical Dermatology; Illinois Council for Mental Retardation; Chicago Association of Retarded Children; Man of the Year, Lincoln University.

Ref: They Set the Pace.
        Who's Who Among Black Americans, 1985, p. 79.
        Jet, Mar. 22, 1982, p. 6.

Bouchet, Edward Alexander   (1852-1918, M)

Physicist. Born in New Haven, CT, Sept. 15, 1852. B.A., Yale, 1874; Ph.D. (physics), Yale 1876. Teacher of Science, Institute for Colored Youth, Philadelphia, PA, 1876-1902; Teacher, Sumner High School, St. Louis, MO, 1902-03; Director of Academics, St. Paul School (now St. Paul's College), Lawrenceville, VA, 1905-1908; Principal, Lincoln High School, Gallipolis, OH, 1908-.

Memberships and awards: Phi Beta Kappa; First black to receive a Ph.D. from an American university; First black Phi Beta Kappa.

Dissertation title: Measuring Refractive Indices.

Ref: Dictionary of American Negro Biography, p. 50-51.
        Ebony, July 1950, p. 18.[p]
        Encyclopedia of Black America, p. 187.
        Holders of Doctorates Among American Negroes, p. 145.
        Who's Who of the Colored Race, 1915, p. 21.
        Negro Year Book, 1952, p. 96.
        Black Collegian, Mar./April 1978, p. 32.

Bourgeois, Marie   (1900s, F)

Nurse. Diploma, Freedmen's Hospital School of Nursing, Washington, DC, 19??; B.S., M.S., Ph.D., Catholic University of America. 1968, Served as Assistant Professor, Nursing Administration Major, Georgetown University, Washington, DC; Chief, Research Training Section, Nursing Research Branch of the Division of Nursing, Bureau of Health Professional; Retired, 1982.

Memberships and awards: American Academy of Nursing as an honorary fellow, 1982; Anthropological Society of DC; American Anthropological Association; Board of Trustees, American Nurses Foundation.

Dissertation title: Present-Day Health & Illness Beliefs and
        Practices of the Seneca Indians.

Pub: The Special Nurse Research Fellow: Characteristics and
        Recent Trends, Nursing Research, 1975.
        Several papers on the relationships between nursing and
        anthropology.

Ref: The Path We Tread, p. 139-141. [p] 140.

Bousfield, Midian Othello   (1885-1948, M)

Physician. Insurance Executive. Military Officer. Born in Tipton, MO, Aug. 22, 1885. B.A., University of Kansas, 1907; M.D., Northwestern University School of Medicine, 1909. Commander of Ft. Huachuca U.S. Army Hospital during WWII, first black to do so. Responsible for blacks being members of State Boards of Health. First black on Chicago Board of Education. Director of Negro Health for Rosenwald Fund and Medical Director of Liberty Life Insurance Co.

Memberships and awards: Kappa Alpha Psi; Sigma Pi Phi; fellow, American Medical Association; Illinois Medical Society; Chicago Medical Society; President, National

Medical Association, 1933–34; Acting Assistant Surgeon, Public Health Service, 1918–1919; fellow, American Public Health Association; AAAS; Advisory Council of the National Association of Colored Graduate Nurses.

Ref: Dictionary of American Negro Biography, p. 51–52.
       Encyclopedia of Black America, p. 187.
       Jet, Aug. 23, 1962. [p]
       Who's Who of the Colored Race, 1915, p. 31.
       Who's Who in Colored America, 1927, p. 19. [p] opp. p. 18.
       Who's Who in Colored America, 1930–32, p. 46–47. [p]
       Who's Who in Colored America, 1933–37, p. 68. [p] opp. p. 65.
       Who's Who in Colored America, 1938–40, p. 67–68. [p] p. 65.
       No Time for Prejudice, p. 189.
       National Medical Association, Journal, v. 25, Nov. 1933, p. 1. [p]
       Dictionary of American Medical Biography, p. 83–84.
       Murray, Peter Marshall. Midian O. Bousfield, M.D. 1885–1948. National Medical Association, Journal, v. 40, 1948, p. 120. [p]
       Who's Who in Colored America, 1941–44, p. 67–68. [p] p. 65.

Boutte, Matthew Virgile   (1884–19??, M)

Pharmacist. Born in Olivier, LA, Mar. 20, 1884. B.A., Fisk University, 1908; Ph.C. and Ph.G., University of Illinois, 1911 and 1914. Teacher of Chemistry, Meharry Medical College, 1911–14; Pharmacist, 1913–17; Captain in the Infantry, 1917–19; Pharmacist, 1920.

Memberships and awards: Alpha Phi Alpha; Sigma Pi Phi; National Medical Association.

Ref: Who's Who of the Colored Race, 1915, p. 31.
       Who's Who of the Colored Race, 1927, p. 19.

Bowen, Clotilde Marian Dent   (1923– —, F)

Military (Army). Lt. Colonel. Physician. Psychiatrist. Born in Chicago, IL, Mar. 20, 1923. B.A., Ohio State University, 1943; M.D., Ohio State University, 1947; Residency in TB, Harlem Hospital, 1948–49. Psychiatrist, V.A. Hospital, 1962–67; Active Reserve, 1959–67; U.S. Army, Chief of Psychiatric Services, 1967–68; Neuropsychiatric Consultant, Vietnam, 1970–71; Chief, Department of Psychiatry, 1971–74; Associate Clinical Professor, Psychiatry, University of Colorado School of Medicine, 1971–.

Memberships and awards: First black woman promoted to Lt. Colonel in the Army, July 1968; American Psychiatric Association; Central Neuropsychiatric Association; Alpha Epsilon Iota; Colorado Psychiatric Society; Oregon Psychiatric Association; Academy of Psychosomatic Medicine; National Medical Association; fellow, Menninger Foundation; Association of Military Surgeons of the United States; Delta Sigma Theta.

Ref: Who's Who Among Black Americans, 1985, p. 80.
       Ebony, Nov. 1958, p. 4. [p]
       Ebony, Dec. 1968, p. 100–101, 104, 106, 108. [p]

Bowie, Walter C.   (1925– —, M)

Physiologist (veterinary). Veterinarian. Born in Kansas City, KS, June 29, 1925. D.V.M., Kansas State College, 1947; M.S., Cornell, 1955; Ph.D. (physiology), 1960. Head, Department of Physiology and Pharmacology; Dean, School of Veterinary Medicine, Tuskegee Institute, AL, 1972–; Consultant, Institute of Medicine, National Academy of Science, 1972–74.

Memberships and awards: Commission on Veterinary Medical Science, National Research Council, 1975; Board of Directors, Alabama Heart Association, 1972–76; President, American Society of Veterinary Physiologists and Pharmacologists, 1966–67; Chairman, Council of Deans of American Association of Veterinary Medical Colleges; Principle Investigator of grants for pentose metabolism in the ruminant, 1956–57; further study on absorption and utilization of pentose sugar in ruminants, Public Health Service, 1956–57; The Cerobrospinal Fluid of Dogs: Its Physiological Diagnostic and Prognostic Evaluation, Mark & L. Morris Foundation, 1961–62.

Dissertation title: In Vitro Studies of Rumen Microorganisms Using a Continuous-flow System.

Ref: American Men and Women of Science, 14th ed., p. 505.
       Who's Who Among Black Americans, 1980–81, p. 76.
       Black Collegian, Mar./April 1979, p. 18. [p]
       Ebony, Feb. 1966, p. 73–76, 78, 80. [p]

Bowles, George William   (1879–1951, M)

Physician. Born in York, PA, July 31, 1879. B.A., Livingston College, 1902; M.D. (valedictorian), Howard University School of Medicine, 1906.

Memberships and awards: Chairman, Executive Board of National Medical Association, 1925–; President, National Medical Association, 1938–39; Chairman, Pennsylvania State Medical, Dental and Pharmaceutical Association; Philadelphia Academy of Medicine; American Medical Association; Omega Psi Phi; Pennsylvania State Medical Society; Advisory Council of the National Association of Colored Graduate Nurses.

Ref: Who's Who of the Colored Race, 1915, p. 32.
       Who's Who in Colored America, 1930–32, p. 50.
       Who's Who in Colored America, 1927, p. 20.
       Who's Who in Colored America, 1933–37, p. 70.
       Who's Who in Colored America, 1938–40, p. 69. (1879 as birth date)
       Who's Who in Colored America, 1941–44, p. 68.
       No Time for Prejudice, p. 189.
       National Medical Association, Journal, v. 44, Jan. 1952, p. 69–70. [p] obit & biog

Bowman, Henry A.   (1800s, M)

Inventor. Born in Worchester, MA. New method of making flags; found a New York firm used his invention. Unable to hire lawyers—had to abandon his business. Feb. 23, 1892, patent #469,395.

Ref: Woodson, *The Negro in Our History*, 5th ed., p. 466.

Bowman, James E., Jr.   (1923- ——, M)

Physician. Pathologist. Human Geneticist. Born in Washington, DC, Feb. 5, 1923. B.S., Howard University, 1943; M.D., 1946. Chief Pathologist, Medical Nutrition Laboratory, U.S. Army, 1953-55; Assistant Professor, Medical Director, Blood Bank, University of Chicago, 1962-67; Associate Professor and Professor, Medicine and Pathology, Director of Laboratories, University of Chicago, 1967-81; Director, Comprehensive Sickle Cell Center, University of Chicago, 1973-84.

Memberships and awards: President, Metropolitan Chicago Blood Council; fellow, College of American Pathologists; American Society of Clinical Pathology; Royal Society of Tropical Medicine and Hygiene; American Society of Human Genetics; AAAS; International Congress on Hematology.

Ref: *American Men and Women of Science*, 14th ed., p. 507.
   Who's Who Among Black Americans, 1985, p. 81.
   The Negro in Science, p. 188.
   Ebony, Sept. 1980, p. 34. [p]

Boyd, Evelyn

See: Collins, Evelyn Boyd.

Boyd, Marie Rozina   (19??- ——, F)

Military (Air Force). Colonel. Nurse. Born in Anderson, SC. Diploma, St. Philip Hospital School of Nursing, Richmond, VA; B.S.N., University of Nebraska, Omaha; M.S.N., University of California, San Francisco. From Staff Nurse to Chief Nurse, U.S. Air Force; Medical Inspector, Headquarters, USAF Inspection and Safety Center; served four months as Chief of a Medical Inspection Team, the only time a nurse has held this position; for two years was President of the Education and Scholarship Committee for improving minority students' educational opportunities.

Memberships and awards: Nominated for the E. A. Hoefly Award in 1978; Consultant to Air Force Surgeon General for Nursing Administration.

Ref: *The Path We Tread*, p. 181-182, [p] p. 181.

Boyd, Robert Fulton   (1858-1912, M)

Physician. Dentist. Surgeon. Pharmacist. Born in Pulaski, TN, July 8, 1858. Graduated from Central State College and Fisk University; M.D., Meharry Medical College, 1886; D.D.S., Meharry Medical College, 1887; P.H.C. (certificate of pharmacy), 1890. Superintendent and Chief Surgeon, Mercy Hospital.

Memberships and awards: First President, National Medical Association, 1895-97; Head, Anti-Tuberculosis League; founded Boyd Infirmary in Nashville, 1893, a teaching hospital for Meharry for many years.

Ref: *Dictionary of American Medical Biography*, p. 86-87.
   Encyclopedia of Black America, 1981, p. 188.
   Jet, July 10, 1969, p. 11.
   History of the Negro in Medicine, p. 67-68, [p] p. 67.
   Cobb, W. Montague. Robert Fulton Boyd. National Medical Association, *Journal*, v. 45, May 1953, p. 233-234. [p] cover
   Progress of a Race or the Remarkable Advancement of the American Negro, p. 586-588. [p]

Boykin, Otis   (1920-1982, M)

Inventor. Born in Dallas, TX, 1920. Attended Fisk University and Illinois Institute of Technology, 1946-47. Invented the electrical device used in all guided missiles and IBM computers, plus 26 other electronic devices including a control unit for artificial heart stimulator (pacemaker); worked as a private consultant for several American firms and three firms in Paris, 1964-82. Died in Chicago of heart failure.

Ref: *African Americans in Science and Invention*, p. 70.
   Black Contributors to Science and Energy Technology, p. 13.
   Journal of African Civilizations, Nov. 1979.
   Jet, Apr. 12, 1982, p. 13.
   Blacks in Science: Ancient and Modern, p. 226.
   Negro Almanac, 4th ed., p. 1055.

Bradley, James T.   (19??- ——, M)

Military (Army). Colonel. B.S., Prairie View A & M College, 1951. Served on Operations Directorate of the Organization of the Joint Chiefs of Staff and Department of the Army Office of Deputy Chief of Staff for Logistics.

Ref: *Afro-American Encyclopedia*, v. 2, p. 373. [p]

Bradley, Lillian Katie   (1921- ——, F)

Mathematician. Born in Tyler, TX, Oct. 15, 1921. B.A. (mathematics), Texas College, 1938; M.A. (mathematics education), University of Michigan, 1946; Ph.D. (mathematics education), University of Texas, 1960; first black woman to receive a doctorate from the University of Texas. Chairman, Mathematics Department, Fouke High School, Hawkins, TX, 1938-46; Assistant Professor, Mathematics and Supervisor, Teacher Education Program in Mathematics, Texas College, 1946-50; Chairman and Associate Professor, Mathematics, Texas College,

1950-60; Professor, Mathematics and Supervisor, Mathematics Program in Teacher Education, Prairie View College, 1960-61; Associate Professor, Mathematics, Texas Southern University, 1961-.

Memberships and awards: Beta Kappa Chi; Kappa Delta Pi; NAM (treasurer and state representative).

Dissertation title: An Evaluation of the Effectiveness of a Collegiate General Mathematics Course.

Pub: (Co-author) *College Algebra.* New York, Pitman Publishing Co., 1956.

Modern Elementary School Mathematics. *Texas Standard,* Spring, 1961.

An Evaluation of the Effectiveness of a General Mathematics Course. *American Mathematic Monthly,* 1962.

(Co-author) The Relationship Between the Performance of the Texas Southern University Freshmen on the Mathematics Placement Test and Their High School Mathematics Background. *American Mathematic Monthly,* v. 73, 1966.

Ref: *Who's Who of American Women.*
Black Mathematicians and Their Works, p. 280. [p]

Bradley, Walter Oswald   (1919- —— , M)

Zoologist. Biologist. Born in High Springs, FL, Mar. 5, 1919. B.S., Florida A & M College, 1941; M.S., Howard University, 1944; Ph.D., Catholic University, 1951. High School Science Teacher, Belle Glade, FL, 1941-45; Biology Assistant Professor, Virginia Union University, 1945-48; Professor, 1950; Director, Division of Natural Science.

Memberships and awards: American Association of University Professors; Sigma Xi; Virginia Academy of Sciences; AAAS; Richmond Medical Society.

Dissertation title: The Effects of Certain Antithyroid Drugs on the Uptake of Radioactive Iodine by the Frog Thyroid.

Ref: *American Men of Science,* 11th ed., p. 542.
The Negro in Science, p. 175.

Bradshaw, Walter H., Jr.   (1938- —— , M)

Physician. Psychiatrist. Born in New York, NY, July 15, 1938. B.S., St. Peter's College, 1960; M.D., State University of New York, 1964. Professor and self-employed Psychiatrist, Department of Psychiatry, Howard University Hospital; Director of Residency Training, Howard University Hospital, 1971-77; Acting Chairman, Department of Psychiatry, Howard University College of Medicine, 1973-74; Staff Psychiatrist, National Institute of Mental Health, 1968-71.

Memberships and awards: American Psychiatric Association, 1968-; fellow, American Psychiatric Association, 1977, Commission of Black Psychiatrists, 1974-77; Chairman and Executive Board, Black Psychiatrists of America, 1976-77; American Psychoanalytic Association Visiting Lectureships, Harlem Hospital, 1974; George Washington University, 1977; American Group Psychotherapists Association, 1973.

Pub: Papers in psychiatric journals.

Ref: *Who's Who Among Black Americans,* 1985, p. 86.
Ebony, Aug. 1960, p. 34. [p]
National Faculty Directory, 1988, p. 400.

Brady, St. Elmo   (1884-1966, M)

Chemist. Born in Louisville, KY, 1884. B.A., Fisk University, 1908; M.A., University of Illinois, 1914; Ph.D., University of Illinois, 1916. First Black to receive a Ph.D. in Chemistry; Professor of Chemistry, Howard University; Professor of Chemistry and Head of the Department, Fisk University.

Memberships and awards: Fellow in Chemistry, 1914-16; Phi Lambda Upsilon; National Chemical Society; Sigma Xi.

Pub: Articles in *Science* and *Industrial and Engineering Chemistry.*

Dissertation title: The Divalent Oxygen Atom.

Ref: *Holders of Doctorates Among American Negroes,* p. 145-146.
Scientists in the Black Perspective.
Crisis, Aug. 1916, p. 190-191. [p]

Bragg, Robert Henry   (1919- —— , M)

Engineer. Physicist. Born in Jacksonville, FL, Aug. 11, 1919. B.S. (physics), Illinois Institute of Technology, 1949; M.S. (physics), 1951; Ph.D. 1960. Assistant Physicist, Research Laboratory of Portland Cement Association, 1951-54; Associate Physicist, 1954-56; Associate Physicist, Illinois Institute of Technology, Research Institute, 1956-57; Research Physicist, 1957-59, Senior Physicist, 1959-61; Research Scientist, Palo Alto Research Laboratory, Lockheed Missile and Space Company, 1961-63; Senior Staff Scientist, 1963-69; Chairman of the Department, 1978-81; Professor of Material Science and Mineral Engineering, University of California, Berkeley, 1969-; Principal Investigator, Materials and Molecular Division, Lawrence Berkely Laboratory, 1969-.

Memberships and awards: American Ceramic Society; American Physical Society; American Crystallography Association; American Institute of Mining and Metallurgical Engineers; American Carbon Society; American Association of University Professors; AAAS; Sigma Xi; Sigma Pi Sigma.

Pub: Numerous publications in scientific journals.

Dissertation title: Studies of Imperfections in Nearly Perfect Crystals.

Ref: *American Men and Women of Science*, 15th ed. p. 647.
Black Engineers in the United States, p. 23–24.
Who's Who Among Black Americans, 1985, p. 87.
Who's Who in America, 1986–87, p. 318.

Braithwaite, John Alexander   (1877–19??, M)

Physician. Born in Barbados, B.W.I., Dec. 17, 1877. B.A., University of Durham, England, 1901; M.D., College of Physicians and Surgeons, Boston, MA, 1912. Founder and first Director of St. Paul's Baby Clinic, Cambridge, MA.

Memberships and awards: President, Bay State Medical, Dental and Pharmaceutical Society, 1925; was an Island Scholar, 1897, Rawle Scholar, 1898 and Coloridge Prizeman, 1899.

Ref: *Who's Who in Colored America*, 1933–37, p. 75.
Who's Who in Colored America, 1930–32, p. 54.
Who's Who in Colored America, 1927, p. 23.
Who's Who in Colored America, 1915, p. 35.
Who's Who in Colored America, 1938–40, p. 74.
Who's Who in Colored America, 1941–44, p. 71.

Branch, Melvyn Clinton   (1944– ——, M)

Engineer (mechanical). Born in Charlotte, NC, June 13, 1944. B.S. (aerospace engineering) Princeton University, 1966; M.S. (mechanical engineering), University of California, Berkeley, 1968; Ph.D., 1972. Mechanical Engineer, University of Colorado, Boulder, 1987.

Memberships and awards: Teaching fellow, University of California, Berkeley, 1968–71; Visiting fellow, Imperial College of London, 1971–72; American Society of Mechanical Engineers; AIAA; AAAS; Combustion Institute; Sigma Xi; Pi Tau Sigma.

Pub: Numerous publications in scientific journals.

Dissertation title: Ammonia Oxidation Kinetics in a High Temperature Flow Reactor.

Ref: *Black Engineers in the United States*, p. 24.
National Faculty Directory, 1988, p. 404.

Brandford, Paul   (19??– ——, M)

Engineer. Helped design bridges and power stations; Department of City Planning Cornell University, NY.

Memberships and awards: California Health Department Award, Bay Area Health Facilities Planning Association for examining regional clinics.

Ref: *Ebony*, July 18, 1968, p. 48.
National Faculty Directory, 1988, p. 405.

Branner, George Richard   (1936– ——, M)

Engineer (electrical). Born in Middletown, OH, Nov. 8, 1936. B.S. (electrical engineering), Ohio University, 1959; M.S.,1962; Ph.D., University of Santa Clara, 1973. Electrical Engineer, U.S. Air Force, Wright-Patterson AF Base, Ohio, 1959–67; Electrical Engineer, Sylvania, 1968–69; Senior Member, Technical Staff, ESL, Inc., Sunnyvale, CA; Electrical Engineering Department, University of California, Davis.

Memberships and awards: IEEE; Tau Beta Pi; Sigma Xi, Eta Kappa Nu.

Dissertation title: Synthesis of Matching Networks for Parametric Amplifiers Using Optimization Techniques.

Ref: *Black Engineers in the United States*, p. 24.
National Faculty Directory, 1988, p. 407.

Branson, Herman Russell   (1914– ——, M)

Physicist. Chemist. Born in Pocahontas, VA, Aug. 14, 1914. B.S. (summa cum laude), Virginia State College, 1936; Ph.D. (physics), University of Cincinnati, 1939. Assistant Professor of Physics and Chemistry, Howard University, 1941–43; Director ESMWT Program in Physics, Howard University, 1942–44; Director, ASTRP courses in Physics, Howard University; Director, Office of Naval Research and Atomic Energy Commission Projects in Physics, Howard University, 1947; Director, Research Corporation Project in Physics, 1946–50; Professor of Physics, Howard University, 1944–; Chairman, Physics Department, Howard University, 1941–68; President, Central State University, 1968–70; President, Lincoln University, 1970–85; Retired; Research in mathematical biology, protein structure.

Memberships and awards: AAAS fellow 1936–37; Sigma Xi; Rosenwald fellow; Senior fellow, National Research Council; Sigma Pi Sigma; American Mathematical Society ; American Chemical Society; American Physical Society; Washington Academy of Science; Philosophical Society of Washington; Carver Research Foundation; National Medical Fellowships, Inc, 1971; National Science Teachers Association; National Research Council, 1972–.

Dissertation title: Part I: The Differential Action of Soft X-Rays on Tubifex. Part II: The Construction and Operation of an X-Ray Intensity Measuring Device. Part III: On the Quantization of Mass.

Ref: *Ebony Success Library*, v. 1, p. 40. [p]
American Men and Women of Science, 16th ed., p. 683.
The Negro in Science, p. 189.
Who's Who in America, 1986–87, p. 323.
Who's Who Among Black Americans, 1985, p. 88.
Holders of Doctorates Among American Negroes, p. 146.
Afro-American Encyclopedia, v. 2, p. 375.
Encyclopedia of Black America, p. 190–191.
Blacks in Science, Astrophysicist to Zoologist, p. 16–17.
[p] after p. 48.

Brewer, Mattie D.   (1900s, F)

Midwife. Born in Tennessee in 1882. Delivered 1,000 babies until she was 81.

Ref: *Contributions of Black Women in America,* v. 2, p. 359–360.

Bright, William Michael   (1901–19??, M)

Zoologist. Biologist. Born in Elizabeth City, NC, Jan. 27, 1901. B.S., Howard University, 1926; M.S., 1931, Ph.D., University of Illinois, 1937. Instructor, Biology, Kentucky State College, 1930–31; Professor, Louisville Municipal College, 1931–50; Chairman, Department of Anatomy, Meharry Medical College, 1950–.

Memberships and awards: General Education Board fellow, Illinois, 1936; Microscopical Society; Association of Biology Teachers; National Institute of Science; Sigma Xi.

Dissertation title: Spermatogenesis in sunfish.

Ref: *Holders of Doctorates Among American Negroes,* p. 186.
American Men in Science, 10th ed., p. 450.
National Register, 1952, p. 251.

Briscoe, Madison Spencer   (1905– ——, M)

Parasitologist. Entomologist (medical). Born in Winchester, VA., Mar. 4, 1905. B.A., Lincoln University (PA), 1926; M.A., Columbia University, 1930; Ph.D., Catholic University, 1950. Professor of Biology, New Orleans College, 1926–29; Storer College, 1930–41; Instructor in Bacteriology and Parasitology, School of Medicine, Howard University, 1941–42; Assistant Professor, 1946–50; Professor, 1950–.

Memberships and awards: Helminthological Society of Washington; American Society of Tropical Medicine, Entomological Society of America; Washington Biological Society; Sigma Xi.

Dissertation title: Some Ecological Aspects of Liberia as Interpreted from the Vegetation on Ground and Aerial Photography with Special Reference to the Distribution of Parasites.

Ref: *American Men and Women of Science,* 12th ed., p. 691.
The Negro in Science, p. 175.

Brookes, E. Luther   (19??– ——, M)

Chemist. Educator. Born in Jamaica, B.W.I. B.A., Lincoln University, (PA), (magna cum laude and valedictorian), 1923; M.A. (chemistry), Columbia University, 1928. Head, Department and Professor of Chemistry, 1928–; Acting Dean, Clark University, 1929–30; Florida A & M College, 1926; taught summers at Alabama State Teachers College, 1927–30; Director, Birmingham Branch, Alabama State Teachers' College, 1931–.

Memberships and awards: Board of Directors, Atlanta Tuberculosis Association, 1932–; Alpha Phi Alpha; American Chemical Society; Founder, Alpha Delta Alpha Scientific Society of Clark University.

Pub: Co-author, A Syllabus for an Orientation Course in the Physical Sciences.

Ref: *Who's Who in Colored America,* 1930–32, p. 56–57. [p]
Who's Who in Colored America, 1933–37, p. 79. [p] p. 71.
Who's Who in Colored America, 1938–40, p. 78. [p] p. 71.
Who's Who in Colored America, 1941–44, p. 75. [p] p. 73.

Brooks, Adrian D.   (1894–1958, M)

Physician. Founder and builder of Brookhaven Hospital in Jackson, TN. Died in Toledo, OH, at age of 64.

Ref: *Jet,* Feb. 13, 1958, p. 20.

Brooks, C. B.   (1800s, M)

Inventor. Street sweeper consisting of large brushed on the bottom of a vehicle, patent #556,711, 1896.

Ref: *At Last Recognition in America,* v. 1, p. 42.

Brooks, Edward B.   (1886–19??, M)

Physician. Born in Paducah, KY, Mar. 11, 1886. M.D., Louisville National Medical College, 1908. 1st Lt., U.S. Army, 1912, the only black Physician in Oklahoma holding a Commission by U.S. Employees Compensation Commission; Medical Examiner for six insurance companies.

Memberships and awards: Pottawatomie County Medical Examining Board; Secretary, Historian, President, Executive Board, Oklahoma State Medical, Dental and Pharmaceutical Association; Chi Delta Mu; Oklahoma County and City Medical Society.

Ref: *Who's Who in Colored America,* 1928–29, p. 49.
Who's Who in Colored America, 1933–37, p. 80.
Who's Who in Colored America, 1938–40, p. 81.
Who's Who in Colored America, 1941–44, p. 76.

Brooks, Harry Williams, Jr.   (1928– ——, M)

Military (Army). Major General. Born in Indianapolis, IN, May 17, 1928. B.A., University of Omaha, 1962; M.A., University of Oklahoma, 1973; Four Military Schools; U.S. Army War College, 1970. Assistant Division Commander, 2nd Infantry, U.S. Army, Brigadier General, 1972; retired, 1976; Department of Military Science, Howard University.

Memberships and awards: Legion of Merit; Bronze Star; Army Commendation Medal; Distinguished Service Medal, 1976.

Ref: *Black Americans in Defense of Our Nation,* p. 121. [p]
Ebony Success Library, v. 1, p. 43. [p]
Who's Who Among Black Americans, 1985, p. 96.
National Faculty Directory, 1988, p. 440.

Brooks, Robert Roosevelt (1930- ——, M)

Engineer (electrical). Born in Richmond, VA, Aug. 9, 1930. B.S. (electrical engineering), Howard University, 1959; M.S., University of Pennsylvania, 1964. Senior Electrical Design and Development Engineer, RCA Corporation, Camden, NJ.

Ref: *Black Engineers in the United States*, p. 26.

Brooks, Roosevelt (1902-1985, M)

Physician. Ophthalmologist. Surgeon. Born in Birmingham, AL, Mar. 1, 1902. M.D., University of Illinois, 1930. First black faculty member, University of Illinois Medical School, 1937.

Memberships and awards: American Medical Association; fellow, American College of Surgeons; fellow, Academy of Ophthalmology and Otolaryngology; National Medical Association; Kappa Alpha Psi; American Board of Ophthalmology, 1940.

Ref: *Jet*, April 15, 1985, p. 19.
Who's Who Among Black Americans, 1985, p. 97.
A Century of Black Surgeons, p. 502.

Brothers, Warren Hill (1915-198?, M)

Mathematician. Born in Talladega, AL, Jan. 15, 1915. B.A.,Talladega College, 1936; M.S., Michigan University, 1937, Ph.D. (mathematics), 1945. Instructor, Mathematics, Talladega College, 1937-39; Professor, 1941-50; Head of the Department, 1944-50. Professor, Dillard University, 1950-; research in solutions of boundary value problems in hyperbolic differential equations.

Memberships and awards: General Education Board fellow, Mathematics Society, Sigma Xi; Phi Kappa Phi; fellow in Actuarial Science, 1957-58; American Mathematical Society; Mathematical Association of America.

Dissertation title: On the Solution of Boundary Valve Problems in Hyperbolic Differential Equations.

Ref: *American Men of Science*, 9th ed., p. 229.
Black Mathematicians and Their Works, p. 280-281.
Crisis, Aug. 1936, p. 235. [p]

Brown, Arthur McKimmon (1867-1939, M)

Physician. Born in Raleigh, NC, Nov. 9, 1867. B.A., Lincoln University, 1888; M.D., University of Michigan, 1891, only black in his class. Made an average of 98.25. Surgeon, 10th Cavalry, 1898-99; the only black Surgeon serving in Cuba during Spanish-American War; First black officer commissioned in the regular army, July 1898; denied a pension. Highest score ever made in the history of the Alabama Medical Examining Board. Practiced medicine in Bessemer, AL, for two years, returned to Cleveland. The next year he opened a practice in Birmingham, AL, where he stayed from 1894-1902, after

which he went to Chicago, IL, to practice Medicine, but returned to Birmingham for his wife's health's sake, although she died soon after.

Memberships and awards: President, National Medical Association, 1914; Tri-State Medical, Dental and Pharmaceutical Association.

Pub: Co-author of *Under Fire with the Tenth U.S. Cavalry.*

Ref: *Dictionary of American Negro Biography*, p. 64-76.
In Black & White, p. 120.
Beacon Lights of the Race, 1911, p. 18-25. [P]
Who's Who of the Colored Race, 1915, p. 40.
A Century of Black Surgeons, p. 615-617. (article about his son, Walter Scott Brown)

Brown, Delores Elaine Robinson (1945- ——, F)

Engineer (electrical). Born in Wildwood, FL, Dec. 10, 1945. B.S., Tuskegee Institute, 1967. Evaluation Engineer, USAEC, General Electric Plant, 1967; Engineer, Florida Power Corporation, 1967-70; Evaluation Engineer, Honeywell Aerospace, Inc., St. Petersburg, FL, 1970-75; Quality Engineer, E-Systems ECI Division, St. Petersburg, FL, 1975-78; Sperry Univac, Clearwater FL, Engineer, 1978-; Baptist Minister, 1981-.

Memberships and awards: IEEE; First female engineering graduate from Tuskegee Institute; Society of Women Engineers, 1973-75; Society of Quality Control, 1975-77; Electronic Excellence, Tuskegee Institute.

Ref: *Black Engineers in the United States*, p. 27.
Who's Who Among Black Americans, 1985, p. 100.

Brown, Dorothy Lavinia (1919- ——, F)

Physician. Surgeon. Born in Philadelphia, PA, Jan. 7, 1919. Spent first 12 years in an orphanage. B.A., Bennett College, 1941; M.D., Meharry Medical College, 1948. Chief of Surgery, Riverside Hospital, Nashville, TN, 1960-83; Clinical Professor of Surgery, Meharry Medical College.

Memberships and awards: Fellow, American College of Medicine; Nashville Academy of Medicine; R.F. Boyd Medical Society; National Medical Association; Award for Outstanding Achievement, Delta Sigma Theta Sorority, 1963; Outstanding Citizen, Davidson County Business and Professional Women's Club, 1966-67; Women of the Year, Nashville Jaycees; Women's building at Meharry Medical College named for her; Honorary Doctor of Science, Russell Sage College, Troy, NY, 1972; Served on American Medical Association Joint Committee on Opportunities for Women in Medicine, 1976; fellow, American College of Surgeons (first black female).

Ref: *Who's Who Among Black Americans*, 1985, p. 100.
Profiles in Black, p. 14-15. [p]
Ebony Success Library, v. 1, p. 43. [p]
Bachelor Mother, Ebony, Sept. 1958, p. 92-96. [p]

National Medical Association, *Journal*, v. 60, Mar. 1968,
    p. 136–137, 163.
Ebony, May 1964, p. 76. [p]
A Century of Black Surgeons, p. 591–593. [p]

Brown, E. P.   (1856–19??, M)

Physician. Born a slave in Holmesville, MS, Dec. 13,
1856. Learned to read although a slave. Taught school
until 1886. B.S., Central Tennessee College; M.D., Meharry Medical College, 1886. Practiced Medicine in Utica,
MS, for three years. Had four children all of whom pur-
sued medical degrees. Moved to Greenville in 1889. President of Delta Savings Bank, Greenville, MS. Had an independent fortune consisting of farms and oil land, the
town of Daisy, OK, named for his only daughter, a physician also. Wealthy business man.

Ref: *Beacon Lights of the Race*, p. 487–499. [p]

Brown, Jesse   (1926–1950, M)

Military (Navy). Ensign. Born in 1926.
    Memberships and awards: Congressional Medal of
Honor, awarded posthumously, April 13, 1951. First
black naval officer to die in an American war.

Ref: *Jet*, April 18, 1963, p. 11 [p]

Brown, John Ollis   (1922– ——, M)

Physician. Born in Colbert, OK, Oct. 23, 1922. University
of Wisconsin, 1939–43; M.D., Meharry Medical College,
1950; Residency V.A. Hospital, Tuskegee, AL, 1951–55.
Physician, Cedars of Lebanon Hospital, Jackson Memorial Hospital and Christian Hospital.
    Memberships and awards: President, National Medi-
cal Association, 1987; American Medical Association;
Sigma Pi Phi; Omega Psi Phi.

Ref: *Jet*, April 13, 1987, p. 16.
    Who's Who Among Black Americans, 1985, p. 103.
    National Medical Association, *Journal*, v. 79, June 1987,
        [p] cover

Brown, Leroy J. H.   (1912– ——, M)

Architect. Born in Charleston, SC, Dec. 14, 1912. B.S.,
South Carolina State College; B.S. (architecture), Howard University; M.S. (architecture), Catholic University
of America. One of 11 black architects and engineers
contracted to survey 5,900 buildings for rehabilitation in
Washington, DC, and one of seven black architects re-
tained to make a preliminary study of the future campus
of Federal City College.
    Memberships and awards: American Institute of Ar-
chitects.

Ref: *Ebony Success Library*, v. 1, p. 45. [p]
    Who's Who Among Black Americans, 1985, p. 104.

Brown, Lucy Hughes   (1863–1911, F)

Physician. Born in North Carolina, 1863. M.D., Women's
Medical College of Pennsylvania, 1894. First black
woman physician in Charleston, South Carolina. Estab-
lished a Hospital and Nursing Training School in 1890 in
Charleston with seven other blacks led by Alonzo C. Mc-
Clellan.

Ref: *Send Us a Lady Physician.* p. 113.

Brown, Randolph Kelly   (1909–1975, M)

Physician. Internist. Gastroenterologist. Born in Holli-
daysburg, PA, April 3, 1909. M.D., Howard University
Medical School, 1938; further study, Tufts University. As-
sociate Professor, Chemistry, Howard University,
1945–1971.
    Memberships and awards: Diplomate, American
Board of Internal Medicine, 1948, American Board of
Gastroenterology, 1950; fellow, American College of
Physicians, 1956.

Ref: *The National Register*, 1952, p. 556–557.

Brown, Roscoe Conklin   (1884–19??, M)

Dentist. Born in Washington, DC, Oct. 14, 1884. D.D.S.,
Howard University, 1906. Practiced dentistry, Richmond,
VA, 1907–15; Office of the Surgeon General, U.S. Army,
1918–19; U.S. Public Health Service, 1919–23; Medical
Examiner, National Medical Association and North Carolina Mutual Life Insurance Company of Durham, NC,
1923–.
    Memberships and awards: Omega Psi Phi, National
Medical Association, Advisory Council, National Association of Colored Graduate Nurses.

Ref: *Who's Who in Colored America*, 1933–37, p. 86.
    Who's Who in Colored America, 1930–32, p. 65–66.
    Who's Who in Colored America, 1915, p. 45.
    Who's Who in Colored America, 1928–29, p. 52.
    Who's Who in Colored America, 1938–40, p. 86.
    No Time for Prejudice, p. 189.
    Who's Who in Colored America, 1941–44, p. 85.

Brown, Russell Wilfred   (1905– ——, M)

Bacteriologist (physiological). Microbiologist (medical).
Born in Gray, LA, Jan. 17, 1905. B.S., Howard University, 1926; M.S., Iowa State University, 1932; Ph.D.
(physiological bacteriology), 1936. Instructor, Biology,
Rush College, 1930–31; Associate Professor, Langston
University, 1932–33; Instructor, Tuskegee Institute,
1936–43; Research Assistant, Iowa State College,
1942–43; Professor, Bacteriology, Tuskegee Institute,
1943–; Head, Division of Natural Science, 1943–46; Director, Carver Foundation, 1944–; Chairman, Graduate
Commission, 1946–; Vice-President and Dean, Tuskegee
Institute, 1962–70; Distinguished Professor, Microbiol-

ogy, School of Medical Sciences, University of Reno, NV, 1970; Emeritus Professor of Biology, Tuskegee Institute, 1979.

Memberships and awards: President, SE section, American Society for Microbiology, late 1960's; Sigma Xi, Phi Kappa Phi, National Institute of Science, President, 1949–50; Society of American Bacteriologists; American Chemical Society; Institute of Food Technology; AAAS; Tissue Culture Association; Beta Kappa Chi; National Education Association; Postdoctoral fellow, Yale University School of Medicine, 1956–57; American Institute of Chemists.

Dissertation title: Physiological Studies & Classification of the Butyric Acid Butyl-Alcohol Bacteria.

Ref: *American Men and Women of Science*, 15th ed., p. 735.
Encyclopedia of Black America, p. 744.
Holders of Doctorates Among American Negroes, p. 118.
The Negro in Science, p. 175.
Negro Year Book, 1947, p. 34.
Who's Who Among Black Americans, 1977, p. 113.

Brown, Solomon G.   (1829–1903, M)

Scientific Technician and Lecturer. Born in Washington, DC, Feb. 14, 1829. Worked in Post Office Department in 1844, assisted Morse in installation of wires on poles between Washington and Baltimore to use his Morse Code. Worked in Smithsonian Institution preparing illustrations for lecturers, 1855–1887. Lectured in churches and clubs using information about telegraph, plants, geology and insects which he had learned while working at the Smithsonian.

Ref: *Dictionary of American Negro Biography*, p. 70–71.
Men of Mark, 1970 ed., p. 193–200; 1968 ed., p. 302–313.

Brown, W. Roderick, Jr.   (1895–1965, M)

Physician. Born in Huntington, WV, Dec. 29, 1895. Virginia Union University, 1915; University of Pittsburgh, 1916–18; M.D., Howard University, 1923; Staff, Tuberculosis League Clinic, 1930 until its closing in 1960; research in diseases of the chest.

Memberships and awards: National Medical Association; Vice-President, Pennsylvania State Medical, Dental and Pharmaceutical Society; Treasurer, Medico-Odonto Pharmaceutical Society; Board of Directors, Livingstone Memorial Hospital; Alpha Phi Alpha; Chi Delta Mu; Gateway Medical Group of Pittsburgh; Honorary D.Sci., Virginia Union University.

Pub: New Control of Tuberculosis, *Crisis*, May 1939, p. 139, 158.

Ref: *Who's Who in Colored America*, 1938–40, p. 89.
Who's Who in Colored America, 1941–44, p. 86.
National Cyclopedia of American Biography, v. 50, p. 539. [p] opp. p. 539.
Crisis, May 1939, p. 139 [p]

Brown, Wesley A.   (1927– ——, M)

Military (Navy). Lt. Commander, Born in Washington, DC, 1927. Commissioned Ensign in U.S. Navy. First black graduate of the Naval Academy, 1949. Instructor, U.S. Naval Academy, Annapolis, MD; retired.

Ref: *Jet*, Mar. 31, 1955.
Ebony, April 1960, p. 71–75. [p]
Black Americans in Defense of Our Nation, p. 153. [p]
Crisis, June 1949. [p] cover.

Brown, Willa B.   (1900s, F)

Pilot. Born in Glasgow, KY. M.A., Northwestern University; Master Mechanic's Certificate and Commercial Pilot's Certificate. Operated a flying school near Chicago which she began and was approved by the U.S. Government (Caffey School). One of the few women to combine aviation and business; instrumental in getting black pilots in the Army Air Force, with backing by Eleanor Roosevelt. She became a lieutenant in the Civil Air Patrol.

Ref: *Strength for the Fight*, p. 143.
Women in Aeronautics, p. 170.
Women in Aviation, p. 35–36, [p] portrait 23

Brown, William Wells   (1816–1884, M)

Physician. Practitioner. Born in Lexington, KY, in 1816. With no formal training, he attended medical lectures and demonstrations in Boston where he opened an office in 1865. Practiced medicine for nineteen years.

Pub: *Narrative of William W. Brown, a Fugitive Slave. Written by Himself*, 1847. Reading, MA, Addison-Wesley, 1969, 98 p.

Ref: *The Black Man: His Antecedents, His Genius, and His Achievements*, 1847.
History of the Negro in Medicine, p. 24–26. [p]
Journal, National Medical Association, v. 83 Sup., Dec, 1981, p. 1209.
William Wells Brown, M.D., 1816–1884. National Medical Association, *Journal*, v. 47, May 1955, p. 207–211. [p] cover

Browne, Frederick   (1901–19??, M)

Chemist. Born in Washington, DC, Aug. 1, 1901. B.S., Howard University, 1926; M.S., Fisk University, TN, 1928. Teacher and fellow in Chemistry, Howard University, 1926–27; Chemistry Teacher, Fisk University, 1928–30; Professor, Chemistry, Claflin College, Orangeburg, SC, 1930–.

Memberships and awards: American Chemical Society; Kappa Mu, Honorary Scholastic Society.

Ref: *Who's Who in Colored America*, 1930–32, p. 67.
Who's Who in Colored America, 1933–37, p. 90.

Who's Who in Colored America, 1938–40, p. 90.
Who's Who in Colored America, 1941–44, p. 87.

Browne, Hugh A.   (1900–1962, M)

Physician. Born in 1900. M.D., Howard University, 1928. Youthful victim of tuberculosis, became an authority on the disease in the United States. As Superintendent, he took charge of the McRae Tuberculosis Sanitarium in McRae, AR, in 1931. He then turned a 26 bed Hospital into a 411 bed capacity hospital by 1962.

Memberships and awards: American College of Chest Physicians; American Thoracic Society; National Medical Association.

Ref: *Jet*, Nov. 29, 1969, p. 13. [p]
National Medical Association, *Journal*, v. 55, May 1963, p. 254. obit.

Browne, Marjorie Lee   (1914–1979, F)

Mathematician. Born in Memphis, TN, Sept, 9, 1914. B.S., Howard University 1935; M.S., University of Michigan, 1939; Ph.D. (mathematics), University of Michigan, 1950. One of the first black females to earn a Ph.D. in Mathematics. Teaching fellow, University of Michigan, 1947–48; Professor, and Chairman, Department of Mathematics, North Carolina Central University, 1949–70.

Memberships and awards: American Mathematical Society, Institutional Nominee, University of Michigan, 1948; Mathematical Association of America; Sigma Xi.

Pub: A Note on the Classical Groups. *American Mathematical Monthly*, v. 62, Aug. 1955.

Dissertation title: Studies of One Parameter Subgroups of Certain Topological & Matrix Groups.

Ref: Kenschaft, Patricia C. Black Women in Math in the United States. *American Mathematical Monthly*, v. 88, Oct. 1981, p. 599–600.
Black Mathematicians and their Works, p. 281.
Black Women Achievers Against All Odds, Smithsonian.
Negroes in Science: Natural Science Doctorates, 1876–1969, p. 60.

Bryant, J. Edmond   (1901–1955, M)

Physiologist. Born in Page, ND, Aug. 24, 1901. B.S., Jamestown College, Jamestown, ND, 1923; B.S. (medicine) and M.S. (physiology), University of North Dakota, 1930; B.S. (medicine), Northwestern University, 1926; B.S., University of Chicago, 1928; M.D., Howard University, 1937; interned at Provident Hospital, Chicago and remained there with remarkable energy despite the fact that he was a victim of tuberculosis. Head, Science Department, Paine College, Augusta, GA, 1928–29; Instructor, Physiology, Howard University Medical College, 1930–34.

Memberships and awards: Cook County Physicians Association; National Medical Association; National Tu-

berculosis Association; Editorial Board, National Medical Association *Journal*.

Pub: *Calcium Determination in Sweat*, 1931, paper presented at a meeting of the American Physiological Society, Montreal, Canada.
Ten articles in various medical journals, many on tuberculosis.

Ref: *Who's Who in Colored America*, 1930–32, p. 68.
Who's Who in Colored America, 1933–37, p. 91–91.
Who's Who in Colored America, 1941–44, p. 88.
National Medical Association, *Journal*, v. 48, Mar. 1956, p. 137–139. [p] & obit

Buggs, Charles Wesley   (1906– ——, M)

Bacteriologist (medical). Biologist. Born in Brunswick, GA, Aug, 6, 1906. B.A., Morehouse College, 1928; M.S., University of Minnesota, 1932; Ph.D., 1934. Professor of Chemistry, Bishop College, 1934–35; Professor, Biology and Chairman, Division of Natural Sciences, Dillard University, 1935–43; Instructor to Associate Professor, School of Medicine, Wayne University, 1943–49; Professor, Biology and Chairman, Division of Science, Dillard University, 1949–56; Professor of Microbiology, College of Medicine, Howard University, 1956–71; Head, Department, 1958–70; Project Director, Faculty of Allied Health Science, Charles R. Drew Postgraduate Medical School, University of California, Los Angeles, 1969–72; Dean, 1972; Professor, Microbiology, California State University, Long Beach, 1973–.

Memberships and awards: AAAS; American Association of Pathologists and Bacteriologists; American Public Health Association; National Institute of Science; New York Academy of Science; Society of American Bacteriologists; Society of Experimental Biology and Medicine; Sigma Xi; Rosenwald fellow for postdoctoral studies in Zoology; Shevlin fellow.

Dissertation title: Cataphoretic Phenomena.

Pub: *Premedical Education for Negroes*, 1949.

Ref: *Holders of Doctorates Among American Negroes*, p. 186.
The Negro in Science, p. 176.
American Men and Women of Science, 16th ed., p. 802.
Negro Year Book, 1947, p. 35. (List of publications up to 1947)
Who's Who Among Black Americans, 1985, p. 116.

Bullard, Eugene Jacques   (1894–1961, M)

Aviator. Born in Columbus, GA, Oct. 9. 1894. He was the world's first black combat aviator.

Memberships and awards: Fought for the French Foreign Legion, earning 15 medals including the Legion of Honor. Following his graduation from Flight School, he won $1,000 from an American who felt blacks were incapable of learning to fly.

Ref: *Black Americans in Defense of Our Nation,* p. 31. (sketch)

Carisella, P.J., and James W. Ryan. *The Black Swallow of Death.* [p] p. 151.

Bullock, Carrie E. (18??–1961, F)

Nurse. Born in St. Lawrence, SC. Scotia Seminary, Conrad, NC; Provident Hospital Training, 1909. Visiting Nurse Association, 1909–49; Assistant Supervisor of Chicago Visiting Nurses' Association.

Memberships and awards: Vice-President, Colored Nurses Association; President, Provident Hospital Alumni, 1922–24; First District, Illinois State Association of Graduate Nurses, 1926–. Received Harriet McCormick scholarship as a delegate to V.N.A. She was the third recipient of the Mary Mahoney Award, 1938.

Ref: *Pathfinders,* p. 17–19. [p] p. 224
Who's Who in Colored America, 1928–29, p. 423.
Who's Who in Colored America, 1933–37, p. 95.
Who's Who in Colored America, 1938–40, p. 92.
The Path We Tread, p. 151–152. [p] p. 152.

Burgess, Landry Edward (1908– ——, M)

Physiologist. Born in Baton Rouge, LA, May 9, 1908. B.A., Morehouse College, 1935; M.S., Atlanta University, 1937; Ph.D. (zoology), University of Iowa, 1948. Instructor, Georgia State Teachers College, 1937–39. Assistant Professor, Arkansas A & M, 1939–40; Instructor, Morehouse College, 1947–48; Assistant Professor, Physiology, Meharry Medical College, 1948–49; Associate Professor, 1949–52; Professor, 1952–; Visiting Professor, Department of Zoology, Tennessee State, 1964; Consultant, Veterans Administration Hospital, Tuskegee, 1964; research in liver cirrhosis, paper read before convention of the Federation of American Societies for Experimental Biology, 1960, on substance from grasshopper eggs.

Memberships and awards: Sigma Xi; American Society of Zoologists; American Association for Laboratory Animal Science; Society of Nuclear Medicine; American Medical Association; American Federation of Societies for Research.

Dissertation title: A Quantitative Study of Pterine Pigments in the Developing Egg of the Grasshopper, Melanoplus Differentialis.

Ref: *American Men and Women of Science,* 12th ed., p. 794.
The Negro in Science, p. 176.
Jet, July 21, 1960, p. 22–24.

Burrell, Montrust Q. (1927– ——, M)

Engineer (mechanical). Born in Houston, TX, Oct. 22, 1927. B.S. (mechanical engineering), Howard University, 1951; M.S., Tulane University, 1968. Design Engineer, U.S. Naval Gun Factory, 1951–55; Instructor, Prairie View A & M College, 1956–59; Acting Dean and Dean,

Engineering School, Southern University, Baton Rouge, LA, 1960s.

Memberships and awards: American Society of Mechanical Engineers; American Society of Electrical Engineers; Louisiana Engineering Society; American Society for Engineering Education; Chairman, Board of Directors of Minority Engineers of Louisiana, Inc.

Ref: *Ebony,* May 1986, p. 98. [p]
National Faculty Directory, 1988, p. 506.
Black Engineers in the United States, p. 31.
Who's Who in Engineering, p. 88.

Burt, Robert Tecumseh (1873–19??, M)

Physician. Surgeon. Born in Kosciusko, MS, Nov. 25, 1873. B.S., Central Mississippi College, 1983; M.S., Meharry Medical College, 1897; course in Surgery, Harvard University, 1899–1902. Owner and Surgeon-in-Charge of Home infirmary, Clarksville, TN, which he founded in 1900. In 25 years, he performed over 5,000 operations and his wife developed over 11,000 X-ray plates as well as giving the anesthesia for the operations. He also had many white patients.

Memberships and awards: Clarksville Board of Health; National Medical Association; President, Tennessee State Medical Association.

Ref: *Who's Who in Colored America,* 1915, p. 52–53.
Who's Who in Colored America, 1927, p. 31–32.
Who's Who in Colored America, 1928–29 p. 60.
Who's Who in Colored America, 1930–32, p. 72.
Who's Who in Colored America, 1933–37, p. 96.
Who's Who in Colored America, 1941–44, p. 95.
The Negro Too, In American History, p. 354–56. [p]

Burton, Aldrich Robert (1892–193?, M)

Physician. Born in 1892. B.A., University of Pennsylvania, 1911; M.D., 1917. U.S. Public Health Service, 1919–22; Chief, Genito-Urinary Department, Mercy Hospital, Philadelphia, PA, 1923–.

Memberships and awards: National Medical Association; Philadelphia Academy of Medicine and Allied Societies; American Medical Association; Clinical Pathological Society; Philadelphia County Medical Society; Alpha Pi Alpha.

Ref: *Who's Who in Colored America,* 1928–29, p. 60.
Who's Who in Colored America, 1930–32, p. 73.
Crisis, May 1933, p. 111.

Burton, John Frederick (1913– ——, M)

Physician. Pathologist (forensic). Pathologist (anatomic). Born in Nashville, TN, Mar. 26, 1913. Fisk University and Tennessee State University, 1933; M.D., Meharry Medical College, 1941. Pathologist, Wayne County, MI, Medical Examiner's Office, 1970; Staff Pathologist, V.A. Hospital, Dearborn, MI, 1952–55; Instructor, Cytology, Wayne University, 1955; Chief, Anatomic Pathology, 1958–62; retired.

Memberships and awards: First black to be certified in forensic pathology by the American Board of Pathology, 1964—at that time, there were less than 100 U.S. Pathologists with that distinction; Exchange Trainee with Scotland Yard, London, 1970; Meritorious Service Unit Award, U.S. Army Medical Corps, 1945.

Ref: *Jet*, May 7, 1964, p. 52.
National Medical Association, *Journal*, v. 58, May 1966, p. 223. [p]
Who's Who Among Black Americans, 1985, p. 122.

Burwell, Alphonso Colfax   (1889–19??, M)

Pharmacist. Born in Washington, DC, July 10, 1889. Armstrong High School, Washington DC, 1909; Phar.C., Philadelphia College of Pharmacy, 1913; President and Dean, Washington College of Pharmacy.

Memberships and awards: National Medical Association.

Ref: *Who's Who in Colored America*, 1928–29, p. 60.

Burwell, T. Spotuos   (18??–19??, M)

Physician. B.S., Lincoln University, 1900; M.D., Jefferson Medical College. 1907.

Memberships and awards: Philadelphia County Medical Association; American Medical Association; President, National Medical Association, 1928–29; Alpha Phi Alpha.

Ref: *Who's Who in Colored America*, 1928–29, p. 63.
National Medical Association, *Journal*, v. 20, Jan.–Mar., 1928. [p]
National Medical Association, *Journal*, v. 20, Oct.–Dec., 1928, p. 194.
Who's Who in Colored America, 1938–40.
Who's Who in Colored America, 1941–44, p. 96.
Crisis, Feb. 1929, p. 52, 55. [p]

Busch, Oliver Roy   (1886–19??, M)

Physician. Surgeon. Born in Independence, MO, Oct. 14, 1886. Lincoln Institute, Jefferson City, MO, 1905; M.D., Meharry Medical College, 1911. Secretary of Clinics in George Hubbard Hospital, 1911–12; Resident Physician and Surgeon, Kansas City General Hospital, 1912; Superintendent, Morgan-Busch Sanitarium, Dallas, TX, 1914–.

Memberships and awards: Lone Star Medical, Dental and Pharmaceutical Association; Dallas Medical Society.

Ref: *Who's Who in Colored America*, 1915, p. 53.

Bush, Gow Max   (1909– ——, M)

Anatomist (vertebrate). Biologist. Zoologist. Born in Cincinnati, OH, Dec. 3, 1909. B.S., West Virginia State College, 1933; M.S., Cornell University, 1934; Ph.D., University of Iowa, 1939; Professor of Zoology, Louisville Municipal College, 1934–35; Professor of Zoology, North Carolina College for Negroes, 1935–.

Memberships and awards: Sigma Xi.

Dissertation title: Adaptations for Burrowing in the Forelimb Anatomy of *Citellus tridecemlineatus* (Mitchell).

Ref: *Holders of Doctorates Among American Negroes*, p. 186–187.
American Men of Science, 7th ed., p. 256.

Butcher, George Hench, Jr.   (19??– ——, M)

Mathematician. B.S., Howard University, 1941; M.A., University of Pennsylvania, 1943; Ph.D., University of Pennsylvania, 1950. Instructor, Howard University, A.S.T.P.; Instructor, Mathematics Department, Howard University, 1946–47; Assistant Professor, Mathematics, Howard University, 1947–58; Phelps-Stokes Foundation Summer Institute, Howard University, summers 1955 and 1956; Associate Professor, Mathematics, Howard University, 1959–.

Memberships and awards: National Science Foundation Science Teaching fellowship; Numerical Analysis Computer Institute, University of North Carolina, 1962.

Dissertation title: An Extension of the Sum Theorem of Dimension Theory.

Ref: *Black Mathematicians and Their Works*, p. 281.

Butler, Henry Rutherford   (1862–1931, M)

Physician. Surgeon. Pediatrician. Born in Cumberland County, NC, April 11, 1862. B.A., Lincoln University, PA, 1887; M.A., 1890; M.D., Meharry Medical College, 1890; Special course in Diseases of Children, Harvard Medical School, 1894; Special course in Surgery, Harvard Medical School, 1895. Grand Medical Director, Knights of Pythias, GA, for 15 years; Superintendent, Fair Haven Infirmary, Atlanta, GA, which he organized.

Memberships and awards: Organizer and first President, Georgia Medical, Dental and Pharmaceutical Association; Omega Psi Phi; First Chairman, Executive Board, National Medical Association, 1895; Atlanta Medical Association.

Pub: *Acute Gastro-Infection of Infants and Children*, 1912.
Special correspondent for Atlanta Constitution for 10 years.
Published papers, pamphlets and articles on medical subjects.

Ref: *Dictionary of American Medical Biography*, p. 109.
Who's Who in Colored America, 1915, p. 54.
Who's Who in Colored America, 1927, p. 33.
Who's Who in Colored America, 1928–29, p. 64.
Who's Who in Colored America, 1930–32, p. 74.
The History of the Negro in Medicine, p. 68, 83, 84. [p] p. 83.

W. Montague Cobb, *Henry Rutherford Butler,* M.D.,
1862–1931. National Medical Association *Journal,* v.
51, Sept. 1959, p. 406–408. [p] cover
Crisis, Feb. 1932, p. 62, 63. [p] obit.

Butteese, Shearman   (1870–19??, M)

Inventor. Born in Richmond, TX, May 15, 1870. Attended
public schools in Richmond and Harrisburg, TX, and a
Methodist Seminary in Houston in 1885. Invented E.Z.
Adjustable Sides, a device used on wheelbarrows, express baggage, motor trucks, etc.

Ref: Who's Who in Colored America, 1915, p. 55.

Byas, A. D.   (1871–19??, M)

Physician. Born in Kosciusko, MS, May 9, 1871. Diploma,
Rust University, Holly Springs, MS, 1895; M.D., Meharry
Medical College, 1899. Practiced in Beujestow, TN, for
five or six years, went to Memphis in 1905, and became
one of the busiest physicians in Memphis. Had several
brothers who became physicians also.

Memberships and awards: President, North Memphis
Drug Company.

Ref: Beacon Lights of the Race, p. 424–428. [p]

Byas, James Spencer, Sr.   (1916– ——, M)

Physician. Surgeon. Born in Millington, TN, Nov. 3,
1916. B.S. (chemistry), Lemoyne-Owen College, 1937;
M.D., Meharry Medical College, 1943. Private practice.

Memberships and awards: Charter fellow, American
Academy of Family Practice, 1975–80; Tennessee Academy of Family Practice, 1980; Vice-Chairman, Lemoyne-
Owen College Board of Trustees, 1980; Omega Psi Phi,
1980; Sigma Pi Phi, 1980; Memphis and Shelby County
Medical Society, 1980; Tennessee Medical Society; Bluff
City Medical Society; South Medical Society, 1980; Secretary, Family Practice Staff, Baptist Memorial Hospital,
1974–78.

Ref: Who's Who Among Black Americans, 1985, p. 126.

Byer, Erroll   (19??– ——, M)

Physician. Obstetrician. Gynecologist. Born in St. George
Parish, Barbados. B.S., Richmond College, Staten Island,
1969; M.D., Downstate Medical College, 1974. While
working at Kings County Hospital Center in 1967, he was
involved in the research and study of the Augustine
Blood Groups, a very rare type.

Memberships and awards: Jonas Salk Scholarship,
1969, for original research.

Ref: Profiles in Black, p. 80–81. [p]

Byrd, David Wellington   (1868–1945, M)

Physician. Pharmacist. Born in Ashland, OH, Nov. 1,
1868. B.A., Baldwin University, Berea, OH; Postgraduate work, Harvard University; M.D., Meharry Medical College; Ph.D. Meharry Medical College. Teacher of
Latin and Greek, Rust University, Holly Springs, MS, four
years; Walden University, Nashville, TN, 10 years;
Teacher of Medical Chemistry, Meharry Medical College,
1904–. He established the first public venereal disease
clinic in the nation in 1933. The clinic was an approved
clinic with relation to the U.S. Marine Hospital at Norfolk, VA; Special consultant to the U.S. Public Health
Service, 1938.

Memberships and awards: President, National Medical Association, 1917–1918; Omega Psi Phi.

*Ref: National Medical Association *Journal,* Oct.–Dec. 1916, p.
190–191.
Who's Who in Colored America, 1928–29, p. 64. [p] p. 65.
Who's Who in Colored America, 1938–40, p. 98. [p] p. 93.
Who's Who in Colored America, 1941–44, p. 97. [p] p.
175.
National Medical Association, *Journal,* v. 37, Nov. 1945,
p. 206.
Crisis, May 1938, p. 138–139, 146.

C

Cabiniss, George Williamson   (1857–19??, M)

Physician. Born in Williamson, VA, Aug. 26, 1857. Graduate, Richmond Collegiate Institute; M.D., Howard University Medical School, 1890.

Memberships and awards: President, National Medical Association, 1918; President, Medico-Chirurgical Society, 1906–07; Vice-President of the staff of the 19th
Street Baptist Free Dispensary, Washington, DC, 1907.

Ref: Howard University Medical Department, p. 153. [p]
National Medical Association, *Journal,* v. 9, Oct.–Dec.
1917, p. 199.

Cabiniss, Charles   (1927–1979, M)

Physician. Surgeon. Obstetrician.

Ref: Ebony, Jan. 1954, p. 73. [p]
National Medical Association, *Journal,* v. 72, Aug. 1980,
p. 793. obit.

Cadoria, Sherian Grace   (1940– ——, F)

Military (Army). Brigadier General. Born in Marksville,
LA, Jan. 26, 1940. B.S. (business education), Southern
University, 1961; Command and Staff College Diploma,
1971; M.A. (human relations), University of Oklahoma,
1974; AUS War College diploma, 1979; National Defense
University Institute of Higher Defense Studies, 1985.
Highest ranking black woman in the U.S. Army; Director

of Manpower and Personnel in the Organization of the Joint Chiefs of Staff; first woman from the Military Police Corps/Combat Support arms promoted to General.

Ref: *Ebony*, Dec. 1985, p. 140, 142, 144, 146. [p]
Who's Who Among Black Americans, 1985, p. 128.
Black Americans in Defense of Our Nation, p. 126. [p] only

Callender, Clive Orville   (1936- ——, M)

Physician. Surgeon. Born in New York, NY, Nov. 16, 1936. B.A., Hunter College, 1959; M.D., Meharry Medical College, 1963. Assistant Resident, Harlem Hospital, 1964–65; Assistant Resident, Memorial Hospital for Cancer and Allied Diseases, 1966–67; Chief Resident, Howard University Hospital, 1968–69; Medical Officer, DC General Hospital, 1970–71; Assistant Professor, Howard University Medical College, 1973–76; Professor, 1982–. Transplant Director, Howard University Hospital, 1973–.

Memberships and awards: District of Columbia Medical Society; Transplantation Society; American Society of Transplant Surgeons; fellow, American College of Surgeons; Alpha Phi Alpha; Diplomate, American Board of Surgery; National Medical Association; Hoffman La Roche Award, 1961. Only black member, Task Force on Organ Procurement and Transplantation.

Ref: *Who's Who Among Black Americans*, 1985, p. 131.
Ebony, April 1977, p. 59–62, 64–66.
A Century of Black Surgeons, p. 47–49. [p]
Black Enterprise, Oct. 1988, p. 90. [p]

Callender, Leroy Nathaniel   (1932- ——, M)

Engineer (structural). Engineer (civil). Born in New York, NY, Feb. 22, 1932. B.C.E., City College of New York, 1958. Draftsman, 1950–52; Project Engineer, Severeid Associates, 1959–68; owns his own firm, Callender Consulting Engineers, 1969–.

Memberships and awards: Engineer on first nuclear power plant built in the East after his discharge from the Army; consultant on $6.3 million Whitney Young Complex and $3.2 million dormitory at Mary Holmes College; $30 million Lindsay-Bushwick House and $14 million Douglas Circle Project.

Ref: *Black Engineers in the U.S.*, p. 33.
Who's Who Among Black Americans, 1985, p. 131.
Ebony Success Library, v. 1, p. 57. [p]; v. 2, p. 36. [p]

Callis, Henry Arthur   (1887–1974, M)

Physician. Internist. Cardiologist. Born in Rochester, NY, Jan. 14, 1887. B.A., Cornell University, 1909; University of Chicago School of Science; M.D., Rush Medical College, 1922. Chemist, 1915–17; Medical Laboratorian, 1917–19; Bacteriologist, 1922–23; Physician, 1923–27; Pathologist, 1927–30; Associate Professor of Medicine,

Howard University, 1930–39. Private Practice, 1939–63. Retired.

Memberships and awards: Founder of Alpha Phi Alpha Fraternity; life member, Association for the Study of Negro History; Henry A. Callis Student Loan Fund established in his honor; National Medical Association; Diplomate, American Board of Internal Medicine; American College of Cardiology.

Pub: Articles on medical subjects in the National Medical Association, *Journal*; U.S. Veterans Bureau, *Medical Bulletin*; *Journal of Urology*; and *Medical Journal of Record*.

Ref: *American Men of Science*, 11th ed., p. 727.
Who's Who in Colored America, 1930–32, p. 78.
Who's Who in Colored America, 1933–37, p. 102.
Who's Who in Colored America, 1938–40, p. 101.
Who's Who in Colored America, 1941–44, p. 101.
National Medical Association, *Journal*, v. 21, Apr./June, 1929, p. 64–65.
Ebony, Oct. 1958, p. 58–59. [p]
National Medical Association, *Journal*, v. 67, July 1975, p. 333–334. obit
Jet, Dec. 5, 1974, p. 18.

Calloway, Nathaniel Oglesby   (1907–1979, M)

Physician. Chemist (organic). Born in Tuskegee, AL, Oct. 10, 1907. B.S., Iowa State College, 1930; Ph.D., 1934; M.D., University of Illinois, 1943. Head, Chemistry Department, Tuskegee Institute, 1933–36; Assistant Professor, Fisk University, 1936–40; Instructor, Pharmacology, University of Chicago, 1940–42; Lieutenant, Medical Corps, 1943–45; appointed Lecturer in Internal Medicine, University of Illinois Medical School, 1945–46; Major, 1950–53; Assistant Chief, Medicine, Percy Jones Army Hospital; Assistant Professor of Internal Medicine and Senior Physician, University of Illinois Medical School, 1947–.

Memberships and awards: Research fellow, Iowa State College, 1930–33; Sigma Xi; AAAS; Phi Lambda Upsilon; American Chemical Society; American Medical Association.

Dissertation title: Condensation Reactions of Furfural and Its Derivatives.

Pub: Over 30 scientific publications and articles as of 1947.

Ref: *American Men of Science*, 11th ed., p. 728.
Holders of Doctorates Among American Negroes, p. 146.
Negro Year Book, 1947, p. 16, p. 37. (list of publications up to 1946)
Ebony, June 1973, p. 76. [p]
Scientists in the Black Perspective.
Jet, Dec. 27, 1979, p. 17.
Medico-Chirurgical Society of the District of Columbia, Inc., *Bulletin*, Nov. 1947, p. 3. [p]
Jet, Aug. 21, 1958, p. 29. [p]
The Negro in Science, p. 176.

Encyclopedia of Black America, p. 213.
In Black and White, p. 156.

Campbell, David Newton Emanuel (1871-19??, M)

Physician. Inventor. Born in Jamaica, B.W.I., Jan. 24, 1871. M.D., Philadelphia Optical College; M.D., Vermont University. Nerve, lung and kidney specialist. Patented a dispenser to prevent tuberculosis and to cure and check insipient cases.

Pub: The X-Ray of Life. Phil., AME Pub. House, 1905.
        Grievance From the Medical Professional For Which Reform Is Imperative.
        Longevity and How to Live Long.
        Tuberculosis and Its Needed Alkali Reserve.
        Many others.

Ref: *Who's Who in Colored America*, 1933-37, p. 105.
        Who's Who in Colored America, 1938-40, p. 102.
        Who's Who in Colored America, 1941-44, p. 102.

Campbell, Haywood (1934- ——, M)

Virologist. Microbiologist. Bacteriologist. Biochemist. Born in Abbeville, LA, April 30, 1934. B.S., Southern University, 1954; M.S., University of Iowa, 1961; Ph.D. (bacteriology), 1962. Biologist, National Institutes of Health, 1956-57; Senior Bacteriologist, 1962-63; Head, Department of Biological Assay Development, 1965-66; Head, Ampoule Pilot Plant, 1966-69; Section Director, Eli Lilly Company, 1969-; Vice-President, Lilly Research Laboratories, Indianapolis, IN.

Memberships and awards: American Society for Microbiological Research.

Dissertation title: Complement Fixing Antigenicity of Coxsackie B Viruses Grown in Tissue Culture.

Ref: *American Men and Women of Science*, 14th ed., p. 617.
        Encyclopedia of Black America, p. 744.
        Ebony Success Library, v. III, p. 38-39. [p]
        Ebony, June 1967, p. 7. [p]
        Ebony, Oct. 1968, p. 17. [p] advertisement
        Ebony, Oct. 1976, p. 6. [p]

Campbell, Robert Lee (1875-19??, M)

Military (Army). Engineer (electrical). Inventor. Born in Athens, GA, Mar. 28, 1875. Tuskegee Institute, AL, 1895; American School of Correspondence, Mathematics and Science. Instructor, A & M College, Huntsville, AL, 1909-12; Instructor, Western University, Kansas City, KS, 1911; Instructor, Machine Shop Practice and Engineering, A & T College, Greensboro, NC, 1913-17, 1919-30; he enlisted in the 49th Volunteer Infantry in the Spanish-American War 1899-1901, was promoted to corporal and sergeant; commissioned 1st Lt. in World War I, 1917; recommended for captaincy in the Battle of Argonne for bravery on the battlefield; invented a valve gear for a

steam engine for which he obtained a patent; had a civil service rating as a steam-electric-engineer.

Memberships and awards: Bronze Medal presented to him for a model locomotive which he built and had on display at the Atlanta Exposition in 1895; Phi Beta Sigma; Legion of Valor.

Ref: *Who's Who in Colored America*, 1930-32, p. 79. [p] opp. p. 74.
        Who's Who in Colored America, 1933-37, p. 106.
        Who's Who in Colored America, 1938-40, p. 103.
        Who's Who in Colored America, 1941-44, p. 102.

Campbell, W. S. (1800s, M)

Inventor. Self-setting animal trap in 1881, patent # 246,368, automatically resetting itself after one animal caught, used extensively by hunters.

Ref: *At Last Recognition in America*, v. 1, p. 3.

Campbell, Wendell Jerome (1927- ——, M)

Architect. Born in East Chicago, IL, April 27, 1927. B.A. (architecture), Illinois Institute of Technology, 1956. Architect—Planner, Purdue-Calumet Development Foundation, 1956-; organized the firm of Wendell Campbell Associates, Inc., 1966, Urban Design Consultants to grassroots organizations working on urban renewal and development in their own communities; design development in multifamily government-assisted programs, schools and institutional buildings; lecturer, Yale University, Illinois University Institute of Technology.

Memberships and awards: American Institute of Architects; National Organization of Minority Architects; Board Director, Chicago American Institute of Architects; Chicago Association of Commerce and Industry; Distinguished Building Award, 1973; Construction Man of the Year, 1973; American Institute of Architects Medal awarded in memory of Whitney Young, Jr., 1976.

Ref: *Profiles in Black*, p. 174-175. [p]
        Who's Who Among Black Americans, 1985, p. 134.

Canady, Alexa I. (1950- ——, F)

Physician. Neurosurgeon (pediatric). Born in Lansing, MI, 1950. B.S., University of Michigan; M.D. (cum laude), University of Michigan, 1975. Pediatric Neurosurgeon, Detroit's Children's Hospital of Michigan; Clinical Instructor, Neurosurgery, Wayne State University.

Memberships and awards: American Medical Association; National Medical Association; Alpha Omega Alpha; Delta Sigma Theta.

Ref: *ABMS Compendium of Certified Medical Specialists*, v. 3, p. 25.
        Ebony, Sept. 1983, p. 72-76. [p]

Canady, Herman George   (1901–1970, M)

Psychologist. Born in Okmulgee, OK, Oct. 19, 1901. B.A., Northwestern University, 1927; M.A. (clinical psychology), 1928; Ph.D. (psychology), 1941. Professor, Psychology and Philosophy, West Virginia State College, 1928–.

Memberships and awards: Sigma Xi; General Education Board fellow for two years; Charter Member, Research Council, West Virginia State College; Chairman, Department of Psychology of the West Virginia Academy of Sciences, 1952–53, 1955–56; Chairman, Department of Psychology of the American Teachers Association, 1936–45; AAAS; American Association of University Professors; Alpha Kappa Delta; Kappa Alpha Psi; Diplomate, American Board of Examiners in Professional Psychology, Inc.

Dissertation title: Test Standing and Social Setting: A Comparative Study of the Intelligence-Test Scores of Negroes Living Under Varied Environmental Conditions.

Pub: The Psychology of the Negro. In *Encyclopedia of Psychology*, edited by P. L. Harriman, Philosophical Library.
The Question of Negro Intelligence and Our Defense Program. *Opportunity*, v. 20.
Many other journal articles.

Ref: *Holders of Doctorates Among American Negroes*, p. 204.
American Men of Science, 11th ed., p. 230. (social & behavioral)
National Register, 1952, p. 252.
Even the Rat Was White, p. 155–157. [p]
Leaders in American Science, 5th ed., 1962–63, p. 103. [p]
Crisis, Aug. 1941, p. 248. [p] only

Cann, John William   (1873–1925, M)

Physician. Born at Somerset Bridge, Bermuda, May 10, 1873. St. James Day School, Bermuda; M.D., Meharry Medical School, 1897; postgraduate work at Harvard Medical School, Boston, MA, 1897–98; Staff, King Edward VII Memorial Hospital, Hamilton, Bermuda.

Memberships and awards: Bermuda Chamber of Commerce, 1905; Colonial Legislature, 1911; Joint Committee House of Assembly and Legislative Council on Tuberculosis; Trustee, Wilberforce University.

Ref: *Who's Who of the Colored Race*, 1915, p. 58–59.
Crisis, April 1925, p. 264. [p]

Cannon, George Dows   (1902–1986, M)

Physician. Radiologist. Born in Jersey City, NJ, Oct. 16, 1902. B.A., Lincoln University, PA, 1924; M.D., Rush Medical College, 1934; Postgraduate studies in Radiology, University of California, New York University, Columbia University, and Albert Einstein Medical School. Radiologist for Daughters of Israel Hospital.

Memberships and awards: Associate Radiologist Emeritus at the Hospital for Joint Diseases; Radiologist, Upper Manhattan Medical Group; fellow, New York Academy of Medicine; New York State Medical Society; American Medical Association; County of New York Medical Society; Chairman, Board of Trustees for Lincoln University for 13 years; Trustee of Barnes Foundation; Honorary L.L.D., Lincoln University; citation from Alumni Association, University of Chicago.

Ref: *Who's Who Among Black Americans*, 1985, p. 135.

Cannon, George E.   (1869–1925, M)

Physician. Born in Carlisle, SC, July 7, 1869. B.A., Lincoln University, (PA), 1893; M.D., New York Homeopathic Medical College and Flower Hospital, 1900; Practiced in New Jersey, 1900–.

Memberships and awards: Chairman, Executive Board, National Medical Association; North Jersey Medical Association; Academy of Medicine of Northern New Jersey; President, Lincoln University Alumni Association.

Ref: National Medical Association, *Journal*, v. 17, Apr.–June 1925, p. 70–71.
National Medical Association, *Journal*, v. 17, July–Sept. 1925, p. 173–174. [p] p. 76.
Who's Who of the Colored Race, 1915, p. 59.

Cannon, Joseph Nevel   (1942– ——, M)

Engineer (chemical). Born in Weldon, AZ, May 2, 1942. B.S. (chemical engineering), University of Wisconsin, 1964; M.S., University of Colorado, 1966; Ph.D. (chemical engineering), 1971. Process Engineer, Dow Chemical Co., 1964–66; Research Engineer, Proctor & Gamble Co., 1965–68; Teaching Associate, University of Colorado, 1970; Assistant Professor, Department of Chemical Engineering, Howard University, 1970–.

Memberships and awards: American Institute of Chemical Engineers; American Society for Engineering Education.

Dissertation title: A Model Study of Transpiration from Broad Leaves.

Ref: *National Faculty Directory*, 1987, p. 538.
Black Engineers in the U.S., p. 33.

Cansler, Charles W.   (1871–19??, M)

Mathematician. Educator. Born in Maryville, TN, May 15, 1871. He had a natural talent for adding four or five columns of numbers and writing the results from left to right almost immediately, and he could give the day of the week of any date. Attended Maryville College, Maryville, TN. Principal of Burnside School in Knoxville, TN, 1896–98; teacher, Austin High School, Knoxville, TN, 1898–1910; Principal of Green School, 1928–3?. He lectured and gave exhibitions of "lightning calculation" in several northern states in 1891 and 1892.

Memberships and awards: The Carnegie Library in Knoxville bears the inscription stating that the library was erected in recognition of Charles Cansler who conceived the idea of the library for his race and assisted materially in securing it.

Pub: Cansler's Short Methods in Arithmetic, 1895.

Ref: *Who's Who in Colored America*, 1930–32, p. 80.
   Who's Who in Colored America, 1933–37, p. 106. [p] p. 103.
   Who's Who in Colored America, 1938–40, p. 105. [p] p. 105.
   Who's Who in Colored America, 1941–44, p. 103. [p] p. 105.

Cardoza, William Warrick   (1905–1962, M)

Physician. Pediatrician. Born in Washington, DC, April 6, 1905. B.A., Ohio State University, 1929; M.D., 1933. Associate Professor of Pediatrics, Freedmen's Hospital; School Medical Inspector for the DC Board of Health; Pioneer investigator of sickle cell anemia.

Memberships and awards: American Academy of Pediatrics; Medical Society of the District of Columbia; Advisory Committee of the District of Columbia Crippled Children Society; National Medical Association; a founder of Alpha Omega Alpha Honorary Society at Howard University, College of Medicine.

Pub: Immunologic Studies in Sickle Cell Anemia, *Archives of Internal Medicine*, Oct. 1937.
   Hodgkin's Disease with Terminal Eosinophilia (co-author), *Journal of Pediatrics*, Feb., 1938.
   Growth and Development of Negro Infants. III. Growth During the First Year of Life. Ibid, 1950.

Ref: National Medical Association, *Journal*, v. 54, Nov. 1962, p. 723–724. obit

Carey, Richard N.   (1953– ——, M)

Physician. Internist. M.D., University of Maryland School of Medicine, 1981. Physician, Harlem Hospital; Clinical Instructor in Medicine, Vanderbilt Clinic of Columbia University—Presbyterian Hospital Medical Center.

Memberships and awards: Received first annual David M. Heyman Award for contribution to development of medical group practice; Diplomate in Internal Medicine.

Ref: *ABMS Compendium of Medical Specialists*, v. 2, p. 256.

Cargill, William Harrison   (1889–19??, M)

Physician. Roentgenologist. Born in Washington, DC, June 22, 1889. Howard University, 1910–13; M.D., Meharry Medical College, 1914. Physician, Provident Hospi-

tal, Baltimore, MD, 1919; Roentgenologist, Provident Hospital, 1932–. The only black X-Ray specialist in Baltimore in 1930's with complete modern X-Ray equipment and offices in 12 rooms. His father was a founder of Provident Hospital in Baltimore (which closed in 1986).

Memberships and awards: President, Kappa Alpha Psi, 1934–46; Maryland Medical, Dental and Pharmaceutical Association.

Ref: *Who's Who in Colored America*, 1933–37, p. 109.
   Who's Who in Colored America, 1938–40, p. 104.
   Who's Who in Colored America, 1941–44, p. 104.

Carnegie, Mary Elizabeth   (1916– ——, F)

Nurse. Nursing Diploma, Lincoln School for Nurses, New York, 1937; B.A., West Virginia State College, 1942; Certificate, University of Toronto, Canada; M.A., Syracuse University, 1952; D.P.A, New York University, 1972. Professor and Dean, School of Nursing, Florida A & M University, Tallahassee; Editorial Staff of the *American Journal of Nursing*, 1953; began the Baccalaureate Nursing Program, Hampton University; retired.

Memberships and awards: Editor Emeritus, *Nursing Research*; nursing archives at Hampton University named for her; President, American Academy of Nursing; Delta Sigma Theta; American Nursing Association; National Black Nurses' Association; American Association for the History of Nursing; Mary Mahoney Award, 1980; Distinguished Service Award, 1985; Chi Eta Phi; Honorary member, Sigma Theta Tau.

Dissertation title: A Comparative Study of the School-Completion Records of Two Groups of Socioeconomically Disadvantaged Students in Programs Leading to Registered Nurse Licensure.

Pub: Contributed chapters to 17 books; published 62 articles in journals.
   The Path We Tread: Blacks in Nursing; 1854–1984. Philadelphia, J. B. Lippincott Co., 1986. 254 p.

Ref: *The Path We Tread*, introduction, back cover, p. 88. [p]
   Ebony, May 1958, p. 4. [p]
   International Directory of Nurses with Doctoral Degrees, 1973, p. 10–11.
   Directory of Nurses with Doctoral Degrees, 1984, p. 11.

Carney, William H.   (1840–1908, M)

Military. Born in Norfolk, VA, 1840. Congressional Medal of Honor for bravery, July 18, 1863, Fort Wagner, Charleston, SC. First black to receive it on May 23, 1900.

Ref: *Jet*, July 22, 1965, p. 11.
   Dictionary of American Negro Biography, p. 90–91.
   Ebony Pictorial History of Black America, p. 305. [p]
   Before the Mayflower, p. 635.
   Black Americans in Defense of Our Nation, p. 58. [p]
   Ebony, Aug. 1968, p. 176. [p]

Carroll, Edward Major   (1916- —— , M)

Mathematician. Born in Corsicana, TX, Dec. 30, 1916. A.A. (mathematics), Butler College, 1937; B.S., Bishop College, 1939; graduate study in mathematics, University of Michigan, 1946-47; M.A. (mathematics), Columbia University, 1952; D.Ed. (mathematics), Columbia University, 1964. Teacher, elementary school, Hallsville, TX, 1939-40; Assistant Professor, Department of Mathematics and Physics, Bishop College, 1940-44, 1946-57; Teacher of Mathematics, D. Morrow High School, Englewood, NJ, 1958-65; Visiting Professor, University of Wisconsin, 1964; Mathematics Consultant and Writer, Educational Services, Inc., 1965 (summer); Referee, *The Mathematics Teacher*, 1970-72; Professor of Mathematics Education, N.Y.U., 1965-.

Memberships and awards: Committee of Examiners (mathematics), National Teachers Examination, Educational Testing Service, 1970-73; Research Advisory Committee, National Council of Teachers of Mathematics, 1968-70; Phi Delta Kappa; Alumni of the Year Award, Bishop College, 1965; Mathematical Association of America.

Dissertation title: Competencies in Mathematics of Certain Prospective Elementary School Teachers.

Pub: Wax Paper Geometry. Watertown, MA, Educational Services, 1965.
Modern School Algebra 1, Morristown, NJ, Silver Burdett, 1971. (Co-author).

Ref: Black Mathematicians and Their Works, p. 281. [p] p. 264.
Who's Who Among Black Americans, 1985, p. 138.
American Men and Women of Science, 15th ed., p. 74.

Carruthers, George R.   (1939- —— , M)

Astrophysicist. Physicist. Engineer (aeronautical). Inventor. Born in Cincinatti, OH, Oct. 1, 1939. B.S. (physics), University of Illinois, 1961; M.S., 1962; Ph.D. (aeronautical and astronomical engineering), 1964. Rocket Astronomy Research Physicist, 1964-82; Head, Ultraviolet Measurements Branch, Naval Research Laboratory; Inventor, lunar surface ultraviolet cameras—a team of engineers used his idea to build it; research in experimental investigations of atomic nitrogen recombination.

Memberships and awards: American Astronomical Society; American Geophysical Union; AIAA; AAAS; National Technical Association; Chairman, Editing and Review Committee and Editor, *Journal of the National Technical Association*, 1983-; Arthur S. Fleming Award, Washington Jaycees, 1971; Exceptional Achievement Scientific Award Medal NASA, 1972; Warner Prize, American Astronomical Society; National Science Foundation fellow; Honorary Doctor of Engineering, Michigan Technological University.

Dissertation title: Experimental Investigations of Atomic Nitrogen Recombination.

Ref: American Men and Women of Science, 12th ed., p. 909.
Blacks in Science, Ancient and Modern, p. 258-262. [p]
Ebony, Sept. 1985, p. 7. [p]
In Black and White, p. 166.
Who's Who Among Black Americans, 1980-81, p. 131.
Who's Who Among Black Americans, 1985, p. 139.
Ebony, Oct. 1970, p. 6. [p]
Ebony, Oct. 1973, p. 61-63. [p]
Blacks in Science: Astrophysicist to Zoologist, p. 13-14. [p] after p. 48.

Carson, Benjamin S.   (1951- —— , M)

Physician. Neurosurgeon (pediatric). B.S., Yale University; M.D., University of Michigan Medical School. Primary Surgeon on the team which separated the German Siamese twins in 1987; Director, Pediatric Neurosurgery and Assistant Professor, Neurosurgery, Oncology, and Pediatrics, Johns Hopkins University School of Medicine.

Memberships and awards: Fellow in Neurological Surgery, Johns Hopkins University; Senior Registrar in Neurosurgery, Sir Charles Gairdner Hospital, Western Australia.

Pub: Factors Affecting Minority Learning in Scientific Fields, *Journal of College Science Teaching*, v. 17, Mar./Apr., 1988, p. 340-341. [p]

Ref: Ebony, Jan. 88, p. 52, 54, 56, 58. [p]
Black Enterprise, Oct. 1988, p. 70. [p]

Carson, Simeon Lewis   (1882-1954, M)

Physician. Surgeon. Born in Marion, NC, Jan. 16, 1882. M.D., University of Michigan, 1903. Founded, owned, and conducted a private hospital in Washington DC, 1919-; Government Physician to Indians at Lower Brule, SD, 1903-08; Assistant Surgeon, Freedmen's Hospital, 1908-18.

Memberships and awards: National Medical Association; Medico-Chirurgical Society of DC; Alpha Phi Alpha; Chi Delta Mu.

Ref: Dictionary of American Medical Biography, p. 123.
Who's Who in Colored America, 1928-29, p. 71.
Who's Who in Colored America, 1930-32, p. 84.
Who's Who in Colored America, 1933-37, p. 110.
Who's Who in Colored America, 1938-40, p. 108.
Who's Who in Colored America, 1941-44, p. 107.
Cobb, W. Montague, Simeon Lewis Carson, M.D., 1882-1954. National Medical Association, *Journal*, v. 46, 1954, p. 414-419. [p] cover

Carswell, Thomas W., Jr.   (1949- —— , M)

Physician. Family Practice. Born in Springfield, IL, Jan. 1, 1949. B.S., Morehouse College, 1972; M.D., University of Illinois School of Basic Medical Science, 1976; University of Illinois Residency in Family Practice, Chief Resident, 1979–80. Medical Director, Peoria, 1978–80; Association for Retarded Citizens, 1978–82; Medical Director, Morehouse Family Practice Center, 1984–.

Memberships and awards: American Board of Family Practice, 1982–; National Medical Association; American Medical Association; Illinois State Medical Society; Peoria Medical Society; Society of Teachers of Family Medicine.

Ref: *Who's Who Among Black Americans*, 1985, p. 139.

Carter, Edward Albert   (1882–1958, M)

Physician. Surgeon. Born in Charlottesville, VA, April 11, 1882. B.Ph., State University of Iowa, 1903; M.D., 1907. Was partner to Dr. R. O. Early (white), bought his interest in 1913. Health Physician for Bluff Creek Township, local Surgeon for C&NW. Railway and for Consolidated Coal Company, Buxton, IA. President of staff of Dunbar Hospital; Surgeon and Medical Examiner for fraternal and insurance agencies.

Memberships and awards: Kappa Alpha Psi; number one of 55 in Medical and State Board Examination; only black M.D. from the State University of Iowa in 1915; only black member in 1915 of Monroe County Medical Society; National Medical Association; Iowa State Medical Society.

Ref: *Who's Who of the Colored Race*, 1915, p. 60.
Who's Who in Colored America, 1927, p. 37.
Who's Who in Colored America, 1930–32, p. 84.
Who's Who in Colored America, 1933–37, p. 113.
Who's Who in Colored America, 1938–40, p. 108.
Who's Who in Colored America, 1941–44, p. 107–108.
Crisis, Aug. 1914, p. 169–170. [p]

Carter, Ellen Woods   (1800s, F)

Nurse. Midwife. Dixie Hospital School of Nursing, 1895. Head Nurse, Good Physician's Hospital in Columbia, SC; became supervisor of black midwives among a population of 4,500 blacks isolated on islands off the coast of SC. She spent 16 years educating the midwives and the population on the value of health and hygiene. Spent several years after traveling to Rome where she was given the trip by the Bureau of Hygiene and Public Health Nursing. She recruited over 55 nurses.

Memberships and awards: Mary Mahoney Award in 1941.

Ref: *The Path We Tread*, p. 154–156. [p]

Carter, Thomas J.   (1900s, M)

Chemist. Inventor. Born in Hopkins, SC. B.S., Benedict College, 19??. Chemist, U.S. Bureau of Standards. Has perfected a leather testing machine which pretests the durability of leather in various kinds of weather.

Memberships and awards: Citation from American Leather Chemists Association.

Ref: *Ebony*, May 1954, p. 4. [p]

Carter, Willie James   (1939– ——, M)

Engineer (civil). Born in Ponchatoula, LA, Oct. 14, 1939. B.S. (civil engineering), Southern University, 1961; M.S., University of Illinois, 1968; Ph.D., 1970. Associate Facilities Engineer, Boeing Company, 1962–64; Assistant Professor, Southern University, 1964–66; Research Assistant, University of Illinois, 1966–69; Associate Professor, Tennessee State University, Department of Civil Engineering, 1969–70; Dean, School of Engineering & Technology, Tennessee State University.

Memberships and awards: American Society of Civil Engineers; American Institute of Aeronautics and Astronautics; Society for Experimental Stress Analysis; Sigma Xi; Tau Beta Pi.

Dissertation title: Parametric Response of Nonlinear Orthotropic Plates.

Ref: *Black Engineers in the U.S.*, p. 35.

Cartwright, Roscoe Conklin   (1919– ——, M)

Military (Army). Brigadier General. Born in Kansas City, MO, May 27, 1919. B.A., San Francisco State College; M.B.A., University of Missouri.

Ref: *Black Americans in Defense of Our Nation*, p. 12. [p]
Ebony Success Library, v. 1, p. 60. [p]

Carver, George Washington   (1864–1943, M)

Agriculturist. Inventor. Born on a Missouri farm near Diamond Grove in 1864. B.S., Iowa Agricultural College, 1894; M.S., 1896. Member of the faculty, Iowa State College of Agriculture and Mechanics in charge of bacterial laboratory work in Systematic Botany. Produced 325 products from peanuts, 108 from sweet potatoes and 75 from pecans. Went to Tuskegee in 1896 as a teacher and remained there until his death. He created 118 products including rubber and over 500 dyes from 28 kinds of plants. He invented a process for producing these paints and stains (1927), for which he received three patents.

Memberships and awards: FDR signed bill in July 14, 1943, for $30,000 for national monument to him—the area of his childhood preserved as a park with a bust of him in Diamond, MO, first national monument to a black; Sc.D., Simpson College, 1928, honorary; was made a member of the Royal Society of Arts in London, England; received the Spingarn Medal in 1923 which is given every year by the National Association for the Advancement of Colored People to the black person who has made the greatest contribution to the advancement of his race.

Ref: *American Men of Science*, 6th ed., p. 230.
      Dictionary of American Negro Biography, p. 92–95.
      Encyclopedia of Black America, p. 218.
      Great Negroes Past and Present, p. 56–57.
      Who's Who Among Black Americans, 1927, p. 38.
      In Spite of Handicaps, p. 45–51. [p] p. 43. biog.
      Black Pioneers in Science and Invention, p. 73–85. [p] p. 74.
      Who's Who in Colored America, 1930–32, p. 87–88. [p] opp. p. 84.
      Who's Who in Colored America, 1933–37, p. 114. [p] p. 111.
      Who Was Who in American History: Science & Technology, p. 98.
      Who's Who in Colored America, 1938–40, p. 112.
      Negro Year Book, 1947, p. 37–39.
      Who's Who in Colored America, 1941–44, p. 111–112. [p] p. 113.
      Afro-American Encyclopedia, v. 5, p. 1277–1280.
      Ebony, Sept. 1963, p. 112. Picture of bust of him in park in Diamond, MO.
      Blacks in Science: Astrophysicist to Zoologist, p. 18–19.

Casey, Edmund Clarence   (1923– ——, M)

Physician. Internist. Born in Marion, IN, 1923. Attended Earlham College, 1942–43; University of Pennsylvania, 1943; M.D., Meharry Medical College, 1948; Postgraduate courses and a course in pulmonary physiology, Cook County Hospital. Assistant Professor of Medicine, University of Cincinnati.

Memberships and awards: Elected member, Board of Trustees, National Medical Association, 1965; Chairman, National Medical Association, 1970; President, National Medical Association, 1971–72; American Medical Association; President, Ohio Thoracic Society, 1970–71; American Lung Association; Academy of Medicine; Chairman, National Advisory Committee, Sickle Cell Anemia Program, National Institutes of Health, Department of Health, Education and Welfare; President, Southwest Ohio Lung Association, 1977; Alpha Phi Alpha.

Ref: *Jet*, Sept. 2, 1965, p. 42. large picture only
      Who's Who Among Black Americans, 1985, p. 145.
      Ebony Success Library, v. 1, p. 61. [p]
      National Medical Association, *Journal*, v. 62, Nov. 1970, p. 486. [p]
      National Medical Association, *Journal*, v. 65, Jan. 1973, p. 1. [p]

Cason, Louis Forrester   (1916– ——, M)

Chemist (organic). Born in St. Paul, MN, June 8, 1916. B.A., Fisk University, 1938. M.S., 1940; Ph.D., Iowa State College, 1949. Instructor, Chemistry, Fisk University, 1941–42; resident fellow, Iowa State College, 1942–45; Research Assistant, 1945–46; Assistant Professor, Tuskegee Institute, 1946–52; Associate Professor, 1952–; research in Medicinal Chemistry, organometallic compounds.

Memberships and awards: American Chemical Society; National Institute of Science; Sigma Xi; Beta Kappa Chi; Phi Lambda Upsilon.

Dissertation title: Some Addition Reactions of Chalcones.

Ref: *The Negro in Science*, p. 181.
      American Men and Women of Science, 12th ed., p. 924.

Cassell, Albert I.   (1895–1969, M)

Engineer. Architect. Born in Townson, MD, 1895. B.A. (architecture), Cornell, 1919. Laid the foundation for a strong Department of Architecture at Howard University where he became head of the department from 1921 through 1928. In 1934 the College of Engineering and Architecture was established at Howard University due greatly to his efforts. Designed most of the buildings at Howard University including Founders Library in 1938. A list of the buildings for which he was architect is in the *Dictionary of American Negro Biography*, p. 97–98.

Ref: *Dictionary of American Negro Biography*, p. 97–98.
      Historical Afro-American Biographies, p. 172–173. [p]
      In Black and White, p. 172.

Catchings, James A. A.   (19??– ——, M)

Dentist. Born in Houston, TX. D.D.S., Howard University, 1944. Taught a Dental Assistants course to hard core inner-city youths in Detroit.

Memberships and awards: Appointed to interim American Dental Association (ADA) Council on Dental Health; Past President (1966–67), (NDA) National Dental Association and Member of its House of Delegates; Executive Council, Detroit District Dental Society; Dentist of the Year; Chi Delta Mu; Omega Psi Phi.

Ref: *Jet*, Jan. 7, 1971, p. 17. [p]
      The Book of Presidents, Leaders of Organized Dentistry N.P.

Cave, Vernal Gordon   (1918– ——, M)

Physician. Dermatologist. Born in Colon, Panama, 1918. B.S., 1941; M.D., Howard University Medical School, 1944. Intern, Harlem Hospital, NY, 1945; Assistant Clinical Professor, NYU Medical College Center for Disease Control, 1972–.

Memberships and awards: President, National Medical Association, 1973–74; American Medical Association; fellow, American College of Physicians; Society for Investigative Dermatology; People to People for Dr. Vernal Cave, Sept. 25, 1970.

Ref: *Who's Who Among Black Americans*, 1985, p. 147.
      Who's Who in America, 1976, p. 537.

Certaine, Jeremiah   (1920- ——, M)

Mathematician. Born in Philadelphia, PA, June 6, 1920. B.A., Temple University, 1940; M.A., Harvard University, 1941; Ph.D., 1945. Staff Member, Radiation Laboratory, M.I.T., 1945–46; Research Mathematician, N.R.L., 1946–48; Assistant Professor, Mathematics, Howard University, 1947–51; Senior Mathematician, Nuclear Development Associates, 1951–58; Manager, Mathematics Department, Research & Development Operation, 1958–64; Science Advisor, Office of the Manager, Research & Development Division, United Nuclear Corporation, 1964–.

Memberships and awards: Rosenwald fellow, Harvard, 1940–43; Mathematical Society; Society for Industrial and Applied Mathematics; Mathematical Association of America; Institute of Management Science.

Dissertation title: Lattice-Ordered Groupoids and Some Related Problems.

Ref: *American Men and Women of Science*, 12th ed., p. 943.
         The Negro in Science, p. 188.

Cesar (Slave)   (1700s, M)

Medical Practitioner. South Carolina slave who was given his freedom by the General Assembly of South Carolina for the discovery of a cure for rattlesnake bite which was published in the *South Carolina Gazette* (Charleston), Feb. 25, 1751. He also was given a stipend of a hundred pounds sterling. The cure was published by Carey in Philadelphia in 1791, and in the *Massachusetts Magazine* in 1792. Cesar described the symptoms and how to prepare and administer the remedy, which consisted of various roots and rum. A reference to his antidote was made in *Domestic Medicine*, published in 1799.

Ref: *History of the Negro in Medicine*, p. 12–13, 207.
         Nine Black American Doctors, p. 7.
             Miller, Kelly. The Historic Background of the Negro Physician, *Journal of Negro History*, v. 1, April 1916, p. 101.

Chambers, Andrew P.   (1931- ——, M)

Military (Army). Major General. Born in Bedford, VA, 1931. Infantry School; Command and General Staff College; Army War College; M.S. (communications), Shippensburg State College, 1974. Commander of Army Readiness and Mobilization Region VII, Fort Sam Houston Texas, 1981–.

Ref: *Ebony*, Nov. 1981, p. 118, 120–122. [p]
         Black Americans in Defense of Our Nation, p. 122. [p] only

Chambers, J. Clarence   (19??- ——, M)

Physician. B.S., Amherst College; M.D., Columbia University College of Physicians and Surgeons. Deputy Medical Superintendent, Harlem Hospital; Superintendent,

Metropolitan Hospital, Welfare Island, NY; Superintendent, James Ewing Hospital, New York.

Memberships and awards: Phi Beta Kappa.

Ref: National Medical Association, *Journal*, v. 43, July 1951, p. 282–283.
         National Medical Association, *Journal*, v. 43, Nov. 1951, p. 407. [p]

Chambers, Lawrence C.   (1929- ——, M)

Military (Navy). Rear Admiral. Born in Bedford, VA, 1929. Second black graduate of the U.S. Naval Academy in Annapolis, MD. First black Annapolis graduate to be commissioned a line officer. Graduated June 6, 1952. B.S. (aeronautical engineering), Naval Postgraduate School, Monterey, CA, 1959. Rear Admiral in 1980. Commander, Naval Air Systems Command; Commanded the carrier Group 3 in the Indian Ocean, including 6,000 personnel and 85 planes; retired.

Ref: *Jet*, June 11, 1964, p. 11.
         Jet, Mar. 13, 1980, p. 57. [p]
         Ebony, May 1978, p. 46. [p] only
         Black Americans in Defense of Our Nation, p. 172. [p] only
         Ebony, Nov. 1981, p. 118, 120–122. [p]

Chambers, Vivian Murray   (1903- ——, M)

Entomologist. Born in Salisbury, NC, June 4, 1903. B.S., Shaw University, 1928; B.A., Columbia, 1931; M.S., Cornell, 1935; Ph.D. (economic entomology), Cornell, 1946. Senior Research Worker, WPA, American Museum of Natural History, 1935–36; Instructor in Science, Lincoln Normal School, AL, 1936–37; Biologist, Alabama Agricultural and Mechanical, 1937–43; Professor of Biology, 1945–; Dean of the School of Arts and Sciences, 1970–.

Memberships and awards: National Institute of Science.

Ref: *American Men and Women of Science*, 12th ed., p. 952.
         In Black and White, p. 176.
         The Negro in Science, p. 176.
         Contributions of Black Women to America, v. 2, p. 425.

Chandler, Edward Marion Augustus   (1887–19??, M)

Chemist. Born in Ocala, FL, April 10, 1887. B.A., Howard University,1913; M.A., Clark College, 1914; Ph.D. (chemistry), University of Illinois, 1917. Chemist, Dicks, David & Heller Company, 1917–21; Plant Chemist, Abbott Laboratories, 1921–24; Consulting Chemist, Lake County, IL, 1924–; research in triphenylmethane dyes.

Memberships and awards: Chemical Society; Second black to earn a Ph.D. in Chemistry, the first being St. Elmo Brady, also from the University of Illinois; fellowship in Chemistry for two years; Phi Lambda Epsilon.

Dissertation title: The Molecular Rearrangement of Carbon Compounds.

Ref: *Holders of Doctorates Among American Negroes*, p. 146.
American Men of Science, 4th ed., p. 170.
Negroes in Science: Natural Science Doctorates, 1876–1969, p. 46.
Crisis, July 1917, p. 155, 118. [p]

Chappelle, Emmett, W.   (1925– ——, M)

Biochemist. Photobiologist. Astrochemist. Born in Phoenix, AZ, Oct. 24, 1925. B.A., University of California, 1950; M.S., University of Washington, 1954. Instructor in Biochemistry, Meharry Medical College, 1950–52; Research Associate, Stanford University, 1955–58; Scientist and Biochemist, Research Institute of Advanced Studies, 1958–63; Biochemist, Hazleton Laboratories, 1963–66; Exobiologist, 1966–70; Astrochemist, 1970–73; Biochemist, Research Center for Space Exploration; Remote Sensing Scientist, Goddard Space Flight Center, 1977–.

Memberships and awards: American Chemical Society; New York Academy of Science; American Society of Photobiology.

Ref: *American Men and Women of Science*, 15th ed., p. 145.
In Black in White, p. 177.
Ebony, Nov. 1961, p. 7. [p]

Charlton, Cornelius H.   (1929–1952, M)

Military (Army). Sergeant. Born in East Gulf, WV, July 24, 1929. Feb. 12, 1952, posthumously awarded the Congressional Medal of Honor for assuming command of his platoon and leading an attack on communist held ridge in North Korea.

Ref: *Jet*, July 25, 1963, p. 11. [p]
Jet, Feb. 13, 1958, p. 11. [p]
Black Americans in Defense of Our Nation, p. 66.

Charlton, Emily C.   (1882–19??, F)

Podiatrist. Born in New York, NY, April 13, 1882. Attended Manual Training School, 1899; graduate of Brooklyn High School; studied at College of City of New York; graduate of First Institute of Podiatry, 1920.

Memberships and awards: First and only black woman honor graduate from First Institute of Podiatry, receiving 99% in physiology; Vice-President and Secretary of New York County Pedic Society.

Ref: *Who's Who in Colored America*, 1927, p. 40. [p] opp. p. 40.
Who's Who in Colored America, 1928–29, p. 74. [p] opp. p. 74.
Who's Who in Colored America, 1930–32, p. 89. [p] opp. p. 90.
Who's Who in Colored America, 1933–37, p. 116. [p] p. 117.

Who's Who in Colored America, 1937–40, p. 116. [p] p. 117.
Who's Who in Colored America, 1941–44, p. 115. [p] p. 117.

Chase, Hyman Yates   (1902– ——, M)

Biologist. Zoologist. Born in Washington, DC, Nov. 24, 1902. B.S., Howard University, 1926; M.S., 1930; Ph.D., Stanford University, 1935. Professor of Zoology, Howard University, 1936–.

Memberships and awards: Society of Zoologists; research in experimental embryology.

Dissertation title: A Comparative Study of Marine Ova and the Effect of Temperature on the Rate of Fertilization Reaction.

Ref: *American Men of Science*, 7th ed., p. 305.
Holders of Doctorates Among American Negroes, p. 187.

Chatman, Donald Leveritt   (1934– ——, M)

Physician. Obstetrician. Gynecologist. Born in New Orleans, LA, Dec. 27, 1934. B.A., Harvard University, 1956; M.D., Meharry Medical College, 1960. Assistant Attending Physician and Vice-Chairman, Department of Obstetrics and Gynecology, Michael Reese Hospital, 1969–74; Associate Professor, Obstetrics and Gynecology, University of Chicago; research in endometriosis and the black female.

Memberships and awards: President, American Association of Gynecologic Laparoscopists (first black); National Medical Association; American Medical Association; fellow, American College of Obstetricians and Gynecologists; Chicago Medical Society; Illinois State Medical Society; Diplomate, American Board of Obstetrics and Gynecology.

Ref: *Jet*, Jan. 11, 1988. p. 20.
Who's Who Among Black Americans, 1985, p. 151.

Chinn, May Edward   (1896–19??, F)

Physician. Born in 1896. B.A., Teachers College of New York; M.D., Bellevue Hospital Medical College, 1892. First black woman to graduate from there and first black woman to intern at Harlem Hospital. M.S. (public health), Columbia University. First woman to ride ambulances on emergency calls. Specialized in cancer research.

Ref: *Send Us A Lady Physician*, p. 112.
American Medical Women's Association, *Journal*, v. 39, Nov.–Dec. 1984, p. 192–195.
New York State Journal of Medicine, April 1985, p. 145–146. [p]

Chissell, R. Garland   (1870–1964, M)

Physician. (Dean of Baltimore Physicians). One of the first staff doctors at Provident Hospital.

Ref: *Jet*, June 4, 1964, p. 50.
National Medical Association, *Journal*, v. 57, Jan. 1965, p. 71. obit

Chisum, Gloria Twine   (1930– ——, F)

Psychologist (experimental). Born in Muskogee, OK, May 17, 1930. B.S., Howard University, 1951; M.S., 1953; Ph.D. (experimental psychology), University of Pennsylvania, 1960. Lecturer, Psychology, University of Pennsylvania, 1958–68; Research Psychologist, Naval Air Development Center, 1960–65; Head, Vision Laboratory, 1965–80; Head, Environmental Physiology Research Team, 1980–.

Memberships and awards: Board member, Arthritis Foundation of Eastern Pennsylvania, 1972–80; Trustee, University of Pennsylvania, 1974; Raymond F. Longacre Award, Aerospace Medicine Association, 1979; AAAS; American Psychological Association; Sigma Xi; Optical Society of America.

Dissertation title: Transposition as a Function of the Number of Test Trials.

Ref: *Who's Who Among Black Americans*, 1985, p. 154.
Ebony, Sept. 1970, p. 7. [p]
American Men and Women of Science, 13th ed., p. 211. (Social & Behavioral)

Christian, Eugenia D.   (19??– ——, F)

Biologist. Born in Henderson, KY. B.S., University of Louisville, 1938; M.S., Atlanta University, 1940. Head, Science Department, Bethune-Cookman College; Head, Biology Department, Spelman College.

Memberships and awards: AAAS; National Science Teachers Association; National Institute of Science Protozoology.

Ref: *The Negro in Science*, p. 176.

Christian, John B.   (1927– ——, M)

Chemist (engineering). Inventor. Born in Marietta, GA, Jan. 2, 1927. B.S. (chemistry), University of Louisville, 1950. Chemist, E. I. Dupont de Nemours and Co., 1952–54; Chemist, U.S. Naval Ordnance Laboratory, 1954–55; Materials Research Engineer, U.S. Air Force, OH, 1955.

Memberships and awards: New York Academy of Sciences; one of ten outstanding engineers in the Ohio and Miami Valley Area, 1970.

Pub: Numerous patents and journal articles.

Ref: *Black Engineers in the U.S.*, p. 36–37.

Cille, Michel Du   (1900s, M)

Photographer. Winner of Pulitzer Prize for spot news photography in 1986 *(Miami Herald).*

Clark, John H.   (1900s, M)

Physician. B.S., Knoxville College; M.D., Meharry Medical College; M.S. (health service and hospital administration), University of California at Los Angeles. Fifteen-year veteran of public health service in California; Chief Physician, Los Angeles County Sheriff's Department; Deputy Director, Public Health of Santa Clara County. Third generation physician.

Ref: *Jet*, May 1986, p. 7. [p]

Clark, Julia V.   (19??– ——, F)

Science Educator. B.S., 19??; M.S., 19??; Ph.D., 19??. Associate Professor of Science Education, Texas A & M University, College Station, TX.

Memberships and awards: Chosen from 800 candidates to receive a fellowship from W. K. Kellogg Foundation for $30,000 to develop leadership potential in various areas.

Pub: Black Women in Science, *Journal of College Science Teaching*, v. 17, Mar./April 1988, p. 348–352. [p] See bibliography.

Ref: *Jet*, Sept. 1, 1986, p. 21.
National Faculty Directory, 1988, p. 669.

Clark, Kenneth Bancroft   (1914– ——, M)

Psychologist. Born in Panama Canal Zone, July 24, 1914. B.A., Howard University, 1935; M.S., 1936; Ph.D., Columbia University, 1940. Professor, Psychology, College of City of New York, 1942–75; Ambredge Visiting Professor, Harvard University; Founder/Director, Northside Center for Child Development.

Memberships and awards: Spingarn Medal for research in Psychology, 1961; President, American Psychological Association; Rosenwald fellow; Sigma Xi; Psychologist Emeritus, City College of New York; Distinguished Professor, 1942–75; New York State Board of Regents, 1966; Trustee, University of Chicago; Kurt Lewin Memorial Award, 1965; Kappa Alpha Psi.

Dissertation title: Some Factors Influencing the Remembering of Prose Material.

Pub: Author of more than 16 books on education and psychology.
Prejudice and Your Child, Boston, Beacon Press, 1963. 247 p.

Ref: *Afro USA*, p. 212.
American Men of Science, 10th ed., p. 192. (Social & Behavioral)
Ebony, Nov., 1985, p. 62. [p]

Jet, Sept. 23, 1971, p. 53. [p]
Holders of Doctorates Among American Negroes, p. 204.
Who's Who Among Black Americans, 1985, p. 158.
Who's Who in America, 1986–87, p. 511.
Jenkins, Betty. *Kenneth B. Clark, A Bibliography*. New York, Metropolitan Applied Research Center, 1970.
Ebony Success Library, v. 1, p. 67. [p]
Even the Rat Was White, p. 150–151. [p]
Ebony, Aug. 1972, p. 162. [p]
Living Black American Authors, p. 28–29.
Current Biography, Sept. 1964, p. 80–83. [p]

Clark, Lillian Atkins   (1897–19??, F)

Physician. Born in Richmond, VA, April 29, 1897. Shaw University, 19??–1916; Howard University, 1916–18; M.D., Women's Medical College of Pennsylvania specializing in women's and children's diseases. She was secretary of her senior class and is said to be the only black woman to receive a diploma from the National Board of Medical Examiners. Chief Resident Physician, Douglas Hospital, 1924–26.

Memberships and awards: Fellow, American Medical Association; National Medical Association; Philadelphia Academy of Medicine and Allied Sciences; Secretary, Clinical-Pathological Society; Delta Sigma Theta. While a student at Women's Medical College, she received the Anatomy Prize for an average of 97%, the only prize offered during four-year course.

Ref: *Who's Who in Colored America*, 1928–29, p. 81.
    Who's Who in Colored America, 1930–32, p. 94.
    Who's Who in Colored America, 1933–37, p. 121.
    Who's Who in Colored America, 1938–40, p. 121.
    Who's Who in Colored America, 1941–44, p. 120, 123.
    Negro Year Book, 1931, p. 180.

Clark, Mamie Phipps   (1917– ——, F)

Psychologist. Born in Hot Springs, AR, Oct. 18, 1917. B.S., Howard University, 1938; M.S., 1939. Ph.D. (psychology), Columbia University, 1944. Research Psychologist, American Public Health Association, 1944–45; Research Psychologist, U.S. Armed Forces Institute, 1945–46; Executive Director, Northside Center for Child Development, New York, NY, 1946–; she is married to Kenneth Bancroft Clark, a fellow Ph.D. in Psychology.

Memberships and awards: American Psychological Association; Phi Beta Kappa; Alumni Achievement Award, Howard University; fellow, American Association of Orthopsychiatry; Alumni Award, Columbia University, 1972; Rosenwald fellow, 1940–43.

Dissertation title: Changes in Primary Mental Abilities with Age.

Pub: The Development of Consciousness of Self and the Emergence of Racial Identification in Negro Pre-School Children.

Skin Color as a Factor in Racial Identification of Negro Preschool Children.

Ref: *Even the Rat Was White*, p. 166–167. [p] p. 167.
    Who's Who Among Black Americans, 1985, p. 158.
    American Men and Women of Science, 12th ed., p. 401.

Clark, Mary Frances   (1873–19??, F)

Nurse. Born in Chesterfield County, VA, Mar. 6, 1873. Graduated Nurse Training Department of Freedmen's Hospital, Washington, DC, 1900. First black nurse in Richmond, VA.

Memberships and awards: Honorary President, National Association of Colored Graduate Nurses; Council of Colored Women.

Ref: *Who's Who of the Colored Race*, 1915, p. 66–67.

Clark, Yvonne Young   (1929– ——, F)

Engineer (mechanical). Born in Houston, TX, 1929. B.S. (mechanical engineering), Howard University, 1952; Engineering Management, Vanderbilt University. Gage Designer, Frankford Arsenal, 1952; Equipment Designer, RCA Tube Division, NJ, 1952–55; Head, Mechanical Engineering Department, Tennessee State University School of Engineering and Technology, 1956–70; Research Consultant, Ford Motor Company, 1971–72; Engineering Department, Tennessee State College, 1972–.

Memberships and awards: Society of Women Engineers; National Science Foundation fellow, 1958; American Association of University Professors.

Ref: *Ebony*, May 1986, p. 96. [p]
    Ebony, July 1964, p. 75–76, 78, 80, 82. [p]
    Black Engineers in the United States, p. 38.
    National Faculty Directory, 1988, p. 672.

Clarke, Richard Claybourne   (1879–19??, M)

Chemist. Bacteriologist. Born in New Brunswick, NJ, Feb. 3, 1879. Chemist and Bacteriologist in psychological laboratory of Dr. E. E. Smith, New York, 1901–.

Ref: *Who's Who of the Colored Race*, 1915, p. 67.

Clarke, Wilbur Bancroft   (1929– ——, M)

Chemist (organic). Born in Colon, Panama, July 22, 1929. B.S., Xavier University, 1950; M.S., Indiana University, 1953; Ph.D. (chemistry), 1962. Instructor, Xavier University, 1950–53; Assistant in Neurology, U.S. Army Chemical Center, MD, 1953–55; Assistant in Chemistry, Indiana University, 1956–58; Chemist, Northern Regional Laboratories, 1958–59; Professor, Chemistry, Southern University, 1960–70; Chairman of the Department, 1970–.

Memberships and awards: Sigma Xi; AAAS; American Chemical Society; British Chemical Society.

Dissertation title: Investigation of the McFadyen-Stevens Reaction.

Ref: *Leaders of American Science,* 5th ed., 1962–63, p. 124.
[p]
American Men and Women of Science, 16th ed., p. 254.

Clarkson, Llayron L.   (19??– ——, M)

Mathematician. B.S., Texas Southern University, 1950; M.S., Texas Southern University, 1953; Ph.D. (mathematics), University of Texas at Austin, 1967. Instructor, Mathematics, Houston Independent School District, 1951–60; Assistant Professor, Texas Southern University, 1960–67; Chairman, Department of Mathematics, Texas Southern University, Houston, TX, 1969–.

Memberships and awards: American Mathematical Society (1969 Committee on Opportunities in Mathematics for Disadvantaged Groups); Mathematical Association of America; National Association of Mathematicians; National Council of Teachers of Mathematics.

Dissertation title: A Theorem Concerning Product Integrals.

Pub: The Mathematical Sciences. Undergraduate Education, National Academy of Science, 1968.
Participated in the preparation of several Mathematical Association of America Publications.

Ref: *Black Mathematicians and Their Works,* p. 281.
National Faculty Directory, 1988, p. 674.

Clayton, Archer A.   (1894–1967, M)

Physician. B.S., Temple University; M.D., Meharry Medical College, TN. Delivered over 4,000 babies by 1959.

Memberships and awards: Received "Foremost Family Physician for 1959-1960" by Michigan Medical Society in Grand Rapids. First black to receive it. Pharmacist before Physician, began practice at 42.

Ref: *Jet,* Feb. 26, 1967, p. 28–29.
Jet, Oct. 15, 1959, p. 17. [p]

Claytor, William Waldron Shiefflin   (1908–1967, M)

Mathematician. Born in Norfolk, VA, Jan. 4, 1908. B.A., M.A, Howard University, 1929; Ph.D., University of Pennsylvania, 1933. Howard University Mathematics Professor, 1947–. Taught, University of Michigan, West Virginia State, Hampton and Southern University.

Memberships and awards: Harrison Scholar, 1931–32; Harrison fellow, 1932–33; Rosenwald fellow, 1935–36.

Dissertation title: Topological Immersion of Paenian Continua in a Spherical Surface.

Pub: Special Studies in Topology, published in *Annals of Mathematics,* 1934 and 1937.

Ref: *American Men of Science,* 11th ed., p. 892.
Holders of Doctorates Among American Negroes, p. 147.
Black Mathematicians and Their Works, p. xv, 282.
Negro Year Book, 1947, p. 40–41.

Clement, Kenneth Witcher   (1920–1974, M)

Physician. Surgeon. Born in Pittsylvania County, VA, Feb. 24, 1920. B.A., Oberlin College, 1942; M.D., Howard University Medical School, 1945. U.S. Army Flight Surgeon, 1951–53; General Surgery Practice, Cleveland, 1953–; Assistant Clinical Professor of Surgery, Case Western Reserve University School of Medicine, Cleveland, OH.

Memberships and awards: First black president of the Cleveland Baptist Association; Presidents Kennedy and Johnson appointed him to assist in the formulation of Medicare Legislation; Board of Directors, Mt. Pleasant Medical Center; Board of Trustees, Howard University; 29 professional and civil organizations; President, National Medical Association, 1963–64; Distinguished Service Medal, National Medical Association, 1965; Board of Directors, Academy of Medicine of Cleveland, 1970.

Pub: Over 36 papers and articles in journals.

Ref: *History of the Negro in Medicine,* p. 161. [p]
Ebony Success Library, v. 1, p. 71. [p]
National Medical Association, *Journal,* v. 54, Nov. 1962, p. 713, 727. [p]
National Medical Association, *Journal,* v. 57, Nov. 1965, p. 505–506. [p]
Who's Who Among Black Americans, 1975, p. 117.
National Medical Association, *Journal,* v. 67, Jan. 1975, p. 87. obit
National Medical Association, *Journal,* v. 67, May 1975, p. 252–255. [p] cover

Clifford, Thomas E.   (1929– ——, M)

Military (Air Force). Major General. Born in Washington, DC, Mar. 9, 1929. B.A., Howard University, 1949; M.B.A., George Washington University, 1963. Emergency Plans Officer, Secretary of Defense, Pentagon, 1967–69; Commander, 26th North American Air Defense Region, Luke Air Force Base, AZ, 1977–; retired.

Memberships and awards: Air Force Association; Air Force Legion of Merit with one Oak Leaf Cluster; Air Medals with four Oak Leaf Clusters; Distinguished Flying Cross; Air Force Commendation Medal with One Oak Leaf Cluster.

Ref: *Black Americans in Defense of Our Nation,* p. 129. [p]
Ebony, May 1978, p. 42. [p]
Who's Who Among Black Americans, 1985, p. 164.

Cobb, Jewel Plummer   (1924– ——, F)

Biologist (cell). Physiologist (cell). Born in Chicago, IL, Jan. 17, 1924. B.A., Talladega College, 1944; M.S., New

York University, 1947; Ph.D, (cellular biology), New York University, 1950. Assistant Professor, New York University, 1956–60; Professor, Biology, Sarah Lawrence College, 1960–69; Dean and Professor, Zoology, Connecticut College, New London, CT, 1969–76; Dean and Professor, Biology, Douglass College—Rutgers University, 1976–81; President, California State University at Fullerton, 1981–.

Memberships and awards: National Academy of Sciences, Institute of Medicine; Board of Trustees, Institute for Education Management, 1973–; Developer and Director of Fifth Year Post Baccalaureate Pre-med Program; Human Resources Commission, 1974–; National Science Foundation, 1974–; Education Committee, Tissue Culture Association, 1972–74; Research Grant, American Cancer Society, 1971–73, 1969–74; Honorary D.Sci, Pennsylvania Medical College; fellow, National Cancer Institute, 1950–52; fellow, New York Academy of Sciences; Sigma Xi.

Pub: Thirty-five papers on cancer research and related areas.

Ref: *American Men and Women of Science,* 15th ed., p. 266.
Minorities in Science, p. 7.
Who's Who Among Black Americans, 1980–81, p. 156.
Who's Who Among Black Americans, 1985, p. 165–166.
Ebony, Aug. 1982, p. 97–98, 100. [p]
Smithsonian Booklet on Black Women Achievements Against Odds.
Who's Who in America, 1986–87, p. 527.
Ebony Success Library, v. 1, p. 72. [p]
Contributions of Black Women to America, v. 2, p. 426–428. [p]

Cobb, William Montague (1904– ——, M)

Physician. Surgeon. Anthropologist (physical). Anatomist. Born in Washington, DC, Oct. 12, 1904. B.A., Amherst, 1925; M.D., Howard University Medical College, 1929; Ph.D., Case Western Reserve, 1932; Director of Howard University Medical School, 1947–69; Distinguished Professor of Anatomy, 1969–73; Emeritus, 1973–.

Memberships and awards: Distinguished Service Medal, National Medical Association, 1955; AAAS, Vice-President; American Association of Anatomists; Recording Secretary and President, Medico-Chirurgical Society of the District of Columbia; Amherst awarded him the Blodgett Scholarship for proficiency in Biology, which permitted him to spend a summer at the Marine Biological laboratory in Woods Hole, MA, upon graduation from college; Emeritus Professor, Howard University; Editor, *Journal of the National Medical Association,* 1949–; cited by Modern Medicine as principal historian of the Negro in Medicine; President, Anthropology Association of Washington; Vice-President, American Association of Physical Anthropologists; President, National Medical Association, 1963–64; Board of Directors, American

Heart Association; Alpha Omega Alpha; Sigma Xi; Omega Psi Phi; numerous honorary degrees.

Dissertation title: Human Archives.

Pub: Index of the American Journal of Physical Anthropology.
Physical Anthropology of the American Negro.
The First Negro Medical Society, 1939.
Over 500 monographs.
Over 200 biographies of black doctors.

Ref: *American Men and Women of Science,* 15th ed., p. 266–267.
Encyclopedia of Black America, 1981, p. 276–277.
Historical Afro-American Biographies, p. 176. [p]
History of the Negro in Medicine, p. 142. [p] p. 143
Who's Who in Colored America, 1941–44, p. 125.
Holders of Doctorates Among American Negroes, p. 118.
The Negro in Science, p. 176.
Leaders in American Science, 5th ed., 1962–63, p. 126.
Nine Black American Doctors, p. 64–77. [p] p. 64.
Who's Who in America, 1986–87, p. 527.
Ebony Success Library, v. 1, p. 73. [p]
National Medical Association, *Journal,* v. 55, Nov. 1963, p. 551–554. [p]
Who's Who Among Black Americans, 1985, p. 166.
Crisis, Mar. 1955, p. 175. [p] only
National Medical Association, Journal, v. 70, June 1978. [p] cover
A Century of Black Surgeons, p. 470–472. [p]

Cobbs, Price Mashaw (1928– ——, M)

Physician. Psychiatrist. Born in Los Angeles, CA, Nov. 2, 1928. B.A., University of California at Berkeley, 1954; M.D., Meharry Medical College, 1958. Psychiatric Research, Langley Porter Neuropsychiatric Institute, 1961–62; President, Pacific Management Systems, 1967–; Consultant, State of California Department of Corrections, 1963–65; Advisor Esalen Institute; Assistant Clinical Professor, University of California, San Francisco, 1966–; Digital Equipment Corporation, 1975–.

Memberships and awards: Fellow, American Psychiatric Association; International Association of Social Scientists; National Medical Association; Institute of Medicine; National Academy of Sciences; International Association of Social Psychiatrists.

Pub: *The Jesus Bag* (with Wm. H. Grier), New York, McGraw-Hill, 1971. 295 p.
Black Rage (with Wm. H. Grier), New York, Basic Books, 1968. 213 p.

Ref: *Ebony Success Library,* v. 1, p. 73. [p]
Who's Who Among Black Americans, 1985, p. 166.
Who's Who in America, 1986–87, p. 527.
Ebony, July 1987, p. 120. [p]
ABMS, *Compendium of Certified Medical Specialists,* v. 5, p. 383.
Ebony, Aug. 1972, p. 197. [p]
Black Enterprise, Oct. 1988, p. 86. [p]

Coffin, Alfred O. (1861–19??, M)

Zoologist. Biologist. B.A., Fisk University, 1885; Ph.D. (zoology), Illinois Wesleyan University, 1889. First black to obtain a Bioscience Ph.D. Professor of Romance Languages, Langston University.

Dissertation title: The Mound Builders (published).

Ref: *Who's Who of the Colored Race*, 1915, p. 71.
Holders of Doctorates Among American Negroes, p. 187.
Negro Year Book, 1952, p. 96.
Negroes in Science: Natural Science Doctorates, 1876–1969, p. 41.

Cole, Rebecca J. (1846–1922, F)

Physician. M.D., Women's Medical College of Pennsylvania, 1867 (first black woman graduate). First or second black woman physician in the United States, controversial with Crumpler; practiced in Philadelphia, 1872–1881; worked for a while with Elizabeth Blackwell, the first white female physician in the United States; founded, with Dr. Charlotte Abbey, the Women's Directory, a medical and legal aid center; her medical career spanned 50 years.

Ref: *History of the Negro in Medicine*, p. 43.
Negro Almanac, 1976, p. 1043.
Jet, Aug. 27, 1964, p. 11.
Medico-Chirurgical Society of DC, Inc., *Bulletin*, Jan. 1949, p. 3.
Send Us a Lady Physician, p. 108, 110, 113.
We Are Your Sisters, p. 440–441.

Cole, Thomas Winston, Jr. (1941– ——, M)

Chemist (organic). Born in Vernon, TX, Jan. 11, 1941. B.S., Wiley College, 1961; Ph.D. (chemistry), University of Chicago, 1966. Assistant Professor, 1966–69, Atlanta University; Filler E. Calloway Professor of Chemistry, 1969–71; Chairman, Department of Chemistry, 1971–; President, West Virginia State College, 1982–; Visiting Professor, Chemistry Department, MIT, 1973–74; President, Clark College, Atlanta, 1988–.

Memberships and awards: AAAS; American Chemical Society; National Institute of Science; Woodrow Wilson fellow, 1961–62; National Organization for the Professional Advancement of Black Chemists and Chemical Engineers; Georgia Academy of Sciences; Sigma Xi; Sigma Pi Phi; Alpha Phi Alpha; Allied Chemical fellow, 1963.

Ref: *American Men and Women of Science*, 16th ed., p. 309.
Who's Who Among Black Americans, 1985, p. 168.

Coleman, Arthur H. (1920– ——, M)

Physician. Born in Philadelphia, PA, Feb. 18, 1920. B.S., Pennsylvania State University, 1941; M.D., Howard University Medical School, 1944; L.L.B., Golden Gate College, 1956; J.D., 1968. President and Co-Founder, American Health Care Plan, 1973; Executive Director, Hunters Point Baypoint Community Health Services, 1968–72.

Memberships and awards: President, National Medical Association, 1975–77; American Medical Association; California Medical Association; President, John Hale Medical Society; fellow, American Academy of Forensic Science, 1958; President, Northern California Medical, Dental, and Pharmaceutical Association, 1964; President, Golden State Medical Association, 1970–74; World Medical Association; California Academy of Medicine; American Cancer Society; Howard University Alumni Award, 1966; San Francisco Department of Health Commendation, 1976; Omega Psi Phi Award for Distinguished Service, 1973.

Ref: *Who's Who Among Black Americans*, 1985, p. 169.
National Medical Association, *Journal*, v. 67, Nov. 1975, p. 481–482. [p]

Coleman, Bessie (1893–1926, F)

Pilot. Born in Atlanta, TX, Jan. 26, 1893. Went to Europe to learn to fly since all doors were closed in the U.S. for teaching a black woman to fly. Shuster, pilot for Fokker Aircraft Corporation in Germany taught her to fly the German Fokker. She earned an International Pilots License, making her one of the first women and the only black woman so qualified. She had plans to open a school in the United States to teach young black men to fly but on April 30, 1926, she was killed in a plane crash in Jacksonville, FL.

Ref: Patterson, Elois. *Memoirs of the Late Bessie Coleman, Aviatrix.* (written by her sister). 1969. [p]
Ebony, May 1977, p. 88–90, 94, 96. [p]

Coleman, John William (1929– ——, M)

Physicist (molecular). Born in New York, NY, Dec. 30, 1929. B.S., Howard University, 1950; M.S., University of Illinois, 1957; Ph.D. (biophysics), University of Pennsylvania, 1963; Physicist, National Bureau of Standards, 1951–53; Instructor in Physics, Howard University, 1957–58; Engineer, RCA, 1958–; research in physics of electrons, etc.; assisted in development of American electron microscope.

Memberships and awards: David Sarnoff Award, RCA, 1962–63; Electron Microscopy Society; Physical Society; Biophysical Society; Society of Cell Biology; Fulbright Scholar.

Dissertation title: The Diffraction of Electrons in Ultramicroscopic Biological Particles of Ordered Structure.

Ref: *American Men of Science*, 11th ed., sup. 2, p. 158.
Encyclopedia of Black America, p. 744.

Coles, Anna Louise Bailey   (1925- ——, F)

Nurse. Born in Kansas City, KS, Jan. 16, 1925. B.S., Avila College, 1958; M.S., Catholic University, 1960; Ph.D., 1967. V.A. Hospital, Topeka, KS; Teacher, 1950–52; V.A. Hospital, Kansas City, 1952–58; Head, Baccalaureate Nursing Program, Howard University College of Nursing since 1969. Was made Dean in 1968 and spent first year developing curriculum and recruiting faculty members. The Diploma Program, in force since 1894 and between then and 1973, graduated 1,700 nurses. A graduate program was introduced in 1980 leading to a Master of Science in Nursing.

Memberships and awards: Board of Directors, Iona Whipper Home for Unwed Mothers, 1970–72; Board of Regents, State University System of Florida, 1977; Sustained Superior Performance Award, HEW, 1962; Sigma Theta Tau; Alpha Kappa Alpha; Nurses Examining Board; DC League of Nursing; Board of National League of Nursing; Advisory Committee of Visiting Nurses Association; American Nurses Association; American Association of Medical Colleges; American Congress of Rehabilitation Medicine; DC Health Planning Advisory Commission, 1968–71.

Dissertation title: Doctoral Education of Nurses in the United States.

Ref: *Jet*, Aug. 1, 1968, p. 45. [p]
The Path We Tread, p. 40. [p]
Who's Who Among Black Americans, 1985, p. 171.
Who's Who in America, 1986–87, p. 546.
American Men and Women of Science, 16th ed., p. 314.
National Faculty Directory, 1988, p. 708.

Colley, Edward Duval   (1873–1960, M)

Physician. Born in Starksville, MS, May 8, 1873. St. Joseph, MO, High School, 1893; M.D., Howard University, 1897; Postgraduate course, Vienna Clinic, Austria, 1927. Owner of Colley Private Hospital of Cincinnati; Founder, Mercy Hospital and Peter Faucett Memorial Hospital.

Memberships and awards: National Medical Association; Cincinnati Medical Academy; President, Cincinnati Medical Society; Ohio State Medical, Dental and Pharmaceutical Association.

Ref: *Who's Who in Colored America*, 1930–32, p. 102.
Who's Who in Colored America, 1933–37, p. 129.
Who's Who in Colored America, 1938–40, p. 129.
Who's Who in Colored America, 1941–44, p. 129.

Colleymore, Errold Duncan   (1892–19??, M)

Dentist. Born in Bridgetown, Barbados, B.W.I., Oct. 25, 1892. B.S., Howard University, 1919; D.D.S., 1923. Assisted in the organization of the North Harlem Dental Clinic for Children.

Memberships and awards: Secretary, North Harlem Dental Association; Secretary, Westchester Academy of Medicine, 1928–; Omega Psi Phi.

Ref: *Who's Who in Colored America*, 1930–32, p. 102.
Who's Who in Colored America, 1938–41, p. 129.
Crisis, June/July 1952, p. 386. [p]

Collins, Daniel A.   (1916- ——, M)

Dentist. Researcher. Pathologist (oral). Health Educator. Born in Darlington, SC, Jan 11, 1916. B.A., Paine College, 1936; D.D.S., Meharry Medical College, 1941; M.S. (dentistry), University of California, 1944, Certification in Children's Dentistry, Guggenheim Dental Clinic, New York, NY, 1941. Instructor, College of Dentistry, University of California; Research Assistant to Assistant Professor, 1942–60; research in the action of hormones and dental health and the pituitary gland.

Memberships and awards: Named to California State Board of Health and to National Advisory Committee for Selection of Physicians, Dentists and Allied Specialists to National Selective Board in one day; Omicron Kappa Upsilon; Sigma Chi Iota; House of Delegates, California State Dental Association; Board of Trustees, Meharry Medical College; American Academy of Oral Pathology; National Dental Association.

Ref: *Jet*, Nov. 2, 1961, p. 50.
Nine Black American Doctors, p. 909–107. [p] p. 90.
Who's Who Among Black Americans, 1985, p. 173.
Crisis, Aug. 1941, p. 248. [p] only

Collins, Elmer Ernest   (1908- ——, M)

Physician. Pathologist. Born in 1908. B.A., M.D., University of Iowa, 1933; Ph.D., Western Reserve University, 1936. Assistant Professor, Pathology.

Memberships and awards: Ranking student (four years) in medicine; Sigma Xi; Alpha Omega Alpha, honorary medical society.

Dissertation title: The Interstitial Cells of the Testicles—Relationship to Carcinoma.

Ref: *Holders of Doctorates Among American Negroes*, p. 118.

Collins, Margaret Strickland   (1922- ——, F)

Zoologist. Born in Institute, WV, Sept. 4, 1922. B.S., West Virginia State College, 1943; Ph.D. (zoology), University of Chicago, 1950. Instructor, Zoology, Howard University, 1947–50; Assistant Professor, 1950–51; Professor, Biology, Florida A & M University, 1951–; Head, Biology Department, Florida A & M University, 1953–; Department of Zoology, Howard University; presented paper to 125th meeting of AAAS on difference in toleration of drying and rate of water loss between species of Florida termites; research on termites.

Memberships and awards: Society of Zoologists.

Dissertation title: Difference in Toleration of Drying Between Species of Termites (Reticulitermes).

Ref: *Jet*, Feb. 5, 1959, p. 25.
American Men of Science, 11th ed., p. 942.
National Faculty Directory, 1988, p. 713.

Comer, James Pierpont (1934- ——, M)

Physician. Psychiatrist. Surgeon. Public Health Administrator. Born in East Chicago, IN, Sept. 25, 1934. B.A., Indiana University, 1956; M.D., Howard University, 1960; M.P.H., University of Michigan, 1964. Staff Physician, National Institute of Mental Health, 1967-68; Co-Director, Baldwin-King School Program, 1968-73; Assistant Professor, 1968-70, Associate Professor, 1970-75; Professor, Yale University, 1975-76; Maurice Falk Professor of Child Psychiatry, Child Study Center, Yale University, 1976-; Associate Dean of Student Affairs, Medical School, Yale University, 1969-.

Memberships and awards: NIMH fellow, 1967-68; Markle Scholar, 1969; Professional Advisory Council, National Association of Mental Health, 1971-; National Advisory Mental Health Council, HEW, 1976; Assembly of Behavioral and Social Science; National Research Council, 1980; American Psychiatric Association; American Orthopsychiatric Association; American Academy of Child Psychiatry (Council member, 1977-80); Co-Founder, Black Psychiatrists of America; National Medical Association; Outstanding Service to Mankind, Alpha Phi Alpha, Eastern Region, 1972.

Pub: *Beyond Black & White.* New York, Quadrangle Books, 1972. 272 p.
Black Child Care: How to Bring up a Healthy Black Child in America. New York, Simon & Schuster, 1975. 408 p.
School Power: Implications of an Intervention Project. New York, Free Press London, 1980. 285 p.

Ref: *Black Collegian*, v. 5, Sept./Oct. 1974, p. 16, 18. [p] p. 16.
American Men and Women of Science, 16th ed., p. 330.
Who's Who Among Black Americans, 1985, p. 175-176.
Ebony Success Library, v. 1, p. 77. [p]
Ebony, July 1975, p. 69-70, 72-75. [p]
In Black and White, p. 206.
Black Enterprise, Oct. 1988, p. 95.

Conliffe, Calvin Hughes (1926- ——, M)

Engineer (mechanical). Born in Washington, DC, Nov. 21, 1926. B.S. (mechanical engineering), Howard University, 1951. Consultant, Educational Relations, General Electric Co., CT.

Ref: *Black Engineers in the U.S.*, p. 41.

Cooke, Herman Glen (1918- ——, M)

Zoologist. Entomologist. Born in Petersburg, VA, Nov. 28, 1918. B.S., Virginia State College, 1936; M.S., University of Pennsylvania, 1939; Ph.D. (zoology), University of Wisconsin, 1962. Taxonomist Entomologist, Agricultural Research Center, 1944-45; Assistant Professor, Biology, Hampton Institute, 1946-53; Professor, Biology, Elizabeth City State University, 1961-.

Memberships and awards: AAAS; American Entomological Society; International Association of Theoretical and Applied Limnology.

Dissertation title: The Ecology, Life-Histories and Systematics of the Tendipedid (Chironomid) Midges of the Vicinity of Madison, Wisconsin.

Ref: *American Men and Women of Science*, 14th ed., p. 948.
Leaders in American Science, 2nd ed., p. 95.

Cooke, Lloyd Miller (1916- ——, M)

Chemist (industrial). Born in La Salle, IL, June 7, 1916. B.S., University of Wisconsin, 1937; Ph.D. (organic chemistry), McGill University, 1941. Section Leader, Corn Product Refining Co., 1942-47; Group Leader, The Visking Corp., 1947-50; Manager, Cellulose and Casing Research Department, 1950-54; Assistant to Manager, Technical Division, 1954-57; Assistant Director of Research, 1957-65; Manager, Market Research, 1965-67; Manager of Planning, 1967-70; Director of Urban Affairs, New York, NY, 1970-78; Senior Consultant, 1978-81; retired; research on the structure of lignin, carbohydrate chemistry.

Memberships and awards: Honorary L.L.D., College of Ganado; National Science Board, 1970-82; President, National Action Council on Minorities in Engineering, 1981-83; Phi Kappa Phi; Phi Lambda Upsilon; Sigma Xi; American Chemical Society (Councilor); Chicago Section, American Chemical Society (Director, Secretary, Vice-Chairman); Chicago Chemical Library Foundation (Trustee, Treasurer).

Dissertation title: High Pressure Hydrogenation Studies on Lignin and Related Materials.

Pub: Articles to professional journals.

Ref: *American Men and Women of Science*, 16th ed., p. 349.
In Black and White, p. 210.
Who's Who Among Black Americans, 1980-81, p. 168.
The Negro in Science, p. 181.
Who's Who Among Black Americans, 1985, p. 178.
Who's Who in America, 1986-87, p. 569.

Cooper, Chauncy Ira (1906- ——, M)

Pharmacist. Born in St. Louis, MO, May 31, 1906. B.S., University of Minnesota, 1934; M.S., 1935. Professor, Dean, Howard University College of Pharmacy, 1940-72.

Memberships and awards: Executive Secretary, District of Columbia Pharmaceutical Association; Founder and First President, National Pharmaceutical Association; Washington Pharmaceutical Association; American Pharmaceutical Association; AACP; National Advisory Commission Pharmacy Careers, 1960; Outstanding Achievement Award, University of Minnesota, 1964; Honorary D.Sci., Philadelphia College of Pharmacy and Science, 1970.

Ref: *Negro Year Book,* 1947, p. 84.
    Who's Who in America, 1976, p. 650.
    Who's Who Among Black Americans, 1977, p. 189.

Cooper, Dolores Janet

See: Shockley, Dolores Cooper

Cooper, Edward Sawyer   (1926- ——, M)

Physician. Internist. Born in Columbia, SC, Dec. 11, 1926. B.A., Lincoln University (PA), 1946; M.D. (first in his class), Meharry Medical College, 1949; Internship and Residency, Philadelphia General Hospital, 1949–54; President, Medical Staff, 1969–71; Chief of Medical Service, 1972–76; Professor of Medicine, University of Pennsylvania, 1933–; Chairman, Member of the Board, Director, Stroke Council; research in stroke prevention.

Memberships and awards: American Heart Association; 1982–; National Medical Association, 1959–; Council, College of Physicians of Philadelphia, 1970–84; Hartley Gold Medal, Meharry Medical College, 1949; Distinguished Alumni Award, Meharry Medical College, 1971; Alpha Omega Alpha; Charles Drew Award for Distinguished Contributions to Medical Education, 1979; fellow in Cardiology, 1956–57.

Ref: *Who's Who Among Black Americans,* 1985, p. 180.
    Black Enterprise, Oct. 1988, p. 68. [p]

Cooper, John R.   (1900s, M)

Chemist. Inventor. E. I. DuPont de Nemours, Chemical Department. Several patents.

Ref: *In Black and White,* p. 211.
    Ebony, May 1970, p. 6. [p]

Cooper, Lois Louise   (1931- ——, F)

Engineer (transportation). Mathematician. Born in Vicksburg, MS, Nov. 25, 1931. B.A. (mathematics), Los Angeles State University, 1954. Engineering Aide, Division of Highways (Caltrans), 1953–58; Junior Civil Engineer, 1958–61; California Department of Transportation Assistant Engineer, 1961–83.

Memberships and awards: Los Angeles Council of Black Professional Engineers, President, 1975–76; Trail Blazer Award, 1964; fellow, Institute for the Advancement of Engineers, 1982.

Ref: *Black Engineers in the U.S.,* p. 42.
    Who's Who Among Black Americans, 1985, p. 180.

Cooper, Stewart Rochester   (1893–19??, M)

Chemist (analytical). Born in Baltimore, MD, July 24, 1893. B.S., Howard University, 1916; M.S., Cornell, 1924; Ph.D., 1934. Professor, Howard University, 1922–59; retired.

Memberships and awards: American Chemical Society; Sigma Xi; AAAS; Washington Academy of Science, National Institute of Science; Beta Kappa Chi.

Dissertation title: The Germanium-Germanium Dioxide Electrode.

Pub: Articles in science journals.

Ref: *American Men of Science,* 11th ed., p. 983.
    The Negro in Science, p. 181.
    Holders of Doctorates Among American Negroes, p. 147.

Cordice, John Walter Vincent   (1881–1958, M)

Physician. Born in St. Vincent, B.W.I., Nov. 21, 1881. Studied Pharmacy at St. Vincent; M.D., Howard University Medical School, 1911. Examiner for Life Extension Medical of New York; founded the first private sanitarium in Greensboro, NC.

Memberships and awards: North Carolina State Medical, Dental, Pharmaceutical Association.

Ref: *Who's Who in Colored America,* 1928–29, p. 89.
    Who's Who in Colored America, 1930–32, p. 107.
    Who's Who in Colored America, 1933–37, p. 135.
    Who's Who in Colored America, 1938–40, p. 135.
    Who's Who in Colored America, 1941–44, p. 135.

Cornely, Paul Bertau   (1906- ——, M)

Physician. Public Health Officer. Born in French West Indies, Mar. 9, 1906. Naturalized U.S. citizen. B.A., University of Michigan, 1928; M.D., 1931; Ph.D. (public health), 1934. Assistant Professor, 1934–35; Associate Professor, 1935–47; Director of Health Service, 1937–47; Head, Department of Community Health Practice, 1955–70; Professor, 1947–73; Emeritus Professor of Preventive Medicine and Public Health, College of Medicine, Howard University, 1973–; Staff Member, Health Services Evaluation Systems Science, Inc., 1973.

Memberships and awards: President, American Public Health Association, 1969–70; fellow, American College of Preventive Medicine; received Sedgewick Memorial Medal, 1972; research in black health problems, student health programs and health motivation among low-income families; first black to receive a Ph.D. in Public Health.

Dissertation title: A Survey of Post-Graduate Medical Education in the United States and an Inquiry into the Educational Needs of the General Practioner.

Pub: The Economics of Medical Practice and the Negro Physician. National Medical Association, *Journal,* v., Mar. 1951.
Contribution to journals.
100 scientific and popular articles.

Ref: *History of the Negro in Medicine,* p. 99–100. [p]
American Men and Women of Science, 15th ed., p. 372.
Holders of Doctorates Among American Negroes, p. 119.
Who's Who Among Black Americans, 1985, p. 183.
Who's Who in Colored America, 1941–44, p. 135.
Negroes in Science; Natural Science Doctorates, 1876–1969, p. 41.
Who's Who in America, 1986–87, p. 582.
Ebony Success Library, v. 1, p. 79. [p]
Encyclopedia of Black America, p. 288.

Coruthers, John Milton   (1900– ——, M)

Agriculturist. Born in Austin, TX, April 15, 1900. B.S., Hampton Institute, 1926; M.S.,University of Wisconsin, 1928; Ph.D. (agricultural economics), Cornell University, 1934. Professor of Dairying, Southern University, 1925–29; Director and Professor, Agricultural Economics, Arkansas Agricultural, Mechanical and Normal College, 1929–37; Professor, Agricultural Economics, Prairie View A & M. 1937–.

Dissertation title: One Variety Cotton Communities.

Ref: *American Men of Science,* 11th ed., p. 1000.
Holders of Doctorates Among American Negroes, p. 119.

Cotton, Carol Blanche   (1904– ——, F)

Psychologist. B.A., Oberlin College; M.A., Columbia University; Ph.D. (psychology), University of Chicago, 1940.
Memberships and awards: Sigma Xi.

Dissertation title: A Study of the Reactions of Spastic Children to Certain Test Situations.

Ref: *Holders of Doctorates Among American Negroes,* p. 204–205.
Even the Rat Was White, p. 126.

Cotton, Donald   (1935– ——, M)

Chemist. Born in Cleveland, OH, Dec. 6, 1935. B.S., Howard University, 1957; M.S., Yale, 1959; Ph.D., Howard University, 1967. Research Chemist, U.S. Naval Propellant Plant, Indian Head, MD, 1960–64; U.S. Naval Ship Research & Development Laboratory, Annapolis, MD, 1964. Has several patents. Department of energy technical head for nuclear chemistry research.
Memberships and awards: AAAS; The Chemical Society; American Chemical Society.

Dissertation title: A General Theory of Interfacial Tension and Its Application to Adsorption Phenomena.

Ref: *Black contributors to Science and Energy Technology,* p. 22–23.
American Men and Women of Science, 12th ed., p. 1193.

Cotton, Norman Therkeil   (1885–1953, M)

Physician. Born in Greensboro, NC, Aug. 25, 1885. B.A., Lincoln University, PA, 1904; M.D., College of Surgeons and Physicians, Boston, MA, 1908. Commissioner of Health, City of Paterson, NJ, 1924–30.

Memberships and awards: President, State, County Negro Welfare League, 1923; Ex-President, North Jersey Medical Society; National Medical Association, American Medical Association; Alpha Phi Alpha.

Ref: *Who's Who in Colored America,* 1933–37, p. 136. [p] p. 139.
Who's Who in Colored America, 1930–32, p. 108. [p] opp. p. 108.
Who's Who in Colored America, 1928–29, p. 89–90, [p] opp. p. 90.
Who's Who in Colored America, 1938–40, p. 136. [p] p. 137.
Who's Who in Colored America, 1941–44, p. 136. [p] p. 137.

Courtney, Samuel E.   (1855–19??, M)

Physician. Born in Maiden, WV, 1855. B.S., Hampton Institute, 1879; State Normal School, Westfield, MA; M.D., Harvard Medical School, 1894. House Physician, Boston Lying-in-Hospital.

Memberships and awards: Vice-President, National Medical Association several terms; one of the founders of the Negro Business League, 1900.

Ref: *Who's Who in Colored America,* 1928–29, p. 90.
Who's Who in Colored America, 1930–32, p. 108.
Who's Who in Colored America, 1933–37, p. 136.
Who's Who in Colored America, 1938–40, p. 136.

Covington, Benjamin Jesse   (1869–1961, M)

Physician. Born in Marlin, TX, 1869. No college education. Hearne Baptist Academy, TX, 1892; M.D., Meharry Medical School, 1900. Established with four other physicians the Houston Negro Hospital, 1925, now Riverside General Hospital. Still practiced at 90 in 1961—started practicing in 1900.

Memberships and awards: Helped reorganize the Lone Star Medical Association of which he was Secretary-Treasurer for 10 years and President, 1929.

Ref: *Dictionary of American Medical Biography,* p. 161–162.
Bell, Howard H. "Benjamin Jesse Covington, M.D., 1869–1961." National Medical Association, *Journal,* v. 55, Sept. 1963, p. 462–463. [p] cover
Crisis, Aug. 1946, p. 242. [p] only

Cowan, James Rankin   (1919– ——, M)

Physician. Surgeon. Born in Washington, DC, Oct. 21, 1919. B.S., Howard University, 1939; M.A., Fisk University, 1940; M.D., Meharry Medical College, 1944. Captain in Armed Forces, Chief of Surgery, 26th Station Hospital in Germany; worked East Orange General Hospital; first black appointed State Commissioner Health in New Jersey, 1970–74; research, Freedmen's Hospital, 1945–48.

Memberships and awards: Howard University fellow, 1948–50; American Medical Association; American College of Preventive Medicine; American Association of Public Health; Academy of Medicine of New Jersey; Association of Military Surgeons of the United States; Academy of Medicine of Washington, DC; American Hospital Association; National Cancer Advisory Board; National Advisory on Mental Health Council; National Advisory on Neurological Diseases and Stroke Council; Essex County Medical Society; New Jersey Chapter, Medical Committee on Human Rights.

Ref: *Encyclopedia of Black America*, p. 291.
　　Who's Who Among Black Americans, 1985, p. 185.
　　Ebony Success Library, v. 1, p. 81. [p]
　　National Medical Association, *Journal*, v. 63, Mar. 1971, p. 151. [p]
　　National Medical Association, *Journal*, v. 66, July 1974, p. 336–338. [p] cover

Cowings, Patricia   (19??– ——, F)

Psychologist. B.S., M.S., Ph.D. (psychology), University of California, Davis, 1973. Postdoctoral work in Aerospace Medicine, Bioastronautics, Psychophysiological and Biological problems of long duration space flights.

Dissertation title: Combined Use of Autogenic Theory and Biofeedback in Conditioned Autoregulation of Autonomic Responses in Humans: Development of Technique.

Ref: *Blacks in Science, Ancient and Modern*, p. 252–254. [p]

Cox, Elbert Frank   (1895–1969, M)

Mathematician. Born in Evansville, IN, Dec. 5, 1895. B.A., Indiana University, 1917; Ph.D., Cornell University, 1925. First black to earn a Ph.D. in pure mathematics. Instructor, Shaw University, 1921–23; Professor, Physics and Mathematics, West Virginia State College, 1925–29; Associate Professor of Mathematics, Howard University, 1929–47; Professor, 1947–.

Memberships and awards: Brooks fellow, 1924–25; Mathematical Society; Physical Society; University Scholars (two years); Erastus Brooks fellow.

Dissertation title: The Polynomial Solutions of Difference Equations, $AF(X+1) + BF(X) = \text{Phi}(X)$

Ref: *American Men and Women of Science*, 11th ed., p. 1018.
　　Black Mathematicians and Their Works, p. 282.
　　Holders of Doctorates Among American Negroes, p. 147.

Cox, Wendell   (1914– ——, M)

Dentist. Born in Charleston, SC, Nov. 7, 1914. B.A., Talladega College, AL; D.D.S., Meharry Medical College, 1944; attended graduate courses at Fisk University and Boston University. Dentist in Inkster, MI, 1946–; Vice-President of Radio Stations WCHB and WCHD in Detroit, MI.

Memberships and awards: American Dental Association; National Dental Association; Detroit Mayor's Committee on Human Relations.

Ref: *Ebony Success Library*, v. 1, p. 81. [p]
　　Who's Who Among Black Americans, 1985, p. 187.

Craig, Arthur   (1871–19??, M)

Engineer (electrical). Born in Weston, MO, Dec. 1, 1871. B.S., University of Kansas School of Electrical Engineering. First black electrical engineer graduate in the United States. First black to graduate from Kansas University. Taught students at Tuskegee Institute to build electrical wiring into student built buildings at Tuskegee. Studied in Sweden under Otto Soloman, Principal of Armstrong Manual Training Night School. Taught at old M Street (Dunbar) High School, Washington, DC. Introduced Mechanical and Architectural Drawing in black schools in Washington, DC.

Ref: *Who's Who of the Colored Race*, 1915, p. 79–80.

Craig, George   (1915– ——, M)

Engineer (chemical). Heath Missionary to Liberia. Air pollution researcher.

Ref: *In Black and White*, p. 219.

Craig, Suzanne   (19??– ——, F)

Mathematician. Born in Chicago, IL. Attended the University of Chicago High School; B.A., University of Michigan, 1969; M.A., 1975; Ph.D., University of Southern California, 1980. Taught high school Mathematics in Detroit, 1969–1979; Senior Engineer, Jet Propulsion Laboratory, Pasadena, CA, 1980–.

Memberships and awards: Phi Beta Kappa.

Dissertation title: Strong Trichotomies and the Splitting Index for Linear Differential Systems.

Ref: Kenschaft, Patricia C. Women in Mathematics in the U.S., *American Mathematical Monthly*, v. 88, Oct. 1981, p. 599–600.

Crawford, Charles Linwood   (1929- —, M)

Engineer (civil). Born in Fordwick, VA, April 3, 1929. B.S. (civil engineering), Howard University, 1956; M.S. (engineering mechanics), Catholic University of America, 1964. Bridge Construction Engineer, DC Department of Highways and Traffic, 1956; Senior Civil Engineering Assistant, Los Angeles Department of Public Works, Sewer Design Division, 1956–61; Bridge Design Engineer, DC Department of Highways and Traffic, 1961–65; Structural Research Engineer, Naval Ship Research and Development Center, 1965–68; Associate Professor, Federal City College, School of Engineering, Washington, DC, 1968–72; Chief, Engineering Division, Bureau of Design and Engineering, Department of Environmental Services.

Memberships and awards: American Society of Civil Engineers; American Public Works Association; National Society of Professional Engineers.

Pub: Naval Ship R & D Center Report #2532. Buckling of Web-Stiffened Sandwiched Cylindrical Shells, 1967.

Ref: *Black Engineers in the United States,* p. 43–44.
Who's Who Among Black Americans, 1985, p. 188.

Cromartie, Eugene R.   (1936- —, M)

Military (Army). Brigadier General. Born in Wabasso, FL, Oct. 3, 1936. B.S., Florida A & M University, 1957; M.S., University of Dayton, 1968; U.S. Army Command and General Staff College, 1970; National War College, 1977. Assistant Professor, Military Science, University of Dayton; Faculty Member, Command and General Staff College; Special Assistant to the Commanding General, U.S. Army Criminal Investigation Command, Washington, DC.

Memberships and awards: Alpha Phi Alpha; FAMU Meritorious Achievement Award, 1982; City of Tallahassee and Leon County declared May 1, 1982 as Brigadier General Eugene R. Cromartie Day; Two Bronze Stars; Three Meritorious Service Medals; Two Army Commendation Medals.

Ref: *Who's Who Among Black Americans,* 1985, p. 191.
Black Americans in Defense of Our Nation, p. 122. [p] only.
Ebony, Oct. 1986, p. 72. [p]

Crooks, Kenneth Bronstorph M.   (1905- —, M)

Parasitologist. Biologist. Born in Jamaica, B.W.I., May 25, 1905. B.A., Harvard, 1927; M.A., 1928; Ph.D., 1940. Graduate Assistant, Harvard Biology Laboratory, 1927–28; Instructor, Biology, Hampton Institute, 1928–33; Assistant Professor to Professor, 1933–41; Headmaster, Happy Grove College, Jamaica, B.W.I., 1941–53; Professor, Zoology and Department Head, Fort Valley State College, 1953–.

Memberships and awards: General Education Board fellow, Harvard, 1937–38; Vice-President, Science Masters' Association, Jamaica, 1952; Vice-President, National Historical Society, Jamaica, 1941–53; American Association of Physical Anthropology; AAAS; VA Society for Research; Helminthological Society of Washington; Harvard Club.

Dissertation title: The Effect of Attrahents on Mosquitoes with Special Reference to Oviposition in Certain Common Species.

Ref: *American Men of Science,* 9th ed., p. 238.
Holders of Doctorates Among American Negroes, p. 188.
The Negro in Science, p. 176.
Who's Who in Colored America, 1938–40, p. 140.

Crossley, Frank Alphonso   (1925- —, M)

Engineer (metallurgical). Born in Chicago, IL, Feb. 19, 1925. B.S. (chemical engineering), Illinois Institute Technology, 1945; M.S., 1947; Ph.D. (metallurgical engineering), 1950—first doctorate in metallurgical engineering given by Illinois Institute of Technology. Manager, Lockheed Missile Systems; Leader in Research of a Submarine Launched Intercontinental Ballistic Missile; Senior Metallurgist, Illinois Institute of Technology Research; Consulting Engineer, Lockheed Missiles and Space Co.; Specialist in Titanium Science and Technology, 1979–.

Memberships and awards: Sigma Xi; American Institute of Mechanical Engineers; Tau Beta Pi; Phi Lambda Upsilon; Pi Delta Epsilon; fellow, American Society for Metals; Metallurgical Society; AIAA; Society for Advancement of Materials and Process Engineering.

Dissertation title: Grain Refinement by the Peritectic Reaction in Aluminum and Aluminum Base Alloys.

Ref: *American Men and Women of Science,* 16th ed., p. 452.
In Black and White, p. 228.
Who's Who Among Black Americans, 1985, p. 193.
Who's Who in Engineering, p. 137.
Black Engineers in U.S., p. 44–46. (list of publications)
Ebony, May 1958, p. 22. [p]
Ebony, April 1966, p. 7. [p]
Ebony, Sept. 1975, p. 158, 160–161. [p]

Crosthwait, David Nelson, Jr.   (1898–1976, M)

Engineer (mechanical). Engineer (electrical). Inventor. Born in Nashville, TN, May 27, 1898. B.S., Purdue University, 1913; M.E., 1920. An authority on heat transfer, ventilation and air conditioning. Research Engineer, Director of Research Laboratories, C. A. Dunham Company, 1925–30; Technical Advisor of Dunham-Bush, Inc., 1930–71; Past President, Michigan City Redevelopment Commission; received 39 patents; designed Radio City Music Hall heating system.

Memberships and awards: N. W. Comprehensive Health Planning Executive Committee; fellow, AAAS;

American Society of Heating, Refrigerating and Air Conditioning Engineers; American Chemical Society; National Society of Professional Engineers; Alpha Phi Alpha.

Ref: *American Men and Women of Science*, 12th ed., p. 1246.
Historical Afro-American Biographies, p. 175–176.
In Black and White, p. 223.
Who's Who in Colored America, 1930–32, 112.
Who's Who in Colored America, 1938–40, p. 140.
Blacks in Science: Astrophysicist to Zoologist, p. 45.

Crouch, Hubert Branch   (1906– , M)

Zoologist. Born in Jacksonville, TN, Dec. 1, 1906. B.A., Texas College, 1927; M.S., Iowa State University, 1930; Ph.D. (parasitology), 1936. Dean, Graduate School and Director of Division of Science, Tennessee State University, 1958–; research on parasitic protozoa and nematodes.

Dissertation title: The Animal Parasites of the Woodchuck (*Marmota monax*L.) with Special Reference to the Protozoa.

Ref: *American Men and Women of Science*, 13th ed., p. 888.
Holders of Doctorates Among American Negroes, p. 188.
Who's Who Among Black Americans, 1977–78, p. 203.

Crummie, John H.   (1936– , M)

Military (Air Force). Captain. Inventor. Engineer (electronics). Space balloon scientist. Developed a locating system for tracking launched balloons.

Ref: *Ebony*, Mar. 1967, p. 44–46, 50. [p]

Crump, Edward Perry   (1910– , M)

Physician. Pediatrician. Allergist. Born in Vicksburg, MS, Aug. 7, 1910. B.S., Fisk University, 1934; M.S., Minnesota, 1947; M.D., Meharry Medical College, 1941. Instructor, Anatomy, Meharry Medical College; Assistant Professor, Pediatrics, to Professor and Chairman, Department; research on the mechanism of convulsive seizures, umbilical hernia, prematurity.

Memberships and awards: Chairman, R. F. Boyd Medical Society; Vice-Chairman, Pediatrics Section, National Medical Association; American Academy of Pediatrics; Kappa Pi; Volunteer State Medical Society.

Ref: *American Men of Science*, 11th ed., p. 1058.
The Negro in Science, p. 176–177.
Ebony, Nov. 1961, p. 48. [p]
National Medical Association, *Journal*, v. 63, July 1971, p. 302–303. [p] cover

Crump, Walter Gray   (1869–1945, M)

Physician.

Pub: The Art and Science of Medicine, National Medical Association, *Journal*, v. 26, May 1934, p. 52.

Ref: National Medical Association, *Journal*, v. 26, May 1934, first page. [p]

Crumpler, Rebecca Lee   (1858–19??, F)

Physician. B.S., First black woman to graduate, New England Female Medical College. First black female physician (controversial with Cole).

Pub: Book of Medical Discourses, in two parts, 144 p., Boston, Cushman, Keating & Co., 1883.

Ref: *Ebony*, Feb. 1948, p. 22.
History of the Negro in Medicine, p. 43.
A Century of Black Surgeons, p, 108, 584.
Medico-Chirurgical Society of DC, Inc. *Bulletin*, Jan. 1949, p. 3.

Cuff, John Reginald   (1896–1958, M)

Physician. Pathologist. Born in Jamaica, B.W.I., May 27, 1896. Attended City College of New York and Howard University; M.D., Meharry Medical College, 1926. Assistant in Pathology, Peter Brent Brigham Hospital and Infants' and Children's Hospital, 1927–28; Research fellow, Harvard Medical School, 1928–29; Associate Professor, Pathology, Meharry Medical College, 1929; Acting Head, 1948–58.

Memberships and awards: AAAS; R. F. Boyd Medical Society; Alpha Omega Alpha Medical Society; National Medical Association.

Ref: *American Men of Science*, 9th ed., p. 241.
National Medical Association, *Journal*, v. 51, Jan. 1959, p. 71. [p] obit.

Cuffee, Paul   (1759–1817, M)

Ship Captain. Navigator. Born in Cuttyhunk near New Bedford, MA. At 16, he went on a whaling voyage to the Gulf of Mexico, working as a common seaman. At the age of 20, he and his brother built an open boat which they used to trade with merchants in Connecticut and Nantucket. At 25, he was master of a 12-ton vessel. By the time he was 46, he owned three ships and expanded his trade to Europe and Africa. In 1816, he transported 38 free blacks to the British Colony of Sierra Leone in West Africa. He was the first to implement the back-to-Africa idea. He captained and navigated the ship which belonged to him, the "Traveller," in 55 days to Sierra Leone.

Ref: Harris, Sheldon. *Paul Cuffee, Black American and the African Return*. New York, Simon & Schuster, 1972.

Salvador, George. *Paul Cuffe, The Black Yankee, 1759–1817.* New Bedford, Mass., 1969.

Sherwood, Henry Noble. Paul Cuffe. *Journal of Negro History,* v. 8, April 1923, p. 153–229.

Thomas, Lamont D. *Rise to Be a People,* Urbana, University of Illinois Press, 1986.

Howard, Horatio. *A Self-made Man: Capt. Paul Cuffee.* New York, 1912.

Dictionary of American Negro Biography, p. 147–148.

Harbison, David *Reaching for Freedom.* Scholastic Book Services, 1972, p. 11–37. Silhouette, p. 10.

Taylor, Olive. Before the Civil War: History of Commitment, Paul Cuffee, 1759–1817. *Negro History bulletin,* Jan.–Mar. 1981, p. 9.

National Cyclopedia of American Biography.

Curby, Norma   (1952–   , F)

Engineer (structural design). Born in 1952. B.S., University of Missouri, 1972. Design Engineer, Monsanto Company, 1973–.

Ref: *Black Women Makers of History; A Portrait,* p. 199. [p] p. 200 (drawing).
Ebony, Oct. 1973, p. 135–138, 140. [p]

Curtis, Austin Maurice, Sr.   (1868–1939, M)

Physician. Surgeon. Born in Raleigh, NC, Jan. 15, 1868. B.A., Lincoln University, PA, 1888, M.A., 1898; Sc.D., 1929 (honorary); Northwestern, 1891. Professor of Surgery at Howard University for 25 years; Chief Surgeon, Freedmen's Hospital, 1898–1938; initiated and directed a six-week postgraduate course for rural surgeons; first intern, Provident Hospital, Chicago; first black surgeon on staff of Cook County Hospital, Chicago, 1896; with one of his three sons, he operated a surgical hospital for black patients in Washington, DC, 1925–33.

Memberships and awards: American Medical Association; Medico-Chirurgical Society of DC; President, National Medical Association, 1911; Alpha Phi Alpha.

Ref: *Dictionary of American Medical Biography,* p. 171.
Dictionary of American Negro Biography, p. 153–154.
The History of the Negro in Medicine, p. 78–79. [p] p. 79.
Who's Who of the Colored Race, 1915, p. 84.
Who's Who in Colored America, 1928–29, p. 94.
Who's Who in Colored America, 1930–32, p. 113.
Who's Who in Colored America, 1933–37, p. 141.
Cobb, W. Montague. Austin Maurice Curtis, 1868–1939. National Medical Association, *Journal,* v. 46 (1954), p. 294–298.

Curtis, Austin Maurice, Jr.   (1890–1959, M)

Physician. Surgeon. Born in Chicago, IL, June 21, 1890. Son of Dr. Austin Curtis, Sr. Brother of Dr. Leo Curtis. University of Michigan, 1909–1910; M.D., Howard University School of Medicine, 1914. Physician and Surgeon, Freedmen's Hospital, Washington, DC.

Ref: *Who's Who in Colored America,* 1915, p. 84.

Curtis, Namahyoke Sockum   (18??–1935, F)

Nurse. Registered 32 black nurses, who, like herself, had had yellow fever and were thus immune, to work among the troops in Santiago during an outbreak of yellow fever; worked with Clara Barton, head of the American Red Cross, during the Galveston flood in Texas in 1900. Because of her excellent work and the work of others, bills were introduced and later passed which provided for an Army Nurse Corps which was established in 1908. Received government pension and is buried in Arlington Cemetery. Wife of Austin M. Curtis Sr., first Intern at Provident Hospital in Chicago, and Surgeon-in-Chief, Freedmen's Hospital, Washington, DC.

Ref: Elmore, Joyce Ann. Black Nurses: Their Struggle, *American Journal of Nursing,* v. 76, Mar. 1976, p. 435–437.
The Path We Tread, p. 12–13. [p] p. 13.
Black Americans in Defense of Our Nation, p. 97.

D

Dabney, Maurice B.   (1895–19??, M)

Pharmacist. Born in Gloucester, VA, Mar. 9, 1895. Philadelphia College of Pharmacy, 1917; Phg., Phc., Philadelphia College of Pharmacy.

Memberships and awards: President, Cooperative Retail Druggists' Association, 1925–; Chairman, Pharmaceutical Section of the National Medical Association, 1927; Philadelphia Academy of Medical Sciences; Kappa Alpha Psi.

Ref: *Who's Who in Colored America,* 1928–29, p.97.
Who's Who in Colored America, 1933–37, p. 145.

Dacons, Joseph Carl   (1912–   , M)

Chemist (organic). Born in Wilkesboro, NC, May 22, 1912. B.A., Ohio State University, 1937; M.S., 1948; Ph.D., 1952. Associate Professor, Chemistry and Chairman, Chemistry Department, Fisk University, 1950–53; Chairman, Chemistry Department, A & T College, 1953–55. Research Chemist, U.S. Naval Ordnance Lab., 1956–.

Memberships and awards: Research fellow, Ohio State University, 1948–50; American Chemical Society; Sigma Xi; National Institute of Science.

Dissertation title: Cellulose Oligosaccharides.

Ref: *American Men and Women of Science,* 13th ed., p. 915–916.
The Negro in Science, p. 182.

Dailey, Ulysses Grant   (1885–1961, M)

Physician. Surgeon. Born in Donaldsonville, LA, Aug. 3, 1885. B.S., Dillard University; M.D., Northwestern University, 1902. Established Dailey Hospital and Sanitarium in 1926 and was its Surgeon-in-Chief for six years; Lecturer at Northwestern University; Surgeon Emeritus, Provident Hospital, Chicago.

Memberships and awards: Fellow, American Medical Association; President, National Medical Association, 1915; Co-Founder and fellow, International College of Surgeons; Distinguished Service Medal, National Medical Association, 1949; One of the first four black members of the American College of Surgeons; fellow, Institute of Medicine of Chicago; American Medical Association; Editor-in-Chief, National Medical Association, *Journal*, after Charles Victor Roman.

Pub: Total Congenital Absence of the Vermiform Appendix in Man. *Surgery, Gynecology and Obstetrics*, Oct. 1910. Numerous articles in the *Journal* of the National Medical Association of which he was the consulting editor.

Ref: *Historical Afro-American Biographies*, p. 176–177. [p]
American Men of Science, 7th ed., p. 403.
Dictionary of American Negro Biography, p. 155–156.
In Black and White, p. 231.
Negro Almanac, 1976, p. 790.
The Negro in Science, p. 177.
History of the Negro in Medicine, p. 135.
National Medical Association, *Journal*, v. 42, Mar. 1950, p. 39–40. [p]
National Medical Association, *Journal*, v. 52, July 1960, p. 309–310. [p] cover
Negro Scientists Past & Present, p. 60.
Who's Who in Colored America, 1928–29, p. 97. [p]
Who's Who in Colored America, 1930–32, p. 115. [p]
Who's Who in Colored America, 1933–37, p. 146. [p]
Who's Who in Colored America, 1938–40, p. 145.
Who's Who in Colored America, 1941–44, p. 145.
Jet, May 4, 1961, p. 51.
National Medical Association, *Journal*, v. 7, Jan.–Mar. 1915, p. 290. [p]
Dictionary of American Medical Biography, p. 176.
National Medical Association, *Journal*, v. 35, Mar. 1943, p. 64–65.
National Medical Association, *Journal*, v. 41, May 1949, p. 134.
A Century of Black Surgeons, p. 280–298. [p] p. 281.

Daly, Marie Maynard   (1921– ——, F)

Biochemist. Born in Corona, NY, April 16, 1921. B.S., Queens College, 1942; M.S., New York University, 1943; Ph.D. (chemistry), Columbia University, 1948. The first black female to earn a Ph.D. in chemistry. Instructor in Physical Science, Howard University, 1947–48; Research Assistant, Rockefeller Institute, 1951–55; Associate, Columbia University Research Service, Goldwater Memorial Hospital, 1955–59; Assistant Professor of Biochemistry, 1960–61; Associate Professor of Biochemistry and Medicine, Albert Einstein College of Medicine, 1971–; research on nucleic acids.

Memberships and awards: Sigma Xi; American Chemical Society; New York Academy of Science.

Disseration title: A Study of the Products formed by the Action of Pancreatic Amylase on Corn Starch.
American Men and Women of Science, 15th ed., p. 488.
The Negro in Science, p. 182.
National Faculty Directory, 1986, p. 741.
Who's Who Among Black Americans, 1985, p. 199.
Negroes in Science: Natural Science Doctorates, 1876–1969, p. 60.

Daniel, Walter Thomas   (1908– ——, M)

Engineer (structural). Born in 1908. B.S., University of Arizona, 1929; M.S., Iowa State University, 1932; Ph.D., 1941. Professor of Mechanical Engineering, Prairie View State College and Howard University, 1943–. First black to earn a Ph.D. in Engineering. First black engineer licensed in Louisiana.

Memberships and awards: American Society of Civil Engineers; American Concrete Institute; American Society for Engineering Education; Prestressed Concrete Institute; Tau Beta Pi; Sigma Xi.

Dissertation title: Deflection in Rigid Frames Stressed Beyond the Yield Point.

Ref: *American Men of Science*, 9th ed., p. 427.
Black Collegian, Jan./Feb. 1979, p. 136–138.
Holders of Doctorates Among American Negroes, p. 119.
Black Engineers in the United States, p. 47.

Darden, Christine Mann   (1942– ——, F)

Engineer (aerospace). Born in Monroe, NC, Sept. 10, 1942. B.S. (mathematics), Virginia State College, 1962; M.S., 1967; D.Sc. (mechanical engineering), George Washington University, 1983. Brunswick County School Teacher, 1962–63; Mathematics Instructor, Virginia State College, 1966–67; Data Analyst, NASA Langley Research Center, 1967–73; Aerospace Engineer, NASA, Langley.

Memberships and awards: President, Hampton Roads Chapter, National Technical Association, 1984; AIAA; Alpha Kappa Alpha; National Langley Exchange Council, 1979–; Outstanding Woman of America, 1975; Twenty Year Alumnus Award, Hampton Institute, 1982; Who's Who in Aviation and Aerospace, 1983.

Disseration title: An Analysis of Shock Coalescence Including Three-Dimensional Effects with Application to Sonic Boom Prediction.

Pub: Over 20 technical reports and articles.

Ref: *Blacks in Science, Ancient & Modern*, p. 255–257. [p]
Who's Who Among Black Americans, 1985, p. 202.
Profiles in Excellence, (NASA), p. 24. [p]
Ebony, July 1977, p. 7. [p]

Darden, Geraldine Claudette (1936- ——, F)

Mathematician. Born in Nansemond County, VA, July 22, 1936. B.S., Hampton Institute, 1957; M.S. (mathematics education), University of Illinois, 1960; M.S., Syracuse University, 1965; Ph.D. (mathematics), 1967. Mathematics Instructor, S. H. Clarke Junior High School, Portsmouth, VA, 1957–59; Instructor of Mathematics, Hampton Institute, 1960–63; Associate Professor to Head, Department of Mathematics, Hampton Institute, 1963–.

Memberships and awards: Departmental Honors, Hampton Institute; Alpha Kappa Mu National Honor Society; Beta Kappa Chi; National Science Foundation; Science Faculty fellow; United College Fund fellow; IBM fellow; Mathematical Association of America.

Dissertation title: On the Direct Sums of Cyclic Groups.

Ref: Kenschaft, Patricia C. Black Women in Mathematics in U.S. *American Mathematical Monthly*, v. 88, p. 599.
Black Mathematicians and Their Works, p. 282. [p]
American Men and Women of Science, 16th ed., p. 521.

Darden, James Benjamin (1881–1951, M)

Physician. Born in Wilson, NC, July 17, 1881. D.Pharm., Howard University School of Pharmacy; M.D., Meharry Medical College. Practiced medicine in Petersburg, VA; first physician employed by Virginia State College.

Memberships and awards: Reorganized and developed the Old Dominion Medical Society into one of the largest component societies of the National Medical Association and served as President and Chairman of the Executive Board; Omega Psi Phi; Sigma Pi.

Ref: National Medical Association, *Journal*, v. 44, Jan. 1952, p. 72–73. [p]

Darity, William Alexander (1924- ——, M)

Health Administrator. Born in Flat Rock, NC, Jan. 15, 1924. B.S., Shaw University, 1948; M.S.P.H, North Carolina Central University, 1949; Ph.D. (public health), 1964. Community Health Educator, City Department of Public Health, Charlotte, NC, 1949–50; Public Health Department, Danville, VA, 1950–52; Antituberculosis League, Norfolk, VA, 1952–53; Consultant, World Health Orgnization, 1953–56; Professor, Public Health, University of Massachusetts, Amherst, 1968–; Director, Division of Public Health, 1976–

Memberships and awards: NIMH grant, 1969–70; Board of Directors, Planned Parenthood Federation of American, Inc., 1967–; Board of Directors, Drug Abuse Counsel, Inc., 1972–; American Public Health Association.

Dissertation title: Contraceptive Education: The Relative Cultural and Social Factors Related to Applied Health Education with Special Reference to Oral Contraceptives.

Ref: Who's Who in the East, 1972, p. 161. [p]
American Men and Women of Science, 14th ed., p. 1071.
Complete Guide to Selected Health and Related Careers, p. 18–19. [p]
Who's Who Among Black Americans, 1985, p. 202.

Darlington, Ray Clifford (1908- ——, M)

Pharmacist. B.S., M.S., and Ph.D., Ohio State University, 1948. First black to receive Ph.D. in Pharmacy in the United States.

Dissertation title: An Investigation of Bentonite as a Major Component of Ointment Bases.

Ref: Encyclopedia of Black America, 1981, p. 301–302.

Davidson, Ezra C., Jr. (1933- ——, M)

Physician. Obstetrician. Gynecologist. Born in Water Valley, MS, Oct. 21, 1933. B.S., Morehouse College, 1954; M.D., Meharry Medical College, 1958. Professor and Chairman, Department of Obstetrics and Gynecology, Drew Postgraduate Medical School, 1971–; Professor, UCLA, 1979–; Professor, University of Southern California School of Medicine, 1971–80; Chairman, Roosevelt Hospital, 1970.

Memberships and awards: Member, Consultant, National Foundation, March of Dimes, 1970–; Examiner, American Board of Obstetrics and Gynecology, 1973–; Member, Board of Directors, National Alliance for School Age Parents, 1975–; fellow, American College of Surgeons; Alpha Omega Alpha.

Pub: Numerous articles in medical journals.

Ref: Who's Who Among Black Americans, 1985, p. 205.
Black Enterprise, Oct. 1988, p. 72. [p]

Davidson, Frederick Ellis (19??- ——, M)

Military (Army). Major General. B.S. Highest ranking black officer in the U.S. Army when promoted to Major General on April 25, 1972; Commander of the 8th Infantry Division in Europe; first black officer to lead an Army Division. Retired.

Ref: Black Americans in Defense of Our Nation, p. 122. [p] only
Blacks in America, 1492–1976, p. 69.

Davidson, Shelby J. (1800s, M)

Inventor. Born in Lexington, KY, May 10, 1868. B.A., Howard University, 1893. Lawyer. Invented a mechanical tabulator or adding machine.

Pub: Several Articles on Adding Machines.

Ref: Negro in Our History, 5th ed., p. 462.
Who's Who of the Colored Race, 1915, p. 86.

Davis, Abraham Isaiah (1877–1973, M)

Physician. Born in Sturgis, MS, Mar. 4, 1877. B.S., Rust College; M.D., Meharry Medical College, 1902. Private practice and drug store operator, 1910, Ardmore, OK, and Oklahoma City, 1910–73. One of the first black physicians in Oklahoma; practiced for 70 years, often without payment.

Ref: *Dictionary of American Medical Biography*, p. 184.
Cobb, W. Montague. Abraham Isaiah Davis, M.D., 1877–1973. National Medical Association, *Journal*, v. 66, Mar. 1974, p. 176–178. [p] cover.

Davis, Albert Porter (1890–1976, M)

Physician. Surgeon. Born in Palestine, TX, Nov. 13, 1890. M.D., Meharry Medical College, 1913. Appointed Assistant Health Director of Kansas City, KS, 1926–32. He was the founder and organizer of the Davis Maternity Sanitarium and was on the staffs of Wheatley, Provident and Old City Hospitals of Kansas City, MO; had the oldest pilot's license in the U.S. among black pilots. He was a First Lieutenant in the Medical Reserve Corp., U.S. Army, 1917–22.

Memberships and awards: President, Kansas Medical, Dental and Pharmaceutical Association, 1924–25; Treasurer, Missouri Pan Medical Association, 1924–25; President, National Medical Association, 1952–53.

Ref: *Who's Who in Colored America*, 1927, p. 52. [p]
Who's Who in Colored America, 1928–29, p. 98.
Who's Who in Colored America, 1930–32, p. 119. [p]
Who's Who in Colored America, 1933–37, p. 147.
Who's Who in Colored America, 1938–40, p. 147.
Who's Who in Colored America, 1941–44, p. 149. [p]
National Medical Association, *Journal*, v. 44, Nov. 1952, p. 477.
National Medical Association, *Journal*, v. 46, Sept. 1954, p. 364.
National Medical Association, *Journal*, v. 49, Nov. 1957, p. 424. [p] only
National Medical Association, *Journal*, v. 68, Nov. 1976, p. 547–548. [p] obit

Davis, Alonzo Joseph (1909– ——, M)

Psychologist. Born in Washington, DC, July 18, 1909. B.S., Howard University, 1931; M.S., 1932; Ph.D. (psychology), University of Minnesota, 1947. Instructor, Psychology, Howard University, 1932–33; Tuskegee Institute, 1934–44; Associate Professor, 1945–47; Professor, 1947–59; Professor, Florida A & M University, 1959–62; Chairman, Psychology Department, North Carolina Central University, 1962–69.

Memberships and awards: American Psychological Association.

Dissertation title: Status Factors in Personality Characteristics of Negro College Students.

Ref: *Even the Rat Was White*, p. 127.
Directory of the American Psychological Association, 1985, p. 226.
American Men and Women of Science, 12th ed., p. 507.

Davis, Benjamin O., Sr. (1877–1970, M)

Military (Army) Brigadier General. Born in Washington, DC, July 1, 1877. First black General, U.S. Army (1940), attended Howard University, enlisted in 1899. He became a Second Lieutenant in 1901, full Colonel in 1930, and retired in 1948. He taught Military Science at Wilberforce University and Tuskegee Institute. Promoted to Brigadier General in 1940, serving as Commander of NY National Guard's 369th Infantry. From 1944–45 he was Special Advisor to European Theatre Commander and from 1945–47 he was the Assistant to the Inspector General.

Ref: *Encyclopedia of Black America*, p. 303–304.
Historical Afro-American Biographies, p. 177–178.
Negro Medal of Honor Men, p. 98–99.
Great Negroes, Adams. p. 112.
Jet, July 8, 1971, p. 10. [p]
Current Biography, 1942, p. 180–181. [p]
Who's Who of the Colored Race, 1915, p. 86.
Crisis, Dec. 1940, p. 383, 388. [p]

Davis, Benjamin O., Jr. (1912– ——, M)

Military (Air Force). Lt. General. Born in Washington, DC, Dec. 18, 1912. First black General (Oct. 27, 1954) in the United States Air Force. B.S., U.S. Military Academy, West Point, 1936. Fourth black to finish. In 1942 he received wings in the Air Force. Chief of Staff, U.S. Forces in Korea; Chief of Staff, United Nations Command, 1965–67; Commander, 13th Air Force, Clark AF Base, Phillipines; Deputy Commander in Chief, U.S. Strike Command, MacDill AF Base, Tampa, FL; retired, 1970.

Memberships and awards: Silver Star and Distinguished Flying Cross; President's Commission on Campus Unrest; Honorary Dr.Sci., Morgan State College; Honorary Dr.Mil.Sci., Wilberforce University; Honorary L.L.D., Tuskegee Institute; many other military decorations.

Ref: *Current Biography*, Sept. 1955, p. 150–152.
Ebony, Mar. 1960, p. 27–39. [p]
Encyclopedia of Black America, p. 303.
Great Negroes, Adams, p. 113.
Historical Afro-American Biographies, p. 178–179. [p]
Ebony Success Libray, v. 1, p. 87. [p]
Who's Who Among Black Americans, 1985, p. 206.
Ebony, Aug. 1968, p. 56–58. [p]

Davis, Charles Alexander (1936– ——, M)

Engineer (electrical). Born in Petersburg, VA, Aug. 20, 1936. B.S. (electrical engineering), Michigan State University, 1959; M.S., 1963; Ph.D., 1975. Research Associate, University of Michigan, 1960-63; Engineer, Bendix Corporation, 1963-64; Engineer, Ford Motor Company, 1964-67; Professor, Western Michigan University, 1967-.

Memberships and awards: Kappa Alpha Psi; National Society of Professional Engineers, 1976-; Institute of Electrical and Electronics Engineers, 1984-; Registered Professional Engineer, 1976-; Tau Beta Pi; Eta Kappa Nu.

Dissertation title: An Experimental Study of the Effects of Quantitative Management Information on the Generation and Selection of Alternative Actions in Individual Decision-Making Under Uncertainty.

Ref: *Who's Who Among Black Americans*, 1985, p. 207.

Davis, De Wayne France   (1897-19??, M)

Physician. Born in Covington, KY, Dec. 25, 1897. B.S., West Virginia State College, Institute, WV; M.D., Meharry Medical College, TN; Physician, West Virginia State College; Assistant Health Commissioner, Charleston, WV.

Memberships and awards: Vice-President, State Medical Society; Alpha Phi Alpha.

Ref: *The National Register*, 1952, p. 566.

Davis, Elizabeth Bishop   (1920- ——, F)

Physician. Psychiatrist. Born in Pittsburgh, PA, April 26, 1920. B.A., Columbia University, 1941; M.D., 1949. Director of Psychiatry, Harlem Hospital Center, 1962-78; Professor of Clinical Psychiatry, Columbia University, 1972-78. Distinguished Visiting Professor, Puerto Rican Institute of Psychiatry, San Juan, 1978-.

Memberships and awards: Professor Emeritus in Clinical Psychiatry, Columbia University; American Psychiatric Association; Academy of Physical Medicine.

Ref: *American Men and Women of Science*, 14th ed., p. 1090.
In Black & White, p. 241.
ABMS Compendium of Certified Medical Specialists, v. 5, p. 401.
Ebony, May 1964, p. 68. [p]
Biographical Directory of the Fellows and Members of the American Psychiatric Association, 1983, p. 264.

Davis, Francis Reed Elliott

See: Elliott, Francis Reed.

Davis, Jackson Lee   (1890-19??, M)

Dentist. Born in Mansfield, LA, Jan. 18, 1890. B.A., New Orleans University, 1910; University of Chicago; L.L.B., Howard University, 1916; D.D.S., 1923. Teacher of Mathematics, New Orleans University, 1910-12; Clerk, Bureau of the Census, 1912-20; Instructor in Dentistry, Howard University, 1928-.

Memberships and awards: Treasurer, Robert T. Freeman Dental Society, 1929-; Interstate Dental Association.

Ref: *Who's Who in Colored America*, 1930-32, p. 120.
Who's Who in Colored America, 1933-37, p. 151.
Who's Who in Colored America, 1938-40, p. 148.
Who's Who in Colored America, 1941-44, p. 151.

Davis, Murray B.   (1907-1963, M)

Physician. Born in High Point, NC, Nov. 1, 1907. B.S., Howard University, 1930; M.D., 1934; New York Post-Graduate School of Medicine for study of venereal diseases. Worked on the staff of City Health Department and directed a venereal disease clinic.

Memberships and awards: Chairman, National Medical Association Board of Trustees; President, National Medical Association (6,000 members), 1962. Only black member of State Prison Commission; Old North State Medical Society.

Ref: *Jet*, Aug. 23, 1962, p. 23.
National Medical Association, *Journal*, v. 55, Sept. 1963, p. 460-461. [p] obit & biog

Davis, Rodney Maxwell   (1942-1967, M)

Military (Marine). Sergeant. Born in Macon, GA, April 7, 1942. Threw himself upon a grenade thrown into his trench, absorbed the explosion with his body and saved his comrades, enabling his platoon to hold its position.

Memberships and awards: Medal of Honor, 1967; U.S. Navy warship named for him, USS Rodney M. Davis is 453 feet long, 3,800 tons and 47 feet wide.

Ref *Jet*, June 1, 1987, p. 38.
Black Americans in Defense of Our Nation, p. 72. [p]

Davis, Stephen Smith   (1910- ——, M)

Engineer (mechanical). Inventor. Born in Philadelphia, PA, Oct. 24, 1910. B.S. (engineering), Howard University, 1936; M.S., Harvard University, 1947. Professor, Mechanical Enginering, Howard University, 1938; Department Head, 1962; Dean, School of Engineering and Architecture, 1964-70; Consultant, Naval Ordnance Laboratory, 1953-63.

Memberships and awards: AAAS; Washington Academy of Sciences; ASME; American Society for Engineering Education; Tau Beta Pi; American Society of Mechanical Engineers; National Society of Professional Engineers; Inventor with patent for wind tunnel nozzle.

Ref: *Who's Who Among Black Americans*, 1985, p. 214.
Who's Who in America, 1976, p. 754.
American Men and Women of Science, 15th ed., p. 538.
Black Engineers in the United States, p. 50-51.

Davis, Toye George   (1909- ——, M)

Parasitologist. Zoologist. Born in 1909. B.A., Lincoln University, PA, (cum laude); M.S., Pennsylvania University, 1932; M.A., Harvard University, 1939; Ph.D., 1940; M.D., Howard University, 1947. Professor of Hygiene and University Physician, Lincoln University, 1948-. Research in morphology and division in ciliate parasites.

Memberships and awards: Beta Kappa Chi; Sigma Xi.

Dissertation title: Morphology and Division in Spirodinium, Tetratoxum and Ditoxum.

Ref: American Men of Science, 11th ed., p. 1144.
Holders of Doctorates Among American Negroes, p. 188.

Davis, Walter Strother   (1905- ——, M)

Agriculturist. Born in Canton, MS, Aug. 9, 1905. B.S., Tennessee Agricultural and Industrial State College, 1931; M.S., Cornell, 1933; Ph.D., 1941. Professor of Agriculture and Director of the Department, Tennessee State University, 1933-34; President, 1943-1970, Emeritus President, 1970-.

Memberships and awards: National Executive Secretary of New Farmers of America, 1941-43; Trustee, Meharry Medical College, 1951-; Interim Metropolitan Board of Education, 1963.

Dissertation title: The Establishment of Negro Young Men in Farming: A Study of Opportunities and Qualifications of Negro Young Men for Becoming Established in Farming in West Tennessee.

Ref: American Men and Women of Science, 12th ed., p. 1351.
Holders of Doctorates Among American Negroes, p. 119-120.
Crisis, Oct. 1933, p. 233. [p] only
Crisis, Aug. 1941, p. 248. [p] only
Crisis, Nov. 1943, p. 350. [p] only

Davis, William Allison   (1902- ——, M)

Anthropologist. Born in Washington, DC, Oct. 14, 1902. B.A., Williams College, 1924; M.A., Harvard, 1925; Ph.D. Chicago University, 1942. Professor of Anthropology, Dillard University, 1935-38; Director of Research Intelligence Tests, Chicago, 1942; Lecturer, Harvard, 1948.

Memberships and awards: Phi Beta Kappa.

Dissertation title: The Relation Between Color Caste and Economic Stratification in Two "Black" Plantation Counties.

Ref: American Men of Science, 8th ed., p. 581.
In Black & White, p. 207.
Holders of Doctorates Among American Negroes, p. 55.
Who's Who in Colored America, 1927, p. 54.

Davison, Frederic Ellis   (1917- ——, M)

Military (Army). Major General. Born in Washington, DC, Sept. 28, 1917. B.S., Howard University, 1938; M.S., 1940; M.A., 1963. Commander, Military District of Washington, DC, 1973-.

Memberships and awards: First black to lead an army division. Distinguished Alumnus, Howard University, 1973; Honorary L.L.D., Eastern Michigan University, 1974; retired; Distinguished Service Medal; Legion of Merit; Bronze Star; Army Commendation Medal.

Ref: Ebony, Nov. 1985, p. 326. [p]
Black Americans in Defense of Our Nation, p. 122. [p]
Who's Who Among Black Americans, 1985, p. 215.
Ebony, Jan. 1969, p. 96. [p]
Current Biography, 1974, p. 100-102. [p]
Ebony, Nov. 1968, p. 128-130, 132-134. [p]

Dawson, Robert Edward   (1918- ——, M)

Physician. Opththalmologist. Surgeon. Born in Rocky Mount, NC, Feb. 23, 1918. B.S., Clark College, 1939; M.D., Meharry Medical College, 1943. Attending Staff, Ophthalmology Department, Lincoln Hospital, 1946-55; Chief, Ophthalmology and Otolaryngology, 3310 Hospital Scott AF Base, 1955-57; Ophthalmic Pathology, Armed Forces Institute of Pathology, 1956; Chief, Ophthalmology and Otolaryngology, Lincoln Hospital, 1959-76.

Memberships and awards: President, National Medical Association, 1978-79; fellow, American College of Surgeons; fellow, American Academy of Ophthalmology; Chi Delta Mu; Society of Eye Surgeons; Board of Trustees, Meharry Medical College; Distinguished Service Award.

Pub: Equal Access to health care delivery for blacks: A challenge for the NMA. National Medical Association, *Journal*, Jan. 1981.
Crisis in the medical arena: A challenge for the black physician. National Medical Association, *Journal*, Dec. 1979.

Ref: Who's Who Among Black Americans, 1985, p. 216.
ABMS Compendium of Certified Medical Specialists, v. 3, p. 1013.
National Medical Association, *Journal*, v. 72, May 1980, p. 431. [p]
National Medical Association, *Journal*, v. 72, June 1980. [p] cover
National Medical Association, *Journal*, v. 75, Mar. 1983, p. 321.

De Grasse, John Van Surley   (1825-1868, M)

Physician. Surgeon. Born in New York City, NY, 1825. Attended Oneida Institute, NY; later entered Aubuk College in Paris, spent two years; M.D., Bowdoin College, Brunswick, ME, 1849, with honors.

Memberships and awards: Became member of Massachusetts Medical Society in 1854, first black to belong to a medical association. Served as Assistant Surgeon with 35th U.S. Colored Troops in 1863. One of the first eight blacks to be commissioned a surgeon in the U.S. Army. One of the two first blacks to finish Bowdoin Medical College, the other being Thomas J. White.

Ref: *Dictionary of American Negro Biography*, p. 169.
History of the Negro in Medicine, p. 30, 38. [p]
Jet, Aug. 25, 1960, p. 9.

Deconge, Sister Mary Sylvester (1933- ——, F)

Mathematician. Born in Wickliff, LA, 1933. B.A. (mathematics and science), Seton Hill College, 1959; M.A. (mathematics), Louisiana State University, 1962; Ph.D. (mathematics and French), St. Louis University, 1968. Elementary School Teacher, parochial schools, Baton Rouge and Lafayette Dioceses, 1952–55; Teacher, Holy Ghost High School, Opelousas, LA, 1959–64; Teacher, Holy Ghost High School and Delisle Junior College, 1962–64; Assistant Professor of Mathematics, Loyala University, 1968–71; Mathematics Faculty, Southern University, Baton Rouge, LA, 1971–.

Dissertation title: 2-Normed Lattices and 2-Metric Spaces.

Pub: A Singular Abstract Cauchy Problem. *PNAS, USA*, v. 66, 1970, p. 269. (With R. Hersh)
A Perturbation Series for Cauchy's Problem for Higher-Order Abstract Parabolic Equation. *PNAS USA*, v. 67, 1970, p. 21.
An Operational Calculus for a Class of Abstract Operator Equations. *J. Math. Anal. Appl.*, v. 37, Jan. 1972.
New Integral Representations for Solutions of Cauchy's Problems for Abstract Parabolic Equations. *PNAS, USA*, Sept. 1971.
(With A. Gibson and R. Hersh) On the Invariance Principle of Scattering Theory. University of New Mexico Technical Report No. 259, Aug. 1972.
D_2Lattices. American Mathematical Society, *Notices*, Jan. 1971.

Ref: *Black Mathematicians and Their Works*, p. 283. [p]

Deese, Dawson Charles (1931- ——, M)

Biochemist. Born in Raleigh, NC, Dec. 7, 1931. B.S., North Carolina A & T, 1952; M.S., Tuskegee Institute, 1954; Ph.D., University of Wisconsin, 1960. Chemistry and Laboratory Instructor, North Carolina A & T, 1952; Biochemistry Research Assistant, University of Wisconsin, 1954–57; 1958–60; Research Associate, Department of Veterinary Sciences and Biochemistry, 1960–64; Instructor, 1964–68; Chairman of the Department, 1969–71; Associate Professor, Nutrition, 1969–80; Associate Professor, Human Biology, 1980–.

Memberships and awards: American Chemical Society; Phi Sigma Biological Society; Sigma Xi; American Society of Plant Physiologists; Alpha Phi Alpha; AAAS; New York Academy of Sciences; American Institute of Biological Science.

Dissertation title: The Role of Pectic Ezymes in Susceptibility and Resistance of Plants to Fusarium and Verticillium Wilt Diseases.

Ref: *Leaders in American Science*, 1960–61, p. 200. [p]
American Men and Women of Science, 15th ed., p. 565.

Delaney, Martin Robison (1812–1885, M)

Physician. Born in Charlestown, WV, May 6, 1812. Studied as apprentice Physician under A. N. McDowell, J. P. Gazzan, and F. J. Lemoyne. Attended Harvard Medical School, 1850–51, but left due to protest of fellow students. Practiced as a Physician remainder of his life. First black major in the U.S. Army, 1865; instrumental in putting down cholora epidemic in Pittsburgh, PA, where he practiced.

Pub: *Blake; or the Huts of America.* Boston, Beacon Press, 1970. Reprint.
Principia of Ethnology: The Origin of Races and Color, 1879.

Ref: *Dictionary of American Medical Biography*, p. 193–194.
Dictionary of American Negro Biography, p. 169–172.
Encyclopedia of Black America, 1981, p. 306–307.
Great Negroes Past and Present, p. 54.
History of the Negro in Medicine, 1967, p. 27–29. [p] p. 35.
Jet, May 10, 1932, p. 19.
Jet, April 10, 1958, p. 11. [p]
Men of Mark, p. 720–725 [p]
National Medical Association, *Journal*, v. 73 (Supplement), Dec. 1981, p. 1205–1206.
Nine Black American Doctors, p. 8–9.
Historical Afro-American Biographies, p. 72. [p]
Cobb, W. Montague. Martin Robison Delaney. National Medical Association, *Journal*, v. 44, May 1952, p. 232–238.
Miller, Kelly. Historic Background of the Negro Physician. *Journal of Negro History*, v. 1, 1916, p. 105–106.
Negro History Bulletin, v. 36, Feb. 1973, p. 37–39. [p]
Fleming, Robert E. Black, White & Mulatto in Martin R. Delany's *Blake*.
Crisis, Nov. 1926, p. 9–13. [p]

Dennar, Ezenwa A. (1943- ——, M)

Engineer (mechanical). Born in Nigeria, June 8, 1943. B.S.E. (mechanical engineering), University of Connecticut, 1966; M.S. (english), Brown University, 1967; Ph.D. (engineering), 1970.

Memberships and awards: AIAA; Pi Tau Sigma; Phi Kappa Pi; Sigma Xi.

Dissertation title: Radiating Hypervelocity Boundary Layers.

Pub: Several scientific journal articles.

Ref: *Black Engineers in the U.S.*, p. 51–52.

Dennis, Joseph J., Jr.   (1905–1977, M)

Mathematician. Born in Gainesville, FL, April 11, 1905. B.A., Clark College, 1925; M.A., Northwestern University, 1935; Ph.D. (mathematics), Northwestern University, 1944. Former Chairman, Department of Mathematics, Clark college.

Dissertation title: Some Points in the Theory of Positive Definite J-Fractions.

Pub: Some Points in the Theory of Positive Definite J-Fractions. American Math. Soc., *Bulletin*, 1944. Numerous other articles in scientific journals.

Ref: *Black Mathematicians and Their Works*, p. 283. [p] p. 86.

Dent, Anthony L.   (1943– ——, M)

Engineer (chemical). Born in Indian Head, MD, April 19, 1943. B.S. (chemistry), Morgan State College; 1966; Ph.D. (physical chemistry), Johns Hopkins University, 1970.

Memberships and awards: American Chemical Society; American Institute of Chemical Engineers; American Society for Engineering Education; American Association of University Professors; AAAS; Phi Beta Kappa; Phi Lambda Epsilon; Beta Kappa Chi; Sigma Xi; Alpha Kappa Mu.

Dissertation title: The Adsorption and Hydrogenation of Ethylene and Propylene by Zinc-Oxide as studied by Conventional and Infrared Spectroscopic Techniques.

Ref: *Who's Who Among Black Americans*, 1985, p. 222.

Dent, Carl Ashley   (1914– ——, M)

Physician. Born in St. Simon's Island, GA, May 27, 1914. B.S., Union Pacific College, 1934; M.D., Loma Linda University, 1939. Medical Director of Riverside Hospital, Nashville, TN, 1950–69.

Memberships and awards: American Society of Abdominal Surgeons; Society of Nuclear Medicine.

Ref: *Who's Who Among Black Americans*, 1985, p. 222.
Ebony, May 1951, p. 98. [p]

Dent, Samuel George   (1919– ——, M)

Chemist (organic). Born in Brunswick, GA, Sept. 22, 1919. B.S., Dillard University, 1941; M.S., University of Cincinnati, 1942; Ph.D. (organic chemistry), 1944. Instructor in Chemistry, Dillard University, 1944; Research Chemist, Eastman Kodak Co., 1946–.

Memberships and awards: Laws fellow, 1942–44; Chemical Society.

Dissertation title: Benzoxozodiones and Benzoxodiones: Their Syntheses and Pharmacological Properties.

Ref: *American Men of Science*, 8th ed., p. 604.

Derbigny, Irvin Anthony   (1900–1957, M)

Chemist. B.A., Talladega College, 1921; M.A., Cornell, 1925; Ph.D., Columbia University, 1932. Head, Chemistry Department, Talladega College, 1931–36; Vice-President of Tuskegee Institute, 1950; researched vitamins; died in hospital in Tuskegee, 1957.

Memberships and awards: Sigma Xi, Phi Lambda Upsilon.

Dissertation title: Studies on Vitamin A, with Special Reference to Protein Intake.

Pub: *A Survey of Physical Science.*
A Survey of Biological Science.

Ref: *American Men of Science*, 9th ed., p. 460.
Holders of Doctorates Among American Negroes, p. 148.
Jet, Dec. 19, 1957, p. 20.
Crisis, May 1931, p. 165.
Crisis, Aug. 1932, p. 247. [p]

Derham (Durham), James   (1757–18??, M)

Physician. Born a slave in Philadelphia, PA, May 1, 1757. First black man to practice medicine in the United States. Learned from working with Dr. John Kearsley, who taught him how to mix medicines and perform other minor chores. Dr. George West, Surgeon, purchased him, and under Dr. West, he performed many duties of a doctor. He was later sold to Dr. Robert Dove who employed him as an assistant and was so pleased with his progress he freed him. Derham secured a license and practiced medicine in New Orleans during the 1780s. He was fluent in English, French, and Spanish. Dr. Benjamin Rush read his paper entitled "An Account of the Putrid Sore Throat" before the College of Physicians of Philadelphia in 1789.

Ref: *Dictionary of American Medical Biography*, p. 220.
Dictionary of American Negro Biography, p. 205–206. (see Durham)
Encyclopedia of Black America, 1981, p. 308.
Toner, Philip S. *History of Black Americans from Africa to the Emergence of the Cotton King.* vol. 1.
History of the Negro in Medicine, p. 8–10.
Woodson, C. G. *Negro Makers of History*, 5th ed., p. 73–74.
History of the Negro Race in America 1619–1880, Williams, GW, p. 400–401.
Medico-Chirurgical Society of the District of Columbia, *Bulletin*, Dec. 1947, p. 1.
Miller, Kelly. Historic Background of the Negro Physician. *Journal of Negro History*, v. 1, 1916, p. 103–104.
National Medical Association, *Journal*, v. 4, Jan.–Mar. 1912, p. 50.
National Medical Association, *Journal*, v. 34, May 1942, p. 118.
Historical Afro-American Biographies, p. 14.
Nine Black American Doctors, p. 7–8.

Dibble, Eugene Heriot   (1893–1968, M)

Physician. Surgeon. Born in Camden, SC, Aug. 14, 1893. B.A., Atlanta University, 1919; M. D., Howard University Medical College, 1920. Assistant Medical Director of J. A. Andrew Memorial Hospital, 1920–23; Chief Surgeon, U.S. Veterans Administration Hospital, Tuskegee, AL, 1924–25. Medical Director, John A. Andrew Memorial Hospital, 1925–36; Manager and Medical Director, V.A. Hospital, Tuskegee, 1936–46; Medical Director, John A. Andrew Memorial Hospital, 1946–65.

Memberships and awards: 17th Distinguished Medalist of the National Medical Association, 1962; Alpha Phi Alpha; John A. Andrew Clinical Society; C. V. Roman Distinguished Service Medal, 1943.

Ref: *Dictionary of American Medical Biography*, p. 199.
Encyclopedia of Black America, 1981, p. 308.
Who's Who in Colored America, 1928–29, p. 109.
Who's Who in Colored America, 1930–32, p. 126.
Jet, Sept. 2, 1966, p. 42. large [p]
Who's Who in Colored America, 1933–37, p. 156.
Cobb, W. Montague. Eugene Heriot Dibble, M.D., Perspective and Profile. National Medical Association, *Journal*, v. 57, Sept. 1965, p. 435–437. [p]
National Medical Association, *Journal*, v. 35, 1943, p. 175.
Who's Who in Colored America, 1941–44, p. 156.
National Medical Association, *Journal*, v. 54, Nov. 1962, p. 711. [p]
National Medical Association, *Journal*, v. 60, Sept. 1968, p. 446. obit
Crisis, Nov. 1924, p. 30. [p] p. 31–32.
A Century of Black Surgeons, p. 347. [p] p. 348.

Dibble, Joseph Edgar   (18??–19??, M)

Physician. Surgeon. Born in Houston, TX. B.S., Wiley College, Marshall, TX, 1892; M.D., Meharry Medical College, 1895; postgraduate work, University of Pennsylvania, 1899–1900. Surgical staffs of Wheatley Provident Hospital, General Hospital no. 2, Kansas City, MO; Kansas City Southern Hospital; U.S. Government Staff of Designated Surgeons; Assistant Surgeon, U.S. Army Foreign Service, 1916–; Chief Medical Inspector, Kansas City Colored Schools.

Memberships and awards: Research club to encourage, foster, and promote research by surveys, studies and discussions; Missouri Pan Medical Society; Kansas City Medical Society; in an exam for Assistant Surgeon in the Philippines, he won first place in Missouri and fifth in the nation.

Ref: *Who's Who in Colored America*, 1930–32, p. 126.
Who's Who in Colored America, 1933–37, p. 156.
Who's Who in Colored America, 1938–40, p. 156.
Who's Who in Colored America, 1941–44, p. 156.
Crisis, Aug. 1916, p. 190–191. [p]

Dickens, Helen Octavia   (1909– —— , F)

Physician. Surgeon. Obstetrician. Gynecologist. Born in Dayton, OH, 1909. B.S., University of Illinois, 1932; M.D., University of Illinois, 1934; M.M.Sc., University of Pennsylvania Graduate School of Medicine, 1945; Resident in Obstetrics and Gynecology, Provident Hospital, Chicago, 1934–35, 1942–43; Associate Dean, University of Pennsylvania Hospital, Philadelphia; Director, Department of Obstetrics and Gynecology, Mercy Douglas Hospital, 1948–67; Director, Teen Clinic, University of Pennsylvania School of Medicine, 1969–, Professor of Obstetrics and Gynecology and Associate Dean.

Memberships and awards: President, Pan American Women's Alliance, 1970–73; College of Physicians; Obstetrics Society of Philadelphia; Philadelphia County Medical Society; American Medical Association; National Medical Association; Board of Directors, American Cancer Society, 1963; Illini Achievement Award from the University of Illinois, 1982; first black woman admitted to the American College of Surgeons, 1950; fellow, American College of Obstetrics and Gynecology, 1953.

Ref: *Ebony*, April 1951, p. 5. [p]
ABMS Compendium of Certified Medical Specialists, v. 3, p. 500.
Who's Who Among Black Americans, 1985, p. 224.

Dickenson, J. H.   (1800s, M)

Inventor. Dickenson, S. L., of New Jersey. A dozen patents for mechanical appliances used in player piano machinery.

Dickerson, Spencer Cornelius   (1871–1948, M)

Physician. Otolaryngologist. Ophthalmologist. Military (Army). Brigadier General. Born In Austin, TX, Dec. 1, 1871. B.S., University of Chicago, 1897; M.D., Rush Medical College, 1901. Staff, Provident Hospital, Chicago, 1907–48; Chairman, Department of Ophthalmology; Brigadier General, Commander of all Black Regiment, 8th, Illinois, 1930–37; Emeritus, 1937–48.

Ref: *Dictionary of American Medical Biography*, p. 201.
National Medical Association, *Journal*, v. 34, 1942, p. 119.
Crisis, June 1930, p. 204–205. [p]

Dillard, Oliver Williams   (1926– —— , M)

Military (Army). Major General. Born in Margaret, AL, Sept. 28, 1926. B.G.E. (general education), Omaha University, 1959; M.S. (international affairs), George Washington University, 1965. Inducted into the Army in 1945; Second Lieutenant, 1947; Brigadier General, 1972; now a Major General.

Memberships and awards: Purple Heart; Silver Star; Bronze Star; Distinguished Service Medal; legion of Merit with two oak leaf clusters; Combat infantry Badge.

Ref: *Ebony Success Library*, v. 1, p. 95. [p]
  Black Americans in Defense of Our Nation, p. 122. [p]
  Ebony, May 1978, p. 42. [p]

Diuguid, Lincoln I. (1917- ——, M)

Chemist (organic). Born in Lynchburg, VA, Feb. 6, 1917. B.S., West Virginia State College, 1938; M.S., Cornell University, 1939; Ph.D. (organic chemistry), 1945. Head, Chemistry Department, Arkansas State College, 1939-43; Analytical Chemist, Pine Bluffs Arsenal Chemical Warfare Service, U.S. Army, 1943; Merrill Research fellow, Cornell University, 1943-45; Office of Scientific Research and Development, Research fellow, 1945-46; Professor, Chemistry, 1954-74; Professor, Physical Sciences, Harris-Stowe College, 1974-; Chairman of the Department, 1977-.

Memberships and awards: Vice-President, Leukemia Guild, MO and IL, 1964-; American Chemical Society.

Dissertation title: Benzothiazole Derivatives for Antimalarial Studies.

Ref: *American Men of Science*, 16th ed., p. 680.

Dixon, Russell Alexander (1898-1976, M)

Dentist. Born in Kansas City, MO, 1898. D.D.S., Northwestern University, 1929; M.S. (dentistry), 1933. Dean, Howard University Dental School, 1931-19.

Memberships and awards: Board of Regents, National Library of Medicine, 1963-67; Board of Overseers, Visiting Committee of Harvard College for the Medical and Dental Schools; Executive Council, American Association of Dental Schools; fellow, AAAS; fellow, American College of Dentists; Omicron Kappa Upsilon (founder).

Ref: *Jet*, Aug. 26, 1965, p. 22.
  National Medical Association, *Journal*, v. 55, Nov. 1963, p. 562. [p]
  Ebony, Jan. 1960, p. 21. [p]
  Who's Who Among Black Americans, 1977, p. 241.
  Jet, Jan. 22, 1976, p. 44.

Doman, James Richard, Jr. (1937- ——, M)

Architect. Born in New York, NY, 1937. B.A. (architecture), 1965; M.A. (architecture), Columbia University, 1971. Founder of Doman & Associates Architectural Firm in New York; taught at Columbia University, New York University, Opportunities Industrial Center and Architects Renewal Committee in Harlem; Professor of Architecture, City College of New York.

Ref: *Profiles in Black*, p. 74-75. [p]

Donaldson, James Ashley (1941- ——, M)

Mathematician. Born in Madison County, FL, April 17, 1941. B.A., Lincoln University, 1961; M.S. (mathematics), University of Illinois, 1963; Ph.D. (mathematics), 1965. Assistant Professor, Mathematics, Howard University, 1965-66; Assistant Professor, Mathematics, University of Illinois, 1966-69; Associate Professor, Mathematics, University of New Mexico, 1970-71; Professor, Howard University, 1971-; Chairman of the Department of Mathematics, Howard University, 1972-; research in the perturbation theory.

Memberships and awards: American Mathematical Society (member of the reviewing staff of Mathematical Reviews); Mathematical Association of America; AAAS; Sigma Xi; New York Academy of Science; National Association of Mathematicians.

Dissertation title: Integral Representations of the Extended Airy Integral Type for the Modified Bessel Function.

Pub: Integral Representation of the Extended Airy Integral Type of the Modified Bessel Function. *Journal of Mathematics and Physics*, v. 46, no. 1, 1967.
  Expansions for Kv(e) Involving Airy's Function. *Proc. Cambridge Philosophical Society*, v. 66, 1969.
  A Singular Abstract Cauchy Problem, *PNAS, USA*, v. 66, 1970, p. 269.

Fef: *Black Mathematicians and Their Works*, p. 283.
  American Men and Women of Science, 16th ed., p. 704.

Donnell, Clyde (1890-1971, M)

Physician. Roentgenologist. Physiotherapist. Born in Greensboro, NC, Aug. 4, 1890. B.S., North Carolina A & T College, 1907; B.A., Howard University, 1911; M.D., Harvard University, 1915. He was third in exams but was offered no internship because of his race. Dr. Richard C. Cabot arranged for him to work as Junior House Officer on Medical Service of Boston City Hospital under the auspices of Harvard Graduate School, 1915-16; postgraduate work in Internal Medicine, Roentgenology and Physical Therapy, Harvard University, 1918-11, 1924, 1932; postgraduate in X-ray and physiotherapy, Harvard University, 1922-24, 1926. Second Medical Director and a Chairman of the Board of Directors of the North Carolina Mutual Life Insurance Co. He pioneered in the study of the causes of mortality and morbidity in the black population.

Memberships and awards: National Medical Association; Secretary, Old North State Medical Society for 32 years.

Ref: *Who's Who in Colored America*, 1941-44, p. 162. [p] p. 163.
  Jet, Oct. 28, 1971, p. 28. [p]
  Cobb, W. Montague. Clyde Donnell, M.D., 1890-. National Medical Association, *Journal*, v. 52, Sept. 1960, p. 382. [p] cover

Dictionary of American Medical Biography, p. 210.
National Medical Association, *Journal*, v. 73 (Supplement), Dec. 1981, p. 207.

Dooley, Thomas Price   (1904- —— , M)

Geneticist. Zoologist. Born in Elberton, GA, Oct. 12, 1904. B.A., Morehouse College, 1927; Detroit, 1929; M.S., University of Iowa, 1931; Ph.D. (zoology), 1939. Professor, Prairie View A & M College, 1934-; Head, Department of Natural Science, 1941-49; Dean, School of Arts and Sciences, 1949-68.

Memberships and awards: Sigma Xi; General Education Board fellow; AAAS; Genetics Society of America; American Microscopical Society; National Association of Research Scientists Teaching; National Institute of Science.

Dissertation title: Influence of Colchicine on the Germ Cells of Insects, *Gryllus Assimilis* and *Melanoplus Differentialis*, with Special Reference to the Mitochondria and Dictysomes.

Ref: *American Men and Women of Science*, 12th ed., p. 1498.
Holders of Doctorates Among American Negroes, p. 189.

Dorman, Linnaeus Cuthbert   (1935- —— , M)

Chemist (organic). Inventor. Born in Orangeburg, SC, June 28, 1935. B.S., Bradley University, 1956; Ph.D., Indiana University, 1961. Chemist, U.S. Department of Agriculture, Pioria, IL, summers, 1956-59; Research Chemist, Dow Chemical Co., Midland, MI, 1960-68; Research Specialist to Associate Scientist, Dow Chemical Co., 1968-83.

Memberships and awards: Trustee, Midland Foundation, 1980-; Board fellow, Saginaw Valley State College, 1975-, Vice-President, 1981-83, President, 1983-85; Co-Recipient, Bond Award, American Oil Chemists Society, 1960; Central Research Inventor of the Year Award, Dow Chemical Co., 1982; National Organization of Black Chemists and Chemical Engineers; AAAS; American Chemical Society; Sigma Xi; Phi Lambda Upsilon; Pi Kappa Delta; Omega Psi Phi.

Dissertation title: Synthesis of Heterocyclic Nitrogen Compounds of the Tetrahydroimidazole and Hexahydropyrimidine Series—Reduction of Aromatic Ketones with alloys of Magnesium.

Pub: Several articles in professional journals.

Ref: *Who's Who in America*, 1986-87, p. 737.
Who's Who Among Black Americans, 1985, p. 231.
Ebony Success Library, v. 1, p. 97. [p]
American Men and Women of Science, 15th ed., p. 688.

Dorn, Stephen E.   (1900s, M)

Physician. Director of the Bureau of Membership of the American Hospital Association; Executive Director of Chicago's Provident Hospital, 1971-.

Ref: *Jet*, Sept. 2, 1971, p. 17.

Dorsette, Cornelius Nathaniel   (1852-1897, M)

Physician. Born in 1852, a slave. B.A., Hampton Institute, 1878; worked for Dr. Vosburgh of Syracuse who encouraged him to become a physician; M.D., University of Buffalo Medical School, 1882. Alabama's first licensed black practitioner. Founded Hale Infirmary which was enlarged several years after his death, operated from 1890-1958. He also was a teacher of Booker T. Washington.

Memberships and awards: Board of Trustees, Tuskegee Institute, 1883-1397.

Ref: *History of the Negro in Medicine*, p. 83-84, 281. [p] p. 84.
Dictionary of American Medical Biography, p. 211.
Cobb, W. Montague. Cornelius Nathaniel Dorsette, M.D., 1852-1897. National Medical Association, *Journal*, v. 52, Nov. 1960, p. 452-459. [p] cover

Douglas, Aurelius William, Jr.   (1934- —— , M)

Engineer (metallurgical). Born in Gary, IN, Aug. 3, 1934. B.S. (metallurgical engineering), Illinois Institute of Technology, 1963; Ph.D., 1967. Research Engineer, Inland Steel, East Chicago, IN.

Memberships and awards: American Institute of Mining, Metallurgical Engineers; American Metal Powder Institute; Alpha Sigma Mu; Foundry Educational Foundation Award; National Science Foundation Award.

Dissertation title: Heterogeneous Nucleation.

Ref: *Black Engineers in the United States*, p. 54.

Douglas, Janice Green   (1944- —— , F)

Physician. Internist. Born in 1944. B.A., M.D., Meharry Medical College. Director, Department of Hypertension and Endocrinology, Case Western Reserve University, Cleveland, OH.

Memberships and awards: Fellow, National Institute of Health, Vanderbilt University, Department of Medicine, 1973.

Ref: *Black Enterprise*, Oct. 1988, p. 94-95.
ABMS Compendium of Certified Medical Specialists, v. 2, p. 423.

Douglas, Joseph Francis   (1926- —— , M)

Engineer (electrical). Born in Indianapolis, IN, Oct. 31, 1926. B.S. (electrical engineering), Purdue University, 1948; M.S., University of Missouri, 1962. Project Engineer, U.S. Department of Agriculture, 1948-56; Head and Associate Professor, Southern University Department of Electrical Engineering 1956-64; Project Engineer, American Machine and Foundry Co., 1964-66; Group Leader in Electrical Technology and Engineering, 1966-74; Associate Dean of Academic Instruction, 1974-77; Associate Professor of Electrical Technology, Bachelor Technology Program, 1977-; Associate Professor of Engineering and Head of Electrical Engineering, Pennsylvania State University, York, PA, 1970-.

Memberships and awards: Institute of Electrical and Electronics Engineers; American Society for Engineering Education; Lindback Award for Distinguished Teaching, 1972.

Ref: *Black Engineers in the United States*, p. 54.
American Men and Women of Science, 15th ed., p. 697.
Who's Who Among Black Americans, 1985, p. 233.

Douglas, Samuel Horace   (1928- ——, M)

Mathematician. Born in Ardmore, OK, May 10, 1928. B.S., Bishop College, 1950; B.S., Oklahoma State University, 1959; M.S., Oklahoma State University, 1963; Ph.D., 1967. Assistant Professor of Mathematics, Prairie View A & M, 1959-63; Department Chairman, 1962-63; Professor and Chairman of the Department of Mathematics, Grambling College, 1967-.

Memberships and awards: American Mathematical Society; London Mathematical Society; Mathematical Association of America; Pi Mu Epsilon; Alpha Phi Alpha; fellow, Science Faculty, 1963-67.

Dissertation title: Convexity Lattices Related to Topological Lattices and Incidence Geometries.

Ref: *Black Mathematicians and Their Works*, p. 284.
Who's Who Among Black Americans, 1985, p. 233.

Douglas, William   (1800s, M)

Inventor. Kansas, AR, six patents for inventions of self-binding harvesting machinery.

Ref: *Negro in Our History*, 5th ed., p. 464.

Douglas, William R.   (19??- ——, M)

Biomedical specialist. Born in Indianapolis, IN. B.S., M.S., Ph.D., Columbia University. Director of Biomedical Sciences Division of American Standard Testing Bureau, Inc., New York, NY; Expert in Aerospace Medicine.

Memberships and awards: Chairman of Second United National Conference on the Exploration and Peaceful Uses of Outer Space, 1982.

Ref: *Ebony*, July 1982, p. 7. [p]

Dove, Lillian Elizabeth Singleton   (1895-1971, F)

Physician. Born in Roanoke, VA, May 23, 1895. B.A., Morgan College, 1913; M.D., Meharry Medical College, 1917. Editor, "Health Briefs," Chicago Defender; Chairman, Scientific Staff of the Woman's World Fair, Chicago, 1928; House Physician for Orphan Children's Home; Attending and Examining Physician for Friendly Big Sisters Home; Ex-Field Physician, Health, City of Chicago.

Memberships and awards: National Medical Association; Cook County Physicians Association; Chairman, Health and Hygiene Federated Clubs of Chicago; Alpha Kappa Alpha.

Ref: *Who's Who in Colored America*, 1928-29, p. 114. [p] opp. 114.
Who's Who in Colored America, 1930-32, p. 134. [p] opp. 136.
Who's Who in Colored America, 1933-37, p. 163.
Who's Who in Colored America, 1938-40, p. 164.
Who's Who in Colored America, 1941-40, p. 165. [p] p. 163.

Dove, Ray Allen   (1921- ——, M)

Chemist. Born in Rockmart, GA, Aug. 17, 1921. B.S., University of Akron, 1947; M.S., 1953. From Junior Research Chemist to Senior Research Chemist, Goodyear Tire & Rubber Co., 1958-75; Section Head, Goodyear Tire & Rubber Co., 1975-; research in ion exchange chromatography.

Memberships and awards: American Chemical Society.

Ref: *American Men and Women of Science*, 15th ed., p. 701.
In Black & White, p. 274.

Dowdy, William Wallace   (1895-19??, M)

Ecologist. Biologist. Born in Eastover, SC, Oct. 10, 1895. B.A., Iowa State University, 1923; M.S., Cornell University, 1928; Ph.D. (ecology), Western Reserve University, 1942. Professor, Biology, Shaw University, 1923-27; Langston University, 1929. Professor and Head of Department, Lincoln University, 1929-; Summer Professor, Fisk University, 1928; Emeritus Professor and Head, Biology Department, Lincoln University (Jefferson City), 1974-; Community studies of disturbed areas, with emphasis on invertebrates; striatal and seasonal societies of invertebrates.

Memberships and awards: AAAS; Ecological Society of America; American Institute of Biological Sciences; Sigma Xi, Science Research Society of American; National Institute of Science; Missouri Academy of Science.

Dissertation title: A Community Study of a Disturbed Deciduous Forest Area near Cleveland, Ohio, with Special Reference to Invertebrates.

Ref: *American Men and Women of Science*, 13th ed., p. 1075.
Holders of Doctorates Among American Negroes, p. 189.
Negroes in Science, p. 177.

Downing, Lewis King   (1896–1967, M)

Engineer. Born in Roanoke, VA, Jan. 2, 1896. B.S., Johnson C. Smith, 1916; B.S. (civil engineering), Howard University, 1921; B.S. (engineering administration), M.I.T., 1923; M.S. (highway transport and traffic control), University of Michigan, 1932. Helped set up School of Engineering and Architecture at Howard University. Named Dean of the School in 1936 until his retirement in 1964; Dean Emeritus, 1964–67; Chairman, Engineering Commission, DC Commissioners Traffic Advisory Board, 1958–.

Memberships and awards: Distinguished Alumni Award, Howard University, 1953; fellow, American Society of Civil Engineers; Washington Academy of Sciences; American Society of Engineering Education; National Teacher Association; Alpha Phi Alpha; Beta Kappa Chi; Tau Beta Pi.

Ref: *American Men of Science*, 7th ed., p. 470.
Dictionary of American Negro Biography, p. 189–190.
Who Was Who in American History—Science & Technology, p. 164–165.
Ebony, Mar. 1955, p. 18 [p]

Downing, Lylburn Clinton   (1889–1965, M)

Physician. Surgeon. Born in Danville, VA, Mar. 18, 1889. B.A., Johnson C. Smith University, 1907; M.A., 1916; M.D., Howard University Medical School, 1912; Harvard Graduate School, 1919 and 1930; Marquette University, 1927; University of Pennsylvania, 1919. Superintendent of Burrell Memorial Hospital, Roanoke, VA, 1915–.

Memberships and awards: National Medical Association; National Hospital Association; President, Old Dominion State Medical Society; President, Magic City Medical Society; President, Former Internes of Freedmen's Hospital; Philadelphia County Medical Society; Alpha Phi Alpha.

Ref: *Who's Who in Colored America*, 1930–32, p. 135.
Who's Who in Colored America, 1933–37, p. 164.
Who's Who in Colored America, 1938–40, p. 165.
Who's Who in Colored America, 1941–44, p. 165. [p] p. 163.

Doyle, James   (1800s, M)

Inventor. Pittsburgh; automatic serving system so as to dispense with the waiters in cafes.

Ref: *Negro in Our History*, 5th ed., p. 464.

Dozier, Richard K.   (1939– —— , M)

Architect. Born in Buffalo, NY, Jan. 18, 1939. B.S., Lawrence Institute of Technology, Yale University, 1969; M.A., Yale University, School of Architecture, 1970; work toward Ph.D., University of Michigan, 1974. Professor of Architecture, Yale University, 1970–76; Historic Preservation Architect, Tuskegee Institute, Chairman, Department of Architecture, 1976–79; History of Afro-American Architects and Architecture, Teaching and Professional Specialization; was a high school dropout, went into the Navy and changed his outlook.

Memberships and awards: American Institute of Architects; National Organization of Minority Architects; Honor Award, Yale University; Leadership Award, Yale University, 1969; Research fellow, Graham Foundation, 1970; National Endowment of the Arts Award, 1974.

Ref: *Black Collegian*, v. 5, Sept./Oct. 1974, p. 18, 61. [p] p. 61.
Who's Who Among Black Americans, 1985, p. 235.

Drew, Charles Richard   (1904–1950, M)

Physician. Surgeon. Born in Washington, DC, June 3, 1904. B.A., Amherst, 1926; M.D. and C.M. (master of surgery), McGill, 1933; Dr. of Sci. in Medicine, 1940, Columbia University. Instructor in Pathology, Howard University, 1936; Assistant in Surgery, 1936; Professor of Surgery and Chief Surgeon, Freedmen's Hospital; Organizer of Blood Bank; researched in blood plasma for transfusion due to longer life of the blood with cells removed (plasma) while at Presbyterian Hospital in New York, NY; Organized a blood bank in London during World War II.

Memberships and awards: Rockefeller fellow, in Surgery, College of Physicians and Surgeons, Columbia; Washington Medical Director, 1946–47; Surgical Consultant, ETO (Army); Director of first Plasma Division, Blood Transfusion Association, supplying plasma to the British, 1940–41; first Director, A.R.C. Blood Bank, supplying blood plasma to U.S. forces, 1941; America-Soviet Science Commission, 1944; Distinguished Service Medal, National Medical Association (posthumously), 1950; General Education Board fellow in Surgery; Spingarn Medal, 1944; Postage stamp issued in his honor, 1981.

Ref: *American Men of Science*, 8th ed., p. 653.
Blood Brother, p. 131–174.
Hardwick, Richard. *Charles Richard Drew*, New York, Scribner, 1967.
Dictionary of American Biography, Supplement 4, p. 242.
Dictionary of American Medical Biography, p. 215–216.
Dictionary of American Negro Biography, p. 190–192.
Encyclopedia of Black America, p. 325–326. [p]
History of the Negro in Medicine, p. 107–109. [p] p. 108.
They Showed the Way, Rollins, p. 53–54.
Historical Afro-American Biographies, p. 184–185. [p]

Negro History Bulletin, v. 36, Nov. 1973, p. 144–150. family [p] p. 147.
Jet, June 5, 1980, p. 26. [p]
Holders of Doctorates Among American Negroes, p. 120.
Black Pioneers of Science & Invention, p. 151–167. [p] p. 152.
National Medical Association, *Journal*, v. 63, Mar. 1971, p. 156–157. The Red Cross Leaflet.
Ebony, Feb. 1974, p. 88–90, 92–94, 96. [p]
Scott, C. Waldo. Biography of a Surgeon. *Crisis*, Oct. 1951, p. 501–506, 555.
National Medical Association, *Journal*, v. 71, Sept. 1979, p. 893–895.
National Medical Association, *Journal*, v. 74, June 1982, p. 561–565. (stamp issue article)
National Medical Association, *Journal*, v., Mar. 1956. [p] cover
National Medical Association, *Journal*, v. 69, June 1977. [p] cover
A Century of Black Surgeons, v. 1, p. 63–102. [p]

Drew, James William   (1894–1965, M)

Mathematician. B.A., Virginia Union University, 1918; M.S., Cornell, 1927. Professor of Mathematics, Storer College, 1922–35; Emeritus Professor of Mathematics, Virginia Union University.

Memberships and awards: Mathematics Association.

Ref: *American Men of Science*, 11th ed., p. 1291.

Duke, Charles Sumner   (1879–1952, M)

Engineer (structural). Engineer (architectural). Born in Selma, AL, July 21, 1879. B.A., Harvard, 1904; C.E., University of Wisconsin, 1913. Served as Construction Engineer with GSA in the Virgin Islands; Structural Engineer in independent practice, 1922–; designed Seventh Day Adventist Church, 46th & St. Laurence in Chicago and Walter AME Church 38th & Dearborn; worked as an Engineer for Pennsylvania Railroad, Missouri Pacific Railroad, Chicago & Northwestern Railroad and George W. Jackson, Inc.

Memberships and awards: Helped form National Technical Association and was its President; Chicago Zoning Commission; Western Society of Engineers; Structural Engineers Society; Kappa Alpha Psi; Sigma Pi Phi.

Ref: *Encyclopedia of Black America*, 1981, p. 329.
Who's Who in Colored America, 1928–29, p. 117.
Who's Who in Colored America, 1930–32, p. 136–137.
Who's Who in Colored America, 1933–37, p. 166.
Who's Who in Colored America, 1938–40, p. 166.
Who's Who in Colored America, 1941–44, p. 169.

Dukes, Lamar   (1925– ——, M)

Engineer (electrical). Born in Pensacola, FL, Nov. 6, 1925. Attended Florida A & M University., 1943–45; B.S. (electrical engineering), University of Pittsburg, 1953; advanced studies, New York University, St. Johns Uni-

versity, NY, and West Coast University, CA. Assisted in the design of an airborne warning and control system and an air-to-surface missile under a Douglas Aircraft government contract; contributed to the development of the landing and rendevous radars for the Apollo lunar lander. Manager of advanced communications and avionics engineering at Douglas Aircraft in Long Beach, CA.

Memberships and awards: Rumor Control Advisory Board of Long Beach.

Ref: *Ebony Success Library*, v. 1, p. 99. [p]
Who's Who Among Black Americans, 1977, p. 252.

Dumas, Albert W., Sr.   (1876–19??, M)

Physician. Inventor. Born in Terrebonne Parish, LA, Sept. 9, 1876. Houma Academy, 1896; Flint Medical College, New Orleans University, three years; M.D., Illinois Medical College, 1899. Passed Mississippi State Board and practiced at Natchez for 40 years; Inventor of a nonstopping Trocar and Canula manufactured by Max Wocher Company, Cincinnati, OH.

Memberships and awards: Chairman, Medical Section, National Medical Association, two years; Vice-President, National Medical Association; President, National Medical Association, 1939–40; Mississippi Medical and Surgical Association, President twice; Supervisor of Clinics, John A. Andrew Clinical Society.

Ref: National Medical Association, *Journal*, v. 31, Sept. 1939, p. 191. [p]

Dumas, Rhetaugh   (1930– ——, F)

Nurse. B.S., Dillard University, Division of Nursing; M.S.N., Yale University; Ph.D., Union Graduate School, Yellow Springs, OH. Chief, Psychiatric Nursing Education Branch, Division of Manpower and Training Programs, NIMH; Deputy Director, NIMH, 1979; Dean, University of Michigan School of Nursing, 1981–.

Memberships and awards: Charter fellow, American Academy of Nursing; Honorary Doctorates, University of Cincinnati and Simmons College; Distinguished Alumnae Award, Yale University.

Pub: The Effect of Nursing Care on Postoperative Vomiting.

Ref: *The Path We Tread*, p. 109–110, p. 242. [p]
Ebony, Feb. 1967, p. 54. [p]

Dummett, Clifton Orin   (1919– ——, M)

Dentist. Born in Georgetown, Guyana, May 20, 1919. B.S., Roosevelt University, 1941; D.D.S., Northwestern University, 1941; M.S.D., 1942; M.P.H., 1947. One of the first three dentists to get a Ph.D. in Dentistry. Chief, Dental Services, V.A. Hospital, Tuskegee, 1949–65; V.A. Research Hospital, Chicago, 1965–66; Dean and Director, Dental Education, Meharry Medical College, 1942–47.

Memberships and awards: Julius Rosenwald fellow; American Public Health Association; American College of Dentists; International College of Dentists; Honorary Member, American Dental Association; International Association for Dental Research; National Dental Association; American Academy of Dental Medicine; Sigma Xi; Delta Omega; Sigma Pi Phi; Alpha Phi Alpha.

Pub: *The Growth and Development of the Negro in Dentistry in the United States.* Chicago, National Dental Association, 1952.

Ref: *Chicago Black Dental Professionals,* p. 100.
Medico-Chirurgical Society of the District of Columbia, Inc., *Bulletin,* April 1949, p. 1. [p]
Who's Who Among Black Americans, 1985, p. 239.

Dupre, Ernest Frank   (19??- ——, M)

Physiologist. B.S., University of Chicago; Ph.D., University of Edinburgh, 1932.

Memberships and awards: Earl of Moray Research Fund Grant.

Dissertation title: Distribution of Calcium in Blood.

Ref: *Holders of Doctorates Among American Negroes,* p. 120.
Crisis, Oct. 1932, p. 325. [p]

Durham, J.

Physician. See Derham.

Dutton, Benson Leroy   (1910- ——, M)

Engineer. Born in Philadelphia, PA, Jan. 7, 1910. B.S. (civil engineering), Pennsylvania State College, 1933. Chief of Party, Bureau of Engineering and Surveys, Philadelphia, PA, 1933-34; Construction Engineer, Philadelphia, 1933-36; Project Engineer, U.S. Department of the Interior, National Park Service, 1937-40; Instructor, Hampton Institute, 1940-47; Plant Engineer, Hampton Institute, 1942-44; Director of Engineering, Tennessee A & I State College, Nashville.

Memberships and awards: American Society of Civil Engineers; National Society of Professional Engineers; American Concrete Institute; National Technical Institute.

Ref: *The National Register,* 1952, p. 568.
Black Engineers in the United States, p. 56.

Duvalle, Sylvester Howard   (1890-19??, M)

Chemist. Born in Indianapolis, IN, Jan. 4, 1890. B.A. (chemistry), Butler College, 1912; M.A., Indiana University, 1919; Ed.D., New York University, 1942. Head, Chemistry Department, Lincoln University, MO, 1917-18; Assistant in Chemistry, Claremont Men's College, 1962; research in salt effect of weak electrolytes and indicators.

Memberships and awards: Kappa Alpha Psi.

Dissertation title: An Evaluation of the Standards of Chemistry Teaching in the Universities and Colleges for Negroes in the United States.

Ref: *American Men of Science,* 11th ed., p. 1331.
Holders of Doctorates Among American Negroes, p. 148.
Who's Who in Colored America, 1933-37, p. 169.

Dwight, Edward J.   (19??- ——, M)

Astronaut candidate. Born in. First black candidate for astronaut. B.S. (cum laude) (aeronautics), Arizona State College, 1957.

Ref: *Jet,* April 18, 1963, p. 14-18. [p]
Ebony, June 1965, p. 19-32, 34-36. [p]
Ebony, July 1963, p. 71-, 74-76, 78, 80-81. [p]

Dyce, Barbara Jeanne   (1928- ——, F)

Biochemist. Born in Chicago, IL, Feb. 17, 1928. Attended Loyola University, University of Illinois, University of Chicago, University of Illinois Medical School; M.S., University of Southern California School of Medicine, 1971. Instructor, Trade Technical Community College; Assistant Professor, Pharmacology, University of Southern California Medical School; President and Technical Director, Radioimmunoassay Laboratory of Southern California.

Memberships and awards: AAAS; Founder and Past-President, Feminine Touch, Inc.

Pub: Numerous papers in scientific journals.

Ref: *Ebony Success Library,* v. 1, p. 101. [p]
Who's Who Among Black Americans, 1985, p. 243.

Dyer, Joseph Francis, Sr.   (1888-1960, M)

Physician. Otolaryngologist. Born in Washington, DC, 1888. M.D., Howard University Medical School, 1912. Clinical Professor, Otolaryngology, Howard University Medical College.

Memberships and awards: President, Medico-Chirurgical Society of the District of Columbia; National Medical Association; Association of Former Internes and Residents of Freedmen's Hospital; Diplomate, American Board of Otolaryngology, 1940; fellow, American Academy of Otolaryngology.

Ref: National Medical Association, *Journal,* v. 52, Sept. 1960, p. 380. [p] obit

Dyer, W. H.   (18??-1958, M)

Physician. Surgeon. B.A., Lincoln College, University of Illinois, 1916. Medical Examiner for the Standard Life Insurance Company. Doctor for Kansas City Police Department since 1929 and Surgeon for Santa Fe Railroad.

Ref: *Who's Who in Colored America*, 1928–29, p. 425.
        Jet, Feb. 13, 1958, p. 20.

E

Eagleson, Halson Vashon   (1903– ——, M)

Physicist (experimental). Born in Bloomington, IN, Mar. 14, 1903. B.A., Indiana University, 1926; M.A., 1931; Ph.D. (physics), 1939. Professor of Mathematics and Physics, Morehouse college, 1927–35; Head, Department of Physics, 1935–47; Professor of Physics, Howard University, 1947–; Chairman, Department of Physics and Astronomy, 1961–71; University of Maryland Visiting Professor, 1967–73.

Memberships and awards: Philosophical Society of Washington; American Association of Physics Teachers; Acoustical Society of America; Grantee NSF, 1968–80; Alpha Phi Alpha; Alpha Phi Omega; General Education Board fellow.

Dissertation title: The Influence of Certain Atmospheric Conditions upon Sound Intensity.

Ref: *Who's Who Among Black Americans*, 1985, p. 244.
        American Men and Women of Science, 15th ed., p. 776.
        Holders of Doctorates Among American Negroes, p. 148.

Eagleson, Oran Wendle   (1910– ——, M)

Psychologist. Born in Unionville, IN, 1910. B.A., Indiana University, 1931; M.A., 1932; Ph.D., 1935. Psychology Professor, Spelman College, 1936–70; Calloway Professor of Psychology, 1970–.

Dissertation title: Comparative Studies of White and Negro Subjects in Learning to Discriminate Visual Magnitude.

Ref: *Holders of Doctorates Among American Negroes*, p. 205.
        American Men of Science, 9th ed., p. 182. (Social & Behavioral)
        Even the Rat Was White, p. 141. [p] p. 142.

Earles, Lucius C., III   (1935– ——, M)

Physician. Dermatologist. Born in New Orleans, LA, 1935. B.S. (physical education), Howard University, 1956; M.D., 1963. Private practice with Dr. T. K. Lawless, 1969–70; single practice, 1970–78; dermatologist for several clinics, 1971–77; Assistant Professor, Chicago College of Osteopathic Medicine, 1977–79.

Memberships and awards: President, National Medical Association, 1983; American Medical Association; Chicago Medical Association; Illinois State Medical Society; Cook County Physicians Association; National Medical Association; Prairie State Medical Society.

Ref: National Medical Association, *Journal*, v. 76, Jan. 1984, p. 83. [p]

Earls, Julian Manley   (1942– ——, M)

Engineer. Born in Portsmouth, VA, Nov. 22, 1942. B.S., Norfolk State College, 1964; M.S., University of Rochester, 1965; M.S., University of Michigan, 1972; Ph.D., 1973; P.M.D. (administration), Harvard Business School, 1979. NASA Physicist, 1965–67; Radiation Specialist, Nuclear Regulatory Agency, 1967–68; NASA Physicist and Chief, Office of Environmental Health, 1968–.

Memberships and awards: President, National Technical Association, Inc., 1976–77; American Nuclear Society, 1966–; U.S. Nuclear Regulatory Commission, Radiation Emergency Team, 1971–; Environmental Pollution Control Board, NASA, 1970–; Kappa Alpha Psi; Distinguished Young Black American, 1973; U.S. Atomic Energy fellow, 1964; NASA fellow, 1971; Federal Executive Board Certificate of Merit, 1973; Technical Achievement Award, Society of Black Manufacturers, Engineers and Technologists, 1978.

Dissertation title: Volume I. Radiation Protection Guides for Long-Range Space Missions. Volume II. Radiological Health Aspects of Fabricating Operations with Thoriated Metals.

Ref: *Who's Who Among Black Americans*, 1985, p. 244–245.

Early, Benjamin Nathaniel   (1944– ——, M)

Engineer (electrical). Born in Washington, DC, Sept. 29, 1944. B.S. (electrical engineering), Howard University, 1966; M.S., California Institute of Technology, 1967; Ph.D., 1969. Technical Staff, NAR Electronics Division, 1969–71; Chairman, Electrical Engineering Department, Howard University.

Memberships and awards: RCA Scholarship; Robert H. Goddard Scholarship; Two years National Science Foundation Scholarship; Sigma Xi; Tau Beta Pi; Sigma Pi Sigma; Pi Mu Epsilon.

Dissertation title: Stochastic Optimal Control.

Ref: *Black Engineers in the United States*, p. 57.

Easley, Annie   (1933– ——, F)

Mathematician. B.S., Cleveland State University, 1977. Works for NASA, Lewis Research Center, Cleveland. Develops and implements computer codes used in solar, wind and other energy projects.

Ref: *Black Contributors to Science and Energy Technology*, p. 18–19.
        In Black and White, 3rd ed., p. 289.

Edelin, Kenneth Carlton   (1939– ——, M)

Physician. Obstetrician. Gynecologist. Born in Washington, DC, Mar. 31, 1939. B.S., Columbia University, 1961; M.D., Meharry Medical School, 1967. Associate Director, Chairman, and Professor, Department of Obstetrics and

Gynecology, Boston University School of Medicine, 1974-.

Memberships and awards: President, Gynecological Association of Boston; Board of Trustees, Fuller Mental Health Center; Board of Trustees, Planned Parenthood League of Massachusetts; American Association of Gynecologists and Laparoscopists.

Ref: *Black Enterprise*, Oct. 1988, p. 95.
Who's Who Among Black Americans, 1985, p. 246-247.

Edwards, Cecile Hoover   (1926- ——, F)

Nutritionist. Born in East St. Louis, IL, Oct. 20, 1926. B.S., Tuskegee Institute, 1946; M.S., 1947; Ph.D. (nutrition), Iowa State University, 1950. American Board of Nutrition, 1963. Research Associate in Nutrition, Iowa State University, 1949-50; Head, Department of Food and Nutrition and Research Associate, The Carver Foundation, Tuskegee Institute; Dean, School of Human Ecology, Howard University, 1974-; research in amino acid content of food, utilization of protein from vegetable sources.

Memberships and awards: Sigma Xi; Phi Kappa Phi; Beta Kappa Chi; Alpha Kappa Mu.

Dissertation title: Utilization of Nitrogen by the Animal Organism: Influence of Caloric Intake and Methionine Supplementation on the Protein Metabolism of Albino Rats Fed Rations Low in Nitrogen and Containing Varying Proportions of Fat.

Ref: *American Men and Women of Science*, 14th ed., p. 804.
In Black & White, p. 292.
Who's Who Among Black Americans, 1985, p. 248.
The Negro in Science, p. 177.

Edwards, Donald Anderson   (1905- ——, M)

Physicist. Born in Calhoun, AL, Jan. 5, 1905. B.A., Talladega College, AL, 1926; M.S., University of Chicago, 1931; Ph.D., University of Pittsburg, 1952. Prairie View College, 1935-36; Instructor, Physics and Mathematics, Louisville Municipal College, 1936-42; Physics Department, Virginia State College, 1943-45; Research Associate, Pittsburgh, 1952-53; editor, Publications Agency, Signal Corps, Ft. Monmouth, NJ; Head, Department of Physics, Lincoln University, 1952-53; Head, Department of Physics, The Agricultural College of North Carolina, 1954-.

Memberships and awards: Sigma Xi.

Dissertation title: The Structural Characteristics of some Magnesium-Cadmium Alloys. Between 25 and 300 Degrees C as Determined by X-Ray Diffraction.

Ref: *Negro in Science*, p. 189-190.
Crisis, Aug. 1931, p. 277. [p] only

Edwards, Gaston Alonzo   (1875-19??, M)

Architect. Born in Belvoir, NC, Apr. 12, 1875. B.S., Agricultural and Mechanical College, 1901; M.S., Cornell University, 1909; President, Kittrell College, 1917-29; Principal, Hillside Park High School, Durham, NC, 1929-1941. First black to design and construct buildings for American Baptist Home Mission Society and first black architect licensed in North Carolina.

Ref: *Who's Who in Colored America*, 1930, 32, p. 140.
Jet, April 18, 1963, p. 11.

Edwards, Lena Frances   (1900-1986, F)

Physician. Born in Washington, DC, Sept. 17, 1900. B.S., Howard University, 1921; M.D., Howard University Medical School, 1924. Professor, Howard University Medical School, 1954-60. In 1961 she gave up a lucrative practice in New Jersey to build a maternity clinic for migrant Mexican workers in Hereford, TX, with $14,500 of her money. Mother of six children.

Memberships and awards: Citizen of the Year at 36th Annual Chamber of Commerce dinner, 1963. In 1964 she was awarded the Presidential Medal of Freedom by President Johnson; Honorary Doctor of Humane Letters, St. Peters College; Dr. Lena Edwards Park, Jersey City, named for her.

Ref: *Ebony*, Feb. 1962, p. 59-60, 62, 64, 66, 68. [p]
Jet, Mar. 11, 1963, p. 42.
Washington Post, Dec. 5, 1986, B11. obit.
Lady Doctor. American Medical Women's Association, *Journal*, v. 39, p. 192-195.
Medicine, Motherhood and Mercy: The Story of a Black Woman Doctor, 1979.
Who's Who Among Black Americans, 1985, p. 249.
National Medical Association, *Journal*, v. 79, July 1987, p. 785-786. obit & biog

Edwards, Robert Valentino   (1940- ——, M)

Engineer (chemical). Born in Baltimore, MD, Dec. 15, 1940. B.S. (mathematics), Johns Hopkins University, 1962; M.S. (chemical engineering), 1964; Ph.D., 1968. From Research Associate to Senior Research Associate, 1968-70; From Assistant Professor to Associate Professor, 1970-79; Professor and Chairman of Chemical Engineering, Case Western Reserve University, 1979-.

Memberships and awards: AAAS; American Institute of Chemical Engineers; American Chemical Society; American Optical Society; American Physical Society; Sigma Xi; Phi Lambda Epsilon; over $1 million in research grants, 1968-85.

Dissertation title: The Temperature Dependence of the Collision Induced Predissociation Rate Constant of 1 Sub 2.

Pub: Over 100 scientific papers and lectures.

Ref: *American Men and Women of Science*, 16th ed., p. 836.
Black Engineers in the United States, p. 58.
Who's Who Among Black Americans, 1985, p. 250.

Elam, Lloyd Charles   (1928-——, M)

Physician. Psychiatrist. Born in Little Rock, AR, Oct. 27, 1928. B.S., Roosevelt University, 1950; M.D., University of Washington, Seattle, 1957. American Board of Neurology and Psychiatry Diploma, 1965. President, Meharry Medical College, 1968–81. Established its Psychiatry Department and became its first Head, 1961–68.

Memberships and awards: fellow, Center for Advanced Study of Behavioral Science, Palo Alto, CA, 1981–82; Distinguished Service Professor, Meharry Medical College, Nashville, TN, 1982–; National Medical Association; American College of Psychiatrists; American Medical Association; American Psychiatric Association; Distinguished Service Medal, 1976; Group for the Advancement of Psychiatry; Governor's Commission on Alcoholism; Nashville Mental Health Association.

Ref: *American Men and Women of Science*, 15th ed., p. 832.
In Black & White, p. 295.
Who's Who Among Black Americans, 1980–81, p. 237.
Biographical Directory of the American Psychiatric Association, 1983, p. 322.
ABMS Compendium of Certified Medical Specialists, v. 5, p. 423.
Ebony Success Library, v. 1, p. 105. [p]
National Medical Association, *Journal*, v. 60, Mar. 1968, p. 150–151. [p]
Ebony, Oct. 1976, p. 32. [p]

Elder, Clarence L.   (1935-——, M)

Inventor. Born in 1935. Attended Morgan State College. Has patent for "occustat" energy conservation system designed to get up to 30% in energy saving.

Memberships and awards: Received plaque at New York International Patent Exposition in 1969 for "Outstanding achievement in the field of electronics."

Ref: *Black Contributors to Science and Energy Technology*, p. 20–21.

Elders, Minnie Joycelyn   (1933-——, F)

Physician. Pediatrician. Endocrinologist. Born in Schaal, AR, Aug. 13, 1933. B.S., Philander Smith, 1952; M.D., University of Arizona Medical College, 1960; M.S., University of Arkansas Medical College, 1967. Professor, University of Arkansas Medical College, Department of Pediatrics, 1976–; National Advisor to Food and Drug, FDA, 1977–; National Pituitary Agency, 1977–; research in metabolism and research in growth hormone and somatomedin in acute leukemia.

Memberships and awards: Academy of Pediatrics; AAAS; Arkansas Academy of Pediatrics; American Diabetes Association; Lawson Wilkins Endocrine Society; American Federation of Clinical Research; The Endocrine Society; American Physical Society; Society for Pediatric Research.

Ref: *Who's Who Among Black Americans*, 1980–81, p. 237.
American Men and Women of Science, 15th ed., p. 834.
Who's Who Among Black Americans, 1985, p. 252.
ABMS Compendium of Certified Medical Specialists, v. 4, p. 811.
Ebony, April 1964, p. 27–30, 33–35. [p]

Eldridge, Henry Madison   (1924-——, M)

Mathematician. Born in Montgomery, AL, Dec. 15, 1924. B.S., Alabama State College; M.A., Columbia University; Ph.D., University of Pittsburgh. Instructor, Mathematics and Science, Westside High School, Talladega, AL; Associate Professor, Mathematics, Alabama State College, 1950; Graduate Assistant, University of Pittsburgh, 1954–55; Chairman, Science and Mathematics, Fayetteville State Teachers College, 1956–; Consultant, Science Workshops, Southeastern Section, North Carolina Teachers' Association, 1956–68; Professor, Mathematics, A & T State University; Field Researcher, School Mathematics Study Group, 1960–63; Professor, Mathematics, North Carolina State University, Fort Bragg Branch, 1966–72; Associate Vice-Chancellor for Academic Affairs, Fayetteville State University.

Memberships and awards: Beta Kappa Chi; National Institute of Science; Mathematical Association of America; American Mathematical Society.

Dissertation title: A Study in the Variation in Accomplishment and Subject Preference in Different Secondary Schools.

Pub: Relative Difficulties of Students in Elementary College Mathematics. *North Carolina Teachers Record*, Oct. 1957.
Experience and Success in Mathematics. *North Carolina Teachers Record*, Mar. 1958.
Performance in College General Mathematics. *North Carolina Teachers Record*, May 1962.
Mathematics and the Deprived Child. *Proc. Education for the Disadvantaged*, Mar. 28, 1966.
The Impact of "Modern Mathematics" in the Secondary and Elementary Schools. *Quarterly Review of Higher Education Among Negroes*, Johnson C. Smith University, April 1967.

Ref: *Black Mathematicians and Their Works*, p. 284. [p]
Crisis, Mar. 1956, p. 179. [p]

Elfe, Wilcie   (1800s, M)

Pharmacist. Slave. Worked in a pharmacy for his master who was a drunkard. Elfe kept a prescription book dated 1853, which proved he was the formulator of many of the drug recipes. He assumed the management of the drug store and concocted many drugs which he sold throughout South Carolina.

Ref: History of the Negro in Medicine, p. 12.

Elkins, T.   (1800s, M)

Inventor. Refrigerating apparatus, cooling metal coils maintained perishable food in a chamber where temperature was below that of the outside. Prior to his invention, perishables were kept in cellars between blocks of ice. Patent #221,222 in 1879.

Ref: At Last Recognition in America, p. 6.

Elliott, Frances Reed   (1882–1964, F)

Nurse. Born in 1882. Freedmen's Hospital School of Nursing; one-year course, Teachers College, Columbia University (first black to take the Course). First black to be accepted inthe American Red Cross Nursing Service, 1918; her first assignment was in Jackson, TN.

Ref: The Path We Tread, p. 91. [p]
    Petrone, Jean. *Trailblazer: Negroe Nurse in the American Red Cross,* New York, Harcourt Brace & World, 1969. 191 p.

Elliott, Irvin Wesley, Jr.   (1925-   , M)

Chemist (organic). Born in Newton, KS, Oct. 21, 1925. B.S., University of Kansas, 1947; M.S., 1949; Ph.D., 1952. Eastman Kodak Company, 1948; Instructor, Southern University, 1949–50; Research Chemist, Kansas Geological Survey, 1950–51; Associate Professor, Chemistry, Florida A & M, 1952–53; Professor, 1953–; Fisk University, 1958–.

Memberships and awards: American Chemical Society; fellow, Chemical Society London; Sigma Xi; Beta Kappa Chi; Omicron Delta Kappa.

Dissertation title: I. Hydrogenation Studies on Reissert Compounds. II. Synthesis of Some Hexadecanes and Octadecanes.

Ref: American Men and Women of Science, 16th ed., p. 873.
    The Negro in Science, p. 182.
    Who's Who Among Black Americans, 1985, p. 252.

Ellis, Effie O'Neal   (1913-   , F)

Physician. Pediatrician. Public Health Specialist. Born in Pulaski County, GA, June 15, 1913. B.A., Spelman College, 1933; M.S., Atlanta University, 1935; M.D., University of Illinois, 1950; Director of Medical Education, Provident Hospital, Baltimore, MD, 1953–61; Pediatric Consultant and Director of Maternal and Child Health, Ohio Department of Health, Columbus, OH, 1961–65; Regional Medical Director, U.S. Children's Bureau, HEW, Chicago, 1961–67; Regional Commissioner of Social and

Rehabilitation Service, Chicago, 1967–70; Special Assistant for Health Services, AMA, 1970–.

Memberships and awards: Outstanding Service Award, American Association of Maternal and Child Health, 1967; Golden Plate Award, American Academic Achievement, 1970; Distinguished Service Award, National Medical Association; Institute of Medicine; National Academy of Sciences; Honorary fellow, American School Health Association; American Public Health Association; American Public Welfare Association; American Association on Mental Deficiency; Women's Medical Association; Alpha Gamma Phi; Delta Sigma Theta; Liaison for the American Medical Association with the National Medical Association.

Ref: American Men and Women of Science, 15th ed. , p. 847.
    In Black & White, p. 298–299.
    Who's Who Among Black Americans, 1980–81, p. 239.
    Who's Who Among Black Americans, 1985, p. 253.
    Ebony Success Library, v. 1, p. 106. [p]
    Ebony, Aug. 1974, p. 38. [p]

Ellis, James R.   (19??-   , M)

Mathematician. Born in Oklahama. B.S., Langston University; M.S., University of New Mexico; D.Ed., University of Tulsa, 1961. Professor and Chairman, Mathematics Department, Langston University, OK.

Memberships and awards: Mathematical Association of America; National Association of Mathematicians.

Dissertation title: The Characteristics of Junior High School Pupils Associated With Academic Achievement in the Tenth Grade.

Ref: Black Mathematicians and Their Works, p. 284.

Ellis, James Riley, Jr.   (1940-   , M)

Engineer (electrical). Born in Ardmore, OK, Mar. 17, 1940. B.S. (electrical engineering), MIT, 1962; M.S., 1964. Research Engineer, North American Aviation, 1966; Research Engineer, Esso Production Research Company, 1968–69; Research Assistant, Massachusetts Institute of Technology, 1969–.

Memberships and awards: IEEE, Eta Kappa Nu; Tau Beta Pi; Sigma Xi; National Merit Scholarship.

Ref: Black Engineers in the United States, p. 59.

Ellis, Wade   (1909-   , M)

Mathematician. Born in Chandler, OK, June 9, 1909. B.S., Wilberforce University, 1928; M.S. (mathematics), University of New Mexico, 1938; Ph.D. (mathematics), University of Michigan, 1944. Teacher in segregated schools of Oklahoma, 1928–37. Instructor, summer school, Fort Valley State College; Instructor, Fisk University, 1938–40; Special Instructor, University of Michigan, 1943–45; Staff Member, Radiation Laboratory, MIT, 1945;

Mathematician, Air Force Laboratories, Cambridge, MA, 1946–48; Professor, Mathematics, Oberlin College, 1948–67; Professor, Mathematics and Associate Dean, Horace H. Rockham School of Graduate Studies, University of Michigan, 1967–77; Emeritus Professor of Mathematics, University of Michigan, 1977–; Vice-Chancellor of Academic Affairs, University of Maryland, Eastern Shore, 1978–79; Interim President, Marygrove College, Detroit, 1979–80; Consultant, Mathematician Computers, 1980–.

Memberships and awards: Kappa Mu Epsilon; Phi Beta Kappa; Sigma Xi; Ford Foundation Science Faculty fellow, India and France, 1954–55; National Science Foundation Science Faculty fellow, 1961–62; Visiting Lecturer on Mathematics, Mathematical Association of America, 1955–62 and 1967–; American Mathematical Society; Educational Testing Service, Committee Writing Graduate Record Examinations in Mathematics, 1964–69; decorated by the government of Peru in 1964 as Comendador de la Order de Los Palmas Magisteriales del Peru; Mathematics Workshop, Uganda, East Africa, 1962; Observer, First National Mathematics Congress (Mexican), Satillo, Mexico, 1967; Observer, Commonwealth (British) Conference on Mathematics Education, Trinidad, Sept. 1968; Doctor of Humane Letters, Marygrove College.

Dissertation title: On Relations Satisfied by Linear Operators on a Three Dimensional Linear Vector Space.

Ref: *Black Mathematicians and Their Works*, p. 285. [p]
Crisis, Aug. 1943, p. 234. [p] only
American Men and Women of Science, 15th ed., p. 850.
Who's Who Among Black Americans, 1985, p. 254.

Emanuel, Jonah   (1858–19??, M)

Chiropodist. Born in Bibb County, GA, Sept. 9, 1858. Public schools, Arkansas, night high school, New York, private instruction. Farm hand, bellboy. Went to work for a Chiropodist and learned the profession. Later bought out the business.

Memberships and awards: Was the only black Charter Member of the New York State Pedic Society, joined in 1896. Was one of the oldest in New York City in 1929.

Ref: *Who's Who in Colored America*, 1928–29, p. 125.
Who's Who in Colored America, 1933–37, p. 175.
Who's Who in Colored America, 1938–40, p. 175.

Embree, Earl Owen   (1924– ——, M)

Mathematician. Born in Alton, IL, Feb. 17, 1924. B.S., Morgan State College, 1950; M.S., 1952; Ph.D. (mathematics), 1963. Mathematician, Ballistics Research Laboratories, MD, 1953–55; Teacher, 1955–58; from Assistant Professor to Associate Professor, 1960–74; Professor of Mathematics, Morgan State College, 1974–.

Memberships and awards: American Mathematical Society; Mathematical Association of America.

Dissertation title: A Class of Linear Differential Equations Involving Distributions.

Ref: *American Men and Women of Science*, 15th ed., p. 859.
National Faculty Directory, 1988, p. 1065.

Epps, Anna Cherrie   (1930– ——, F)

Immunologist. Zoologist. Born in New Orleans, LA, July 8, 1930. B.S., Howard University, 1951; M.S., Loyola University, 1959; Ph.D., Howard University, 1966. Technologist, Clinical Laboratories, Our Lady of Mercy Hospital, Cincinnati, OH, 1953–54; Clinical Laboratories, Flint-Goodridge Hospital, New Orleans, 1954–55; Assistant Professor of Microbiology, School of Medicine, Howard University, 1961–69; Director of Medical Education, Tulane University, 1969–; U.S. Public Health Service fellow and Assistant Professor of Medicine, 1969–71; Associate Professor, 1971–75; Director of Medicine, Medical Center, 1975–80; Assistant Dean of Student Services, Tulane Medical Center, New Orleans, LA, 1980–.

Memberships and awards: American Society of Clinical Pathologists; American Society of Medical Technologists; American Society of Bacteriologists; Sigma Xi; American Society of Tropical Medicine and Hygiene; American Association of Blood Banks; American Association of University Professors; Musser Burch Society; Leaders in American Science, 1960; Award for Meritorious Research, Interstate Postgraduate Medical Association of North America.

Dissertation title: Immunological Responses in the Chick Embryo to Chick and Mouse Limb Bud Grafts.

Ref: *American Men and Women of Science*, 15th ed., p. 880.
Smithsonian. *Black Women Achieve Against All Odds*
Who's Who Among Black Americans, 1985, p. 256.
Who's Who of American Women: 1979.

Epps, Charles Harry, Jr.   (1930– ——, M)

Physician. Surgeon. Born in Baltimore, MD, July 24, 1930. B.S., Howard University, 1951; M.D., Howard University, 1955. Director, Howard University Orthopaedic Residency Training Program; Chief, Orthopedic Surgery; Professional Residency Review Committee for Orthopaedic Surgeons, 1971–; Examiner, American Board of Orthopedic Surgeons, 1974–.

Memberships and awards: Diplomate, American Board of Orthopedic Surgeons, 1964; American Orthopaedic Association; American Academy of Orthopaedic Surgeons; Kappa Alpha Psi; Distinguished Service Medal, National Medical Association, 1978; American Medical Association; fellow, American College of Surgeons.

Pub: *Complications in Orthopaedic Surgery*, 2 vols., Philadelphia, Lippincott, 1978. 1206 p.

Ref: Who's Who Among Black Americans, 1980–81, p. 242.
      Who's Who Among Black Americans, 1985, p. 256.
      Best Doctors in the U.S.A., p. 136 (orthopedic surgeon, fraction repair)
      ABMS Compendium of Certified Medical Specialists, v. 3, p. 1385.
      National Medical Association, Journal, v. 49, Sept. 1957, p. 341. [p]
      A Century of Black Surgeons, p. 37–38. [p]

Epps, Roselyn P.   (1930– —— , F)

Physician. Pediatrician. Born in Little Rock, AR, 1930; B.S., Howard University, 1951; M.D., Howard University School of Medicine, 1955. Chief Resident in Pediatrics, Freedmen's Hospital; District of Columbia Department of Public Health, 1961–81; Director, Clinic for Retarded Children; Director, Howard University Child Development Center, 1985–.

Memberships and awards: Chairwoman, National Medical Association, Council on Maternal and Child Health.

Pub: More than 35 articles.

Ref: Black Enterprise, Oct. 1988, p. 84. [p]
      ABMS Compendium of Certified Medical Specialists, v. 4, p. 816.

Esogbue, Augustine Onwuyalim   (1940– —— , M)

Engineer (industrial). Born in Kaduna, Nigeria, Dec. 25, 1940. B.S. (electrical engineering), University of California, Los Angeles, 1964; M.S. (industrial engineering and operations research), Columbia University, 1965; Ph.D. (operations research and systems engineering), University of Southern California, 1968. Research Associate in Engineering Medicine, University of Southern California, 1966–68; Assistant Professor in Operations Research, Case Western Reserve University, 1968–72; Associate Professor of Engineering, 1972–77; Professor of Engineering, Georgia Institute of Technology, 1977–; Professor in Residence, Morehouse College and Howard University School of Engineering.

Memberships and awards: Operations Research Society of America; Sigma Xi; fellow, AAAS.

Dissertation title: Optimal and Adaptive Control of a Stochastic Service System with Applications to Hospitals.

Pub: Integrative Procedures for Coordinated Urban Land and Water Measurement. Atlanta, GA, School of Industrial and Systems Engineering, Georgia Institute of Technology, 1975. 219 p.
      (With Bellman, Richard Ernest). Mathematical Aspects of Scheduling and Applications. Oxford, New York, Pergamon Press, 1982. 329p.

Ref: American Men and Women of Science, 16th ed., p. 927.
      Black Engineers in the United States, p. 60.
      Who's Who Among Black Americans, 1985, p. 257.
      Who's Who in Engineering, 1985, p. 186.

Estep, Roger D.   (1930– —— , M)

Veterinarian. Born in Clarksville, MD, Mar. 2, 1930. B.S., Maryland State College, 1951; M.S., Pennsylvania State University, 1957; D.V.M., Tuskegee Institute, 1962. Instructor, Poultry Husbandry, Pennsylvania State College, 1957–58; Research Veterinarian and Instructor, Physiology, Howard University, 1962–70; Director, Division of Research Services, National Institutes of Health, 1971–.

Memberships and awards: President, National Capital Area Branch, American Association for Laboratory Animal Science, 1965–66; Board of Directors, American Association for Laboratory Animal Science, 1967–; Council on Accreditation of the American Association for the Accreditation of Laboratory Animal Care; Intergovernmental Ad Hoc Committee of the National Academy of Sciences.

Ref: National Medical Association, Journal, v. 64, May 1972, p. 267. [p]

Eubanks, Robert Alonzo   (1926– —— , M)

Engineer (civil). Born in Chicago, IL, June 3, 1926. B.S. (mathematics), Illinois Institute of Technology, 1950; M.S. (engineering mechanics), 1951; Ph.D. (mathematics), 1953. From Instructor to Assistant Professor of Mechanics, Illinois Institute of Technology, 1950–54; Senior Engineer, Bulova Research Lab., NY, 1954–55; Research Engineer, American Machine and Foundry Co., IL, 1955–56; Scientist, Borg-Warner Research Center, 1956–60; Senior Scientist, Armour Research Foundation, 1960–62; Manager in Vibration, 1962–64; Scientific Advisor in Mechanics and Structural Engineering, Illinois Institute, 1964–65; Professor of Civil Engineering and Theoretical and Applied Mechanics, University of Illinois, Urbana, 1965–; Consultant, Continental Can Co., 1968–75.

Memberships and awards: American Society of Mechanics; American Mathematical Society; Society of Industrial and Applied Mathematics; American Society of Civil Engineers; Acoustical Society of America; Sigma Xi; American Association of University Professors; Sigma Pi Sigma.

Dissertation title: Stress Concentration Due to a Hemispherical Pit at a Free Surface.

Pub: Articles in various scientific journals.

Ref: American Men and Women of Science, 16th ed., p. 935.
      Black Engineers in the United States, 1985, p. 60–61.
      Who's Who Among Black Americans, 1985, p. 259.
      Who's Who in Engineering, p. 186.

Evans, Armon Gloster   (1895–1975, M)

Physician. Pediatrician. Born in Cleveland, OH, July 20, 1895. Adelbert College of Western Reserve, undergraduate and graduate degrees; M.D., 1920. Private practice, 1921–74.

Memberships and awards: President, Western Reserve School of Medicine Alumni Association, 1960–61; Cleveland Academy of Medicine; Ohio State Medical Association; American Medical Association; National Medical Association; fellow, American Academy of Pediatrics.

Ref: National Medical Association, *Journal*, v. 68, Jan. 1976, p. 76–77. (autobiography) [p] cover
National Medical Association, *Journal*, v. 68, Jan. 1976, p. 87. obit

Evans, Harold Bethuel   (1907– ——, M)

Chemist. Born in Brazil, IN, Oct. 31, 1907. B.A., Michigan State College, 1931; M.S., 1932. Instructor, Chemistry, Georgia State College; Research Chemist, Kankakee Ordnance Works 1941–43; Associate Chemist, Argonne National Laboratory, 1943–.

Memberships and awards: American Chemical Society; Science Research Society of America.

Ref: *American Men of Science*, 11th ed., p. 1450
The Negro in Science, Taylor, p. 182.
Ebony, Nov. 1949, p. 27. [p]

Evans, James Carmichal   (1900– ——, M)

Engineer. Born in Gallatin, TN, July 1, 1900. B.A., Roger Williams University, 1921; B.S., MIT, 1925; M.S., 1926; L.L.D., Virginia State College, 1955; L.H.D., Agricultural & Technical College, 1961. Rose E. Electrical Engineering Construction, Miami, FL, 1926–28; Administrative Assistant to the President, West Virginia State College, 1937–42; Assistant Civilian Aide to Secretary of War, 1943–47; Civilian Aide, 1947–48; Professor, Electrical Engineering, Howard University, 1946–70.

Memberships and awards: National Institute of Science; American Institute of Electrical Engineering; Institute of Radio Engineers; American Association of University Professors; National Technical Association; Tau Beta Pi; Epsilon Pi Tau; Alpha Phi Alpha.

Ref: *American Men of Science*, 11th ed., p. 1451
Who's Who Among Black Americans, 1977, p. 277.
Crisis, Aug. 1926, p. 169. [p] only

Evans, Matilda Arabella   (1872–1935, F)

Physician. Born in Aiken County, SC, May 13, 1872. Preparatory Department, Oberlin College, 1887–91; M.D., Women's Medical College of Pennsylvania, 1897. Opened Taylor Lane Hospital and Nurse's Training School. After it was destroyed by fire, built St. Luke's Hospital. She conducted three clinics where she treated both white and black patients. First black woman physician in Columbia, SC.

Memberships and awards: Negro Health Association of South Carolina, which she organized.

Ref: *Dictionary of American Medical Biography*, p. 234–235.
We Are Your Sisters, p. 444–445. [p] p. 444.
Send Us a Lady Physician, p. 110. [p]
Smithsonian. *Black Women Achievers Against All Odds*, p. 27.

Evans, Therman Eugene   (1944– ——, M)

Physician. Public Health Officer. Born in Henderson, NC, Aug. 20, 1944. B.S., Howard University, 1966; M.D., Howard University School of Medicine, 1971; Harvard University College of Medicine Peter Bent Brigham Hospital Medical Externeship; M.S., Howard University. Executive Director of Health Manpower Development Corp; Program Development Specialist, Office of Health and Resources Opportunity, 1973–74; Mayor's Advisory Committee of Emergency Medical Service, 1974–76; Clinical Instructor in Pediatrics, Howard University, 1974–75.

Memberships and awards: DC Black Assembly Meriotorious Award, Graduate School, Howard University, 1975.

Pub: Health Care and the Black Community. *Black Collegian*, v. 5, Sept./Oct. 1975, p. 4, 6, 66. [p] p. 6.
Is Your Doctor Ripping You Off? *Ebony*, Sept. 1977, p. 45–46, 48, 50–52.

Ref: *Who's Who Among Black Americans*, 1985, p. 262.
Ebony, Sept. 1977. [p] p. 52.

Evans, Wilson Lovett   (1899–19??, M)

Engineer (electrical). Born in Winchester, VA, June 3, 1889. Riverdale Military Academy, Poughkeepsi, NY, 1902–04; B.S. (electrical engineering), MIT, 1908. Proprietor of "Evans Live Wire Service," Atlantic City, NJ, 1920–1940s.

Ref: *Who's Who in Colored America*, 1928–29, p. 126.
Who's Who in Colored America, 1930–32, p. 145.
Who's Who in Colored America, 1933–37, p. 179.
Who's Who in Colored America, 1938–40, p. 179.
Who's Who in Colored America, 1941–44, p. 178.

Ewell, Cleve Winfield   (1922–1966, M)

Physician. Internist. Hematologist. Born in Wichita, KS, June 20, 1922. B. S., Yale University, 1943; M.D., Meharry Medical College, 1947. Assistant to Instructor to Professor of Internal Medicine and Hematology and Director of Hematology Laboratory and Blood Bank, Meharry Medical College, TN, 1948–57.

Memberships and awards: Rockefeller Foundation fellow in Hematology, Simpson Memorial Institute, Michigan, 1953–54; Diplomate, American Board of Internal Medicine, 1956; National Medical Association.

Ref: *American Men of Science*, 11th ed., p. 1460
           Jet, Aug. 25, 1966, p. 51.

Ewell, John Albert, III   (1928–   , M)

Mathematician. Born in Newellton, LA, Feb. 28, 1928. B.S. (chemistry), Morehouse College, 1948; University of Colorado, 1951; M.A. (mathematics), University of California at Los Angeles, 1955; Ph.D. (mathematics), University of California at Los Angeles, 1966. Instructor, Assistant Professor, Southern University, 1955–57; Part-time Lecturer, UCLA Extension, 1959–61; Assistant Professor, Associate Professor, California State College, Long Beach, 1961–66; post-doctoral fellow, University of Manitoba (Canada), 1966–67; Assistant Professor, York University (Canada), 1967–70; Associate Professor, Mathematics, California State University, Sonoma, 1970–.

Dissertation title: On the Determination of Sets by Sets of Sums of Fixed Order.

Pub: On the Determination of Sets by Sets of Sums of Fixed Order. *Canadian Journal of Mathematics*, 1968.
        Partition Recurrences. *Journal of Combinational Theory*, Series A, 1973.
        Consequences of a Gaussian Identity. *Indian Journal of Pure and Applied Mathematics*, 1973.
        On Sets and Their Sum Sets. *Duke Journal of Mathematics*, 1973.

Ref: *Black Mathematicians and Their Works*, p. 285.

F

Fairchild, Halford H.   (1949–   , M)

Psychologist. Born Mar. 16, 1949. Ph.D. (social psychology), University of Michigan, 1977. Assistant Professor, Psychology, University of California at Los Angeles, 1978–.

Memberships and awards: President, Association of Black Psychologists.

Dissertation title: An Ecological Analysis of Interracial Attitudes and Behaviors in American High Schools.

Ref: *Ebony*, May 1987, p. 120. [p]
        American Psychological Association, *Directory*, 1985, p. 292.
        National Faculty Directory, 1988, p. 1107.

Falconer, Etta Zuber   (1933–   , F)

Mathematician. Born in Tupelo, MS, Nov. 21, 1933. B.A., Fisk University, 1953; M.S., University of Wisconsin, 1954; Ph.D. (mathematics), Emory University, 1969. Instructor, Okolona Junior College, 1954–63; Teacher, Chattanooga Public Schools, 1963–64; Assistant Professor, Spelman College, 1965–71; Assistant Professor in Mathematics, Norfolk State College, 1971–72; Associate Professor and Chairman of the Department of Mathematics, Spelman College, 1972–; research in quasigroups and loops.

Memberships and awards: Phi Beta Kappa; Secretary, National Association of Mathematics, 1970–73; Mathematical Association of America; American Mathematical Society; National Science Foundation Faculty Fellowship, 1967–69.

Dissertation title: Quasigroup Identities Invariant Under Isotopy.

Pub: Isotopy invariants in quasigroups. American Mathematical Society, *Transactions*, v. 151, 1970, p. 511–526.

Ref: *American Men and Women of Science*, 15th ed., p. 934.
        Black Mathematicians and Their Works, p. 286. [p]
        National Faculty Directory, 1988, p. 1109.
        Kenschaft, Patricia C. Black women in Mathematics in the United States. *American Mathematical Monthly*, v. 88, Oct. 1981, p. 599–600.

Falls, Arthur Grand Pre   (1901–   , M)

Physician. Surgeon. Born in Chicago, IL, Dec. 25, 1901. B.S. (medicine), Crane Junior College, 1924; M.D., Northwestern University, 1925. Junior Surgical Staff, Wilson Hospital; Surgical Staff of Provident Hospital, Chicago; Editor of the *Bulletin*, Publication of Cook County Physicians Association, 1930–.

Memberships and awards: Kappa Alpha Psi; Illinois State Medical Association; Chicago Medical Society; National Medical Association; Cook County Physicians' Association; American College of Chest Physicians.

Pub: Author of numerous articles and editorials in the *Journal* of the National Medical Association and the *Bulletin* of the Cook County Physicians' Association.

Ref: *Who's Who in Colored America*, 1930–32, p. 146.
        Who's Who in Colored America, 1933–37, p. 180.
        History of the Negro in Medicine, p. 167. [p]
        Who's Who in Colored America, 1941–44, p. 178.
        National Medical Association, *Journal*, v. 54, Jan. 1962, p. 117. [p]

Farley, James   (1854–????, M)

Photographer. Born in Prince Edward County, VA, Aug. 10, 1854. First black to attain prominence as a photographer. Work exhibited at the World Exposition in New Orleans in 1885.

Ref: *Jet*, Aug. 12, 1954.
        Men of Mark, 1970 ed., p. 563–565. [p] p. 564.

Ferebee, Dorothy Boulding   (1897–1980, F)

Physician. Obstetrician. Born in Norfolk, VA, 1897. B.S., Simmons College; M.D., Tufts Medical School, with honors, 1927. Founded and directed Southeast Settlement House in 1960s in Washington, DC; worked among sharecroppers in Mississippi on health projects sponsored by Alpha Kappa Alpha Sorority; Instructor, Obstetrics, Howard University, 1928–68.

Memberships and awards: President, National Council of Negro Women; Howard University Medical Health Director; named to Board of Action, a Better Housing Group; Vice-President, Medico-Chirurgical Society of the District of Columbia; Board of Trustees, District of Columbia Social Hygiene Society; Washington Housing Association; Council of Social Agencies.

Ref: Brodie, J. L. Dorothy Boulding Ferebee, M.D. American Medical Women's Association, *Journal*, v. 15, 1960, p. 1095.
Negro Almanac, 1976, p. 1006.
Roy, J. H. Pinpoint Portrait of Dr. Dorothy Boulding Ferebee. *Negro History Bulletin*, v. 25, April 1962, p. 160.
Medico-Chirurgical Society of the District of Columbia, Inc., *Bulletin*, Feb. 1948, p. 4. [p]
Smithsonian, *Black Women Achievers Against All Odds*, p. 30.
Ebony, Feb. 1948, p. 22.
In Black & White, p. 314.
National Medical Association, *Journal*, v. 62, Mar. 1970, p. 177. [p] cover
National Medical Association, *Journal*, v. 73, Sept. 1981, p. 896–897. obit

Ferguson, Angela Dorothea   (1925– ——, F)

(Mrs. Charles M. Cabanis). Physician. Pediatrician. Born in Washington, DC, Feb. 15, 1924. B.S., Howard University, 1945; M.D., 1949. Sickle cell anemia researcher since early 1940s with Dr. Roland Scott; Associate Professor, Howard University Pediatric Department, 1953–.

Memberships and awards: Society of Pediatric Research; Society of Nuclear Medicine; National Medical Association; Certificate of Merit, American Medical Association.

Ref: *In Black & White*, p. 314.
American Men of Science, 11th ed., Suppl 3, p. 99.
Who's Who of American Women, 1970, p. 392.
Ebony, Jan. 1954, p. 73.
Ebony, Aug. 1960, p. 44. [p]
Ebony, Sept. 1963, p. 86, 92. [p]
Ebony, May 1964, p. 70. [p]
Blacks in Science: Astrophysicist to Zoologist, p. 58.
National Faculty Directory, 1988, p. 1138.

Ferguson, David Arthur   (1875–19??, M)

Dentist. Born in Portsmouth, OH, June 8, 1874. D.D.S., Howard University Dental College, 1899. Assistant to demonstrators in dental laboratories at Howard University; Assistant of seven dentists in Washington; practiced in Richmond, VA; first black applicant before Virginia State Board of Dental Examiners; Instructor in Anatomy and Physiology, Richmond Hospital and Training School for Nurses.

Memberships and awards: Vice-President and President, National Medical Association, 1919; President Tri-State Dental Association.

Ref: *Who's Who of the Colored Race*, 1915, p. 101.
Who's Who in Colored America, 1927, p. 65.
Crisis, April 1917, p. 282–283. [p]

Ferguson, Edward, Jr.   (1907–1968, M)

Biologist. Zoologist (invertebrate). Born in Dawson, GA, Jan. 6, 1907. B.A., University of Illinois, 1929; M.S., 1933; Ph.D., 1942. Professor of Biology, South Carolina State College, 1929–36; Associate Professor, Southern University and A & M College, 1936–40; Instructor, Sumner High School, St. Louis, MO, 1940–41; Assistant Professor, Stowe College, 1941–46; Professor, Tennessee State College, 1946–48; Professor and Chairman, Division of Arts & Sciences, Maryland State College, 1948–51; Professor and Head, Biology Department, South Carolina State A & M College, 1951–56; Grambling College, 1956–60; Lincoln University, MO, 1960–68.

Memberships and awards: American Society of Zoology; AAAS; Sigma Xi; Phi Sigma Biological Society; Beta Kappa Chi; National Science Foundation Grant, 1963–66; Ecological Society.

Dissertation title: Studies on the Seasonal Life History of Three Species of Fresh Water Ostracods.

Ref: *American Men of Science*, 11th ed., p. 1514.
Holders of Doctorates Among American Negroes, p. 190.
The Negro in Science, p. 177.

Ferguson, George Alonzo   (1923– ——, M)

Engineer (nuclear). Born in Washington, DC, May 25, 1923; B.S. (physics), Howard University, 1947; M.S., 1948; Ph.D. (physics/nuclear engineering), Catholic University of America, 1965. Research Assistant in Physics, University of Pennsylvania, 1948–50; Chairman, Department of Physics, Clark College, GA, 1950–53; Research Scientist, Naval Research Lab., Washington, DC, 1954–67; Professor of Physics, 1967–80; Professor of Engineering, Howard University, 1980–.

Memberships and awards: American Physical Society; AAAS; American Nuclear Society; American Association of Physics Teachers; Sigma Xi; AEC fellow; Thomas Edison fellow.

Dissertation title: A Neutron Diffraction Study of Palladium Containing Absorbed Hydrogen.

Pub: Numerous articles in scientific journals.

Ref: *American Men and Women of Science*, 16th ed., p. 1019.
Black Engineers in the United States, p. 63.

Who's Who Among Black Americans, 1985, p. 268.
Who's Who in Engineering, 1985, p. 196.
National Faculty Directory, 1988, p. 1139.

Ferguson, Joseph (1800s, M)

Physician. Born prior to 1861, lived in Richmond, VA, working as leecher, cupper, and barber. He later studied medicine, M.D., University of Michigan Medical School and practiced medicine for many years.

Ref: Miller, Kelly. The Historic Background of the Negro Physician. *The Journal of Negro History*, v. 1, 1916, p. 103.

Ferguson, Lloyd Noel (1918- ——, M)

Chemist. Born in Oakland, CA, Feb. 9, 1918. B.S., University of California, 1940; Ph.D. (chemistry), University of California, 1943. Research Assistant, National Defense Project, University of California, Berkeley, 1941–44; Associate Professor to Professor and Head, Chemistry Department, Howard University, 1945–65; Chairman of the Department, 1958–65; Professor of Chemistry, California State University, Los Angeles, 1965–.

Memberships and awards: Honorary D.Sc., Howard University, 1970; American Chemical Society; Sigma Xi; AAAS; Washington Academy of Science; American Association of University Professors; Phi Kappa Phi; fellow, Chemical Society of London; National Cancer Institute, Chemotherapy Advisory Commission, 1972–75; National Organization of Black Chemists and Chemical Engineers; Alpha Phi Alpha.

Dissertation title: Absorption Spectra of Some Linear Conjugated Compounds.

Pub: *Electron Structures of Organic Molecules*, 1952. New York, Prentice Hall, 1952, 335 p.
Modern Structural Theory of Organic Chemistry. Englewood Cliffs, NJ, Prentice-Hall, 1963. 600 p.
Textbook of Organic Chemistry. New York, Van Nostrand, 1965. 755 p.

Ref.; *Encyclopedia of Black America*, p. 385.
The Negro in Science, p. 182.
American Men and Women of Science, 15th ed., p. 987.
Who's Who Among Black Americans, 1985, p. 268.
Leaders in American Science, 1955–56, p. 139. [p]

Ferrell, Frank J. (1800s, M)

Born in New York. Obtained a dozen patents for improvements in valves for steam engines.

Ref: Woodson, *Negro in Our History*, 5th ed., p. 464.

Fields, Victor Hugo (1907–197?, M)

Chemist (analytical). Born in Milwaukee, WI, July 11, 1907. B.A., Fisk University, 1931; M.S., 1935; Ph.D., Marquette, 1944. Instructor and Assistant Professor of

Chemistry, Fisk University, 1935–47; Professor and Chairman of the Department, Florida A & M College, 1947–49; Professor and Chairman of the Department, Hampton Institute, 1949–56; Professor of Natural Science and Mathematics and Chairman of the Department, Hampton Institute, 1956–; Director, Division of Science and Mathematics, 1967–73.

Memberships and awards: Virginia Academy of Sciences; AAAS; National Institute of Science; Beta Kappa Chi; Omega Psi Phi.

Dissertation title: Preparation and Properties of Substituted Brom-Methyl-Fluoresceins.

Ref: *American Men and Women of Science*, 13th ed., p. 1287.
The Negro in Science, p. 182.
Who's Who in America, 1978, p. 1036.
Who's Who Among Black Americans, 1977, p. 288.

Finley, Harold Eugene (1905–1975, M)

Parasitologist. Protozoologist. Born in Palatka, FL, Nov. 30, 1905. B.S., Morehouse, 1928; M.S., University of Wisconsin, 1929; Ph.D. (zoology), 1942. Professor, Atlanta University, 1938–47; Howard University, 1947–. Head, Zoology Department, 1947–69.

Memberships and awards: Editor, Transactions of the National Institute of Science; Editorial Board and President, Society of Protozoologists, 1966–67; AAAS; President, American Microscopic Society, 1971; Biological Society, Washington, DC; New York Academy of Science; Sigma Xi; Phi Sigma; Beta Kappa Chi; delivered 3rd Honor Paper of the National Institute of Science; Postdoctoral fellow, Johns Hopkins, 1955; Principle Investigator, USPHS research grants, 1959–.

Dissertation title: The Conjugation of Vorticella Microstoma.

Ref: *American Men and Women of Science*, 12th ed., p. 1826.
Encyclopedia of Black America, p. 745.
The Negro in Science, p. 177.
Holders of Doctorates Among American Negroes, p. 190.
Drew. Negro Scholar in Scientific Research. *Journal of Negro History*, v. 35, 1950, p. 145.
Who's Who Among Black Americans, 1977.
Crisis, Aug. 1929, p. 260. [p] only
National Medical Association, *Journal*, v. 67, Sept. 1975, p. 414. obit

Finney, Essex Eugene, Jr. (1937- ——, M)

Engineer (agricultural). Born in Powhatan, VA, May 16, 1937. B.S. (agricultural engineering), Virginia Polytechnic Institute, 1959; M.S., Pennsylvania State University, 1961; Ph.D., Michigan State University, 1963. Research Agricultural Engineer, Science and Education Administration of the Agricultural Research Service, Beltsville, MD, 1965–77; Assistant Director, Beltsville Agricultural Research Center, 1977–.

Memberships and awards: American Society of Agricultural Engineers; Institute of Food Technologists; American Society for Testing Materials; Princeton fellow in Public Affairs, 1973–74; American Society of Agricultural Engineers Paper Award, 1969; Tau Beta Pi; Alpha Phi Alpha; Phi Kappa Phi; Omicron Delta Kappa; Sigma Xi.

Dissertation title: The Viscoelastic Behavior of the Potato, Solanum Tuberosum, Under Quasi-Static Loading.

Pub: Numerous publications in scientific journals.

Ref: *American Men and Women of Science*, 16th ed., p. 1054.
Black Engineers in the United States, p. 64–65.
Who's Who in Engineering, 1985, p. 199.
Who's Who Among Black Americans, 1977, p. 289.

Fisher, D. A.   (1800s, M)

Inventor. Furniture caster, making it easy to roll heavy furniture. Previously all furniture had to be picked up to be moved. Patent #174,794 in 1876.

Ref: *At Last Recognition in America*, p. 6.

Fisher, Rudolph   (1897–1934, M)

Physician. Author. Born in Washington, DC, 1897. B.A., Brown University, 1919; M.A., 1920. Taught Biology one year; M.D., Howard University Medical College. X-ray Division of the Department of Health, New York, NY.

Memberships and awards: Phi Beta Kappa; Sigma Xi; Delta Sigma Rho.

Ref: *Historical Afro-American Biographies*, p. 190–191. [p]
Black American Writers Past and Present, p. 296–298.
Crisis, Sept. 1932, p. 293. [p]

Fitzbutler, William Henry   (1842–1901, M)

Physician. Born in Ontario, Canada, Dec. 22, 1842. Detroit Medical College, Jan.–June 1871 (first black); M.D., University of Michigan Medical School, 1872 (first black). Practiced medicine in Louisville, KY (first black); founded and was Dean of Louisville National Medical College, 1888–1901; cured a girl burned over five-eighths of her body; many of the successful physicians of Kentucky were trained by him.

Ref: *Encyclopedia of Black America*, p. 388.
History of the Negro in Medicine, p. 65–66. [p]
Dictionary of American Medical Biography, p. 250–251.
Cobb, W. Montague. Henry Fitzbutler. National Medical Association, *Journal*, v. 44, Sept. 1952, p. 403–407.
National Cyclopedia of American Biography, v. 14, p. 317.

Fletcher, Douglas Wellington   (1919– —— , M)

Engineer (sanitary). Born in Gary, IN, May 20, 1919. B.S. (sanitary engineering), Purdue University, 1942. Field Engineer, Alschuler-Friedman Engineers, 1942–43; Associate Engineer, White & Griffen Associates, 1943–44; Engineer of Water Systems and Contract Administration, Detroit, MI; designed reservoirs, tunnels and pumping stations, Department of Water Supply, Detroit, MI, 1944–.

Memberships and awards: American Public Works Association; American Society of Civil Engineers; Chi Epsilon; National Civil Engineering Honorary Service Award.

Ref: *Black Engineers in the United States*, p. 66
Ebony, Sept. 1950, p. 20. [p]

Fletcher, William Thomas   (1934– —— , M)

Mathematician. Born in Durham, NC, Aug. 19, 1934. B.S. (mathematics), North Carolina Central University, 1956; M.S. (mathematics), 1958; Michigan State University, 1960–63; Ph.D. (mathematics), University of Idaho, 1966. From Associate Professor to Professor, Mathematics, LeMoyne-Owen College, 1957–72; Professor, Mathematics and Chairman, Mathematics Department, North Carolina Central University, 1972–.

Memberships and awards: American Mathematical Society; Mathematical Association of America.

Dissertation title: On the Decomposition of Associative Algebras of Prime Characteristic.

Ref: *American Men and Women of Science*, 15th ed., p. 1056.
Black Mathematicians and Their Works, p. 286. [p] p. 114.
National Faculty Directory, 1988, p. 1183.

Flipper, Henry Ossian   (1856–1940, M)

Military. Born a slave in Thomasville, GA, Mar. 21, 1856. Attended Atlanta University from which he was appointed to the U.S. Military Academy in 1873. He was not the first black to attend the Academy but the first to graduate, in 1877, and discharged in 1882. He held many jobs in engineering and surveying including a job in the court of Private Land Claims as a special agent of the Department of Justice between 1892 and 1903.

Memberships and awards: A bust of him was unveiled at West Point.

Pub: *The Colored Cadet at West Point*, New York, H. Lee, 1878. 322 p.
Negro-Frontiersman; The Western Memoirs of Henry O. Flipper. Edited by T. D. Harris, 1963.
Other publications.

Ref: *Dictionary of American Negro biography*, p. 227–228.
Jet, May 9, 1963, p. 11. [p]
Historical Afro-American Biographies, p. 80–81. [p]
Negro History Bulletin, v. 19, April 1956, p. 148–149.

Florant, Leroy Frederic   (1919-——, M)

Engineer (mechanical). Born in New York, NY, July 15, 1919. B.S. (mechanical engineering), Howard University, 1943; Columbia University, 1944–45. Research Assistant with Manhattan Project, 1943–46; Chief Engineer of Rocket Test Laboratory, Ohio State University, 1946–50; Owner of Florant Mechanical Laboratory, 1950–53; Chief Engineer, Process and Instruments Corporation, Brooklyn, NY specializing in instrumentation, electro/optical and mechanical.

Memberships and awards: Federation of Science; Association of Science Workers; National Technical Association; Tau Beta Phi.

Ref: American Men of Science, 8th ed., p. 796.
Drew. Negro Scholars in Scientific Research. *Journal of Negro History*, v. 35, 1950. p. 143.
Black Engineers in the United States, p. 66.
Ebony, April 1958, p. 122–125. [p]

Forbes, Dennis Arthur   (1887–19??, M)

Chemist (physical). Inventor. Born in Baltimore, MD, June 16, 1887. B.A., Howard University, 1912. Instructor, Physics and Chemistry, Livingstone College, 1918–21; Shaw University, 1921–24; Professor, Physical Science, Tennessee A & I University, Nashville, 1924–40; Vocational Educator, American Youth Administration, Nashville, TN, 1941–; design patent for a cheulls game.

Memberships and awards: General Education Board scholar, 1926–27; Tennessee Negro Education Association, Executive Committee, 1940.

Ref: American Men of Science, 7th ed., p. 583.
Downing, Lewis K. Contribution of Negro Scientists. *Crisis*, June 1939, p. 169.

Ford, Charles Marion   (1910-——, M)

Bacteriologist. Born in Chicago, IL, Mar. 29, 1910. B.S., University of Illinois, 1932; M.S., 1936; Ph.D., University of Wisconsin, 1948. Instructor in Chemistry, Claflin College, 1936–37; Instructor, Virginia State College, 1939–40; Instructor in Biology, Bennett College, 1940–44; Associate Professor of Bacteriology and Research Associate, Carver Foundation, Tuskegee Institute, 1944–48; Head, Department of Biological Sciences, 1948–; Professor of Bacteriology, 1954–.

Memberships and awards: National Institute of Science; Society of American Bacteriologists; Sigma Xi; Phi Sigma Biological Society; Beta Kappa Chi.

Dissertation title: Certain Environmental Agents Affecting the Action of Penicillin on Streptococcus Agalactiae.

Ref: American Men of Science, 9th ed., p. 360.
The Negro in Science, p. 177.

Ford, Denise Annette   (1900s, F)

Engineer (geological). First black graduate, University of Missouri—Rolla, with a degree in Geological Engineering. Working at Gulf Oil in Odessa, TX, as a petroleum engineer trainee.

Ref: *Jet*, May 31, 1982.

Ford, Leonard A.   (1904–1967, M)

Chemist. Born in 1904. B.A., Morgan; M.S., Howard University. First black analytical chemist in the Department of Agriculture.

Ref: *In Black and White*, p. 326.
Ebony, April 1960, p. 7. [p]

Foreman, Madeline Clark   (1900s, F)

Biologist. Biology teacher, Hampton Institute; Head, Biology Department, William Penn College, Oskaloosa, IA, 1945– (one of the first black department heads in a white college).

Ref: *Negro Year Book*, 1947, p. 16.

Forney, Claudius Langdon   (1898–19??, M)

Physician. Surgeon. Ophthalmologist. Born in Columbus, OH, Sept. 12, 1898. B.A., Ohio State University, 1923; M.D., 1925. Medical Examiner, Cook County Bureau of Public Welfare, 1927; Director, Department of Eye, Ear, Nose and Throat, Provident Hospital, Chicago, 1927–; performed cataract surgery on a man 103 years old who had been blind for 30 years, enabling him to see again a few hours after surgery. This was done at the Andrews Hospital Clinic in Tuskegee, AL, where he removed cataracts from other patients.

Memberships and awards: Fellowship in Ophthalmology, University of Chicago, 1931; Kappa Alpha Psi; Diplomate of the American Board of Ophthalmology, 1936; Association of Military Surgeons of the United States; National Medical Association; Cook County Physicians Association; American Medical Association; Chicago Medical Society; Illinois Medical Society; Chicago Ophthalmological Society.

Ref: *Who's Who in Colored America*, 1930–32, p. 154.
Who's Who in Colored America, 1933–37, p. 189.
The National Register, 1952, p. 569.
Who's Who in Colored America, 1941–44, p. 187.
Ebony, Jan. 1963, p. 40. [p]

Fort, Marron William   (1906-——, M)

Engineer (chemical). Chemist. Born in Boston, MA, June 11, 1906. B.S., MIT, 1926; M.S., 1927; Ph.D (chemical engineering), 1933. Chief Chemist and Plant Superintendent of A. G. Caldwell Co., MA, 1934–38; Deputy Chief, Industrial and Transportation Division, U.S. Operations

Mission, International Co-Op Administration, Turkey, 1957–59; Chief in Pakistan, 1959.

Memberships and awards: Chemical Society; Rosenwald Foundation fellow, 1933.

Dissertation title: Heat of Dilution of Hydrochloric Acid by Continuous Flow Calorimetry.

Ref: *American Men of Science*, 10th ed., p. 1244.
Holders of Doctorates Among American Negroes, p. 149.

Forten, James, Sr.   (1766–1842, M)

Inventor. Born free in Philadelphia, PA, 1766. Invented a device for handling sails while working in a sailmaking factory which he later owned. By 1832 he had a fortune of $100,000 from his work and his invention.

Ref: *Dictionary of American Negro Biography*, p. 234–235.
Encyclopedia of Black America, p. 390.
Historical Afro-American Biography, p. 19–20.
In Black and White, p. 328.
McGraw-Hill Encyclopedia of Biography.
Negro Impact on Western Civilization, p. 55.
Douty, Ester M. *Forten the Sailmaker, Pioneer, Champion of Negro Rights*, 1968.
Johnston, Brenda A. *Between the Devil & the Sea: the Life of James Forten*, 1974.
Encyclopedia of American Biography, p. 375–376.
Webster's American Biographies, p. 358.

Foster, William Clarence   (1905– ——, M)

Chemist (physiological). Born in Providence, RI, Jan. 27, 1905. Ph.B., Brown University, 1929; M.S., University of Minnesota, 1939. Instructor, Morehouse College, 1930–32; Laboratory Assistant, Medical School, University of Minnesota, 1934–36; Research Assistant, 1936–39; Research Associate, Physiology, Hanemann Medical College, 1939–56; Director, Clinical Chemistry Laboratory, Misericordia Hospital, Philadelphia, 1957; Professor, Physiology, University of Pennsylvania, 1960–; Professor, Morehouse College, 1961–. One of the first three men in the United States to conduct tests for protein-bound iodine in the blood.

Memberships and awards: Chemical Society; Physiological Society; Society for the Study of Arteriosclerosis; Association of Clinical Chemistry; Heart Association.

Ref: *Ebony*, Feb. 1961, p. 6. [p]
American Men of Science, 10th ed., p. 1250–1251.

Francis, Grossi Hamilton   (1885–1963, M)

Physician. Born in St. Christopher, B.W.I., Nov. 29, 1885. Berkeley Institute, Hamilton, Bermuda; M.D., Meharry Medical College, 1910. He was the first intern at Hubbard Hospital in Nashville, TN.

Memberships and awards: Highest honors, Obstetrics, awarded the W. H. Basskett prize at Meharry; President, Tidewater Medical Society; President, Old Dominion Medical Society; Assistant Secretary, National Medical Society; Executive Board, National Medical Association; President, National Medical Association, 1933–34; Distinguished Service Medal, National Medical Association, 1953; Founder, House of Delegates, National Medical Association.

Ref: Cobb, W. Montague. Dr. G. Hamilton Francis. National Medical Association, *Journal*, v. 41, Sept. 1949, p. 232.
Dictionary of American Medical Biography, p. 262–263.
Who's Who in Colored America, 1933–37, p. 191. [p] p. 187.
National Medical Association, *Journal*, v. 24, Nov. 1932, before p. 1.
National Medical Association, *Journal*, v. 45, Nov. 1953, p. 433–434. [p]
Cobb, W. Montague. Grossi Hamilton Francis, M.D., 1885–. National Medical Association, *Journal*, v. 51, Nov. 1959, p. 489. [p] cover
National Medical Association, *Journal*, v. 55, Sept. 1963, p. 461. [p] obit, biog

Francis, John Richard   (18??–19??, M)

Dentist. Born in Washington, DC, April 29, 18. D.D.S., University of Pennsylvania, Philadelphia, PA, 1906. Teacher in the Dental School at Howard University, 1908–14; Dental Inspector, Public Schools, Washington, DC, 1909–15; Dental Clinician, Montgomery County, MD, 1928–31; One of the physicians who in 1891 applied to join the white Medical Society of the District of Columbia. Although they received a majority of the votes, they did not receive the two-thirds majority needed for election.

Ref: *Who's Who in Colored America*, 1930–32, p. 156–157.
Who's Who in Colored America, 1933–37, p. 191.
History of the Negro in Medicine, p. 57–58. [p]

Francis, Marie Jones   (1900s, F)

Midwife. Nurse. Born in Dublin, GA. Claims to have delivered 40,000 babies in 32 years. Attended Florida A & M and Tuskegee and became a nurse. Founder, Jones Francis Maternity Home, Sanford, FL.

Ref: *Contributions of Black Women to America*, v. 2, p. 360.

Francis, Milton A.   (1882–1961, M)

Physician. Urologist. Born in Washington, DC, 1882. M.D., Howard University, 1906. First black specialist in genito-urinary diseases. Chief, Genito-Urinary Unit, Freedmen's Hospital, 1917–22; With $100,000 cash he created the "Milton A. Francis Trust Fund," the income is to aid medical students by loans and scholarships. At the time this was the largest single gift by a living alumnus of Howard University.

Ref: *Dictionary of American Negro Biography*, p. 241.
        National Medical Association, *Journal*, v. 70, Dec. 1978,
            p. 945–946.

Francis, Richard Louis   (1919–   , M)

Physician. Psychiatrist. Born in Millerton, NY, Oct. 10,
1919. B.S., Howard University, 1941; M.D., 1944. Intern,
Sydenham Hospital, 1945; Veterans Administration Medical Center, Tuskegee, AL, 1947–51; Psychiatric Residency, Harlem Valley Psychiatric Center, Wingdale, NY,
1955–57; Vanderbilt Clinic, Columbia Presbyterian Medical Center, 1958–59; first black Assistant Director, New
York State Department of Mental Hygiene Facility,
Harlem Valley Psychiatric Center, 1961–67; Chief of Medical Services, Sunmount Development Center, 1968–81.

Memberships and awards: Secretary, Mid-Hudson
District Branch, American Psychiatric Association,
1963–67; Member of the Advisory Commission, North
City Community College, 1968–77; Chairman, Ethics
Committee of the American Association on Mental Deficiency, 1971–72; Chairman, Narcotic Guidance Council
of Tupper Lake, NY, 1971–76; National Medical Association; American Association of Psychiatric Administration; New York State Medical Society; Franklin City Medical Society; Community Leaders of America Award,
1973.

Pub: *Further Studies in EKG Changes in Old Age.* 1947.

Ref: *In Black and White*, p. 333.
        Who's Who Among Black Americans, 1985, p. 285.
        Who's Who in the East, 1979, p. ?
        American Psychiatric Association, *Biographical Direc-
            tory*, p. 375.
        ABMS Compendium of Certified Medical Specialists, v. 5,
            p. 443.

Frank, Rudolph Joseph   (1943–   , M)

Engineer (electrical). Born in New Orleans, LA, Feb. 24,
1943. B.S., Seattle University, 1966; M.S., Oregon State
University, 1970; Ph.D. (electrical engineering), 1972;
M.S. (business management), Stanford University. Director of 5ESS, an Electronic Switching Telecommunication
System at AT&T Bell Laboratories in Naperville, IL,
1964–.

Memberships and awards: Thomas Lee Memorial
Scholarship; National Science Foundation Trainee.

Dissertation title: A Feasibility Study on the Use of
        Arithmatic-Memory Registers in the Design of Digital
        Computer Systems.

Ref: *Ebony*, May 1987, p. 6. [p]
        Black Engineers in the United States, p. 69.

Franklin, Benjamin   (1934–   , M)

Engineer (architectural). Engineer (mechanical). Born in
Pilot Point, TX, Jan. 12, 1934. B.S. (architectural engineering), Prairie View A & M College, 1957; B.S. (architecture), University of Washington, 1969. Senior Design
Engineer, The Boeing Corporation, 1957–70; Director of
Programs, Seattle Opportunities and Industrial Center,
1971–74.

Memberships and awards: Northern California Council of Black Professional Engineers; American Institute
of Architects; Employee Award, The Boeing Company,
1980; Pride in Excellence Award, The Boeing Company,
Seattle, 1969; Artist Award, Prairie View A & M College,
1956–57.

Ref: *Black Engineers in the United States*, p. 69.
        Who's Who Among Black Americans, 1985, p. 285.

Franklin, Eleanor   (1929–   , F)

Zoologist. Endocrinologist. Born in Dublin, GA, Dec. 24,
1929. B.S. (magna cum laude), Spelman College, 1948;
M.S. (zoology), University of Wisconsin, 1951; Ph.D. (endocrinology), 1957. Instructor, Biology, Spelman College,
1948–49, 1951–53; Assistant Professor, Physiology and
Pharmacology, Tuskegee Institute, 1957; Associate Professor, 1960; Assistant to Associate Professor, Physiology,
Howard University, 1963–66; first female administrative
officer in the College of Medicine.

Ref: National Medical Association, *Journal*, v. 62, Sept. 1970,
            p. 369. [p]

Franklin, Hal Addison II   (1939–   , M)

Physician. Photographer. Born in Milledgeville, GA, Dec.
30, 1939. B.S., Allen University, 1960; M.D., State University of New York, Buffalo, 1975. Cancer Research Scientist, Roswell Park Memorial Hospital, 1961–68; Staff
Photographer, *Ebony* magazine, 1968–71; Clinical Instructor of Medicine, North Carolina School of Medicine,
1978–.

Memberships and awards: Alpha Phi Alpha; American College of Physicians; American Society of Internal
Medicine; fellow, George Washington Carver Foundation, 1959; David K. Miller Internal Medicine Award,
State University of New York.

Pub: Co-author with Darwin Walton. *What Color Are You?* Chi-
        cago, Johnson Publishing Company, 1969–70. 63 p.

Ref: *Ebony*, Dec. 1980, p. 100–102, 104, 106. [p]
        Who's Who Among Black Americans, 1985, p. 286.

Franklin, Martha   (1870–1968, F)

Nurse. Born in Connecticut in 1870. Graduate of Wom-
en's Hospital, Philadelphia, 1897. Second black nurse to
graduate and the only black in her class.

Memberships and awards: Organized the National Association of Colored Graduate Nurses in New York City in 1908.

Ref: *The Path We Tread*, p. 93, 95. [p] p. 93.

Franks, Cleveland James   (1912– ——, M)

Chemist. Born in Darlington, SC, July 15, 1912. B.A., Morehouse College, 1934; Atlanta University, 1935–36; M.A., New York University, 1939; M.S., McKinley-Roosevelt, 1944; Ph.D. (chemistry), 1945; M.A., Columbia, 1951. Instructor in Science, Florida Memorial College, 1934–35; Walker Institute, 1935–36; Professor of Chemistry and Head of the Science Department, Texas College, 1945–47; Associate Professor of Chemistry, Morgan State College, 1947–.

Memberships and awards: Chemical Society; fellow, Institute of Chemistry; National Institute of Science; National Science Teachers Association.

Dissertation title: The Organization, Installation, Implementation and Administration of a Course in Physical Science Designed for General Education.

Ref: *American Men of Science*, 9th ed., p. 628.

Fraser, Sarah Logan   (18??–1933, F)

Physician. Born in New York, NY. M.D., Medical School of Syracuse University, 1876. For 20 years she was the only female physician in Santo Domingo.

Ref: *Send Us a Lady Physician*, p. 111.
Crisis, June 1933, p. 139. obit

Fraser, Thomas Petigru   (1902– ——, M)

Science Educator. Science Writer. Born in Georgetown, SC, June 24, 1902. B.S., Caflin College, 1926; M.A., 1930; Ed.D., 1948; Ph.D., Columbia University. High School Science Department Chairman in Miami before going to Morgan State University as Science Department Head.

Memberships and awards: Inducted into South Carolina Hall of Science and Technology, fifth to receive the honor and the first black; elected 26th President of the National Association for Research in Science Teaching, elected at the 31st meeting in the Sherman Hotel in Chicago in 1958.

Pub: Author of widely used science textbook series.

Ref: *American Men and Women of Science*, 13th ed., p. 1373.
Jet, Mar. 13, 1958, p. 58.
Jet, May 3, 1982, p. 38. [p]
Who's Who in the East, 1977, p. 255

Frazier, Thyrsa

See: Svager, Thyrsa Frazier

Frederick, Lafayette   (1923– ——, M)

Mycologist. Born in Friarspoint, MS, Mar. 19, 1923. B.S., Tuskegee Institute, 1943; M.S., Rhode Island State College, 1950; Ph.D. (plant pathology), State College of Washington, 1952. From Associate Professor to Professor of Biology, Southern University, 1952–62; Professor of Biology, Atlanta University, 1962–76; Professor of Botany and Chairman of the Department, Howard University, 1976–; research in vascular wilt diseases of plants.

Memberships and awards: Carnegie Research Grant, 1953; General Research Support Advisory Committee, NIH and Biological Achievement Test Committee, Educational Testing Service; AAAS; American Phytopathological Society; Mycology Society of America; Botanical Society of America; American Institute of Biological Sciences.

Dissertation title: Growth Variations in Bacteria-Free Crown-Gall Tissue.

Ref: *American Men and Women of Science*, 15th ed., p. 1131.
Encyclopedia of Black America, p. 745.
Who's Who Among Black Americans, 1977, p. 308.

Frederick, Rivers   (1873–1954, M)

Physician. Surgeon. Born in Pointe Coupee Parish, LA, May 22, 1873. Completed the English Course, New Orleans University, 1893; M.D., University of Illinois College of Medicine, Chicago, 1897. Surgeon-in-Chief, Government Hospital, El Roi Tan, Spanish Honduras, 1901–04; Chief Surgeon, Flint-Goodrich Hospital, New Orleans, 1904–53. Deeply involved in teaching and improving the facilities and services of Flint-Goodrich Hospital.

Memberships and awards: Fellow, International College of Surgeons; diplomate, International Board of Surgery; Distinguished Service Award, National Medical Association, 1951; Louisiana and Orleans Parish Medical Societies; Society Losco Umbra di Italia; Award of Merit, American Cancer Society; Executive Committee of the New Orleans Tuberculosis Association; Associate Medical Advisor to the Selective Service Board; Chi Delta Mu; Phi Beta Sigma.

Ref: Dr. Rivers Frederick Receives Distinguished Service Award for 1951. National Medical Association, *Journal*, v. 43, Nov. 1951, p. 400. [p]
Dictionary of American Medical Biography, p. 264.
Who's Who in Colored America, 1941–44, p. 195.
National Medical Association, *Journal*, v. 46, Nov. 1954, p. 434–435. [p]
National Medical Association, *Journal*, v. 48, Nov. 1956. [p] cover

Freeman, C. V.   (18??–19??, M)

Dentist.

Memberships and awards: President, National Medical Association, 1927–28.

Ref: National Medical Association, *Journal*, v. 19, Oct.–Dec. 1927, p. 162; July–Sept. [p] last page

Freeman, C. Wendell   (1900–1982, M)

Physician. Dermatologist. Born in Washington, DC in 1900. B.S., M.D., Howard University Medical College, 1926. Instructor, Anatomy, Howard Medical Faculty. Studied in Europe for two years after which he became a Dermatologist; Chief, Division of Dermatology, Freedmen's Hospital, 19–; Chief, Venereal Disease Control Division, DC Health Services Administration; retired, 1970.

Memberships and awards: Diplomate, American Board of Dermatology; President, Medico-Chirurgical Society of the District of Columbia.

Ref: National Medical Association, *Journal*, v. 63, Jan. 1971, p. 74.

Freeman, Harold P.   (1933– ——, M)

Physician. Surgeon. Oncologist. Born in Washington, DC, Mar. 2, 1933. B.A., Catholic University, 1954; M.D., Howard University College of Medicine, 1958. Resident in General Surgery, 1959–64, Howard University Hospital; Resident, Sloane Kettering Cancer Center, 1964–67; Surgeon, Harlem Hospital, NY, 1973–74; Director of Surgery, Harlem Hospital, 1974–. Established the Breast Examination Center of Harlem, a free cancer screening clinic.

Memberships and awards: President-Elect, American Cancer Society, 1988; Prize in Psychiatry, Howard University, 1958; Daniel Hale Williams Award for Outstanding Achievement as Chief Resident, Howard University Hospital, 1964.

Ref: *Health*, Dec. 1987, p. 32. [p]
    Who's Who Among Black Americans, 1985, p. 289.
    ABMS Compendium of Certified Medical Specialists, v. 6, p. 227.
    Ebony, July 1974, p. 94. [p]
    Black Enterprise, Oct. 1988, p. 95.

Freeman, Robert Tanner   (1847–19??, M)

Physician. Dentist. Born in North Carolina in 1847 to slave parents. First black American to receive a Dental Doctorate, Harvard University, Mar. 6, 1867.

Ref: *Afro-Americans in Dentistry; Sequence and Consequence of Events*, p. 6.
    Nine Black American Doctors, p. 12–13.

Fuller, Joseph Everett   (1905– —— M)

Mathematician. Born in Murphysboro, IL, June 1, 1905. B.A., Bradley College, 1926; M.A., University of Michigan, 1931; Ed.D., University of Pennsylvania, 1945. Head, Department of Science, Selma, 1926–37; Professor of Mathematics and Head of the Department, Tuskegee Institute, 1937–.

Memberships and awards: National Institute of Science.

Dissertation title: Basic College Mathematics for Prospective Elementary School Teachers.

Ref: *American Men of Science, 11th ed. P. 1692.*

Fuller, Solomon Carter   (1872–1953, M)

Physician. Neurologist. Psychiatrist. Pathologist. Born in Monrovia, Liberia, Aug. 11, 1872. B.A., Livingstone College, 1893; M.D., Boston University Medical School, 1897; postgraduate study, University of Munich, Germany. Instructor in Neurology and Psychiatry at Boston University Medical School in 1899, serving more than 30 years; Head Pathologist, Westborough State Hospital during this time; he studied under Dr. Alzheimer in Germany in 1904; while still there in 1905, he spent a chance afternoon with Paul Ehrlich, winner of the 1908 Nobel Prize for his work in immunology, which he said was one of the most profitable and lasting memories of his life; research in degenerative disease of the brain, including Alzheimers Disease; acknowledged as the first black psychiatrist.

Memberships and awards: Massachusetts Psychiatric Society; New York Psychiatric Society; American Psychiatric Society; American Medical Association; Black Psychiatrists of America presented his portrait to the American Psychiatric Association in Washington, DC, 1971; see: National Medical Association, *Journal*, v. 66, Jan. 1974, p. 84–86, Boston University School of Medicine memorialized him in an all-day conference, Oct. 1973; Boston Society for Psychiatry and Neurology; Massachusetts Medical Society; New England Medical Society; Solomon Carter Fuller Mental Health Center in Boston is named for him.

Pub: Special Studies on the Histopathology of the Brain Cortex.
    Nervous and Mental Diseases. *Domestic and Foreign Journal.*

Ref: *Dictionary of American Negro Biography*, p. 247.
    Encyclopedia of Black America, p. 400.
    Who's Who in Colored America, 1927, p. 70.
    Who's Who in Colored America, 1928–29, p. 139.
    Who's Who in Colored America, 1930–32, p. 159–160.
    Who's Who in Colored America, 1933–37, p. 196.
    Who's Who in Colored America, 1941–44, p. 196.
    History of the Negro in Medicine, p. 104–105. [p] p. 104.
    Dictionary of American Medical Biography, p. 268.

Cobb, W. Montague. Solomon Carter Fuller, 1872–1953. National Medical Association, *Journal*, v. 46, Sept. 1954, p. 37–72. [p] cover

National Medical Association, *Journal*, v. 64, Jan. 1972, p. 93.

Fuller, Thomas   (1710–1790, M)

Mathematician. Born in Africa, sold into slavery in Virginia at 14. (Virginia Calculator). Could neither read nor write but could perform calculations in this head. Could calculate the number of days, weeks, seconds for any period of time in less time than most men could do with pens.

Ref: *Dictionary of American Negro Biography*, p. 247–248.
In Black and White, p. 342.
Needle's History Memoir of the Pennsylvania Society for Promoting the Abolition of Slavery, p. 32.
History of the Negro Race in America, 1619–1880, Williams, G. W., p. 398–400.
Time Union, Rochester, NY, Feb. 16, 1987. Daily, Monday.

Funderburk, William Watson   (1931– ——, M)

Physician. Surgeon. Born in Lancaster, SC, Aug. 26, 1931. B.S., Johnson C. Smith University, 1952; M.D., Howard University, 1956. Associate Professor of Surgery, Howard University, 1971–77; Medical Director of Center for Ambulatory Surgery, 1977.

Memberships and awards: District of Columbia Medical Society, Executive Board, 1974–77; District of Columbia Cancer Society, 1967–74; Alpha Omega Alpha; Diplomate, American Board of Surgery.

Ref: *Who's Who Among Black Americans*, 1985, p. 293.
ABMS Compendium of Certified Medical Specialists, v. 6, p. 231.
National Medical Association, *Journal*, v. 60, Jan. 1968, p. 65. [p]
National Medical Association, *Journal*, v. 62, Sept. 1970, p. 370–371. (list of publications as of 1970)
Ebony, Mar. 1968, p. 65–66, 68, 70. [p]
Ebony, July 1974, p. 98. [p]

G

Gainer, Frank Edward   (1938– ——, M)

Chemist (analytical). Born in Waynesboro, GA, June 18, 1938. B.S., Morehouse College, 1960; M.S., Tuskegee, 1962; M.S., Iowa State University, 1964; Ph.D. (chemistry), 1967. Senior Analytical Chemist, Analytical Development Department, 1967–73; Antibiotic Assay Coordinator, Antibiotic Assay Department, 1973–80; Manager, Antibiotic Analytical and Qualitative Control, Eli Lilly & Co., 1980–.

Memberships and awards: American Chemical Society; National Research Council Conference on Electrical Insulation; Sigma Xi; Beta kappa Chi.

Dissertation title: Coulometric Titration of Acids in Nonaqueous Solvents.

Pub: In science journals.

Ref: *Ebony Success Library*, v. 3, 72–73. [p]
Who's Who Among Black American, 1985, p. 295.
American Men and Women of Science, 16th ed., p. 9

Gamble, Henry Floyd   (1862–1932, M)

Physician. Surgeon. Born in Albermarle County, VA, Jan. 16, 1862. B.S., Lincoln University, 1888. M.D., Yale University, 1891. Spoke Greek and Hebrew fluently. Private and surgical practice, 1891–1932.

Memberships and awards: President, National Medical Association, 1911–1912; West Virginia State Medical Society which he organized; Upsilon Boule; Kappa Alpha Psi; Director, Supreme Liberty Life Insurance Co.

Ref: National Medical Association, *Journal*, Feb. 1933, p. 35–36. obit & biog.
Dictionary of American Medical Biography, p. 273–274.
Gamble, Robert L. Henry Floyd Gamble, M.D., 1862–1932. National Medical Association, *Journal*, v. 64, Jan. 1972, p. 85–86. [p] cover (article written by his grandson also an M.D.)

Gans, Louis H.   (1902–1962, M)

Dentist. Born in 1902. B.S. Chief of Oral Surgery Department of Chicago Board of Health.

Ref: *Jet*, Feb. 22, 1962, p. 17.

Gant, Virgil Arnett   (1897–19??, M)

Pharmacologist. B.S., M.S., University of Illinois; Ph.D., College of Medicine, University of Illinois, 1938. Pharmacology.

Dissertation title: Lead Poisoning in Human Beings.

Ref: *Holders of Doctorates Among American Negroes*, p. 121

Garland, Cornelius N.   (18??–19??, M)

Physician. Surgeon. Born in Alabama. B.S., Livingstone College, 1897; M.D., Leonard Medical College, 1901; Postgraduate, London University Medical College, England, 1902–03. Founded in 1908, Plymouth Hospital and Training School for Nurses, was Surgeon-in-Chief, 1915.

Memberships and awards: National Medical Association; Massachusetts Medical Society; Boston Society for Medical Improvement; Boston Business League.

Ref: *Who's Who in Colored America*, 1933–37, p. 200.
Who's Who of the Colored Race, 1915, p. 112.
Who's Who in Colored America, 1928–29, p. 140–141.

Who's Who in Colored America, 1930–32, p. 163.
Who's Who in Colored America, 1941–44, p. 197.

Garland, J. O.   (1893–1963, M)

Physician. Born in 1893. B.S., Bishop College, TX; M.D., Howard University Medical College, 1925.

Memberships and awards: Vice-President, National Medical Association; Charles Drew Medical Society; Medical Dental, and Pharmaceutical Society of Southern California; Los Angeles County Medical Society; American Medical Association.

Ref: *Jet,* Dec. 5, 1963, p. 52.
National Medical Association, *Journal,* v. 58, May 1966, p. 244–255. [p]

Garrott, Alva Curtis   (1866–19??, M)

Dentist. Born in Marion, AL, Sept. 18, 1866. B.S., Talladega College, 1886; Phar.D., Howard University, 1895; D.D.S., 1899. Went to California in 1901 and became the first black Dentist in southern California, second on the west coast; teacher in Henderson and Carlisle, TX, 1886–90; government clerk, 1890–1901; dentist after 1901.

Memberships and awards: Sigma Pi Phi.

Ref: *Who's Who of the Colored Race,* 1915, p. 112–113.
Who's Who in Colored America, 1927, p. 73.
Who's Who in Colored America, 1928–29, p. 427.
Who's Who in Colored America, 1930–32, p. 164.
Who's Who in Colored America, 1933–37, p. 200–201.
Who's Who in Colored America, 1941–44, p. 201.

Garvin, Charles Herbert   (1890–1968, M)

Physician. Surgeon. Born in Jacksonville, FL, Oct. 27, 1890. B.A., Howard University, 1911; M.D., 1915. Assistant Visiting Surgeon at Freedmen's Hospital, 1916; first black member of the staff of the Genito-Urinary Department of Lakeland Hospital of Western Reserve University, 1920; Captain in the Medical Corps, U.S. Army, 367th Infantry and Commanding Officer of the 368th Ambulance Company during World War I; first black to receive a commission in the Army in World War I, 1st Lieutenant, 1917.

Memberships and awards: Cleveland Academy of Medicine; American Venereal Disease Society; American Medical Association; National Medical Association; Alpha Phi Alpha; Sigma Pi Phi; William A. Warfield Award, Howard University, 1963.

Pub: Author of numerous articles in the *Journal* of the National Medical Association, *Ohio State Medical Journal,* and others.
Index Medicus of Negro Authors, 1924–34. National Medical Association, *Journal,* v. 27, 1935, p. 146–153. Numerous other articles.

Ref: *Who's Who in Colored America,* 1933–37, p. 201.
Jet, Oct. 30, 1969, [p]
Who's Who in Colored America, 1930–32, p. 164–165.
Who's Who in Colored America, 1927, p. 73.
Who's Who in Colored America, 1928–29, p. 141.
Medico-Chirurgical Society of the District of Columbia, *Bulletin,* April 1949, p. 12. [p]
The National Register, 1952, p. 572.
Dictionary of American Medical Biography, p. 280–281.
Who's Who in Colored America, 1941–44, p. 201.
National Medical Association, *Journal,* v. 49, July 1957, p. 257–258. [p]
National Medical Association, *Journal,* v. 56, Mar. 1964, p. 208.
National Medical Association, *Journal,* v. 61, Jan. 1969. [p] cover

Garvin, Walter B.   (18??–1958, M)

Dentist. Served Board of Dental Examiners Freedmen's Group since 1920; taught at Howard University for 20 years; taught in clinics in New York, Detroit and other cities. Died of heart attack.

Ref: *Jet,* Feb. 7, 1957.

Gasaway, Sadie Catherine   (1916– ——, F)

Mathematician. Born in Memphis, TN, Oct. 6, 1916. B.A., LeMoyne College, 1941; M.A., University of Illinois, 1945; Ph.D., Cornell University, 1961. Faculty member, Tennessee State University, 1949–62; Professor, Mathematics, 1962–68; Chairman, Department of Physics and Mathematics, 1968–.

Memberships and awards: Mathematics Association; American National Council of Teachers of Mathematics; American Association of University Women; Alpha Kappa Alpha; Beta Kappa Chi.

Dissertation title: The Effectiveness of Continued Testing.

Ref: *Who's Who in America,* 1976.
Who's Who Among Black Americans, 1975, p. 226.
Jet, July 19, 1976, p. 14.

Gaston, Marilyn Hughes   (1939– ——, F)

Physician. Pediatrician. Born in Cincinnati, OH, Jan. 31, 1939. B.A., Miami University, 1960; M.D., University of Cincinnati, 1964. Residency, Children's Hospital Medical Center, 1967; Assistant Director, Children's Hospital Medical Center, 1968; Assistant Professor of Pediatrics, 1972–; Director, Cincinnati Comprehensive Sickle Cell Center, 1972–; Medical Director, Lincoln Heights Health Center, 1973–.

Memberships and awards: American Academy of Pediatrics; United Black Faculty Association; American Public Health Association; Pi Kappa Epsilon; Outstanding Young Women of America, 1973; Outstanding Black Women of Cincinnati, 1974.

Ref: ABMS Compendium of Certified Medical Specialists, v. 4, p. 853.
Who's Who Among Black Americans, 1985, p. 302.
Who's Who of American Women, 1974, p. 330.

Gathings, Joseph Gouverneur (1898–1965, M)

Physician. Dermatologist. Born in Richmond, TX, July 11, 1898. B.A., Howard University, 1924; Meharry Medical College, 1924–25; M.D., Howard University Medical College, 1928. Private practice, 1929–41; Dermatologist, Washington, DC, 1946–65; Clinical Faculty in Dermatology and Syphilology, Howard University Medical College, 1946–65.

Memberships and awards: President, National Medical Association, 1952; addressed the American Medical Association at their 101st convention; Rosenwald fellow in Dermatology and Syphilology, New York Skin and Cancer Hospital; Diplomate, American Board of Dermatology and Syphilology; fellow, American Academy of Dermatology and Syphilology; President, Board of Trustees, National Medical Association, 1947–49; Medico-Chirurgical Society of the District of Columbia; Kappa Alpha Psi; Chi Delta Mu; National Medical Committee of the NAACP.

Pub: Speech to AMA from NMA. National Medical Association, Journal, v. 44, July 1952, p. 313–314. [p]
Physician Heal Thyself. National Medical Association, Journal, v. 44, Sept. 1952, p. 333–358. [p]

Ref: National Medical Association, Journal, v. 42, Nov. 1950, p. 396. [p]
Jet, June 19, 1952, p. 58. [p]
Dictionary of American Medical Biography, p. 283.
Cobb, W. Montague. "Joseph Gouverneur Gathings, M.D., 1898–1965."
National Medical Association, Journal, v. 57, Sept. 1965, p. 427–428. [p] cover
Medico-Chirurgical Society of the District of Columbia, Inc., Bulletin, May–Sept. 1949, p. 12. [p]

Gay, Edward Charles (1940– ——, M)

Engineer (chemical). Born in Starksville, MS, May 13, 1940. B.S. (chemical engineering), Washington University, MO, 1962; Ph.D., 1967. Assistant Engineer, Argonne National Lab., 1968–69; Lithium-Chalcogen Cell Development Problem Leader, Argonne National Lab., 1969–71; Battery Program Group Leader, Argonne National Lab., 1941–75; Program Manager, 1975–.

Membership and awards: Electrochemical Society; American Institute of Chemical Engineers; Sigma Xi; President, National Organization for the Professional Advancement of Black Chemists and Chemical Engineers; Thesis Award, Argonne National Lab.

Dissertation title: Flow Properties of Liquid Sodium Suspensions with High Solid Concentration.

Ref: Black Engineers in the United States, p. 74–75.
Who's Who Among Black Americans, 1985, p. 303.

Gayle, Helene D. (1955– ——, F)

Physician. Epidemiologist. Born in 1955. B.S. (psychology), Barnard College, 1976; M.D., University of Pennsylvania School of Medicine; M.S. (public health), Johns Hopkins. Two years at the CDC Epidemic Intelligence Service learning how to track the spread of AIDS.

Ref: Black Enterprise, Oct. 1988, p. 62. [p]

Gee, Fannie (19??– ——, F)

Mathematician. Born in Carthage, MS. B.S., Alcorn State College; MS, 1967; M.A. (mathematics), DePauw University, 1969; Ph.D., University of Pittsburgh, 1979; Mathematics Faculty, Alcorn University.

Dissertation title: A Characterization of a Class of LaGrangian Groups.

Ref: Kenschaft, Patricia C. "Black Women in Mathematics in the United States." American Mathematical Monthly, v. 88, Oct. 1951, p. 601–602.
National Faculty Directory, 1988, p. 1308.

Gibbs, James Albert (1917– ——, M)

Chemist (organic). Born in Montgomery, AL, Oct. 1, 1917. B.A., Fisk University, 1938; M.A., 1940; M.A., Harvard University, 1947. Instructor, Chemistry, Fisk University, 1943–44; Assistant Professor, Hampton Institute, 1945–46; Research Chemist, Tufts Medical School, 1947–49; Chemist, Tracerlab, Inc., 1949–57; Technical Director and Treasurer, Volk Radiochem Co., IL, 1958–60; Manager of Chemical Labs., 1960–67; Manager of Chemicals & Supplies, 1967–74; Regulatory Affairs Manager, Packard Instrument Co., Inc., 1974–; research in synthesis of isotopically labeled compounds, carbon-14, hydrogen-2, etc.

Memberships and awards: American Chemical Society; AAAS; New York Academy of Sciences.

Ref: American Men and Women of Science, 16th ed., p. 111.
The Negro in Science, p. 182.

Gibbs, William Walden (1890–1948, M)

Physician. Obstetrician. Gynecologist. Surgeon. Born in Mobile, AL, July 12, 1890. B.A., Knoxville College, 1912; B.S., M.D., Indiana University, 1917. Junior Gynecologist, 1926–30; Acting Senior Surgeon, 1930–32; Senior Gynecologist and Chairman of the Division of Gynecology, 1933–39; Co-Chairman, Department of Obstetrics and Gynecology, 1939–47, all at Provident Hospital.

Memberships and awards: Only black member of the Physical Education Committee of all Chicago YMCA; Association Vice-Chairman and member of the Executive Committee, Cook County Physician's Association; Ex-President, Cook County Medical Association; National Medical Association; American Medical Association; Chicago Medical Association; Diplomate, American Board of Surgery.

Ref: *Who's Who in Colored America*, 1928–29, p. 145.
         Who's Who in Colored America, 1930–32, p. 166.
         Who's Who in Colored America, 1933–37, p. 205.
         National Medical Association, *Journal*, v. 34, May 1942,
              p. 119.
         National Medical Association, *Journal*, v. 40, May 1948,
              p. 131. obit
         Who's Who in Colored America, 1941–44, p. 203.

Gibson, Walter William   (1907–19??, M)

Zoologist. Biologist. Born in Charleston, SC, Feb. 24, 1907. B.A., Morehouse College, 1930; M.S., University of Iowa, 1934; Ph.D. (zoology), Ohio State, 1944. From Assistant Professor to Professor of Biology, LeMoyne-Owens College, 1934–48; Chairman of the Department of Biology, 1939–48; Head of the Biology Department, Texas Southern University, 1948–51; Acting President of the College, 1954–59; Professor of Biology and Chairman of the Division of Natural Science, 1951–54 and 1959–77; Emeritus Professor of Biology, LeMoyne-Owen College, 1977–.

Memberships and awards: American Association for the Advancement of Science; American Entomological Society; Tennessee Academy of Sciences; Sigma Xi; National Institute of Science.

Dissertation title: An Ecological Study of the Spiders of a Riverterrace Forest in Western Tennessee.

Ref: *The Negro in Science*, p. 178.
         American Men and Women of Science, 14th ed., p. 1717.

Gier, Joseph Thomas   (1910–19??, M)

Engineer (thermal). Inventor. Born in 1910. B.S., University of California, 1934; M.S., 1940. Professor of Engineering, University of California, Los Angeles, 1958–. World authority on thermal radiation; research engineering consultant and manufacturer of Gier and Dunkle Thermal Instruments.

Memberships and awards: Illuminating Engineering Society.

Ref: *American Men of Science*, 10th ed., p. 1391.
         In Black and White, 3rd ed., p. 358.

Gilbert, Artishia Garcia   (1869–19??, F)

Physician. Obstetrician. Born in Manchester, KY, 1869. M.A., State University, Louisville, KY, 1892; M.D., Louisville National Medical College, 1893. She is said to have been the first black woman physician to pass the State Board and register in Kentucky. Attended Howard University Medical College, 1896–97 with M.D., 1897. Assistant to the Professor of Obstetrics, Medical Department,

State University and Superintendent of the Red Cross Sanitarium in Louisville, KY.

Ref: *Howard University Medical Department.* 1971 reprint, p.
              168.

Gilbert, John Wesley   (1864–1923, M)

Archeologist. Born in Hephzibah, Richmond County, GA, July 6, 1864. B.S. Greek scholar; first graduate and first black faculty member, Paine Institute, 1888–; President, Miles College; Minister; Missionary to Africa.

Memberships and awards: American Philological Association.

Ref: *Afro-American Encyclopedia*, v. 4, p. 1063.
         In Black and White, p. 359.
         *Progress of a Race or the Remarkable Advancement of the
              American Negro*, p. 519–522.

Giles, Julian Wheatley   (1921–1969, M)

Physician. Otolaryngologist. Born in Washington, DC, July 21, 1921. B.S., Howard University, 1942; M.D., Howard University School of Medicine, 1946; postgraduate study in Otolaryngology, Washington University, St., Louis, Chief, Otolaryngology Service, Tuskegee V.A. Hospital, 1951; Associate Chief of Staff, Research and Education, Tuskegee V.A. Hospital, 1960–; Director, 1962–; Discovered chloraseptic with Dr. A. L. Bookhardt, Tuskegee V.A. Hospital.

Memberships and awards: Fellow, American Academy of Ophthalmology and Otolaryngology; Diplomate, American Board of Otolaryngology; Medical Society of the District of Columbia; Medico-Chirurgical Society of the District of Columbia; National Medical Association; American Medical Association; University of Alabama Advisory Committee on Medical Programs in heart disease, cancer and stroke.

Ref: *Jet*, Jan. 19, 1961, p. 15.
         National Medical Association, *Journal*, v. 55, May 1963,
              p. 247. [p]
         National Medical Association, *Journal*, v. 61, July 1969,
              p. 373. obit & biog

Giles, Roscoe Conkling   (1890–1970, M)

Physician. Surgeon. Born in Albany, NY, May 6, 1890. B.A., Cornell University, 1911; M.D., Cornell Medical College, 1915. Supervisor of City Health Department of Chicago in 1916; Surgeon, Provident Hospital, 1916–26; Assistant Professor of Surgery, Chicago Medical School, 1946; Attending Surgeon, Cook County Hospital, 1953. First black graduate of Cornell Medical School.

Memberships and awards: President and member of the Executive Board, National Medical Association, 1936–37; President, Alpha Phi Alpha Fraternity; Chicago Medical Society; fellow, American Medical Association; President of John A. Andrews Clinical Society; elected a member of the Executive Committee of the American Medical Association of Vienna while he was in Vienna studying under a Rosenwald Fund and the University of Chicago; Nov. 19, 1938, became Diplomate of the American Board of Surgery by competitive examination; first black surgeon to be granted a certificate. One of the first four black members of the American College of Surgeons. He was chairman of the National Medical Association Committee which succeeded in removing "Col." from the names of black members listed in the American Medical Association Directory.

Pub: See list on pages 308–309, *A Century of Black Surgeons.*

Ref: *Dictionary of American Medical Biography,* p. 292.
 Encyclopedia of Black America, p. 404.
 Chicago Defender, Feb. 21–27, 1970. C2, p. 1. Obituary.
 Who's Who in Colored America, 1951, p. 74–75. [p] opp. p. 72.
 Who's Who in Colored America, 1928–29, p. 145.
 Who's Who in Colored America, 1930–32, p. 169–170. [p] opp. p. 166.
 Who's Who in Colored America, 1933–37, p. 206. [p] p. 203.
 Who's Who in Colored America, 1927, p. 74–75.
 Who's Who in Colored America, 1941–44, p. 204. [p] p. 205.
 History of the Negro in Medicine, p. 135.
 National Medical Association, *Journal,* v. 31, May 1939, p. 122.
 Cobb, W. Montague. Rosco Conkling Giles. National Medical Association, *Journal,* v. 62, 1970, p. 254–256.
 National Medical Association, *Journal,* v. 41, Sept. 1949, p. 266–267.
 National Medical Association, *Journal,* v. 62, May 1970, p. 254.
 National Medical Association, *Journal,* v. 62, May 1970. [p] cover
 A Century of Black Surgeons, p. 297–306. [p] p. 298

Gillam, Isaac Thomas, IV   (1932– ——, M)

Mathematician. Born in Little Rock, AR, Feb. 23, 1932. B.S. (mathematics), Howard University, 1953; Tennessee A & I State University, 1957–61. NASA Director of shuttle operations at Dryden Flight Research Center at Edwards Air Force Base in California, 1977–78. He joined NASA in 1963 and by 1973 headed the Delta and Scout Small Missile Launch Programs; NASA Headquarters Special Assistant, 1981–82; Assistant Associate Administrator, 1982–84; 10 years in Air force, pilot during the Korean War and a launch missile commander for the Strategic Air Command; under his direction NASA put up several satellites for RCA, Comsat, and Western Union, as well as some foreign countries.

Memberships and awards: Fellow, American Astronautical Society, 1978; American Management Association; American Defense Preparedness Association; NASA Distinguished Service Medal, 1976; NASA Exceptional Service Medal, 1982–83; Tau Beta Pi; named one

of four distinguished Howard University Alumni for his successful pursuits in Space Engineering, 1981.

Ref: *Blacks in Science: Ancient and Modern,* p. 246–248.
 Ebony, Aug. 1985, p. 174. [p]
 Who's Who Among Black Americans, 1985, p. 309.
 Jet, April 30, 1978, p. 4. [p] p. 5.
 Ebony, April 1977, p. 124–126, 128–129. [p]

Gipson, Joella Hardeman   (1929– ——, F)

Mathematician. Born in Los Angeles, CA, Jan. 8, 1929. B.M., Mount Saint Mary's College, 1950; M.A., State University of Iowa, 1951; University of Southern California, 1960–63; Ph.D., University of Illinois, 1971. Instructor, Southern University, Baton Rouge, 1954–56; Assistant Professor, Jackson State College, 1956–58; Teacher, Superintendent, Administrator, Los Angeles City Schools, 1958–69; Visiting Lecturer, University of Georgia, summer, 1969; Assistant Professor, University of Illinois, 1969–71; Consultant, Unified Science and Mathematics, Elementary School Program, Educational Development Corp., Newton, MA, 1970–71; Researcher, Southwest Regional Laboratory for Educational Research and Development, 1971; Visiting lecturer, Grambling College, summer, 1972; Professor and Coordinator, Master of Arts in Teaching Program, College of Education, Wayne State University, 1972–.

Memberships and awards: Mathematics Association of America; National Council of Teachers of Mathematics; American Association of University Women; National Alliance of Black School Administrators; Delta Sigma Theta.

Dissertation title: Teaching Probability in the Elementary School: An Exploratory Study.

Pub: In-Service Education in the Los Angeles City Schools. California Mathematics Council, *Bulletin,* Spring 1968.
 Use of Computer Assisted Instruction in Mathematics for Disadvantaged Seventh Grade Youth. *Research in Education,* July 1971.
 An Experiment in Teaching Decimal Fractions to Second-Grade Children. *Primary Math.,* Nov. 1971.
 Why Teach Probability and Statistics to Elementary School Children? California Math Council, *Bulletin,* Winter 1971.
 An Everyday Approach to Mathematics. *Instructor,* Mar. 1972.
 (Contributing author) Mathematics Target System Grades K–6, Textbook Series, American Book Company, 1972–73.

Ref: *Black Mathematicians and Their Works,* p. 286–287. [p] p. 268
 Who's Who Among Black Americans, 1977, p. 333–334.

Gipson, Mack, Jr.,   (1931– ——, M)

Geologist. Born in Trenton, SC, Sept. 15, 1931. B.A., Paine College, 1953; M.S., University of Chicago, 1961;

Ph.D., University of Chicago, 1963. Professor of Geology and Head of the Department, Virginia State College, 1964; Senior Research Specialist for Exxon.

Memberships and awards: Geological Society of America, fellow; American Geophysical Union; National Association of Geology Teachers; Sigma Xi; Beta Kappa Chi; J. Elmer Thomas fellowship in Geology, 1961–63; Distinguished Science Award, National Consortium for Black Professional Development, 1976.

Dissertation title: A Study of the Relations of Depth, Porosity, and Clay Mineral Orientation in Pennsylvanian Shales.

Ref: *In Black and White,* 3rd ed., p. 362.
Who's Who Among Black Americans, 1985, p. 312.
American Men and Women of Science, 13th ed., p. 1519.
Blacks in the Geosciences, *Black Collegian,* Mar./April 1978, p. 68, 70, 72. [p] p. 70.
Ebony, May 1976, p. 7. [p]

Givens, John Talmadge   (1890–1977, M)

Physician. Born in Aiken, SC, 1890. B.S., Claflin College, SC; M.D., Meharry Medical College, 1912.

Memberships and awards: Executive Secretary, National Medical Association, 1936–69; citation for 20 years work in polio prevention, National Medical Association, 1959.

Ref: National Medical Association, *Journal,* v. 52, Jan. 1960, p. 63. [p]
National Medical Association, *Journal,* v. 67, Nov. 1975, p. 486–487. [p] on cover

Gladden, James Robert   (1911–1969, M)

Physician. Orthopedic Surgeon. Born in Charlottesville, NC, 1911. B.S., Long Island University; M.D. (cum laude), Meharry Medical College, 1938. First Resident, Freedmen's Hospital Orthopedic Residency Program; Chief, Division of Orthopedic Surgery, Howard University College of Medicine, 1950–64.

Memberships and awards: First black certified by the American Board of Orthopedic Surgery, 1949; American Academy of Orthopedic Surgeons; American College of Surgeons; Washington Orthopedic Club; National Medical Association.

Ref: *A Century of Black Surgeons,* p. 502–504. [p] p. 503.

Gleason, Eliza Veleria Atkins   (1909– ——, F)

Librarian. Born in Winston Salem, NC, 1909. B.A., Fisk University, 1930; B.S., University of Illinois, 1931; M.A., University of California, 1936; Ph.D., University of Chicago, 1940. Assistant Librarian, Louisville Municipal College, 1931–32; Librarian, 1932–36; Assistant Professor, Fisk University, 1936–37; Director of Libraries, Talladega College, 1940–41; Professor, Atlanta University,

1941–46; Associate Professor, Chicago Teachers College, 1954–65; Professor, Illinois Institute of Technology, 1967–70; Assistant, John Crerar Library, 1967–70; Assistant Chief Librarian, Chicago Public Library, 1970–73; Professor, Northern Illinois University, 1974–75; Self-employed Library Consultant.

Memberships and awards: Phi Beta Kappa; Beta Phi Mu; American Library Association; first black female to receive Ph.D. in Library Science.

Dissertation title: The Government and Administration of Public Library Service to Negroes in the South.

Ref: *Holders of Doctorates Among American Negroes,* p. 121.
Who's Who Among Black Americans, 1985, p. 313.
Who's Who of American Women, 1974.
Who's Who in America, 1978, p. 1214.

Glover, Israel Everett   (1913– ——, M)

Mathematician. Born in Oxford, NC, Feb. 13, 1913. B.S., Johnson C. Smith University, 1935; M.A., University of Michigan, 1937; Ph.D. (mathematics), Oklahoma State University, 1959. Flutter Engineer, Bell Aircraft Corp. 1944–46; Aeronautical Research Engineer, Wright-Patterson Air Force Base, 1946–48; Associate Professor of Mathematics, Langston, 1948–55; Professor and Head of the Department, Prairie View A & M College, 1955–62; Florida A & M, 1962–67; Visiting Professor, Teachers College, Columbia, 1967–68; Professor and Head of the Department, Albany State College, 1968–69; Professor, Norfolk State College, 1969–71; Mathematics, DC Teachers College, 1971–.

Memberships and awards: General Education Board fellow, 1939–40; John Hay Whitney fellow, Oklahoma State, 1953–54; Visiting Scientist, Texas Academy of Science, 1959–62 and Florida Academy of Science, 1964–67; National Science Foundation, 1961–69; Director—Coordinator, Minnesota Mathematics and Science Teaching Project, Tallahassee Center, 1963–67; Director of Physical Science for Non-Scientists Project, Florida A & M, 1966–67; Visiting Lecturer, Mu Alpha Theta; fellow in History and Mathematics, University of Michigan, summer, 1962; Consultant in Mathematics, Gujarat University, India, 1969; AAAS; New York Academy of Science; American Mathematical Society; Mathematical Association of America.

Dissertation title: On Analytic Functions Having as Singular Sets Certain Closed and Bounded Sets.

Ref: *American Men and Women of Science,* 12th ed., p. 2173–2174.

Goin, Logwood Ulysses   (1873–19??, M)

Physician. Surgeon. Born in Florence, AL, Nov. 24, 1873. B.A., Fisk University, 1896; M.D., Meharry Medical College, 1899. Surgeon at Home Hospital in Birmingham, AL.

Memberships and awards: National Association of Negro Physicians, Dentists, and Pharmacists; Medical Examiner of the Knights of Pythias, United Brothers of Friendship and the Grand United Order of Odd Fellows of Birmingham; Medical Examiner for Reliance Life Insurance Co. and Old Colony Life Insurance Company of Chicago, IL.

Ref: *Beacon Lights of the Race,* p. 933–936. [p] biog
Who's Who of the Colored Race, 1915, p. 117.

Goins, William Fauntleroy, Jr.   (1916- ——, M)

Science Educator. Born in Charlottesville, VA, Dec. 4, 1916. B.S., Hampton Institute, 1937; M.A., Ohio State, 1947. Ph.D., 1950. Assistant Professor, Chemistry, Hampton Institute, 1942–50; Professor and Head, Science Education, Tennessee A & I State, 1951–.

Memberships and awards; AAAS; National Science Teachers Association; National Association of Research in Science Teaching; Tennessee Academy of Science; Beta Kappa Chi; Alpha Kappa Mu.

Dissertation title: An Evaluation of Science Courses Offered for General Education in Selected Negro Colleges.

Ref: *The Negro in Science,* p. 178.
Crisis, Aug. 1937, p. 238. [p]

Goldson, Alfred Lloyd   (1946- ——, M)

Physician. Radiotherapist. Born in New York, NY, April 9, 1946. B.S., Hampton Institute, 1968; M.D., Howard University College of Medicine, 1972. Resident, Department of Radiotherapy, Howard University Hospital, 1973–75; Assistant Radiotherapist, 1976–79; Chairman of the Department, 1979–.

Memberships and awards: Board of Trustees, District of Columbia Division, American Cancer Society, 1979; Chairman, Advisory Commission, College of Allied Health Radiation Therapy, Howard University, 1977–78; National Medical Association; American Medical Association, 1978–; Certificate of Merit, Radiological Society of North America, 1978; among top 50 scientists and researchers in cancer for 1978.

Ref: *Who's Who Among Black Americans,* 1985, p. 315.
Ebony, Nov. 1978, p. 96–96. [p]
National Faculty Directory, 1988, p. 1379.

Goodlett, Carlton B.   (1914- ——, M)

Psychologist. Physician. Born in Chipley, FL, July 23, 1914. B.S., Howard University, 1935; Ph.D., University of California, 1938; M.D., Meharry Medical College, 1944.

Memberships and awards: Sigma Xi; Research Council, West Virginia State College; Beta Kappa Chi; Kappa Sigma Prize.

Dissertation title: A Comparative Study of Adolescent Interests in Two Socioeconomic Groups.

Pub: The Mental Abilities of Twenty-nine Deaf and Partially Deaf Negro Children, The Reading Abilities of the Negro Elementary School Child in Kanawha County, West Virginia.
Journal Articles.

Ref: *Holders of Doctorates Among American Negroes,* p. 206–207.
Who's Who Among Black Americans, 1985, p. 317.

Gourdine, Meredith C.   (1929- ——, F)

Physicist. Engineer. Born in Newark, NJ, Sept. 26, 1929. B.S. (engineering physics), Cornell University, 1953; Ph.D. (engineering physics), California Institute of Technology, 1960; pioneered in electrogasdynamics; developed "Incineraid" for removing smoke from buildings; developed technique for dispersing fog from airport runways; Technical Staff, Ramo-Woolridge Corporation, 1957–58; Senior Research Scientist, Caltech Jet Propulsion Lab., 1958–60; Lab Director, Plasmodyne Corp., 1960–62; Chief Scientist, Curtiss-Wright Corp., 1962–64; owner of Gourdine Laboratories in Livingston, NJ, with a staff of over 150. Several patents on gasdynamic products.

Memberships and awards: Daniel & Florence Guggenheim fellowship; Ramo-Woolridge fellowship.

Dissertation title: On Magnetohydrodynamic Flow over Solids.

Pub: Numerous articles in scientific journals on electrogasdynamics.

Ref: *Black Contributors to Science, Energy, and Technology,* 1979, p. 16–17.
In Black and White, 3rd ed., p. 371.
Black Engineers in the United States, p. 78–79.
Blacks in Science: Astrophysicist to Zoologist, p. 50–51. [p] after p. 48.
Ebony, April 1967, p. 52–54, 56, 58, 60–62. [p]
Ebony, Aug. 1972, p. 125. [p]
Ebony, Feb. 1974, p. 74, 77. [p]

Govan, Charles   (1900s, M)

Engineer (heating). M.E., Ecole Technique, Montreal, Canada, 1917. Associated with Black Star Line as Marine Engineer, 1919–20; organized Harlem Mechanical Works, 1920–22; Foreman, Lehigh Valley R.R. Co., Coston, PA, 1922–23; proprietor of Lehigh Heating Co., heating engineers and contractors, 1924–.

Memberships and awards: Phi Beta Sigma.

Ref: *Who's Who in Colored America,* 1928–29, p. 149.

Grand, George F.

See: Grant, George F.

Grant, Ernest A.   (1900s, M)

Agriculturist. B.S., Tuskegee Institute; M.S., Cornell University, 1930; Ph.D., 1940. Professor of Agriculture, Tuskegee Institute.

Dissertation title: A Proposed Program for the Improvement of Pre-employment Teacher Training in Agriculture for Negroes in Alabama Based Upon an Analysis and Evaluation of What Teachers of Agriculture Do.

Ref: *Holders of Doctorates Among American Negroes,* p. 121–122.
Crisis, Aug. 1930, p. 268. [p] only

Grant, George F.   (1800s, M)

Inventor. Dentist. D.D.S., Harvard Dental School, 1870 and was the Dental School's first black Instructor, renowned for his dental bridgework; expert in cleft palate; golf tee, patent #638,920 in 1899, small wooden peg to hold golf ball for initial drive.

Ref: *At Last Recognition in America,* v. 1, p. 13.
In Black and White, 3rd ed., p. 374; Supplement, p. 159.
Black Collegian, Mar./April 1978, p. 30.
Minorities in Science: The Challenge for Change in Biomedicine, p. 3.
Blacks in Science: Astrophysicist to Zoologist, p. 23.

Grant, William H.   (1900's, M)

Physician. Pathologist. Professor of Clinical Pathology and Director of Clinical Laboratories, Meharry Medical College, 1940s. Has studied Tropical Medicine, Army Medical School, Washington, DC, special field and hospital work in Central America.

Ref: *The Negro Too, in American History,* p. 450.

Granville, Evelyn Boyd   (1924- ——, F)

Mathematician. Born in Washington, DC, May 1, 1924. B.A., Smith College (summa cum laude), 1945; M.A., Yale University, 1946; Ph.D. (mathematics), Yale University, 1949. Research Assistant, New York University Institute of Mathematics and Mechanics, 1949–50; Associate Professor of Mathematics, Fisk University, 1950–52; Mathematician, Bureau of Standards, U.S. Department of Commerce, 1952–53; Diamond Ordnance Fuse Laboratory, Ordnance Corps, U.S. Department of the Army, 1953–56; International Business Machines Corporation, 1956–60; Space Technology Laboratories, research on space trajectories, 1962–63; North American Aviation Space and Information Systems Division, Research Specialist on Apollo Project in celestial mechanics and trajectory and orbit computation, 1963–67; Department of Mathematics, California State University, 1967–.

Memberships and awards: First black woman to earn a Ph.D. in pure Mathematics; Rosenwald fellow, 1946–48; Atomic Energy Commission predoctoral fellow, 1946–48; Phi Beta Kappa; American Mathematical Society; Sigma Xi; Mathematical Association of America.

Dissertation title: On Laguerre Series in the Complex Domain.

Pub: Wrote on Laguerre series in the Complex Domain, Numerical Analysis. *Theory of Applications of Math for Teachers.* Belmon, CA, Wadsworth, 1978. 498 p.

Ref: *American Men of Science,* 10th ed., under Boyd, Evelyn, p. 410. (also known as Evelyn B. Collins)
Black Mathematicians and Their Works, p. 287. [p]
Black Women in Mathematics in the United States. *American Mathematical Monthly,* v. 88, no. 8, Oct. 1981, p. 592–604.
National Faculty Directory, 1986, p. 1266.
The Negro in Science, p. 188.
Profiles of Negro Womanhood, v. 2, p. 82–86.
Negroes in Science: Natural Science Doctorates 1876–1969, p. 60.
Ebony, Aug. 1960, p. 7. [p] only
In Black & White, p. 103, 204.

Gravely, Samuel Lee, Jr.   (1922- ——, M)

Military (Navy). Vice-Admiral. Born in Richmond. VA, June 4, 1922. B.A., Virginia Union, 1948. First black admiral, promoted April 15, 1971. Commander U.S.S. Falgout, 1962 (first warship under black command); Third Fleet Commander, 1967–78; retired as director of the Defense Communications Agency. One of the first two black officers to attend the Naval War College and to earn a 3-star vice-admiral's rank.

Memberships and awards: Navy League, 1982–; Major Richard R. Wright Award of Excellence, from Savannah State College, 1974; Alpha Phi Alpha Award of Merit; World War II Victory Medal; Korean President's Unit Citation; Korean Service Medal with two Bronze Stars; United Nations Service Medal.

Ref: *Encyclopedia of Black America,* p. 408.
Jet, Feb. 15, 1962, p. 5.
Jet, Aug. 28, 1980, p. 7.
Who's Who Among Black Americans, 1985, p. 324.
Ebony Success Library, v. 1, p. 129. [p]
In Black and White, 3rd ed., p. 375.
Black Americans in Defense of Our Nation, p. 127. [p]
Ebony, Nov. 1985, p. 290. [p]
Ebony, July 1966, p. 25–28, 30, 32, 34. [p]
Ebony, Sept. 1977, p. 66–68, 70, 72, 74, 76. [p]

Graves, Artis P.   (1907-19??, M)

Zoologist. Embryologist. Born in Hiawatha, WV, Sept. 23, 1907. B.S., Bluefield State College, 1931; M.S., University of Iowa, 1938; Ph.D. (zoology), 1943. Instructor in

Biology, Morristown College, 1931–35; Instructor, Shorter College, 1935–36; Instructor, Morris Brown College, 1936–41; Professor and Chairman of the Department, 1942–50; Professor of Biology and Chairman of the Department, North Carolina State University, 1950–.

Memberships and awards: National Science Foundation Science Faculty fellow, 1959–60; AAAS; President, National Institute of Science, 1950–51; National Association of Biology Teachers; American Society of Zoologists; Society of Experimental Biology and Medicine.

Dissertation title: Development of the Golden Hamster, *Cricetus auratus* Waterhouse, During the First Nine Days.

Ref: *American Men and Women of Science,* 14th ed., p. 1841.
Holders of Doctorates Among American Negroes, p. 274.

Gray, Ida   (1867–1913, F)

See: Nelson, Ida Gray.

Green, Henry M.   (1876–1939, M)

Physician. Surgeon. Born in Georgia, Aug. 26, 1876. B.S., Knoxville College; University of Michigan; Roger-Williams University; M.D., Knoxville Medical College; Post-Graduate, University of Illinois; University of Berlin. Specialized in nervous diseases and surgery.

Memberships and awards: President, National Medical Association, 1921–22; President, National Hospital Association, which he helped found in 1923. Succeeded in getting a black hospital unit attached to the Knoxville General Hospital.

Ref: *Who's Who in Colored America,* 1928–29, p. 151.
Who's Who in Colored America, 1930–32, p. 177.
Who's Who in Colored America, 1933–37, p. 216.
National Medical Association, *Journal,* v. 13, Oct.–Dec. 1921, p. 248. [p] p. 250.
Crisis, Feb. 1915, p. 185–187. [p]

Green, Harry James, Jr.   (1911– ——, M)

Chemist. Engineer (chemical). Born in St. Louis, MO, Dec. 7, 1911. B.Ch.E., Ohio State University, 1932; M.S., MIT, 1938; Ph.D. (chemical engineering), Ohio State University, 1943. Instructor in Chemistry, North Carolina A & T College, 1934–37; Assistant Professor, 1938–41; Professor, 1943–44; Senior Engineer, Stromberg-Carlson Co., 1944–59; Supervisor, Manufacturing Research and Development Production Engineering Department, 1959–67; Staff, Xerox Corporation after 1970; research in materials engineering, metals, polymer applications, wire and insulation, telephone transmitter materials, electrical properties of plastics, microelectronic packaging of thick and thin film hybrid circuits, and xerographic materials development; application of the film concept to dialysis (Principal Engineer, Electronics Division, General Dynamics, 1967–70.)

Memberships and awards: Sigma Xi; American Chemical Society; American Society of Metals.

Dissertation title: Application of the Film Concept to Dialysis.

Ref: *Encyclopedia of Black America,* p. 408.
American Men and Women of Science, 15th ed., p. 282.
Holders of Doctorates Among American Negroes, p. 122.
Drew, Charles Richard. Negro Scholars in Scientific Research, *Journal of Negro History,* v. 35, 1950, p.
Crisis, Aug. 1932, p. 248. [p] only

Greene, Bettye Washington   (1935– ——, F)

Chemist (physical). Chemist (colloid). Born in Palestine, TX, Mar. 20, 1935. B.S. (chemistry), Tuskegee Institute, 1955; Ph.D. (physical chemistry), Wayne State University, 1956; Research Chemist, 1965–70; Senior Research Chemist, Dow Chemical Corporation, 1970–85; Research Associate, 1975–81.

Memberships and awards: AAAS; American Chemical Society; Sigma Xi.

Dissertation title: Determination of Particle Size Distributions in Emulsions By Light Scattering.

Ref: *American Men and Women of Science,* 15th ed., p. 293.
In Black and White, p. 379.
Ebony, July 1973, p. 6. [p]

Greene, Clarence Sumner   (1901–1957, M)

Dentist. Physician. Neurosurgeon. Born in Washington, DC, Dec. 26, 1901. D.D.S., University of Pennsylvania, 1926; B.A., 1932; M.D., Howard University Medical School, 1936. Assistant Resident in Surgery, Freedmen's Hospital, 1939–41; Resident, Freedmen's Hospital, under Dr. Charles Drew, 1942; two-year residency, McGill University, Montreal Neurological Institute; Chief, Neurosurgery, Freedmen's Hospital, 1955–57.

Memberships and awards: Kappa Pi; Diplomate, National Board of Medical Examiners, 1938; American Board of Surgery, 1943, first Howard graduate to pass the Surgical Board; American Board of Neurosurgery, first black diplomate, 1953.

Ref: Cobb, W. Montague. Clarence Sumner Greene, A.B., D.D.S, M.D., 1901–1957. National Medical Association, *Journal,* v. 60, May 1968, p. 253–255. [p] cover
Medico-Chirurgical Society of the District of Columbia, Inc., *Bulletin,* Nov. 1949, p. 9. [p]
A Century of Black Surgeons, p. 493–496. [p] p. 494.

Greene, Frank S., Jr.   (1938– ——, M)

Engineer (electrical). Born in Washington, DC, Oct. 19, 1938. B.S. (electrical engineering), Washington University, MO, 1961; M.S., Purdue University, 1962; Ph.D., University of Santa Clara, 1970. Technical Staff, Fairchild R & D, 1965–71; President and Chairman of the Board, Technology Development of California, 1971–; Board of Regents, University of Santa Clara, 1983–.

Memberships and awards: IEEE Computer Society Governing Board; IEEE, 1960–; Eta Kappa Nu; Sigma Xi.

Dissertation title: Low-Field Magnetometer Using Orthogonal Drive of the Ferromagnetic Films.

Pub: Ten technical articles in journals; two textbooks.

Ref: *Black Engineers in the United States*, p. 81–82.
Who's Who Among Black Americans, 1985, p. 330.

Greene, Lionel Oliver, Jr.   (1948– ——, M)

Neurophysiologist. Born in Brooklyn, NY, April 28, 1948. B.A., California State University, Los Angeles, 1970; Ph.D., Stanford University, 1978. Research Scientist, NASA, 1973–77, 1979–81; Research Associate, MIT, 1977–79; Research Scientist, Lockheed Missiles and Space Company, 1981–84; Senior Engineer/Scientist, MacDonald Douglas Astronautics, 1984–.

Memberships and awards: Society for Neuroscience; Aerospace Medicine Association; Association of Black Psychologists; Mission Specialist Astronaut Candidate, 1978; Ford Foundation fellow, Washington, DC; NASA Postdoctoral fellow; National Research fellow, National Academy of Sciences.

Dissertation title: Visually Induced Reorganization of Vestibular Influences in the Rhesus Primate.

Pub: Nine research publications, 1975.

Ref: *Who's Who Among Black Americans*, 1985, p. 331.
Ebony, June 1980, p. 144. [p] only

Greener, Richard Theodore   (1844–1923, M)

Metaphysician. Born in Philadelphia, PA, Jan. 30, 1844. B.A., Harvard College, 1870; while at Harvard he won more prizes than any classmate. Principal in the male department of the Institute for Colored Youth, Philadelphia, PA, Sept. 1870–Dec. 1872; Principal, Sumner High School, Washington, DC, Jan. 1873–July 1873; Professor of Metaphysics, University of South Carolina, Columbia, SC, 1873–1877, also Librarian, May–Oct. 1875 where he rearranged 30,000 volumes and prepared a catalogue; he also wrote a paper on the rare books in the library which he read before the American Philological Association in 1877.

Memberships and awards: First black graduate of Harvard College; American Philological Association.

Ref: *Blacks in America, 1492–1976*, p. 21.
In Black and White, 3rd ed., p. 381. many refs.
Men of Mark, 1970 ed., p. 210–216. [p] p. 210.
National Cyclopedia of American Biography, v. 13, p. 577.
Who's Who of the Colored Race, 1915, p. 121–122.
Dictionary of American Biography, v. 4, p. 578–579.

Greenidge, Robert Isaac   (1888–19??, M)

Physician. Born in Georgetown, British Guiana (now Guyana), Oct. 27, 1888. B.S., Battle Creek College, MI, 1910; M.D., College of Medicine, Detroit, 1915; further study Cook County Hospital, Chicago; Illinois Post Graduate Hospital. Superintendent, Fairview Sanatorium, Detroit, 1930; Director, East Side Medical laboratory, 1927–; Medical Director, Vice-President, Great lakes Mutual Life Insurance, 1928–.

Memberships and awards: Alpha Phi Alpha; Wayne County Medical Society; Michigan State Medical Society; American College of Radiology; American Medical Association; National Medical Association.

Ref: *The National Register*, 1952, p. 575.
Ebony, Oct. 1950, p. 41. [p]
Who's Who in Colored America, 1941–44, pp. 217–218.

Greer, Edward   (1924– ——, M)

Military (Army). Major General. Born in Gary, WV, Mar. 8, 1924. B.S., West Virginia State College, 1948; M.S., George Washington University, 1967.

Memberships and awards: Distinguished Service Medal; Silver Star; Legion of Merit; Oak Leaf Cluster; Bronze Star and Medal, Oak Leaf Cluster; Air Medal; Joint Service Commendation Medal; Army Commendation Medal; Alumnus of the Year, West Virginia State College, 1963.

Ref: *Who's Who Among Black Americans*, 1985, p. 332.
Ebony Success Library, v. 1, p. 133, [p]
Black Americans in Defense of Our Nation, p. 122. [p]

Gregg, Anna D.   (18??–19??, F)

Physician. One of the first two women graduates of Meharry Medical School, 1893. The other doctor was Georgia E. Lee Patton-Washington.

Ref: *Send Us a Lady Physician*, p. 110.

Gregg, Arthur James   (1928– ——, M)

Military (Army). Lt. General. Born in Florence, SC, May 12, 1928. B.S. (summa cum laude), St. Benedict College, 1964; Post-Graduate, Command and General Staff College, 1964; attended Army War College, 1968. Advanced in grade to Brigadier General, 1949–81, then to Lt. General.

Memberships and awards: Legion of Merit, two Oak Leaf Clusters; Joint Service Commendation Medal; Army Commendation Medal, two Oak Leaf Clusters; Meritorious Unit Citation; Defense Distinguished Service Medal; Army Distinguished Service Medal.

Ref: *Ebony Success Library*, v. 1, p. 133. [p]
Black Americans in Defense of Our Nation, p. 121. [p]
Who's Who Among Black Americans, 1985, p. 333.
Ebony, May 1978, p. 40. [p]

Gregory, Frederick Drew   (1941– ——, M)

Astronaut. Military (Air Force). Colonel. Born in Washington, DC, Jan. 7, 1941. B.S., USAF Academy, 1964; M.S.A., George Washington University, 1977. Research test pilot for USAF, 1971–78; more than 40 different aircraft, including helicopters and fighter pilot, 1965–70; Astronaut, 1978–. Nephew of Dr. Charles Drew. First black commander of a space shuttle.

Memberships and awards: Society for Experimental Test Pilots; Graduate of U.S. Naval Test Pilot School; Tuskegee Airmen, Inc.; American Helicopter Society; National Technical Association; Omega Psi Phi; Sigma Pi Phi; Distinguished National Scientist, National Society of Black Engineers, 1979.

Ref: *Jet,* Mar. 9, 1978, p. 22–26.
  Blacks in Science, Ancient & Modern, p. 239–245. [p]
  Ebony, Aug. 1985, p. 62–63.
  Who's Who Among Black Americans, 1985, p. 333.
  Ebony, Mar. 1979, p. 54–56, 58, 60, 62. [p]

Grier, Eliza Anna   (18??–1902, F)

Physician. B.A., Fisk University, 1890; M.D., Women's Medical College of Pennsylvania, 1897. A former slave who worked her way through college and medical school, working every other year to earn the next year's tuition. She took seven years to finish. Had an office in Greenville, SC.

Ref: *We Are Your Sisters,* p. 445–447. [p] p. 446.
  Send Us a Lady Physician, p. 110, 112. [p] p. 112.

Griffin, Clarence W.   (195?–1983, M)

Photographer. B.A., Richard Stockman State College, Pomona, CA; enlisted in Navy in 1976.

Memberships and awards: First black Navy photographer to win Military Photographer of the Year, 1981, from 108 photographers in the competition which was sponsored by the University of Missouri School of Journalism and the Defense Department.

Ref: *Jet,* April 30, 1981, p. 46. [p]
  Jet, May 9, 1983, p. 53.

Griffin, Joseph Howard   (1888–19??, M)

Physician. Surgeon. Born in Stewart County, GA, Feb. 1, 1888. B.S. (first in his class), Georgia State Industrial College for Negroes, 1911; M.D., Meharry Medical College, 1915. In 1930, he built an 18-bed hospital and in 1950 a 50-bed hospital. For over 60 years, he worked in Bainbridge, GA.

Ref: Cotton, Barbara R. *Non Verba Opera, Not Words But Works; The Biography of Joseph Howard Griffin, M.D.* Tallahassee, FL, B. R. Cotton, 1980. 216 p.

Griffith, Booker Taliaferro   (1905–19??, M)

Biologist. Zoologist. Cytologist. Born in Prentiss, MS, April 18, 1905. B.S., Pittsburgh University, 1926; M.S., 1929; Ph.D. (zoology), 1939. Professor and Chairman of the Department, Savannah State College, 1946; research in the study of antibiosis between wind-borne molds and insect larvae from wind-borne eggs.

Memberships and awards: AAAS; National Institute of Science; Beta Kappa Chi; National Association of Biology Teachers.

Dissertation title: A Study of Seasonal Changes in the Gonads of the Male English Sparrow (*Passer domesticus*).

Ref: *American Men of Science,* 11th ed., p. 1959.
  Holders of Doctorates Among American Negroes, p. 190.
  The Negro in Science, p. 178.

Griffiths, Norman Henry Campbell   (1916–1978, M)

Dentist (prosthetic). Born in Costa Rica, C.A., April 16, 1916. D.D.S., Howard University Dental School, 1947; M.S.D., Northwestern University, 1948; D.Sci., University of Pennsylvania, 1957. Assistant Professor to Associate Professor, College of Dentistry, Howard University, 1949–61; Acting Department Head, 1967–68; Professor of Prosthodontics, 1961–; Chairman, Department of Removable Prosthodontics, 1970–.

Memberships and awards: Rotating staff, American Hospital Ship, Guinea; Fulbright Professor, Alexandria University, 1966–67; Visiting Professor, University of Baghdad, 1967; WHO Consultant, Government of India; AAAS; American Medical Writers Association; International Association for Dental Research; New York Academy of Sciences.

Ref: *American Men and Women of Science,* 13th ed., p. 1645–1646.
  Leaders of American Science, 1960–61, p. 333. [p]

Grigsby, Margaret E.   (1923– ——, F)

Physician. Born in Prairie View, TX, Jan. 16, 1923. B.S., Prairie View College, 1943; M.D., University of Michigan, 1948; D.T.M.&H., University of London, 1963. Intern to Assistant Resident, Homer G. Phillips Hospital, St. Louis, MO, 1948–50; Assistant Resident, Freedmen's Hospital, Washington, DC, 1950–51; Instructor to Associate Professor, Howard University Medical College, 1952–66; Professor of Medicine, Howard Medical School, 1966–; research in internal medicine, tropical medicine, and infectious diseases, antibiotic research, electrophoresis of proteins.

Memberships and awards: Rockefeller Foundation Research fellow, Harvard Medical School, 1951–52;

China Medical Board fellow, School of Tropical Medicine, University of Puerto Rico, 1956; fellow, American College of Physicians; American Medical Association; National Medical Association; Medical Society of DC; Sigma Xi; Medico-Chirurgical Society of DC; Alpha Epsilon Iota; American College of Physicians, fellow, 1962; Alpha Kappa Alpha.

Ref: *American Men and Women of Science,* 15th ed., p. 321.
          In Black and White, 3rd ed., p. 387.
          who's Who Among Black Americans, 1985, p. 336.
          ABMS Compendium of Certified Medical Specialists, v. 2,
             p. 650.
          Ebony, May 1964, p. 72. [p]

Grooms, Henry Randall   (1944– ——, M)

Engineer (civil). Born in Cleveland, OK, Feb. 10, 1944. B.S. (civil engineering), Howard University, 1965; M.S., Carnegie-Mellon University, 1967; Ph.D., 1969. Highway Engineer, District of Columbia Highway Department, 1965–66; Structural Engineer, Peter F. Loftus Corporation, 1966; Consultant, Blaw-Knox Corporation, 1967–68; Structural Engineer, Rockwell International, Downey, CA, 1969–.

Memberships and awards: Tau Beta Pi, 1964–; Sigma Xi; Kappa Alpha Psi; American Society of Civil Engineers; Engineer of the Year, Rockwell International Space Division, 1980; Alumni Merit Award, Carnegie Mellon University, 1985.

Dissertation title: A Simulation Model for the Patient Treatment System in General Hospitals.

Ref: *Black Engineers in the U.S.,* p. 83–84.
          Who's Who Among Black Americans, 1985, p. 337.

Gwaltney, John Langston   (1928– ——, M)

Anthropologist. Born in Orange, NJ, Sept. 25, 1928. B.A., Upsala College, 1952; M.A., New School of Social Research, 1957; Ph.D., Columbia University, 1967. Associate Professor of Anthropology, Maxwell Graduate School, Syracuse University. Is Blind.

Memberships and awards: Participant, Seminar, American Foundation for the Blind, 1971; fellow, American Anthropological Society; Society for Applied Anthropology; National Science Foundation School-College Program in African Studies; Committee on Opportunities in Science and Research Group; National Institutes of Health, 1963–67; American Philosophical Society; Ansley Dissertation Award, Columbia University, 1967.

Dissertation title: Role of Blindness in a Claxaca Village.

Ref: *American Men and Women of Science,* 13th ed., p. 1688.
          In Black and White, p. 391.
          Jet, Dec. 14, 1967, p. 43.
          Who's Who Among Black Americans, 1985, p. 340–341.
          Living Black American Authors, p. 63.
          National Faculty Directory, 1988, p. 1487.

Gwynn, John Austin   (1857–19??, M)

Physician. Born in Yanceyville, NC, Feb. 15, 1857 of slave parents. B.A., Hampton Institute, VA, 1879. Taught near Petersburg, VA, became Principal of Clover Hill School, 1882. In 1883, he entered Howard University and graduated, 1886; M.D., Howard University Medical College, 1889; postgraduate course, Bellevue Hospital Medical College, NY. Practiced in Ashland, KY, 1891–92; Richmond, VA, 1893–.

Memberships and awards: Board of Pension Examining Surgeons, Secretary.

Ref: *Howard University Medical Department,* 1971. Reprint,
             p. 173. [p]

H

Hale, John Henry   (1879–1944, M)

Physician. Surgeon. Born in Tullahoma, TN, June 4, 1879. B.A., Walden University, Nashville, TN, 1903; M.D., Meharry Medical College, 1905. Chief of Surgery, Meharry Medical College, 1938; Performed 30,000 operations during his career; Medical Examiner for Rock City Academy of Medicine; life member of Mayo Clinic; Co-founder of Millie E. Hale Hospital which was named for his wife, a Fisk University Graduate and Registered Nurse, 1916; Surgeon-in-Chief, Millie E. Hale Hospital, 1916–38; Medical Advisor and Head, Student Health Service, Tennessee A & I State College for 33 years.

Memberships and awards: Vice-President, National Medical Association; President, National Medical Association, 1934–35; low-rent housing project in Nashville named for him after his death.

Ref: National Medical Association, *Journal,* v. 36, July 1944,
             p. 130–131.
          Dictionary of American Medical Biography, p. 316.
          The History of the Negro in Medicine, p. 93–94. [p] p. 94.
          Who's Who of the Colored Race, 1915, p. 127.
          National Medical Association, *Journal,* v. 46, Jan. 1954.
             [p] cover.
          A Century of Black Surgeons, v. 1, p. 113–116. [p]

Hall, George Cleveland   (1864–1930, M)

Physician. Surgeon. Gynecologist. Born in Ypsilanti, MI, Feb. 22, 1864. B.A., Lincoln University, 1886; M.D., Bennett College of Medicine, Chicago, 1888. Helped organize and was Surgeon-in-Chief, Provident Hospital, Chicago, IL, 1890, with Daniel Hale Williams. Helped establish infirmaries throughout cities in the south. Organized first postgraduate course at Provident Hospital.

Memberships and awards: Founded Cook County Physicians Association; National Medical Association; Illinois State Medical Society; Cook County Surgical Society; Chicago Medical Society; Chicago Gynecological Society; Alpha Phi Alpha; Leading black Physician in Chicago, 1900–30; Board of Trustees, Lincoln University; Board of Trustees, Provident Hospital, Chicago.

Ref: *Encyclopedia of Black America*, p. 412.
Historical Afro-American Biographies, p. 87.
The History of the Negro in Medicine, p. 77–78. [p] p. 77.
Jet, Feb. 24, 1955, p. 10. [p]
Who's Who of the Colored Race, 1915, p. 128.
Who's Who in Colored America, 1928–29, p. 158.
Who's Who in Colored America, 1930–32, p. 187.
National Medical Association, *Journal*, v. 22, July–Sept. 1930, p. 170–171. obit
Dictionary of American Medical Biography, p. 316-317.
Crisis, Sept. 1915, p. 240–241. [p]
Crisis, Sept. 1930, p. 311. [p]
National Medical Association, *Journal*, v. 46, May 1954. [p]
A Century of Black Surgeons, p. 271–274.

Hall, James Lowell   (1892–1965, M)

Physician. Allergist. Born in Waxahachie, TX, Dec. 30, 1892. B.A., Prairie View College, 1911; B.S., University of Chicago, 1923; M.D., Rush Medical College, 1925. Director of Medical Research Laboratory, University of Chicago, 1932–40; Director of Clinics, Provident Hospital, Chicago, 1936–41; Department of Medicine, Howard University Medical School (chairman), 1941–44; Superintendent, Freedmen's Hospital, 1944–47; private practice, Chicago, 1947–65.

Memberships and awards: National Medical Association; Chicago Medical Society; Illinois State Medical Society; American Medical Association; President, Cook County Physicians Association; Alpha Phi Alpha.

Ref: *Howard University: The First Hundred Years*, p. 5.
Dictionary of American Medical Biography, p. 318.
National Cyclopedia of American Biography, v. 53, p. 137.
Lawlah, John W. James Lowell Hall, Sr., M.D., 1892–1965.
National Medical Association, *Journal*, v. 58, Jan. 1966, p. 82–83. [p] cover

Hall, Japheth, Jr.   (1926– ——, M)

Mathematician. Born Aug. 1, 1926. B.S. (mathematics), Alabama State College, 1952; M.S. (mathematics), University of Illinois, 1957; Ph.D. (topology, algebra and analysis), University of Alabama, 1970. Instructor, Alabama Public School System, 1952–57; Teacher, Chairman, Division of Mathematics and Science, Stillman College, 1960–70; Professor and Chairman, Mathematics Department, Stillman College, 1970–.

Memberships and awards: Educational Association; University Associates of Washington, DC, 1971; Program Association, Institute for Services to Education, 1972; Director, Secondary Science Training Program, Stillman College, summers, 1967–70; Associate Director, Alabama Mathematics Talent Search, 1968–71; American Mathe-

matical Society; Alabama Academy of Science; National Association of Mathematicians; Alabama Association of College Teachers of Mathematics.

Dissertation title: On the Theory of Structures in Sets.

Pub: A Condition for Equality of Cardinals of Minimal Generators Under Closure Operations. *Canadian Mathematic Bulletin*, v. 14, 1971.
The Independence of Certain Axioms of Structures in Sets. *Proceedings* American Mathematics Society 31, no. 2, 1972.
Independence in Geometry. *Canadian Mathematics Bulletin*, 1973.

Ref: *Black Mathematicians and Their Works*, p. 287. [p] p. 126.

Hall, John B., Sr.   (1876–1959, M)

Physician. Born in 1876. M.D. University of PA, 1901.

Memberships and awards: Advisory Council of Massachusetts Department of Public Health; Medical Examiner for Massachusetts State Insurance Department and Medical Inspector for Public Schools.

Ref: *Jet*, May 21, 1959, p. 53.

Hall, Lloyd Augustus   (1894–1971, M)

Chemist (food). Inventor. Born in Elgin, IL, June 20, 1894. Ph.C., Northwestern University, 1914; B.S., Northwestern, 1916; D.Sc., Virginia State College, 1944. Technical Director and Chief Chemist, Griffith's Laboratories, Chicago, 1925–46; held more than 100 patents in the United States, Great Britain, and Canada.

Memberships and awards: Board of Directors, American Institute of Chemists; Honor Scroll Award, American Institute of Chemists, 1956; first black to hold office in 32-year history of Food Chemists; member, NRC; New York Academy of Sciences; Sigma Xi; Honorary Secretary and Chairman of the Constitution and Bylaws Committee, Institute of Food Chemistry; American Chemical Society; Alpha Phi Alpha; American Public Health Association; AAAS; American Oil Chemists' Society; Illinois State Academy of Science; American Association of Cereal Chemists.

Ref: *American Men of Science*, 11th ed., p. 2050.
Black Pioneers of Science and Invention, p. 102–111. [p] p. 102.
Encyclopedia of Black America, p. 745, 412.
Historical Afro-American Biographies, p. 197–198.
Who's Who in Colored America, 1933–37, p. 226.
In Black and White, p. 396.
The Negro in Science, Taylor, p. 182.
Jet, May 26, 1955, p. 20. [p]
Jet, Dec. 24, 1959, p. 53.
Drew, Charles Richard. Negro Scholars in Scientific Research. *Journal of Negro History*, v. 35, 1950, p. 135–189.
Jet, Jan. 21, 1971, p. 27. obit

Jet, June 25, 1981, p. 16. [p]
Who's Who in Colored America, 1938-40, p. 225.
The National Register, 1952, p. 578.
Who's Who in Colored America, 1941-44, p. 223-224.
Blacks in Science: Astrophysicist to Zoologist, p. 27-28.
[p] after p. 48.

Hall, Raymond E.   (19??- ——, M)

Micropaleontologist. Geologist. B.S., St. Joseph's College; M.S. (geology), Brown University. Board member for Unified Research and Development Laboratories.

Ref: *Ebony,* Aug. 19, 1985, p. 7.

Hamblin, Adolf Putnam   (1896-19??, M)

Biologist. Born in Galesburg, IL, Jan. 11, 1896. B.S., Knox College, 1920; M.S., Ohio State, 1946. Assistant in Biology, Knox College, 1920-21; Head, Department of Biology, West Virginia State College, 1921-.

Memberships and awards: Sigma Xi; Beta Kappa Chi; National Association of Biology Teachers; West Virginia Academy of Science; American Teachers' Association; West Virginia Teachers' Association.

Ref: *The Negro in Science,* p. 178.

Hamlet, James Frank   (1900s, M)

Military (Army). Major General. Retired. Born in Alliance, OH. Commissioned a First Lieutenant, through Officers Candidate School, 1944. Parachutist and Aviator, spent three years in Vietnam; Commanding Officer, Eleventh Aviation Group, First Cavalry Division, Vietnam.

Memberships and awards: Distinguished Service Medal; Army Commendation Medal with three Oak Leaf Clusters; Combat Infantryman Badge.

Ref: *Black Americans in Defense of Our Nation,* p. 122. [p]
Ebony, May 1978, p. 42. [p]
The Negro Almanac, 4th ed., p. 893.

Hammond, Benjamin Franklin   (1934- ——, M)

Dentist. Microbiologist. Bacteriologist. Born in Austin, TX, Feb. 23, 1934. B.A., University of Kansas, 1954; D.D.S., Meharry Medical College, 1958; Ph.D. (microbiology), University of Pennsylvania, 1962. From Instructor to Chairman, Department of Microbiology, School of Dentistry, University of Pennsylvania, 1958-84; Associate Dean for Academic Affairs, 1984-; research in oral microbiology with emphasis on physical and molecular biology of oral lactic acid bacteria.

Memberships and awards: International Association for Dental Research, 1959; Lindback Award for Distinguished Teaching, University of Pennsylvania, 1969; Medaille D'Argent City of Paris, France, 1976; President, Lecture University of Pennsylvania, 1981; USPHS Career Development Awards, 1966; Hatton Award, International Association for Dental Research; American Society for Microbiology.

Dissertation title: Studies on Capsule Formation in Lactobacillus Casei.

Ref: *American Men and Women of Science,* 15th ed., p. 450.
Encyclopedia of Black America, p. 745.
Who's Who Among Black Americans, 1985, p. 348.
National Faculty Directory, 1988, p. 1526.

Hampton, Delon   (1933- ——, M)

Engineer (civil). Born in Jefferson, TX, Aug. 23, 1933. B.S. (civil engineering), University of Illinois, 1954; M.S., Purdue University, 1958; Ph.D., 1961. Instructor, Civil Engineering, Prairie View College, 1954-55; Assistant Professor, University of Kansas, 1961-64; Senior Research Engineer, Illinois Institute of Technology Research Institute, 1964-68; Professor of Civil Engineering, Howard University, 1968-85; President, Delon Hampton & Associates, 1973-.

Memberships and awards: American Society of Civil Engineers; Highway Research Board; National Academy of Sciences—National Research Council; American Society for Engineering Education; American Society of Testing and Materials; American Consulting Engineers Council; Sigma Xi; Washington Board of Trade; U.S. National Committee for Tunneling Technology; Transportation Research Board.

Dissertation title: Statistical Analysis of Soil Variability.

Pub: Numerous articles in technical journals.

Ref: *American Men and Women of Science,* 16th ed., p. 463.
Black Engineers in the United States, p. 86-87.
Who's Who in Engineering, 1985, p. 262.
Who's Who Among Black Americans, 1977, p. 375.
Ebony, June 1963, p. 157. [p]

Hansborough, Louis Armstead   (1908-19??, M)

Embryologist. Biologist. Born in Washington, DC, Jan. 23, 1908. B.S., Howard University, 1928; M.S., University of Chicago, 1931; Ph.D., Harvard University, 1938. Assistant Professor, 1938-46; Professor and Head of the Department, Biology, Fort Valley State College, 1946-47; Professor, Zoology, Howard University, 1947-69; Associate Provost, University of Connecticut, 1969-.

Memberships and awards: Special Research fellow, National Institutes of Health, 1953-54; Visiting Professor, Genetics, Connecticut, 1953-54; A.E.C. Research Grant, 1950-54; American Society of Zoology, American Federation of Science; AAAS; National Institute of Science; American Association of Biology Teachers; A.A.U.P.; New York Academy of Science; Sigma Xi; Kappa Mu.

Dissertation title: The Influence of Vitamins on the Development of the Chick.

Ref: *American Men and Women of Science,* 12th ed., p. 2475.
The Negro in Science, p. 178.
Holders of Doctorates Among American Negroes, p. 190–191.

Hansen, Austin   (1900s, M)

Photographer. Born in U.S. Virgin Islands. Taught Photography by Clair Taylor and his son. Took pictures of a hurricane in 1924 and sold them for $4.00. In 1928 he moved to New York. Took pictures in nightclubs and churches with his brother; worked into quite a business. In the Navy he was sent to California to learn combat/war photography with the rank of Photographer's Mate, 2nd Class. In his studio in Harlem he had pictures of most famous black persons. Photographer for *Amsterdam News, Peoples Voice, New York Age,* and *African Opinion.*

Ref: *Profiles in Black,* p. 20. [p] p. 21.

Hargrave, Charles William   (1929- ——, M)

Physicist. Mathematician. Born in Dandridge, TN, May 12, 1929. B.S., Johnson C. Smith University, 1949; M.A., Washington University, St. Louis, 1952. Navy Department Physicist, 1954–55; U.S. Atomic Energy Commission Scientific Analyst, 1955–62; Technical Information Specialist, NASA, 1962–75; Assistant Chief, Systems and Retrieval Division, 1975–. Captain, US Navy Reserve, retired.

Memberships and awards: Award of Merit, Johnson C. Smith University Alumni Association, 1979; Spaceship Earth, NASA, 1982; UNCF Alumni Award, 1983; American Chemical Society; AAAS; American Society for Information Science; AIAA.

Ref: *Who's Who Among Black Americans,* 1985, p. 353.
Who's Who in Government, 1977, p. 253.
Crisis, Aug./Sept. 1949, p. 240. [p] only

Hargrave, Frank Settle   (1874–1942, M)

Physician. Surgeon. Born in Lexington, N.C., Aug. 27, 1874. B.S., Shaw University, Raleigh, NC; M.D., Shaw University, 1901. Founder and Medical Director, Wilson Hospital and Tubercular Home, which later became Mercy Hospital, Wilson, N.C., 1913–23.

Memberships and awards: President, North Carolina Medical, Dental, and Pharmaceutical Association, 1912; Executive Committee, National Medical Association, 1913–14; President, National Medical Association, 1914–15; Chairman, Committee on Medical Education, National Medical Association, 1927; Honorary Master of Art, 1930; New Jersey Medical Society.

Ref: *Who's Who in Colored America,* 1941–44, p. 228.

Dictionary of American Medical Biography, p. 325.
Who's Who in Colored America, 1928–29, p. 162, [p] opp. p. 162.
Who's Who in Colored America, 1931–32, p. 190. [p] opp. p. 190.
Who's Who in Colored America, 1938–40, p. 230. [p] opp. 226.
National Medical Association, *Journal,* v. 6, Jan.–Mar. 1914. [p] p. 215.
National Medical Association, *Journal,* v. 34, July 1942, p. 174. obit
Dr. Frank S. Hargrave, An Assemblyman. National Medical Association, *Journal,* v. 21, Oct.–Dec. 1929, p. 165–166.

Harper, Marilyn E. Hill   (1938- ——, F)

Physician. Anesthesiologist. Born in Seneca, SC, Mar. 19, 1938. B.A., Tallodega College, 1958; M.D., Howard University, 1963.

Ref: *Who's Who of American Women,* 1974, p. 392.

Harper, Mary Starke   (1919- ——, F)

Nurse. Psychologist. Born in Fort Mitchell, AL, Sept. 6, 1919. Diploma R.N., Tuskegee Institute, 1941; B.S., University of Minnesota, 1950; M.S., 1952; Ph.D., St. Louis University, 1963. Credentials for four professions—clinical psychology, nursing, sociology, and secondary education. Assistant Chief, Center for Minority Group Mental Health Programs; Positions in Nursing (Supervisory, Administration), Veterans Administration for 30 years.

Memberships and awards: Meritorious Award, Tuskegee Institute, Administration on Alcohol, Drug Abuse and Mental Health and Veterans Administration; American Association on International Aging; National Council on Home Health; President, Hillcrest Children's Center.

Dissertation title: Changes in Concepts of Mental Health, Mental Illness, and Perceptions of Interpersonal Relationships as a Result of Patient, Family and Members of Family-Friend System Participation in Conjoint Family Therapy in a Hospital.

Pub: Several government publications on mental health.

Ref: *Who's Who Among Black Americans,* 1985, p. 354.
Who's Who in American Nursing, 1986–87, p. 210.
The Path We Tread, p. 120–121. [p] p. 121.

Harris, Edward Lee   (1902–1974, M)

Chemist. Born in Big Bend, LA, Sept. 28, 1902. B.S., University of Pittsburgh, 1926; Ph.D. (chemical engineering), 1935. Head, Department of Chemistry, Bishop College, 1927–30; Professor and Head of the Department, Wilberforce, 1937–; Chairman, Division of the National Science and Mathematics, 1939–; Chief Chemist, Rocket Propellant Section, Wright-Patterson Air Force Base,

1942–; rocket fuel research, Consultant, Wright Air Development Center, 1943; Air Force Major, 1951–53.

Memberships and awards: Chemical Society, Organic and Analytical Chemistry.

Dissertation title: Preparation of the Derivatives of 4-Phenylsalicylaldehyde.

Ref: *American Men of Science,* 11th ed., p. 2124.
Holders of Doctorates Among American Negroes, p. 149.
Ebony, May 1958, p. 20. [p]

Harris, Gary L.   (1954– ——, M)

Engineer. B.A., M.S., Ph.D. (engineering), Cornell University, 1980. Operates a low pressure/high pressure temperature silicon carbide reactor which allows scientists to grow silicon carbide; Department of Electrical Engineering, Howard University.

Dissertation title: An Experimental Study of Capless Annealing of Ion Implanted Gallium-Arsenide.

Ref: *Ebony,* Aug. 1985, p. 64.
National Faculty Directory, 1988, p. 1562.

Harris, Harry C.   (1897–19??, M)

Physician. Urologist. Born in Birmingham, AL, Aug. 10, 1897. B.S., Northwestern University, 1921; M.D., University of Illinois, 1926; Instructor, Department of Genito-Urinary Diseases, University of Illinois, 1926–27; first black physician to be appointed Coroner in Cook County, IL.

Memberships and awards: Fellowship, Rosenwald Foundation of Chicago to study Urology, Billings Hospital of the University of Chicago; Cook County Medical Association; Kappa Alpha Psi.

Ref: *Who's Who in Colored America,* 1938–40, p. 233.
Who's Who in Colored America, 1941–44, p. 231–232.

Harris, James Andrew   (1932– ——, M)

Chemist (nuclear). Born in Waco, TX, Mar. 26, 1932. B.S. (chemistry), Houston-Tillotson College, 1953; M.P.A., California State University, Haywood, CA, 1975. Worked in heavy isotope production, Lawrence Berkeley Laboratory; Head, Engineering and Technical Services Division, Lawrence Berkeley Laboratory, 1977–; worked with the team who discovered elements 104 and 105.

Memberships and awards: National Society of Black Chemists and Chemical Engineers; Nuclear Target Society; American Chemical Society; AEC Transplutonium Program; Alpha Phi Alpha; numerous certificates of merit; Honorary Ph.D. from Houston-Tillotson College, 1973; Scientific Merit Award from the Mayor of Richmond, CA; Certificate of Merit from the Black Dignity Science Association.

Ref:

Black Contributors to Science and Energy Technology, p. 18–19.
In Black and White, p. 410.
Who's Who Among Black Americans, 1980–81, p. 342.
Who's Who Among Black Americans, 1985, p. 358.
Black Collegian, v. 5, Sept./Oct. 1974, p. 16. [p]
Ebony, May 1973, p. 144–148, 150. [p]
Blacks in Science: Astrophysicist to Zoologist, p. 46–47. [p] after p. 48.

Harris, Jean Louise   (1931– ——, F)

Physician. Internist. Born in Richmond, VA, Nov. 24, 1931. B.S., Virginia Union University, 1951; M.D., Medical College of Virginia, 1955. First black graduate, Medical College of Virginia, Internal Medicine. Secretary, Human Resources, Commonwealth of Virginia, 1977–; Vice-President, Control Data Corp., 1982–; Director, Bureau of Resources Development, DC Department of Health, 1967–69; Executive Director, National Medical Association Foundation, 1969–73; Professor of Family Practice, Medical College of Virginia, 1973–78; Secretary of Human Resources, Commonwealth of Virginia.

Memberships and awards: National Academy of Sciences; Institute of Medicine; Recombinant DNA Commission, NIH; Board of Trustees, University of Richmond; Distinguished Service, National Governors Association, 1981; Outstanding Woman in Government, YWCA, 1980; named to list of 100 Top Black Business and Professional Women, *Dollars & Sense Magazine,* 1986; Delta Sigma Theta; American Public Health Association.

Ref: *American Men and Women of Science,* 16th ed., p. 519.
In Black and White, p. 410.
Who's Who Among Black Americans, 1980–81, p. 343.
Who's Who Among Black Americans, 1985, p. 359.
Who's Who of American Women, 1987–88, p. 339.
Ebony, Nov. 1981, p. 108, 110. [p]
Ebony, July 1955. [p] cover

Harris, Mary Styles   (1949– ——, F)

Biologist. Geneticist. Born in Nashville, TN, June 26, 1949. B.A. (biology), Lincoln University, 1971; Ph.D. (genetics), Cornell University, 1975; Rutgers Medical School Post-Doctoral Study, 1977; Executive Director, Sickle Cell Foundation of Georgia, 1977–79; Assistant Professor, Morehouse College School of Medicine, 1978–; Scientist in Residence, WGTV Channel 8, University of Georgia, 1979–80; Assistant Professor of Biology, Atlanta University, 1980–81; Director of Genetic Services, Georgia Department of Human Resources.

Memberships and awards: Public Health Association; American Society of Human Genetics, 1977; Georgia Board of Regents, University of Georgia, 1979–80; Congressional Black Caucus Health Brain Trust; Governor's Advisory Council on Alcohol and Drug Abuse; General Research Support Grant, Rutgers Medical School, 1975–77; honored at White House reception as one of *Glamour Magazine*'s Outstanding Young Women for

1980; she wrote, produced and narrated an educational science series for Georgia TV through a grant from the National Science Foundation.

Dissertation title: An Investigation of Several Aspects of the Killer Character in Saccharomyces Cerevisiae.

Ref: *American Men and Women of Science*, 16th ed., p. 521.
Who's Who Among Black Americans, 1985, p. 360.
Jet, Feb. 21, 1980, p. 27. [p]

Harris, Robert McCants   (1891–19??, M)

Chemist. Pharmacist. Born in Sparta, GA, June 4, 1891. Tuskegee Institute, Al, 1907–11; Phar. C., Leonard College of Pharmacy, Shaw University, Raleigh, NC, 1914. Druggist and Pharmaceutical Chemist, Waycross, GA, 1916–; Founder and President, The Union Mercantile Corp.

Ref: *Who's Who in Colored America*, 1930–32, p. 194.
Who's Who in Colored America, 1928–29, p. 429.
Who's Who in Colored America, 1941–44, p. 232. [p] p. 233.

Harris, Wesley Leroy, Sr.   (1941– ——, M)

Engineer (aerospace). Born in Richmond, VA, Oct. 29, 1941. B.S. (aerospace engineering), University of Virginia, 1964; M.A., Princeton University, 1966; Ph.D., 1968. NASA Trainee Aerospace Engineer, Princeton University, 1964–66; Assistant Professor, Aerospace Engineering, University of Virginia, 1968–70; Associate Professor of Physics, Southern University, 1970–71; Assistant Professor of Aerospace Engineering, University of Virginia, 1971–72; Associate Professor of Aeronautics and Astronautics and Ocean Engineering, 1972–81; Professor of Aeronautics and Astronautics, Massachusetts Institute of Technology, 1981–; Consulting in area of isotope separation in gas mixtures, computational fluid dynamics; current research in areas of external transonic flow and wind turbine aerodynamics.

Memberships and awards: Tau Beta Pi; Sigma Xi; American Institute of Aeronautics and Astronautics; American Physical Society; Society of Industrial and Applied Mathematics.

Dissertation title: An Asymptotic Theory of Shock Structure in Binary Gas Mixtures of Disparate Masses.

Pub: Over 80 technical publications.

Ref: *American Men and Women of Science*, 16th ed., p. 525.
Black Engineers in the United States, p. 89–90.
Who's Who Among Black Americans, 1985, p. 362.
Who's Who in Engineering, 1985, p. 270.

Harris, William Henry   (1867–1934, M)

Physician. Born in Augusta, GA, June 15, 1867. B.A., Clark University; M.D., Meharry Medical College, 1893; Postgraduate course in medicine, New York School of Clinical Medicine and Massachusetts General Hospital, 1906. Private practice, 1893–1934.

Memberships and awards: Co-founded Georgia State Medical Association, 1893; founded in Athens, GA, a Black Burial and Fraternal Insurance Society; Board of Trustees, Morris Brown College.

Ref: Robinson, Henry S. William Henry Harris, M.D., 1867–1934. National Medical Association, *Journal*, v. 62, Nov. 1970, p. 474–477. [p]

Harrison-Ross, Phyllis Ann   (1936– ——, F)

Physician. Pediatrician. Psychiatrist. Born in Detroit, MI, Aug. 14, 1936. B.S., Albion College, 1956; M.D., Wayne State University College of Medicine, 1959. Instructor of Pediatrics, Cornell Medical School, 1961–62; Instructor in Pediatrics and Psychology, Albert Einstein College of Medicine, 1966–68; Assistant Professor, 1968–72; member of President's National Advisory Council on Drug Abuse Prevention; Professor of Clinical Psychiatry, New York Medical College, 1972–.

Memberships and awards: Fellowship in Adult Psychiatry, Albert Einstein College of Medicine, 1964–66; Medical Review Board, New York State Commission of Corrections, 1976; New York State Alcoholism Advisory Committee, 1977; Minority Advisory Committee to the Secretary of HEW; Chairman, Advisory Council of Minority Affairs, 1979; Achievement Award, Greater New York Links, 1973; Distinguished Alumnus, Albion College, 1976; Leadership in Medicine Award, Susan Smith McKinney Stewart Medical Society, 1978; Award of Merit, Public Health Association of New York City, 1980; President, Black Psychiatrists of America, 1976–78.

Pub: The Black Child—A Parents' Guide. New York, P. H. Wyden, 1973. 360 p.

Ref: *Wise Women*, Rayner, p. 90–102. [p] p. 90.
Women Scientists from Antiquity to the Present: An Index.
Who's Who Among Black Americans, 1985, p. 728 (under Ross)
Who's Who of American Women, 1974, p. 396.
National Faculty Directory, 1988, p. 1570.

Harvey, Burwell Towns, Jr.   (1892–1971, M)

Chemist. Born in Griffin, GA, July 18, 1892. B.S., Colgate University, 1916; M.A., Columbia University, 1927. Professor of Chemistry, Morehouse College, 1916–57; Chairman of the Department, 1950–57; Editor, *Morehouse Journal of Science*, 1929–57.

Memberships and awards: Electrochemical Society; New York Academy of Chemical Education in Negro Schools.

Ref: *American Men of Science*, 10th ed., p. 1670.
Jet, Nov. 11, 1971, p. 18.

Harwell, William   (1953- —— , M)

Engineer (mechanical). Born in 1953. Designs tools for NASA in Crew Systems Division at the Johnson Space Center in Houston, TX. Designs special power packs worn by the astronauts during space walks.

Ref: *Ebony,* Aug. 1985, p. 63.

Haskell, Roscoe Chester   (1881-1972, M)

Physician. Born in St. Louis, MO, Sept. 12, 1881. Genner Medical College, Chicago, 1905-06; Howard University, 1908-10; M.D., Meharry Medical College, 1911.

Ref: *Jet,* Oct. 26, 1972, p. 42.

Haskins, Alma Mary   (1894-19??, F)

Podiatrist. Born in Newport News, VA, July 7, 1894. New York University, 1917; First Institute of Podiatry, NY, M. Chiropody, 1921. Established Podiatry in Okolona Industrial School, MS, 1921-22.

Memberships and awards: President, New York County Pedic Society, 1927-; Founder, Pi Delta Mu Sorority; one of two women practicing podiatry in the 1920s in New York; National Association of Chiropodists.

Ref: *Who's Who in Colored America,* 1933-37, p. 239.
      Who's Who in Colored America, 1928-29, p. 169. [p] opp. p. 170.
      Who's Who in Colored America, 1930-32, p. 197. [p] opp. p. 194.
      Who's Who in Colored America, 1941-44, p. 236.

Haskins, Ethelbert William   (1921- —— , M)

Mathematician. Born in Freeman, WV, Oct. 12, 1921. B.A., Bluefield State College, 1949; M.S., University of Pittsburgh, 1950; Benedict College, 1950-53. Assistant Professor, Prairie View A & M College, 1953-.

Memberships and awards: Treasurer, Pittsburgh Rocket Society, 1949-50; Beta Kappa Chi; Texas Academy of Sciences.

Ref: *The Negro in Science,* p. 188.

Hastings, Alicia Elizabeth   (1934- —— , F)

Physician. Psychiatrist. Physical Medicine and Rehabilitation. Born in Tuskegee, AL, 1934. B.S.; M.D., Howard University, 1959. Intern, General Rose Memorial Hospital, Denver, 1959-60; Physical Medicine and Rehabilitation, University of Colorado, 1960-63; Professor, Howard University; Department of Physical Medicine and Rehabilitation, Howard University Health Sciences Center.

Memberships and awards: American Academy of Physical Medicine and Rehabilitation, American Congress of Rehabilitation Medicine; American Medical Women's Association.

Ref: *ABMS Compendium of Certified Medical Specialists,* v. 5, p. 33.

Hatcher, Warren   (1900s, M)

Nurse. B.S., Mills School for Men at Bellevue Hospital in New York; Ph.D. (public administration), New York University, 1967. He was the first black male nurse to earn a Ph.D.

Dissertation title: Inservice Education: A Means for Improving Administration and Patient Care in a Nursing Home.

Ref: *The Path We Tread,* p. 241.

Haughton, James G.   (1925- —— , M)

Physician. Public Health Administrator. Born in Panama City, Mar. 30, 1925. B.A., Pacific Union College, 1947; M.D., Loma Linda University, 1950; Postgraduate, New York University Medical School, 1959-60; M.P.H., Columbia University, 1962. Child Health Clinician, New York City Health Department, 1958-60; Assistant Director and Assistant Executive Director, Demonstration Project and other positions, 1962-70; Director, Cook County Health and Hospital Governing Commission, 1970-79; Executive Vice-President, Charles R. Drew Postgraduate Medical School, 1980-82; Director, Public Health, City of Houston, 1983-.

Memberships and awards: American Public Health Association; Advisory Council on Aging; American Medical Association; Hospice, Inc.; Illinois Hospital Association; Institute of Medicine; National Academy of Science; Honorary D.Sci., Chicago Medical School, 1972; many other citations and awards.

Ref: *Who's Who Among Black Americans,* 1985, p. 367.
      Ebony, Mar. 1978, p. 25. [p]
      American Men and Women of Science, 16th ed., p. 562.

Hawkins, Charles Clinton   (1900s, M)

Physical Education. B.S., Morehouse College; M.P.E., Springfield College; Ph.D., New York University, 1937. Research Associate, Safety Education Division, New York University.

Dissertation title: The Effects of Conditioning and Training Upon the Differential White Cell Count.

Pub: *Fire Prevention Education.*

Ref: *Holders of Doctorates Among American Negroes,* p. 98.

Hawkins, Walter Lincoln   (1911- —— , M)

Chemist (polymer). Chemist (organic). Engineer. Born in Washington, DC, Mar. 21, 1911. Ch.E., Rensselaer Polytechnic Institute, 1932; M.S., Howard University, 1934; Ph.D. (cellulose chemistry), McGill University, 1939. Chemical Research Laboratories, McGill University Lecturer, 1938-41; Bell Laboratories Technical Staff,

1942–63; Supervisor of Applied Research, 1963–72; Department Head, 1972–74; Assistant Director of the Chemical Research Laboratory, 1974–76; Research Director, Plastics Institute of America, 1976–84; Bell Laboratories, 1974–; research in the degradation and stabilization of high polymers and research in plastics for telecommunications; Research Staff of Bell Telephone.

Memberships and awards: L.L.D. (honorary), 1975 and 1981; Board of Trustees, Montclair State, 1963–74; Board of Directors NACME, 1980–; Sigma Xi; Honorary Scroll, American Institute of Chemistry, 1970; Percy Julian Award, 1977; International Award, Society of Plastics Engineering, Inc., 1984; National Academy of Engineering; fellow, New York Academy of Sciences.

Dissertation title: The Structure of Lignin Obtained from Hard Woods.

Ref: *American Men and Women of Science*, 15th ed., p. 369.
Who's Who Among Black Americans, 1985, p. 369.
Holders of Doctorates Among American Negroes, p. 149.
Who's Who in Engineering, 1985, p. 275.

Hawthorne, Edward William   (1921–1986, M)

Physiologist. Physician. Born in Port Gibson, MS, Nov. 30, 1921. B.S., Howard University, 1941; M.D., 1946; M.S., University of Illinois, 1949; Ph.D. (physiology), 1951. Laboratory Assistant, Howard University, 1942–44; Intern, Freedmen's Hospital, 1946–47; Special Consultant, National Institutes of Health, 1954–57; Assistant Resident in Internal Medicine; Dean, Graduate School, Howard University, 1974; research in cardiovascular-renal physiology.

Memberships and awards: AAAS; Vice-President at Large, American Heart Association, 1970; American Physiological Society; National Academy of Science; Washington Heart Association; Society for Experimental Biology and Medicine; New York Academy of Sciences; Alpha Omega Alpha; Award of Merit, American Heart Association, 1969; Gifted Teacher Award, College of Cardiology, 1972; Helen B. Taussig Award, 1975.

Dissertation title: Effects of Preliminary Renal Ischemia on Experimental Renal Hypertension.

Ref: *American Men and Women of Science*, 14th ed., p. 2074.
In Black and White, p. 419.
Who's Who Among Black Americans, 1980–81, p. 352.
Who's Who Among Black Americans, 1985, p. 369.
Ebony, Feb. 1966, p. 73–76, 78, 80. [p]
Ebony, Aug. 1972, p. 124. [p]

Haynes, Moses Alfred   (1921–——, M)

Physician. Born in Guyana, Nov. 11, 1921. U.S. Citizen, 1955. B.S., Columbia University, 1951; M.D., State University of New York, 1954; M.P.H., Harvard University, 1963. Physician, U.S. Public Health Service Indian Hospital, Cheyenne Agy, SD, 1955–59; Assistant Professor,

Community Medicine, University of Vermont, 1959–64; Associate Professor, School of Public Health, Johns Hopkins, 1966–69; Professor, Preventive and Social Medicine and Public Health, UCLA, 1969–77; Associate Dean, Drew Postgraduate Medical School, Los Angeles, 1969–77; Chairman, Department of Community Medicine, 1969–74; Acting Dean, 1975–76; Dean, 1979–.

Memberships and awards: Cancer Review Committee, National Cancer Institute; President's Commission on Health Education, 1972; Executive Director, National Medical Association Foundation, 1968–69; Member, Advisory Committee, National Center for Health Statistics, 1974–76; fellow, American College of Preventive Medicine, President, 1983–85; AAAS; Alpha Omega Alpha; Association of Teachers of Preventive Medicine.

Ref: *Who's Who in America*, 1986–87, p. 1229.
Living Legends in Black, p. 25. [p]

Hazzard, James William, Jr.   (1905–1944, M)

Zoologist. Born in Gainesville, FL, Sept. 18, 1905. B.S., Clark College, 1929; M.S., University of Iowa, 1936; Ph.D., Cornell University, 1940. Instructor in Biology, New Orleans, 1929–32; Professor and Head of the Department of Zoology, Arkansas State College, 1932–40; Southern University and Agricultural and Mechanical College, 1940–44.

Memberships and awards: American Geographical Society.

Dissertation title: A Comparative and Functional Study of the Osteology and Myology of the Limbs in Lepus Californicus, Texianus, Sylvilagus Floridanus, Alacer, Sylvilagus Palustris Palustris, and Oryctolagus Cuniculus (Lepus).

Ref: *American Men of Science*, 7th ed., p. 774. 8th ed., obit.
Holders of Doctorates Among American Negroes, p. 191.
Crisis, Aug. 1940, p. 233. [p] only

Hedrick, Robert Milton   (1898–19??, M)

Physician. Surgeon. Born in Port Gibson, MS, July 29, 1898. B.S., Alcorn A & M College, MS, 1912; M.D., Meharry Medical College, 1918; Postgraduate, Chicago, IL, 1912–14. One of the first black physicians to receive Reciprocity License from Mississippi, he began practice in Gary, IN; Chief Surgeon, St. Mary's Mercy Hospital for two years after serving four years at McMitchell's Sanitarium. When St. Mary's Hospital closed its staff to black physicians, he opened a small hospital, Hedrick Hospital, which remained open for five years; opened a larger hospital, St. John's in 1929; supervised the annual clinics at Tuskegee Institute in connection with the John A. Andrew Memorial Hospital.

Memberships and awards: Indiana State Medical Society, President; President, John A. Andrew Clinical Society; National Medical Association; American Medical

Association; Lake County Medical Society; Kappa Alpha Psi.

Ref: *Who's Who in Colored America*, 1941–44, p. 245. [p] p. 247.

Heins, Henry L., Jr.   (1931– ——, M)

Physician. Pediatrician. Cardiologist. Born in New Orleans, LA, Feb. 8, 1931. B.S., University of Pittsburgh, 1951; M.D., 1955. Clinical Staff in Pediatrics, Cedars-Sinai Medical Center, 1961; Member, Cardiac Team, UCLA Medical Center, 1961; Assistant Attending Physician, Cardiology Division, Children's Hospital, 1961–; Associate Clinical Professor in Pediatrics.

Memberships and awards: American Medical Association; National Medical Association; Los Angeles Heart Association; Charles Drew Medical Society; California Medical Association; California Society for Pediatric Cardiology; fellow, American Academy of Pediatrics; fellow, American College of Cardiology; fellow, American College of Chest Physicians; Scientific Achievement Award, 1976.

Ref: *Jet*, Dec. 12, 1961, p. 15.
   Who's Who Among Black Americans, 1985, p. 374.

Henderson, Henry Fairfax, Jr.   (1928– ——, M)

Engineer. Born in Paterson, NJ, Mar. 10, 1928. State University of New York, Alfred A. Paterson Seton Hall, and New York University, certified 1950. Engineer, 1950–67; President, H. F. Henderson Industries, 1967–.

Membership and awards: Board of Trustees, Bloomfield College, Caldwell College, Rutgers, and Stevens Institute of Technology; Outstanding Business Achievement Award; National Association of Negro Business and Professional Women's Clubs, Inc., awards; Company of the Year, Black Enterprise, 1984.

Ref: *Who's Who Among Black Americans*, 1985, p. 376.
   Ebony, Feb. 1977, p. 72–74, 76–78. [p]

Henderson, James Henry Meriwether   (1917– ——, M)

Plant physiologist. Botanist. Born in Falls Church, VA, Aug. 10, 1917. B.S., Howard University, 1939; M.Ph., University of Wisconsin, 1940; Ph.D. (plant physiology), 1943. Chemist, Badger Ordnance Works, 1942–43; Research Assistant, NDRC, UCTL, University of Chicago, 1943–45; Assistant Professor and Research Associate, Plant Physiology, Carver Foundation, Tuskegee Institute, 1945–48; Director, Research Foundation and Chairman of Natural Science Division, Carver Research Foundation, Tuskegee Institute, 1968–75; Chairman, Division of Natural Science, Tuskegee Institute, 1975–; research in tissue culture, physiology of normal and abnormal plant tissues.

Memberships and awards: AAAS; Botanical Society of America; American Society of Plant Physiologists; National Institute of Science; New York Academy of Sciences; Sigma Xi; Phi Sigma; Gamma Alpha; Alumni Award, Howard University, 1964, 1975; Tissue Culture Association; Eminent Faculty Award, Tuskegee Institute, 1965; Faculty Award, 1976, 1980.

Dissertation title: The Effect of Respiratory Intermediates and Inhibitors on the Growth and Respiration of Tomato Roots.

Ref: *American Men and Women of Science*, 14th ed., p. 2120–2121.
   The Negro in Science, p. 178.
   Holders of Doctorates Among American Negroes, p. 191.
   Who's Who Among Black Americans, 1985, p. 376.

Henry, E. Pentoka   (1899–19??, M)

Physician. Neuro-Psychiatrist. Born in Taft, OK, Feb. 17, 1899. B.S., University of West Tennessee, 1917; M.D., University of West Tennessee, 1921. Woodmen Union Hospital, Hot Springs, AR, 1927–28; Staff Surgeon, Hubbard Clinic, Tulsa, OK, 1929–32; Staff Surgeon, Maurice Willow Hospital, Tulsa, OK, 1923–25; Medical Superintendent, State Hospital for Negro Insane, Taft, OK, 1937–.

Memberships and awards: Lunacy Board, State of Oklahoma, 1936–; Vice-Chairman, Commission on Neurology, National Medical Association; Chairman, Psychiatric Section, Oklahoma Medical and Dental Association; Muskogee County Medical Society; National Medical Association; American Psychiatric Association.

Pub: High Lights on Mental Deficiency, State Hospital for Negro Insane, 1939.

Ref: *Who's Who in Colored America*, 1941–44, p. 246. [p] p. 247.

Henry, Robert William   (1883–19??, M)

Physician. Born in Natchez, MS, July 26, 1883. Jackson College, 1900–03; Shaw University, 1903–07; Long Island College Hospital, 1908. Chief, X-Ray Department, Frederick Douglas Hospital; Chief, Dermatological Department, Frederick Douglas Hospital.

Memberships and awards: American Medical Association; National Medical Association; Philadelphia County Medical Society; Philadelphia Academy of Medicine and Allied Science; Clinical Pathological Society; Pennsylvania State Medical, Dental and Pharmaceutical Association; Alpha Phi Alpha.

Ref: *Who's Who in Colored America*, 1933–37, p. 248.
   Who's Who in Colored America, 1938–40, p. 248.
   Who's Who in Colored America, 1941–44, p. 249.

Henry, Walter Lester, Jr. (1915– ——, M)

Physician. Endocrinologist. Internist. Born in Philadelphia, PA, Nov. 19, 1915. B.A., Temple University, 1936; M.D., Howard University Medical School, 1941 (first in his class). Assistant and Associate Professor, Howard University, 1953–63; Chairman, Department of Medicine, 1962–73; John B. Johnson Professor of Medicine, Howard University, 1971–; research in the etiology of diabetes mellitus; research in the mechanism of the action of insulin.

Memberships and awards: American Medical Association; National Medical Association; Endocrine Society; Association of American Physicians; Certified in Endocrinology and Metabolism of the American Board of Internal Medicine; Regent, American College of Physicians (first and only black regent), 1974–; Trustee, Howard University, 1971–75; American College of Physicians; American Federation for Clinical Research.

Ref: *ABMS Compendium of Certified Medical Specialists*, v. 2, p. 721.
Who's Who Among Black Americans, 1985, p. 380.
Best Doctors in the U.S.A., p. 107. (Endocrinologist)
Who's Who in America, 1986–87, p. 1261.
American Men and Women of Science, 16th ed., p. 648.
National Medical Association, *Journal*, v. 54, July 1962, p. 494–495. [p]
Black Enterprise, Oct. 1988, p. 60. [p]

Henry, Warren Elliott (1909– ——, M)

Physicist. Chemist (physical). Born in Evergreen, AL, Feb. 18, 1909. B.S., Tuskegee Institute, 1931; M.S., Atlanta University, 1937; Ph.D. (physical chemistry), University of Chicago, 1941; MIT, 1941–46. Principal, Escambia County Training School, 1931–34; Instructor in Physics, Spelman College and Morehouse College, 1934–36; Instructor, Chemistry, Tuskegee Institute, 1936–38; Lecture Assistant, Chemistry, Chicago, 1939–41; Instructor, Chemistry, Physics, and Radio, Tuskegee Institute, 1941–43; Instructor, Chemistry and Physics, Spelman College, 1943–47; Staff Member, Radiation Laboratory, MIT, 1943–46; Research Associate, Institute for the Study of Metals, Chicago, 1946–47; Acting Head, Department of Physics, Morehouse College and Clark College, 1947–48; Physicist, Naval Research Laboratory, Washington, DC, 1948–.

Memberships and awards: AAAS; American Physical Society; American Chemical Society; Institute of Radio Engineers; Washington Philosophical Society; Lecture Service Committee, Association of Cambridge (MA) Scientists, 1945–46; Secretary, Naval Research Laboratory Branch, Scientific Research Society of America, 1952–54; Sigma Xi; American Association of Physics Teachers; Federation of American Scientists; Presidential Associate, Tuskegee Institute; Carver Award.

Dissertation title: I. Resistance Thermometry. II. An Experimental Investigation of the Possibility of Using Alternating Current Technique in the Measurement of Small Temperature Differences.

Ref: *American Men of Science*, 10th ed., p. 1740.
The Negro in Science, p. 190.
Holders of Doctorates Among American Negroes, p. 149–150.
Negro Year Book, 1947, p. 16.
Who's Who Among Black Americans, 1985, p. 381.
Ebony, May 1958, p. 19.

Henson, Matthew Alexander (1867–1955, M)

Explorer. Born in Charles County, MD, Aug. 6, 1867. Co-discoverer of the North Pole with Admiral Peary, Apr. 6, 1909. Article in *Liberty*, a weekly white magazine stated that Peary's assistant, a Negro, was the first to reach the North Pole, 45 minutes ahead of Peary.

Memberships and awards: Honorary Master of Science conferred by Morgan College, 1924; Congressional Medal; Life membership, Explorers' Club.

Pub: *Negro Explorer at the North Pole.* New York, Fred A. Stokes & Co., 1912. 200 p.

Ref: *Dictionary of American Negro Biography*, p. 308.
Dolau, Edward. *Matthew Henson, Black Explorer.*
Great Negroes Past & Present, p. 55.
Who's Who in Colored America, 1927, p. 91.
Who's Who in Colored America, 1941–44, p. 249. [p] p. 251.
Jet, Mar. 24, 1955, p. 49.
Jet, Aug. 13, 1959, p. 9.
Ebony, Sept. 1985, p. 114.
Who's Who in Colored America, 1933–37, p. 251. [p] p. 249.
Who's Who in Colored America, 1938–39, p. 248. [p] p. 249.
Negro History Bulletin, v. 25, May 1962, p. 195–196.
Ebony, Jan. 1987, p. 51, 52, 56, 59. [p]
Miller, Floyd H. *Ahdoolo: The Biography of Matthew Henson*, 1963.
Ebony, Mar. 1967, p. 133. [p]
Ebony, Nov. 1976, p. 38, 42. [p]
Rogers, J. A. The Negro Explorer. *Crisis*, Jan. 1940, p. 7–9. [p]
World's Great Men of Color, v. 2, p. 313, 490–498.
National Geographic Magazine, Sept. 1988, Entire Section on Peary & Henson.

Hernandez, Marion Pettiford (1900–19??, F)

Nurse. Born in New York, NY, Aug. 6, 1900. R.N., Lincoln School for Nurses, 1920; State Diploma, 1920; Public Health Nursing, Teachers College, Columbia University, 1920–21; Certificate in Public Health, Hospital Social Service Bureau; New School of Social Research, 1927–28; observed preschool clinic and nursery school, Brussels, Belgium, July 1928; Personality Adjustment,

New York University, 1930. Supervisor of Nurses, Henry Street Visiting Nurse Service, 1927-.

Memberships and awards: American Red Cross Nurse Association; American Nurses Association; Gamma Delta Sigma Sorority; Welfare Council to study conditions among black children, the result of which was a Rockefeller Foundation grant to finance the Utopia Children's House and the Columbus Hill Center.

Ref: *Who's Who in Colored America*, 1941-44, p. 249-250.
Who's Who in Colored America, 1930-32, p. 208.
Who's Who in Colored America, 1938-40, p. 251.
Pathfinders, p. 109-111. [p] opp. p. 192.

Hewitt, Gloria Conyers   (1935- ——, F)

Mathematician. Born in Sumter, SC, Oct. 26, 1935. B.A. (mathematics), Fisk University, 1956; M.S. (mathematics), University of Washington, 1960; Ph.D. (mathematics), University of Washington, 1962. Third black woman to be granted Ph.D. in mathematics, 1962. Teaching Assistant, University of Washington, 1959-61; Pre-doctoral Associate, University of Washington, 1961; Assistant Professor, University of Montana, 1961-65; on leave, University of Montana, 1956-66; Associate Professor, Professor, University of Montana, 1966; Director, Office of Education, Summer Institute, University of Montana, 1973-.

Memberships and awards: National Science Foundation post-doctoral Science Faculty Fellowship, University of Oregon, 1966; American Mathematical Society; AAAS; Mathematical Association of America (Committee on Institutes and Visiting Lecturer); Committee on Regional Developments and Centers of Research, Division of Mathematical Sciences, National Academy of Sciences; National Research Council, 1968-71; National Academy of Sciences Advisory Committee to identify scientists and engineers from minority groups for service on its various panels, boards, and committees, 1971-72.

Dissertation title: Direct and Inverse Limits of Abstract Algebras.

Pub: The Existence of Free Unions in Classes of Abstract Algebras. American Mathematical Society, *Proceedings*, v. 14, 1963, p. 417-422.
Limits in Certain Classes of Abstract Algebras. *Pacific Journal of Mathematics*, v. 22, no. 1, 1967.

Ref: *Black Mathematicians and Their Works*, p 287. [p] p. 287.
Kenschaft, Patricia C. Black Women in Mathematics in the United States. *American Mathematical Monthly*, v. 88, Oct. 1981, p. 596.
National Faculty Directory, 1988, p. 1655.

Hicks, William J.   (1948- ——, M)

Physician. Hematologist. Born in Columbus, OH, 1948. B.S. (chemistry), Morehouse College, 1970; M.D., Univer-

sity of Pittsburgh, 1974. Researcher, Grant Medical Center and St. Anthony's Hospital, Columbus, OH.

Memberships and awards: National Medical Association.

Ref: *Black Enterprise*, Oct. 1988, p. 94.
ABMS Compendium of Certified Medical Specialists, v. 2, p. 731.

Higginbotham, Peyton Randolph   (1902- ——, M)

Physician. Born in Lynchburg, VA, Aug. 21, 1902. B.S., Howard University, 1923; M.D., Howard University Medical School, 1926. College Physician for Women, Bluefield State College, 1934-; Public Health Clinician, Mercer County, 1937-; first black man appointed to West Virginia State Board of Health.

Memberships and awards: Kappa Pi Medical Scholarship Society; Alpha Phi Alpha; President, West Virginia State Medical Society, 1930; State Vice-President, National Medical Association, 1945; Sigma Pi Phi; Plaque for Fifty Years of Continuous Service.

Ref: *The National Register*, 1952, p. 580.
Who's Who Among Black Americans, 1985, p. 385.

Higgins, William Harvey   (1872-1938, M)

Physician. Born in Marion, NC, Dec. 14, 1872. B.A., Livingstone College, 1897; M.D., Shaw University Medical Department, 1902; Long Island Medical College, NY, 1903.

Memberships and awards: House of Delegates of Rhode Island Medical Society; Vice-President, National Medical Association, served 12 years on Providence City Committee; American Medical Association; Alpha Phi Alpha; Trustee, Livingstone College, Salisbury, NC; President, National Medical Association, 1930-31; Providence Medical Association.

Ref: *Who's Who of the Colored Race*, 1915, p. 136.
Who's Who in Colored America, 1927, p. 92.
Who's Who in Colored America, 1930-32, p. 211.
Who's Who in Colored America, 1933-37, p. 252.
Who's Who in Colored America, 1938-40, p. 252.
National Medical Association, *Journal*, v. 21, Oct.-Dec. 1929. [p] opp. p. 204.
National Medical Association, *Journal*, v. 22, Oct.-Dec. 1930, p. 204-205.
Who's Who in Colored America, 1941-44, p. 250, 253.

Higgs, Roland Wellington   (1927- ——, M)

Physicist. Born in Philadelphia, PA, Apr. 27, 1927. B.E.E., Villanova, 1947; M.S., Catholic University of America, 1952; Ph.D. (physics), 1959. Instructor in Electrical Engineering, Howard University, 1947-52; Assistant Professor, 1952-55, 1957-59; Associate Professor, 1959-60; Nuclear Physicist, Radiation Division, U.S. Naval Research Laboratory, 1955-57; Research Physicist,

Acoustics Section, ITT Research Institute, 1960–63; Research Specialist, Space Physics Group, Space and Information System Division, North American Aviation, Inc., 1963–64; Senior Research Scientist, Corporate Research Center, Honeywell, Inc., 1964–67; Senior Principal Research Scientist, 1967–.

Memberships and awards: American Physical Society; Acoustical Society of America.

Dissertation title: Measurement of the Ultrasonic Absorption and Velocity in Molten Salts.

Ref: *American Men and Women of Science,* 12th ed., p. 2698. *Ebony,* May 1969, p. 6. [p]

High, Edward Garfield   (1919– ——, M)

Biochemist. Nutritionist. Born in Indianapolis, IN, Jan. 4, 1919. B.A., Indiana University, 1940; M.A., 1941; Ph.D. (chemistry), 1950. Chemistry Teacher, North Carolina College, Durham and Chemistry Professor, ESMWT Program, 1941–44; Chemistry, Prairie View A & M College, 1946–47; Professor, Chemistry and Director of Chemistry Research, 1949–53; Associate Professor, Biochemistry, Meharry Medical College, 1953–59; Acting Head of the Department, 1959–67; Professor of Biochemistry, Meharry Medical College, 1959–; Chairman of the Department, 1967–; Director, Laboratory of Biochemical Research, Prairie View A & M College.

Memberships and awards: Research fellow, Columbia University, 1944–46; National Institutes of Health Research fellow, Indiana, 1948–49; Fulbright Lecturer, University of Tehran, 1965–66; National Academy of Sciences—National Research Council, 1968–; Executive Council, Tennessee Nutrition Council; American Institute of Chemists; American Institute of Nutrition; New York Academy of Sciences; American Chemical Society; AAAS; Texas Academy of Science; International Congress of Pure and Applied Chemistry; Sigma Xi; Beta Kappa Chi; Phi Lambda Upsilon.

Dissertation title: Effect of Certain Polyenes, Vitamin E, and Related Substances on the Utilization of Beta-Carotene and Vitamin A for Storage of Vitamin A in the Kidneys and Livers of Rats.

Ref: *The Negro in Science,* p. 182–183. *American Men and Women of Science,* 15th ed., p. 695.

Hill, Carl McClellan   (1907–19??, M)

Chemist (organic). Born in Norfolk, VA, July 27, 1907. B.S., Hampton Institute, 1931; M.S., Cornell University, 1935; Ph.D. (organic chemistry), 1941; D.Sc., East Kentucky University, 1975. Instructor in high school at Hampton Institute, 1931–39; Assistant Professor of Chemistry, 1939–40; Principal of Laboratory School, 1940–41; Associate Professor, Chemistry, Agricultural and Technical University of North Carolina, 1941–44; worked on chemistry research projects for the Tennessee Valley Authority, 1948–52; Head of the Department, Tennessee State University, 1944–52; Chairman of the Department, 1952–58; Dean of the Faculty and the School of Arts and Sciences, 1958–62; Professor of Chemistry and President of Kentucky State University, 1962–75; President, Hampton Institute, 1976–78; research in organic chemistry with ketenes, aliphatic, alicyclic and arylunsaturated ethers and Grignard reagents, quality levels of fruits and vegetables, low temperature of soft coal.

Memberships and awards: Trustee, Stillman College; Board of Directors, United Virginia Bank; Rosenwald fellow, General Education Board fellow; Honorary L.L.D., University of Kentucky, 1966; AAAS; American Chemical Society; President, National Institute of Science, 1946; American Institute of Chemists; Sigma Xi; numerous other organizations.

Dissertation title: Studies of Ketenes and Their Derivatives.

Pub: Author and co-author of several textbooks and papers.

Ref: *Holders of Doctorates Among American Negroes,* p. 150. *American Men and Women of Science,* 16th ed., p. 701. *Who's Who Among Black Americans,* 1977, p. 417. *Ebony Success Library,* v. 1, p. 152. [p] *Encyclopedia of Black America,* 1984, p. 437.

Hill, Henry Aaron   (1915–1979, M)

Chemist (organic). Born in St. Joseph, MO, May 30, 1915. B.A., Johnson C. Smith University, 1936; Ph.D., MIT, 1942. Research Chemist, Atlantic Research Associates, 1942–43; Director of Research, 1943–44; Vice-President in Charge of Research, Atlantic Research Corp., 1944–46; civilian employee, Office of Scientific Research and Development, 1944; Supervisor of Research, Dewey & Almy Chemical Co., 1946–52; Assistant Manager, National Polychemicals, Inc., 1952–; Founder and President, Riverside Research Laboratory, 1962–; Director, Rohm & Hass Company, 1976; research in fluorocarbons.

Memberships and awards: Rosenwald fellow; AAAS; American Chemical Society; Sigma Xi; First black President, American Chemical Society; American Association of Textile Chemists and Colorists; New York Academy of Sciences.

Dissertation title: Test of Van't Hoff's Principle of Optical Superposition.

Ref: *American Men and Women of Science,* 14th ed., p. 2179. *Holders of Doctorates Among American Negroes,* p. 150. *The Negro in Science,* p. 183. *Encyclopedia of Black America,* 1985, p. 437. *Ebony,* Jan. 1977, p. 86. [p] *Who's Who Among Black Americans,* 1977, p. 419. *Jet,* Apr. 19, 1979, p. 55.

Hill, Julius Wanser   (1917–1983, M)

Physician. Orthopedist. Surgeon. Born in Atlanta, GA, June 12, 1917. B.A., Johnson C. Smith University, 1933; B.S., M.S., University of Illinois, 1973; M.D., Meharr Medical College, 1951; Orthopedic Surgery, University of Southern California, 1956.

Memberships and awards: President, National Medical Association, 1969–70; Board of Directors, National Medical Association, 1965; Distinguished Service Medal, National Medical Association, 1971; Board of Directors, Los Angeles County Hospital Commission, 1963–; National Medical Fellowships, Inc., 1970; President Emeritus, Golden State Medical Association, 1960–72; Board of Directors, Martin Luther King Hospital, Los Angeles; American Medical Association; Phi Beta Kappa; Sigma Xi; Kappa Alpha Psi.

Ref: *Jet*, Sept. 2, 1965, p. 42. [p]
   Who's Who Among Black Americans, 1985, p. 389.
   National Medical Association, *Journal*, v. 76, Apr. 1984, p. 390. [p] in memoriam
   Jet, Nov. 7, 1983, p. 55.

Hill, Lyndon M.   (1880–19??, M)

Physician. Born in Atlanta, GA, Oct. 25, 1880. B.S., Clark University, 1902; M.D., Meharry Medical School (cum laude), 1907. Chemistry teacher, Meharry Medical College while in school. Intern, Hubbard Hospital, 1911. Head, Science Department, Clark University, 1911–14; Medical Director of Atlanta Life Insurance Co., 1915–35.

Memberships and awards: President, National Medical Association, 1936–37; President, Georgia Medical Association, 1935–36; Omega Psi Phi; Executive Board, National Medical Association for two years.

Pub: A Deformed Chick. Scientific Labs of Denison University, *Bulletin*, v. 12, Oct. 1902.

Ref: National Medical Association, *Journal*, Nov. 1936, p. 141, 169–170.

Hill, Mary Elliot   (1907–1969, F)

Chemist (analytical). Chemist (organic). Born in South Mills, NC, Jan. 5, 1907. B.S., Virginia State College, 1929; M.S. Pennsylvania, 1941. Laboratory School, Virginia State College, 1930–32; Hampton Institute, 1932–36; Virginia State College, 1938–42; Bennett College, 1942–43; Assistant Professor, Chemistry, Tennessee A & I State University, 1944–62; Acting Head of the Department, 1951–; Kentucky State College, 1962–; research in ultraviolet spectrophotometry and research in synthesis and properties of monomeric and dimeric ketenes. Mrs. Carl McClellan Hill.

Memberships and awards: American Chemical Society; Tennessee Academy of Science; Beta Kappa Chi; National Institute of Science.

Ref: *American Men of Science*, 11th ed., p. 2295.
   The Negro in Science, p. 183.
   Who's Who Among American Women, 1966, p. 528.

Hill, Walter Andrew   (1946-——, M)

Agronomist. Soil scientist. Born in New Brunswick, NJ, Aug. 9, 1946. B.A., Lake Forest College, 1968; MAT, University of Chicago, 1970; M.S., University of Arizona, 1973; Ph.D. (soil chemistry and fertilization), University of Illinois, Urbana, 1978. Research Assistant in Chemistry, Lake Forest College, 1967–68; Teacher of Chemistry, University of Chicago, 1969–71; Research Assistant in Soil Chemistry/Fertilization, University of Arizona, 1971–73; Irrigation/Fertilization Specialist, University of Arizona Experimental Station, 1973–74; Teaching Assistant in Soils, University of Illinois, 1976–77; Research Assistant in Soil Chemistry, University of Illinois, 1974–77; Assistant Professor, 1978–81; Associate Professor, Soil Science, Tuskegee Institute, 1981–.

Memberships and awards: Soil Science Society of America; American Society of Agronomists; International Society of Soil Science; American Chemical Society; American Society of Horticultural Science; Sigma Xi.

Dissertation title: Leaching and Denitrification Losses of Nitrogen-15 Labeled Fertilizer Nitrogen in Two Illinois Soils.

Ref: *American Men and Women of Science*, 16th ed., p. 709.
   National Faculty Directory, 1988, p. 1671.

Hill, Washington C.   (1900s, M)

Physician. Obstetrician. Gynecologist. Director of Division of Maternal Fetal Medicine, Creighton University School of Medicine. Director of Perinatal Center, 1986–.

Ref: *Jet*, Apr. 7, 1986, p. 20.
   ABMS Compendium of Certified Medical Specialists, v. 3, p. 584.

Hillery, John Richard   (1874–1940, M)

Podiatrist. Inventor. Born in St. Mary's County, MD, Apr. 28, 1874. New York School of Chiropody and Dermatology, 1901. Received a Scroll of Blessing from the Pope for a cure on one of the nuns of the Catholic Church. He gave a lecture and demonstration at the first International Foot Congress, Paris, France, 1929; lectured in Glasgow, Edinburgh, and London; invented the Tarsal Arch Support.

Memberships and awards: One of the organizers of the Institute of Podiatry of New York City; National Association of Chiropodists; Pedic Society of the State of New York.

Pub: Articles on chiropody in various periodicals.

Ref: *Who's Who in Colored America*, 1930–32, p. 212–213.
Who's Who in Colored America, 1933–37, p. 256. [p] p. 253.
Who's Who in Colored America, 1938–40, p. 256. [p] p. 253.
Who's Who in Colored America, 1941–44, p. 254–255.

Hilliard, Robert Lee Moore   (1931– ——, M)

Physician. Surgeon. Born in San Antonio, TX, Jan. 1, 1931. B.S., Howard University, 1951; M.D., University of Texas, Medical Branch, 1956.

Memberships and awards: Director, National Medical fellowships, 1982–; Texas State Board of Medical Examiners, 1984–; Vice-Chairman, United Negro College Fund, 1971–; President, National Medical Association, 1982.

Ref: National Medical Association, *Journal*, v. 75, June 1983. [p] cover
National Medical Association, *Journal*, v. 75, Jan. 1983, p. 81. [p] (inaugural address)
Who's Who Among Black Americans, 1985, p. 391.

Hilyer, Andrew F.   (1859–19??, M)

Inventor. Born in Monroe, GA, Aug. 14, 1859. B.A., University of Minnesota, 1882; LLB, Howard University, 1884; LLM, 1885. Accountant who supervised the work on the study of business and social status of blacks in Washington and compiled the report. Invented two hot-air register attachments.

Memberships and Awards: Trustee, Howard University.

Ref: *Negro in Our History*, 5th ed., p. 463–464.
Who's Who of the Colored Race, 1915, p. 139.

Hinkson, De Haven   (1891–19??, M)

Physician. Gynecologist. Born in Philadelphia, PA, Dec. 5, 1891. M.D., Medico-Chirurgical College of Philadelphia, 1915. First Lieutenant in World War I. After the war became staff member, Philadelphia General Hospital, first black; first black head of a station hospital, Tuskegee; four-time Head, Philadelphia Black American Legion Post; Head, Fort Huachuca, AZ Hospital, second in command to Lt. Colonel Midion Bousfield (which see). Dr. Hinkson retired as Lt. Colonel in 1945. Staff Emeritus, Mercy Douglas Hospital.

Memberships and awards: Fellowship, Barnes Foundation of Merion, PA; first black with Dr. Edward Holloway elected to the College of Physicians of Philadelphia.

Ref: *Ladies Home Journal*, Aug. 1942.
National Medical Association, *Journal*, v. 66, July 1974, p. 339–342. [p]

Hinson, Eugene Theodore   (1873–1960, M)

Physician. Surgeon. Born in Philadelphia, PA, Nov. 20, 1873. Institute for Colored Youth, Philadelphia, PA, 1892; M.D., University of Pennsylvania, 1898. Staff, Frederick Douglas Memorial Hospital, Philadelphia; Staff, Mercy Hospital and Private Practice, 1907–55; one of the Founders and Member, Board of Directors, Mercy Hospital, Philadelphia; Surgeon and Gynecologist, Mercy Hospital; donated part of his family farm at Oxford for site of Lincoln University, PA.

Memberships and awards: Honor Man of his class; Academy of Medicine; County, State, and National Medical Associations; Alpha Phi Alpha; Sigma Pi Phi.

Ref: *Jet*, Nov. 21, 1963, p. 11. [p]
Who's Who in Colored America, 1927, p. 94.
Who's Who in Colored America, 1928–29, p. 182.
Who's Who in Colored America, 1930–32, p. 213.
Who's Who in Colored America, 1938–40, p. 256.
Eugene Theodore Hinson, M.D., 1873–. National Medical Association, *Journal*, v. 52, 1960, p. 454–455. obit & biog
Who's Who in Colored America, 1941–44, p. 255.
National Medical Association, *Journal*, v. 48, May 1956. [p] cover

Hinton, William Augustus   (1883–1959, M)

Physician. Bacteriologist. Pathologist. Born in Chicago, IL, Dec. 15, 1883. B.S., Harvard University, 1905; M.D., Harvard Medical College (with honors), 1912. Director of Wasserman Laboratory, Massachusetts Department of Public Health, 1915; Pathologist and Director of Research, Bost Dispensary; first black to become a professor at Harvard Medical School, teaching Bacteriology for 36 years; originated the Hinton test for syphilis, as effective as the Wasserman; discoverer of the Davies-Hinton tests of blood and spinal fluid.

Memberships and awards: American Medical Association; American Association of Bacteriologists; he would not accept the Spingarn Medal from the NAACP in 1938 because he wanted his work to be accepted on its merit, and he was afraid that if the world knew he was black, they would not accept it. Fifteen years after his death, the Serology Laboratory of the State Laboratory Institute Building of the Massachusetts Department of Public Health was named for him.

Pub: *Syphilis and Its Treatment*. New York, Macmillan, 1936. 321 p. First medical textbook by a black American to be published.

Ref: *American Men of Science*, 8th ed., p. 1132–1133.
Dictionary of American Negro Biography, p. 315–316.
Encyclopedia of Black America, 1981, p. 439.
History of the Negro in Medicine, p. 103–104. [p] p. 103.
Jet, Aug. 27, 1959, p. 12.
Who's Who in Colored America, 1927, p. 93.
Who's Who in Colored America, 1928–29, p. 182.

Who's Who in Colored America, 1930–32, p. 213.
Who's Who in Colored America, 1933–37, p. 257.
Who's Who in Colored America, 1938–40, p. 256–257.
Who's Who in Colored America, 1941–44, p. 255.
Historical Afro-American Biographies, p. 203–240. [p]
Dictionary of American Medical Biography, p. 351.
Coons, Albert, et al. William Augustus Hinton. *Harvard University Gazette*, July 16, 1960, p. 243–244.
National Medical Association, *Journal*, v. 49, 1957, p. 427–428.
Nine Black American Doctors, p. 30–45. [p] p. 30.
National Medical Association, *Journal*, v. 49, Nov. 1957. [p] cover
National Medical Association, *Journal*, v. 51, Nov. 1959, p. 485. [p] obit
Cobb, W. Montague. William Augustus Hinton, M.D., 1883–. National Medical Association, *Journal*, v. 49, Nov. 1957, p. 427–428. (with list of publications)
Blacks in Science: Astrophysicist to Zoologist, p. 58.
Crisis, Sept. 1927, p. 237.
National Medical Association, *Journal*, v. 67, Jan. 1975, p. 81–82. (a tribute)

Hodge, John Edward   (1914- ——, M)

Chemist. Born in Kansas City, KS, Oct. 12, 1914. B.A., University of Kansas (cum laude), 1936; M.A., 1940; Postgraduate studies, Bradley University, 1946–60; Kansas Teachers Certificate, 1936. Principal Chemist in gasoline and oils, Kansas State Department of Inspections and Registration, 1937–39; Chemistry Teacher, Western University, Kansas City, 1939–41; Organic Chemistry of Carbohydrates, Northern Regional Research Laboratory, USDA, Peoria, IL, 1941–73; Supervisory Research Chemist, 1973–81; Adjunct Professor of Chemistry, Bradley University, 1984–.

Memberships and awards: National Academy of Sciences—National Research Council, 1977; Superior Service Award, USDA, 1953; American Chemical Society; American Association of Cereal Chemists; Phi Beta Kappa; Pi Mu Epsilon; Grant Officer, USDA, U.S. and Foreign, 1962–75; Chairman, Division of Carbohydrate Chemistry, American Chemical Society; Consultant in Program Review of the National Research Council, 1964–80; Founding, Honorary, and Emeritus member, Phi Tau Sigma Society; Citation certificate for most cited scientific journal articles in food science.

Ref: *American Men and Women of Science*, 15th ed., p. 746.
   Who's Who Among Black Americans, 1985, p. 394.

Hoffman, John Wessley   (1870–19??, M)

Agriculturist. Born in Barbados, B.W.I., Aug. 11, 1870. B.S., Albion College, MI, 1882; B.S.A., Michigan Agricultural College, 1895; special work in Ontario Agricultural College, Canada, 1895–96; D.Sc., Royal Agricultural College, England, 1905. Director of Southern Nigeria, West Africa, 1902–07; was the means of introducing cotton growing all through the Territory of Africa since he spoke Hausa and Yoruba languages; taught science and agriculture at Tougaloo University, MS, and was the means for changing farm life in the Tougaloo area.

Memberships and awards: Fellow, Royal Agricultural Society; French Agricultural Society; New York Society of Natural History.

Ref: *Who's Who of the Colored Race*, 1915, p. 139–140.

Holland, James Philip   (1934- ——, M)

Biologist. Endocrinologist. Zoologist. Born in Bowling Green, KY, Dec. 31, 1934. B.S., Kentucky State College, 1956; M.S., University of Indiana, 1958; Ph.D. (endocrinology), 1961. Assistant Professor of Zoology, Howard University, 1962–67; Associate Professor, 1967–74; Professor of Zoology and Associate Dean of the Graduate School, 1974–77; Interim Dean, 1977–78; Professor of Biology, Indiana University, Bloomington, 1978–.

Memberships and awards: Fellow, Endocrinology, School of Medicine, University of Wisconsin, 1961–62; Principal Investigator, NIH Research Grants and NSF Research Grants; National Science Foundation Graduate Fellow Evaluation Panel, 1983–; AAAS; American Society of Zoologists; Endocrine Society.

Dissertation title: An Investigation of the Protein-Bound Iodine in the Fowl.

Ref: *American Men and Women of Science*, 15th ed., p. 774.
   National Faculty Directory, 1988, p. 1706.

Holley, Alonzo Potter Burgess   (1865–19??, M)

Physician. Surgeon. Born in Port-au-Prince, Haiti, B.W.I., Sept. 21, 1865. Only black student in Atherstone Grammar School, England, 1881–83, he won the Alumni Prize for best scholarship; certificate for examinations, Cambridge University, England, 1883; M.D., New York Homeopathic Medical College and Flower Hospital, 1888, only black student in class of 50; conducted Bahama Drug Store at Nassau, 1906–12; President, Board of Health, Haiti.

Memberships and awards: National Medical Association; State Medical, Dental and Pharmaceutical Association of Florida; Dade County Medical Association; fellow, American Electro-Therapeutical Association.

Pub: Applied Hygiene, 1913, and other nonmedical publications.

Ref: *Who's Who of the Colored Race*, 1915, p. 141–142.
   Who's Who in Colored America, 1927, p. 94.
   Who's Who in Colored America, 1930–32, p. 217.
   Who's Who in Colored America, 1933–37, p. 258.
   Who's Who in Colored America, 1938–40, p. 257.
   Who's Who in Colored America, 1941–44, p. 256.

Holliday, Alfonso David   (1931- —— , M)

Physician. Surgeon. Born in Gary, IN, June 10, 1931. B.A., Indiana University, 1952; M.D., Indiana University School of Medicine, 1955; M.B.A. (health administration), University of Chicago. Private Physician-Surgeon, 1960–75; Co-Director, Family Nurse Practitioner Program, 1975–; Executive Director, Medical Center of Gary, 1975–78; Assistant Professor, Nursing, Indiana University, 1978–; Medical Director, Lake County Jail, Crown Point, IN, 1982–.

Memberships and awards: Diplomate, American Board of Surgery, 1964; fellow, American College of Surgeons; American Academy of Medicine; American Medical Association; National Medical Association; Indiana State Medical Association; Lake County Medical Society; American College of Physician Executives; Accreditation Surveyor, Accreditation Association for Ambulatory Health Care, Inc.; Distinguished Service Award, Midwest Association of Community Health Centers, Inc., 1979.

Ref: Who's Who Among Black Americans, 1985, p. 396.
Ebony, Mar. 1978, p. 26. [p] only

Holloman, John Lawrence Sullivan, Jr.   (1919- —— , M)

Physician. Health Administrator. Born in Washington, DC, Nov. 22, 1919. B.S. (biochemistry) (cum laude), Virginia Union University, 1940; M.D., University of Michigan, 1943. President, New York City Health and Hospital Corp., 1974–77; research in clinical, pharmaceutical, social, and administration medicine.

Memberships and awards: President, National Medical Association, 1965–66; Board of Trustees, National Medical Association, 1963–66; Secretary, National Medical Association, 1964–65; Medical Society of the County of New York; New York State Medical Society; American Medical Association; Manhattan Central Medical Society; American Geriatric Society; Association of Military Surgeons; Trustee, State University of New York, 1968–85; Sigma Pi; Alpha Phi Alpha; Institute of Medicine, National Academy of Sciences.

Ref: American Men and Women of Science, 15th ed., p. 782.
In Black and White, p. 448.
Who's Who Among Black Americans, 1985, p. 397.
Jet, Aug. 25, 1966, p. 49.
The History of the Negro in Medicine, p. 197. [p] p. 197.
National Medical Association, Journal, v. 57, Nov. 1965, p. 507–508. [p]

Holly, William G.   (19??- —— , M)

Chemist. Chemical Superintendent of the Gypsy Paint and Varnish Co. of New York; formulated a series of interior paints using titanium as the basic pigment, creating a new method for the field.

Memberships and awards: New York and New Jersey Varnish and Paint Plant Managers' Association.

Ref: Drew. Negro Scholars in Scientific Research. Journal of Negro History, v. 35, 1950, p. 142.
Negro Year Book, 1931, p. 185.
Crisis, Nov. 1929, p. 380.
Downing, Lewis K. Contributions of Negro Scientists. Crisis, June 1939, p. 168–169. [p]

Holmes, Beatrice Josephine   (1899–19??, F)

Nurse. Born in Meridian, MS, Sept. 17, 1899. B.S., Philander Smith College, Little Rock, AR; Red Cross Hospital Nursing School. First black nurse stationed in any company in Mississippi; first graduate registered nurse-midwife in Mississippi.

Memberships and awards: National Organization of Public Health Nursing; National Association of Colored Graduate Nurses.

Ref: The National Register, 1952, p. 580.

Hope, Edward Swain, Jr.   (1901–19??, M)

Military (Navy). Lt. Commander. Engineer (civil). Born in Atlanta, GA, Aug. 28, 1901. B.A., Morehouse College, 1923; M.S. (civil engineering), MIT, 1927; Ph.D. (administration), Columbia University, 1942. Engineer, New York State Department of Public Works, 1927–28; Hydraulic Engineer, Electric Bond Share Co., 1928–31; Superintendent, Buildings and Grounds, Howard University, 1932–44; Commissioned Lieutenant in the Navy, 1944, released to inactive duty as a Lieutenant Commander. At one time was the highest ranking black in the Navy. Professor of Civil Engineering, 1947–65; Emeritus Professor, Engineering, American University of Beirut, 1966–.

Memberships and awards: Grant Award Panel member, Office of Education, 1978–; American Society of Civil Engineers; fellow, American Society of Engineering Education.

Ref: American Men and Women of Science, 14th ed., p. 2261.
The Naval Engineer, v. 26, Winter 1986-87, p. 16, 28–32. [p]

Horne, Woody Lemuel   (1893–19??, M)

Dentist. Born in Rocky Mount, NC, Aug. 24, 1893. B.S., Department of Sciences, North Carolina A & T College, Greensboro, NC, 1914; D.D.S., Howard University, 1917. Worked for U.S. Public Health Service and the North Carolina State Board of Health, where he conducted a special clinic in Salisbury, NC, 1924, before the Health Committee of the League of Nations while it was studying the health situation in the United States. He did most of the technical papers and typing for Dr. E. E. Just.

Memberships and awards: Secretary, Old North State Dental Society; National Dental Association.

Ref: *Who's Who in Colored America,* 1941–44, p. 260–261. [p]
        p. 257.

Houser, N. B.   (1869–19??, M)

Physician. Born in Gastonia, NC, Feb. 14, 1869. B.S., Biddle University (now Johnson C. Smith University); M.D., Leonard Medical College, 1891, four years' work in three years. Practice, 1901, Helena, AR; opened Black Diamond Drug Co.

Memberships and awards: President, North Carolina Colored Medical Association for one year and Secretary for two years; Physician in charge of the Samaritan Hospital of Charlotte, NC for three years, only black physician to hold this office by 1911; won first prize for superior knowledge of obstetrics.

Ref: *Beacon Lights of the Race,* p. 351–360. [p] & biog.

Howard, Edwin Clarence Joseph Turpin   (18??–1912, M)

Physician. M.D., Harvard University, 1869. First black to receive an M.D. from Harvard University.

Ref: *Black Collegian,* Mar./Apr. 1978, p. 29–30.
        National Medical Association, *Journal,* v. 73, Dec. 1981, p. 1207.

Howard, Ralph   (1900s, M)

Chemist. Tennessee State University, 1956. Worked with NASA as part of the Bendix Corporation Launch Support Division Program; Head, Chemistry Laboratory, Kennedy Space Center; found a fuel contamination in Apollo 14 which delayed the mission.

Ref: *Jet,* Feb. 25, 1971, p. 40.

Howard, Roscoe Conkling   (1903–1969, M)

Biologist. Zoologist. Born in Petersburg, VA, Oct. 13, 1903. B.S., University of Pittsburgh, 1926; M.S., Cornell, 1931; Ph.D., 1942. Instructor, AAUP; Virginia State College, 1931–35; Dean of Men, 1931–33; Assistant Professor, 1935–38; Associate Professor, 1938–43; Professor of Biology, Virginia State College, 1943–.

Memberships and awards: AAAS; AAUP; Virginia Teachers Association; American Teachers Association.

Dissertation title: Comparative Morphology, Variation, and Seasonal Studies on the Genitalia of Local Species of the Family Polygridae.

Ref: *American Men of Science,* 11th ed., p. 2418.
        The Negro in Science, p. 178.
        Holders of Doctorates Among American Negroes, p. 191–192.

Howard, Ruth

Psychologist. See: Beckham, Ruth H.

Howard, Theodore Roosevelt Mason   (1908–1976, M)

Physician. Surgeon. Born in Murray, KY, Mar. 4, 1908. B.S., Union College, NB, 1931; M.D., College of Medical Evangelists, 1936. Director, Riverside Sanitarium and Hospital, Nashville, 1937–39; Surgeon-in-Chief, Taborian Hospital, Mound Bayou, MS, 1942–47; Surgeon-in-Chief and Medical Director, Friendship Clinic and Hospital, MS, 1947–56.

Memberships and awards: President, National Medical Association, 1956–57; Diplomate, National Board of Examiners, 1937; Mississippi Medical Association; Founder and President Emeritus, Mississippi Regional Council of Negro Leadership; Sigma Psi Phi; Omega Psi Phi.

Ref: *History of the Negro in Medicine,* p. 149–150. [p]
        Ebony Success Library, v. 1, p. 160. [p]
        Who's Who Among Black Americans, 1975–76, p. 307.
        National Medical Association, *Journal,* v. 68, Nov. 1976, p. 544. obit

Hubbard, Philip Gamalieh   (1921– ——, M)

Engineer (electrical). Engineer (mechanical). Inventor. Born in Macon, MO, Mar. 4, 1921. B.S. (electrical engineering), University of Iowa, 1946; M.S. (mechanics), 1949; Ph.D. (mechanics/hydrology), 1954. Research Engineer and Instrumentation Section Head, Institute of Hydraulic Research, 1946–65; from Instructor to Associate Professor of Mechanics and Hydraulics, 1946–59; Professor of Mechanics and Hydraulics, University of Iowa, 1959–; Dean of Academic Affairs, 1966–71; Professor of Energy Engineering, 1977–; Vice-Provost, 1969–; invented an anemometer to measure fluid turbulence.

Memberships and awards: American Society for Engineering Education; Tau Beta Pi; Sigma Xi; Eta Kappa Nu; Phi Lambda Upsilon; Omicron Delta Kappa.

Dissertation title: Constant-Temperature Hot-Wire Anemometry with Application to Measurements in Water.

Ref: *American Men and Women of Science,* 16th ed., p. 869.
        Black Engineers in the United States, p. 98.
        Ebony, Aug. 1959, p. 6. [p]
        Blacks in Science: Astrophysicist to Zoologist, p. 33.

Hubert, Benjamin F.   (1884–1958, M)

Agriculturist. Born in White Plains, GA, Dec. 25, 1884. B.A., Morehouse, 1909; B.S. (agriculture), Massachusetts Agricultural College, Amherst, 1913; Postgraduate work, University of Wisconsin, 1913. Director of Agriculture, Americus Institute, GA, 1909–10; Agricultural Director,

State Agricultural and Mechanical College, Orangeburg, SC, 1912–20; Editor, *Palmetto Farmer*, 1914–15; President, Georgia State Industrial College, 1926–.

Memberships and awards: National Teachers Association in Colored Schools; Chief, Agricultural Department, Tuskegee; President, Georgia State Industrial College, 1926; served during World War I as supervisor for agricultural training for black troops in France; Founder and Executive Secretary, Association for Advancement of Negro Country Life.

Pub: *The Farmer's Garden.*
Text on General Architecture.

Ref: *Who's Who in Colored America*, 1927, p. 98.
Who's Who of the Colored Race, 1915, p. 145.
Who's Who in Colored America, 1928–29, p. 194.
Who's Who in Colored America, 1930–32, p. 223.
Who's Who in Colored America, 1933–37, p. 267.
Who's Who in Colored America, 1938–40, p. 264.
Who's Who in Colored America, 1941–44, p. 265.
Crisis, Nov. 1926, p. 40.

Hubert, Charles Edward   (1918– ——, M)

Anatomist. Born in Mayfield, GA, Aug. 4, 1918. B.A., Savannah State College, 1941; M.S., Atlanta University, 1948. Instructor, Mathematics, Hutcheson High School, Douglasville, GA, 1941–42; Radio Operation Instructor, U.S. Army, 1943–45; Research Assistant, Emory College, 1948–51; Instructor, Hutcheson High School, 1951–53; Instructor in Neurophysiology, V.A. Hospital, Tuskegee, AL, 1949; Instructor, Anatomy, Morehouse College, 1953; research in neuroanatomy and neuroembryology.

Memberships and awards: AAAS; National Education Association.

Ref: *The Negro in Science*, p. 178.

Hudson, Roy Davage   (1930– ——, M)

Pharmacologist. Born in Chattanooga, TN, June 3, 1930. B.S. (biology), Livingstone College, 1955; M.S. (zoology), University of Michigan, 1958; Ph.D. (pharmacology), 1962. Dean of the Graduate School, Brown University, 1966–68; Vice-President, Research Planning & Coordination, Warner-Lambert/Parke Davis Pharmaceutical Research Division, Ann Arbor, MI, 1976–; President, Hampton University, 1970–76; Vice-President, Pharmaceutical and Research Development, Upjohn Company in Europe; research in drug effects on pyramidal and extrapyramidal research; pathophysiological analysis of effects of chronic administration of nicotine.

Memberships and awards: Danforth fellow, 1955–61; NIH Research Grant, 1961; AAAS; American Society of Pharmacology and Experimental Therapeutics.

Dissertation title: Effects of Chlorpromazine on Some Motor Reflexes.

Ref: *American Men and Women of Science*, 13th ed., p. 2315.

In Black and White, p. 463.
Who's Who Among Black Americans, 1980–81, p. 393.
Who's Who Among Black Americans, 1985, p. 411.
Ebony, Dec. 1987, p. 7. [p]
Ebony Success Library, v. 1, p. 161. [p]
Ebony, July 1978, p. 7. [p]

Huggins, Kimuel Alonzo   (1898–19??, M)

Chemist (organic). Born in Whitesburg, GA, May 3, 1898. B.A., Morehouse College, 1923; M.S., Chicago University, 1929; Ph.D. (chemistry), 1937. Instructor in Science, Leland College, 1923–28; Chairman, Division of Sciences and Dean of Men, Arkansas Agricultural and Mechanical College, 1929–31; Assistant Professor of Chemistry, Morehouse College, 1931–32; Chairman, Chemistry Department, Atlanta University, 1933–68; Professor, Bishop College, 1968–; Director, National Science Foundation Academic Year Int., Atlanta, 1966; research in organic microanalysis.

Memberships and awards: American Chemical Society; Sigma Xi.

Dissertation title: Studies in the Dimethylbutadiene Series.

Ref: *American Men and Women of Science*, 12th ed., p. 2886.
In Black and White, p. 464.
Holders of Doctorates Among American Negroes, p. 150–151.

Hughes, Julia Pearl   (1873–19??, F)

Pharmacist. Born in Mebanes, NC, Mar. 19, 1873. Graduate, Scotia Seminary, Concord, NC, 1893; Phar.D., Howard University Pharmaceutical College, 1897. Pharmacist, Frederick Douglass Memorial Hospital Pharmacy, Philadelphia, PA. Opened the Hughes Pharmacy in Philadelphia.

Ref: *Howard University Medical Department*, p. 181–182. [p]

Humphrey, Betty Jean   (1900s, F)

Nurse (psychiatric). B.S., Florida A & M University, 1953; M.S., Catholic University of America, 1963; Ph.D., Nova University, FL, 1981. Director of Godding/Noyes Division, a clinical unit at St. Elizabeth's Mental Hospital, Washington, DC, 1955–.

Ref: *The Path We Tread*, p. 187. [p]
Directory of Nurses with Doctoral Degrees, 1984, p. 35.

Hunt, Fern   (1900s, F)

Mathematician. Born in New York, NY. Attended Bronx High School of Science; B.A., Bryn Mawr College; Ph.D. (mathematical biology), Courant Institute, 1978. Lecturer, City College of New York; Mathematics Faculty, Howard University, 1978–.

Dissertation title: Genetic and Spatial Variation in Some
    Selection-Migration Models.

Ref: Kenschaft, Patricia C. Black Women in Mathematics in
    the United States.
    American Mathematical Monthly, v. 88, Oct. 1951, p.
    601.

Hunter, J. H.   (1800s, F)

Inventor. Portable weighing scales as seen in post offices,
businesses and hospitals today. Patent #570,553, Nov.
1896.

Ref: *At Last Recognition in America,* v. 1, p. 25.

Hunter, Jehu Callis   (1922– ——, M)

Biologist. Zoologist. Born in Washington, DC, Mar. 11,
1922. B.S., Howard University, 1943. Assistant Zoologist,
Howard University, 1947–48; Medical Biological Aide,
National Cancer Institute, 1949–51; Biologist Cyto-
chemist, 1953–62; Research Biologist, 1962–65; Scientist
Administrator, National Institute of Child Health and Human Development, 1965–69; Assistant Director of Planning, 1969–74; Chief, Office of Planning and Analysis,
1975–76; Assistant Director of Program Development,
Center for Research, Mothers and Children, 1976–78;
Head, Public Health Association, 1978–; research in tumor metabolism.

   Memberships and awards: AAAS; American Society
of Cell Biologists; Society of Developmental Biology;
Royal Society of Medicine.

Ref: *American Men and Women of Science,* 16th ed., p. 909.
    Who's Who in the South and Southwest, 1976, p. 374.

Hunter, John Edward   (1866–19??, M)

Physician. Surgeon. Born in Christiansberg, VA, Dec. 31,
1866. B.S., Oberlin College, 1885; M.D., Western Reserve, 1889. Co-founder with Dr. Kenney of the Andrew
Clinical Society at Tuskegee.

   Memberships and awards: President, National Medical Association, 1905–06; Andrew Clinical Society; One
of the founders and organizers of the Florida Surgical
Clinic, Tallahassee, FL; President, Kentucky State Medical, Dental, and Pharmaceutical Association; President,
Blue Grass Medical Society.

Ref: National Medical Association, *Journal,* v. 41, Mar. 1949,
    p. 88.
    National Medical Association, *Journal,* v. 73, Supple-
    ment, Dec. 1981.
    Who's Who in Colored America, 1941–44, p. 269.
    Who's Who of the Colored Race, 1915, p. 147.

Hunter, John McNeile   (1901–19??, M)

Physicist. Chemist. Born in Woodville, TX, Jan. 23, 1901.
B.S., MIT, 1924; M.S., Cornell, 1927; Ph.D. (physics),

1937. Professor and Head, Physics Department, Virginia
State College, 1925–67; research in thermionics.
   Memberships and awards: AAAS; Sigma Xi; Beta
Kappa Chi; Sigma Pi Sigma; American Physical Society;
American Association of Physics Teachers; General Edu-
cation Board fellow.

Dissertation title: The Anomalous Schottky Effect for Oxygen-
    ated Tungsten.

Ref: *American Men and Women of Science,* 12th ed., p. 2912.
    The Negro in Science, p. 179.
    Holders of Doctorates Among American Negroes, p. 151.

Hunter, Norvell Witherspoon   (1911– ——, M)

Zoologist. Protozoologist. Born in Muskogee, OK, Nov.
16, 1911. B.S., Langston University, 1933; M.S., State
University of Iowa, 1945; Ph.D., University of California
at Los Angeles, 1952. Instructor, Biology, North Carolina
College at Durham, 1945–47; Assistant Professor, Morgan
State College, 1947–49; Associate Professor, 1949–;
Teaching Assistant, University of California at Los
Angeles, 1949–52; Associate Professor of Biology, Mor-
gan State College, 1952–59; Professor, 1959–.
   Memberships and awards: Sigma Xi; Society of Pro-
tozoologists; AAAS; American Society of Zoologists.

Dissertation title: Histochemical Studies of Opalina Carolinen-
    sis, Metcalf.

Ref: *The Negro in Science,* p. 179.
    American Men and Women of Science, 12th ed., p. 2913.

Hurd, Joseph Kindall, Jr.   (1938– ——, M)

Physician. Obstetrician. Gynecologist. Ecologist. Born in
Hoisington, KS, Feb. 12, 1938. B.A. (magna cum laude),
Harvard College, 1960; M.D., Harvard Medical School,
1964. Gynecologist, Lahey Clinic Foundation, 1972–.
   Memberships and awards: Treasurer, Obstetrical So-
ciety of Boston, 1979–84; President, New England Medi-
cal Society, 1980; Board of Directors, Freedom House,
Inc., Crispus Attucks Day Care Center; Roxbury Medical
Dental Group; Massachusetts Medical Society; American
Fertility Society; Charles River Medical Society; Ameri-
can Medical Association; National Medical Association;
Army Commendation Medal, 1970–72; National Scholarship Grant.

Ref: *Who's Who Among Black Americans,* 1985, p. 417.
    Ebony, Aug. 1960, p. 33. [p]

Hurst, Charles G.   (1928– ——, M)

Speech pathologist. Audiologist. Born in 1928. B.S.,
Wayne State, 1953; M.A., 1959; Ph.D. (speech), 1961.
Postdoctoral grants from U.S. Office of Education, Stern
Family Fund, United Planning Organization and Howard
University; President, Antioch College, Chicago.

Memberships and awards: AAAS; American Speech and Hearing Association; Acoustical Society of America; President, Malcolm X Education Foundation; Speech Association of America; Central State Speech Association; International Phonetics Association; Certificate of Clinical Competence in Audiology, 1965.

Dissertation title: Speech and Functional Intelligence: An Experimental Study of Educational Implications of a Basic Speech Course.

Pub: *Psychological Correlates in Dialectolalia,* 1965.

Ref: *American Men and Women of Science,* 12th ed., p. 1094.
In Black and White, p. 470.
Who's Who Among Black America, 1980–81, p. 398–399.
Living Black American Authors, p. 76.

Hutcherson, Fred, Jr.   (18??–1962, M)

Pilot. Self-taught. First black to fly across Atlantic. Former Canadian and U.S.A.F. Officer and flying instructor, commercial pilot.

Ref: *Jet,* July 19, 1962, p. 60.

Hutchinson, John E. III   (1932– ——, M)

Physician. Surgeon. Born in Birmingham, AL. 1932. B.A.; M.D., Meharry Medical College, 1957. Cardiac Surgeon. Performed Arthur Ashe's quadruple bypass surgery. Chief of Cardio Surgery, Hackensack Medical Center, NJ.

Memberships and awards: American Association of Thoracic Surgeons; Society of Thoracic Surgery; American College of Surgeons.

Ref: *Jet,* Jan. 10, 1980, p. 9–10.
ABMS Compendium of Certified Medical Specialists, v. 6, p. 685.

Hyde-Rowan, Maxine Deborah   (1949– ——, F)

Physician. Neurosurgeon. Born in Laurel, MS, Jan. 18, 1949. B.S., Tougaloo College, 1970; M.S., Cleveland State, 1973; M.D., University of Cleveland, 1977. One of fewer than 60 black neurosurgeons in America, even fewer women. Guthrie Clinic Neurosurgical Staff, 1982–.

Memberships and awards: Bradford County Medical Society; Pennsylvania Medical Society; Pennsylvania Neurosurgical Society; Congress of Neurological Surgeons; Alpha Omega Alpha Medical Honorary Society.

Ref: *Ebony,* Sept. 1983, p. 72–76. [p]
Mississippi Black History Makers, p. 364–365.
Who's Who Among Black Americans, 1985, p. 419.
American Medical News, 1984. (feature story)

Hytche, William Percy   (1927– ——, M)

Mathematician. Born in Porter, OK, Nov. 28, 1927. B.S. (mathematics), Langston University, 1950; M.S. (mathematics and natural science), Oklahoma State University, 1958; Ed.D. (mathematics and higher education), Oklahoma State University, 1967. Assistant Professor, Associate Professor, Head, Department of Mathematics and Computer Science, and Director, Thirteen-College Curriculum Program, University of Maryland, Eastern Shore, 1960–68; Dean of Student Affairs, 1968–73; Acting Chairman, 1973–74; Acting Chancellor, 1975–76; Chancellor, 1976–.

Memberships and awards: Phi Delta Kappa; Phi Sigma Society; Alpha Phi Alpha; National Science Foundation Grant, 1958–60.

Dissertation title: A Comparative Analysis of Four Methods of Instruction in Mathematics.

Ref: *Black Mathematicians and Their Works,* p. 288. [p]
Who's Who Among Black Americans, 1985, p. 420.
Who's Who in America, 1978, p. 1607.

I

Imes, Elmer Samuel   (1883–1941, M)

Chemist. Physicist. Born in Memphis, TN, Oct. 12, 1883. B.A., Fisk University, 1903; M.A., 1910; Ph.D., University of Michigan, 1918. The second black to receive a Ph.D. in physics, the first being Edward Bouchet from Yale in 1876. Consulting Chemist, New York, 1918–22; Research Physicist, Federal Engineer's Development Corporation, 1922–24; Burrows Magnetic Equipment Corporation, 1924–27; Research Engineer, E. A. Everett Railway Signal Supplies, 1927–30; Professor of Physics and Head of the Department, Fisk University, 1930–41.

Memberships and awards: Fellow, University of Michigan, 1916–18; Physical Society; Society of Testing Materials.

Dissertation title: Measurements on the Near Infra-red Absorption of Some Diatomic Cases.

Ref: *American Men of Science,* 6th ed., p. 710.
Blacks in Science: Ancient and Modern, p. 262–265.
Science, Dec. 26, 1941, p. 600–601.
Holders of Doctorates Among American Negroes, p. 151.
Who's Who of the Colored Race, 1915, p. 149.
Negroes in Science: Natural Science Doctorates, 1876–1969, p. 52.

Imhotep, C.   (3000 BC, M)

Physician. Born in Egypt. Deified 500 years after his death. First person designated as a scientist. Had Negroid features and would today be considered black. Aesclepios, the Greek, born 1,500 years after Imhotep, followed his pattern. Physicians today are traditional descendants of Imhotep through Hippocrates and Aesclepios.

Ref: *Asimov's Biographical Encyclopedia of Science and Technology,* p. 1.
          In Black and White, p. 473.
          World's Great Men of Color, v. 1, p. 38–42.
          National Medical Association, *Journal,* v. 44, Jan. 1952, p. 75–76. [p] cover
          Blacks in Science: Ancient and Modern, p. 129–131. [p]

Inge, Frederick Douglas   (1896–19??, M)

Physiologist (plant). Born in Charlottesville, VA, May 30, 1896. B.S., University of Minnesota, 1924; M.S., Iowa State College, 1937; Ph.D. (plant physiology), 1940. Professor of Pharmacy, Meharry Medical College, 1923–25; Pharmacist, 1924–29; Instructor in Biology, Southern University, 1929–36; Professor of Biology, Florida A & M University, 1938–44; Chairman of the Department, Bennet College, 1944–45; Chairman of the Department of Biology, Hampton Institute, 1945–; Emeritus Professor of Biology, Hampton Institute, 1970–; research in seed germination.

Memberships and awards: Sigma Xi; American Botanical Society; fellow, AAAS; American Institute of Biological Sciences; American Society of Plant Physiology.

Dissertation title: Growth Correlation in Maize Seedlings.

Ref: *American Men and Women of Science,* 13th ed., p. 2084.
          Holders of Doctorates Among American Negroes, p. 123–124.
          The Negro in Science, p. 179.
          Crisis, Aug. 1923, p. 180. [p] only

Irving, Ernest Walker   (1869–19??, M)

Physician. Born in Circleville, OH, Aug. 9, 1896. Diploma from Duckworth Business College, 1893; M.D., Meharry Medical College, 1897. Headed school in Natchez, MS, during which time the enrollment of the school grew from 50 to 500 students. Met a black doctor for the first time (Dr. J. B. Banks) and decided to become a doctor. Practiced in Memphis and became an expert in medical testimony; Medical Examiner for Continental Casualty Insurance Co., Chicago, IL.

Memberships and awards: National Medical Association; Tri-State Medical Association.

Ref: *Beacon Lights of the Race,* p. 402–409. [p] biog.
          Who's Who of the Colored Race, 1915, p. 149.

Ish, George William Stanley, Sr.   (1883–1970, M)

Physician. Surgeon. Born in 1883. B.A., Yale University, 1905; M.D., Harvard Medical School, 1909. Practiced in Little Rock, AR, for 39 years. President, Collins Chapel Hospital; Chief of Surgical Staff, United Friends of American Hospital in Little Rock, AR.

Ref: *Who's Who of the Colored Race,* 1915, p. 149.
          Jet, April 9, 1970, p. 32. [p]
          Ebony, July 1950, p. 18. [p]

Ish, George William Stanley, Jr.   (1919–1965, M)

Physician. Surgeon. Born in Little Rock, AR, Nov. 9, 1919. B.S., Talladega College, AL, 1939; M.D., Howard University, 1944. Chief of Surgery, Collins Chapel Hospital, Memphis, TN, 1962–65.

Memberships and awards: Fellow, American College of Surgeons, first black in Memphis to receive this honor. Won Bronze Star as a member of the Medical Corps in Korea; formed a group of black physicians in Memphis called Medical Associates; Bluff City Medical Society; Alpha Phi Alpha; Sigma Pi Phi.

Ref: *Jet,* May 28, 1964, p. 23.
          National Cyclopedia of American Biography, v. 54, p. 27.

Isibor, Edward Iroguehi   (1940– —— , M)

Engineer (civil). Born in Benin City, Nigeria, June 9, 1940. B.S. (civil engineering), Howard University, 1965; M.S. (civil engineering), MIT, 1963; Ph.D. (civil engineering), Purdue University, 1970. Research Assistant, MIT, 1965–67; Research Assistant, Purdue University, 1967–69; Director, Afro-American Cultural Center, Cleveland, OH, 1970–71; Cleveland Transportation Engineer, 1972; Associate Professor and Head of Urban Systems Program, Florida Int. University, 1973–75; Dean, School of Engineering and Technology, Tennessee State University, 1975– (Specializes in transportation engineering).

Memberships and awards: Highway Research Board; American Society of Civil Engineers; American Society for Engineering Education; Sigma Xi.

Dissertation title: Modeling the Impact of Highway Improvements on the Value of Adjacent Land Parcels.

Ref: *Who's Who Among Black Americans,* 1985, p. 422.
          Ebony, May 1986, p. 96.
          Black Engineers in the United States, p. 100.

Ivy, Mark, III   (1935– —— , M)

Physician. Pharmacist. Obstetrician. Gynecologist. Born in Ocala, FL, April 15, 1935. B.S. (pharmacy), Florida A & M University, 1958; M.D., Meharry Medical College, 1973; Obstetrics and Gynecology Residency, Akron General Medical Center, 1978. Deputy Health Officer, Summit County Health Department, 1973–78; Deputy Health Officer, Akron County Health Department, 1974–78; Director of Obstetrics and Gynecology, Delta Community Hospital and Clinic, Mount Bayou, MS, 1975; Consultant, Planned Parenthood of Summit Co., 1976–78; Medical Director of Planned Parenthood of Central Florida, 1978–.

Memberships and awards: Outstanding Senior Pharmacist of Florida A & M University, 1958; first black president, Department of Obstetrics and Gynecology, Akron General Medical Center, 1973; first black chief, Gynecological Services, Lakeland Regional Medical Center, Lakeland, FL, 1985.

Ref: *Who's Who Among Black Americans*, 1985, p. 422.

J

Jackson, Algernon Brashear   (1878–1942, M)

Physician. Surgeon. Born in Princeton, IN, May 21, 1878. Indiana University; M.D., Jefferson Medical College, Philadelphia, PA, 1900. Assistant Surgeon, Philadelphia Polyclinic Hospital, 1900–12; Superintendent and Surgeon-in-Chief, Mercy Hospital and School for Nurses; described new treatment for acute rheumatism by injections of magnesium sulphate; Professor of Bacterial and Public Health; Director of School of Public Health, Howard University.

Memberships and awards: National Medical Association; Pennsylvania Medical Society; Philadelphia Medical Society; Executive Committee, National Negro Business League; admitted to American College of Physicians at the time of its formation; Supervisor, National Negro Health Week Movement, when it moved to Howard University from Tuskegee; Medico-Chirurgical Society of DC; Public Health Association of DC; John A. Andrew Clinical Society of Tuskegee; National Hospital Association.

Pub: *Evolution of Life*, 1910, F.A.C.P. (Hon.)
   Jim & Mr. Eddy. Washington, DC, Associated Publishers, 1931. Reviewed in the National Medical Association *Journal* April–June 1931, p. 95–96.
   The Man Next Door. Philadelphia, Neaula Publishing Company, 1919.
   Surgical Technique. *New York Medical Journal*, June 1914 (prize essay).

Ref: *Who's Who of the Colored Race*, 1915, p. 149.
   Who's Who in Colored America, 1927, p. 102.
   Jet, Oct. 23, 1958, p. 11.
   National Cyclopedia of American Biography, v. 32, p. 299. [p]

Jackson, Ann Elizabeth   (1922– ——, F)

Photographer. Born in 1922. Only female photographer employed by the Veterans Administration in Columbus, OH, in the 1950s. Assistant Photographer, specializing in line copy work before joining the V.A.

Ref: *Ebony*, Mar. 1955, p. 5. [p]
   Viewfinders, Black Women Photographers, p. 84, 180.

Jackson, Augustus   (1800s, M)

Inventor. Invented ice cream in 1832 in Philadelphia.

Ref: *Ebony Handbook*, p. 371.
   In Black and White, p. 478.
   Negro Almanac, 4th ed., p. 1053.

Jackson, Benjamin F.   (1800s, M)

Inventor. Massachusetts. Invented a heat apparatus, a gas burner, an electrolysers' furnace, a steam boiler, a trolley wheel controller, a tank signal, and a hydrocarbon burner system, Patent #622,482, April 4, 1899.

Ref: *Negro in Our History*, 5th ed., p. 464.

Jackson, Larry Eugene   (1943– ——, M)

Engineer (mechanical). Born in Chicago, IL, Feb. 18, 1943. B.S. (mechanical engineering), Purdue University, 1967; M.S., 1972. Inland Steel Co., Senior Engineer, 1967–75; Project Engineer, Kaiser Engineering, Inc., 1977–.

Memberships and awards: American Institute of Steel Engineers; Board of Directors, Gary and Building; Alpha Phi Alpha.

Ref: *Who's Who Among Black Americans*, 1985, p. 428.
   Black Engineers in the United States, p. 103.

Jackson, Lawrence Waters   (1894–1954, M)

Physician. Anesthesiologist. Born in Washington, DC, Mar. 21, 1894. B.S., Howard University, 1916; M.D., Howard University Medical School, 1919. Chief, Anesthetic Service, Freedmen's Hospital, 1920–26; Resident Physician, 1926–28; Lecturer in Anesthesia, Howard Medical School.

Memberships and awards: President, Medico-Chirurgical Society of DC, 1928; National Medical Association; John A. Andrew Clinical Association.

Ref: *Who's Who in Colored America*, 1928–29, p. 202.
   Who's Who in Colored America, 1930–32, p. 235.
   Who's Who in Colored America, 1933–37, p. 279.
   Who's Who in Colored America, 1938–40, p. 279.
   Who's Who in Colored America, 1941–44, p. 277.
   National Medical Association, *Journal*, v. 46, Sept. 1954, p. 369. obit

Jackson, Richard H.   (1933– ——, M)

Engineer. Born in Detroit, MI, Oct. 17, 1933. Studied, University of Missouri, Lincoln University (MO), and the University of Wichita. He designed the alternate landing gear system and the thrust reverser fail-safe system for the Boeing 747 while an engineer at Boeing Corporation; first black engineer at Beech Aircraft; Consultant to NASA and the DOD experiment team for Gemini Spaceflights V through XII.

Ref: *Ebony Success Library*, v. 1, p. 170. [p]
        Who's Who Among Black Americans, 1985, p. 431.

Jackson, Robert L.   (1894–19??, M)

Physician. Surgeon. Born in Birmingham, AL, Oct. 31, 1894. B.S., Walden University, TN, 1917; M.D., Meharry Medical College, 1921. Practiced medicine in Baltimore for 41 years. First black physician to serve in the chest clinics of the Maryland Tuberculosis Association. One of the founders of Provident Hospital in Baltimore where he was the first President in Surgery and Medical Director. Provident Hospital remained open from 1928–1987.

Memberships and awards: National Medical Association Distinguished Service Medal, 1963; Chief of Surgery Emeritus at Provident Hospital, 1958; National Medical Association; Monument City Medical Society; Baltimore City Medical Society; Medical and Chirurgical Faculty of the State of Maryland; fellow, American College of Surgeons for which he worked hard to get black surgeons admitted; Kappa Alpha Psi.

Ref: National Medical Association, *Journal,* v. 55, Nov. 1963, p. 549–550. [p]

Jackson, Rudolph Ellsworth   (1932– ——, M)

Physician. Pediatrician. Born in Richmond, VA, May 31, 1932. B.S., Morehouse College, 1957; M.D., Meharry Medical College, 1961. Medical Officer, U.S. Navy, 1962–63; Pediatric Resident, U.S. Naval Hospital and Children's Hospital of Philadelphia, 1963–65, 1967–69; Assistant in Hematology, St. Jude Childrens' Research Hospital, 1969–72; Program Coordinator, National Sickle Cell Disease Branch, National Heart and Lung Institute, NIH, 1972–75; Director, Pediatric Hematology and Oncology, Howard University Hospital, 1976–79; Chairman, Department of Pediatrics, Meharry Medical School, 1980–83; Chairman, Department of Pediatrics, Morehouse School of Medicine, 1984–.

Memberships and awards: Diplomate, American Board of Pediatrics; American Academy of Pediatrics; National Medical Association; American Medical Association; Julia Davis Humanitarian Award; Sickle Cell Anemia Award, Indiana Sickle Cell Foundation; DHEW Superior Service Awards; Sigma Xi; Alpha Omega Alpha.

Ref: National Medical Association, *Journal,* v. 72, Mar. 1980, p. 275.
        Who's Who Among Black Americans, 1985, p. 431.

Jackson, Shirley Ann   (1946– ——, F)

Physicist (theoretical). Born in Washington, DC, Aug. 5, 1946. B.S., MIT, 1968; Ph.D. (physics), 1973. First black woman to receive MIT doctorate, Theoretical Solid State Physics. Research Associate in Theoretical Physics, Fermi National Accelerator Laboratory, 1973–74; Visiting Science Associate, European Organization for Nuclear Research, 1974–75; Research Associate in Theoretical Physics, Fermi National Accelerator Laboratory, 1975–76; Stanford Linear Accelerator Center and Aspen Center for Physics, 1976–77; Technical Staff, Bell Telephone Laboratories in theoretical physics, 1976–78; Technical Staff, Scattering and Low Energy Physics Research, Bell Laboratories, 1978–; research in Landau theories of charge density waves in one and two dimensions; two dimensional yang-mills gauge theories; neutrino reactions.

Memberships and awards: Candace Award, National Coalition of 100 Black Women; MIT Educational Council, 1976–; Board of Trustees, Lincoln University, 1980–; Nuclear Regulatory Commission-National Academy of Sciences, 1977–80; Sigma Xi; Delta Sigma Theta; AAAS; New York Academy of Sciences; Scholar, Martin Marietta Aircraft Corporation, 1964–68; National Science Foundation Traineeship, 1968–71; Outstanding Young Women of America Award, 1976, 1981.

Dissertation title: The Study of a Multiperipheral Model with Continued Cross-Channel Unitarity.

Ref: *In Black and White*, p. 489.
        American Men and Women of Science, 15th ed., p. 10.
        Who's Who Among Black Americans, 1985, p. 431.
        Smithsonian. *Black Women Achieve Against Odds*, p. 38.
        Ebony, July 1986, p. 134. [p]
        Blacks in Science: Astrophysicist to Zoologist, p. 60.
        Ebony, Nov. 1974, p. 114–116, 118, 120, 122. [p]

James, Daniel (Chappie)   (1920–1978, M)

Military (Air Force). General (four star). Born in Pensacola, FL, Feb. 11, 1920. Civilian Flying School, Tuskegee Institute, 1938, graduated 1942 and taught Air Force Cadets as a Civilian Instructor, Moton Field, AL, 1942; volunteered for the Army Air Corps in 1943 and won his wings in six months. In 1954 he was the only black commanding a fighter squadron, 437th Fighter Interceptor Squadron, Otis Air Force Base, MA. In 1975, he became the highest ranking black officer when he was promoted to four-star general. Became Commander-in-Chief of the North American Air Defense Command (NORAD).

Memberships and awards: Distinguished Flying Cross; Air Medal with 7 oak leaf clusters; Presidential Unit Citation; about 10 other decorations.

Ref: *Amsterdam News*, Jan. 31, 1970, C4, p. 2, appointment.
        Black Americans in Defense of Our Nation, p. 116–119. [p]
        Ebony, Nov. 1985, p. 332. [p]
        Current Biography, 1976, p. 196–198.
        In Black and White, v. 1, p. 492.
        Ebony Success Library, v. 1, p. 172 [p]
        Ebony, Oct. 1970, p. 152–154, 156. [p]
        Ebony, Dec. 1975, p. 48–51, 54, 58–59, 62. [p] full page
        Who's Who Among Black Americans, 1977–78, p. 466.

James, Grace Marilyn (1923– ——, F)

Physician. Pediatrician. Psychiatrist. Born in Charleston, WV, Aug. 12, 1923. B.A., West Virginia State College, Institute, WV, 1944; M.D., Meharry Medical College, 1950; Instructor in Child Health, University of Louisville School of Medicine, 1953–62; Child Health Physician, Louisville and Jefferson County Department of Health, 1953–55; Public Health Physician, 1962–63; Assistant Visiting Psychiatrist, King's County Hospital Center, Brooklyn, NY, 1965–66; Director of Diagnostic and Evaluation Service, Division of Mental Retardation, Frankfort, KY, 1966–67; Attending Physician, Children's Hospital, 1968–69; Kentucky Kosair Crippled Children's Hospital, 1968–81; 1983–.

Memberships and awards: American Medical Association; National Medical Association; Kentucky Medical Association; Queens Clinical Society, 1964–66; Kentucky Pediatric Society, 1956–; Section II, New York; American Academy of Pediatrics, 1964–66; Action Research Team, University of Louisville Medical School; American Association of Mental Deficiency, 1965–; Chairman, Pediatric Section, National Medical Association, 1962–66; Secretary, Pediatric Section, National Medical Association, 1971–74; fellow, American Academy of Pediatrics; first black appointed to the staff of a Louisville Hospital.

Ref: *Who's Who Among Black Americans*, 1985, p. 434.
Ebony, Feb. 1955, p. 4. [p]
ABMS Compendium of Medical Specialists, v. 4, p. 941.

James, Thomas Leslie (1927– ——, M)

Dentist. Military (Navy). Born in Pensacola, FL, Nov. 7, 1927. B.A., Morehouse; B.S., Fisk University; D.D.S., Meharry Medical College, 1951. Assistant Professor of Oral Biology, University of Miami School of Medicine, 1968–72; First black Regular Commissioned Officer, U.S. Navy, 1951–58.

Memberships and awards: Dade County Dental Society; Dade County Academy of Medicine; Kappa Alpha Psi. Staff of N. Dade Medical Center and Hospital and N. Shore Hospital.

Ref: *Who's Who Among Black Americans*, 1985, p. 436.

Jamison, Francis Trevanian (1892–19??, M)

Dentist. Born in Wrightsville, PA, Oct. 16, 1892. B.A., Lincoln University, PA, 1913; D.D.S., University of Pennsylvania Dental School, 1917. First black dental surgeon at the New Castle County Workhouse in Delaware.

Memberships and awards: Alpha Phi Alpha; won gold medal at Lincoln University for excellence in natural science.

Ref: *Who's Who in Colored America*, 1927, p. 103–104.
Who's Who in Colored America, 1928–29, p. 204.
Who's Who in Colored America, 1930–32, p. 237.

Who's Who in Colored America, 1938–40, p. 283.
Who's Who in Colored America, 1941–44, p. 278.

Jarrett, Bessie (1900s, F)

Military (Army). First black woman in the WAAC, July 11, 1942.

Jason, Robert Stewart (1901–1984, M)

Physician. Pathologist. Born in Santurce, P.R., Nov. 29, 1901. B.A., Lincoln University, PA, 1924 (magna cum laude); M.D., Howard University, 1928; Ph.D. (pathology), University of Chicago, 1932. First black to earn a Ph.D. in Pathology. Dean, Howard Medical School, 1955–65; Emeritus Professor of Pathology, Howard University Medical College, 1970–84; Pathologist, Freedmen's Hospital, 1931–70; research in Histopathology of the palatine tonsils and pathology of syphilis of the aortic valve.

Memberships and awards: Honorary D.Sc., Howard University, 1948; General Education Board fellow, University of Chicago, 1927–31; National Screening Committee, Fulbright Awards, Institute of International Education, 1961–63; National Advisory Council on Education for Health Professionals, 1964–69; Committee on Pathology of the National Academy of Sciences—National Research Council, 1967–71; Consultant of the Advisory Committee for International Health of the Agency for International Development, 1967–72; Distinguished Service Award, National Medical Association, 1969; American Medical Association; American Association of Pathologists and Bacteriologists; fellow, College of American Pathologists; International Academy of Pathologists.

Dissertation title: Studies on the Histopathology of the Palatine Tonsil and on Immunological Reaction of the Adjacent Tissues.

Ref: *American Men and Women of Science*, 12th ed., p. 3015.
Holders of Doctorates Among American Negroes, p. 124.
Jet, May 19, 1955, p. 49.
National Medical Association, *Journal*, v. 47, July 1955, p. 269. [p]
National Medical Association, *Journal*, v. 58, Mar. 1966, p. 131. [p]
National Medical Association, *Journal*, v. 62, Jan. 1970, p. 60.
National Medical Association, *Journal*, v. 76, Sept. 1984, p. 934. [p] obit

Jay, James M. (1927– ——, M)

Biologist. Bacteriologist. Ecologist (microbial). Born in Fitzgerald, GA, Sept. 12, 1927. B.A., Paine College, 1950; M.S., Ohio State University, 1953; Ph.D., Ohio State University, 1956. Assistant Professor, Southern University, 1957–61; Professor, Biology, Wayne State College, 1961–69; owner, Balamp Publishing Company, 1971–; Consultant, Gaines Foods, Inc., 1984–85.

Memberships and awards: Chairman, Food Microbiology Division, American Society for Microbiology, 1983–84; Probus Award, Wayne State University, 1969; Distinguished Alumni Award, Paine College, 1969; AAAS; Sigma Xi; International Association of Milk, Food and Environmental Sanitarians.

Dissertation title: The Effect of Chlortetracycline on the Microflora Which Develops During the Spoilage of Beef, and Studies on the Mode of Action of This Antibiotic in Meat Preservation.

Pub: Negroes in Science, Natural Science Doctorates, 1876–1969. Detroit, Balamp Pub. Co., 1971.
Modern Food Microbiology, New York, Van Nostrand, 1970.

Ref: *American Men and Women of Science,* 16th ed., p. 48.
Who's Who Among Black Americans, 1985, p. 437.
Black Americans in the Sciences. In *Minorities in Science: The Challenge for Change in Biomedicine.* Edited by Melnick, Vijaya and Franklin D. Hamilton. N.Y., Plenum Press, 1977. p. 3–8.

Jearld, Ambrose, Jr.   (1944– ——, M)

Zoologist. Born in Annapolis, MD, Mar. 6, 1944. B.S. (biology), University of Maryland, Eastern Shore, 1965; M.S., Oklahoma State University, 1970; Ph.D. (zoology), 1975. Chemist, Publickers Industries, Inc., 1965–67; Biology Assistant in Medical Research, Army Edgewood Arsenal, 1969–71; Assistant Professor of Biology and Anatomy, Lincoln University, 1975–77; Assistant Professor of Animal Behavior and Ecology, Howard University, 1977–78; Supervisory Research Fishery Biologist, Northeast Fisheries Center, Woods Hole Laboratory, U.S. Department of Commerce, 1978–.

Memberships and awards: Annapolis Environmental Commission, 1977–78; Sigma Xi; Animal Behavior Society; American Fisheries Society; International Association of Fish Ethologists; Residential Citation, National Association for Equal Opportunity in Higher Education as a Distinguished Alumnus, 1984.

Dissertation title: An Ethological Study of the Honey Gourami, Colisa Chuna, and Its Congeners.

Ref: *American Men and Women of Science,* 15th ed., p. 48.
Ebony, 1985, p. 7.

Jefferson, Mildred Fay   (1925– ——, F)

Physician. Born in Pittsburgh, TX. B.A., Texas College; M.S., Tufts College; M.D., Harvard University Medical School, 1951. First black female graduate, Stritch School of Medicine, 1977. Clinical Professor, Boston University.

Memberships and awards: Sword of Loyola; National Right to Life Commission.

Ref: *Who's Who Among Black Americans,* 1985, p. 438.
Crisis, Aug.–Sept., 1951, p. 444. [p]

Jeffries, Jasper Brown   (1912–19??, M)

Physicist. Mathematician. Born in Mocksville, NC, April 15, 1912. B.S., West Virginia State College, 1933; University of Illinois, 1933–35; M.S., University of Chicago, 1940. Instructor in Physics, Public Schools of North Carolina, 1933–35; Physicist, Plutonium Project, Manhattan Atomic Energy Project, Chicago, 1943–46; Professor of Physics and Head of the Department, North Carolina A & T, 1946–49; Senior Engineer, Control Instrument Co., NY, 1951–59; Loral Electronics Corporation, 1959–60; Boland and Boyce, Inc., 1960–63; Assistant Professor of Mathematics, Westchester Community College, 1963–71; Professor and Chairman of the Department, 1971–; worked in general and nuclear physics.

Ref: *American Men and Women of Science,* 12th ed., p. 3021.

Jeffries, Louis Freeman   (1894–19??, M)

Chemist. Born in Jones, TN, April 15, 1894. B.A., Virginia Union University, 1922; B.S., University of Chicago, 1929; M.S., 1930; Michigan, 1937–38; University of Pennsylvania, 1944–45. Instructor in Chemistry and Physics, Roger Williams College, 1922–25; Assistant Professor of Chemistry, Chaflin College, 1925–27; Virginia Union, 1927–34; Director, Division of Material and Natural Sciences, 1934–42; Professor of Chemistry and Head of the Department, 1942.

Memberships and awards: Chemical Society.

Ref: *American Men of Science,* 8th ed., p. 1254.

Jemison, Mae C.   (195?– ——, F)

Physician. Born in Decator, AL. B.S., Stanford University, 1977; M.D., Cornell University Medical School, 1981. Staff Physician for the Peace Corps in Sierra Leone. Oversaw Medical Health Care Program for volunteers in Liberia. Physician with CIGNA Health Plan of California, 1985–87. First black female astronaut trainee for NASA.

Ref: *Ebony,* Oct. 1987, p. 93–95, 98. [p] p. 93.

Jenkins, Charles M.   (1900s, M)

Physician. Allergist. Senior attending physician in charge of Provident Hospital Allergy Clinic, Chicago.

Memberships and awards: President, Chicago Allergy Society, 1961; Chairman, Allergy Section, Illinois State Medical Society; delivered opening lecture on respiratory allergy, sensitivity to soybean and its products, at Mayo Clinic in Minnesota.

Ref: *Jet*, Nov. 27, 1966, p. 21.
    Jet, June 20, 1963, p. 27.
    Jet, Aug. 31, 1961, p. 26. [p]

Jenkins, Melvin E.   (1923- ——, M)

Physician. Pediatrician. Born in Kansas City, MO, June 24, 1923. B.A., University of Kansas, 1944; M.D., 1946. Sickle Cell Disease Specialist; Professor, University of Nebraska, 1969-73; Head, Department of Pediatrics and Child Health, Howard University, 1973-87.

Memberships and awards: Research grant, NIH; Comprehensive Health Association of Omaha (founder); American Academy of Pediatrics; American Pediatric Society; Society for Pediatric Research; Sigma Xi; Student American Medical Association, Golden Apple Award, 1963; AAAS; Medico-Chirurgical Society of the District of Columbia; Alpha Omega Alpha; National Medical Association.

Pub: Over 48 publications.

Ref: National Medical Association, *Journal*, v. 79, Oct. 1987, p. 1104-1106. [p]
    Who's Who Among Black Americans, 1985, p. 441.

Jenkins, N. A.   (1882-1935, M)

Physician. Surgeon. Born in Anderson, SC, June 10 1882. B.S., C.P., Benedict College, 1903; M.D., Shaw University, 1908; Postgraduate courses, Brooklyn School and Hospital, 1909; Rush College, Chicago, 1912. Surgeon-in-Chief and Superintendent of Waverly Fraternity Hospital.

Memberships and awards: National Medical Association; President of Congaree Medical Society and Palmetto Medical Association.

Ref: *Who's Who in Colored America*, 1930-32, p. 237.
    Who's Who in Colored America, 1933-37, p. 283.
    A True Likeness, Portraits by Richard Samuel Roberts, p. 136-137. [p]

Joel, Lawrence   (1928- ——, M)

Military (Army), SP6. Born in Winston-Salem, NC, Feb. 22, 1928.

Memberships and awards: Congressional Medal of Honor for conspicuous gallantry and intrepidity at the risk of his life, Republic of Vietnam, Nov. 8, 1965.

Ref: *Ebony*, Jan. 1968, p. 121.
    Black Americans in Defense of Our Nation, p. 74. [p]

Johnson, Bernard Henry, Jr.   (1920- ——, M)

Chemist (analytical). Born in Washington, DC, Oct. 19, 1920. B.S., Howard University, 1942; M.S., 1944; Ph.D., University of Pittsburgh, 1954. Assistant, Howard University, 1942-44; Instructor, 1944; Assistant Professor of Chemistry, 1946-48; Professor, Central State College,

1951-; Chemistry Specialist and Consultant, USAID, India, University of Vikram, summer, 1966; Research Chemist, Duriron Company, Dayton, OH, 1953, 1955; Research Chemist, Dow Chemical Company, Midland, MI, May-Sept. 1969.

Memberships and awards: American Chemical Society; Beta Kappa Chi; Vice-President, Chemistry Section, Ohio Academy of Science, 1971-72; Research Grant, Air Force, Research and Development Command, Office of Scientific Research, 1956-59; Fulbright Scholar, lecturer and consultant in chemistry, Khon Kaen University, Thailand, 1968-69.

Dissertation title: Microdetermination of Fluorine in Organic Compounds: An Amperometric Approach.

Pub: *Experimental Chemistry*, 1964.

Ref: *The Negro in Science*, p. 183.
    Living Black American Authors, p. 80.

Johnson, Charles E.   (1939- ——, M)

Microbiologist. Born in Dallas, NC, Feb. 28, 1939. B.S., Morgan State College, 1960; Ph.D. (microbiology), University of Cincinnati, 1966. Secondary Head, Dermatology Division, Proctor and Gamble. Former Staff Microbiologist.

Dissertation title: Studies on the Lethal Toxin of Bacillus Cereus.

Ref: *Ebony*, Jan. 1973, p. 6. [p]
    In Black and White, p. 505.

Johnson, Charles William   (1922- ——, M)

Physician. Bacteriologist. Microbiologist. Born in Ennis, TX, Jan. 25, 1922. B.S., Prairie View State College, 1942; M.S., University of Southern California, 1947; M.D., Meharry Medical College, 1953. Instructor in Bacteriology and Parasitology, Meharry Medical College, 1947-48; from Assistant Professor to Chairman of the Department, 1949-73; Dean, Division of Graduate Studies and Research, 1966-81.

Memberships and awards: AAAS; American Society for Microbiology; American Academy of Allergy; American Federation for Clinical Research; Sigma Xi; Kappa Pi; Rockefeller Foundation Fellow, 1957-59.

Ref: *American Men and Women of Science*, 15th ed., p. 81.
    The Negro in Science, p. 179.
    National Medical Association, *Journal*, v. 65, July 1973, p. 307. [p] (article by him)

Johnson, Christine Hedgley   (1900s, F)

Nurse. B.S., Virginia Union University; Nursing diploma, Lincoln School for Nurses, New York; M.S., Boston University. Won rank of Colonel. Twin sister to Hedgley, computer whiz at NASA. Acting Assistant Director of Nursing, Indian Health Service, Santa Fe, NM. Has held key position in USPHS since she joined in 1964.

Ref: *The Path We Tread,* p. 194.

Johnson, Elgy Sibley   (1915–1986, M)

Mathematician. Born in Jacksonville, FL, Nov. 8, 1915. B.A. (mathematics), Johnson C. Smith University, 1935; M.A. (mathematical statistics), University of Michigan, 1938; Ph.D. (pure mathematics), Catholic University of America, 1957. Adjunct Professor, Mathematics and Statistics, American University, 1957–70; Director, Graduate Degree Program, American University, summer, 1967; Professor of Mathematics, University of the District of Columbia, 1964–72; Chairman, Mathematics Department, University of the District of Columbia, 1976–86.

Memberships and awards: National Council of Mathematics Teachers; American Mathematical Society; Mathematical Association of America; Institute for Mathematical Statistics; research in nonlinear differential equations; studies of secondary mathematics teaching, Eugene and Agnes E. Meyer Foundation Grant, England, France, West Germany, and Denmark, summer, 1967; research in Mathematics, National Science Foundation Grant, Michigan State University, summer, 1972; Acting President, Federal City College, 1972–74.

Dissertation title: Properties of Solutions of Nonlinear Differential Equations.

Ref: *Black Mathematicians and Their Works,* p. 288. [p]
Washington Post, Thurs., Mar. 12, 1987, C10. obit
American Men and Women of Science, 14th ed., p. 2455.

Johnson, Frank Bacchus   (1919– ——, M)

Pathologist. Physician. Born in Washington, DC, Feb. 1, 1919. B.S., University of Michigan, 1940; M.D., Howard University Medical College, 1944. From Intern to Resident Pathologist, Medical Center, Jersey City, 1944–46; Director of Clinical Laboratories, Howard University, 1946–48; Research Associate, University of Chicago, 1950–52; Pathologist, 1952–60; Chief, Basic Science Division, 1960–72; Chief, Histochemical Branch, Armed Forces Institute of Pathology, 1972–.

Memberships and awards: AEC fellow in Medical Science, University of Chicago, 1948–50; Citation for Administrative and Technical Proficiency, Veterans Administration, 1958; Commendation for Outstanding Contributions to Histochemistry, 1964; American Crystallography Society; American Medical Association; American Society for Experimental Pathology; American Association of Pathologists and Bacteriologists; Histochemical Society.

Ref: *American Men and Women of Science,* 14th ed., p. 2456.
Drew. Negro Scholars in Scientific Research. *Journal of Negro History,* v. 35, 1950, p. 148.
Medico-Chirurgical Society of the District of Columbia, *Bulletin,* v. 5, May–Sept. 1948, p. 8. [p]

Johnson, Frederick M.   (1800s, M)

Inventor. Born in Washington, DC, in the 1800s. In 1912 he invented a self-feed rifle that fired three hundred shots without stopping (twenty shots per second).

Ref: *Negro Year Book,* 1931, p. 208.

Johnson, Gladys L.   (19??– ——, F)

Dentist. Surgeon (oral). Surgeon (maxillofacial). Ohio State; College of Medicine and Dentistry of New Jersey; Yale; Rutgers. First black female oral and maxillofacial surgeon in the United States.

Ref: *Ebony,* Aug. 1982, p. 5.

Johnson, Hallie Tanner Dillon   (1864–19??, F)

Physician. Born in Pittsburgh, PA, 1864. M.D., Women's Medical College of Pennsylvania, 1891. First woman of any race to practice medicine in Alabama. Wife of John Quincy Johnson, President of Allen University; she served as Resident Physician, Tuskegee Institute, 1891–94, where she taught two classes and had to make her own medicines, serving 450 students and 30 officers and faculty.

Ref: *Profiles of Negro Womanhood,* v. 1, p. 277.
Send Us a Lady Physician, p. 110, 114.

Johnson, Havern H.   (1900s, M)

Physician. Surgeon. Born in New York City. B.S., Lincoln University, PA; M.D., Howard University Medical School. Surgeon-in-Chief, Friendly Clinic and Hospital; operated a 10-bed clinic with a staff of 6.

Memberships and awards: Omega Psi Phi; Volunteer State Medical Association; Beta Kappa Chi Medical Fraternity; President, Bluff City Medical Society.

Ref: *National Register,* 1952, p. 590.

Johnson, Hazel Winifred   (1927– ——, F)

See: Johnson-Brown, Hazel Winifred.

Johnson, John Beauregard, Jr.   (1908–1972, M)

Physician. Cardiologist. Born in Bessemer, AL, April 29, 1908. B.A., Oberlin College; M.D., Western Reserve University, 1935; Postgraduate study in Internal Medicine, University of Rochester, 1939–41. Head, Department of Medicine, Howard University, 1958–61; From Laboratory Assistant to Director, Division of Cardiology, Howard

University Medical College, 1936–72; research in the use of radioactive iodine in hyperthyroidism.

Memberships and awards: Distinguished Service Medal, National Medical Association, 1960; Board of Directors, American Heart Association, 1958–61.

Ref: *American Men and Women of Science*, 12th ed., p. 3063.
Dictionary of American Medical Biography, p. 397.
Ebony, Aug. 1955, p. 84. [p]
National Medical Association, *Journal*, v. 63, July 1971, p. 310.
Ebony, June 1973, p. 75. [p]
National Medical Association, *Journal*, v. 65, Mar. 1973, p. 166–170. Bibliography of his publications, p. 168–170. [p] cover
Medico-Chirurgical Society of the District of Columbia, Inc., *Bulletin*, Nov. 1948, p. 7.

Johnson, John Hayden   (1875–1954, M)

Physician. Born in Washington, DC, Feb. 17, 1875. Certificate, Howard University, 1895; M.D., 1900.

Memberships and awards: Washington, DC, Board of Education, 1916; President, District Medico-Chirurgical Society, 1914; National Medical Association.

Ref: *Howard University Medical Department*, p. 186.
Jet, April 25, 1963, p. 11.
Who's Who in Colored America, 1927, p. 107.
Who's Who in Colored America, 1928–29, p. 212.
Who's Who in Colored America, 1930–32, p. 243.
Who's Who in Colored America, 1933–37, p. 289.
Who's Who in Colored America, 1938–40, p. 290.
Who's Who in Colored America, 1941–44, p. 287.
National Medical Association, *Journal*, v. 46, Sept. 1954, p. 369. obit

Johnson, Joseph Lealand   (1895–19??, M)

Physiologist. Physician. Born in Philadelphia, PA, Jan. 14, 1895. B.A., Pennsylvania State College, 1919; M.D., Ph.D. (medicine and physiology), University of Chicago, 1931. Vice-Principal, Kansas Vocational College, 1919–20; Teacher, Public Schools in Missouri, 1920–26; Professor, Physiology and Head, Physiology Department, Howard University Medical School, 1931–47; Dean, 1946–55; Emeritus, 1969–. He and Arnold H. Maloney were the second and third blacks to earn both the M.D. and Ph.D. degrees.

Memberships and awards: AAAS; American Medical Association; Foundation for Tropical Medicine; fellow, New York Academy of Sciences; International College of Surgeons; Medico-Chirurgical Society of the District of Columbia; Imhotep Conference Chairman, 1960–61.

Dissertation title: Experimental Chronic Hyperparathyroidism.

Ref: *American Men and Women of Science*, 12th ed., p. 3065.
Holders of Doctorates Among American Negroes, p. 125.
History of the Negro in Medicine, p. 138. [p] p. 138.

National Medical Association, *Journal*, v. 45, Jan. 1953, p. 72. [p]
National Medical Association, *Journal*, v. 52, Nov. 1960, p. 449. [p]
Cobb, W. Montague. Joseph Lealand Johnson, B.S., M.D., Ph.D., 1895–. National Medical Association, *Journal*, v. 64, Mar. 1972, p. 176–179. [p] cover

Johnson, Katherine G.   (1918– ——, F)

Physicist. Space Scientist. Mathematician. Born in 1918. Works at NASA with the tracking teams of manned and unmanned orbital missions.

Ref: *Black Contributors to Science and Energy Technology*, p. 11.
Golden Legacy, 1969, v. 5, p. 29.
In Black and White, p. 514.

Johnson, Peter A.   (1851–1914, M)

Physician. Born in Pine Brook, NJ, July 17, 1851. M.D., Long Island College Hospital, 1882. Assistant to Drs. E. I. and Coroner Messener in Mt. Sinai Hospital for seven years. One of the best physicians of his time, serving white and black patients in New York for thirty-two years. Founder and Surgeon-in-Chief McDonugh Memorial Hospital, 1898–1903.

Memberships and awards: President, National Medical Association, 1909; a founder of the Urban League.

Ref: *Dictionary of American Medical Biography*, p. 398.

Johnson, W.   (1800s, M)

Inventor. Eggbeater consisting of a series of formed spring-like wires attached to a handle. The forerunner of today's mixers. Patent #1,292,821, 1884.

Ref: *At Last Recognition in America*, v. 1, p. 7.

Johnson, William H.   (1800s, M)

Inventor. Born in Texas. Invented a device for overcoming dead center in motion, Patent #612,345, Oct. 1898, one for a compound engine, and another for a water boiler.

Ref: *Negro in Our History*, 5th ed., p. 464.

Johnson, William Thomas Mitchell   (1921– ——, M)

Chemist (physical). Physiologist (cardiovascular). Born in Philadelphia, PA, Oct. 22, 1921. B.S., Virginia State College, 1943; M.S., University of Pennsylvania, 1947; Ph.D. (physical chemistry), 1950. Research Chemist, Chemical Division, Fabrics and Finishes Department, E.

I. DuPont de Nemours and Company, 1949–63; Professor of Chemistry, Lincoln University, PA, 1963–72; Program Director, Biomedical Research Programs, Lincoln University, PA, 1972–; research in infrared spectroscopy of blood vessel intima.

Memberships and awards: Roon Award, 1961; Lindback Award for Distinguished Teaching, 1965; John B. Knecht Brotherhood Award, 1965.

Dissertation title: The Mechanism of Acetylene Oxidation by Supported Silver-Nitrate.

Ref: *American Men and Women of Science,* 14th ed., p. 2475.
In Black and White, p. 521.
Who's Who Among Black Americans, 1977, p. 493.

Johnson-Brown, Hazel Winifred   (1927– ——, F)

Military (Army). Brigadier General. Nurse. Born in Pennsylvania in 1927. Basic Nursing Training, Harlem Hospital School of Nursing, New York, NY; B.S. (nursing), Villanova University; M.S. (nursing education), Teachers College, Columbia University; Ph.D. (educational administration), Catholic University of America. First black female general in the U.S. Army. Chief, Army Nurse Corps, 1979; retired, 1983. Adjunct Professor, George Washington University; Director, Washington Office of the American Nursing Association.

Memberships and awards: Anita Newcomb McGee Award given by the DAR to the nurse chosen by the Surgeon General as the U.S. Army Nurse of the Year, 1972; first black female Army General, appointed Sept. 1, 1979; Honorary Doctorates from Villanova University, Morgan State University, and the University of Maryland; Legion of Merit; Meritorious Service Medal; Army Commendation Medal with oak leaf cluster.

Dissertation title: A Description of the Administrative Activities of the Director of Nursing Service in Selected General Hospitals, as Described by the Director of Nursing Service, the Hospital Administrator, and the Medical Director.

Ref: *Jet,* July 17, 1980, p. 60. [p]
Smithsonian. Black Women Achievements Against All Odds. p. 39.
Black Americans in Defense of Our Nation, p. 103. [p]
The Path We Tread, p. 174, 242, 244. [p]
Ebony, Feb. 1980, p. 44–46, 48, 50. [p]
Crisis, v. 91, Jan. 1984, p. 44. [p]

Jones, Edith Mae Irby   (1927– ——, F)

Physician. Born in Conway, AR, Dec. 23, 1927. B.S., Knoxville College, 1947; M.D., University of Arkansas, 1952 (first black); Postgraduate, 1965 and other postgraduate courses.

Memberships and awards: President, National Medical Association, 1986; Board of Trustees, National Medi-

cal Association; Chairman, Council of Scientific Assembly, National Medical Association; Texas Health Association; "Edith Irby Jones" Award Day State of Arkansas, 1979; American Heart Association; President, Arkansas Medical, Dental, and Pharmaceutical Association; Chairman of the Board, Delta Research and Education Foundation; numerous other organizations and awards.

Ref: *Ebony,* May 1986, p. 42. [p]
Ebony, July 1963, p. 52–54, 56, 58–59. [p]
National Medical Association, *Journal,* v. 73, Supplement, Dec. 1981, p. 1128–1129.
Jet, May 26, 1986, p. 13. [p]
Who's Who Among Black Americans, 1985, p. 463.
National Medical Association, *Journal,* v. 67, Mar. 1975, p. 183–184. [p]
National Medical Association, *Journal,* v. 71, Oct. 1979, p. 1025. [p]
National Medical Association, *Journal,* v. 78, June 1986. [p] cover

Jones, Eleanor Green Dawley   (1929– ——, F)

Mathematician. Born in Norfolk, VA, Aug. 10, 1929. B.S. (mathematics), Howard University, 1949; M.S. (mathematics), Howard University, 1950; Ph.D. (mathematics), Syracuse University, 1966. Instructor, Mathematics, Hampton Institute, 1955–62; Associate Professor of Mathematics, Hampton Institute, 1966–67; Professor of Mathematics, Norfolk State College, 1967–.

Memberships and awards: Pi Mu Epsilon; Sigma Xi; Pepsi-Cola Four-Year Scholarship; B.S., cum laude, age 19; National Science Foundation fellow. Mathematical Association of America; V. President, National Association of Mathematicians, 1975–.

Pub: $4' + 4' + 4' =$ aSquare. *American Mathematical Monthly,* Mar. 1969.
A Note on Abelian P-Groups and Their Endomorphism Rings. *American Mathematical Monthly,* May 1967.

Dissertation title: Abelian Groups and Their Endomorphism Rings and the Quasi-Endomorphism of Torsion Free Abelian Groups.

Ref: *Black Mathematicians and Their Works,* p. 288. [p] p. 136.
Kenschaft, Patricia C. Black Women in Math in U.S. *American Mathematical Monthly,* v. 88, p. 593, 598–599.
National Faculty Directory, 1987, p. 1846.
Who's Who Among American Women, 1974, p. 484.
American Men and Women of Science, 16th ed., p. 123

Jones, Ernest J. (1900s, M)

Physician.

Memberships and awards: President, Georgia Academy of Family Physicians. First black to lead the 1200-member group.

Ref: *Jet,* Nov. 17, 1986, p. 52.

Jones, Frank (1900s, M)

Physician. Medical Director, Freedmen's Hospital; testified before Congress urging the government to build a new 500-bed hospital then turn hospital over to Howard University (they did), June 1961.

Ref: *Jet,* June 19, 1961, p. 28.

Jones, Frederick McKinley (1893–1961, M)

Inventor. Born in Cincinnati, OH, 1893. Mastered electronics through self study; invented first portable X-ray machine; had over 60 patents including #2,163,754 for a ticket-dispensing machine for movie-house tickets and when he heard a trucker say he had lost a load of chickens because they were on the road too long, he figured out a way to refrigerate the trucks for long distance travel for which he obtained patent #2,475,841; holds 40 refrigeration patents.

Memberships and awards: American Society of Refrigeration Engineers (first black member); Minnesota Inventors Hall of Fame, 1977.

Ref: *Dictionary of American Negro Biography,* p. 366–367.
Ebony, June 1968, p. 89.
Ott, Virginia, and Gloria Swanson. *Man with a Million Ideas, Fred Jones, Genius/Inventor,* 1977. 109 p.
Ebony, Dec. 1952, p. 41–44, 46. [p] p. 41.
National Cyclopedia of American Biography, v. 50, p. 574.

Jones, George Maceo (1900–19??, M)

Engineer (civil). Architect. Born in Albany, GA, Aug. 25, 1900. B.S.A. and M.S.A., University of Michigan, Ph.D., 1925. Assistant to Dean and Dean, Florida A&M College, 1927–29; Assistant Professor to Associate Professor of Architecture, Howard University, 1930–37; Architect-Engineer, Illinois, 1937–50; Developmental Director, Cook County Housing Authority, 1950–52; Practicing Architect-Engineer, 1952–55; General Engineer, U.S. Government, 1955–. Researched graphical stress analyses of structure.

Memberships and awards: Mathematical Society; Institute of Architects.

Dissertation title: A Study of Various Methods for the Determination of Wind Stresses in Tall Buildings.

Ref: *American Men of Science,* 10th ed., p. 2042.
Holders of Doctorates Among American Negroes, p. 125.

Negroes in Science: Natural Science Doctorates, 1876–1969, p. 52–53.

Jones, Herbert C. (193?– ——, M)

Physician. Otolaryngologist. Surgeon. Attended Talladega College in Alabama three years; B.S., Indiana University, 1957; M.D., 1961. Practices in Atlanta, GA.

Memberships and awards: Examining Board, American Academy of Otolaryngology; American College of Surgeons; Georgia State Medical Association; National Medical Association.

Ref: *Black Enterprise,* Oct. 1988, p. 80. [p]

Jones, Howard St. Claire, Jr. (1921– ——, M)

Engineer (electrical). Inventor. Born in Richmond, VA, Aug. 18, 1921. B.S. (mathematics and physics), Virginia Union University, 1943; M.S. (electrical engineering), Bucknell University, 1973. Electronics Engineer, National Bureau of Standards, 1946–53; Electronic Scientist Microwave Electronics, Diamond Ordnance Freeze Laboratory, Washington, DC, 1953–59; Supervisory Electronic Engineer, Harry Diamond Laboratories, 1959–68; Supervisory Physical Scientist, 1968–80; Technical Consultant, Harry Diamond Laboratories, 1980–; Adjunct Professor, Howard University School of Engineering, 1982–83.

Memberships and awards: Five major awards, Harry Diamond Laboratories; fellow, IEEE; fellow, AAAS; Antenna & Propagation Society; Microwave Theory and Technique Society; Honorary Doctor of Science Degree, Virginia Union University, 1971; Inventor of the Year, Harry Diamond Laboratories, 1972.

Pub: Thirty-five technical publications; thirty-one patents.

Ref: *Who's Who in Engineering,* 6th ed., p. 330.
Black Engineers in the U.S., p. 113.
American Men and Women of Science, 16th ed., p. 125.
Who's Who in America, 1986–87, p. 1441.

Jones, Irving Wendell (1930– ——, M)

Engineer (civil). Engineer (structural). Engineer (mechanical). Born in Washington, DC, Nov. 16, 1930. B.S. (civil engineering), Howard University, 1953; M.S. (applied mechanics), Columbia University, 1957; Ph.D. (applied mechanics), Brooklyn Polytechnic Institute, 1967. Assistant Civil Engineer, Columbia University, 1956–57; Structural Engineer, Grumman Aerospace Corp., 1957–62; Assistant Aerospace and Mechanics, Polytechnic Institute, Brooklyn, 1962–63; Assistant Director and Partner, Applied Technology Associates, Inc., 1963–69; Associate Professor of Civil Engineering, 1969–72; Professor of Civil Engineering and Chairman of the Department, Howard University, 1972–.

Memberships and awards: Pressure Vessel Research Council; Welding Research Foundation, 1964–69; American Society of Civil Engineers; American Society of Mechanical Engineers; American Society of Engineering Education; Award for Teaching Excellence, ASCS, 1970.

Dissertation title: Non-Periodic Vibrations of Layered Viscoelastic Plates.

Ref: *American Men and Women of Science,* 16th ed., p. 125-126.
    Black Engineers in the United States, p. 113.
    Who's Who in Engineering, 6th ed., p. 330.
    Ebony, June 1960, p. 68. [p] only

Jones, J. Loraine   (1900s, F)

Zoologist. B.S., University of Pittsburgh; M.S.; Ph.D. (zoology), 1934. Associate Professor, Biology, West Virginia State College.

Memberships and awards: Sigma Xi.

Dissertation title: Integument and Integumental Glands of the Amphibian, Triturus Viridesceris Viridesceus.

Ref: *Holders of Doctorates Among American Negroes,* p. 192.

Jones, Jane Wright   (1919- —— , F)

See: Wright, Jane Cooke.

Jones, John Leslie   (1913- —— , M)

Chemist (physical). Inventor. Born in Weleetak, OK, Aug. 31, 1913. B.S., M.S., University of California, 1934; Ph.D. (physical chemistry), Stanford University, 1936. Research Chemist, Pennsylvania Salt Manufacturing Co., 1936-37; Instructor in Physical Chemistry, U.S. Department of the Interior, 1937-41; Research Chemist and Section Leader, Plaskon Co., OH, 1941-46; Senior Research Engineer, Jet Propulsion Laboratory, California Institute of Technology, 1946-49; Division Head, U.S. Ordnance Test Station, 1950-59; Patent Agent, 1959-; Industrial Consultant, 1960-; research in plastics, kinetics of the pyrolysis of some alkyl iodides; numerous patents.

Dissertation title: The Kinetics of the Pyrolysis of Some Alkyl Iodides.

Ref: *American Men and Women of Science,* 12th ed., p. 3099.
    Holders of Doctorates Among American Negroes, p. 151.

Jones, Joseph H. N.   (1888-19??, M)

Physician. Born in Richmond, VA, Nov. 1, 1888. B.A., Oberlin College, OH, 1910; M.D., University of Iowa, 1923. Chemist, Dodge Leather Factory, Waukegan, IL, 1916-17; Medical Inspector, Department of Health, New York, NY, 1926-.

Memberships and awards: National Medical Association; American Medical Association; North Harlem Medical Society; Alpha Phi Alpha.

Ref: *Who's Who in Colored America,* 1930-31, p. 246-249. [p]
    Who's Who in Colored America, 1938-40, p. 298. [p] p. 299.
    Who's Who in Colored America, 1941-44, p. 295. [p] p. 297.

Jones, Leroy   (1929-1970, M)

Physician. Surgeon. Born in Kingston, NC, in 1929; B.S., St. Augustine's College, 1951; M.D., Howard University, 1959. Between college and medical school, he was a Supervisor of Chemical Research, Dupont Laboratories, Louisville, KY.

Memberships and awards: Fellow, American College of Surgeons, 1968; National Medical Association; Medico-Chirurgical Society of the District of Columbia; Medical Society of the District of Columbia; Omega Psi Phi.

Ref: National Medical Association, *Journal,* v. 62, May 1970, p. 253. obit & biog.

Jones, Major Boyd   (1909-19??, M)

Mathematician. Physicist. Born in Gloucester, VA, Nov. 3, 1909. B.S., Hampton Institute, VA, 1934; M.S., Cornell University, 1942; Ph.D. (science education, mathematics and physics), 1959. Instructor in Mathematics and Physics, Alabama State College, 1951-55; Acting Professor, Maryland State College, 1956-59; Professor, St. Pauls College, 1959-63; Professor of Mathematics, Norfolk State College, 1963-; Head of the Department, 1977-.

Dissertation title: Techniques, Methods, Procedures and Provisions Used in Selected Maryland Public Secondary Schools in Teaching Mathematics to Rapid Learners.

Ref: *American Men and Women of Science,* 14th ed., p. 2491.

Jones, Robert E.   (18??-19??, M)

Physician. M.D., University of Michigan, 1881.

Memberships and awards: President, National Medical Association, 1906.

Jones, Richard Francis (Frank)   (1897-1979, M)

Physician. Surgeon. Urologist. Born in Washington, DC, Feb. 16, 1897. B.S., Howard University, 1919; M.D., 1922. Instructor, Urology, Howard University Medical School, 1930; Chief of Urology, Freedmen's Hospital, 1933; Clinical Assistant Professor, 1937-42; Clinical Associate Professor, 1942-; Professor, 1945-62; Medical Director, Freedmen's Hospital, 1958-70.

Memberships and awards: President, Medico-Chirurgical Society, 1929-32; National Medical Association; Alpha Phi Alpha; Diplomate, American Board of Urology, 1936, first black; American Urological Association; Sigma Pi Phi; Alpha Omega Alpha.

Pub: Several articles in the *Journal of Urology* and *Journal of* the National Medical Association on Urology and Gonorrhea.

Ref: *Who's Who in Colored America,* 1938–40, p. 302.
The First Negro Medical Society (Cobb).
Who's Who in Colored America, 1941–44, p. 299.
Cobb, W. Montague. Richard Francis Jones, B.S., M.D., 1897–. National Medical Association, *Journal,* v. 64, May 1972, p. 276–279. [p] cover
National Medical Association, *Journal,* v. 71, Sept. 1979, p. 908. obit
A Century of Black Surgeons, p. 516–520. [p] p. 517.

Jones, Sarah Garland Boyd   (1865–19??, F)

Physician. Born in Albemarle County, VA, 1865. Richmond Normal School; M.D., Howard University Medical School, 1893. First woman to pass Virginia Board to practice medicine. Founded the Richmond Hospital and Training School for Nurses, later named Sarah G. Jones Memorial Hospital. She was married to Dr. Miles B. Jones.

Ref: Brown, Hallie Q. *Homespun Heroines and Other Women of Distinction.* 1926. Reprint, 1971.
Send Us a Lady Physician, p. 111.

Jones, Thomas Adolphus   (1983–19??, M)

Physician. Surgeon. Born in British Guiana (now Guyana), S.A., May 6, 1873. Howard University Medical School, 1900; M.D., Boston College of Physicians and Surgeons, Boston, MA, 1903; M.D.C.M., McGill University, 1913. Professor of Bacteriology and Chemistry, Flint Medical College, 1903–04; Medical Examiner, Bergen Lodge no. 43, K. of P. and St. Marks Lodge, Odd Fellows; founded and was Medical Director of an obstetrical school for colored students, Gonzales, TX, 1904; the school graduated the first four females and two males to pass the Texas State Board of Obstetricians.

Memberships and awards: President, Hudson County Physicians Association.

Ref: *Who's Who in Colored America,* 1928–29, p. 219.
Who's Who in Colored America, 1930–32, p. 250.
Who's Who in Colored America, 1933–37, p. 302.
Who's Who in Colored America, 1938–40, p. 302.
Who's Who in Colored America, 1941–44, p. 299.
Who's Who of the Colored Race, 1915, p. 164

Jones, Thomas Edward   (1880–1958, M)

Physician. Surgeon. Anesthetist. Born in Lynchburg, VA, May 26, 1880. Graduated from Lynchburg High School, 1898; M.D., Howard University Medical School, 1912. Anesthetist, Freedmen's Hospital, 1912–17; Resident Assistant Surgeon, Freedmen's Hospital, 1919–36; Surgeon-in-Chief, 1936–42. Successfully operated on a human heart April 7, 1927.

Memberships and awards: Distinguished Service Cross and Croix de Guerre in World War I; National Medical Association; Past Department Surgeon of the American Legion, District of Columbia; Alpha Phi Alpha.

Ref: *Who's Who in Colored America,* 1938–40, p. 305. [p] p. 305.
Who's Who in Colored America, 1941–44, p. 300. [p] p. 301.
National Medical Association, *Journal,* v. 50, Sept. 1958, p. 399. [p] obit

Jones, Verina Morton   (1865–19??, F)

Physician. Born in Cleveland, OH, Jan. 28, 1865. State Normal School, Columbia, SC; M.D., Women's Medical College of Pennsylvania, 1888; served as Resident Physician of Rust College in Holly Springs, MS, upon graduation from medical school; the oldest black Physician in Brooklyn, NY; first woman admitted to practice in Mississippi and first black woman to practice in Nassau County, Long Island, NY.

Memberships and awards: Zeta Phi Beta; Kings County Medical Society.

Ref: *Who's Who in Colored America,* 1928–29, p. 220.
Who's Who in Colored America, 1930–32, p. 250.
Who's Who in Colored America, 1933–37, p. 302.
Send Us a Lady Physician, p. 114.
Who's Who in Colored America, 1938–40, p. 305.
Who's Who in Colored America, 1941–44, p. 303.

Jones, W. Fontaine   (18??–1969, M)

Architect. Architect and Chairman of the Board, West Side Chamber of Commerce of New York. Architectural Consultant on Latin America. Designed Mother AME Zion Church, the oldest black church in New York.

Memberships and awards: American Institute of Architects.

Ref: *Jet,* Aug. 11, 1966, p. 41. (advertisement)
Ebony, May 1968, p. 63. [p] (advertisement)

Jones, William H., Sr.   (18??–1963, M)

Electrical contractor. First black licensed electrician in Louisville, KY.

Ref: *Jet,* Oct. 17, 1963, p. 51.

Jones, William Moses   (1898–19??, M)

Ophthalmologist. Physician. Born in Earle, AR, Nov. 12, 1898. Director, Eye Clinic, Billings Hospital, University of Chicago, 23 years; Ophthalmologist, Consultant, in charge of Student Health Services for 19 years; Department of Surgery, University of Chicago; Ophthalmologist, Chicago Board of Education; Jackson Park Hospital, Woodlawn and Provident Hospitals.

Memberships and awards: Alpha Phi Alpha; American College of Surgeons; fellow, American Academy of Ophthalmology and Otology; New York Academy of Sciences; Chicago Ophthalmological Society; American Medical Association.

Ref: *Negro Year Book*, 1947, p. 17.
  Who's Who Among Black Americans, 1977, p. 368.
  Who's Who Among Black Americans, 1985, p. 473.

Jones, Woodrow Harold   (1913- ——, M)

Bacteriologist. Born in Wewoka, OK, May 29, 1913. B.S., Langston University, 1937; M.A., Columbia University, 1947; Ph.D., University of Oklahoma, 1954. Teacher, Public School, OK, 1941–46; Instructor, Biology, Langston University, 1948–50; Graduate Assistant, University of Oklahoma, 1951–52; Research fellow, 1952–53; Assistant Professor, Biology, Fisk University, 1953–56; Professor, Biology, Southern University, 1956–60; NASA Research Scientist, 1962–69; Professor of Black Studies, San Francisco State College, 1969–; toxicity studies of oil field wastes; uptake of radioactive substances by slime molds.

Memberships and awards: Sigma Xi; AAAS; Oklahoma Academy of Science; American Society of Oceanography and Limnology; Southwestern Association of Naturalists; Postdoctoral fellow, University of the Pacific, 1960–61; National Science Foundation, Postdoctoral fellow, 1960–61; Omega Psi Phi; Ecological Society of America; New York Academy of Sciences.

Dissertation title: Cladocera of Oklahoma.

Ref: *The Negro in Science*, p. 179.
  American Men & Women of Science, 12th ed., p. 3109.

Jones, Yvonne   (1900s, F)

Dentist. D.D.S., University of Pennsylvania.

Memberships and awards: First black woman admitted to the National Dental Honorary Society, Omicron Kappa Upsilon. She was appointed to Springfield, MA, Medical Advisory Board as chief consultant in planning safeguards for dental health. She was appointed for two years by Mayor Daniel Brunton. Daughter of William B. Jones, first black dentist in Springfield, MA.

Ref: *Jet*, Mar. 17, 1955, p. 26. [p]

Joyner, John Erwin   (1935- ——, M)

Physician. Neurosurgeon. Born in Grambling, LA, Feb. 7, 1935. B.S., Albion College, 1955; M.D., Indiana University School of Medicine, 1959. Chairman, Neurology and Neurosurgery, Winona Hospital, 1980–.

Memberships and awards: President, National Medical Association, 1087; National Institutes of Health, Technical Merit Review Commission, 1981–82; Congress

of Neurological Surgeons, 1967; American Medical Association, Physicians Recognition Award.

Ref: *Who's Who Among Black Americans*, 1985, p. 477.
  National Medical Association, *Journal*, v. 79, 1987.

Julian, Percy Lavon   (1899–1975, M)

Chemist (organic). Inventor. Born in Montgomery, AL, April 11, 1899. B.A., DePauw, 1920; M.A., Harvard, 1923; Ph.D. (organic chemistry), University of Vienna, Austria, 1931. Honorary D.Sci., DePauw University, 1947; Fisk University, 1947; West Virginia State College, 1948; Morgan, 1950; Howard, 1951; Northwestern, 1951; Lincoln (PA), 1953. Instructor, Chemistry, Fisk University, 1920–22; Research Assistant, Harvard, 1925–26; Professor, West Virginia State College, 1926–27; Associate Professor and Acting Head Department, Howard, 1927–29; Professor and Head Department, 1931–32; Fellow and Teacher, Organic Chemistry, DePauw, 1932–36; Director of Research, Soya Products Division, The Glidden Co., 1936–45; Director of Research and Manager, Fine Chemicals, 1945–53; Director of Research, Vegetable Oil and Food Division, 1953–54; President, Julian Laboratories, Inc., 1954–; Chemist with 130 chemical patents, 1920; achieved synthesis of physostigmine, developed synthetic drug for glaucoma, developed economical way to extract sterols from soybeans, improved method of producing cortisone; retired from Julian Laboratories, Inc. in 1964 to continue as consultant; chemistry of indoles, of conjugated systems of unsaturated linkages, of soya sterols, of proteins and phosphatides.

Memberships and awards: Austin fellow, Harvard University, 1922–23; George & Martha Derby scholar, 1924–25; Spingarn Medal Award, 1947; Vice-President, Board of Trustees, Provident Hospital, Chicago, 1948; Vice-President, Board of Directors, Roosevelt College, 1948; Trustee, Fisk University; American Chemical Society; Sigma Xi; Phi Beta Kappa; Sigma Xi Procter Prize for outstanding service to science and humanity, 1975.

Dissertation title: Zur Kenntnis Verschiedener Alkaloids und uber ein neues Hererocyclishes, Freies Radikae.

Pub: Articles in American Chemical Society, *Journal*, on physostigmine.

Ref: *American Men and Women of Science*, 12th ed., p. 3126.
  Holders of Doctorates Among American Negroes, p. 152.
  Drew. Negro Scholars in Scientific Research. *Journal of Negro History*, v. 35, 1950, p. 144.
  Jet, May 7, 1964, p. 52. [p]
  The Negro in Science, p. 183.
  Historical Afro-American Biographies, p. 218. [p]
  Black Pioneers of Science and Invention, p. 87–101. [p] p. 86.
  Ebony Success Library, v. 1, p. 187. [p]
  Encyclopedia of Black America, p. 481.
  Ebony, June 1961, p. 70. [p] full page

Cobb, W. Montague. Percy Lavon Julian, Ph.D., Sc.D., L.L.D., L.H.D., 1899–. National Medical Association, *Journal,* v. 63, Mar. 1971, p. 143–150. [p] cover (list of publications)
Ebony, Mar. 1975, p. 94–96, 98, 100, 102, 104. [p]
Who's Who Among Black Americans, 1975, p. 360.
National Medical Association, *Journal,* v. 67, Sept. 1975, p. 413–414. obit

Just, Ernest Everett   (1883–1941, M)

Zoologist. Biologist. Physiologist. Research Scientist. Born in Charleston, SC, Aug. 14, 1883. B.A., Dartmouth College, 1907; Ph.D. (zoology and physiology), University of Chicago, 1916. Instructor in Zoology, Howard University, 1909–10; Assistant Professor, 1910–11; Associate Professor, 1911–12; Professor, 1912–; Spent 20 summers in Woods Hole Marine Biological Laboratory, MA; headed Department of Physiology, Howard University.

Memberships and awards: Vice-President, American Zoological Society; received first Spingarn Medal, 1915, for his research in Biology; National Research Rosenwald fellow, 1920–31; Ecological Society; Phi Beta Kappa; edited the journal *Protoplasm* and the official organ of the Marine Biological Advancement of Science.

Dissertation title: Studies of Fertilization in Platynereis megalops.

Pub: Basic Methods for Experiments in Eggs of Marine Animals, Philadelphia, Blaikston, 1939. 89 p.
Biology of the Cell Surface, Philadelphia, Blakiston, 1939. 392 p.
Published more than 50 papers in his field between 1912 and 1937.

Ref: *Black Pioneers of Science and Invention,* p. 112–121. [p] p. 112.
Manning, Kenneth P., *Black Apollo of Science* (Biography of E. E. Just). New York, Oxford University Press, 1983, 397 p.
Cobb, W. Montague. Ernest Everett Just, 1883–1941. National Medical Association, *Journal,* v. 49, Sept. 1957, p. 349–351. [p] cover (list of publications)
Dictionary of American Negro Biography, p. 372–375.
Encyclopedia of Black America, p. 481. [p]
American Men of Science, 6th ed., p. 752.
Holders of Doctorates Among American Negroes, p. 192.
History of the Negro in Medicine, p. 110. [p] p. 110.
Dictionary of American Medical Biography, p. 402–403.
Who's Who of the Colored Race, 1915, p. 165.
Who's Who in Colored America, 1927, p. 114.
Who's Who in Colored America, 1928–29, p. 430.
Who's Who in Colored America, 1930–32, p. 254.
Who's Who in Colored America, 1933–37, p. 305.
Who's Who in Colored America, 1938–40, p. 307.
Who's Who in Colored America, 1941–44, p. 303.
Historical Afro-American Biographies, p. 218–219. [p]
Ernest Everett Just, 1883–1941. National Medical Association, *Journal,* v. 49, 1957, p. 349–351.
Blacks in Science: Astrophysicist to Zoologist, p. 72–73.
Crisis, Feb. 1932, p. 46. [p] biog

Lovell, J., Jr. In Memoriam. *Crisis,* Dec. 1942, p. 379, 387, 394, 396. [p]
World's Great Men of Color, v. 2, p. 311–312.

K

Kelly, Anguis D.   (1916– ——, M)

Optometrist. Born in Hattiesburg, MS, Mar. 27, 1916. D.O., Northern Illinois College of Optometry, 19??. Clinic Associate, Field of Optometry, Chicago, 1942–45; Staff, Shaw Optical Company, Atlanta, GA, 1945–. Only black optometrist, 1945–50, in the Southeastern United States.

Memberships and awards: Optometric Extension Program.

Ref: *The National Register,* 1952, p. 591.

Kemp, Nancy Lois   (18??–19??, F)

Nurse. Born in Virginia. Attended Howard University for two years before entering Freedmen's Hospital School of Nursing. Private day nursing specializing in massage treatments; became an instructor in the American Red Cross during World War I; after studying Public Health at the University of Pennsylvania, she was appointed staff Nurse at Henry Phipps Institute, which specialized in tuberculosis, 1922; became Supervisor of a public health clinic in northwest Philadelphia in 1923, where she remained for eight years, returning to Phipps Institute where she remained until retirement in 1940.

Memberships and awards: Second recipient of the Mary Mahoney Award in 1937, she was a charter member of the National Association of Colored Graduate Nurses.

Ref: *The Path We Tread,* p. 149–152. [p] p. 152.

Kennedy, Wadaran Latimore   (1905–19??, M)

Agriculturist. Born in Bison, OK, Mar. 3, 1905. B.S., University of Illinois, 1927; M.S., 1929; Ph.D., Pennsylvania State College, 1936. Instructor, Dairy Husbandry and Animal Husbandry, Virginia State College, 1927–29; Instructor, West Virginia State College, 1929–31; Associate Professor, Animal Husbandry, Colored Agricultural and Normal University, 1931–33; Professor of Dairy Husbandry and Chairman of the Department, 1933–70; Emeritus Professor of Agriculture, North Carolina A & T, Greensboro, NC, 1970–.

Memberships and awards: Sigma Xi; Gamma Sigma Delta; Phi Kappa Phi.

Dissertation title: Studies in the Composition of Bovine Blood as Influenced by Age, Gestation, and Location.

Ref: *Holders of Doctorates Among American Negroes,* p. 125–126.
American Men and Women of Science, 13th ed., p. 2291.
Who's Who in the South and Southwest, 1973, p. 398

Kenney, John Andrew, Sr. (1874–1950, M)

Physician. Surgeon. Born in Albemarle County, VA, June 11, 1874. B.A. Hampton Normal and Agricultural Institute, 1897; M.D., Shaw University, NC, 1901. Resident Physician, Tuskegee Institute, AL, 1902–24. Treated Booker T. Washington and George Washington Carver while medical director of the John A. Andrew Memorial Hospital at Tuskegee Institute which he founded. One of the founders of the *Journal* of the National Medical Association; Founder, John A. Andrew Clinical Society; Founder, Kenney Memorial Hospital, Inc., 132 W. Kenney St., Newark, NJ.

Memberships and awards: President, National Medical Association; 1912–13; Secretary, National Hospital Association; Secretary, National Medical Association, eight years; North Jersey Medical Society.

Pub: *Negro in Medicine,* 1912.

Ref: *Jet,* June 13, 1963, p. 11.
Who's Who of the Colored Race, 1915, p. 167–168.
Who's Who in Colored America, 1927, p. 114.
Who's Who in Colored America, 1928–29, p. 223 [p] p. 220.
Who's Who in Colored America, 1930–32, p. 255.
Who's Who in Colored America, 1933–37, p. 306. [p] p. 303.
Who's Who in Colored America, 1941–44, p. 304.
History of the Negro in Medicine, p. 87. [p] p. 87.
Dictionary of American Medical Biography, p. 411–412.
National Medical Association, *Journal,* v. 31, Nov. 1939, p. 254–55.
National Medical Association, *Journal,* v. 41, Mar. 1949, p. 88.
National Medical Association, *Journal,* v. 48, Jan. 1956, p. 75. [p] cover

Kenney, John Andrew, Jr. (1914– ——, M)

Physician. Dermatologist. Born in Tuskegee, AL, 1914. M.D., Howard University Medical School, 1945. Specialist in pigmentation, Department of Dermatology, Howard University.

Memberships and awards: President, National Medical Association, 1961–62; American Medical Association; Society for Investigative Dermatology; fellow, American Academy of Dermatology.

Ref: *History of the Negro in Medicine,* p. 173. [p]
Best Doctors in the U.S.A., p. 169.
ABMS Compendium of Certified Medical Specialists, v. 1, p. 528.

Kenniebrew, Alonzo H. (1875–19??, M)

Physician. Surgeon. Born in Macon County, AL, May 5, 1875. B.S., Tuskegee Institute, 1892; M.D., Meharry Medical College, 1897. Founder and Surgeon-in-charge of the New Home Sanitarium, Inc., 1908–.

Ref: *Who's Who in Colored America,* p. 223.
Who's Who of the Colored Race, 1915, p. 168.

Kent, Elizabeth Lipford (1919– ——, F)

Nurse (psychiatric). Born in 1919. B.S., Spelman College, 1942; Nurses training, RN, St. Phillips Hospital School of Nursing, Richmond, VA, 1945; M.P.H., University of Michigan, 1946; Ph.D. (public health), University of Michigan, 1955. First black nurse to earn a Ph.D. Director of Nursing and Psychiatric Nurse Executive, Lafayette Clinic, Detroit, MI; Assistant Professor, Psychology, College of Nursing, Wayne State University.

Dissertation title: Teachers' Beliefs About Health Appraisal.

Ref: *The Path We Tread,* p. 57–58. [p] p. 58.
International Directory of Nurses with Doctoral Degrees, 1973, p. 34.
Directory of Nurses with Doctoral Degrees, 1984, p. 38.

Keyser, George Ficklin (1932– ——, M)

Engineer (electrical). Engineer (biomedical). Born in Washington, DC, Sept. 27, 1932. B.S. (electrical engineering), San Jose State College, 1965; M.S., University of Maryland, 1968; D.Sci. (biomedical engineering), Washington University, St. Louis, 1972. Electronics Design Engineer, McDonnell Astronautics, St. Louis, 1968–70; Assistant Professor, Washington University, 1973–74; Associate Professor, Electrical Engineering, 1974–.

Memberships and awards: Sigma Xi; AAAS; IEEE.

Dissertation title: Quantitative Analysis of the Spontaneous Activity of Smooth Muscle from the Urinary Bladder of Rabbit.

Ref: *Black Engineers in the United States,* p. 119.
Who's Who Among Black Americans, 1985, p. 485.

Kildare, Albert Alexander (1897–19??, M)

Physicist. Born in Kingston, Jamaica, B.W.I., Dec. 16, 1897. B.S., Boston University, 1921; M.S., 1927; Ph.D., 1934. Instructor in Chemistry and Physics, Virginia State College, 1921–26; Assistant Professor of Physics, Wilberforce University, 1927–28; Professor of Physics, Lincoln University, MO, 1928; research on interferometric measurements of the lines in the secondary spectrum of hydrogen.

Memberships and awards: Missouri Academy of Science.

Dissertation title: A Determination of the Wave Lengths of Certain Lines Between Lambda 4155 and 4380 a, i.e. in the Secondary Spectrum of Hydrogen.

Ref: *American Men of Science*, 7th ed., p. 966.
Holders of Doctorates Among American Negroes, p. 152.

King, Calvin Elijah   (1928- ——, M)

Mathematician. Born in Chicago, IL, June 5, 1928. B.A., Morehouse College, 1949; M.A., Atlanta University, 1950; Ph.D., Ohio State University, 1959. Instructor, Mathematics, Jackson College, 1953–55; Assistant Instructor, Ohio State University, 1955–58; Head, Department of Physics and Mathematics, Teachers College, Lagas, Nigeria, 1962–64; Professor of Mathematics, Tennessee State University, 1964–74; research in teaching remedial Mathematics and elementary Mathematics by television, and the relation of modern Mathematics to traditional Mathematics.

Memberships and awards: Beta Kappa Chi Honorary Scientific Society; Omega Psi Phi.

Dissertation title: A Comparative Study of the Effectiveness of Teaching a Course in Remedial Mathematics to College Students by Television and by the Conventional Method.

Ref: *American Men and Women of Science*, 15th ed., p. 323.
National Faculty Directory, 1987, p. 1960.

King, James, Jr.   (1933- ——, M)

Chemist. Physicist. Born in Columbus, GA, April 23, 1933. B.S., Morehouse College, 1953; M.S., California Institute of Technology, 1955; Ph.D. (chemistry and physics), 1958. Research Engineer, Electrochemistry, Jet Propulsion Laboratory, California Institute of Technology, 1956; Senior Research Engineer, Thermal Properties, Atomics International Division, North American Aviation, Inc., 1958–60; Senior Scientist, Electro-Optical Systems, Inc., 1960–61; Senior Scientist, Jet Propulsion Laboratory, California Institute of Technology, 1961–69; Section Manager, Physics, 1969–74; Director, Space Shuttle Environmental Effects, NASA, 1974–75; Director, Upper Atmospheric Science Program, 1975–76; Manager, User Program Development Office, Jet Propulsion Laboratory, 1976–78; Manager, Space Science and Application, 1981–.

Memberships and awards: American Chemical Society; American Physical Society; Sigma Xi; AAAS; American Geophysical Union.

Ref: *Current Black Man Decade 70*, p. 96. [p]
American Men and Women of Science, 16th ed., p. 333.

King, John Quill Taylor   (1921- ——, M)

Mathematician. Born in Memphis, TN, Sept. 25, 1921. B.A., Fisk University, 1941; Diploma, Landig College of Mortuary Science, 1942; B.S., Samuel Houston College, 1947; M.S., DePaul University, 1950; Ph.D. (statistics), University of Texas, Austin, 1957; L.L.D., Southwest University, 1970. Instructor in Mathematics and Business, Samuel Houston College, 1946–49; Assistant Professor, Houston-Tillotson College, 1950–52; Associate Professor of Mathematics, 1952–54; Professor, 1954–65; Dean of Instruction, 1960–65; President, 1965–.

Memberships and awards: Honorary Degrees, Southwestern, St. Edwards and Fisk Universities; Distinguished Service Award, Texas Lutheran College.

Dissertation title: A Statistical Analysis of the Economic Aspects of Nineteen Protestant Church-Related Colleges in Texas.

Ref: *American Men and Women of Science*, 12th ed., p. 3294.
National Faculty Directory, 1987, p. 1963.
Who's Who Among Black Americans, 1985, p. 488.
Crisis, Dec. 1978, p. 347–349. [p]

King, John Wesley   (1914- ——, M)

Botanist. Biologist. Born in Wilmington, NC, May 7, 1914. B.A., Tuskegee, 1936; M.S., University of Pittsburgh, 1944; Ph.D., 1947. Teacher, High School, Wilmington, NC, 1936–40; Teacher, High School, Pittsburgh, PA, 1940–44; Professor, Biology, Morgan State College, 1946; research in virus diseases of plants; plant growth substance; parasitism among marine algae.

Memberships and awards: Research fellow, California Institute of Technology, 1952; Visiting Research Professor, University of Hawaii, 1953; American Botanical Society; American Phytopathological Society; AAAS; Sigma Xi; Beta Kappa Chi; Maryland Association of Biology Teachers.

Dissertation title: Studies on the Rate of Aster Yellows Virus Transmission by Cusuta Campestris.

Ref: *American Men and Women of Science*, 12th ed., p. 3295.
The Negro in Science, p. 179.

King, Wendell   (1900s, M)

Engineer (electrical). B.S., Union College of Schenectady. Worked for a while for General Electric Company; after World War I, worked for an electrical manufacturing firm in Cleveland; Radio Station of Ashtabula which was moved to Erie in 1927 under his supervision; Chief Engineer of radio station WEDH in Erie, PA.

Memberships and awards: Institute of Radio Engineers.

Ref: *Negro Year Book*, 1931, p. 185.

Kittrell, Flemmie Pansy   (1904–1980, F)

Nutritionist. Home Economist. Born in Henderson, NC, Dec. 25, 1904. B.S., Hampton Institute, 1928; M.S., Cornell University, 1930; Ph.D. (nutrition), 1935. First black female to earn a Ph.D. in Nutrition. Teacher and Director of Nutrition, Bennett College, 1928–40; Chairman, Department of Home Economics and Dean of Women, Hampton Institute, 1940–44; Head Nutritionist at Howard University, 1944–73; Emeritus Professor of Nutrition, Howard University, 1973–80. Research in levels of protein requirements in adults; feeding of Negro infants; enriching preschool experience of children.

Memberships and awards: Fulbright Award, 1950–51; Lecturer and Researcher, State Department Grant to Africa, 1958; Nutrition Consultant for Project Head Start, 1965–; Trustee, Hampton Institute and Sibley Hospital, D.C.; Home Economics Council, Cornell University, 1971; Consultant for various other institutions; AAAS; American Dietetic Association; American Home Economics Association; American Academy of Arts and Sciences; World Population Society; Sigma Xi; Omicron Nu; First International Award, Century Club, 1965; Pi Lambda Theta; Phi Kappa Phi; Beta Kappa Chi.

Dissertation title: A Study of Negro Infant Feeding Practices in a Selected Community of North Carolina.

Ref: *American Men and Women of Science,* 14th ed., p. 2669.
Smithsonian, *Black Women Achieve Against All Odds,* p. 35.
Holders of Doctorates Among American Negroes, p. 126–127.
Negroes in Science: Natural Science Doctorates, 1876–1969, p. 41, 60.
Ebony, Jan. 1958, p. 59. [p]
Who's Who Among Black Americans, 1977, p. 528.

Knight, Genevieve Madeline (1939– ——, F)

Mathematician. Born in Brunswick, GA, June 18, 1939. B.S. (mathematics), Fort Valley State College, 1961; M.S. (mathematics), Atlanta University, 1963; Ph.D. (mathematics), University of Maryland, 1970. Professor, mathematics, Hampton Institute, 1970–.

Dissertation title: The Effect of a Sub-Culturally Appropriate Language upon Achievement in Mathematical Content.

Ref: *Black Mathematicians and Their works,* p. 289 [p]
Who's Who Among American Women, 1974, p. 523.

Knox, Lawrence Howland (1907–19??, M)

Chemist (organic). Born in New Bedford, MA, Sept. 30, 1907. B.S., Bates College, 1928; M.A., Stanford University, 1931; Ph.D., Harvard University, 1940. Instructor, Chemistry, Morehouse College, 1928–30; Professor, A & T College, Greensboro, NC, 1931–33; Head, Department of Chemistry, North Carolina College, 1933–44; Research Scientist, Division of War Research, Columbia University, 1944–45; Research Chemist, Nopco Chemical Company, 1945–48; Research Chemist, Hickrill Chemical Research

Foundation, Katanah, NY, 1948–; research in synthetic organic chemistry.

Memberships and awards: Chemical Society of London; American Chemical Society.

Dissertation title: Bicyclic Structures Prohibiting the Walden Inversion: Replacement Reactions in 1-Substituted 1-Apochamphanes.

Ref: *American Men of Science,* 9th ed., p. 1063.
Holders of Doctorates Among American Negroes, p. 152–153.
The Negro in Science, p. 183–184.

Knox, William Jacob, Jr. (1904–19??, M)

Chemist (surface). Chemist (physical). Born in New Bedford, MA, Jan. 5, 1904. B.S., Harvard, 1925; M.S., MIT, 1929; Ph.D. (physical chemistry), 1935. Instructor, Chemistry, Johnson C. Smith University, 1925–28; Instructor, Howard University, 1929–30; Professor, Atlanta University, 1933–34; Professor and Head of Department, A & T College, 1935–36; Head, Chemistry Department, Talladega College, 1936–43; Research Associate, Group Leader, Manhattan Project, Columbia University, 1943–45; Research Associate, Research Laboratories, Eastman Kodak Co., 1945–70.

Memberships and awards: Sigma Xi; American Chemical Society; Honor Roll of Race Relations, Schomburg Collection, for work on Atomic Bomb Project, Columbia University, 1945; Alpha Phi Alpha.

Dissertation title: Absorption Coefficients of Nitrogen-Dioxide and Dinitrogen-Tetroxide.

Ref: *American Men of Science,* 11th ed., p. 2852.
Encyclopedia of Black America, p. 745.
Holders of Doctorates Among American Negroes, p. 261.
The Negro in Science, p. 184.
Who's Who Among Black Americans, 1985, p. 494.

Koontz, Roscoe L. (1922– ——, M)

Physicist (radiological). Born in St. Louis, MO, Dec. 16, 1922. B.S., Tennessee State, 1948. Research Assistant, University of Rochester, 1949–51; Research Engineer, North American Aviation, 1951–; Engineer, Atomics International; research in instrumentation and development in radiation detection.

Memberships and awards: National Research Council fellow, AEC, 1948–49; Beta Kappa Chi.

Ref: *The Negro in Science,* p. 190.
Blacks in Science: Astrophysicist to Zoologist, p. 32–33.
[p] after p. 48.

Kountz, Samuel Lee, Jr. (1930–1981, M)

Physician. Surgeon. Biochemist. Born in Lexa, AR, 1930. B.S., Arkansas University, Pine Bluff, 1952; M.S. (biochemistry), University of Arkansas, Fayetteville, 1956;

M.D., University of Arkansas, Little Rock, 1958. Associate Professor of Surgery, Stanford University, 1965–67; Associate Professor, University of California, 1967–72; Professor of Surgery and Chairman of the Department, State University of New York, Downstate Medical Center, Brooklyn, NY, 1972–; Surgeon-in-Chief, Kings County Hospital; authority on kidney transplantation; performed an operation on NBC *Today Show*.

Memberships and awards: Diplomate, American Board of Surgeons, 1966; Institute of Medicine of the National Academy of Science; fellow, American College of Surgeons; Fulbright Professor to UAR, 1965–66; Investigator Award, American College of Cardiology; Honorary Juris Doctor, University of Arkansas, 1973; President, Society of University Surgeons, 1974.

Pub: Author or co-author of 172 articles in scientific publications.

Ref: *American Men and Women of Science*, 14th ed., p. 2743.
In Black and White, p. 565.
Who's Who Among Black Americans, 1980–81, p. 470–71.
National Medical Association, *Journal*, v. 73, Supl., Dec. 1981, p. 1229.
Ebony, July 1974, p. 61. [p]
Blacks in Science: Astrophysicist to Zoologist, p. 40–41.
Crisis, Dec. 1965, p. 665.
National Medical Association, *Journal*, v. 70, Sept. 1978, p. 683–684. [p]
Negro Almanac, 4th ed., p. 1059. [p]
A Century of Black Surgeons, p. 661–695. [p] p. 662.

Kreamer, Henry (1800s, M)

Inventor. Born in New York. He made seven different inventions in steam traps.

Ref: Woodson, *Negro in Our History*, 5th ed., p. 464.

Kyle, George Thomas (1904–19??, M)

Psychologist. Born in East St. Louis, IL, Mar. 31, 1904. B.A., University of Illinois; M.A.; Ph.D. (psychology), New York University, 1949.

Dissertation title: A Comparison of Normal and Schizophrenic Subjects in Level of Aspiration, Frustration, and Aggression.

Ref: *Even the Rat Was White*, p. 127.
Who's Who in the Southwest, 1973, p. 417.

L

Lacey, Archie L. (1923– ——, M)

Science Educator. Born in Boothton, AL, Jan. 21, 1923. B.S., Alabama State College, 1947; M.A., Howard University, 1953; Ph.D., Northwestern University, 1955. Science Instructor, Alabama State Branch Junior College, Mobile, 1949–52; Associate Professor, Alabama State Col-

lege, 1955–57; Professor, Grambling College, 1957–60; Assistant to Associate Professor, Hunter College, 1960–68; Chairman, Teacher Education, Federal City College (now UDC), 1967–70; Chairman, Teacher Education, Professor, Herbert H. Lehman College, 1972–75.

Memberships and awards: Board of Trustees, Beacon Press, 1968–71; Board of Directors, National Science Teachers Association, 1958–60; New York Academy of Sciences; Scholarship Education and Defense Fund for Racial Equality, 1965–73; AAAS; Director, National Science Foundation Institute, Grambling College, 1960–61; Beta Kappa Chi; Phi Delta Kappa.

Dissertation title: A Study of the Programs for the Preparation of Science Teachers for Secondary Schools at Selected Colleges and Universities.

Pub: *Chemistry of Life.*
Guide to Science Teaching in Secondary Schools. Belmont, Calif., Wadsworth Pub. Co., 1966.
Numerous articles in professional journals.

Ref: *Who's Who Among Black Americans*, 1985, p. 495.
Profiles in Black, p. 16, [p] p. 17.

Lambright, Middleton Hughes, Sr. (1865–1959, M)

Physician. Obstetrician. Born in Summerville, SC, Aug. 3, 1865. Claflin University; M.D., Meharry Medical College, 1908. Practiced medicine, Kansas City, MO, 1908–; Chief, Obstetrical Division, Kansas City General Hospital No. 2, only black in the department at that time.

Memberships and awards: Founder, Forest City Hospital Association; Cleveland Medical Association.

Ref: National Medical Association, *Journal*, v. 51, Nov. 1959, p. 483.

Lambright, Middleton Hughes, Jr. (1908– ——, M)

Physician. Surgeon. Born in Cleveland, OH, Nov. 7, 1908. B.S.; M.D., Meharry Medical College, 1938. Senior Clinical Instructor in Surgery, Western Reserve Medical School, 1946; Senior Visiting General Surgeon, Cleveland City Hospital, 1946–.

Memberships and awards: Diplomate, American Board of Surgery, 1946; fellow, American College of Surgeons, 1947; Board of Directors and President, Academy of Medicine of Cleveland, 1952, 1964; American Medical Association; National Medical Association.

Ref: National Medical Association, *Journal*, v. 44, 1952, p. 315. [p]
ABMS Compendium of Medical Specialists. v. 6, p. 374.
Ebony, June 1964, p. 6. [p]
A Century of Black Surgeons, p. 625–628. [p]

Landry, Eldridge Percival   (1881–19??, M)

Pharmacist. Born in New Orleans, LA, Feb. 1881. New Orleans University; Pharmacy, Flint Medical College; technical course, Southern University, New Orleans. Pharmacist in U.S. Food and Drug Inspection Laboratory, Savannah, GA, 1912–.

Ref: *Who's Who of the Colored Race*, 1915, p. 170.

Landry, Lord Beaconsfield   (1878–19??, M)

Physician. Born in Donaldsville, LA, Mar. 11, 1878. B.A., Fisk University, 1902; M.D., Meharry Medical College, 1908. Teacher of Medicine, Flint Medical College, New Orleans, LA.

Ref: *Who's Who of the Colored Race*, 1915, p. 170.

Lane, Willard Mercer   (1887–193?, M)

Physician. Surgeon. Born in Raleigh, NC, Mar. 28, 1887. B.A., Lincoln University, 1908; B.A., Oberlin College, 1910; M.D., University of West Tennessee, 1914; M.D., Howard University Medical School, 1916. Orthopedic specialty. Visiting Surgeon, Freedmen's Hospital, 1917–; Associate Professor of Surgery, Howard University Medical School.

Memberships and awards: Medico-Chirurgical Society of the District of Columbia; National Medical Association.

Ref: *Who's Who in Colored America*, 1933–37, p. 315.

Laney, Lucey Craft   (1854–1933, F)

Nurse. Born a slave in Macon, GA, April 13, 1854. Graduated from Atlanta University after being taught to read by her master's sister. Introduced trained nurses to Augusta, GA.

Memberships and awards: President and Founder of Normal and Industrial Institute, Augusta, GA.

Ref: *Who's Who in Colored America*, 1930–32, p. 261.
        Blacks in America, 1492–1977: A Chronology and Fact Book. 4th ed. by Irving J. Sloan, p. 16.
        Afro USA, p. 880.

Langston, Theophilus Steward   (1890–19??, M)

Dentist. Born in Bridgeton, NJ, Nov. 4, 1890. B.S., Howard University, 1914; Eckels Embalming School, Philadelphia, PA; D.D.S., Temple University, 1919. Medical Reserve Corps, U.S. Army, 1918–19; Dental Examiner, United Veterans Bureau, Johnstown, PA, 1920–26.

Memberships and awards: Phi Beta Sigma (charter member and secretary); National Medical Association; State Medical, Dental and Pharmaceutical Association; Lincoln Dental Society.

Ref: *Who's Who in Colored America*, 1933–37, p. 315.
        Who's Who in Colored America, 1941–44, p. 311.

Lankford, John Anderson   (1874–19??, M)

Architect. Engineer (mechanical). Born in Potosi, MO, Dec. 4, 1874. Student, Lincoln Institute, Jefferson City, MO; Tuskegee Normal and Industrial Institute, AL; Architectural College, Scranton, PA; B.S., Shaw University, 1898; M.S., Wilberforce University, 1902; M.M.S., Agricultural and Mechanical College, AL. First black to enter this profession in the United States; Supervising Architect for National Negro Fair Association, Mobile, AL; Directing General at Jamestown Exposition for the District of Columbia; Supervising Architect for A.M.E. Church in 1908; designed St. John's in Norfolk, VA, St. Phillips at Savannah, GA, John Wesley in Washington, DC, and many other churches in the United States, Africa, and South America; Architect and Supervisor of Construction under the U.S. Government during World War I.

Memberships and awards: Vice-President, National Technical Association.

Ref: *Who's Who of the Colored Race*, 1915, p. 172.
        Who's Who in Colored America, 1930–32, p. 261.
        Who's Who in Colored America, 1933–37, p. 315–316. [p] p. 312.
        Who's Who in Colored America, 1941–44, p. 311. [p] p. 305.

Lassiter, Norman   (18??–1929, M)

Dentist. In charge of the Dental Clinic at Hampton Institute for many years.

Ref: National Medical Association, *Journal*, v. 21, June 1929, p. 71. obit

Lathen, John William   (1916– ——, M)

Physician. Psychiatrist. Born in Hackensack, NJ, July 6, 1916. B.S., Virginia State College, 1938; attended Columbia University, 1938–39; M.D., Howard University Medical School, 1949. Dean of Men and Instructor, Manassas Industrial School, 1939–41; Metallurgical Chemist, Bendix Corporation, 1943–45; Psychiatrist in Private Practice, 1949–80; Adolescent Psychiatrist, Essex Company, 1980–84; Assistant Medical Director, Greystone Hospital, 1977.

Memberships and awards: Elected President of Bergen County, NJ, Mental Health Association—first black in its 10-year history; American, National, World Medical Association; first black chemist for Bendix Corporation.

Ref: *Jet*, Feb. 22, 1962, p. 26.
        Who's Who Among Black Americans, 1985, p. 502.

Latimer, Lewis Howard   (1848–1928, M)

Inventor. Engineer (mechanical). Engineer (electrical). Born in Chelsea, MA, Sept. 4, 1848. Learned mechanical drawing in office of Crosby and Gould, Boston, MA. Invented "water closet for railroad cars" in 1873, electric lamp with an inexpensive carbon filament and a wooden socket. Supervised installation of electric lights in New York, Philadelphia, and London. Prepared drawings for Alexander Bell's application for patent on the telephone. Only Black member of the "Edison Pioneers"; Engineer for Edison Company.

Memberships and awards: In 1968, the Lewis H. Latimer Public School in Brooklyn was named for him.

Pub: Incandescent Electric Lighting, a guide for lighting engineers. New York, Van Nostrand, 1890. 140 p.

Ref: *At Last Recognition in America*, v. 1, p. 16–17.
   Black Pioneers of Science and Invention, p. 49–60. [p] p. 50.
   Dictionary of American Negro Biography, p. 385–386.
   Encyclopedia of Black America, p. 497.
   Van Sertima, *Blacks in Science, Ancient and Modern*, p. 229–237.
   Who's Who of the Colored Race, 1915, p. 172.
   Negro Year Book, 1931, p. 185–186.
   Eight Black American Inventors, p. 78–92.
   Hidden Contributors: Black Scientists and Inventors in America, p. 97–108.
   Ebony, July 1967, p. 57. [p]
   Crisis, June 1924, p. 76. [p]
   Crisis, Feb. 1929, p. 52. [p]
   Crisis, Dec. 1929, p. 424. biog
   Crisis, June/July 1984, p. 32–33. [p] advertisement

Lattimer, Agnes   (1928– ——, F)

Physician. Pediatrician. Born in Memphis, TN. B.A.; M.D. Specialist in effects of lead poisoning on childhood development. Presently she is head of Cook County Hospital, Chicago, IL. She is believed to be the only black woman to hold the top job in a major hospital, monitoring 355 physicians who supervise 475 interns and residents.

Ref: *Ebony*, Sept. 1986, p. 44, 46, 48. [p] p. 44.

Lattimore, John Aaron Cicero   (1876–1959, M)

Physician. Born in Shelby, NC, June 23, 1876. B.A., Bennett College, NC, 1897; M.D., Meharry Medical College, 1901; Postgraduate course, Cook County Hospital. Practiced medicine in Louisville, KY for 58 years.

Memberships and awards: Vice-President, National Medical Association, 1920; President, Kentucky State Medical Society; President and one of the organizers of Fall City Medical Society; President, Negro Health Committee; President, Alpha Lambda Chapter of Alpha Phi Alpha; President, National Medical Association, 1947; Advisory Committee of the American National Red Cross; worked successfully for amendment of the Day Law which prevented integrated classes in Kentucky and opened medical and nursing schools of the state to blacks.

Ref: *Dictionary of American Medical Biography*, p. 436.
   Who's Who in Colored America, 1930–32, p. 262.
   Who's Who in Colored America, 1933–37, p. 3161.
   National Medical Association, *Journal*, v. 40, 1948, p. 223–224.
   Who's Who in Colored America, 1941–44, p. 316–317.
   National Medical Association, *Journal*, v. 53, Sept. 1961, p. 536. [p] obit

Laurey, James Richard   (1907–1964, M)

Physician. Surgeon (thoracic). Born in East St. Louis, IL, Aug. 5, 1907. B.A., Wayne University, 1929; M.B., 1932; M.D., 1933. Resident Surgeon, Parkside Hospital, Detroit, MI, 1934–35; Faculty, Surgery, Howard University Medical School, 1935–39, 1941–64, specializing in Thoracic Surgery.

Memberships and awards: Diplomate, American Board of Surgery, 1942; Founders Group, Board of Thoracic Surgery, 1949–; Medico-Chirurgical Society of the District of Columbia; Vice-Chairman, Surgical Section, National Medical Association, 1950; National Tuberculosis Association; American Trudeau Society; American Association for Thoracic Surgery; Society of Thoracic Surgeons.

Ref: National Medical Association, *Journal*, v. 56, Nov. 1964, p. 548–550. [p] obit & biog.
   A Century of Black Surgeons, p. 513–515. [p]

Lawlah, Clyde Avery   (1903–1968, M)

Physician. Born in Bessemer, AL, May 6, 1903. B.S., Morehouse College, 1925; M.D., 1932. College Physician and Science Teacher, A M & N College, Pine Bluff, Arkansas, 35 years.

Memberships and awards: Board of Trustees, National Medical Association; Treasurer, Arkansas State Medical, Dental, and Pharmaceutical Association; Treasurer, Southwestern Medical, Dental, and Pharmaceutical Association; Secretary-Treasurer, Jefferson County Medical Society, first black to hold such an office in Arkansas; award for 30 years of continuous service, Arkansas Medical, Dental, and Pharmaceutical Society; Honorary Sci.D., A M & N College, 1967; Sigma Pi Phi; Alpha Phi Alpha.

Ref: National Medical Association, *Journal*, v. 60, July 1968, p. 345. obit & biog.

Lawlah, John Wesley   (1904–19??, M)

Physician. Radiologist. Surgeon. Born in Bessemer, AL, Aug. 12, 1904. B.S., Morehouse College, 1925; M.S., University of Wisconsin, 1929; M.D., Rush Medical College,

1932. Radiologist, Provident Hospital, Chicago, 1935–36; Assistant Medical Director/Director, and Superintendent, Provident Hospital, 1935–41; Clinical Professor, Radiology and Dean, Howard University College of Medicine, 1941–46; Radiologist, Freedmen's Hospital, 1946–; Cardiovascular Research Project, 1952–.

Memberships and awards: D.Sci., 1941; Diplomate, National Board of Medical Examiners; American Board of Radiologists; AAAS; Roentgen Ray Society; Radiological Society of North America; National Medical Association.

Ref: *American Men of Science*, 11th ed., p. 3033.
National Medical Association, *Journal*, v. 60, July 1968, p. 345 (note only).
National Medical Association, *Journal*, v. 66, Jan. 1974, p. 78–81, 89. [p] on cover

Lawless, Theodore Kenneth   (1894–1971, M)

Physician. Dermatologist. Born in New Orleans, LA, Dec. 6, 1892. B.A., Talladega College, 1914; M.D., Northwestern University School of Medicine, 1919; M.S., 1920; Columbia University, Harvard University, 1920–21; Paris, 1921–22; Freiburg, 1922–23; Clinics in Vienna, 1923–24. In charge of Medical Laboratories, Medical School, Northwestern, 1919–20; Instructor in Dermatology, 1926–; Associate Examiner, National Board of Medical Examiners, 1928–; in 1921 he served at St. Louis Hospital in Paris, France. After three years he returned to Chicago and was an Instructor at Northwestern University School of Medicine from 1924–41. He donated a research laboratory to Provident Hospital.

Memberships and awards: Spingarn Medal, 1954 for his research in Dermatology; fellow, American Medical Association; Harman Award in 1929; Honorary D.Sci., Talladega, 1945; Honorary D.Laws, Bethune-Cookman College, 1952; Clinic in Israel named in his honor; National Advisory Committee on Selection of Physicians, Dentists and Allied Specialists appointed by President Kennedy; President, Board of Trustees, Dillard University, 1959; Diplomate, American Board of Dermatology.

Ref: *American Men of Science*, 7th ed., p. 1036.
Blacks in Science: Astrophysicist to Zoologist, p. 22–23.
Crisis, April 1924, p. 263. [p]
Encyclopedia of Black America, 1981, p. 48–49.
Historical Afro-American Biographies, p. 221. [p]
History of the Negro in Medicine, p. 109–110. [p] p. 110.
In Black and White, p. 577.
Black Winners, p. 55–56.
Jet, May 20, 1971, p. 12–14.
Dictionary of American Medical Biography, p. 437.
Cobb, W. Montague. Theodore Kenneth Lawless. National Medical Association, *Journal*, v. 62, July 1970, p. 310–312. [p] cover (list of publications)
Ebony, May 1962, p. 131. [p] only
National Medical Association, *Journal*, v. 63, Sept. 1971, p. 405. obit

Lawrence, Margaret Morgan   (1914– ——, F)

Physician. Psychiatrist. Born in New York, NY, Aug. 19, 1914. B.A., Cornell University, 1936; M.D., Columbia University, 1940; M.S. (public health), College of Physicians and Surgeons, Columbia University, 1943; Certificate in Psychoanalytic Medicine, 1951. Supervising Child Psychiatrist and Psychoanalyst, 1963–; Associate Clinical Professor of Psychiatry, Columbia College of Physicians and Surgeons, 1963–; Director, Child Development Center, 1969–74 and various other directorships of children's psychiatric centers; Associate Professor in Pediatrics, Meharry Medical College, 1943–47.

Memberships and awards: American Psychoanalytic Association; Academy of Psychoanalysis; Orthopsychiatric Association; National Medical Association; Medical Society, County of Rockland; Rosenwald fellow, 1942–43; National Research Council fellow, 1947–48; U.S. Public Health Service fellow, 1948–50; Joseph R. Bernstein Mental Health Award, Rockland County, NY, 1975.

Pub: *Mental Health Team in the Schools*, New York, Behavioral Publications, 1971. 169 p.
Young Inner City Families: the Development of Ego Strength Under Stress, see above 1975. 139 p.

Ref: *Who's Who Among Black Americans*, 1985, p. 504.
Who's Who of American Women, 1974, p. 552.
Crisis, Aug. 1940, p. 233. [p] only

Lawrence, Montague Schiels   (1923– ——, M)

Physician. Surgeon (thoracic). Surgeon (cardiovascular). Born in Laurel, MS, April 22, 1923. B.S., Alcorn Agricultural and Mechanical College, 1943; M.D., Meharry Medical College, 1946; Homer G. Phillips Hospital, 1946–66 (Intern to Associate Professor of Thoracic Surgery); Professor of Surgery, College of Medicine, University of Iowa, 1966–; research in congenital and acquired cardiac disease.

Memberships and awards: Diplomate, American Board of Surgery and American Board of Thoracic Surgery; National Tuberculosis Association; National Medical Association; American Heart Association; fellow, American College of Surgeons; fellow, American College of Chest Physicians.

Ref: *American Men and Women of Science*, 14th ed., p. 2880.
Ebony, June 1976, p. 44–50. [p] p. 50.
Who's Who Among Black Americans, 1985, p. 504.
A Century of Black Surgeons, p. 628–629. [p] p. 628.

Lawrence, Robert Henry, Jr.   (1935–1967, M)

Military. Major. Astronaut. Born in Chicago, IL, Oct. 2, 1935. B.A. (chemistry), Bradley University, 1956; Ph.D. (physical chemistry), Ohio State University, 1965.

Memberships and awards: First black astronaut selected; killed in a training flight, Dec. 8, 1967.

Dissertation title: The Mechanism of the Tritium Beta-Ray Induced Exchange Reactions of Deuterium with Methane and Ethane in the Gas Phase.

Ref: *Ebony*, Feb. 1968, p. 90–92, 94. [p]
Jet, July 20, 1967, p. 14–19.
Who Was Who in American History—Science and Technology, p. 350.
Negroes in Science: Natural Science Doctorates, 1876–1969, p. 48.
Ebony, Nov. 1985, p. 312. [p]
Ebony, Jan. 1968, p. 121. [p]

Lawson, James Raymond   (1915- —, M)

Physicist. Born in Louisville, KY, Jan. 15, 1915. B.A., Fisk University, 1935; M.S., University of Michigan, 1936; Ph.D. (physics), 1939. Instructor in Physics and Mathematics, St. Augustine College, 1936–37; Assistant Professor, Southern University, 1939–40; Associate Professor, Physics, Langston University, 1940–42; Professor of Physics and Chairman of the Department, Fisk University, 1942–49; Tennessee State College, 1949–51; Tennessee State University, 1951–57; Professor, Fisk University, 1957–66; President, 1967–77; research in infrared and ultraviolet spectroscopy.

Memberships and awards: Julius Rosenwald fellow, Michigan, 1937–39; American Physical Society; American Association of Physics Teachers; Sigma Xi; Phi Beta Kappa; Optical Society of America; Society of Applied Spectroscopy.

Dissertation title: The Infra-red Absorption Spectra of a Number of Heavy Tetrahedral Molecules with Substituted Groups and a Study of Hindered Rotation in Methyl Alcohol.

Ref: *American Men and Women of Science*, 12th ed., p. 2589.
The Negro in Science, p. 190.
Holders of Doctorates Among American Negroes, p. 153.
Ebony Success Library, v. 1, p. 198. [p]
Who's Who Among Black Americans, 1977, p. 541.

Lawson, John   (1837-19??, M)

Military (Navy). Born in Pennsylvania, 1837. Landsman on the Admiral Farragut flagship, Hartford. Won the Navy Medal of Honor during the Battle of Mobile Bay, refused to go below though badly wounded, and stayed in action throughout the engagement.

Memberships and awards: Naval Medal of Honor in the Civil War. Awarded the medal for action of Aug. 5, 1864, awarded Dec. 31, 1864.

Ref: *Negro History Bulletin*, v. 36, Oct. 1973, p. 137–139. [p] p. 138.
Black Americans in Defense of Our Nation, p. 60. [p]
Negro Medal of Honor Men, p. 45–48.

Lawson, Katheryn Emanuel   (1926- —, F)

Chemist. Born in Shreveport, LA, Sept. 15, 1926. B.A., Dillard University, 1945; M.S., Tuskegee Institute, 1947; Ph.D. (chemistry), University of New Mexico, 1957. Assistant Professor of Chemistry, Bishop College, A & T College, Savannah State College, Talladega College, and Grambling College, 1947–51; from Assistant Professor to Associate Professor of Chemistry, Central State College, 1951–54; Research Assistant in Chemistry, University of New Mexico, 1954–57; Staff member in Biochemistry, Veterans Hospital, Albuquerque, NM, 1957–58; staff member in Materials Science, Sandia Laboratories, 1958–; research in quantitative television microscopy.

Dissertation title: Behavior of Indium at Tracer Concentrations.

Ref: *American Men and Women of Science*, 13th ed., p. 2532.
Ebony, June 1965, p. 67–70, 72–72. [p]

Lawson, William Hiram   (1891–1966, M)

Optometrist. Born in Windsor, Ont., May 27, 1891. Windsor Collegiate Institute; Detroit Business College, Opt.D., Gilch Practical Institute of Optometry. First black optometrist in the United States. Retired in 1958 at the age of 65.

Memberships and awards: Michigan State Society of Optometrists; American Optical Association.

Ref: *Jet*, Jan. 5, 1967, p. 49. death notice
Who's Who in Colored America, 1930–32, p. 265.
Who's Who in Colored America, 1933–37, p. 320.
Jet, April 3, 1958, p. 45. [p]
Who's Who in Colored America, 1941–44, p. 316.

Ledbetter, Ruth Pope   (1900s, F)

Nurse. Born in Indianapolis, IN. B.S.N.E., American University, 1958; R.N., Marion County General Hospital, 1958; Graduate Studies, U.D.C. and Catholic University of America, Washington, DC, 1974–80. Supervisor, St. Elizabeth's Hospital, 1950–69; Area B., Alcoholism Center, Mental Health Nurse, 1969–70; Community Mental Health Specialist, Congress Heights Health Center, 1970–73; Senior Community Health Specialist, Employee Counseling Services, 1973–76; Transactional Analysis Instructor, Department of Human Resources, 1975–77; State Prevention Coordinator, Bureau of Alcohol RX, 1976–80; Sex Education, Alcohol, Drug Abuse, Woodson Senior High School, 1978–80; Vice-President, Trifax Corporation, Washington, DC.

Memberships and awards: Second Vice-President, American Association of Black Women Entrepreneurs; Outstanding Achievement Award, C.I.C.; American Association of Sex Educators, Counselors and Therapists; American Nurses Association.

Ref: *Who's Who Among Black Americans*, 1985, p. 507.
       Who's Who in American Nursing, 1986–87, p. 295.

Lee, Charles Bruce   (1921– ——, M)

Zoologist. Born in Buffalo, NY, Nov. 16, 1921. B.S., University of Michigan, 1947; M.S., 1948; Ph.D. (zoology), 1952. Assistant in Zoology, Michigan, 1948–50; Director, Microbiology Laboratory, U.S. Department of the Army, Detroit Arsenal, 1952–58; Chief, Microbiology Section, Research Division, Ordnance Tank Automotive Command , 1958–63; Head, Office of International Activities, National Academy of Sciences; Science Specialist, Science and Technology Division, Library of Congress, 1964–65; Chief, Office for Activities, Bureau of Sport Fisheries and Wildlife, U.S. Fish and Wildlife Service, 1966–67; Grants Program Officer, Water Supply and Sea Resources, Office of Grants Administration, U.S. Public Health Service, National Center for Urban and Industrial Health, OH, 1967–69; Scientist Administrator, Research and Development, Office of Environmental Control Administration, U.S. Public Health Service, 1969–71; Special Projects Branch, National Institute of Alcohol Abuse and Alcoholism, NIMH, 1971–; research in deterioration of ordnance materials, especially synthetic elastomers, etc.

Memberships and awards: Meritorious Civilian Service Award from U.S. Army for developing method of decontamination of missiles.

Dissertation title: The Molluscan Family Succineidae in Michigan, Considerations of Anatomy, Early Embryology and Distribution.

Ref: *American Men and Women of Science*, 12th ed., p. 3610.

Lee, H.   (1800s, M)

Inventor. Animal trap, patent #61,941, 1867. Made of metal and capable of imprisoning large animals such as bears and deer. The old wooden trap could only imprison small animals.

Ref: *At Last Recognition in America*, v. 1, p. 3.

Lee, Henry Eugene   (1880–1959, M)

Physician. Born in Texas, 1880. B.S., Tillotson College, TX; M.D., Meharry Medical College, 1902. Attended Mayo Clinic for further study and for 18 years at the John A. Andrew Clinical Society, Tuskegee, where he was President for two years; Chief of Staff, Houston Negro Hospital; Clinical Staff, Jefferson-Davis City-County Hospital.

Memberships and awards: President, National Medical Association, 1941–42; President, John A. Andrew Society, 1929–30; President, Houston Medical Forum; Julius Rosenwald Clinical Society, Dallas, TX; Lone Star State Medical, Dental, and Pharmaceutical Society; Trustee, Tillotson College, TX.

Ref: National Medical Association, *Journal*, v. 52, Mar. 1960, p. 146. obit & biog.
        National Medical Association, *Journal*, v. 57, May 1965, p. 260. [p]

Lee, James Sumner   (1903–19??, M)

Bacteriologist. Born in Lancaster, SC, Dec. 7, 1903. B.A., Lincoln, 1927; M.S., University of Michigan, 1934; Ph.D., 1938. Professor of Biology, Shaw University, 1930–37; Professor and Head of Department of Bacteriology, North Carolina College, Durham, NC, 1938–; research in bacterial cytology and cytochemistry.

Memberships and awards: General Education Board fellow, 1936–37; Society of Bacteriologists.

Dissertation title: A Study of the Distribution and Viability of Rabies Virus in the Animal Body following its Introduction Into the Blood Stream.

Ref: *American Men of Science*, 10th ed., p. 2361.
        Holders of Doctorates Among American Negroes, p. 193.

Lee, James Warren   (1909–1960, M)

Protozoologist. Zoologist. Born in New Orleans, LA, Oct. 6, 1909. B.S., Morehouse, 1931; M.S., Iowa University, 1932; Ph.D., 1941. Head, Biology Department, Arkansas State College, 1935–41; Instructor in Biology, Southern University A & M College, 1941–44; Head, Biology Department, Southern University A & M College, 1944; researched motor activities of protozoa.

Memberships and awards: Louisiana Academy; Sigma Xi.

Dissertation title: Factors Which Influence Food Vacuole Formation in Paramecium.

Ref: *American Men of Science*, 9th ed., p. 663.
        Holders of Doctorates Among American Negroes, p. 193.

Lee, Joseph   (1800s, M)

Inventor. Born in Boston. Patented inventions for kneading dough. Patent #524,042 and #540,553 for bread crumbing machine.

Ref: Woodson, *Negro in Our History*, 5th ed., p. 464.

Lee, Rebecca   (1800s, F)

See, Crumpler, Rebecca. Physician. First black woman to earn a degree in Medicine. M.D., New England Female Medical College, Boston, 1864. Practiced in Richmond, VA. Her degree came fifteen years after that of Elizabeth Blackwell, the first white woman to finish medical school.

Ref: *Jet*, Feb. 13, 1958, p. 28.
  Medico-Chirurgical Society of the District of Columbia,
   Inc., *Bulletin*, Jan. 1949, p. 3.
  Haber, Louis. *Women Pioneers in Science*, p. 8–9.

Lee, Roseau Franklin   (1897–19??, M)

Dentist. Born in Washington, DC, May 30, 1897. B.S., Howard University; D.D.S., Howard University, 1922. Oral Surgeon at Freedmen's Hospital, 1924–; first black in oral surgery, he organized the Oral Surgery Department at Freedmen's Hospital in 1926.

Memberships and awards: Robert T. Freeman Dental Society; Dental Reading Club.

Ref: *Who's Who in Colored America*, 1930–32, p. 269.
  Who's Who in Colored America, 1933–37, p. 324.
  Jet, July 30, 1964, p. 11.
  Who's Who in Colored America, 1941–44, p. 323.

Leevy, Carroll Moton   (1920– ——, M)

Physician. Internist. Nutritionist. Hepatologist. Born in Columbia, SC, Oct. 13, 1920. B.A., Fisk University, 1941; M.D., University of Michigan, 1944. Director of Clinical Investigation Outpatient Department, Jersey City Medical Center, 1948–58; Research Associate, Harvard University, 1958–59; Associate Professor, 1959–62; Acting Chairman, Department of Medicine, 1966–68; Professor of Medicine, Seton College of Medicine of New Jersey, 1962–; Director, Division of Hepatic Metabolism and Nutrition, 1959–; research in pathogenesis of cirrhosis of alcoholics, mechanism of portal hypertension and malutilization of vitamins and proteins.

Memberships and awards: USPHS Research fellow, 1958–59; Consultant and Member of the Advisory Committee, V.A. Hospital, East Orange, NJ; Mod. Medicine Award, 1972; AAAS; Society for Experimental Biology and Medicine; National Medical Association; fellow, American Medical Association; fellow, American College of Physicians; President, American Association for the Study of Liver Diseases.

Pub: Over 400 articles and six books on liver disease.

Ref: *American Men and Women of Science*, 15th ed., p. 655.
  In Black and White, p. 586.
  Who's Who Among Black Americans, 1985, p. 511.
  National Medical Association, *Journal*, v. 63, Nov. 1971,
   p. 499.
  Blacks in Science: Astrophysicist to Zoologist. p. 33.
  Leaders in American Science, 1960–61, p. 504. [p]
  National Medical Association, *Journal*, v. 65, May 1973,
   p. 259. [p]
  Black Enterprise, Oct. 1988, p. 94.

Leffall, La Salle Doheney, Jr.   (1930– ——, M)

Physician. Surgeon. Oncologist. Born in Tallahassee, FL, May 22, 1930. B.S., Florida A & M University, 1948; M.D., Howard University, 1952. Assistant Dean, Howard University College of Medicine, 1964–70; Acting Dean, 1970; Professor and Chief of Surgery, College of Medicine, Howard University, 1970–; research in cancer diseases.

Memberships and awards: Alpha Omega Alpha, 1972; National Medical Association, 1962; President, Society of Surgeons of Oncology, 1978; SE Surgeons Congress, 1970; Society of Surgeons; Commission on Cancer; Secretary, American College of Surgeons, 1983; Institute of Medicine, National Academy of Sciences, 1973; President, American Cancer Society, 1979; American Surgeons Association, 1976; Alpha Phi Alpha; Sigma Pi Phi; National Cancer Advisory Board, 1980; Diplomate, American Board of Surgery, 1980; Cosmos Club; First Prize, Charles R. Drew Fundamental Forum, 1954; Outstanding Young Man of the Year, 1965; Outstanding Educator in America, Florida A & M, 1971, 1974; William H. Sinkler Memorial Award, 1972; Distinguished Service Medal, National Medical Association, 1979; Medico-Chirurgical Society of the District of Columbia; Medical Society of the District of Columbia; James Ewing Society; Society of Head and Neck Surgeons.

Ref: *American Men and Women of Science*, 15th ed., p. 656.
  In Black and White, p. 586–587.
  Who's Who Among Black Americans, 1985, p. 511.
  National Medical Association, *Journal*, v. 62, May 1970,
   p. 248–249. [p] biog (list of publications as of 1970)
  National Medical Association, *Journal*, v. 63, Nov. 1971,
   p. 499.
  Ebony, Feb. 1974, p. 94. [p] only
  Contemporary Black America, p. 264–266. [p]
  National Medical Association, *Journal*, v. 66, Nov. 1974,
   p. 528. [p]
  Ebony, July 1974, p. 93. [p]
  Ebony, April 1978, p. 127–130, 132, 134, 136. [p]
  Black Enterprise, Oct. 1988, p. 76. [p] & on cover
  A Century of Black Surgeons, p. 697–731. [p], p. 884–913.

Leftenant, Nancy C.   (1900s, F)

Military (Army). First Lieutenant. Nurse. Born in Amityville, NY. Graduated from Lincoln School for Nurses. First black integrated into the Regular Army Nurse Corps at Lockbourne Air Base in Ohio, Feb. 12, 1948. She had been in the Nurse Corps since 1945.

Ref: *Jet*, 1955.
  The Path We Tread, p. 239.
  Blacks in America 1492–1976, p. 36.

Lester, John Angelo   (1864–19??, M)

Physician. Surgeon. Born in Lebanon, TN, Oct. 29, 1864. B.A., Fisk University, 1890; M.D., Meharry Medical College, 1895; he began teaching at Meharry Medical College in 1896; postgraduate work, Physicians and Surgeons College, Chicago, IL; Professor of Botany, Zoology, Physics, and Assistant Professor of Agriculture at Alcorn

A & M College, 1891–93; House Physician in Provident Hospital, Chicago, IL, 1895; Professor, Meharry Medical College Faculty, 1916.

Memberships and awards: State Medical Society (TN); Rock City Academy Medical Society; Meharry Alumni Association.

Ref: *Educating Black Doctors*, p. 40, 229(4).
Who's Who of the Colored Race, 1915, p. 175–176.

Lester, William Alexander, Jr.   (1937– —— , M)

Chemist. Born in Chicago, IL, April 24, 1937. B.A., B.S., University of Chicago, 1958; M.S., 1959; Ph.D. (chemistry), Catholic University, 1964. Project Assistant, Physics, University of Chicago, 1957–59; Assistant, Chemistry, Washington University, 1959–60; Catholic University, 1960–62; Physical Chemist, Physical Chemistry Division, National Bureau of Standards, 1961–64; Theoretical Chemist, University of Wisconsin, 1964–65; Assistant Director, 1965–68; Permanent Professional Staff, Theoretical Chemistry Research Laboratory, IBM, 1968–75; Technical Planning Staff, T. J. Watson Research Center, IBM, 1975–76; Associate Director, Lawrence Berkeley Laboratory, 1978–81; Professor, University of California, Berkeley, 1981–.

Memberships and awards: Consultant, National Science Foundation, 1976–77, 1980–83, 1985; American Physical Society; Percy Julian Award, National Organization of Black Chemists and Chemical Engineers; National Executive Board, National Organization of Black Chemists and Chemical Engineers, 1984–87; American Chemical Society; Sigma Xi; AAAS.

Ref: *American Men and Women of Science*, 16th ed., p. 709.
Who's Who Among Black Americans, 1985, p. 514.
AAAS Election Pamphlet. 1988. [p]

Levert, Francis Edward   (1940– —— , M)

Engineer (mechanical). Engineer (nuclear). Born in Tuscaloosa, AL, Mar. 28, 1940. B.S. (mechanical engineering), Tuskegee Institute, 1964; M.S. (nuclear engineering), University of Michigan, 1966; Ph.D., Pennsylvania State University, 1971. Instructor, Tuskegee Institute, 1966–68; Acting Head, Mechanical Engineering, Tuskegee Institute School of Engineering, 1972–73; Principal Engineer, Commonwealth Edison Company, 1973–74; Nuclear Engineer, Applied Physics Division, Argonne National Laboratory, 1974–.

Memberships and awards: American Nuclear Society; American Society Mechanical Engineers; Phi Beta Phi; Pi Tau Sigma; Beta Kappa Chi; American Society for Engineering Education.

Dissertation title: Local Power Measurements Using Gamma-Ray Fluctuations.

Pub: Seventeen technical journal articles.

Ref: *Black Engineers in the United States*, p. 124–125.
Who's Who Among Black Americans, 1985, p. 514.

Levy, James R.   (1861–1936, M)

Physician. Born in Camden, SC, 1861. B.S., Fisk University, 1891; M.D., University of Illinois School of Medicine, 1894. Practiced medicine in Florence, SC.

Memberships and awards: Treasurer, National Medical Association for 25 years; Trustee, Claflin University and Voorhees Institute, both in South Carolina.

Ref: National Medical Association, *Journal*, v. 28, May 1936, p. 75–76.

Lewis, H. Donell   (1900s, M)

Speech Pathologist. Audiologist. B.S., Shaw University; Ph.D., University of Illinois. Director of the Speech Pathology/Audiology Division of North Carolina Central University.

Dissertation title: Speech Reception Threshold in Noise.

Pub: Several articles on the speech and hearing disorders of blacks.

Ref: *Ebony*, Dec. 1986, p. 7. [p]

Lewis, Harold Ralph   (1931– —— , M)

Physicist (plasma). Physicist (nuclear). Engineer. Born in Chicago, IL, June 7, 1931. B.S. (physics), University of Chicago, 1953; M.S., University of Illinois, 1955; Ph.D. (physics), 1958. Research Associate, University of Heidelberg, 1958–60; Instructor, Princeton University, 1960–63; Research Physicist, Los Alamos National Laboratory, 1963; Laboratory fellow, 1983–; Deputy Group Leader, Los Alamos National Laboratory, 1981–; research in fusion power as an energy source.

Memberships and awards: American Physical Society; President, Student Concerts, Inc., 1973–75; Los Alamos Sinfonietta, 1963–; fellow, University of Illinois, 1953–58.

Dissertation title: A Method for Measuring Magnetic Fields in Superconductors.

Ref: *American Men and Women of Science*, 16th ed., p. 740.
Black Engineers in the United States, p. 125.
Who's Who Among Black Americans, 1985, p. 516.
Blacks in Science: Astrophysicist to Zoologist, p. 51–52.

Lewis, James Earl   (1931– —— , M)

Engineer (electrical). Inventor. Born in Jackson, MS, June 2, 1931. B.S. (electrical engineering), Howard University, 1955; M.S. (physics), 1976. Electrical Scientist, Naval Research Laboratory, 1957–66; Principle Engineer, Lockheed Electronics Company, 1966–69; Senior Electronics Engineer, Westinghouse Electric Company, 1969–75.

Memberships and awards: IEEE; Co-founder, Naylor-Dupont Community Assembly, 1973; U.S. Patent # 3,388,399, Antenna Feed for Two Coordinate Tracking Radars, 1968; Invention award, "Technique for Reduced Sidelobes on Radar Antennas," Westinghouse, 1972.

Ref: *Black Engineers In the United States*, p. 125.
   Who's Who Among Black Americans, 1985, p. 517.

Lewis, Julian Herman   (1891– ——, M)

Physician. Pathologist. Born in Shawneetown, IL, May 26, 1891. B.A., University of Illinois, 1911; M.A., University of Chicago, 1912; Ph.D. (physiology), University of Chicago, 1915; M.D., Rush Medical College, 1917. Associate Professor of Pathology, University of Chicago, 1917–43.

Memberships and awards: John Simon Guggenheim Fellow, 1926–27; Society for Experimental Pathology; American Association of Pathologists and Bacteriologists; Chicago Pathological Society; Chicago Institute of Medicine; Chicago Society of Internal Medicine; National Tuberculosis Association; National Medical Association; Cook County Physicians Association; American Association of Immunologists; AAAS; Illinois Academy of Science; Alpha Omega Alpha; Sigma Xi; Alpha Phi Alpha; Phi Beta Kappa; first black to earn the Ph.D. in Physiology; Benjamin Rush Medal, 1971.

Dissertation title: Lipids in Immunity. The Absorption of Substances Injected Subcutaneously and the Inhibitory Action of Heterologous Protein Mixtures on Anaphylaxis.

Pub: *The Biology of the Negro*, Chicago, University of Chicago Press, 1942. 433 p.
   Many articles on immunity in scientific journals.

Ref: *American Men and Women of Science*, 12th ed., p. 3697.
   Encyclopedia of Black America, p. 505.
   Who's Who in Colored America, 1933–37, p. 328.
   Negro Builders and Heroes, p. 229–230.
   Negroes in Science: Natural Science Doctorates, 1876–1969, p. 41.
   Who's Who in Colored America, 1930–32, p. 271.
   Holders of Doctorates Among American Negroes, p. 127.
   National Medical Association, *Journal*, v. 33, July 1941, p. 174–175. (review of *Biology of the Negro*)
   Who's Who in Colored America, 1941–44, p. 324–325.
   Crisis, July 1922, p. 108, 110. [p]
   Who's Who Among Black Americans, 1985, p. 517.

Lewis, Lillian Burwell   (1904–19??, F)

Zoologist. Born in Meridian, MS, Aug. 13, 1904. B.S., Howard University, 1925; M.S., University of Chicago, 1931; Ph.D. (endocrinology), 1946. From Assistant Professor to Associate Professor of Zoology, State A & M College of South Carolina, 1926–29; Morgan State College, 1929–31; Associate Professor, Tillotson College, 1931–47; Professor, Winston Salem State University, 1947–71.

Memberships and awards: AAAS; American Society of Zoology; Sigma Xi.

Dissertation title: A Study of the Effects of Hormones upon the Reproductive System of the White Pekin Duck.

Ref: *American Men and Women of Science*, 12th ed., p. 3697.
   Crisis, Aug. 1946, p. 243. [p] only

Lewis, Matthew, Jr.   (1930– ——, M)

Photographer. Born in McDonald, PA, Mar. 8, 1930. Assistant Manager, Editor, and Photographer, *Washington Post* newspaper; Instructor, Morgan State College, 1957–65.

Memberships and awards: Pulitzer Prize for Photography, 1975, for feature photography (*Washington Post*); National Press Photographers' Association; First Prize, National Newspaper Publishers' Association, 1964; Washington-Baltimore Newspaper Guild, 1971–72; White House News Photographers' Association.

Ref: *Who's Who Among Black Americans*, 1977, p. 554.
   Who's Who Among Black Americans, 1985, p. 518.

Lewis, Richard Hanna   (1887–19??,M)

Chemist (analytical). Born in Chicago, IL, April 7, 1887. B.S., University of Illinois, 1910. Analytical Chemist with Allaire and Woodward, Peoria, IL; Assistant Chemist to Senior Chemist in Office of Public Roads, Department of Agriculture, Washington, DC, 1911–.

Memberships and awards: Association of Asphalt Paving Technologists.

Pub: Co-author of a paper before the 1912 Congress of Applied Chemistry on the application of demethyl sulphate test for detection of small amount of asphalt in tar.

Ref: *Who's Who of the Colored Race*, 1915, p. 177.
   American Men of Science, 7th ed., p. 1062.

Lewis, Roscoe Warfield   (1920– ——, M)

Nutritionist (animal). Biochemist. Born in Beaumont, TX, Dec. 22, 1920. B.S., Prairie View State College, 1939; M.S., Kansas State University, 1952; Ph.D., 1955. Professor, Nutrition and Biochemistry, Texas Agricultural Experiment Station and Prairie View Experimental Station, 1955–69; Southwest Texas State University, 1969–70; research in chicken flavor.

Memberships and awards: Fribourg Award, 1955; AAAS; Poultry Science Association; Institute of Food Technologists; American Chemical Society; New York Academy of Science; research in chicken flavor.

Dissertation title: The Influence of Certain Dietary Feed Ingredients on Organoleptic Characteristics, Chemical Properties, and Histological Appearance of Specific Tissues from Broilers.

Ref: *Leaders in American Science,* 1955–56, p. 244. [p]
         American Men and Women of Science, 16th ed., p. 745.

Lewis, Stephen J.   (1900s, M)

Dentist. D.D.S., Howard University, 1909. Founder and author of the Interstate Free Lecture Courses for Howard University and Meharry Medical College. Dental editor, *Journal of the National Medical Association.*

Memberships and awards: American Dental Association; Pennsylvania State Dental Association; Harrisburg Dental Society; Interstate Dental Association; National Medical Association.

Ref: *Who's Who in Colored America,* 1927, p. 123.
         Who's Who in Colored America, 1928–29, p. 237–238.
         Who's Who in Colored America, 1941–44, p. 325.

Ligon, Claude Matthew   (1935– ——, M)

Engineer (civil). Born in Baltimore, MD, June 28, 1935. B.S. (mathematics), Morgan State College, 1957; B.S. (civil engineering), University of Illinois, 1965; M.S. (civil engineering), University of Maryland, 1971; Ph.D., 1984. U.S. Army Corps of Engineers, Lt. Col., 1957–79; Manager of Civil Engineering and Transportation Systems Division, AMAF Industries, 1979–85; Maryland Public Service Commissioner, 1985–.

Memberships and awards: American Society of Civil Engineers; fellow, Institute of Transportation Engineers; Transportation Research Board; Kappa Alpha Psi; Howard County Public Transportation Board, 1976–79; Chi Epsilon, National Civil Engineering Honors Fraternity.

Ref: *Black Engineers in the United States,* p. 126.
         Who's Who Among Black Americans, 1985, p. 520.
         Who's Who in Engineering, 6th ed., p. 395.

Linder, J. W. E.   (18??–1939, M)

Physician. Born in Dublin, GA. B.S., Morris Brown College, Atlanta, GA; M.D., Meharry Medical College.

Memberships and awards: President, Atlanta Medical Association; President, Georgia State Medical Association; Executive Board of the National Medical Association, 1931–39; Phi Beta Sigma.

Ref: National Medical Association, *Journal,* v. 31, Sept. 1939, p. 226. obit & biog.

Lion, Jules   (1810–1866, M)

Photographer. Born in Paris, France. First black photographer. He studied the daguerreotype in Paris and brought his knowledge to New Orleans.

Memberships and awards: Honorable Mention in Paris, 1833, for his lithograph "Affut aux Canards" (The Duck Blind). Only one of his photographs exists. He was famous for views of New Orleans Streets and portraits of New Orleans leaders. Did a portrait of Audubon.

Ref: New York History Society, *Dictionary of Artists of America.* p. 400.
         Black Photographers, 1840–1940, a Bio-Bibliography, p. 5.

Lislet, Geoffrey Jean Baptiste   (1755–1836, M)

Botanist. Zoologist. Geologist. Astronomer. Born in 1755. French Academy of Science correspondent, 1786, to which he sent meteorological observations.

Ref: *Historical Negro Biographies,* p. 25–26.
         In Black and White, p. 601.
         Men of Mark, 1970 ed., p. 709–710.

Liston, Hardy, Jr.   (1920– ——, M)

Engineer (mechanical). Born in Winston Salem, NC, Sept. 27, 1920. B.S. (mechanical engineering), Howard University, 1943; M.E.A. (engineering administration), George Washington University, 1967. Junior Engineer, U.S. Navy, Bureau of Ordnance, 1943–46; Assistant Professor, Howard University, Department of Mechanical Engineering, 1957–58; Professor, Oak Ridge Associated Universities, 1969–70; Associate Vice-Chancellor for Academic Affairs and Professor of Mechanical Engineering, University of Tennessee, Knoxville, 1970–.

Memberships and awards: American Association for Higher Education; American Society for Engineering; Education Society of Manufacturing Engineers; Doctor of Humane Letters, Knoxville College, 1972; Phi Kappa Phi; Danforth Foundations fellowship, 1959–60; Scholarships from Howard University and Knoxville College.

Ref: *Black Engineers in the United States,* p. 126.
         National Faculty Directory, 1987, p. 2210.

LittleJohn, Clarence G.   (1900s, M)

Physician. Cardiologist. Pediatrician. Pediatric Cardiologist. Born in Los Angeles. Teaches University of Southern California School of Medicine which denied him admission ten years before, only black child heart specialist at meeting of American Academy of Pediatrics, 1961.

Memberships and awards: Admitted to American Academy of Pediatrics, attended annual meeting in Chicago, 1961, delivered a paper on birth defects of the heart.

Ref: *Jet,* Dec. 21, 1961, p. 15.
         Jet, Oct. 19, 1961, p. 52. [p]
         Jet, Dec. 6, 1973, p. 48. [p]

Lloyd, Birtill Arthur   (1905–19??, M)

Chemist (physical). Born in Jamaica, B.W.I., June 9, 1905. B.S., University of Illinois, 1930; M.A., University of Toronto, 1934; Ph.D. (physical chemistry), 1944. Instructor in Physics and Chemistry, Kentucky State College, 1931–32; Mathematics and Physics, Philander Smith College, 1935–38; Special Research Assistant in Chemistry, University of Illinois, 1942–44; Physical Chemist, Picatinny Arsenal, 1944–; research in acoustic phenomena in gases; application of science and technology to the development of novel ordnance end items.

Ref: *American Men of Science,* 9th ed., p. 1172.

Lloyd, Frank P. (1919– —, M)

Physician. Obstetrician. Surgeon. Gynecologist. Born in Charleston, SC, Oct. 20, 1919. B.S. (chemistry), South Carolina State College, 1941; M.D., Howard University Medical College, 1946. U.S. Medical Corps, Chief of Obstetrics and Gynecology, 6th Evacuation Hospital, Nuremburg, Germany, 1950–52; Director, Medical Research, Methodist Hospital of Indiana, Inc., 1963–81; Chief Executive Officer and President, Methodists Hospital of Indiana, Inc., 1981–.

Memberships and awards: Fellow, Obstetrics and Gynecology, Columbia Presbyterian Medical Center, New York, NY; American Board of Obstetrics and Gynecology; American Academy of Medical Directors; American Hospital Association; National Medical Association; District of Columbia Medical Society; American Fertility Society; American College of Surgeons; American Medical Association; Indiana Hospital Association; Indiana State Obstetrics and Gynecology Society; National Medical Association, Distinguished Service Medal, 1983.

Ref: National Medical Association, *Journal,* v. 76, May 1984, p. 541–542. [p]

Lloyd, Ruth Smith (1917– —, F)

Anatomist. Born in Washington, DC, Jan. 25, 1917. B.A., Mount Holyoke, 1937; M.S., Howard University, 1938; Ph.D. (anatomy), Western Reserve University, 1941; first black female to earn a Ph.D. in anatomy. Assistant in Physiology, College of Medicine, Howard University, 1941–41; Instructor in Zoology, Hampton Institute, 1941–42; Technician in Physiology, Howard University, 1952; from Instructor to Assistant Professor of Anatomy, 1942–58; Associate Professor of Anatomy, Graduate School, Howard University, 1958–; research in female sex cycle and relation of sex hormones to growth.

Dissertation title: Adolescence of Macaques (Macacus Rhesus).

Ref: *American Men and Women of Science,* 14th ed., p. 3030.
Holders of Doctorates Among American Negroes, p. 193.
Negroes in Science: Natural Science Doctorates, 1876–1969, p. 60.

Lockett, John L. (1900s, M)

Microbiologist (soil). B.S., M.S., Iowa State College; Ph.D., Rutgers University, 1937.
Memberships and awards: Sigma Xi.

Dissertation title: Microbiological Aspects of the Use of Legumes Versus Non-Legumes for Green Manure Purposes.

Pub: Nitrogen and Phosphorous Changes in the Decomposition of Rye and Clover at Different Growth Stages.

Ref: *Holders of Doctorates Among American Negroes,* p. 127–128.
National Register, 1952, p. 217.

Lofton, William Garvin (1898–19??, M)

Physician. Obstetrician. Born in Jacksonville, FL, Sept. 5, 1898. B.S., Howard University, 1920; M.D., 1923. Assistant Visiting Obstetrician, Freedmen's Hospital, Washington, DC, 1928–; Clinical Instructor in Obstetrics, Howard University Medical School, 1928–; Medical Director, National Life Insurance Company, 1931–.

Memberships and awards: National Medical Association; Medical Chirurgical Association of Washington, DC; Alpha Phi Alpha.

Ref: *Who's Who in Colored America,* 1930–32, p. 275.
Who's Who in Colored America, 1933–37, p. 333.
Who's Who in Colored America, 1941–44, p. 329.

Logan, Arthur C. (1909–1973, M)

Physician. Surgeon. Born in Tuskegee, AL, Sept. 8, 1909. B.A., Williams College, MA, 1930; M.D., Columbia University College of Physicians and Surgeons, 1934; graduate study in Surgery, New York Postgraduate Medical School, 1941–46. Associate Medical Director of the Upper Manhattan Medical Group; Attending Physician at Sydenham Hospital and Associate Attending Surgeon, Harlem Hospital; he was Duke Ellington's doctor for 37 years.

Memberships and awards: Phi Beta Kappa; Downstate Medical Center, State University of New York, 1971–74; fellow, American College of Surgeons; Knickerbocker Hospital in New York named Arthur C. Logan Memorial Hospital in his honor; Charter member, Institute of Medicine, National Academy of Sciences.

Ref: *Jet,* April 7, 1966, p. 54.
Jet, Feb. 28, 1974, p. 41.
Nine Black American Doctors, p. 78–89. [p] p. 78.
National Medical Association, *Journal,* v. 66, May 1974, p. 272–273. [p] obit

Logan, Joseph G. Jr. (1920– —, M)

Physicist. Inventor. Born in Washington, DC, 1920. B.S., D.C. Teachers College, 1941; Ph.D. (physics), University of Buffalo, 1955; U.S. Bureau of Standards; Research Physicist, Cornell Aeronautical Laboratories, Buffalo, NY; in 1950 he developed a new small jet engine that had relatively low fuel consumption and was applicable to guided missiles and helicopters; Vice-President, Research and Development, West Coast Research Corporation, 1978–.

Dissertation title: The Effect of Isotopic Substitution on Vibrational Wave Functions and Dissociation Probability of Diatomic and Linear Triatomic Molecules.

Ref: *American Men and Women of Science,* 14th ed., p. 30–41.
Ebony, Sept. 1950, p. 16.
Negro History Bulletin, April 1955, p. 158. [p]
Who's Who in America, 1978, p. ?

Logan, Myra Adele   (1908–1977, F)

Physician. Surgeon. Born in Tuskegee, AL, 1908. B.A., Atlanta University, GA, 1927; M.S. (psychology), Columbia University; M.D., New York Medical College, 1933. Served her internship and residency at Harlem Hospital under Dr. Louis T. Wright. First female Surgeon to operate on the heart. She did research on aureomycin and other antibiotics.

Memberships and awards: First black woman surgeon to be elected a fellow of the American College of Surgeons; charter member of the Upper Manhattan Medical Group of the Health Insurance Plan; received a $10,000 scholarship for four years, New York Medical College.

Ref: *Women Pioneers of Science* (Haber), p. 97–104.
New York Times Biography Service, 1977. Jan., p. 100.
National Medical Association, *Journal,* v. 69, July 1977, p. 527. obit

Lomax, Eddie, Jr.   (1923– ——, M)

Chemist (organic). Born in Atlanta, GA, Aug. 12, 1923. B.S., Morehouse College, 1948; M.S., Atlanta University, 1951. Development Chemist, Puritan Chemical Company, 1951-Technical Director, 1973–; he develops and improves products made by the firm; first black to be given such a position.

Memberships and awards: American Chemical Society.

Ref: *Ebony,* Dec. 1956, p. 5. [p]
American Men and Women of Science, 16th ed., p. 836.

Lomax, Eugene W.   (1877–1927, M)

Physician. Born in 1877. M.D., Shaw University Medical School. Founded the Lomax Hospital in Bluefield, WV, 1911 and at his death had completed a $25,000 addition to the hospital.

Memberships and awards: National Medical Association; President, Flat Top Medical Association of West Virginia.

Ref: National Medical Association, *Journal,* v. 19, Oct.-Dec. 1927, p. 164–165. obit & biog.

Long, Irene   (1951– ——, F)

Physician. Surgeon. Born in Cleveland, OH, 1951. Northwestern University and St. Louis University School of Medicine. Chief of NASA's Medical Operations and Human Research Branch of the Biomedical Office, 1982–. First black woman to hold this office.

Ref: *Ebony,* Sept. 1984, p. 61–62, 64. [p]
Who's Who Among Black Americans, 1985, p. 527.

Love, Theodore Arceola   (1909–19??, M)

Mathematician. Born in Columbus, GA, May 25, 1909. B.A., Talladega College, 1929; M.A., University of Michigan, 1932; Ph.D. (mathematics), New York University, 1951. Instructor, Mathematics, Southern Normal School, Brewton, AL, 1924–33; Director, Academic Department and Dean, Principal Demonstration High School, Montgomery, AL, 1938–42; Captain, U.S. Army Corps of Engineers, 1946–51; Instructor, Mathematics, University Training Command MTOSA, FLorence, Italy, while serving in E.T.O.; Chairman, Department of Mathematics, Alabama State University; Dean of the College and Dean of the Graduate Division, Alabama State University; Chairman of Mathematics Department, Fisk University, 1956–77; Emeritus Professor, Fisk University, 1977–.

Memberships and awards: Phi Delta Kappa; American Mathematics Society; Omega Psi Phi.

Dissertation title: The Relation of Achievement in Mathematics to Certain Abilities in Problem Solving.

Ref: *American Men and Women of Science,* 14th ed., p. 3065.
Black Mathematicians and Their Works, p. 289. [p]
Leaders in American Science, 1958–59, p. 229. [p]

Lowden, Fred J.   (1800s, M)

Inventor. A Fisk Jubilee Singer. In 1893 he patented a fastener for the meeting rails of sashes and a key fastener.

Ref: Woodson, *Negro in Our History.* 5th ed. p. 464.

Lowery, John Edward   (1898–19??, M)

Physician. Obstetrician. Gynecologist. Born in Flushing, NY, July 26, 1898. B.S., University of Pennsylvania; M.D., Howard University Medical School, 1923. Instructor, Obstetrics and Gynecology, Freedmen's Hospital School of Nursing; Private Practice.

Memberships and awards: Medical Society of Queens County, 1928; Vice-President, Medical Society of the

State of New York, 1971; fellow, New York Academy of Medicine; Founder, Queens Clinical Society; very active in all of the above organizations serving as committee chairman of several important committees or as President.

Ref: National Medical Association, *Journal,* v. 67, 1975, p. 404–407. [p] on cover.

Lowery, Samuel R.   (1830–??, M)

Silkworm Culturist. Born in Nashville, TN, 1830. Worked at Franklin College and studied privately under Reverend Talbot Fanning. Became a pastor and preached until 1857. Studied Law and practiced in Nashville, TN. His daughter, Annie, persuaded him to purchase silkworm eggs for her and she began the enterprise which her father continued.

Memberships and awards: He devoted all of his time to this and won the highest prize at the World's Exposition in New Orleans. He also received for two years the highest medals from the Southern Expositions in Louisville, KY. These he won over 18 competitors from China, France, Japan, Italy, Mexico, and others from the United States raising over 100,000 worms and cacoons. This was written up in the Birmingham, AL, *Manufacturer and Tradesman.*

Ref: *Men of Mark,* p. 77–80. [p]

Lu Valle, James Ellis   (1912– ——, M)

Chemist (physical). Chemist (photographic). Born in San Antonio, TX, Nov. 10, 1912. B.A., UCLA, 1936; M.A., 1937; Ph.D., California Institute of Technology, 1940. Instructor, Chemistry, Fisk, 1940–41; Senior Chemist, Kodak Research Laboratory, 1941–42; OSRD, University of Chicago, 1942; OSRD, California Institute of Technology, 1942–43; Senior Chemist, Eastman Kodak Research Laboratory, 1943–45; Research Associate, 1945–53; Project Director, Technical Operations, Inc., 1953–59; Director of Basic Research, Fairchild Camera and Instrument, Syosset, NY, 1959; Laboratory Administrator, Chemistry Department, Stanford University, 1975–; research in photochemistry; electron defraction; magnetic resonance.

Memberships and awards: President, Blue Key, UCLA, 1936; U.S. Olympic Track Team, 1935; American Chemical Society; American Physical Society; AAAS; Faraday Society; Sigma Xi; Phi Lambda Upsilon; Pi Mu Epsilon.

Dissertation title: An Electron-Diffraction Investigation of Several Unsaturated Conjugated Organic Molecules.

Ref: *American Men and Women of Science,* 13th ed., p. 2717.
The Negro in Science, p. 184.
Holders of Doctorates Among American Negroes, p. 153.
Leaders in American Science, 1960–61, p. 540. [p]

Lucas, Wendell M.   (1920–1966, M)

Physician. Urologist. Surgeon. Born in 1920. B.S., Howard University, 1940; M.S., 1942; M.D., 1950. Professor of Surgery, Howard University; Chief, Urology Division, Howard University.

Ref: *American Men of Science,* 11th ed., p. 3243.
In Black and White, p. 614.
Jet, Feb. 22, 1968, p. 11.

Lushington, Augusta Nathaniel   (1869–1939, M)

Veterinarian. Born in 1869. University of Pennsylvania, 1897. First black veterinarian graduate.

Ref: *The Black Man in Veterinary Medicine,* p. 28.

Lynk, Beebe Steven   (1872–19??, F)

Chemist. Pharmacist. Born in Mason, TN, Oct. 24, 1872. Graduate, Lane College, 1892; Ph.C., University of West Tennessee, 1903. Professor of Pharmacy and Chemistry, University of West Tennessee, 1903–. Married to Dr. Miles Lynk.

Pub: *Advice to Colored Women,* 1896.

Ref: *Who's Who of the Colored Race,* 1915, p. 181.

Lynk, Miles Vandahurst   (1871–1957, M)

Physician. Born in Brownsville, TN, June 3, 1871. M.D., Meharry Medical College, 1891; M.S., Walden University, 1900; A & M College, Norman, AL, 1901. Practiced Medicine, 1891–1901. L.L.B., University of Tennessee, 1902. Publisher of *Medical and Surgical Observer,* 1892, first medical journal issued by a black man in the United States. President, University of West Tennessee, 1900, which he founded. Married Beebe Lynk, a Chemist. One of the organizers of the National Medical Association. Founder of Lyn-Krest Sanitarium.

Memberships and awards: Distinguished Service Medal, National Medical Association, 1952. First suggested the organization of black physicians which became the National Medical Association.

Pub: *Black Troopers or Daring Deeds of the Negro Soldiers in the Spanish American War,* New York, AMS Press, 1971. 163 p. Reprint.
Sixty Years of Medicine. Memphis, Twentiety Century Press, 1951. 125 p. (autobiography)

Ref: *History of the Negro in Medicine,* p. 64–65, 67. [p] p. 65.
Who's Who of the Colored Race, 1915, p. 181.
Who's Who in Colored America, 1927, p. 127.
Who's Who in Colored America, 1933–37, p. 341.
National Medical Association, *Journal,* v. 73, Dec. 1981, Supplement. p. 1219–1225.
National Medical Association, *Journal,* v. 33, Jan. 1941, p. 46–47.
National Register, 1952, p. 595.

Autobiography, Miles Vandahurst Lynk. National Medical Association, *Journal*, v. 44, Nov. 1952, p. 475–476. [p] cover

National Medical Association, *Journal*, v. 35, Nov. 1943, p. 205–206.

M

Maben, Hayward C., Jr.   (1922– ——, M)

Physician. Surgeon (thoracic). Born in Augusta, GA, June 3, 1922. B.S., Wayne State University, 1942; M.D., Meharry Medical College, 1945. Clinical Assistant to Professor, Wayne State University School of Medicine; Cardiovascular and Thoracic Surgeon, first black in Michigan.

Memberships and awards: American College of Surgeons; American Board of Surgery; American Board of Thoracic Surgery; fellow, American College of Chest Physicians; Society of Thoracic Surgeons; American Medical Association.

Ref: *Who's Who Among Black Americans*, 1985, p. 535. *ABMS Compendium of Certified Medical Specialists*, v. 6, p. 407, 881.

Mabrie, Herman James, III   (1948– ——, M)

Physician. Otolaryngologist. Surgeon. Born in Houston, TX, July 10, 1948. B.S., Howard University, 1969; M.D., Meharry Medical College, 1973. First black Otolaryngologist; private practice; Resident, Baylor Affiliated Hospital, 1975–78.

Memberships and awards: Houston Medical Forum; Alpha Phi Omega Service Fraternity; Deafness Research Foundation; American Medical Association; National Medical Association; Harris County Medical Association; American Council on Otolaryngology; Houston Otolaryngologist Association; one of the first 10 National Achievement Scholarships, 1965.

Ref: *Who's Who Among Black Americans*, 1985, p. 535.

Mackey, Howard Hamilton, Sr.   (1901–1987, M)

Architect. Born in Philadelphia, PA, Nov. 25, 1901. B.Arch., University of Pennsylvania, 1924; M.Arch., 1937. Registered Architect in DC, MD, VA, PA, and NJ; Teacher of Architecture, Design, and Tropical Architecture, Howard University, 1924–73; Acting Head of the Department of Architecture, 1930–37; Head, 1937–71; Associate Dean of the School of Engineering and Architecture, Howard University, 1964–65; Founder and Dean of the School of Architecture and City Planning, 1970–71; Staff of the Civil Engineering Department, University of Maryland.

Memberships and awards: L.H.D. (honorary), Howard University, 1980. Advisory Board of the Associa-

tion of Building Research; Housing and Town Planning Consultant to Guyana and Surinam, 1954–57; Architectural Consultant, U.S.G.S.A., 1971; Consultant to embassies of Ghana, Nigeria, and India; Pioneered National exhibits by black architects, 1930; Distinguished Service Award, National Technical Association, 1961; Whitney M. Young, Jr. Citation, American Institute of Architects, 1983; fellow, American Institute of Architects, National Council for Advancement of the Negro in Architecture; National Technical Association; National Builders Association; Omega Psi Phi.

Pub: *Architecture as a Career.* 1931 *Progressive Architecture.* 1944, 1950.

Ref: *Who's Who Among Black Americans*, 1985, p. 537 *Who's Who in America, 1986–87*, p. 1764. *Who's Who in the World*, 1984, p. 646

Maddox, Elton Preston, Jr.   (1946– ——, M)

Dentist. Born in Kingston, MD, Nov. 17, 1946. B.S., Morgan State College, 1968; D.D.S., University of Maryland Dental School, 1972. Clinical Director, Acting Director, Team Clinic, 1976–77; Assistant Professor, Dental School, University of Maryland, 1973–77; Admissions Committee, University of Maryland Dental School, 1974–77; Clinical Competency Committee, 1975–77.

Memberships and awards: Alpha Phi Alpha.

Pub: A Guide to Clinical Competency. *Journal, of Dental Education*, 1976. Why Not? University of Maryland, 1976.

Ref: *Who's Who Among Black Americans*, 1985, p. 537.

Madison, Eugene W.   (1933– ——, M)

Mathematician. Born in 1933. B.S. (mathematics), Le-Moyne College, 1956; M.S. (mathematics), Michigan State University, 1958; Ph.D (mathematics), University of Illinois, 1966. Instructor, Mathematics, Fisk University, 1958–60; Assistant Professor, Mathematics, California State College, Long Beach, 1963–66; Assistant Professor, University of Iowa, 1966–69; Visiting Assistant Professor, Mathematics, Yale University, 1969–70; Associate Professor, Mathematics, University of Iowa, 1970–.

Dissertation title: Computable Algebraic Structures and Non-Standard Arithmetic.

Pub: Structures Elementarily Closed Relative to a Model for Arithmetic. *Journal of Symbolic Logic*, v. 33. 1968. (With A. Lachlan) Computable Fields and Arithmetically Definable Ordered Field. American Mathematical Society, *Proceedings*, v. 24, 1970. A Note on Computable Real Fields. *Journal, of Symbolic Logic*, v. 35, 1907. Real Fields with Characterization of the Natural Numbers. London Mathematical Society, *Journal*, 1970.

(With D. A. Alton) Computable ?? of Boolean Algebras and Their Extension. Submitted to *Annals of Mathematical Logic,* 1971.

The Existence of Non-Simple Constructive Extensions of the Boolean Algebra of Open Sets of the Cantor Space. Submitted to the *Journal, of Symbolic Logic.*

Ref: *Black Mathematicians and Their Works,* p. 289.

Madison, Robert Prince (1923- ——, M)

Architect. Born in Cleveland, OH, July 28, 1923. B.A. (architecture), Western Reserve, 1948; M.A. (architecture), Howard University, 1952. President of Madison—Madison, International, an architectural firm in Cleveland, OH; has designed several buildings including the U.S. Embassy Office Building in Dakar, Senegal and the Engineering and Nuclear Facility at Tuskegee Institute.

Memberships and awards: American Institute of Architects; Fulbright fellowship under which he studied in Paris.

Ref: *Ebony, Success Library,* v. 1, p. 214. [p].
Who's Who in America, 1986-87, p. 1771.
Who's Who Among Black Americans, 1977, p. 402.
American Architects' Directory, 1970.
Who's Who in the Midwest, 1974, p. 419.

Madison, Shannon L. (1927- ——, M)

Engineer (mechanical). Born in Dallas, TX, June 21, 1927. B.S., Howard University, 1954. Development Engineer, York Division, Borg Warner Corporation, 1954-59; Chief Test Engineer, Emerson Radio and Phonograph Company, 1959-61; Senior Project Engineer, Delco Appliance Division, GM, 1961-65; Senior Manufacturing Research Engineer, Whirlpool Corporation, MI, 1965-.

Memberships and awards: National Technical Association; ASHRAE; Society of Mechanical Engineers; Society of Professional Engineers; Sigma Xi; Comprehensive State Health Planning Advisory Council.

Ref: *Black Engineers in the United States,* p. 130-131.
Who's Who Among Black Americans, 1985, p. 38.

Mahoney, Mary Elizabeth, (1845-1926?, F)

Nurse. Born in Boston, MA, April 16, 1845 (unverified). Enrolled in the New England Hospital for Women and Children, 1878, graduated, 1879. Forty years a Nurse improving the status of graduate Nurses; first black professional Nurse. Made welcoming address at First Meeting of the National Association of Colored Graduate Nurses (NACGN) in Boston in 1909. In July, 1936, the *American Journal of Nursing* announced that the NACGN would present the Mary Mahoney Medal to the person who had contributed the most to nursing. Adah B. Thoms received the first.

Memberships and awards: Award given in her name beginning in 1936; Family Life Center in Roxbury, MA, named for her.

Ref: *Encyclopedia of Black America,* p. 543.
Dictionary of American Negro Biography, p. 420-421.
Goodnow's *History of Nursing,* p. 249-250.
Jet, Mar. 24, 1955, p. 14. [p]
Pathfinders: A History of the Progress of Colored Graduate Nurses, by Adah B. Thoms, R.N., p. 9-11.
Chayer, Mary Ella. Mary Eliza Mahoney, *American Journal of Nursing,* v. 54, p. 429-431.
The Path We Tread, p. 17-19. [p] p. 18.
Notable American Women, 1607-1950, p. 486-487.

Majors, Monroe Alpheus (1864-1960, M)

Physician. Surgeon. Born in Waco, TX, Oct. 12, 1864. B.S., Central Tennessee College, 1886; M.D., Meharry Medical College, 1886. Practiced Austin, TX, 1886, Los Angeles, CA, 1888; first black physician west of the Rockies and first black to pass the Medical Boards of California. Lecturer in hygiene and sanitation, Paul Quinn College, 1891-1894; organized and was superintendent of Colored Hospital in Waco, 1899-1901.

Memberships and awards: Went to Chicago in 1901 and helped form a medical society there and became a charter member, 1908; he became editor of *Chicago Conservator;* organized the Lone Star Medical Association, the first black medical association in the United States, having its first meeting in Galveston, TX.

Pub: *First Steps and Nursery Rhymes,* the first book for black children published in 1921.
Noted Negro Women: Their Triumphs and Activities, published in 1893 and reprinted in Books for Libraries Press in 1971.

Ref: *Who's Who of the Colored Race,* 1915, p. 183.
Who's Who in Colored America, 1927, p. 135-136.
Who's Who in Colored America, 1928-29, p. 252-253. [p]
Dictionary of American Medical Biography, p. 491-492.
Cobb, W. Montague. Monroe Alpheus Majors, 1864-. National Medical Association, *Journal,* v. 47, Mar. 1955, p. 139-141. [p] cover
Who's Who in Colored America, 1941-44, p. 350, 353.
History of the Negro in Medicine, p. 58. [p]

Malone, Huey Perry (1935- ——, M)

Engineer (chemical). Engineer (petroleum). Born in Bude, MS, Feb. 3, 1935. B.S., Roosevelt University, 1958; Ph.D., University of Illinois, 1970. Research Fuels Engineer, Gulf Oil Corporation; Research Chemist, Gulf Oil Corporation.

Memberships and awards: American Chemical Society; American Petroleum Institute.

Dissertation title: The Synthesis and Conformational Analysis of 1,5-Diazabicyclo (3.1.0).

Ref: *Ebony Success Library,* v. 1, p. 215. [p]
       Who's Who Among Black Americans, 1986–87, p. 540.

Maloney, Arnold Hamilton (1888–1955, M)

Pharmacologist. Physician. Born in San Fernando, Trinidad, B.W.I., July 4, 1888. B.S., Naparima College, 1909, M.A., Columbia University, 1910; M.D., Indiana University, 1929; Ph.D. (pharmacology), University of Wisconsin, 1931. Head, Department of Pharmacology, Howard University in the 1930s during which time he contributed over 20 articles to scientific periodicals in the United States and Belgium. Discovered the antidotal action of Picrotoxin to Barbiturate poisoning. He and Joseph L. Johnson were in 1931 the second and third blacks to earn both the M.D., and the Ph.D. degrees. He was the first black Professor of Pharmacology in the United States.

Memberships and awards: fellow, AAAS, General Education Board Fellow; Society of Experimental Biology; National Medical Association; New York Academy of Sciences.

Dissertation title: Studies on Respiratory Stimulants and Depressants. A Study of the Effect of Morphine on the Respiratory Center.

Pub: *Amber Gold,* Boston, Meador Pub. Co., 1946, 448 p. (autobiography)
       Adequate norm. Indianapolis. Pauley, 1914. no. p.
       Over 20 articles contributed to scientific journals.

Ref: *Negro Builders and Heroes,* p. 230–231.
       American Men of Science, 8th ed., p. 1625.
       Holders of Doctorates Among American Negroes, p. 128–129.
       Dictionary of American Medical Biography, p. 493–494.
       Crisis, Aug. 1931, p. 276. [p] only
       Crisis, Aug, 1938, p. 258. [p] only
       National Medical Association, *Journal,* v. 47, Nov. 1955, p. 424–426. [p] only

Maloney, Kenneth Morgan (1941– ——, M)

Chemist (physical). Born in New Orleans, LA, Oct. 11, 1941. B.S., Southern University, 1963; Ph.D. (physical chemistry), University of Washington, Seattle, 1968. Research Assistant in Physical Chemistry, University of Washington, 1963–68; Senior Research Scientist in Reaction Dynamics, Pacific Northwest Laboratories, Battelle Memorial Institute, 1968–70; Senior Scientist and Technical Leader, Lamp Division, General Electric Company, 1970–74; Manager, Advanced Engineering Material Science, 1974–76; Manager, Material Technology and Material Engineering, Xerox Corporation, 1976–81; Associate Director, Forward and Contract Research, Allied Corporation, 1981–; Phillip Morris Research and Development.

Memberships and awards: National Research Council Advisory Committee to U.S. Army Research Office, 1974–, fellow, American Institute of Chemists; American Chemical Society; Sigma Xi; General Electric's Corning Award, 1972.

Dissertation title: The Thermal Unimolecular Isomerization of Ethyl Isocyanide.

Pub: Scientific papers in the *Journal of Physical Chemistry.*

Ref: *American Men and Women of Science,* 16th ed., p. 162.
       Ebony Success Library, v. 1, p. 215. [p]
       Who's Who Among Black Americans, 1977, p. 577.

Malveaux, Floyd (194?– ——, M)

Physician. Immunologist. B.S., Creighton University, NB, 1961; M.S., Loyola University, LA; Ph.D. (public health), Michigan State University, 1968; M.D., Howard University, 1974. Associate Professor, Johns Hopkins University; Professor, Medicine, Howard University Hospital.

Memberships and awards: Medical Service Award, National Medical Association, 1986.

Ref: *Black Enterprise,* Oct. 1988, p. 94.

Mann, Frank (1918– ——, M)

Engineer (aerospace). Built "Baby LeSabre" sports car. 1st Lt. World War II, Wing Commander.

Ref: *In Black and White,* p. 644.

Mann, Marion (1920– ——, M)

Physician. Pathologist. Military (Army Reserve). Brigadier General. Born in Atlanta, GA, Mar. 29, 1920. B.S., Tuskegee Institute, 1940; M.D., Howard University, 1954; Ph.D., Georgetown University Medical Center, 1961. Dean, College of Medicine, Howard University, 1970–79; Assistant to Full Professor of Pathology.

Memberships and awards: Diplomate, National Board of Medical Examiners; American Medical Association; National Medical Association; Institute of Medicine; National Academy of Sciences; Washington Society of Pathologists; Medical Society of the District of Columbia; American Society of Clinical Pathology; International Academy of Pathology.

Dissertation title: The Cranial Nerve Nuclei and Selected Relay Nuclei of the Human Brain Stem Following Transtentorial Herniation.

Ref: *American Men and Women of Science,* 14th ed., p. 3173.
       Black Enterprise, Feb. 1975, p. 23–24.
       Encyclopedia of Black America, p. 545–546.
       Who's Who Among Black Americans, 1980–81, p. 514.
       Who's Who Among Black Americans, 1985, p. 514.
       National Medical Association, *Journal,* v. 62, Sept. 1970, p. 368–369. [p] (list of publications as of 1970)
       Who's Who in America, 1978, p. 2071.

National Medical Association, *Journal*, v. 67, May 1975, p. 248. [p]

Mannings, Gwendolyn Cooper   (19??–1977, F)

Physician. Internist. First black woman physician on visiting staff of Grady Hospital in Atlanta, 1962. Assistant Chief of Medical Service at Tuskegee, AL, before moving to Atlanta.

Ref: *Jet*, May 17, 1962, p. 25.
         Jet, Dec. 15, 1977, p. 12.

Manuey, Nan Phelps   (1926– ——, F)

Mathematician. Statistician. Born in Annapolis, MD, Jan. 30, 1926. B.A., Morgan State College; M.S., Howard University. Statistician, Bureau of Educational Research, Wilberforce State College; Assistant in Mathematics Department. Boston University; Statistical Analyst, Time and Life Company; Assistant Professor of Mathematics, A & T College, NC.

Memberships and awards: American Statistical Association; Beta Kappa Chi; Mathematical Association.

Ref: *The Negro in Science,* p. 188.

Mapp, Frederick Everett   (1910– ——, M)

Zoologist. Born in Atlanta, GA, Oct. 12, 1910. B.S., Morehouse College, 1932; M.S., Atlanta University, 1934; M.A., Harvard University, 1942; Ph.D., University of Chicago, 1950. Booker T. Washington High School, Atlanta, GA, 1933–40; Professor, Biology and Chairman of the Department, Knoxville College, 1944–46; Roosevelt College, 1948–50; Professor, Biology, Tennessee A & I State College, 1951–52; Professor, Biology and Chairman of the Department, Morehouse College, 1952–; research in problems of growth.

Memberships and awards: AAAS; Sigma Xi; New York Academy of Sciences; Tennessee Academy of Sciences; General Education Board fellowship, 1946–48; David Packard Professor of Biology, 1973–82.

Dissertation title: Descriptive and Experimental Studies on Regeneration of the Anuran Notochord.

Ref: *The Negro in Science,* p. 179.
         Ebony, May 1961, p. 27. [p]
         Who's Who Among Black Americans, 1985, p. 543.

Marble, Harriett Beecher Stowe   (1885–19??, F)

Pharmacist. Born in Yazoo City, MS, May 2, 1885. B.Pharm., Meharry Medical College, 1906. Passed examination and licensed in several states, made best mark of 77 applicants before the Mississippi State Board of Examiners, 1908. In charge of drug store for Jeter and Jeter, Oklahoma City, 1907–09; Brown & Fisher Drug Company,

Laurel, MS, 1909–11; Hospital Pharmacist, Tuskegee Institute, AL, 1911–13. In business for herself, 1915–.

Memberships and awards: Pharmaceutical Section of the National Medical Association; Medical, Dental, and Pharmaceutical Association.

Ref: *Who's Who of the Colored Race,* 1915, p. 184.

Marchbanks, Vance Hunter   (1905–1973, M)

Physician. Born in Fort Washikie, WY, 1905. B.A., University of Arizona, 1931; M.D., Howard University, 1937. Medical Staff, V.A. Hospital, Tuskegee, AL, until 1941 when he entered U.S. Air Force; Major, Group Surgeon for 332nd Fighter Group; Space doctor, medical monitor for Project Mercury. Collected data and evaluated John Glenn in orbit.

Memberships and awards: Received William Alonzo Warfield Award of the Association of Former Interns and Residents of the Freedmen's Hospital in Washington, DC. Had received Bronze Star and four Air Force commendations; was cited for noteworthy contributions to aviation medical research during a 20-year military career. One of 23 aeromedical monitors for the Mercury Project.

Pub: Black Physician and the USAF. National Medical Association, *Journal*, v. 64, Jan. 1972, p. 73–74. (read at NMA Convention, Aug. 10, 1971)

Ref: *Ebony,* April 1962, p. 35, 38–40, 42. [p]
         In Black and White, p. 646.
         Wheadon, *Negro from 1863 to 1963.*
         Jet, Dec. 21, 1961, p. 16–17.
         Jet, May 4, 1961, p. 27.
         Ebony, Oct. 1974, p. 6. [p]
         National Medical Association, *Journal*, v. 47, July 1955, p. 284. [p]

Mark, Jessie Jarue   (1906–19??, F)

Plant Physiologist. Botanist. Born in Apple Springs, TX, Sept. 24, 1906. B.S., Prairie View State College, 1929; M.S., Iowa State University, 1931; Ph.D., 1935. First black to earn a Ph.D. in Botany. Professor, Kentucky State Industrial College, 1931.

Memberships and awards: Alpha Pi Mu; Sigma Xi; Society of Plant Physiologists; Forestry Association; Society of Agronomy.

Dissertation title: The Relation of Root Reserves to Cold Resistance in Alfalfa.

Ref: *American Men of Science,* 7th ed., p. 1167.
         Holders of Doctorates Among American Negroes, p. 129.
         Negroes in Science: Natural Science Doctorates, 1876–1969, p. 60

Marsh, Alphonso Howard   (1938– ——, M)

Engineer (electrical). Born in Mobile, AL, Sept. 22, 1938. B.S. (electrical Engineering), Howard University, 1961;

Engineer, R.C.A., 1961–63; Design Engineer, General Dynamics, 1963–66; Research and Development Engineer, Rochester Instrument Systems, 1966–67; Electrical Engineer, Raytheon Company, 1967–73; Digital Equipment Corporation, 1973–77; Managing Engineer, L.F.E. Corporation, 1977–.

Memberships and awards: National Society of Professional Engineers, 1984–; National Director, Massachusetts Society of Professional Engineers, State President, 1983–84; Tau Beta Pi Honor Society, 1960; IEEE; Registered Professional Engineer, State of Massachusetts; several awards from the Massachusetts Society of Professional Engineers.

Pub: Twelve articles in professional journals.

Ref: *Black Engineers in the United States*, p. 132.
Who's Who Among Black Americans, 1985, p. 544.

Marshall, Charles Herbert, (1898–1983, M)

Physician. Gynecologist. Pediatrician. Born in Washington, DC, June 26, 1898. B.S., Howard University, 1921; M.D., Howard University Medical College, 1924. Member of the Department of Gynecology and Department of Pediatrics, Freedmen's Hospital, 1925–28; Instructor, Department of Medicine, Howard University Medical School, 1928–32.

Memberships and awards: President, National Medical Association, 1949–50; President, Medico-Chirurgical Society of DC; Omega Psi Phi; Board Members, Whipper Home; Board of Directors, Citizen's Association of Georgetown, 1969–72.

Ref: National Medical Association, *Journal*, v. 40, Nov. 1948, p. 261. [p]
National Medical Association, *Journal*, v. 41, Sept. 1949, p. 231. [p]
Who's Who Among Black Americans, 1985, p. 545.
Jet, July 18, 1983, p. 22.

Marshall, Lawrence Marcellus (1910–1977, M)

Biochemist. Born in Pittsburgh, PA, Mar. 31, 1910. B.S., Duquesne University, 1932; M.S., 1940; Ph.D., Wayne University, 1949. Assistant Professor, Biology, Arkansas A M & N College, 1940–44; Assistant Chemist, Chemical Warfare Service, 1942–44; Associate Chemist, Quartermaster, Army, 1944–45; Assistant Professor, Biochemistry, Medical School, Howard University, 1948–53; Associate Professor, 1954–; Chairman, Biochemistry Department, Howard University, 1959–; research in terminal respiratory mechanism (Heibs cycle) in physiological systems, chromatography, radioactive tracers, and spectroscopy.

Memberships and awards: Teaching and U.S.P.H. fellow, Wayne Medical School, 1945–48; American Society of Biological Chemistry; Sigma Xi; American Chemical

Society; Lederle Medical Faculty Award, 1953; fellow, American Institute of Chemists.

Dissertation title: Application of Partition Chromatography to the Determination of Fumeric Acid in Biological Materials.

Ref: *The Negro in Science*, p. 184.
American Men and Women of Science, 13th ed., p. 2810.
National Medical Association, *Journal*, v. 69, Oct. 1977, p. 731. [p] obit
Jet, Sept. 1, 1977, p. 11.

Marshall, Vereen Marion (1890–1963, M)

Dentist. Born in Cheraw, SC, Nov. 7, 1890. B.S., Claflin University, Orangeburg, SC, 1909; D.D.S., Meharry Medical College, TN, 1914. Taught French and Science. Claflin College, 1910. Teacher, Meharry Medical College, 1914–17. First black dentist in Gary, IN.

Memberships and awards: Indiana Dental Society (vice-president, 1928–30); National Medical Association.

Ref: *Who's Who in Colored America*, 1933–37, p. 364.
Who's Who in Colored America, 1938–40, p. 364
Jet, Oct. 24, 1963, p. 50.

Marshall, W. (1800s, M)

Inventor. Grain binder, patent #341,599, 1886. Device used to gather grain, form it into bundles and tie the bundles automatically.

Ref: *At Last Recognition in America*, v. 1, p. 3.

Martin, Alfred E. (1911–19??, M)

Physicist. Born in New York, NY, Sept. 15, 1911. B.S., College of the City of New York, 1932; M.S., Michigan University, 1933. Physics Department, Shaw University, 1933–36; Fisk University, 1936–42; Signal Corps Laboratory, Eatontown, NJ, 1942–44; A. D. Cardwell Manufacturing Corporation, Brooklyn, NY, 1944–46; Physics, Hunter College, 1944–; Head, Photonics Section, Physics Laboratories, Sylvania Electric Products, Inc., Bayside, NY, 1946–57; Technical Editor, McGraw-Hill Publishing Company, Inc., 1957–59; Director of Engineering Training, Polaroid Electronics Corporation, New York, NY, 1959–60; Engineer, Arinc Research Corporation, 1961–64; Senior Reliability Engineer, Grumman Aircraft Engineering Corporation, 1964–67; Assistant Professor of Physics, Manhattan Community College, 1967–; work in radiometry, luminescence of inorganic phosphors.

Memberships and awards: American Physical Society; American Association of Physics Teachers; Institute of Radio Engineers; Optical Society of America; Electrochemical Society of Colorimetry; IEEE; Scientific Research Society of America.

Ref: *The Negro in Science*, p. 190.
American Men and Women of Science, 12th ed., p. 4107.
Ebony, April 1954, p. 5. [p]
Crisis, Aug. 1933, p. 184. [p] only

Martin, Benjamin Joseph (1900s, M)

Mathematician. B.S., Morehouse College, 1963; M.S. (applied mathematics), Purdue University, 1966; Ph.D. (applied mathematics), Purdue University, 1969. Student Instructor, Morehouse College, 1962–63; Graduate Assistant, Purdue University, 1963–67; Mathematician, Naval Avionics Facility, 1967–68; Assistant Professor, Southern University, summer, 1966; Associate Professor and Chairman, Department of Mathematics, Morehouse College.

Memberships and awards: Merrill Early Admission Scholarship, 1959–63; U.S. Steel, Woodrow Wilson fellow, 1963–64; Pi Mu Epsilon; American Mathematical Society; Committee on Undergraduate Program in Mathematics; Society for Industrial and Applied Mathematics; Mathematical Association of America (Vice-Chairman, Louisiana-Mississippi Section and Committee on Assistant to Developing Colleges); Subcommittee on Center of Excellence.

Dissertation title: On a New Integral Equation Arising in the Theory of Radiative Transfer.

Pub: On a New Integral Equation Arising in the Theory of Radiative Transfer. *SIAM Journal of Applied Mathematics*, v. 20, June 1971.

Ref: *Black Mathematicians and Their Works*, p. 290, 141–151.

Martin, Hamilton St. Clair (18??–19??, M)

Physician. M.D., Howard University Medical College, 1905. Professor of Otology, Laryngology, Howard University.

Ref: *Who's Who in Colored America*, 1927, p. 137.

Martin, James L. (1882–19??, M)

Physician. Roentgenologist. Born in Jonesville, VA, Nov. 2, 1882. B.S., Swift Memorial College; Shaw University, 1906; M.D., Shaw University, 1906; Graduate School of Medicine, University of Pennsylvania, specializing in X-ray and medicine, 1921–23. Chief, X-Ray Department, Mercy Hospital; Staff Member, Graduate School of Medicine, University of Pennsylvania.

Memberships and awards: American Medical Association; Philadelphia County Medical Society; National Medical Association; Clinical Pathological Society; Academy of Medicine; Alpha Phi Alpha.

Ref: *Who's Who in Colored America*, 1930–32, p. 296.
Who's Who in Colored America, 1933–37, p. 365–366.
Who's Who in Colored America, 1938–40, p. 365.
Crisis, Jan. 1923, p. 126 [p]

Martin, W. A. (1800s, M)

Inventor. Lock, patent #407,735, 1889, an improvement over the 4,000-year-old bolt invented by the Chinese that could be fastened or unfastened from either side—A forerunner of modern door locks.

Ref: *At Last Recognition in America*, v. 1, p. 23.

Mason, Clarence Tyler (1908–1968, M)

Chemist. Born in Chicago, IL, April 21, 1908. B.S., Northwestern University, 1931; M.S., McGill University, 1933; Ph.D. 1935. Associate Professor, Chemistry to Professor and Head, Division of Science, Dillard University, 1935–44; Research Associate to Director of Research and Professor of Chemistry, Carver Foundation, Tuskegee Institute, 1944–; Director, Carver Foundation, 1957–; Abstractor, Chemical Abstracts; research in halogenated ethers, fungicides, plastics, inks.

Memberships and awards: Rosenwald fellow, summer, 1936; American Chemical Society (member-at-large, Auburn section); Sigma Xi; Beta Kappa Chi (council member); Vice-President, National Institute of Science; American Institute of Science, fellow.

Dissertation title: Studies in conductivity.

Ref: *American Men of Science*, 11th ed., p. 2504.
The Negro in Science, 184.
Holders of Doctorates Among American Negroes, p. 153.
Crisis, Sept. 1933, p. 209. [p]

Mason, Ulysses Grant (1872–19??, M)

Physician. Surgeon. Born in Birmingham, AL, Nov. 20, 1872. Alabama A & M University; M.D., Meharry Medical College, 1895; special surgery course, University of Edinburgh, Scotland, 1899. Assistant City Physician, Birmingham, eight years; Chairman and Surgeon, George C. Hull Hospital.

Memberships and awards: Trustee Central Alabama College; Clinical Congress of Surgeons of North America; National Medical Association; State Medical, Dental, and Pharmaceutical Association; Jones Valley Medical, Dental, and Pharmaceutical Association; Alpha Phi Alpha.

Ref: *Who's Who of the Colored Race*, 1915, p. 186.
Who's Who in Colored America, 1928–29, p. 261.
Who's Who in Colored America, 1930–32, p. 299.

Mason, Vaughn Carrington (1915–1970, M)

Physician. Obstetrician. Gynecologist. Surgeon. Born in Pocahontas, VA, May 17, 1915. B.A., University of Pennsylvania, 1936; M.D., McGill University, 1941. Director, Obstetrics and Gynecology, Sydenham Hospital.

Memberships and awards: President, National Medical Association, 1961; Diplomate, American Board of Obstetrics and Gynecology, 1949; fellow, American College of Surgeons, 1950; founding fellow, American College of Obstetrics and Gynecology; founding fellow, New York Gynecological Society; National Medical Association; President, Manhattan Central Medical Society; Harlem Surgical Society; Alpha Phi Alpha; President, Medical Society of the County of New York.

Ref: *Jet,* Aug. 24, 1961, p. 49.
National Medical Association, *Journal,* v. 62, Nov. 1970, p. 480. [p] obit

Mason, William Alfred Madison   (1898–   , M)

Physician. Born in New Orleans, LA, Aug. 25, 1898. B.S., Ohio State University; M.D., Meharry Medical College, 1929; M.P.H., Yale Medical College, 1945; Postgraduate, Vanderbilt University, NIH, Harvard Medical School, University of Pennsylvania, University of Georgia, Emory University. Complex Family Planning Service Consultant, Atlanta University; Medical Director, Atlanta Planned Parenthood Association; Physician Department of Public Health, 1942–74; Associate Professor, Meharry Medical College.

Memberships and awards: Alpha Phi Alpha; Chi Delta Mu; American Association of Sex Educators, Counselors, and Therapists; Meritorious Service Award, Georgia Department of Human Resources; Alan Guttmachet Medallion for Distinguished Service in Contraceptive Practice, Planned Parenthood Association.

Pub: *An Odyssey in Black and White,* New York, Vantage Press, 1978. 162 p.

Ref: *Who's Who Among Black Americans,* 1985, p. 550.
Black Americans in Autobiography, p. 54.
Who's Who in the South and Southwest, 1978, p. 467.

Massey, Walter Eugene   (1938–   , M)

Physicist (theoretical). Physicist (solid state). Born in Hattiesburg, MS, April 5, 1938. B.S., Morehouse, 1958; M.A. & Ph.D. (physics), Washington University, 1966. Associate Professor, Physics, Brown University, 1970–; Professor, 1975–; Director, Argonne National Laboratory, 1979–84; Vice-President for Research, Argonne National Laboratory, 1984–; research in many-body problems, quantum liquids and solids.

Memberships and awards: President, AAAS; Distinguished Service Citation of the American Association of Physics Teachers, 1975; Member of the National Science Board, 1978–84; Trustee, Brown University and the Rand Corporation; Visiting Committee for the Physics Departments of MIT and Harvard; Superconducting Super Collider Site Evaluation Committee of the National Academies of Sciences and Engineering; Co-Chairman, AAAS Steering Committee for the Project to Strengthen the Scientific and Engineering Infra-structure in Sub-Saharan Africa.

Dissertation title: Ground State of Liquid Helium-Boson Solutions for Mass 3 and 4.

Ref: *American Men and Women of Science,* 14th ed., p. 3233.
In Black and White, p. 655.
Who's Who Among Black Americans, 1985, p. 551.
Ebony, Nov. 1985, p. 339. [p]
Ebony, Oct. 1987, p. 84. [p]
Science, Dec. 18, 1987, p. 1657–1658. [p] biog
Ebony, May 1968, p. 6. [p]
Ebony, Nov. 1979, p. 89–92, 94. [p]
Black Collegian, v. 35, Aug./Sept. 1980, p. 172–177. [p]

Massie, Samuel Proctor, Jr.   (1919–   , M)

Chemist (organic). Born in Little Rock, AR, July 3, 1919. B.S., Agricultural Mechanical and Normal College, 1938; M.A., Fisk University, 1940; Ph.D. Iowa University, 1946. Associate Professor, Mathematics and Physics, Arkansas A M & N College, 1940–41; Research Associate, Iowa State College, 1943–46; Instructor, Chemistry, Fisk University, 1946–47; Professor, Chemistry and Chairman of the Department, Langston University, 1947–53; Professor, Chemistry and Chairman of the Department, Fisk University, 1953–60; Program Director, National Science Foundation, 1960; Chairman and Professor, Chemistry, Howard University, 1961–63; Professor, Chemistry, U.S. Naval Academy, 1966–; Chairman, Chemistry Department, 1977–.

Memberships and awards: Represented American Chemical Society at International Conference in Zurich, Switzerland; elected National Chairman of Visiting Scientists for the 90,000-member American Chemical Society; American Chemical Society; National Institute of Science; President, Oklahoma Academy of Sciences, 1953; Tennessee Academy of Science; Sigma Xi; Phi Lambda Upsilon; First of six winners of 1961 College Chemistry Teachers Award.

Dissertation title: High-Molecular Weight Compounds of Nitrogen and Sulfur as Therapeutic Agents.

Ref: *American Men and Women of Science,* 16th ed., p. 250.
The Negro in Science, p. 184.
Jet, Mar. 3, 1960, p. 45.
Jet, Aug. 10, 1961, p. 41. [p]
Who's Who Among Black Americans, 1985, p. 551.

Matory, William Earle   (1928–   , M)

Physician. Surgeon. Born in East St. Louis, IL, Oct. 1, 1928. B.S., Howard University, 1949; M.D., 1953. Chief Resident in Surgery, Freedmen's Hospital.

Memberships and awards: Received first D. Hale Williams Award for outstanding achievement, 1960; American College of Surgeons; American Association for the Surgery of Trauma; National Medical Association, Surgery Section Chairman.

Ref: A Century of Black Surgeons, p. 629–631 [p] p. 630.

Matzeliger, Jan Earnst (1852–1889, M)

Inventor. Born in Dutch Guiana, Sept. 15, 1852. Invented the shoe lasting machine without the aid of a formal education, patent #459,899, 1891; nailing machine, patent # 421,954, Feb. 25, 1896. Made Lynn, MA, the shoe capital of the world. His shoe lasting machine revolutionized the shoe industry. In exchange for a block of stock the Consolidated Lasting Machine Company took over his patents. By 1897 Sidney W. Winslow, who put up some of the original money, formed the United Shoe Machinery Corporation with $20 million and in 12 years, the corporation earned over $50 million. Matzeliger died of tuberculosis in 1889 at the age of 37 not knowing how the industry would grow because of his invention.

Ref: *Black Inventors in America*, p. 429–430.
     Jan Earnst Matzeliger and the Making of the Shoe. *Journal of Negro History*, Jan. 1955, p. 8–33.
     Dictionary of American Negro Biography, p. 429–430.
     They Showed the Way, p. 93–96.
     Negro Almanac, p. 637–638.
     Negro in Our History, 5th ed., p. 461–463.
     Great Negroes: Past and Present, p. 63.
     Jet, Mar. 24, 1986, p. 19. [p]
     Historical Afro-American Biographies, 1969, p. 99. [p]
     Afro USA, p. 730–731.
     The Role of the American Negro in the Field of Science, p. 25–28.
     Black Pioneers of Science and Invention, p. 24–33. [p]
     World's Great Men of Color, p. 350–355.
     Ebony, Jan. 1967, p. 121. [p]
     Cleveland Call & Post, Feb. 26, 1977, B3, col. 4.
     Webster's American Biographies, p. 701.

Maxwell, Ucecil Seymour (1896–19??, M)

Biochemist. Chemist. Born in Fort Scott, KN, Feb. 18, 1896. B.A., University of Colorado, 1921; M.S., University of Chicago, 1928; Ph.D. 1943. Professor, Chemistry, Philander Smith College, Dean of College, 1921–26; Instructor, Fisk University, 1926; Professor, Chemistry, Arkansas State College, 1928; Professor, Lincoln University, MS, 1928; Director, summer session, 1943; Visiting Professor, Biochemistry, Meharry Medical College, 1944.

Memberships and awards: American Chemical Society; American Association of University Professors; National Institute of Science; Beta Kappa Chi; Sigma Xi.

Dissertation title: The Basal Metabolic Rates of Normal Negro Women.

Ref: *American Men of Science*, 10th ed., p. 2710.
     The Negro in Science, p. 184.
     Holders of Doctorates Among American Negroes, p. 154.

Mayes, Vivienne Lucille Malone (1900s, F)

Mathematician. B.A. (mathematics), Fisk University, 1952; M.A. (mathematics), Fisk University, 1954; Ph.D. (mathematics), University of Texas, 1966. Associate Professor, Mathematics, Paul Quinn College, 1954–61; Associate Professor, Mathematics, Baylor University, 1966–.

Memberships and awards: American Association of University Women fellowship, 1964–65; Research College Teachers, summers 1967, 1968; American Mathematical Society; Mathematical Association of America (Resolution Committee, 1972 and Program Committee, 1973); National Council of Teachers of Mathematics; ASL.

Dissertation title: A Structure Problem in Asymptotic Analysis.

Pub: Some Steady State Properties of $(^x_0 (t)dt) - (x)$. American Mathematical Society, *Proceedings*, v. 22, Sept. 1969.
     (Faculty Consultant with Howard Rolf) *Pre-Calculus: Algebraic and Trigonometric Functions*. Individual Learning Systems, 1971.

Ref: Kenschaft, Patricia C. Black Women in Mathematics in the U.S. *American Mathematical Monthly*, v. 88, Oct. 1981, p. 596–597.
     Black Mathematicians and Their Works, p. 152–157, 290. [p] p. 152.
     National Faculty Directory, 1988, p. 2448.

Maynard, Aubre De L. (1901–19??, M)

Physician. Surgeon (thoracic). Born in Georgetown, Guyana, 1901. B.S., College City of New York, 1922; M.D., New York University Medical College, 1926. Surgical Director, Harlem Hospital, NY, 1952–; Surgeon in charge of the removal of the knife from the chest of Dr. Martin Luther King, Jr., Harlem Hospital, 1958.

Memberships and awards: New York Academy of Medicine; New York Thoracic Surgical; New York Surgical Society; Diplomate, American Board of Surgery.

Ref: *Crisis*, June/July 1954, p. 354–356. [p]
     Crisis, June/July 1956, p. 337. [p]
     A Century of Black Surgeons, p. 171–179. [p]

Mazique, Douglas Wilkerson (1909–1964, M)

Physician. Surgeon. Otolaryngologist. Born in Natchez, MS, 1909. B.A., Morehouse College; M.D., Meharry Medical College. Pioneer in Stapendectomy. First black on the staff, Alexian Bros. Hospital, Chicago; Assistant Ear Specialist, University of Illinois Infirmary for 19 years.

Ref: *Jet*, July 23, 1946, p. 44.
     National Cyclopedia of American Biography, v. 50, p. 554.

Mazique, Edward C. (1911–1988, M)

Physician. Internist. Born in Natchez, MS, Mar. 21, 1911. B.S., Morehouse College, 1933; M.A., Atlanta University, 1934; M.D., Howard University, 1941. Private practice, Washington, DC, 1943–.

Memberships and awards: President, National Medical Association, 1959; American Medical Association; American Public Health Association; Medical Society of the District of Columbia; American Geriatric Society; President, Medico-Chirurgical Society of the District of Columbia, 1951; Royal Society of Health, London; Health Advisory Council, Washington Technical Institute; American Association of Medical Assistants; Medical Advisory Board of the Visiting Nurses Association; Omega Psi Phi; Chi Delta Mu; Afro-American Outstanding Citizen Award, 1952; Certificate of Achievement Award, National Medical Association, 1960, 1965; Honorary Degree of Science, Morehouse College, 1974.

Ref: *Who's Who Among Black Americans*, 1985, p. 557.
Medico-Chirurgical Society of the District of Columbia, Inc., *Bulletin*, Jan.–Dec. 1950, p. 1–2. [p]
National Medical Association, *Journal*, v. 60, Nov. 1968, p. 534.

McAfee, Leo Cecil, Jr.   (1945- ——, M)

Engineer (electrical). Born in Marshall, TX, Dec. 15, 1945. B.S., (electrical engineering), Prairie View A & M College, 1966; M.S., University of Michigan, 1967; Ph.D. 1970. Technical staff, Bell Telephone Laboratories, NJ, summer 1968; IBM Thomas J. Watson Research Laboratories, NY, 1971 and 1978; Associate Senior Research Engineer, Semiconductor Group, Electronics Department of General Motors Research Laboratories, 1973–74; Associate Professor of Electrical Engineering, University of Michigan.

Memberships and awards: Eta Kappa Nu; Tau Beta Pi; Sigma Xi; Phi Kappa Pi; Alpha Kappa Nu; Outstanding Engineering Student, Prairie View College, 1956–66; National Science Foundation Trainee, University of Michigan, 1966–68; University of Michigan Predoctoral fellow, 1969–70.

Dissertation title: Techniques for the Optimization of Numerical Models of Semiconductor Devices.

Ref: *Black Engineers in the United States*, p. 135–136.
Who's Who Among Black Americans, 1985, p. 557.

McAfee, Walter Samuel   (1914- ——, M)

Physicist (theoretical). Born in Ore City, TX, Sept. 2, 1914. B.S., Wiley College, 1934; M.S., Ohio State, 1937; Ph.D. (physics), Cornell University, 1949. One of the Mathematicians working on the radar contact of the moon from earth in the 1940s. Teacher, Jr. High School, 1937–43; Physicist in Theoretical Studies Unit, Engineering Laboratories, U.S. Army Electronics Command, 1942–45; Physicist and Supervisor, 1945–46; Physicist in Radiation Physics, 1948–53; Section on Electromagnetic Wave Propagation, 1953–57; Consultant Physicist, Applied Physics Division, 1958–65; Technical Director, Passive Sensing Technical Area, 1965–71; Scientific Advisor

to Director of Research, Development and Engineering, Engineering Laboratories, 1971–78; Scientific Advisor, U.S. Army Electronics Research and Development Command, 1978–; Lecturer, West Long Branch Monmont College, NJ, 1958–75; research in theoretical nuclear physics.

Memberships and awards: Secretary of the Army fellow, Harvard University, 1957–58; AAAS; American Astronomical Society; American Physical Society; American Association of Physics Teachers; Senior Member, IEEE; Eta Kappa Nu; Sigma Pi Sigma; Rosenwald fellow in nuclear physics, Cornell University, 1946; cited for contribution to Project Diana, First Radar to the Moon, 1946, 1971; Wiley College Science Hall of Fame, 1982.

Dissertation title: On the Production of Mesons by Collisions of Nucleons Having Non-Relativistic Energies.

Ref: *American Men and Women of Science*, 16th ed., p. 4.
Drew. Negro Scholars in Scientific Research. *Journal of Negro History*, v. 35, 1950: p. 147.
Who's Who Among Black Americans, 1985, p. 557.
Blacks in Science: Astrophysicist to Zoologist. p. 47

McArthur, Barbara Martin   (1900s, F)

Nurse. Born in Dubuque, IA. Diplomate in Nursing, Provident Hospital and Training School; B.S.N., M.S., DePaul University; M.S., Ph.D., University of Washington, 1976. Nurse and Assistant Professor of Biology and Science Education, Knoxville College; Associate Professor, Wayne State University, 1976–79; Professor and Director of Graduate Program in Institutional Epidemiology, Wayne State University, 1976–83.

Memberships and awards: Delta Sigma Theta; Planned Parenthood League, Inc.; Wayne State University Minority Biomedical Support Program, 1979–81; first certification, Board of Infection Control, 1981–83; American College of Epidemiology; Review Board of Nursing Research; Consultant, University of Alabama School of Nursing Infection Control Program, 1984–85; A. Wilberforce Williams Award, Provident Hospital; fellow, American Academy of Nursing; Sigma Theta Tau Nursing Honor Society, 1980; fellow, New York Academy of Sciences, 1980.

Dissertation title: An Epidemiological Study of Nosocomial Infections Attributed to Acinetobacter Calcoaceticus (Herellea Vaginicola) Featuring a Bacteriocin Typing System.

Pub: Numerous journal articles and chapters in books.

Ref: *Who's Who Among Black Americans*, 1985, p. 558.
The Path We Tread, p. 122–123. [p]

McArthur, Rutherford Benjamin   (1884-1958, M)

Physician. Surgeon. Otorhynolaryngologist. Born in Ridge Springs, NC, July 9, 1884. B.A., Bennett College, NC, 1908; M.D., Meharry Medical College, TN, 1913;

Postgraduate, Indiana University, 1930. Eye, Ear, Nose and Throat Specialist, 1921–.

Memberships and awards: Executive Board of the Escalapian Medical Society; President, East Tennessee Medical Council; Director of Exhibits, National Medical Association; Omega Psi Phi.

Ref: *Jet,* Feb. 13, 1958, p. 20.
   Who's Who in Colored America, 1930-32, p. 281.
   Who's Who in Colored America, 1933-37, p. 341.
   Who's Who in Colored America, 1938-40, p. 343.
   Who's Who in Colored America, 1941-44, p. 335.

McArthur, William Henry   (1922- ——, M)

Protozoologist (parasitic). Zoologist. Born in Selma, AL, Oct. 15, 1922. B.A., Morehouse College, 1947; M.S., Atlanta University, 1948; Ph.D. State University of Iowa, 1955. Instructor, Morehouse College, 1948–51; Associate Professor, Knoxville College, 1951–53; Assistant in Zoology, State University of Iowa, 1954–55; Professor, Knoxville College, 1955–.

Memberships and awards: Sigma Xi; National Institute of Science; Gamma Alpha; Beta Kappa Chi; Tennessee Academy of Sciences, American Association of University Professors; Iowa Academy of Sciences; Four McBride Scholarships; Two Carnegie Grants.

Dissertation title: Observations of the Enteric Protozoa of Rana Pipiens During Larval Development and Metamorphosis.

Ref: *Leaders in American Science,* 1955-56, p. 266. [p]
   American Men and Women of Science, 15th ed., p. 7.

McBay, Henry Cecil Ransom   (1914- ——, M)

Chemist (organic). Born in Mexia, TX, May 29, 1914. B.S., Wiley College, 1934; M.S., Atlanta University, 1936; Ph.D. University of Chicago, 1945. Instructor, Chemistry, Wiley College, 1936–38; Instructor, Western University, Kansas City, 1938–39; Instructor to Professor, Morehouse College, 1945–81; Chairman of the Department of Chemistry 1960–81; Professor of Chemistry, Atlanta University, 1981–.

Memberships and awards: Technical Expert, Unesco Mission to Liberia, W. Africa, 1951; Outstanding Teaching Award, National Association for Black Chemists and Chemical Engineers, 1976; Charles H. Henry Awards, Georgia Section of the American Chemical Society, 1976; James Flack Norris Award, Northeastern Section of the American Chemical Society, 1978; Lamplighter Award, National Beta Kappa Chi Society, 1983; American Chemical Society; Research Fellow, Carver Foundation, 1941–42, Sigma Xi.

Dissertation title: Reactions of Atoms and Free Radicals in Solution. I. The Methyl Free Radical as a Tool for Organic Syntheses. II. The Relative Reactivities of Some Low Molecular Weight Aliphatic Free Radicals.

Ref: *National Faculty Directory,* 1987, p. 2395.
   Who's Who Among Black Americans, 1985, p. 558.
   The Negro in Science, p. 185.
   American Men and Women of Science, 15th ed., p. 7.
   Ebony, May 1961, p. 27. [p]
   Ebony, Dec. 1978, p. 110. [p]

McBay, Shirley Mathis   (1935- ——, F)

Mathematician. Chemist. Born in Bainbridge, GA, May 4, 1935. B.A., (chemistry), Paine College, 1954; M.S. (chemistry), Atlanta University, 1957; M.S. (mathematics), Atlanta University, 1958; Ph.D. (mathematics), University of Georgia, 1966. Instructor, Spelman College, 1955–63; Assistant Professor, University of Georgia, 1965–66; Associate Professor/Professor of Mathematics and Chief, Division of the Natural Sciences, Spelman College, 1966–75; Associate Academic Dean, Spelman College, 1973–75; National Science Foundation, Program Director, 1975–80; MIT, Dean for Student Affairs, 1980–.

Memberships and awards: Evaluation Teams for Southern Association of Colleges and Schools; American Mathematical Society; AAAS; Summa Cum Laude, Paine College, 1952; Outstanding Educator of America, 1975; Presidential Distinguished Alumni Award, 1977; IBM Faculty Fellowship Grant.

Dissertation title: The Homology Theory of Metabelian Life Algebras.

Ref: *Who's Who Among Black Americans,* 1985, p. 558.
   Black Mathematicians and Their Works, p. 290. [p] p. 290.
   Ebony, Nov. 1975, p. 10. [p] (advertisement)

McBroom, Fletcher Pearl Riley   (1926- ——, M)

Physician. Cardiologist. Born in Louisville, MS, Mar. 16, 1926. B.A., University of Chicago, 1946; B.S., Columbia University, 1949; M.D., College of Physicians and Surgeons, 1953. Heart specialist in Cedars of Lebanon Hospital where he developed new method in 1960 of observing changes in coronary blood vessel tissues affected by hardening of the arteries. First black doctor accepted by UCLA Medical Center. Presidency, Columbia University Wing, Goldwater Hospital, NY, 1954–55; Los Angeles, 1955–57.

Memberships and awards: Fellowship in Cardiology, USC, 1957–58; cardiovascular and preventive medicine, independent research, 1962–85; NIH Grants Research fellow, 1958–62; Board Member, Frederick Douglas Child Development Center, 1958–62; Sidoha Yoda Foundation, 1974–80.

Ref: *Jet,* Feb. 11, 1960, p. 18.
   Who's Who Among Black Americans, 1985, p. 558.
   Ebony, May 1964, p. 70. [p]
   Who's Who of American Women, 1975, p. 624.

McCane, Charles Anthony   (1899– ——, M)

Physicist. Born in Jefferson, TX, Oct. 24, 1899. B.A., Wiley College, 1922; M.S., Northwestern University, 1931. Instructor in Natural Science, Wiley College, 1922–28; Professor of Physics and Head of the Department, Wiley College, 1928–32; Head of the Physics Department, D.C. Teachers College, 1932–55; Professor, 1955–; Lecturer at Howard University, 1957–66; Cape Cod Community College, 1968–72; specialist in spectrum analysis and thermionics; retired.

Memberships and awards: Physical Society; Association of Physics Teachers; fellow, New York Academy; Phi Beta Sigma; American Chemical Society; American Association of University Professors; Rosenwald fellow, Northwestern University, 1928–29.

Ref: Who's Who in Colored America, 1930–32, p. 281.
        American Men of Science, 10th ed., p. 2529.
        Who's Who in Colored America, 1933–37, p. 342.
        Who's Who in Colored America, 1938–40, p. 343.
        Who's Who Among Black Americans, 1985, p. 559.

McCarroll, E. Mae   (1898–19??, F)

Physician. Born in Birmingham, AL, 1898. B.A., Talladega College, 1917; M.S. (public health), Columbia University; M.D. Women's College of Pennsylvania, 1925. First black appointed to the staff of Newark City Hospital, 1946–; Deputy Health Officer, Newark, NJ, 1953–.

Memberships and awards: Board of Trustees and Publications Committee, National Medical Association, over 20 years; President, North Jersey Medical Society; Essex County Medical Society; American Medical Association; American Public Health Association; Delta Sigma Theta.

Ref: National Medical Association, Journal, v. 46, Jan. 1954, p. 76. [p]
        National Medical Association, Journal, v. 47, Nov. 1955, p. 416. [p]
        National Medical Association, Journal, v. 55, 1963, p. 367–368.
        Ebony, May 1964, p. 76. [p]
        Who's Who of American Women, 1968, p. 791.
        National Medical Association, Journal, v. 65, Nov. 1973, p. 544–545. [p] cover

McCauley, Lewyn Eugene (1883–19??, M)

Physician. Surgeon. Born in Wilmington, NC, Jan. 28, 1883. B.S., Kittrell College, NC, 1901; M.D., Shaw University Medical Department, Raleigh, NC, 1905; Postgraduate, Philadelphia Polytechnic, 1905; Postgraduate, Freedmen's Hospital, Washington, DC; observation work, Philadelphia General Hospital and Harlem Hospital, New York; postgraduate course, Medical College of Virginia, 1933; founded McCauley Hospital in Raleigh, NC, 1923, with 12 beds and three basinettes.

Memberships and awards: President, North Carolina Medical, Dental, and Pharmaceutical Association; Chairman, Surgical Department, National Medical Association; President, Raleigh Medical, Dental, and Pharmaceutical Association; President, Phi Beta Sigma.

Ref: Who's Who in Colored America, 1930–32, p. 281.
        Who's Who in Colored America, 1933–37, p. 342.
        Who's Who in Colored America, 1938–40, p. 343. [p] p. 339.
        Who's Who in Colored America, 1941–44, p. 335. [p] p. 337.

McCellan, Alonzo C.   (1900s, M)

Physician. Surgeon. Started a hospital and nursing school in 1896 leading a group including Lucy Hughes Brown, a woman Physician, Hospital and Training School for Nurses, Charleston, SC; Surgeon-in-Chief of the hospital.

Ref: National Medical Association, Journal, v.33, Jan. 1941, p. 15–16.

McCoo, Mary Holloway   (1913– ——, F)

Physician. Anesthesiologist. B.S., Hunter College; M.D., Meharry Medical College, 1938; Anesthesiology Residency, Los Angeles County General Hospital; Postgraduate courses in electrocardiography.

Ref: Ebony, May 1964, p. 73. [p]
        Who's Who of American Woman, 1968, p. 794.

McCown, Ira   (1900s, M)

Physician. Gynecologist. The only black examinee for the position of Gynecological Advisor to the Workmen's Compensation Board of New York, received the highest marks in a run-off oral examination between himself and the second highest to receive the appointment.

Ref: National Medical Association, Journal, v. 31, May 1939, p. 123.

McCoy, Caldwell   (1933– ——, M)

Engineer (electrical). B.S., University of Connecticut; M.S., Ph.D. (telecommunications), George Washington University. Designed and tested systems for detecting and tracking submarines; since 1976, has been part of the Magentic Fusion Energy Program at the Department of Energy.

Dissertation title: Improvements in Routing for Packet-Switched Networks.

Ref: Black Contributors to Science and Energy Technology, p. 20–21.
        Who's Who in the East, 1977.

McCoy, Elijah   (1844–1929, M)

Inventor. Engineer. Born in Colchester, Ontario, Canada, May 2, 1844. The son of former slaves who had fled from Kentucky after the Civil War, he returned to the United States and settled in Michigan. He invented a lubricator for steam engines, patent #129,843, July 12, 1872, the first of his inventions. Patents assigned to others, Hamlin, Hodges, etc., 57 in all. The "real McCoy" applies to his oiling device. Other inventions included ironing table and lawn sprinkler. Vice-President, McCoy Manufacturing Company, Detroit, MI.

Ref: *At Last Recognition in America,* v. 1, p. 31–32.
Dictionary of American Negro Biography, p. 413–414.
Negro Almanac, p. 639.
Who's Who in American History—Science and Technology, p. 400.
Negro in Our History, 5th ed., p. 465–566.
Great Negroes, p. 61.
Jet, May 7, 1981, p. 18.
The Role of the American Negro in the Fields of Science, p. 17–18.
Afro USA, p. 732. (Ploski)
Black Pioneers of Science and Invention, p. 34–40. [p] p. 34.
Afro-American Encyclopedia, v. 5, p. 1275.
Ebony, Dec. 1966, p. 157. [p]
Dictionary of American Biography, v. VI, p. 617.
Crisis, Oct. 1920, p. 286–287. [p]

McCreadie, Rada Higgins   (1900s, F)

Mathematician. Born in Columbus, OH. B.A., Miami University, Coral Gables, FL, 1969; Ph.D., Ohio State University, 1974. Visiting Assistant Professor, Ohio State University 1974–76; Research Assistant, Delft University, Holland.

Dissertation title: On the Asymptotic Behavior of Certain Sequences.

Ref: Kenschaft, Patricia C. Black Women in Mathematics in the United States. *American Mathematical Monthly,* v. 88, Oct. 1981. p. 601.

McCree, D.   (1800s, M)

Inventor. Patent #440,322, Nov. 11, 1890, for a portable fire escape consisting of a wooden device with parallel steps used to escape from fires in two or three story buildings, similar to the metal ones used today.

Ref: *At Last Recognition in America,* v. 1, p. 9.

McDaniel, Reuben Roosevelt   (1902–19??, M)

Mathematician. Born in Fairfax, VA, July 27, 1902. B.S., Rutgers University, 1928; M.S., Cornell University, 1931; Ph.D. (mathematics), 1938. Instructor in Physics, Shaw University, 1928–31; Professor of Mathematics, Virginia State College, 1931–36; Professor of Mathematics and Director of the School of Arts and Sciences, 1938; Head of Department, 1953–68; retired; research in algebraic number, matrix approximations.

Memberships and awards: Phi Beta Kappa; Sigma Xi; Erastus Brooks fellow in Mathematics; American Mathematics Society; Mathematical Association of America; American Association of University Professors; Virginia Conference of Science and Mathematics Teachers; Virginia Academy of Sciences; National Honor Society; Sigma Pi Sigma National Honorary Physics Society.

Dissertation title: Approximation to Algebraic Numbers by Means of Periodic Sequences of Transformations in Quadratic Forms.

Ref: *American Men and Women of Science,* 12th ed., p. 3918.
Holders of Doctorates Among American Negroes, p. 154.
The Negro in Science, p. 188.

McDonough, David K.   (1800s, M)

Physician. Slave-born Negro, whose master sent him to school as a bet that he could succeed. B.A., Lafayette College in Pennsylvania, third in his class and attended College of Physicians and Surgeons, graduating and working at New York Eye and Ear Infirmary.

Memberships and awards: First private hospital founded by blacks in New York was named after him.

Ref: *History of the Negro in Medicine,* p. 13.

McKane, Alyce Woodby   (1865–19??, F)

Physician. Born in Bridgewater, PA, 1865. Hampton Institute, 1886; Institute for Colored Youth, PA, 1892; M.D., Women's Medical College of Pennsylvania, 1892. Teacher of Natural Sciences and Instructor of Nurses at Haines Institute, August, GA; established first Training School for Nurses in South East Georgia, Sept. 1893; first class graduated in 1895; Assistant, U.S. Pension Medical Examiner for Civil War Veterans in Liberia; Co-organizer and in charge of Department of Diseases of Women, Private Hospital, Monrovia, Liberia; established the McKane Hospital for Women and Children and Training School for Nurses (now Charity Hospital), Oct. 1896, Savannah, GA; orphaned before seven, lost her eyesight for three years; passed her medical exams winning competitive prizes in literature, science, and English, graduating with highest honors.

Pub: *Fraternal Society Sick Book,* 1913. Boston,

Ref: *Who's Who in Colored America,* 1928–29, p. 250–251.
Who's Who in Colored America, 1930–32, p. 287–288.
Who's Who in Colored America, 1933–37, p. 353.
Who's Who in Colored America, 1938–40, p. 353.
Who's Who in Colored America, 1941–44, p. 347.
Contributions of Black Women to America, v. 2, p. 366.

McKenzie, Bertha B.   (19??- ——, F)

Nurse. Born in Jamaica. Founded Good Samaritan private hospital in Detroit, 1928; for 13 years it catered to tuberculosis patients; in 1944, it became convalescent home for chronically ill and aged patients.

Ref: *Jet*, 1950, p. 38. [p]

McKinney, Roscoe Lewis   (1900–1978, M)

Anatomist. Born in Washington, DC, Feb. 8, 1900. B.A., Bates College, 1921; Ph.D. (anatomy), University of Chicago, 1930. First black to earn a Ph.D. in Anatomy. Professor, Anatomy and Head of the Department, Howard University, 1930–47; Vice-Dean, School of Medicine, Howard University, 1944–46; Emeritus Professor, Howard University Medical School, 1968–78.

Memberships and awards: Sigma Xi; Phi Beta Kappa; Beta Kappa Chi; American Association of Anatomists; AAAS.

Dissertation title: Studies on Fibres in Tissue Culture, III, The Development of Reticulum into Collagenous Fibres in Cultures of Adult Rabbit Lymph Nodes.

Ref: *American Men and Women of Science*, 12th ed., p. 3975.
Holders of Doctorates Among American Negroes, p. 130.
Negroes in Science: Natural Sciences Doctorates, 1876–1969, p. 41.
Crisis, Sept. 1930, p. 309–310. [p]
Jet, Nov. 9, 1978, p. 18.
National Medical Association, *Journal*, v. 71, May 1979, p. 518. obit

McKinney, Susan Smith

See: Steward, Susan Smith McKinney.

McKinney, Thomas Theodore   (1869–1946, M)

Physician. Surgeon. Born in Van Alstyne, Grayson City, TX, Aug. 16, 1869. Rural schools, 1876–1886; Central Tennessee College, 1894; M.D., Meharry Medical College, 1895; Philadelphia Polyclinic, Surgery, 1901; Postgraduate, Medical School and Hospital of Chicago, 1909; University of Michigan; postgraduate course, 1911. Physician and Surgeon, 1895–1926; staff of Denver General Hospital.

Memberships and awards: Supreme Physician for the American Woodmen, 1924, and elected in 1925 for a four-year term; Lone Star Medical Pharmaceutical Association of Texas; National Medical Association; American Public Health Association.

Pub: *Sparks from the Medical World*, National Baptist Publishing Co., 1922.

Ref: *Who's Who in Colored America*, 1927, p. 133–134. [p] opp. p. 134.
Who's Who in Colored America, 1928–29, p. 251–252.
Who's Who in Colored America, 1930–32, p. 288–289.

Who's Who in Colored America, 1933–37, p. 354. [p] p. 355.
Who's Who in Colored America, 1938–40, p. 354. [p] 355.
National Medical Association, *Journal*, v. 38, 1946, p. 106.
Who's Who in Colored America, 1941–44, p. 348–349. [p] p. 351.

McLinn, Harry Marvin   (1921- ——, M)

Dentist. Orthodontist. Born in Huntsville, AL, 1921. D.D.S., Howard University, 1947. Chairman, Department of Orthodontics and Dental Anatomy, Howard University, 1948–50; Panel, New York City Department of Health, 1950–60; Assistant-Associate Professor, New York City Medical Dental College, 1973–75; Head, Orthodontics, Howard University, second black, first, Earl Renfrow.

Memberships and awards: Elected to American Board of Orthodontists in New York; Graduate of Howard and Coleman; Certificate of Proficiency; Diplomate, American Board of Orthodontics; American Dental Association; National Dental Association; Columbia University Dental Alumni.

Ref: *Jet*, May 22, 1958, p. 26. [p]
Who's Who Among Black Americans, 1985, p. 576.

McMillan, Julius Augustus   (1871–1949, M)

Physician. Surgeon. Chemist. Born in Quinlan, TX, Dec. 27, 1871. Wiley College, TX, 1892; New Orleans University, 1893; B.S., Central Tennessee College, Nashville, 1898; M.D., Meharry Medical College, TN, 1904. Instructor, Chemistry, Wiley College, TX, 1898–1901; Professor, Chemistry, Meharry Medical College, TN, 1904–11; Professor, Gynecology, Meharry Medical College, 1912–38; Medical Director, Hubbard Hospital (part of Meharry Medical College), 1925–38.

Memberships and awards: Kappa Alpha Psi; National Medical Association; Tennessee State Medical, Dental, and Pharmaceutical Association.

Ref: *Who's Who in Colored America*, 1930–32, p. 290.
Who's Who in Colored America, 1933–37, p. 358.
Who's Who in Colored America, 1938–40, p. 357. [p] p. 351.
Who's Who in Colored America, 1941–44, p. 349–350, [p] p. 345.
National Medical Association, *Journal*, v. 48, Sept. 1956. [p] cover
A Century of Black Surgeons, v. 1, p. 112–113. [p]

McNair, Ronald Erwin   (1950–1986, M)

Astronaut. Physicist. Born in Lake City, SC, Oct. 21, 1950. B.S., North Carolina A & T State University, 1971; Coles d'-t-Taheorque de Physique, 1975; Ph.D. (physics), MIT, 1976. Physicist, Hughes Research Laboratories,

1976–78; Mission Specialist Astronaut, NASA, 1978–; killed January 1986 in explosion of shuttle.

Memberships and awards: AAAS; Black Belt Karate; Distinguished Natural Scientist. National Society of Black Professional Engineers, 1979; Science Building at MIT named for him.

Dissertation title: Energy Absorption and Vibrational Heating in Molecules Following Intense Laser Excitation.

Ref: *Jet,* Mar. 9. 1978, p. 22–26.
Ebony, May 1986, p. 82–84, 88, 90, 92, 94.
Jet, Mar. 31, 1986, p. 14–17. [p] family
Ebony, Mar. 1979, p. 54–56, 58, 60, 62. [p]
Who's Who Among Black Americans, 1985, p. 578.
Black Collegian, Dec. 1980/Jan. 1981, p. 31, 134–138. [p]

McNeil, Phillip Eugene   (1941– ——, M)

Mathematician. Born in Cincinnati, OH, May 13, 1941. B.S., Ohio State University, 1963; M.A., Pennsylvania State University, 1965; Ph.D., Pennsylvania State University, 1968. Assistant Professor, Mathematics, Xavier University, 1968–70; Assistant Professor, Mathematics, University of Cincinnati, 1970–71; Program Associate in Mathematics, Institute for Services to Education, Washington, DC.

Dissertation title: The Structure of Certain Semigroups with Two Idempotents.

Pub: Group Extension of Null Semigroups. *Duke Mathematical Journal,* v. 38 (1971).
Finite Commutative Subdirectly Irreducible Semigroups. American Mathematics Society, *Transactions,* 172 (1972).

Ref: *Black Mathematicians and Their Works,* p. 158–165, 291. [p] p. 158.
American Men and Women of Science, 16th ed., p. 116.

McNeill, William Clarence   (1878–19??, M)

Physician. Gynecologist. Surgeon. Born in Lake Waccamow, NC, Feb. 16, 1878. B.S., Howard University, 1900; M.D., 1904. Assistant to Dr. Furman J. Shadd, appointed Assistant Surgeon, Freedmen's Hospital, 1905; Secretary-Treasurer, College of Medicine, Howard University, 1907–17; Professor, Gynecology, 1910–43.

Memberships and awards: National Medical Association; Phi Delta Mu.

Ref: Cobb, W. Montague. William Clarence McNeill, M.D., 1878–. National Medical Association, *Journal,* v. 50, July 1958, p. 314. [p] cover

McPherson, Gertrude Elizabeth Curtis   (18??–19??, F)

Dentist. Born in Franklin, PA. D.D.S., New York College of Dental and Oral Surgery, 1909; While at College, she won a Gold Medal for her thesis "Pyorrhea alveolaris."

She was the first black women to pass the New York State Board of Dentistry.

Ref: *Who's Who in Colored America,* 1927, p. 135.
Who's Who in Colored America, 1928–29, p. 25.

McSwain, Berah Davis   (1935– ——, M)

Engineer (biophysical). Engineer (optical). Born in Albany, NY, Feb. 6, 1935. B.S., (optics), University of Rochester, 1956; M.S., 1962; Ph.D. (biophysics), University of California, 1968. Optical Engineer, Northrup Aircraft, Inc., CA, 1956–58; Optical Physicist, U.S. Naval Ordnance Laboratory, 1958–60; Research Associate in Chemical Engineering, University of Rochester, 1960–62; Research Assistant in Cell Physiology, 1962–68; Assistant Biophysicist and Lecturer in Cell Physiology, University of California, Berkeley, 1968–.

Memberships and awards: AAAS; American Chemical Society; Optical Society of America, American Society of Plant Physiology; Society of Photo-Optical Instrument Engineering.

Dissertation title: Quantum Requirements and Enhancement Effects of Photosynthetic Electron Transport in Chloroplasts.

Ref: *Black Engineers in the United States,* p. 139.
American Men and Women of Science, 14th ed., p. 3354.

Meaddough, Ray James   (1869–19??, M)

Dentist. Born in Fernandina, FL, Feb. 23, 1869. D.D.S. Meharry Dental College, 1901. Practiced Dentistry in Little Rock, AR, 1901–.

Memberships and awards: On graduation from Meharry, he received the only two gold medals awarded class of 1901, Singleton Medal for highest examination in Metallurgy and the Morrison Medal for excellency in Prosthetic Dentistry; he organized the Dental Unit of the Arkansas Colored Medical Association and was its president for six years; President, Arkansas Dental Association.

Ref: *Who's Who of the Colored Race,* 1915, p. 190–191. [p] opp. p. 142.
Who's Who in Colored America, 1927, p. 140–141.
Who's Who in Colored America, 1928–29, p. 262. [p] opp. p. 262.
Who's Who in Colored America, 1930–32, p. 300–310. [p] opp. p. 296.
Who's Who in Colored America, 1933–37, p. 368. [p] p. 374.
Who's Who in Colored America, 1938–40, p. 368.
Who's Who in Colored America, 1941–44, p. 362.

Means, Curtis S.   (19??– ——, M)

Mathematician. B.S. (mathematics and chemistry), St. Augustine College, 1960; M.S. (mathematics), Union College, Schenectady, 1967; Ph.D. (applied mathematics),

Rensselaer Polytechnic Institute, 1971. Assistant Professor, Mathematics, Southern University, Baton Rouge, 1971–.

Dissertation title: Initial Value Problems for a class of Higher Order Partial Differential Equations Which are Related to the Heat Equation.

Pub: (With J. B. Diaz) An Initial Value Problem for a Class of Higher Order Partial Differential Equations Related to the Heat Equation. To appear in *Annali di Mathematica*, Italy.

Ref: *Black Mathematicians and Their Works*, p. 291. [p]

Means, James Horatio (1910–19??, M)

Mathematician. Born in Pine Bluff, AK, July 16, 1910. B.S., Arkansas Agricultural, Mechanical & Normal, 1933; D.Ed. Oklahoma State, 1958. Professor of Physics and Mathematics and Head, Department of Physical Sciences, Huston-Tillotson College, 1938–.

Memberships and awards: Consultant, National Science Foundation; National Institute of Science; Mathematical Association.

Ref: *American Men of Science*, 11th ed., p. 3547

Method, William Arthur (1881–193?, M)

Physician. Surgeon. Born in Bainbridge, OH, Feb. 18, 1881. M.A., Wilberforce University, 1900; M.D., Ohio Medical University, Columbus, OH, 1906; Postgraduate, Harvard University, 1920. Founder and Surgeon-in-Chief, Alpha Hospital, Columbus, OH, 1920–23.

Memberships and awards: National Medical Association; Ohio State Medical, Dental, and Pharmaceutical Association; Columbus Academy of Medicine; Ohio State Medical Association; American Medical Association; Alpha Phi Alpha.

Ref: *Who's Who in Colored America*, 1930–32, p. 302.

Mickens, Ronald Elbert (1943– ——, M)

Physicist (theoretical). Born in Petersburg, VA, Feb. 7, 1943. B.A., Fisk University, 1964; Ph.D. (physics), Vanderbilt University, 1968; MIT Center for Theoretical Physics post doctoral researcher, 1968–70; Assistant Professor, Fisk University Department of Physics, 1970–81; Chairperson and Professor, Atlanta University.

Memberships and awards: Research fellow, Joint Institute for Laboratory Astrophysics, Boulder, CO, 1981–82; AAAS; American Physical Society; Sigma Xi; Beta Kappa Chi; National Society of Black Physicists; American Mathematical Association; Woodrow Wilson fellowship, 1965–68; Ford Foundation Postdoctoral fellowship, 1980–81.

Dissertation title: Branch Points in the Complex Angular-Momentum Plane.

Pub: Over 150 published papers.

Ref: *American Men and Women of Science*, 16th ed., p. 366.
Who's Who Among Black Americans, 1985, p. 586.
Who's Who in the South and Southwest, 1978, p. 500.

Miller, Dorie (1919–1943, M)

Military (Navy). Born in 1919.

Memberships and awards: The Frigate, U.S.S. Miller, named for him; Won Navy Cross, May 27, 1942.

Ref: *Jet*, June 1, 1961, p. 11. [p]
Historical Afro-American Biographies, p. 227–228. [p]
Black Americans in Defense of Our Nation, p. 52.

Miller, Dublin B. (18??–19??, M)

Physician. Born in Pittsburgh, PA. M.A., Lincoln University, 1895. Principal of the public school in Martinsville, VA; M.D., Meharry Medical College. Practiced in Memphis.

Ref: *Beacon Lights of the Race*, p. 525–527. [p] & biog.

Miller, Kelly (1863–1939, M)

Mathematician. Born in Winnsboro, SC, July 23, 1863. B.A., Howard University, 1886; M.A., 1901; LL.D., 1903; Postgraduate work in Mathematics and Physics. Professor of Mathematics, Howard University, 1890; retired as Howard University Administrator, 1935.

Memberships and awards: Vice-President, American Negro Academy of Experimental Geometry.

Pub: Enumerations of Errors in Negro Population. *Scientific Monthly*, Feb. 1922.
The Education of the Negro. U.S. Bureau of Education, *Report*, 1901.

Ref: *Dictionary of American Negro Biography*, p. 435–438.
Encyclopedia of Black America, p. 562.
In Black and White, p. 672.
Negro Almanac, 1976, p. 246.
Who's Who in Colored America, 1927, p. 142.
Who's Who of the Colored Race, 1915, p. 192–193.
Who's Who in Colored America, 1928–29, p. 266.
Who's Who in Colored America, 1930–32, p. 304.
Who's Who in Colored America, 1933–37, p. 373.
Who's Who in Colored America, 1938–40, p. 372.
Who's Who in Colored America, 1941–44, p. 367.

Miller, Lloyd (1874–1951, M)

Physician. Surgeon. M.D., Meharry Medical College, 1893. Co-founder of the first black owned and operated hospital in Mississippi.

Dissertation title: Synergic Solvent Extraction and Thermal Studies of Flourinated Beta-Diketone-Organophosphorus Adduct Complexes of Lauthanide and Related Elements.

Pub: *Contamination Control in Trace Element Analysis.* New York, Wiley-Interscience. 1975. 262 p.
Forty journal articles.

Ref: *American Men and Women of Science,* 16th ed., p. 430.
Ebony, Sept. 1979, p. 50-51. [p]
Who's Who Among Black Americans, 1985, p. 597.

Mitchell, Matthew (1900-1965, M)

Dentist. Born in Vicksburg, MS, 1900. Ph.D., Howard University, 1945. Assistant Professor of Orthodontics, Howard University for 15 years.

Memberships and awards: President, National Dental Association, 1964; Dentist of the Year, 1964; Editor, *D.C. Dental Journal;* Ohio State University Gold Key in Dental Journalism, 1964; American College of Dentistry fellow, 1966.

Ref: *Jet,* Aug. 20, 1964, p. 48.
Jet, Jan. 11, 1968, p. 41. obit

Monroe, Clarence Lee Edward (1901-19??, M)

Biologist. Born in 1901. B.A., Pennsylvania University, 1925; M.S., 1926; Ph.D. (bacteriology), 1940. Professor of Biology and Head of Department, Morris Brown College, 1930-42; Morgan State College, 1941-71; retired; research in nutrition of Neisseria, airborne infection.

Dissertation title: A Study in Airborne Infection with Special Reference to Tuberculosis Infection.

Ref: *American Men and Women of Science,* 12th ed., p. 4347.
Holders of Doctorates Among American Negroes, p. 130.
Crisis, Aug. 1940, p. 233. [p] only

Montague, William Henry (1883-19??, M)

Physician. Otolaryngologist. First black otolaryngologist in Baltimore. Founded and owned Montague Sanitorium in Baltimore.

Ref: *Who's Who in Colored America,* 1928-29, p. 269-270.

Montez, Billy V. (1928- ——, M)

Inventor. Self-taught engineer. Made small radios, tape and wire recorders, an electronics expert. At eight years old he could take apart and reassemble a 250-part radio set. He also made sending and receiving sets for professional football players. No degree in engineering; learned by reading. He has studied at Temple University and Swarthmore College.

Ref: *Ebony,* Sept. 1962, p. 54-58. [p]
Ebony, Oct. 1964, p. 76.

Moore, Aaron McDuffie (1863-1923, M)

Physician. Born in Whiteville, NC, Sept. 6, 1863. M.D., Leonard Medical College, Shaw University, Raleigh, NC, 1888. Medical Director and Secretary-Treasurer and President of North Carolina Mutual and Provident Association, 1899-; Founder and Superintendent, Lincoln Hospital, Durham, NC; Director, Mechanics Farmers' Bank; Bull City Drug Co., Trustee, Shaw University; first black physician in Durham, NC, 1888; assisted in many black business ventures.

Memberships and awards: National Medical Association; Chairman Board of Trustees, Shaw University for ten years; Board of Trustees, Colored Orphan Asylum and North Carolina Reform School.

Ref: *Dictionary of American Medical Biography,* p. 533.
Who's Who of the Colored Race, 1915, p. 195.
National Medical Association, *Journal,* v. 16, Jan.-Mar. 1924, p. 72-74. obit & biog.
Crisis, Dec. 1916, p. 76. [p]

Moore, George Sheppard (1883-19??, M)

Physician. Born in Nashville, TN, Sept. 27, 1883. B.A., Fisk University, 1906; M.D., Northwestern University Medical College, 1910. Professor of Mental and Nervous Diseases, Meharry Medical College.

Ref: *Who's Who of the Colored Race,* 1915, p. 196.

Moore, James A. (1900s, M)

Physical Health. B.A., University of Pittsburgh; M.A., University of Cincinnati, Ph.D. 1938.

Ref: *Holders of Doctorates Among American Negroes,* p. 104-105.

Moore, John E. (1900s, M)

Herbologist. Nutritionist. Born in Caddogap, AK.
Memberships and awards: Honorary Doctorate, New York University Weinstein Center for Student Living.

Ref: *Profiles in Black,* p. 120-121. [p]

Moore, Paul Joaquin (1902-19??, M)

Chemist (organic). Pharmacist. Born in Pasadena, CA, May 18, 1902. Ph.G., University of Southern California, 1923; B.A., 1925; M.S., 1926. Pharmacist, 1922-26; Instructor, Chemistry and Physics, Virginia State College, 1926-27; Associate Professor, Chemistry, West Virginia State College, 1927-33; Head of Department, 1933-; Professor, 1945-.

Memberships and awards: West Virginia Academy of Sciences; American Chemical Society; Beta Kappa Chi; American Association of University Professors.

Ref: *The Negro in Science*, p. 185.
American Men of Science, 11th ed., p. 3712.

Moore, Ruth Ella   (1903–19??, F)

Bacteriologist. Born in 1903. B.S., Ohio State University, 1926; M.A., 1927; Ph.D. (bacteriology), 1933. First black female to earn a Ph.D. in Bacteriology. Head, Department of Bacteriology, Howard University Medical College, 1947–58; Part-time, 1971–; research in blood grouping and enteriobacteriaceae.

Dissertation title: (a) Studies on Dissociation of Mycobacterium Tuberculosis; (b) A New Method of Concentration on the Tubercle Bacilli as Applied to Sputum and Urine Examination.

Ref: *American Men and Women of Science*, 12th ed., p. 4370.
Holders of Doctorates Among American Negroes, p. 193–194.
Crisis, Aug. 1933, p. 181. [p] only

Moragne, Lenora   (1931– ——, F)

Nutritionist. Born in Evanston, IL, Sept. 29, 1931. B.S., Iowa State University; M.S., Cornell University; Ph.D., 1969. Professor of food and nutrition, Hunter College in New York City; Lecturer at Columbia University; Head of Nutrition Education and Training, Food and Nutrition Service, U.S. Department of Agriculture, DC.

Memberships and awards: American Public Health Association; National Council of Women; American Dietetic Association; Society of Nutrition Education; Cornell Club of DC; Distinguished Alumni Award, Iowa State College, 1981; certificate of appreciation, U.S. Department of Agriculture.

Dissertation title: Influence of Household Differentiation on Food Habits Among Low-Income Urban Negro Families.

Pub: Jr. H. S. Nutrition text, *Focus on Food*.
Our Baby's Early Years.
Several articles on food-nutrition in professional journals.

Ref: *Who's Who Among Black Americans*, 1985, p. 608.
Black Women Makers of History: A Portrait, 198–199, 1977. Rev. ed. List of publications, p. 198.

Morgan, Charles L.   (1878–19??, M)

Physician. Born in Oxford, AL, Aug. 9, 1878. Graduate, Dallas High School, TX; M.D., Meharry Medical College, 1909. President, Mecca Sanitarium, Dallas, TX. President and Treasurer, Morgan-Busch Sanitarium; Medical Examiner for American Woodmen.

Memberships and awards: Treasurer, Negro Medical, Dental, and Pharmaceutical Society.

Ref: *Who's Who of the Colored Race*, 1915, p. 198.

Morgan, Don   (1900s, M)

Photographer. Only black member of the Cincinnati Professional Photographers of America, Inc.

Ref: *Jet*, Aug, 23, 1962, p. 25.

Morgan, Garrett Augustus   (1875–1963, M)

Inventor. Born in Paris, KY, Mar. 4, 1875. Invented the gas mask in 1912, patent #1,113,675 issued in 1914. Used by firemen and saved countless lives in World War I from chlorine gas fumes. Patent #1,475,024 for three-way traffic signal in 1923. Sold his rights to the traffic signal to General Electric for $40,000. Received patents in England and Canada. In 1916 waterwork crib to shore tunnel disaster, he entered tunnel twice rescuing two men using the gas mask. He invented the first hair straightner and marketed it under the name G. A. Morgan Hair Refining Cream.

Memberships and awards: Received Carnegie Medal and a Medal for Bravery from the city for his bravery 250 ft. down in Lake Erie, 1916. First grand prize at the 2nd International Exposition of Safety and Sanitation in 1914 for his gas mask. Also founded the *Cleveland Call* in 1920. He was cited in 1963, three months before his death, by the U.S. Government for inventing the first traffic signal.

Ref: *At Last Recognition in America*, v. 1, p. 27–28.
Biographical History of Blacks in America Since 1528, p. 371–372.
Dictionary of American Negro Biography, p. 453.
Encyclopedia of Black America, p. 567.
Great Negroes Past and Present, p. 53.
Jet, Aug. 5, 1954, p. 51.
Jet, Aug. 15, 1963, p. 11. [p]
Jet, July 3, 1964, p. 11. [p]
Historical Afro-American Biographies, p. 230.
Black Pioneers of Science and Invention, p. 61–72. [p] p. 62.
Ebony, Nov. 1966, p. 111. [p]

Morman, William Daniel   (1901–1951, M)

Physician. Otolaryngologist. Surgeon. Born in Augusta, GA, Dec. 20, 1901. B.S., Morehouse College, 1925; M.D., Howard University Medical School, 1929. Hygiene Inspector in the Public Schools of St. Louis, 1931–45.

Memberships and awards: Diplomate, American Board of Otolaryngology, 1940; fellow, American Academy of Otology, Rhinology, and Larynogology, 1941; American College of Surgeons, 1948; one of two first Black Physicians admitted to St. Louis Medical Society, 1949; Missouri State Medical Society, 1949; American Medical Association, 1950.

Ref: National Medical Association, *Journal*, v. 44, Jan. 1952, p. 70–73. [p]

National Medical Association, *Journal*, v. 51, Jan. 1959. [p] cover

Morris, Joel M.   (1944- ——, M)

Engineer (electrical). Born in Washington, DC, Aug. 11, 1944. B.S. (electrical engineering), Howard University, 1966; M.S., Polytech Institute of Brooklyn, 1970; Ph.D. Johns Hopkins University, 1975. Electrical Engineer, Bell Telephone Laboratories, 1966-70; Electrical Engineer, Bendix Corporation; Research Engineer, Naval Research Laboratory, Communications Science Division, 1975; Science Officer, Office of Naval Research Electronics and Solid State Science Program, 1979-.

Memberships and awards: IEEE; Sigma Xi; International Union of Radio Science; The Research Society; Kappa Alpha Psi; Tau Beta Pi; Johns Hopkins fellowship Grant; awarded a patent for work at Bell Laboratories.

Dissertation title: Source Encoding of a Class of Discrete-Time Signal Sources by Robust Quantization.

Ref: *Black Engineers in the United States,* p. 146.
Who's Who Among Black Americans, 1985, p. 612.

Morris, Kelso Bronson   (1909-19??, M)

Chemist (physical). Chemist (inorganic). Born in Beaumont, TX, Feb. 6, 1909. B.S., Wiley College, 1930; M.S., Cornell, 1937; Ph.D. (inorganic chemistry), 1940. Instructor, Chemistry and Mathematics, Wiley College, 1930-37; Associate Professor, Chemistry, 1937-42; Professor and Head of Department, 1942-46; Associate Professor, Howard University, 1946-; Professor of Chemistry, Howard University, 1946-77; research in Electrochemistry, Chemistry of Hydroxylamine.

Memberships and awards: Fellow, Texas Academy of Science; American Chemical Society; AAAS; Sigma Xi; Texas Academy of Sciences; Electrochemistry Society; American Association of University Professors; Beta Kappa Chi; National Institute of Science; Alpha Phi Alpha.

Dissertation title: The Action of the Complex Delectronator, Potassium Permanganate, upon Hydroxylamine in Sulfuric Acid Solution.

Ref: *American Men and Women of Science,* 13th ed., p. 3101.
The Negro in Science, p. 185.
Holders of Doctorates Among American Negroes, p. 154.
Who's Who in Colored America, 1941-44, p. 373.
Leaders in American Science, 1960-61, p. 610-611.
Who's Who Among Black Americans, 1985, p. 612.

Morrison, Harry L.   (1932- ——, M)

Physicist. Born in Arlington, VA, Oct. 7, 1932. Ph.D. (physics), Catholic University, 1960. Taught physics in AF Academy and guest scientist, Bureau of Standards in Boulder Laboratory.

Ref: *Jet,* Aug. 24, 1961, p. 27.
Who's Who Among Black Americans, 1985, p. 613.

Morton, James Thomas, Jr.   (1911-1974, M)

Psychologist Born in Greenwood, NC, 1911. B.A., University of Illinois, 1934; M.A., Northwestern University, 1935; Ph.D. (psychology), Northwestern University, 1942. Dean of Instruction, Bennett College, 1942; Professor and Counselor, Dillard University, 1945-46; Chief Psychologist, Tuskegee Veterans Hospital, 1946-53; Psychologist, Downey V.A. Hospital in Illinois, 1953-74.

Memberships and awards: Diplomate in Clinical Psychology, American Psychological Association; fellow, American Psychological Society.

Dissertation title: The Distortion of Syllogistic Reasoning Produced by Personal Convictions.

Ref: *Even the Rat Was White,* p. 164-165. [p] p. 165.

Moss, Leon Wilson   (1937- ——, M)

Engineer (mechanical). Born in Beckley, WV, April 8, 1937. B.S., Michigan State University, 1958; M.S., University of Washington, Seattle, 1962; Ph.D. (mechanical engineering), 1969. Test and Development Engineer, Missile Division, Chrysler Corporation, 1958-60; Instrumentation Design Engineer, Bendix Systems Divisions, Ann Arbor, 1961; Research Engineer, Boeing, 1961-62; Technical Staff, Rockwell International Space Division, Downy, CA, 1962-72; President, Moss Autoelectric Corporation, Beckley, WV, 1972-.

Memberships and awards: Omega Psi Phi.

Dissertation title: Analysis of Axisymmetric Problems in Fracture Mechanics.

Ref: *Ebony,* Sept. 1970, p. 34. [p]
In Black and White, p. 700.

Mossell, Nathan Francis   (1856-1946, M)

Physician. Born in Hamilton, Canada, July 27, 1856. B.A., Lincoln University, 1879; M.D., University of Pennsylvania, 1882. First black to finish at the University of Pennsylvania Medical School. Founded Frederick Douglas Memorial Hospital, Philadelphia, 1895.

Memberships and awards: American Hospital Association; first black member, Philadelphia County Medical Society; Philadelphia Academy of Medicine and Allied Sciences; National Medical Association, President, 1907-08; winner, Bradley Medal for excellence in natural science, Lincoln University.

Pub: Hospital Construction, Organization and Management (pamphlet).

Ref: *Dictionary of American Medical Biography,* p. 541.
Dictionary of American Negro Biography, p. 457-458.
History of Negroes in Medicine, p. 79-82.

Who's Who of the Colored Race, 1915, p. 202.
Who's Who in Colored America, 1927, p. 145.
Who's Who in Colored America, 1928–29, p. [p] opp. p. 272.
Who's Who in Colored America, 1930–32, p. 312.
Who's Who in Colored America, 1933–37, p. 383.
Cobb, Montague. Nathan Francis Mossell, M.D., 1856–1946. National Medical Association, *Journal,* v. 46, Mar. 1954, p. 118–130. [p] cover
National Medical Association, *Journal,* v. 39, Jan. 1947, p. 38.
Who's Who in Colored America, 1941–44, p. 375. [p] p. 377.

Moten, Edwin Donerson (1876–1955, M)

Physician. Born in Winchester, TX, 1876. B.A., Hampton Institute; M.D., Leonard Medical School, 1906. Private practice.

Memberships and awards: Organized the Aesculapian Medical Society and Indiana State Medical, Dental, and Pharmaceutical Society, 1923; Organized with Dr. J. J. Hoover and others the Hoosier State Medical Society whose Bulletin he edited; Omega Psi Phi; Plaque from the Meharry Alumni Club of Indiana for Outstanding Medical Service to the Community, 1953; Vice-President, National Medical Association and long time member of its House of Delegates.

Ref: National Medical Association, *Journal,* v. 47, May 1955, p. 306–307. [p] obit

Mtingwa, Sekazi (1950– ——, M)

Physicist. Ph.D., Princeton. Fermi National Accelerator Laboratory in Batavia, IL, working on the Tevatron I, now considered the most powerful accelerator in the United States.

Dissertation title: Asymptotic Chiral Invariance and Its Consequences.

Ref: *Ebony,* Aug. 1985, p. 66. [p]
Ebony, Nov. 1988, p. 6. [p]

Mulzac, Hugh Nathaniel (1886–1971, M)

Sea Captain.

Ref: *Historical Afro-American Biographies,* p. 232–233.
Jet, Feb. 18, 1971, p. 12.

Munday, Reuban A. (1900–19??, M)

Poultry Geneticist. Born in Berea, KY, Feb. 10, 1900. B.S., Hampton Institute, 1927; M.S., Iowa State University, 1935; Ph.D. (poultry genetics), Massachusetts University, 1947. Instructor, Poultry Husbandry, Tuskegee Institute, 1928–37; Director of Agriculture, Tennessee A & I State College, 1937–40; Professor and Head, Division of Animal Science, Tuskegee, Institute, 1940–.

Memberships and awards: Sigma Xi; Poultry Science Association.

Dissertation title: External Characters of Hens' Eggs in Relation to Their Fertility, Hatchability and the Sex Ratio.

Ref: *National Register,* 1952, p. 218.
American Men of Science, 11th ed., p. 3788.

Murray, Beatrice L. (19??– ——, F)

Nurse (psychiatric). Diploma, Kansas City, MO, School of Nursing; Certificate, University of Minnesota School of Public Health; B.S.N., Wayne State University School of Nursing; M.S.N. Veterans Administration, 1941–; Chief nurse trainee, 1963; Chief Nurse, V.A. Hospital, Pittsburgh, 1964–; retired, 1981, after serving three other V.A. Hospitals.

Memberships and awards: Represented V.A. Nursing Service at the International Congress for Psychiatry and Social Change, Jerusalem, 1971; Honor Award, Department of Medicine and Surgery, 1975.

Ref: *Path We Tread,* p. 217.
Ebony, Mar. 1963, p. 73. [p]

Murray, Diane P. (19??– ——, F)

Mathematician. B.A., Spelman College; Cornell University. First of seven women profiled in National Science Foundation film "Science, Women's Work." Is head of the Engagement Simulation Sky (operations research department) of TRW, Inc. in Redondo Beach, CA. Works on command and control of space satellites, earthquake detection and other technological advances.

Ref: *Ebony,* Aug. 1982, p. 6.

Murray, George W. (1800s, M)

Inventor. Politician. Former member of Congress from South Carolina. Patented eight inventions of agricultural implements.

Ref: *Negro in Our History,* 5th ed., p. 464.

Murray, Peter Marshall (1888–1969, M)

Physician. Surgeon. Gynecologist. Born in Houma, LA, June 9, 1888. B.A., Dillard University, 1910; M.D., Howard Medical School, 1914. Assistant Surgeon-in-Chief, Freedmen's Hospital, Washington, DC and Dean and Professor of Surgery, Howard University Medical School, 1918; Clinical Instructor in Surgery, 1915–20, Howard University; Director of Gynecology, Harlem Hospital, retired, 1953, after 25 years.

Memberships and awards: First black member, House of Delegates, American Medical Association; President, Medical Board of Sydenham Hospital; President, New York County Medical Society, 1954–57—first black to serve as its president; Founder, Howard Medical Reading Club of New York; President National Medical Association, 1932–33.

Ref: *American Men of Science*, 11th ed., p. 3804.
Who's Who in Colored America, 1930–32, p. 315. [p] p. 319.
Who's Who in Colored America, 1928–29, p. 275.
Who's Who in Colored America, 1933–37, p. 387. [p] p. 381.
Jet, May 25, 1961, p. 9. [p]
Jet, June 12, 1968, p. 18.
Dictionary of American Negro Biography, p. 465–467.
Dictionary of American Medical Biography, p. 548–549.
History of Negroes in Medicine, p. 119–120.
Cobb, W. Montague. Peter Marshall Murray, M.D., 1888–. National Medical Association, *Journal*, v. 59, Jan. 1967, p. 71–74.
National Medical Association, *Journal*, v. 62, Mar. 1970, p. 161.
National Medical Association, *Journal*, v. 41, Sept. 1949, p. 232.
National Medical Association, *Journal*, v. 44, July 1952, p. 315. [p]
Who's Who in Colored America, 1941–44, p. 379. [p] p. 376.
A Century of Black Surgeons, p. 497–500. [p]

Murray, Robert F. (1931– ——, M)

Physician. Geneticist. Surgeon. Born in Newburgh, NY, Oct. 19, 1931. B.S., Union College of New York, 1953; M.D., University of Rochester, 1958. Senior Surgeon, U.S. Public Health Service, NIH, 1962–65; Assistant Professor to Associate Professor, Pediatrics and Medicine, University of Washington, 1967–74; Professor, Genetics, School of Arts and Sciences, 1976; Professor, Oncology, 1977; Professor, Pediatrics and Medicine, College of Medicine, Howard University, 1974–.

Memberships and awards: Diplomate, American Board of Internal Medicine, 1966; Chairman, Ad Hoc Committee on the Sickle Cell Trait, Armed Forces, 1972; Committee on Inborn Errors in Metabolism, National Research Council, National Academy of Science, 1972–75; Board of Directors, Institute of Social Ethics and Life Science; National Institute of Medicine; American Society of Human Genetics; AAAS fellow; fellow, American College of Physicians.

Ref: *American Men and Women of Science*, 16th ed., p. 576.
Black Enterprise, Oct. 1988, p. 94.

Myles, Marion Antoinette Richards (1917– ——, F)

Physiologist (plant). Pharmacognosist. Botanist. Zoologist. Born in Philadelphia, PA, June 22, 1917. B.S., Pennsylvania University, 1937; M.S., Atlanta University, 1939; Ph.D. Iowa State College, 1945. Head, Department of Biology, Philander Smith College, 1941–43; Associate Professor, Biology, Tennessee A & I State College, 1945–48; Associate Professor, Agronomy, 1948–51; Professor, Botany and Zoology, Acting Head, Science Division, Fort Valley State College, 1951–59; Professor, Botany, Head, Division of Science and Mathematics, 1953–54; Research Associate in Enzymology, Vanderbilt University, 1959–61; Assistant Professor, Pharmacology, Medical Center of Mississippi, 1965–.

Memberships and awards: Research fellow, Plant Physiology, Iowa State College, Ames, 1943–45; Carnegie Research Grant, 1952–54; Sigma Delta Epsilon; Phi Kappa Phi; Beta Kappa Chi; American Society of Plant Physiologists; Botany Society of America; AAAS; Botanical Society; Society of Pharmacognosy; Alpha Kappa Alpha.

Ref: *The Negro in Science*, p. 179.
American Men of Science, 11th ed., p. 3816–3817.
Leaders in American Science, 1955, p. 495. [p]

N

Nabrit, Samuel Milton (1905– ——, M)

Physiologist. Embryologist. Born in Macon, GA, Feb. 21, 1905. B.S., Morehouse College, 1925; M.S., Brown University, 1928; Ph.D. (biology), 1932. Professor, Biology, Morehouse College, 1925–31; Professor, Biology and Chairman of the Department, Atlanta University, 1932–; Dean, Graduate School of Arts and Sciences, 1932–55; President, Texas Southern University, 1955–66 at the same time his brother, James, was President of Howard University, two of the largest black colleges in the country.

Memberships and awards: Coordinator, Carnegie Foundation for Advancement of Teaching, Atlanta University; Grants-in-aid Program for Research, 1948–53; Screening Committee, Ford Foundation Fellowship Program; Sigma Xi; American Society of Zoologists; Beta Kappa Chi; Pi Delta Phi; Omega Psi Phi; Phi Beta Kappa; AAAS; National Institute of Science, President, 1945; National Committee for Research in Higher Education.

Dissertation title: Regeneration in the Tail-Fins of Fishes.

Ref: *American Men and Women of Science*, 16th ed., p. 593.
Current Biography, 1963, p. 295–297.
Encyclopedia of Black America, p. 611–612.
Holders of Doctorates Among American Negroes, p. 194.
Many Shades of Black, p. 159–172.
The Negro in Science, p. 179–180.
Ebony Success Library, v. 1, p. 234. [p]
Who's Who Among Black Americans, 1977, p. 662.

Ndefo, Ejike D. (1939– ——, M)

Engineer (mechanical). Born in Awka, Nigeria, Aug. 6, 1939. GCE (mathematics), Federal College of Science, Nigeria, 1962; B.S. (mechanical engineering), University of

California, Berkeley, 1965; M.S., 1967; Ph.D. (mechanical engineering), 1969. Research Scientist, Northrop Corporate Laboratories, 1969–71; Senior Technical Staff, Marshall Industries, Dynamic Systems Division, 1971–72; Senior Technical Staff, TRW Systems, Redondo Beach, CA, 1972.

Memberships and awards: Sigma Xi; American Institute of Aeronautics and Astronautics.

Dissertation title: A Numerical Method for Calculating Steady Unsymmetrical Supersonic Flow Past Cones.

Ref: *Black Engineers in the United States*, p. 149.

Neal, Homer Alfred   (1942– ——, M)

Physicist (high energy). Born in Franklin, KY, June 13, 1942. B.S., Indiana University, 1961; M.S. (physics), University of Michigan, 1963; Ph.D. (physics), 1966. Professor, Physics, Indiana University, 1967–70; Associate Professor, 1970–72; Professor, 1972–81; Dean of Research and Graduate Development, 1977–81; Provost, State University of New York Stoneybrook, 1981–; Chairman and Professor, Physics, University of Michigan, 1987–.

Memberships and awards: Honorary D.Sc., Indiana University, 1984; fellow, American Physical Society, 1972; National Science Board, 1980–86; New York Seagrant Institute Board of Directors, 1982–; fellow, AAAS, 1983–; SUNY Research Foundation Board of Directors, 1983–; Scientists Institute for Public Information Board of Trustees, 1985–87; fellow, National Science Foundation, 1966–67; fellow, Sloan Foundation, 1968; Chairman, Argonne Zero Gradient Synchrotron Users Group, 1970–72; Trustee, Argonne University Association, 1971–74; Physics Advisory Panel, National Science Foundation, 1976–; High Energy Physics Advisory Panel, U.S. Department of Energy, 1977–81; Sigma Xi.

Dissertation title: The Polarization Parameter in Elastic Proton-Proton Scattering from .75 to 2.84 GEV.

Ref: *American Men and Women of Science*, 15th ed., p. 604.
Who's Who Among Black Americans, 1985, p. 625.
1988 AAAS Election Pamphlet [p]

Neal, Xenophon Lamar   (1906–19??, M)

Chemist. Born in Okmulgee, OK, Aug. 2, 1906. B.S., Morehouse College, 1931; M.S., Atlanta University, 1943; Ph.C., Meharry Medical College, 1927. Instructor, Morehouse College, 1945–46; Atlanta University Summer School, 1945–47; Professor and Chairman of the Chemistry Department, Spelman College, 1947–.

Memberships and awards: Beta Kappa Chi; National Science Teachers Association; AAAS.

Ref.: *The Negro in Science*, p. 185.

Neblett, Richard Flemon   (1925– ——, M)

Chemist (organic). Born in Cincinnati, OH, Mar. 3, 1925. B.S., University of Cincinnati, 1949; M.S., 1951; Ph.D. (chemistry), 1953. Laboratory Director, Exxon Corporation, 1966–; research in gasoline and lubricant additives.

Memberships and awards: American Chemical Society; Member and President, Board of Education, Plainfield, 1963–74.

Dissertation title: Some Applications of Acenaphtene to the Chemistry of Cancer.

Ref: *American Men and Women of Science*, 12th ed., p. 4517.
In Black and White, p. 713.
Who's Who Among Black Americans, 1985, p. 625.
Ebony, July 1965, p. 6. [p]

Nelms, Ann T.   (192?– ——, F)

Mathematician. Physicist (nuclear). Born in Washington, DC. B.S., Howard University. Nuclear Physicist, U.S. National Bureau of Standards.

Pub: *Energy Loss and Range of Electrons.* Washington, U.S. Govt. Print. Off., 1956. 30 p.
Graphs of the Compton Energy Angle Relationship and the Klein-Nishina Formulas from 10 KEV to 500 MEV. Washington, U.S. Govt. Print. Off., 1953. 89 p.

Ref: *Ebony*, May 1954, p. 5 [p]

Nelson, Edward O.   (1925– ——, M)

Engineer (test). Born in Johnsonville, TN, Feb. 2, 1925. Attended St. Louis University and Rankin Technical Institute. Engineering Technician, U.S. Environmental Protection Agency, St. Louis; Rockwell International Monitoring Services Center.

Memberships and awards: American Radio Relay League; first black admitted to International Brotherhood of Electrical Workers.

Ref: *Ebony Success Library*, v. 1, 235. [p]
Who's Who Among Black Americans, 1985, 626.

Nelson, Ida Gray   (1867–1953, F)

Dentist. Born in Clarksville, TN. B.S., Ann Arbor College, 1899; D.D.S., University of Michigan, Ann Arbor Dental School, 1890.

Memberships and awards: First black female D.D.S. Practiced in Chicago.

Ref: *Chicago Black Dental Professional*, 1850–1983, p. 22–23.
Profiles of Negro Womanhood, v. 1, p. 260–261.
Smithsonian. *Black Women Achievers Against All Odds*, p. 26.
In Black and White, 3rd ed., p. 376–377.
Blacks in Science: Astrophysicist to Zoologist, p. 23.
Contributions of Black Women to America, p. 395.

Nelson, William Thomas   (1875–19??, M)

Physician. Born in Maineville, OH, May 23, 1875. B.A., Howard University, 1899; M.D., Howard University, 1904. Physician for Aged Colored Women's Home and Day Nursery; Grand Medical Registrar, Knights of Phthias of Ohio; Examining Physician for Cincinnati Lodges; Physician for Orphan Asylum for two years.

Memberships and awards: Vice-President, Ohio Branch, National Medical Association.

Ref: *Who's Who of the Colored Race*, 1915, p. 204.

Newman, Rogers   (1926– ——, M)

Mathematician. Born in Ramer, AL, Dec. 22, 1926. B.A., Morehouse College, 1948; M.A., Atlanta University, 1949; Ph.D., University of Michigan, 1961. Instructor, Mathematics and Physics, Bishop College, 1950–51; Instructor, Mathematics, Grambling College, 1951; Instructor, Mathematics and Physics, 1951–53; Teaching fellow, Junior Instructor, University of Michigan, 1957–60; Professor, Mathematics, Southern University, 1960–; Chairman, Mathematics Department, Southern University, 1961–; Committee on Educational Media Writing Team, 1964; Reviewer, Mathematical Reviews, 1962–65.

Memberships and awards: Mathematical Association of America; National Council of Teachers of Mathematics; American Mathematical Society; National Institute of Science.

Dissertation title: Capacity and Tchebycheff Polynomials.

Ref: *Black Mathematicians and Their Works*, p. 292.
American Men and Women of Science, 15th ed., p. 647.

Nichols, Barbara Lauraine   (1900s, F)

Nurse. Born in Waterville, ME. B.S., Case Western Reserve University, Cleveland; M.S., University of Wisconsin, Madison; Diploma, Massachusetts General Hospital School of Nursing, Boston. Director, In-Service Education for all employees, St. Mary's Hospital, Madison, WI.

Memberships and awards: First black president, American Nursing Association, 1978–82; Secretary, Wisconsin Department of Regulation and Licensing, a cabinet-level post, first black in Wisconsin; Honorary Ph.D.s from University of Wisconsin, Rhode Island College, Providence, and Lowell University, MA; one of eight women to receive Outstanding Women of Color Award, sponsored by the National Institute for Women of Color, 1984; Scroll of Merit, 1984; National Medical Association; Secretary, American Journal of Nursing Board of Directors.

Ref: *In Black and White*, 3rd ed., Suppl., p. 279.
Jet, Sept. 7, 1978, p. 21.
The Path We Tread, p. 80–81, 83–84. [p] p. 80.
Ebony, Sept. 1981, p. 56–57. [p]

Nichols, Victoria   (1900s, F)

Physician. Obstetrician/Gynecologist. Residency at Mayo Clinic. Faculty of Southern Illinois University; Faculty, Illinois Department of Public Health.

Ref: *Contribution of Black Women to America*, v. 2, p. 386.

Noel, H. T.   (18??–1916, M)

Physician. First black physician, Nashville, TN. Member, Meharry Medical School Faculty for 36 years.

Memberships and awards: Second President, National Medical Association, 1899–1900.

Ref: *Crisis*, Jan. 1917, p. 145. Obit.

Norman, John C.   (1930– ——, M)

Physician. Surgeon (thoracic). Born in Charleston, WV, May 11, 1930. B.A. (magna cum laude), Harvard University, 1950; M.D., Harvard Medical School, 1954. Physician, Heart Institute of St. Luke's Episcopal and Texas Children's Hospital, Houston, TX; Director, Cardiovascular Surgery Research Laboratories; Professor, Surgery, University of Texas Health Science Center; Visiting Professor, Biomedical Engineering Seminar Program, University of Miami; Department of Surgery, Harvard University Medical School.

Memberships and awards: Phi Beta Kappa; Massachusetts Medical Society; New York Academy of Sciences; AAAS; American College of Surgeons; Society of University Surgeons; Society of Thoracic Surgeons; American Physiological Society; Sigma Xi; Thoracic and Cardiovascular NIH fellow, University of Birmingham, England, 1962–63; fellow, American College of Cardiology, 1965.

Ref: *Who's Who Among Black Americans*, 1985, p. 634.
Ebony, Sept. 1965, p. 57–58, 60, 62. [p]

Norris, Ernest M.   (1903– ——, M)

Agriculturalist. B.S., Prairie View State College; Ph.D., Cornell University, 1934. Director of Graduate Studies, Prairie View State College.

Dissertation title: Determining Implications for Vocational Education from certain Characteristic Trends of the Negro Population in Kentucky. Published Ithaca, N.Y., 1934. 5 p.

Ref: *Holders of Doctorates Among American Negroes*, p. 131.

Northcross, Daisy Hill   (1881–19??, F)

Physician. Born in Montgomery, AL, 1881. B.A., Temple College, Philadelphia, PA, 1902; M.D., Loyola Medical College, Chicago, IL, 1913. One of the founders of Mercy Hospital, Detroit, 1917–. Married to Dr. David C. Northcross with whom she had a team practice.

Memberships and awards: National Medical Association; Allied Medical Association. In 1944, became Superintendent of Mercy Hospital, a community center with 50 beds at the time.

Ref: *Who's Who of the Colored Race*, 1915, p. 206.
Who's Who in Colored America, 1933–37, p. 393. [p] p. 385.
Who's Who in Colored America, 1938–40, p. 393. [p] p. 385.
Who's Who in Colored America, 1941–44, p. 386. [p] p. 381.
Contributions of Black Women to America, v. 2, p. 405.
Ebony, Oct. 1950, p. 38. [p]

Norwood, William R.   (1936–   , M)

Pilot. Born in Centralia, IL, Feb. 14, 1936. B.A., University of Southern Illinois, 1959; M.B.A., University of Chicago, 1974. U.S. Army Pilot of B-52s, Captain, 1959–65; first black pilot for United Air Lines, 1965; first officer, 1968–.

Memberships and awards: Board of Trustees, Southern Illinois University; Aviation Board of Elk Grove Village, IL; Air Line Pilots' Association; United Air Lines Speakers Panel; Charter Member, Organization of Black Air Line Pilots.

Ref: *Who's Who Among Black Americans*, 1985, p. 636.
Profiles in Black, p. 12. [p]

Nwude, Joseph Kanayo   (1940–   , M)

Engineer (mechanical). Born in Awka, Nigeria, Nov. 28, 1940. B.S. (mechanical engineering), Purdue University, 1964; M.S., MIT, 1966; Ph.D. (engineering), Dartmouth College, 1969. Engineer, General Electric, 1969–70; Professor, Department of Mechanical Engineering, Drexel University, Philadelphia, 19.

Ref: *Black Engineers in the United States*, p. 152.

O

O'Hara, Leon P. (1888–19??, M)

Physiologist. Born in Louisville, KY, April 24, 1888. B.A., Fisk University, 1911; M.S., Yale, 1915. Professor of Biology, Talladega College, 1923–1953. Retired.

Memberships and awards: American Geographical Society.

Ref: *American Men of Science*, 9th ed., p. 837.
Who's Who Among Black Americans, 1977, p. 678.

Olden, Georg   (1921–   , M)

Designer. First black to design a postage stamp.

Ref: *Ebony*, Nov. 1960, 79–85.
Jet, Aug. 1967, p. 11.
In Black and White, p. 729.

Olive, Milton Lee   (1947–1965, M)

Military. Born in 1947.

Memberships and awards: Congressional Medal of Honor awarded posthumously. First black congressional medal winner in Vietnam, the eighth black American.

Ref: *Jet*, Sept. 5, 1968, p. 49.
Ebony, Nov. 1985, p. 310. [p]
Ebony, June 1966, p. 160–161. [p]
Crisis, May 1966, p. 247–248. [p] cover

Oliver, Edwin E.   (1926–   , M)

Pharmacist. Born in Montgomery, AL, Feb. 15, 1926. Xavier University College of Pharmacy, 1950. Owns Oliver's Pharmacy, Spartanburg, SC.

Memberships and awards: Omega Psi Phi; American Pharmaceutical Association; Palmetto Medical and Dental Association; South Carolina Pharmaceutical Association; President, National Pharmaceutical Association.

Ref: *Who's Who Among Black Americans*, 1977, p. 679.
Ebony Success Library, v. 1, p. 238. [p]

O'Neal, Kenneth   (1908–19??, M)

Architect. Born in Union, MO, July 30, 1908. B.A., University of Indiana, 1931; B.S., 1935; Graduate study, Illinois Institute of Technology; Graduate study, University of Chicago, 1956–58. Engineer, Illinois Division of Highways, 1935–43; Architect, private practice, 1945–50; Architect, Skidmore, Owings and Merril, 1950–51; Schmidt, Garden, Erickson, 1951–54; City of Chicago Project Manager, Architect, 1975.

Memberships and awards: American Institute of Architects; Board Member, Chase House, 1967–75; Board Member, Hyde Park Co-op, 1967–68; Creator of detail plates on architectural details for *American Builder Magazine;* Certificate of Recognition, *Opportunity Magazine*.

Ref: *Who's Who Among Black Americans*, 1985, p. 638.

Onesimus (Slave)   (1700s, M)

Provided Americans with antidote for smallpox in 1721. Explained to Cotton Mather, his master, how he had been inoculated against it, a common practice in Africa. Cotton Mather wrote about it to Dr. Boylston who tried it on his son and two slaves. Boylston was called to London and honored by being made a fellow of the Royal Society.

Ref: *Encyclopedia of Black America*, p. 670.
Great Negroes Past and Present, p. 49.
Yale Journal of Biology and Medicine, v. 22, Dec. 1949, p. 130.
History of the Negro in Medicine, p. 11–12.
Nine Black American Doctors, p. 5–6.
National Medical Association, *Journal*, v. 44, 1952, p. 219.

Organ, Claude H., Jr.   (1927–   , M)

Physician. Surgeon. Born in Denison, TX, Oct. 16, 1927. B.S., Xavier University, 1948; M.D., Creighton University School of Medicine, 1952. Department of Surgery, Creighton University, 1960–71.

Memberships and awards: Allen Whipple Surgical Society; American Burn Association; American Medical Association; Midwest Clinical Society; National Medical Association; Alpha Omega Alpha; Board of Directors and Senior Member, American Board of Surgery; fellow, American College of Surgeons; Society of Head and Neck Surgeons; American Burn Association; Society of University Chairmen; National Medical Association; Douglas County Medical Association; San Diego Surgical Society; Association of Military Surgeons of the United States.

Ref: *Ebony,* Jan. 1987, p. 88, 90, 92, 95. [p] p. 88.
   Ebony Success Library, v. 1, p. 238. [p]
   Who's Who Among Black Americans, 1977, p. 681.
   A Century of Black Surgeons, p. 775–809, 884–914. [p] p. 776.

Osborne, Estelle Massey Riddle   (1901–1981, F)

Nurse. Born in Palestine, TX, May 3, 1901. B.S., Teachers College of Columbia University, 1930; M.A., 1981. Kansas City General, Harlem, Lincoln and Freedmen's Nursing Schools. Consultant, National Nursing Council for War Service, 1943–48; Faculty member, School of Education, New York University, 1946–52; Associate General Director of National League for Nursing, 1946–57.

Memberships and awards: Julius Rosenwald Fund, 1934–36; First Vice-President, National Council of Negro Women, 1952; Chairman, National Health Project, Alpha Kappa Alpha Sorority; first black nurse on the Board of Directors of the American Nurses Association, 1948; American delegate, International Council of Nurses Assembly, Stockholm, Sweden, 1949; Nurse of the Year Award, New York University, 1959; first black nurse inducted into American Academy of Nursing as an Honorary fellow; American Nurses Association Hall of Fame, 1984; first black nurse with Rosenwald Fund.

Ref: *The Path We Tread,* p. 137–139. [p] p. 137.
   Yost, Edna. *American Women of Nursing.* Lippincott, 1955. p. 96–118.
   Contributions of Black Women to America, v. 2, p. 367–368.
   Who's Who Among Black Americans, 1985, p. 640.
   Encyclopedia of Black America, p. 731.
   Jet, Sept. 1957, p. 5. [p]
   Who's Who of American Women, 1968.

Osborne, Muriel   (1900s, F)

Podiatrist. 1967, Chief of Freedmen's (now Howard University) Hospital Podiatry Clinic.

Memberships and awards: President, District of Columbia Podiatry Society, an organization of 50 foot specialists—first woman and first black.

Ref: *Jet,* Aug. 3, 1967, p. 52.
   Who's Who in Government, 1972.

Oseni, Hakeem O.   (1938–   , M)

Engineer. Born in Lagos, Nigeria, May 26, 1938. B.A., 1965; M.S., 1969; Ph.D., 1974. Research Engineer, E.I. DuPont Yerkes Research Laboratory, 1969–70; State University of New York, Buffalo, Corporate College Center Lecturer, 1972–74; Research Engineer, Exxon Production Research Company, 1974.

Memberships and awards: American Institute of Chemical Engineers; Society of Petroleum Engineers; President, African Students Union of Buffalo, 1972–73.

Ref: *Who's Who Among Black Americans,* 1985, p. 641.

Overton, Norris Webster   (1926–   , M)

Military (Air Force). Brigadier General. Born in Clarksville, TN, Jan. 6, 1926. B.S., University of Indiana, 1951; M.B.A., Air Force Institute of Technology, 1958; A.M.P., Harvard Graduate School of Business, 1972. Comptroller Executive Officer, Pentagon, 1969–72; Associate Professor, Aerospace Studies, University of Iowa, 1964–68; Comptroller, Air Force Academy, CO, 1973–76; Comptroller, Pacific Air Forces, Hawaii, 1976–79; Deputy Commander, Air Force Exchange Services, 1979–.

Memberships and awards: Harvard Alumni Association; Kappa Alpha Psi; Bronze Star, USAF, 1953 and 1958; Commendation Medal, USAF, 1964; Legion of Merit, USAF, 1972, 1976, and 1979; Brigadier General, 28 years; retired.

Ref: *Who's Who Among Black Americans,* 1985, p. 642.
   Black Americans in Defense of Our Nation, p. 130. [p] only
   Ebony, June 1966, p. 138. [p] only

Owens, Hugo, Sr.   (1916–   , M)

Dentist. Born in Chesapeake, VA, Jan. 21, 1916. President Elect, National Dental Association, 1987.

Ref: *Jet,* Mar. 16, 1987, p. 20. [p]
   Who's Who Among Black Americans, 1985, p. 643.
   Who's Who Among Black Americans, 1977.

Owens, O'Dell M.   (1947–   , M)

Physician. Endocrinologist. Obstetrician. Gynecologist. Born in Cincinnati, OH, 1947. M.D., Yale University, 1976. Director, Endocrinology and Infertility Division, University of Cincinnati Medical Center; Assistant Professor, University of Cincinnati Medical School.

Memberships and awards: Fellow, Reproductive Endocrinology and Infertility, Yale, 1976–80; American Laser Society; American Medical Association; Obstetric Gynecology Society.

Ref: *Black Enterprise,* Oct. 1988, p. 88 [p]
    ABMS Compendium of Certified Medical Specialists, v. 3, p. 724.
    Directory of Medical Specialists, v. 1, p. 1881.

Oxley, Lucy Orintha   (1912– ——, F)

Physician. Family Physician. Born in Harrisburg, PA, Aug. 19, 1912. B.S., University of Cincinnati, 1936; D.N.B., 1938.

Memberships and awards: Fellow, American Academy of Family Physicians.

Ref: *Who's Who Among Black Americans,* 1985, p. 644.

P

Paige, Emmett, Jr.   (1931– ——, M)

Military (Army). Lt. General. Born in Jacksonville, FL, Feb. 20, 1931. B.A., University of Maryland, 1972; M.P.A., Pennsylvania State University, 1974; Army War College, 1974. Enlisted age 16. Did not attend a military academy. Commander of the U.S. Information Systems Command, Fort Huachuca, AZ. Three-star general, the Army's senior ranking black officer.

Memberships and awards: Legion of Merit, three times; only black Signal Corps officer ever promoted to General, 1979.

Ref: *Ebony,* May 1986, p. 64, 66, 68, 70. [p]
    Who's Who Among Black Americans, 1985, p. 645.
    Ebony, May 1978, p. 46. [p] only
    Black Americans in Defense of Our Nation, p. 121. [p] only
    Who's Who in America, 1986–87, p. 2137.

Palmer, Doreen Pamela   (1949– ——, F)

Physician. Gastroenterologist. Internist. Born in Kingston, Jamaica, June 1, 1949. B.S., Lehman College, Bronx, NY, 1972; M.D., Brooklyn's Downstate Medical College, 1976; Specialized in Gastroenterology, Johns Hopkins Hospital. Head, Gastroenterology Department, Metropolitan Hospital, Manhattan, NY.

Ref: *Black Enterprise,* Oct. 1988, p. 64 [p]
    ABMS Compendium of Certified Medical Specialists, v. 2, p. 1256.
    Directory of Medical Specialists, v. 1, p. 1185.

Palmer, Edward   (1937– ——, M)

Physician. Ophthalmologist. Surgeon. Born in New York, July 25, 1937. B.S., Adelphi University, Garden City, NY,

1960; M.D., Meharry Medical School, 1964. Battalion Surgeon, U.S. Navy, two years.

Ref: *Black Enterprise,* Oct. 1988, p. 95.
    Who's Who Among Black Americans, 1985, p. 645.

Papan (Slave)   (1700s, M)

Medical Practitioner. Born in Virginia. His treatment of skin and venereal diseases was so effective, that the Virginia Legislature bought him from his master in 1729 and freed him. He practiced medicine in Virginia.

Ref: *Nine Black American Doctors,* p. 7.

Parker, Charles Stewart   (1882–19??, M)

Botanist. Born in Corinne, UT, Mar. 31, 1882. B.A., Trinity College, 1905; B.S., 1922; M.S., State College of Washington, 1923; Ph.D., Pennsylvania State College, 1932. Professor of Botany, Howard University, 1924–27; described new sub-genus and section of the genus carex; discovered and described 39 species of plants; his research ended the blight of stoned fruits in Washington State in the 1920s. Director of a field expedition to Mexico, 1908–12.

Memberships and awards: Botanical Survey Party, Washington, 1921–22; Mycology Society; Botanical Society; Phytopathological Society; Torrey Botanical Club; British Mycology Society.

Dissertation title: A Taxonomic Study of the Gene Hypholoma in North America.

Ref: *Afro-American Encyclopedia,* v. 7, p. 1977.
    American Men of Science, 8th ed., p. 1891.
    Holders of Doctorates Among American Negroes, p. 194.

Parker, John P.   (1827–1900, M)

Inventor. One of few blacks to obtain patents in the United States before 1900 for a screw for tobacco presses in 1884 and a similar one a year later. Ripley Foundry and Machine Co., Ripley, OH, established business.

Ref: *Dictionary of American Negro Biography,* p. 480–481.
    Negro in Our History, 5th ed., p. 464.

Parker, Neville Anthony   (1939– ——, M)

Engineer (civil). Born in Tobago, B.W.I., Nov. 22, 1939. B.S. (civil engineering), City University of New York, 1965; M.S. (transportation engineering), Cornell University, 1966; Ph.D. (environmental engineering), 1971. Instructor, U.S. Army Corps of Engineers, 1970–71; Professor, Howard University School of Engineering, 1971–.

Memberships and awards: American Society of Civil Engineers; Highway Research Board; Operations Research Society of America; National Society of Professional Engineers; Chi Epsilon; Outstanding Civil Engineering Instructor, 1971–72.

Dissertation title: A Systems Analysis of Route Location.

Ref: *Black Engineers in the United States,* p. 156.

Parks, Gordon Alexander Buchanan   (1912- —, M)

Photographer. Born in Ft. Scott, KS, Nov. 30, 1912. Chose photography as a career in 1937. Moved to Chicago and was inspired and influenced by artists of the South Side Community Art Center. Went to Farm Security Administration directed by Roy Stryker and after a year joined Elmer Davis in OWI's Overseas Division, 1944. Made documentaries for Standard Oil of New Jersey, 1945–48. Staff Photographer, *Life,* 1949. Wrote and directed a documentary film on Flavio; lived in Paris a year as a European staff photographer for *Life.*

Memberships and awards: Won a Rosenwald Fellowship, first in photography as a result of his one man exhibit at the Community Art Center. The ASMP named him "Magazine Photographer of the Year" in 1961 and he received the Newhouse Award in Photography from Syracuse University; Spingarn Medal for his multifaceted creative achievement including the field of photography, 1972; Sterling Silver Pagoda Award by the makers of Nikon cameras; winner of the 1965 International Understanding Through Photography Award, Photography Society of America; Frederick W. Brehm Award, 1962.

Pub: *A Choice of Weapons.* New York, Harper & Row, 1966. 274 p.

Ref: *Great Negroes: Past and Present,* Adams, p. 205.
Jet, Sept. 16, 1965, p. 55. [p]
Who's Who Among Black Americans, 1985, p. 649.
Black Americans in Autobiography, p. 61.
Ebony, Sept. 1987, p. 50. [p]
Ebony Success Library, v. 1, p. 240. [p]
Ebony, April 1978, p. 108. [p]
Living Black American Authors, p. 121–122.
Who's Who in America, 1986–87, p. 2153.
Crisis, Oct. 1972, p. 269, 274–275, 282–283.

Parnell, John Vaze, Jr.   (1915–1963, M)

Embryologist. Biologist. Born in Boston, MA, Feb. 11, 1915. B.S., Boston University, 1938; M.S., 1940; M.A., Harvard University, 1946; Ph.D., 1948. Instructor, Virginia State College, 1940–43; Professor, Bennett College, 1943–44; Associate Professor, Virginia State College, 1944–49; Professor, 1949–; Coordinator, Mathematics and Electronics, Bay State Community College, Boston.

Memberships and awards: AAAS; Sigma Xi; American Association of University Professors; National Institute of Science; National Association of Biology Teachers.

Dissertation title: Metamorphosis of the Nervous System in the Lumbosacral and Caudal.

Ref: *Jet,* Nov. 21, 1963, p. 49.
The Negro in Science, p. 180.
American Men of Science, 10th ed., p. 3097.

Parsons, James A.   (1900s, M)

Electrochemist. Metallurgist. Inventor. Rensselaer Polytechnic Institute. Worked in aluminum bronze, contributing to the resources of Aluminum Bronze Foundation. Became, at 27 years old, Chief Chemist and Metallurgist of the Duriron Company of Dayton, OH; patented austenitic alloy steels, which are corrosion resistant to sulfuric and nitric acids and other industrial chemicals.

Memberships and awards: award for achievement, Harman Foundation, 1927; President, National Technical Association.

Ref: *Negro Builders and Heroes,* p. 253.
Drew. Negro Scholars in Scientific Research. *Journal of Negro History,* v. 35, p. 142, 1950.
Blacks in Science: Astrophysicist to Zoologist, p. 45.

Passon, Myrtle Ashe   (1891–19??, F)

Nurse. Born in Austin, TX, Nov. 27, 1891. M.A., Tillotson College, 1909. Freedmen's Hospital Training School for Nurses, 1917–20; Registered Nurse, Wiley Wilson Sanitarium, NY, 1923–.

Ref: *Who's Who in Colored America,* 1928–29, p. 431.

Patrick-Yeboah, Jennie R.   (1949- —, F)

Engineer (chemical). Born in Gadsden, AL, Jan. 1, 1949. B.S., University of California, Berkeley, 1973; Ph.D., Massachusetts Institute of Technology, 1979. Assistant Engineer, Dow Chemical Company, 1972; Stauffer Chemical Company, 1973; Research Associate, MIT, 1973-79; Engineer Chevron Research, 1974; Engineer, Arthur D. Little, 1975; Research Engineer, General Electric Company, 1979–83; Phillip Morris, Inc., 1983–.

Memberships and awards: First black woman to earn a doctorate in chemical engineering; Sigma Xi; American Institute of Chemical Engineers; Outstanding Women in Science and Engineering Award, 1980.

Dissertation title: Superheat-Limit Temperatures for Nonideal-Liquid Mixtures and Pure Components.

Ref: *Ebony,* May 1981, p. 6. [p]
Who's Who Among Black Americans, 1985, p. 651.

Patterson, Annie Elizabeth   (1892–19??, F)

Nurse. Born in Baton Rouge, LA, May 14, 1892. Laurenburg Normal and Industrial Institute, NC; Tuskegee Institute, AL. Head Nurse, Bigelow Memorial Hospital, Laurenburg, NC, 1925–29.

Memberships and awards: Tuskegee Institute Club; Graduate Nurses of New York Association.

Ref: *Who's Who in Colored America,* 1930–32, p. 329.

Patterson, Frederick Douglas   (1901–1988, M)

Veterinarian. Born in Washington, DC, Oct. 10, 1901. Prairie View State College, TX, 1915–19; D.V.M., Iowa State College, 1923; M.S., 1927; Ph.D. (veterinary medicine), Cornell, 1932. Instructor, Director of Agriculture, Virginia State College, 1923–28; Director, School of Agriculture; President, Tuskegee Institute for 25 years; founder, United Negro College Fund; founded the only black school of veterinary medicine in the United States at Tuskegee Institute.

Memberships and awards: Iowa Chapter of Veterinary Medical Society; National Honor Society of Phi Kappa Phi; Alpha Phi Alpha.

Dissertation title: Avian Coccidiosis: A Study of Some of the Factors Concerned in Its Control.

Pub: *College Endowment Funding Plan.* Washington, American Council on Education, 1976. 120 p.
Contributor of articles to scientific magazines.

Ref: *Who's Who Among Black Americans,* 1980–81, p. 619.
Holders of Doctorates Among American Negroes, p. 132.
Who's Who in Colored America, 1933–37, p. 403.
National Register, 1952, p. 606.
Black Family International Journal, 1985, p. 19.[p]
Who's Who in Colored America, 1941–44, p. 396.
Ebony, Nov. 1985, p. 72. [p]
Washington Post, April 28, 1988, D4. obit
Who's Who in America, 1986–87, p. 2162.
Chronicles of Faith, Autobiography of Frederick D. Patterson.

Patterson, Raymond Frederick   (195?– ——, M)

Physician. Psychiatrist (forensic). Born in Chicago, IL. B.S.; M.D.; Howard University Medical School.

Ref: *Washington Post Magazine,* Nov. 23, 1986, p. 34–37. [p]

Patton-Washington, Georgia Esther Lee   (1864–1900, F)

Physician. Surgeon. Born in Grundy County, TN, April 15, 1864. M.D., Meharry Medical School, 1893. One of the first two women to finish Meharry Medical School. The other doctor was Dr. Anna D. Gregg. She was the first black woman to receive a license to practice Medicine and Surgery in Tennessee. In 1897 she married Davis W. Washington and practiced under the name Washington until her death in 1900.

Ref: *Educating Black Doctors,* p. 32.
Noted Negro Women, p. 117–121.
Send Us a Lady Physician, p. 110.

Payne, Betty J.   (1950– ——, F)

Pilot. In 1977 became first black woman to receive navigator wings in the United States Air Force.

Ref: *Smithsonian Women Achievements Against All Odds,* p. 39.

Payne, Clarence H.   (1892–1965, M)

Physician. Surgeon. Born in Hopkinsville, KY, Jan. 23, 1892. M.D., University of Chicago Medical School, 1920. Head of Interns, Provident Hospital for 10 years; elected Surgeon General of the Veterans of Foreign Wars of Illinois twice, was called to a conference on racial integration of the Armed Forces by President Roosevelt during World War II; was the first of two blacks appointed to the staff of the Municipal Tuberculosis Sanitarium of Chicago. One of the three physicians to appear before the American Medical Association requesting the removal of "col." behind the names of black physicians in the *AMA Directory.* They succeeded. (Dr. C. G. Roberts and Dr. Roscoe Giles were the other two).

Memberships and awards: Fellow, American College of Chest Physicians and Surgeons; first President, Chicago Chapter, Alpha Phi Alpha.

Ref: *Jet,* July 22, 1965, p. 24.
Jet, Jan. 26, 1987, p. 39.
National Medical Association, *Journal,* v. 57, Nov. 1965, p. 525. obit

Payne, Fitz-Melvin Carrington   (1890–19??, M)

Physician. Surgeon. Born in Barbados, B.W.I., Nov. 18, 1890. Virginia Union University, Richmond, VA; M.D., Meharry Medical College, 1918; Postgraduate work in Surgery, 1930. Vice-President, Tulsa County Public Health Association; Superintendent, Nurse's Training School and Director and Surgeon, Willow Hospital; Superintendent, Hubbard Memorial Hospital and Surgical Clinic.

Memberships and awards: National Medical, Dental, and Pharmaceutical Association; Honorary member, Kansas State Medical Association; Chi Delta Mu; Alpha Phi Alpha.

Ref: *Who's Who in Colored America,* 1930–32, p. 329–330. [p] p. 331.
Who's Who in Colored America, 1933–37, p. 404.
Who's Who in Colored America, 1938–40, p. 403. [p] p. 405.
Who's Who in Colored America, 1941–44, p. 399. [p] p. 402.

Payne, Howard Marshall   (1907–1961, M)

Physician. Internist. Pathologist. Born in Washington, DC, Aug. 18, 1907. B.A., Dartmouth College, 1928; Education Certificate, Dartmouth Medical College, 1929;

M.D., Howard University Medical College, 1931. Assistant Resident in Pathology, Sea View Hospital, Staten Island, NY, 1935–36; Resident in Medicine (tuberculosis), 1936; Medicine Faculty Professor, Howard University, 1937–58; Tuberculosis Specialist, Superintendent, Middlesex County Sanitarium, Waltham, MA, 1958–61.

Memberships and awards: First black president, National Tuberculosis Association, 1951–52.

Ref: Jet, Sept. 28, 1961, p. 54.
   National Medical Association, Journal, v. 53, Nov. 1961, p. 653–655. [p] obit
   Who's Who in Colored America, 1950, p. 410–411.
   Dictionary of American Medical Biography, p. 586.

Pease, Joachim (1800s, M)

Military. Born in Long Island, NY.

Memberships and awards: Congressional Medal of Honor. June 19, 1864.

Ref: Jet, June 25, 1964, p. 11.
   Negro Medal of Honor Men, p. 42–45.

Peck, David John (1800s, M)

Physician. First black to graduate from an American Medical School, M.D., Rush Medical Center, 1847. Settled and practiced in Philadelphia, PA.

Ref: History of Negroes in Medicine, p. 29–30.
   Medico-Chirurgical Society of the District of Columbia, Inc., Bulletin, v. 6, Feb. 1949, p. 3.
   Medico-Chirurgical Society of the District of Columbia, Inc., Bulletin, Oct. 1949, p. 4.

Peebles-Meyers, Helen Marjorie (1915- ——, F)

Physician. Born Oct. 6, 1915. B.S. (physics and chemistry), Hunter College, 1937; M.A. (psychology), Columbia University; M.D., Wayne State University School of Medicine, 1943 (first black woman graduate). First black woman Intern, Resident, and Chief Resident, Detroit Receiving Hospital; Chief Physician, World Headquarters of the Ford Motor Company, 1977–85; retired.

Memberships and awards: Distinguished Warrior Award from the Detroit Urban League; named one of America's top 100 citizens by Newsweek Magazine; Board of Trustees, Founders Society of the Detroit Institute of Arts; American Medical Association; American Diabetes Association; Medical Advisory Committee, Visiting Nurses Association; Alpha Omega Alpha.

Ref: Ebony, Dec. 1986, p. 68, 70, 72, 74. [p] p. 68.
   Who's Who Among Black Americans, 1985, p. 657.

Peele, Amanda E. (1908–19??, F)

Biologist. Born in Jackson, NC, Jan. 10, 1908. B.S., Hampton Institute, VA, 1930; M.S., Cornell University,

NY, 1934. Professor of Biology, Hampton Institute, 1930–.

Memberships and awards: Secretary-Treasurer, Virginia Conference of College Science Teachers; AAAS; Phi Lambda Theta; Virginia Academy of Science; Virginia Research Society. In May, 1939, she presented a research paper before the Virginia Academy of Science, the first black female to do so.

Ref: Who's Who in Colored America, 1941–44, p. 399–400. [p]

Peery, Benjamin Franklin, Jr. (1922- ——, M)

Astronomer. Physicist. Born in St. Joseph, MO, Mar. 4, 1922. B.S. (physics), University of Minnesota, 1949; M.A., Fisk University, 1955; Ph.D. (astronomy), University of Michigan, 1962. Instructor in Physics, Agricultural and Technical College of North Carolina, 1951–53; Instructor, University of Michigan, 1958; Associate Professor, Indiana University, 1959–74; Professor of Astronomy, Indiana University, 1974–76; Professor of Astronomy, Howard University, 1977–; Visiting Associate, California Institute of Technology, 1967–70; Visiting Associate, Harvard University, 1971; Visiting Research Astronomer, Kitt Peak National Observatory, 1975–76.

Memberships and awards: Astronomical Society; Advisory Panel of the National Science Foundation, 1974–78; Chairman, Committee on Manpower and Employment, 1977; U.S. National Committee of the International Astronomical Union, 1972–77; Consultant, National Science Foundation, NASA; Visiting Professor Program, American Astronomical Society, 1964–; Trustee, Adler Planetarium; Astronomical Society of the Pacific; fellow, AAAS.

Dissertation title: The System VV Cephei.

Pub: Published a number of articles in astrophysical journals.

Ref: American Men and Women of Science, 14th ed., p. 3410.
   In Black and White, p. 752.
   Who's Who Among Black Americans, 1985, p. 657.
   Negroes in Science: Natural Science Doctorates, 1876–1969, p. 53.

Pelham, Robert A., Jr. (1859–1943, M)

Inventor. Born in Petersburg, VA, Jan. 4, 1859. Invented a pasting machine, a tabulating machine used in the census of manufacturers, and a tallying machine used in the population division; worked on the Detroit Post, 1884–1891; active in politics.

Ref: Negro in Our History, 5th ed., p. 462.
   Dictionary of American Biography, Suppl. 3, p. 595–596.
   Men of mark, 1970 ed., p. 732–735. [p]

Penn, Irvine Garland (1867–1930, M)

Physician. Born in Lynchburg, VA, Oct. 7, 1867. Educated in Lynchburg, VA. Principal of a public school at age 19; Commissioner, Negro Division, Cotton States and International Exposition.

Memberships and awards: Chaired the first meeting of the group of 12 doctors who began the National Medical Association in 1895.

Pub: *The Afro-American Press and Its Editors.* New York, Arno Press, 1969. 565 p.
   The United Negro: His Problems and His Progress. New York, Negro Universities Press, 1969. 600 p.
   The Southern College of Life and University Educator. Philadelphia, National Publishing Co., 1902. 897 p.
   The College of Life. Chicago, Chicago Publication & Lithography Co., 1895. 80 p.

Ref: *History of the Negro in Medicine,* p. 68. [p]
   Crisis, Mar. 1918, p. 231. [p]
   Crisis, Feb. 1931, p. 56. [p]

Penn, William   (1900s, M)

Physician. Surgeon. First black to earn M.D. from Yale Medical School. Step-grandfather of Dr. Jane Cook Wright. Stepfather of Dr. Louis T. Wright.

Ref: *Current Biography,* 1968, p. 443.
   Who's Who in Colored America, 1928–29, p. 288.
   A Century of Black Surgeons, p. 161.

Perdue, Omer Felix   (1884–19??, M)

Physician. Surgeon. Born in Fort Smith, Ark., Dec. 10, 1884. B.S., Williams Industrial College, Little Rock, AR, 1906; Ph.C., Meharry Medical College, Nashville, TN, 1911; M.D., 1916. Superintendent, City Hospital, St. Louis, MO, 1926.

Memberships and awards: National Medical Association; Tri-State Medical, Dental, and Pharmaceutical Association.

Ref: *Who's Who in Colored America,* 1938–40, p. 407.
   Who's Who in Colored America, 1941–44, p. 400, 403.

Perry, Ervin Sewell   (1935– ——, M)

Engineer (civil). Born in Coldspring, TX, Dec. 22, 1935. B.S., Prairie View A & M College, 1956; M.S., University of Texas, 1961; Ph.D. (civil engineering), 1964. Instructor in Civil Engineering, Southern University, 1958–59; Assistant Professor, Prairie View A & M College, 1959–60; University of Texas, 1964–.

Memberships and awards: Society of Civil Engineers; Society of Testing and Materials; Society of Engineering Education; Society of Professional Engineers.

Dissertation title: A Study of Dynamically Loaded Composite Members.

Ref: *Jet,* May 28, 1964, p. 24.
   American Men of Science, 11th ed., p. 4130.

Perry, John Edward   (1870–1962, M)

Physician. Surgeon. Born in Clarksville, TX, April 27, 1870. B.A., Bishop College, Marshall, TX, 1891; M.D., Meharry Medical College, 1895. Founder of Wheatly-Provident Hospital in Kansas City; Founder, Perry Sanitarium, 1910; 1st Lt. Army Medical Corps, 1898; Chief of Surgery, Municipal Hospital No. 2 for over 23 years; Surgeon, Kansas Southern Railroad.

Memberships and awards: Distinguished Service Medal, National Medical Association, 1947; President, Medico-Chirurgical Society of the District of Columbia; President, National Medical Association, 1923–24; President, Pan-Missouri Medical Association; Board of Trustees, Meharry Medical College.

Pub: *Forty Cords of Wood: Memoirs of a Medical Doctor* (sketches of faculty of Meharry) (autobiography)

Ref: *History of the Negro in Medicine,* p. 47. [p] p. 47.
   Who's Who in Colored America, 1928–29, p. 289.
   Who's Who in Colored America, 1927, p. 155.
   Who's Who of the Colored Race, 1915, p. 215.
   Who's Who in Colored America, 1930–32, p. 334.
   Jet, May 31, 1962, p. 52.
   Who's Who in Colored America, 1933–37, p. 408.
   Who's Who in Colored America, 1938–40, p. 408.
   Dictionary of American Medical Biography, p. 592.
   Cobb, W. Montague. John Edward Perry, M.D., 1870–. National Medical Association, *Journal,* v. 48, 1956, p. 292–296.
   National Medical Association, *Journal,* v. 41, May 1949, p. 135.
   National Medical Association, *Journal,* v. 54, Sept. 1962, p. 526. [p]
   A Century of Black Surgeons, p. 439–440.

Perry, John Sinclair   (1889–19??, M)

Physician. Psychiatrist. Born in Fayetteville, NC, Sept. 9, 1889. B.A., Shaw University, 1910; M.D., University of West Tennessee, 1915; studied at St. Elizabeth's Hospital, 1936–38. Owned and operated a small hospital, Hamlet, NC, 1915–18; Clinical Assistant, Neuropsychiatry, Freedmen's Hospital, 1938–39; Psychiatric Division, Ft. Myer Medical Examining Board, National Selective Service, 1940s.

Memberships and awards: President, Medico-Chirurgical Society of the District of Columbia, Inc., 1948–.

Ref: Medico-Chirurgical Society of the District of Columbia, Inc., *Bulletin,* Jan. 1948, p. 1, 5–6. [p]

Perry, Rufus Patterson   (1903–1984, M)

Chemist (organic). Born in Brunswick, GA, June 4, 1903. B.A., Johnson C. Smith University, 1925; M.S., University of Iowa, 1927; Ph.D. (organic chemistry), 1939. Professor of Chemistry, Head and Chairman of the Department of Natural Science, Prairie View State College,

1927–43; Director, Division of Arts and Sciences, 1939–43; Professor of Chemistry and Vice-President and Administrative Dean, Langston University, 1943–57; President, Johnson C. Smith University, 1957–69; Emeritus Professor of Chemistry, Washington Technical Institute, 1970–; research in synthesis of local anesthetics and analgesics.

Memberships and awards: AAAS; American Chemical Society; National Institute of Science; American Institute of Chemistry; Sigma Xi.

Dissertation title: Behavior of Certain Vanillin Substitution Products and Some of Their Alkyl Derivatives Toward Potassium-Permanganate.

Ref: *American Men and Women of Science*, 13th ed., p. 3429.
Holders of Doctorates Among American Negroes, p. 155.
Who's Who Among Black Americans, 1980.

Perry, Thomas Gilbert   (1890–19??, M)

Veterinarian. Born in Higginsville, MO, June 8, 1890. D.V.M., Kansas State Agricultural College, 1921.

Memberships and awards: Phi Beta Sigma; Gamma Sigma Delta, Honorary Agricultural Fraternity.

Ref: *Who's Who in Colored America*, 1928–29, p. 289. [p] opp. p. 290.
Who's Who in Colored America, 1930–32, p. 335.
Who's Who in Colored America, 1941–44, p. 404. [p] p. 405.
The Black Man in Veterinary Medicine, p. 115. [p] only

Perry, Wayne Deroyce   (1944– ——, M)

Engineer (mechanical). Born in Denton, TX, Oct. 14, 1944. B.S., Tuskegee Institute, 1967; M.S., University of New Mexico, Ph.D., Carnegie Mellon University, 1975. Staff Engineer, Sandia Laboratories, Albuquerque, NM, 1967–71; Manpower Studies Project, Carnegie Mellon University, 1971–75; Rand Corporation, 1975–.

Memberships and awards: American Statistical Association; The Institute of Management Science; Econometric Society of North America; American Society of Mechanical Engineers; Omega Psi Phi; Co-founder, Concerned Black Employees of Sandia Laboratories; Sandia Laboratory Service Award; Research Paper winner, American Society of Mechanical Engineers, 1967; Scholarship, Tuskegee Institute, 1962–67; Graduate fellowship, Carnegie-Mellon University, 1971–75.

Dissertation title: General Quantitative Models and Policy Analysis of Turnover and Attendance in Manpower Programs.

Ref: *Who's Who Among Black Americans*, 1985, p. 662.
Black Engineers in the United States, p. 159.
Ebony, May 1986.

Person, Waverly   (1922– ——, M)

Geophysicist. Born in Lawrenceville, VA. B.S., St. Pauls College. Became Technician with earthquake services in 1960; Chief, NEJC, 1977.

Ref: *Ebony*, Sept. 1987, p. 134, 136, 138. [p]

Peters, Henry R.   (1900s, M)

Pharmacist.

Memberships and awards: First black member of the District of Columbia Pharmacy Board. National President, Vice-President, and Executive Committee, National Pharmaceutical Association; Past President, Washington Pharmaceutical Association.

Ref: *Jet*, Aug. 23, 1962, p. 38.
Jet, Sept. 8, 1960, p. 50.

Petersen, Frank E., Jr.   (19??– ——, M)

Military (Marines). General. First black general in the Marine Corps.

Ref: *Ebony*, Nov. 1985, p. 339. [p]
Ebony, Dec. 1986, p. 140, 144, 146. [p]

Peyton, Thomas R.   (1900s, M)

Physician. Proctologist. Born in Brooklyn, NY. M.D., Long Island School of Medicine; only black in a class of 100. Refused admission to a large New York hospital because of his race, he took postgraduate course in proctology in Paris and London, but was still refused membership in the American Proctologic Society.

Pub: *Quest for Dignity: An Autobiography of a Negro Doctor.* Los Angeles, Publishers Western, 1963. 160 p. Reprint.

Ref: *History of Negroes in Medicine*, p. 95–99.

Phillips, Charles Henry, Jr.   (1882–19??, M)

Physician. Surgeon. Internist. Born in Tullahoma, TN, May 5, 1882. Lane College, Jackson, TN, Fisk University, 1901; B.Pd., Walden University, 1904; M.D. Meharry Medical College, 1908. Famous as an Internist and Diagnostician, specialized in diseases of women and children.

Pub: Contributed articles to the *New York Medical Journal*.

Ref: *Who's Who in Colored America*, 1927, p. 157.
Who's Who of the Colored Race, 1915, p. 217.

Phillips, Clyde W.   (1923– ——, M)

Physician. Surgeon. Born in Chicago, IL, Mar. 22, 1923. B.S., Morehouse College, 1943; M.D., Howard University Medical College, 1946. Internship and Residency in Surgery, Provident Hospital, 1947–50; Faculty, Howard University Medical School as Assistant in Thoracic Surgery, 1950–; Chairman, Department of Surgery, Provident

Hospital, Chicago, 1957–; in 1970, he was appointed Medical Director, Cook County Hospital, IL; resigned Nov. 1971; Clinical Professor, Surgery, University of Illinois, Abraham Lincoln School of Medicine, 1980–.

Memberships and awards: John Hale Surgical Award, 1949; National Medical Association; Chicago Medical Society; Illinois State Medical Society; Society for Experimental Biology and Medicine; Junior Candidate Group of the American College of Surgeons; American Medical Association, fellow; Editorial Board, National Medical Association, *Journal*, Diplomate, American Board of Surgery.

Ref: National Medical Association, *Journal*, v. 49, May 1957, p. 186. [p]
National Medical Association, *Journal*, v. 43, 1951, p. 129–130.
Jet, Dec. 17, 1970, p. 19. [p]

Phillips, Edward Martin   (1935–   , M)

Engineer (chemical). Born in Philadelphia, PA, Dec. 23, 1935. B.S. (chemical engineering), Lafayette College, 1958; M.S. (chemical engineering), Northwestern University, 1959; Ph.D. (chemical engineering), University of Pittsburgh, 1969. Research Engineer, Atlantic Richfield Company, 1959–64; Project Engineer, Exxon Engineering Company, 1968–72; Associate Professor, Tufts University, 1972–74; Engineering Associate, Air Products and Chemicals, Inc., 1974–. Memberships and awards: American Institute of Chemical Engineers, 1958–; American Chemical Society, 1969–; NASA Predoctoral fellow, University of Pittsburgh, 1964–68; Instrument Society of America; Tau Beta Pi; Sigma Xi.

Dissertation title: An Experimental Study of Velocity Profiles and Pressure Losses During Pulsating Newtonian Flow in a Rigid Tube.

Ref: *Black Engineers in the United States*, p. 160.
Who's Who Among Black Americans, 1985, p. 666.

Phillips, Frederick Brian   (1946–   , M)

Psychologist. Born in Philadelphia, PA, Sept. 2, 1946. B.A., Pennsylvania State University, 1968; M.S.W., 1970; Psy.D., The Fielding Institute, 1978. Psychologist, Washington, DC, Government, 1978–81; Associate Director, Institute for Life Enrichment, 1981–83; Director/President, Progressive Life Institute.

Memberships and awards: Kappa Alpha Psi; Association of Black Psychologists, 1978–.

Ref: *Ebony*, July 1987, p. 120. [p]
Who's Who Among Black Americans, 1985, p. 667.

Phillips, Jasper Tappan   (1884–19??, M)

Physician. Born in Jackson, TN, May 17, 1884. B.A., Fisk University, 1907; M.D., Meharry Medical College, 1913.

First black man in the United States to serve as monitor over medical applicants and assist Tennessee State Medical Board of Examiners, 1913–14.

Memberships and awards: Vice-President, Rock City Academy of Medicine and Surgery.

Ref: *Who's Who of the Colored Race*, 1915, p. 218.

Phillips, Joseph R., Sr.   (1931–   , M)

Physician. Psychiatrist. Born in Clarksville, TN, Dec. 28, 1931. B.S., Tennessee State University, 1954; M.S., 1956; M.D., Meharry Medical College, 1963. General Psychiatric Research, 1968; Acting Department Chairman, Clark College, 1956–58; Assistant Professor, Anatomy, Meharry Medical College, 1969–72; Associate Professor, Psychiatry and Staff Psychiatrist, V.A. Medical Center, Tuskegee, 1980.

Memberships and awards: National Medical Association; American Psychiatric Association; Omega Psi Phi; Black Psychiatrists of America; Beta Kappa Chi; Advisory Board, National Association for Sickle Cell Disease, 1973–76; National Institute of Mental Health, 1969–73.

Ref: *Who's Who Among Black Americans*, 1985, p. 667.
Biographic Directory of the American Psychiatric Association, 1983, p. 932.

Phillips, Mildred E.   (1928–   , F)

Physician. Pathologist. Born in New York, NY, May 21, 1928. B.A., Hunter College, 1946; M.D., Howard University Medical College, 1950. Resident in Pathology, Mt. Sinai Hospital, NY, 1952–54; Resident Assistant Surgical Pathology, Presbyterian Hospital, 1954–55; Instructor in Pathology, State University of New York, Downstate Medical Center, 1955–56; from Instructor to Assistant Professor, 1957–68; Associate Professor of Pathology, Medical Center, New York University, 1965–; State University of New York, Stony Brook.

Memberships and awards: American Association of Pathologists and Bacteriologists; American Association of Experimental Pathology; New York Pathologic Society; American Medical Association; College of American Pathologists; Transplantation Society; New York Academy of Sciences; International Academy of Pathologists; fellow in Surgical Pathology; Presbyterian Hospital, NY, 1954–55.

Ref: *Contributions of Black Women to America*, v. 2, p. 385.
American Men and Women of Science, 16th ed., p. 966.

Pickens, Harriet F.   (1900s, F)

Military (Navy). New York. First Black Wave, 1944.

Ref: *Jet*, Dec. 14, 1961, p. 11.
Black Women Achievements Against All Odds, p. 32.

Pickering, J. F.   (1900s, M)

Inventor. Patent #643,975, Feb. 20, 1900, for an airship (dirigible) powered by an electric motor. It was the first to have directional control. The first airship (1852) was developed in France but was filled with hydrogen gas (very combustible).

Ref: *At Last Recognition in America,* v. 1, p. 44.
Negro in Our History, 5th ed., p. 464.

Pickrum, Harvey   (1943- ——, M)

Microbiologist. Born in Springfield, OH, Nov. 13, 1943. B.S., Ohio State University, 1970; M.S., 1972; Ph.D. (microbiology), 1975. Research Scientist, Food Microbiology, Proctor & Gamble Company, 1975-.

Memberships and awards: American, Society of Microbiology.

Ref: *American Men and Women of Science,* 14th ed., p. 3947.

Pierce, Joseph Alphonso   (1902-1969, M)

Mathematician. Born in Waycross, GA, Aug. 10, 1902. B.A., Atlanta University, 1925; M.S., University of Michigan, 1930; Ph.D., 1938. Instructor in Mathematics, Texas College, 1925-27; Chairman of the Department, Booker T. Washington High School, Atlanta, GA, 1927-29; Professor, Wiley College, 1930-38; Professor and Chairman of Mathematics Department, Atlanta University, 1938-48; Dean and President of Texas Southern University, 1948-67; research in mathematical statistics and derivation of random stratified sampling formulas.

Memberships and awards: Institute of Mathematical Statistics; American Statistical Association; President, National Institute of Science, 1946-47; Beta Kappa Chi.

Dissertation title: A Study of a Universe of Finite Population with Applications to Moment Function.

Ref: *Holders of Doctorates Among American Negroes,* p. 155.
American Men of Science, 11th ed., p. 4177.
Encyclopedia of Black America, p. 676-677.
In Black and White, p. 766.
The Negro in Science, p. 188.
Black Mathematicians and Their Works, p. 292.
Crisis, Aug. 1930. [p] only

Pierre, Percy Anthony   (1939- ——, M)

Engineer (electrical). Born in St. James Parish, LA, Jan. 3, 1939. B.S. (electrical engineering), Notre Dame, 1961; M.S., 1963; Ph.D., Johns Hopkins University, 1967; Postdoctoral, University of Michigan, 1968. Dean, School of Engineering, Howard University, 1971-77; U.S. Department of the Army, Assistant Secretary for Research, Development, and Regulation, 1977-81; Engineering Management Consultant, 1981-; President, Prairie View A & M University, 1985-.

Memberships and awards: Senator Proxmire's Award of Merit, 1979; Outstanding Notre Dame Alumni; Sigma Xi; Scientific Research Society of America; Honorary Doctor of Engineering, University of Notre Dame; Tau Beta Pi; Outstanding Black Engineer, National Conference for Black Professionals; Board of Trustees, University of Notre Dame; IEEE; White House fellow; Institute of Mathematical Statistics; Board of Trustees, Chesapeake Research Consortium.

Dissertation title: Properties of Non-Gaussian, Continuous Parameter, Random Processes as Used in Detection Theory.

Ref: *Black Engineers in the United States,* p. 161-162.
In Black and White, p. 767.
Who's Who Among Black Americans, 1985, p. 669.
Black Mathematicians and Their Works, p. 166-180, 292-293. [p] p. 16.
Who's Who in Engineering, 1985, p. 519.
Jet, April 15, 1985, p. 16.
Who's Who in America, 1986-87, p. 2216.

Pinderhughes, Charles Alfred   (1919- ——, M)

Physician. Psychiatrist. Born in Baltimore, MD, Jan. 28, 1919. B.A., Dartmouth College, 1940; M.D., Howard University, 1943; Boston Psychoanalytic Society and Institute, 1955. Chief, Psychiatry, Boston V.A. Hospital, 1960-65; Psychiatrist, Psychoanalyst, Boston University School of Medicine, 1950-72; Professor, Psychiatry, Boston University School of Medicine, 1971-.

Memberships and awards: Surgeon General's Advisory Committee on TV and Social Behavior, 1970-74; Task Force on Aggression and Violence, 1972-75; American Psychiatric Association.

Ref: *American Men and Women of Science,* 12th ed., (Soc. & Behav.), p. 1944.
American Psychiatric Association, Biographical Directory, 1983, p. 936.
In Black and White, p. 768.
Who's Who Among Black Americans, 1985, p. 670.
Ebony, Aug. 1973, p. 174. [p]

Pinn, Petra Fitzalieu   (1881-1958, F)

Nurse. Born in Zanesville, OH, Feb. 9, 1881. B.S., Tuskegee Institute, 1906; Postgraduate courses for Nurses, John A. Andrew Memorial Hospital, Tuskegee, 1922. Nurse in charge of Hale Infirmary, Montgomery, AL, 1906-09; Superintendent, Red Cross Sanitarium and Nurse Training School, Louisville, KY, 1909-11; Private nurse, 1911-16; Relief nurse, District Nurses Association, 1914; Superintendent, Pine Ridge Hospital, West Palm Beach, FL, 1916-25; Superintendent, Christian Hospital, Miami, FL, 1926-.

Memberships and awards: President, Tuskegee Nurses Alumni; Treasurer, National Hospital Association; President, National Association of Colored Graduate

Nurses; fourth winner of the Mary Mahoney Medal given in 1939 to the person who contributed the most to nursing.

Ref: *Who's Who in Colored America,* 1927, p. 159.
      Who's Who in Colored America, 1928–29, p. 294.
      Who's Who in Colored America, 1930–32, p. 341.
      Who's Who in Colored America, 1933–37, p. 416, 419.
      The Path We Tread, p. 151–153. [p]

Pinn-Wiggins, Vivian Winona   (1941– ——, F)

Physician. Pathologist. Born in Halifax, VA., 1941. B.A., Wellesley College, MA; M.D., University of Virginia School of Medicine, 1967; research with Martin Flax, Massachusetts General.

Memberships and awards: Teaching fellow in Pathology, Harvard Medical School; Diplomate in Anatomic Pathology from American Board of Pathology.

Ref: *Contributions of Black Women to America,* v. 2, p. 388–389. [p]

Pittman, William Sidney   (1875–1958, M)

Architect. Born in Montgomery, AL, 1875. Certificate of Apprenticeship, Wheel-Wrighting Trade, Tuskegee Institute, transferred to Architectural Drawing, Graduating in 1897. Married Booker T. Washington's daughter in 1907. Designed the Washington, DC, YMCA, 12th Street Branch; the National Training School, Durham, NC, among others.

Ref: *Jet,* April 3, 1958, p. 29.
      Crisis, Sept. 1916, p. 239–240. [p]

Pitts, Raymond Jackson   (1911–19??, M)

Mathematician. Born in Macon, GA, June 21, 1911. B.A., Talladega College, 1932; M.A., Michigan University, 1938; Ph.D. (mathematics education), 1956. Instructor in Mathematics, Georgia State Teachers College, 1933–34; High School in Florida, 1934–37; Fort Valley State College, 1938–40; Assistant Professor, 1942–44; Professor, 1945–54; Assistant Professor, Los Angeles State College, 1956–60; Associate Professor, 1960–61; Director, Santa Barbara County Mathematics Projects, 1961–63; Assistant Director, Center for Coordinated Education, Santa Barbara, CA, 1963–64; Director, Intergroup Education, Pasadena City School, 1964–66; Project Specialist, California State Department of Education, 1966–.

Memberships and awards: Mathematical Society; Mathematical Association; President, National Institute of Science, 1955–56.

Dissertation title: An Analysis and Evaluation of Supplementary Teaching Materials Found in Selected Secondary School Textbooks.

Ref: *American Men of Science,* 11th ed., p. 4197.
      Who's Who in the West, 1978, p. 573.

Plummer, John Owens   (1880–1958, M)

Physician. Otolaryngologist. Ophthalmologist. Born in Warrenton, NC, May 19, 1880. B.S., Shaw University, 1904; M.D., Leonard Medical School, 1910 (valedictorian). Otolaryngologist and Ophthalmologist to St. Agnes Hospital, 1905; Physician to State Deaf, Dumb and Blind Institute, Raleigh, NC, 1906–18; Chairman of Anatomy, Leonard Medical School, 1910–13; the V.A. Hospital at Tuskegee was consummated while he was President of the National Medical Association, 1924; in 1937, he had the largest Eye, Ear, Nose and Throat practice of any black physician in the country.

Memberships and awards: President, 1915, North Carolina Medical Association; President, National Medical Association, 1924–25; Phi Beta Sigma.

Ref: *Who's Who in Colored America,* 1927, p. 159–160.
      Who's Who in Colored America, 1928–29, p. 294, [p] opp. p. 160.
      Who's Who in Colored America, 1930–32, p. 341–342. [p] p. 339.
      Who's Who in Colored America, 1933–37, p. 419. [p] p. 417.
      Who's Who in Colored America, 1938–40, p. 419. [p] p. 417.
      Who's Who in Colored America, 1941–44, p. 412, 415. [p] p. 413.
      National Medical Association, *Journal,* v. 41, July 1949, p. 189.

Poindexter, Hildrus A.   (1901–1987, M)

Physician. Bacteriologist. Malariologist. Born in Memphis, TN, May 10, 1901. B.A., Lincoln University (cum laude), 1924; M.D., Harvard University, 1929; M.S., Columbia University, 1930; Ph.D. (bacteriology), 1932; M.P.H., Columbia University. 1937. Professor of Microbiology, Howard University, 1931–43; Professor of Community Health, Howard University; Surgical and Medical Director, U.S. Public Health Service, 1947–65; Medical Mission to Liberia.

Memberships and awards: Bronze Star, four Battle Stars; National Civil Service League Award; Browning Alpha Award; Aid to International Development, for which he was Chief Public Health Advisor, presented him with Distinguished Public Service Award; Rockefeller Foundation traveling fellow; National Medical Association; Society of Bacteriology; fellow, Society of Parasitology; Board of Trustees, Lincoln University; Browning Alpha Award.

Dissertation title: Observations on the Defense Mechanism in Trypanosoma Equiperdum and Trypanosoma Lewisi Infections in Guinea-Pigs and Rats.

Pub: *My World of Reality.* (an autobiography) Detroit, Balamp Publishing, 1973. 342 p. [p] p. iv.

Extensive bibliography in *Who's Who in Colored America,* 1941–44, p. 415.

Ref: *American Men of Science,* 8th ed., p. 1964.
Encyclopedia of Black America, p. 678–679.
Holders of Doctorates Among American Negroes, p. 132–133.
Who's Who in Colored America, 1941–44, p. 415.
National Medical Association, *Journal,* v. 46, Jan. 1954, p. 76. [p]
Ebony, Jan. 1957, p. 61. [p]
National Medical Association, *Journal,* v. 53, July 1961, p. 409. [p]
National Medical Association, *Journal,* v. 55, May 1963, p. 244. [p]
National Medical Association, *Journal,* v. 56, Nov. 1964, p. 537. [p]
Who's Who Among Black Americans, 1985, p. 674.
Who's Who in America, 1986–87, p. 2230–2231.
Crisis, April 1945, p. 95. [p]
National Medical Association, *Journal,* v. 65, May 1973, p. 243. (list of publications, p. 245–248) [p] cover.

Pollard, Nathaniel, Jr.   (1939– —— , M)

Mathematician. Born in Bessemer, AL, Sept. 27, 1939. B.A. (natural science and mathematics), Miles College, 1960; M.S. (mathematics), Atlanta University, 1964; Ph.D. (mathematics education), University of Oklahoma, 1970. Instructor, Mathematics, Atlanta University, summer 1968; Instructor, Mathematics, Fort Valley State College, 1964–65; Instructor, Mathematics, Lawson State College, 1965–1967; Assistant Professor, Mathematics, University of Alabama, 1970–72; Chairman, Natural Science Division and Professor, Mathematics, Miles College, 1972–.

Memberships and awards: National Teaching fellow, Miles College, 1967–68; College Honor Society; Pi Mu Epsilon; Outstanding American Educator Award, 1972–73; National Council of Teachers of Mathematics.

Dissertation title: An Empirical Investigation of Some Effects of Non-Normality on Bartlett's Test of Significance in Principal Component Analysis.

Ref: *Black Mathematicians and Their Works,* p. 293.

Porter, E. S.   (1848–19??, M)

Physician. Born in Delaware, Oct. 19, 1848. B.A., Lincoln University, PA, 1873; M.D., Brooklyn Medical College, 1876. Sanitary Force, Louisville, KY, where he practiced medicine, 1882–1884; Physician in the Orphans' Home, 1882–; Lecturer, State University of Kentucky, 1881–.

Ref: *Men of Mark,* 1970 ed., p. 287–289. [p]

Porter, James Hall   (1933– —— , M)

Engineer (chemical). Born in Portchester, NY, Nov. 11, 1933. B.S. (chemical engineering). Rensselaer Polytechnic Institute, 1955; D.Sc. (chemical engineering), MIT, 1963. Manager of Computer Applications Design, 1967–72; Associate Professor of Chemical Engineering, MIT, 1972–; President, Energy and Environmental Engineering.

Memberships and awards: Co-founder, member of the Executive Board, and President, National Organization for the Professional Advancement of Black Chemists and Chemical Engineers; American Institute of Chemical Engineers; Jesse Smith Noyes Foundation fellowship, 1953–54; Chevron Research fellowship, 1962; Outstanding Professor Award, MIT, 1974.

Dissertation title: Formation and Growth of Voids in Fluidized Beds.

Pub: Numerous publications in technical journals.

Ref: *Who's Who in Engineering,* 1985, p. 525.
Black Engineers in the United States, p. 162.
Who's Who Among Black Americans, 1985, p. 677.

Porter, James Reynolds   (1865–1960, M)

Dentist. Born in Savannah, GA, Feb. 6, 1865. B.A., Atlanta University, 1886; D.D.S., Meharry Medical College, 1889.

Memberships and awards: President, Dental Section, National Medical Association; Georgia Medical, Dental, and Pharmaceutical Association; President, Atlanta Medical Association.

Ref: *Who's Who in Colored America,* 1930–32, p. 342.
Who's Who in Colored America, 1928–29, p. 295.
Who's Who in Colored America, 1933–37, p. 420.
Who's Who in Colored America, 1941–44, p. 416.
Jet, Jan. 12, 1961, p. 46. [p]

Porter, Otho Dandrith   (1864–19??, M)

Physician. Born in Logan County, KY, Dec. 16, 1864. B.S., Fisk University, 1891; M.D., Meharry Medical College, 1894.

Memberships and awards: National Medical Association, President, 1901–02; one of the organizers of Kentucky Medical Society of Negro Physicians and Dentists.

Ref: *Who's Who of the Colored Race,* 1915, p. 221.

Posey, Leroy Raadell, Jr.   (1915– —— , M)

Physicist. Born in Hopkinsville, KY, July 4, 1915. B.A., Ohio State University, 1936; M.S., 1937; Ph.D. (physics), University of Michigan, 1942. Professor of Physics, Florida A & M College, 1939–40 and 1942–43; Acting Head of Physics Department, Fisk University, 1943; Research Physicist, University of Michigan, 1943–45; Professor of

Physics and Head of the Department, Tennessee A & I, 1945–47; Professor and Head of the Department, Morgan State College, 1947–49; Head, Department of Mathematics and Physics, Southern University, 1949–55; from Assistant to Associate Professor, 1955–60; Professor of Physics, San Jose State College, 1960–; research in infrared spectroscopy and molecular structure.

Memberships and awards: American Physical Society.

Dissertation title: The Infra-Red Spectrum of Ethane, Mono-Deutero-Ethane, and Hexa-Deutero-Ethane.

Ref: *American Men and Women of Science,* 14th ed., p. 4006.
Holders of Doctorates Among American Negroes, p. 155–156.

Potter, Mary Etta   (1900s, F)

Physician. Born in Bowling Green, KY. Attended Simmons University, Louisville, KY, Hampton Institute, and Dixie Hospital, VA; Citizens National Hospital, Louisville, KY; M.D., Louisville, National Medical College, 1907. Superintendent, Citizens National Hospital; Faculty, Louisville National Hospital; one of the organizers of State Society of Registered Nurses; organized the Fraternal Hospital Training School for Nurses, 1922; Medical Examiner for five female organizations in Louisville, KY.

Ref: *Who's Who in Colored America,* 1928–29, p. 295.

Poussaint, Alvin Francis   (1934– ——, M)

Physician. Psychiatrist. Born in East Harlem, NY, May 15, 1934. B.A., Columbia College, 1956; M.D., Cornell University Medical College, 1960; M.S., UCLA, 1964. Instructor to Assistant Professor, Tufts University Medical School, 1965–69; Associate Dean of Students and Associate Professor of Psychiatry, Harvard Medical School, 1969–; Consultant for Bill Cosby Show.

Memberships and awards: Certified, American Board of Psychiatry and Neurology, 1970; Board of Trustees, Weslyan College, 1968–69; Board of Trustees, National Afro-American Artists, 1968; fellow, American Psychiatric Association, 1972–; National Medical Association; several honorary doctoral degrees; Michael Schwerner Award, 1968.

Pub: *Why Blacks Kill Blacks,* 1972.

Ref: *American Men and Women of Science,* 14th ed., p. 4015.
Encyclopedia of Black America, p. 696.
History of the Negro in Medicine, p. 172. [p] p. 172.
In Black and White, p. 778.
Who's Who Among Black Americans, 1980–81, p. 644.
Who's Who Among Black Americans, 1985, p. 679.
Ebony, Aug. 1987, p. 76. [p] article by him
Ebony Success Library, v. 1, p. 253. [p]
Who's Who in America, 1986–87, p. 247.
Ebony, Oct. 1964, p. 6. [p]

Ebony, Aug. 1979, p. 7. [p] only
Living Black American Authors, p. 129.

Powell, C. Clayton   (1927– ——, M)

Optometrist. Born in Dothan, AL, April 11, 1927. B.A., Morehouse College; B.S., Illinois College of Optometry; O.D., College of Optometry; Graduate Study, University of Michigan, Master of Public Health Program; M.Ed., Atlanta University. Executive Director, Atlanta Southside Comprehensive Health Center, 1973–76.

Memberships and awards: Founder and President, National Optometric Association, which received a grant of $150,000 for recruitment of black college students to optometry; American Public Health Association; National Eye Institute; Beta Kappa Chi National Science Honor Society; Omega Psi Phi.

Ref: *Who's Who Among Black Americans,* 1985, p. 679.
Ebony Success Library, v. 1, p. 253. [p]

Powell, Charles William   (1879–1939, M)

Physician. Surgeon. Born in Gumridge, MS, Oct. 3, 1879. B.S., Shaw University, Raleigh, NC; M.D., Leonard Medical College, 1910. He established a private hospital in Atlanta, GA, 1928 (William A. Harris Memorial Hospital with 30 beds, the only private hospital for blacks in Atlanta at the time).

Memberships and awards: Charter member, John A. Andrew Clinical Society, Tuskegee; Executive Board, National Medical Association.

Ref: *Who's Who.*

Powell, Clilan Bethany   (1894–19??, M)

Physician. Radiologist. Roentgenologist. Born in Suffolk, VA, Aug. 8, 1894. B.S., Virginia Normal University, 1913; M.D., Howard University Medical College, 1920. First black roentgenologist in New York; one of the founders of FEPC law in the United States.

Memberships and awards: Distinguished Achievement, Howard University, 1968; fifty years in medical service, Howard University Alumni Association, 1970; numerous other awards and plaques.

Ref: *Who's Who Among Black Americans,* 1985, p. 680.

Powell, Colin   (1937– ——, M)

Military (Army). Lt. General. Born in New York, NY, April 5, 1937. B.S., City College of New York, 1958; M.B.A., George Washington University, 1971; National War College, 1976. Military Expert to Defense Secretary Weinberger; Commander of Army's 5th Corps in Frankfurt, Germany, –1986; second in command, National Security Council, Washington, DC, 1987–.

Memberships and awards: White House fellow; Purple Heart; Bronze Star; Legion of Merit, 1969 and 1971; Distinguished Service Medal.

Ref: *Jet,* Jan. 12, 1987, p. 24. [p]
     Who's Who Among Black Americans, 1985, p. 680.

Powell, Robert Lee   (1923– ——, M)

Physicist. Holographer. Born in Kerns, TX, Nov. 4, 1923. B.A., Fisk University, 1944; M.S., 1951. Research Associate, Fisk University, 1950–51; Physicist, Lincoln Laboratory, MIT, 1951–.

     Memberships and awards: American Association of Physics Teachers; research in semiconductors, vibration spectra of molecules.

Ref: *The Negro in Science,* p. 190.
     American Men and Women of Science, 11th ed., p. 4247.
     Blacks in Science: Astrophysicist to Zoologist, p. 33.

Presnell, J. H.   (1885–19??, F)

Physician. Surgeon. Obstetrician. Born in Knoxville, TN, Nov. 13, 1885. B.S., Knoxville College, TN, 1910; M.D., Meharry Medical College, TN, 1913. Chairman of the Committee of the Beverly Hills Negro Sanitarium, the only black tubercular sanitarium in Tennessee.

Ref: *Who's Who in Colored America,* 1930–32, p. 343. [p]
     Who's Who in Colored America, 1933–37, p. 423. [p]
     Who's Who in Colored America, 1938–40, p. 423. [p]

Presnell, Walter Madison   (1925– ——, M)

Psychologist. Born in Knoxville, TN, Sept. 23, 1925. Medical Director, International Federation of Internal Freedom, a new psychic research started by Harvard Psychologists Timothy Leary and Richard Alpert; research on "mind-altering" and "consciousness expanding" drugs LSD-25 and psilocybin after being dropped from Harvard because drugs in IFIF Center, designed to help people live according to whatever they can dream about.

Ref: *Jet,* April 11, 1963, p. 23. [p]

Price, Jessie Isabelle   (1930– ——, F)

Microbiologist (veterinary). Bacteriologist. Born in Montrose, PA, Jan. 22, 1930. B.S., Cornell University, 1953; M.S., 1958; Ph.D. (veterinary bacteriology), 1959; Laboratory Technician, Poultry Diseases, Cornell University, 1953–56; Teaching Assistant, Veterinary Bacteriology, 1956–59; Research Specialist, Microbiology, Duck Research Laboratory, New York State Veterinary College, Cornell University, 1959–; research in organisms causing bacterial infections in the white Pekin duck on Long Island.

Memberships and awards: AAAS; American Association of Avian Pathologists; American Institute of Biological Sciences; American Society for Microbiology.

Dissertation title: Studies on Pasteurella Antipestifer Infection in White Pekin Ducks.

Ref: *American Men and Women of Science,* 14th ed., p. 4036.
     Ebony, Sept. 1964, p. 76–78, 80, 82. [p]

Primas, H. Raymond   (192?– ——, M)

Dentist.
     Memberships and awards: President, National Dental Association, 1965.

Ref: *Jet,* Aug. 19, 1965, p. 48.

Primus (Slave)   (1700s, M)

Physician. Born in New England, slave of a surgeon. He often assisted his master in surgery and in his general practice. When the physician died, Primus took over his practice serving both white and black patients.

Ref: *Nine Black American Doctors,* p. 6.

Prince, Frank Rodger   (1941– ——, M)

Chemist (organic). Chemist (polymer). Born in St. Thomas, Virgin Islands, Nov. 1, 1941. B.S., Philadelphia College of Pharmacy, 1963; Ph.D., Brooklyn Polytechnic Institute, 1968. Senior Research Chemist, Atlantic Richfield Chemical Company, 1967–69; Allied Chemical Corporation, 1969–.

Dissertation title: Effects of Side Chains on the Conformation of Polypeptides and N-Substituted Polypeptides.

Ref: *American Men and Women of Science,* 12th ed., p. 5031.
     Ebony, July 1970, p. 7. [p]

Proctor, Charles D.   (1922– ——, M)

Pharmacologist. B.A., Fisk University, 1943; M.A., 1946; Ph.D., Loyola University, 1950. Member, National Institutes of Health Research Grant Advisory Group; Visiting Associate Professor of Pharmacology, Chicago Medical School; Professor and Chairman of Pharmacology Department, Meharry Medical College, 1968–; work on tranquilizers, neurochemistry, gave paper before national convention in 1961.

     Memberships and awards: Chicago Catholic Archdiocesum School Board.

Dissertation title: Some Applications of Polarography to Pharmacological, Toxicological and Physiological Studies.

Ref: *American Men and Women of Science,* 15th ed., p. 1088.
     Encyclopedia of Black America, p. 745.
     Jet, Nov. 16, 1961, p. 27.
     Jet, Oct. 27, 1963, p. 51.

Proctor, Nathaniel Kipling   (1914– —— , M)

Physiologist. Born in Baltimore, MD, Oct. 17, 1914. B.S., Morgan State College, 1934; M.A., Pennsylvania University, 1941; Ph.D., 1951. Research Assistant, Department of Embryology, Carnegie Institution of Washington, 1946–47; Instructor in Biology, Morgan State College, 1950–51; Associate Professor, 1951–53; Professor, 1954–.

Memberships and awards: Fellow, National Institutes of Health, 1947–48; Corporation member, Marine Biological Laboratory, 1953–; Sigma Xi, AAAS; Beta Kappa Chi.

Dissertation title: The Effects of the Four Major Cations on Arthropod Muscle.

Ref: The Negro in Science, p. 180.

Pugh, Roderich Wellington   (1919– —— , M)

Psychologist. Born in Richmond, KY, June 1, 1919. B.A., Fisk University, 1940; M.A., Ohio State University, 1941; Ph.D. (psychology), University of Chicago, 1949. Staff Psychologist, Hines V.A. Hospital, Chicago, 1949–54; Assistant Chief, Clinical Psychology for Psychotherapy, 1954–58; Chief, 1958–60; Supervisor of Psychology and Coordinator of Psychological Internship Training, 1960–66; Associate Professor, Loyola University of Chicago, 1966–73; Professor of Psychology, 1973–.

Memberships and awards: American Psychological Association and National Institute of Mental Health Visiting Psychological Program, 1968–; Juvenile Problems Research Review Committee, National Institute of Mental Health, 1970–74; fellow, American Psychological Association; Society for Psychological Study of Social Issues; Association of Black Psychologists; Illinois Psychological Association; Alpha Phi Alpha; Sigma Xi; Diplomate of Clinical Psychology; American Board of Professional Psychologists, 1957; Psi Chi.

Dissertation title: An Investigation of Some Psychological Processes Accompanying Concurrent Electric Convulsive Therapy and Nondirective Psychotherapy with Paranoid Schizophrenia.

Ref: Who's Who in America, 1986–87, p. 2267.
American Men and Women of Science, 13th ed., p. 966.
Even the Rat Was White, p. 127.
Who's Who Among Black Americans, 1985, p. 688.
Ebony Success Library, v. 1, p. 257. [p]
Ebony, April 1960, p. 7. [p]
Ebony, Jan. 1962, p. 114. [p]

Purvis, Charles Burleigh   (1842–1929, M)

Physician. Surgeon. Born in Philadelphia, PA, April 14, 1842. Oberlin College, 1860–62; M.D., Medical College of Western Reserve, 1865; M.A., Howard University, 1868; L.L.D., 1914. 1882, appointed surgeon in charge of Freedmen's Hospital; First black Surgeon in charge of a civilian hospital; Emeritus Professor of Obstetrics and Gynecology, Howard University, attended President Garfield after he was attacked by an assassin; first black physician to serve on D.C. Board of Medical Examiners; second to become an instructor in an American Medical School. (Alexander Augusta was the first, at Howard University).

Ref: Afro-American Encyclopedia, v. 7, p. 2129.
Encyclopedia of Black America, 1981, p. 708.
In Black and White, p. 789.
Jet, Apr. 14, 1955, p. 10, [p] p. 163.
Men of Mark, 1970 ed., p. 476–479. [p]
Who's Who in Colored America, 1927, p. 163.
Dictionary of American Medical Biography, p. 612–613.
History of the Negro in Medicine, 1968, p. 51–52. [p]
Dictionary of American Negro Biography, p. 507–508.
Howard University Medical Department: Historical Biographical and Statistics Souvenir, p. 113. [p]
Cobb, W. Montague, Charles Burleigh Purvis, National Medical Association, *Journal*, v. 45, Jan. 1953, p. 79–82.

Purvis, William B.   (1800s, M)

Inventor. Invented machine for making paper bags (10 patents) in 1884–1894. Has patent for fountain pen, patent #419,065, three patents on electrical railway, one on a hand stamp in 1883. Sold paper bag machine to Union Paper Bag Co. of New York.

Ref: Afro-American Encyclopedia, v. 7, p. 2128–2129.
At Last Recognition in America, p. 8, 36, 37.
In Black and White, p. 790.

Q

Quaterman, Lloyd Albert   (1918–1982, M)

Physicist (nuclear). Chemist (nuclear). Chemist (fluoride). Born in Philadelphia, PA, May 31, 1918. B.S., St. Augustine's College, NC, 1943; M.S., Northwestern University, 1952. One of six black scientists who worked on the atomic bomb (Manhattan Project). Assistant to Associate Research Scientist and Chemist, Argonne National Laboratories, 1943–49; student under Enrico Fermi.

Memberships and awards: Society of Applied Spectroscopy; Sigma Xi; American Chemical Society; AAAS; Honorary Doctorate of Science, St. Augustine's College, 1971; Scientific Research Society of America.

Ref: Ebony, Sept. 1949, p. 28.
The Negro in Science, p. 185.
Ebony, Nov. 1949, p. 28. [p]
Blacks in Science: Ancient and Modern, p. 266–272. [p]

Quinland, William Samuel   (1885–1953, M)

Physician. Pathologist. Bacteriologist. Born in Antigua, B.W.I., Oct. 12, 1885. B.S., Oskaloosa College, 1918;

M.D., Meharry Medical College, 1919; Harvard Medical School Graduate Certificate in Pathology and Bacteriology, 1921. Harvard University offered him a Professorship in the Medical College, but he refused saying Meharry needed him more. Professor and Head, Department of Pathology, Meharry Medical College, 1922–47; Chief, Laboratory Service, V.A. Hospital, Tuskegee, 1947–.

Memberships and awards: First Rosenwald fellow, postgraduate study in pathology and bacteriology, Harvard Medical School, 1919–22; first black named to the American Association of Pathologists and Bacteriologists; first black diplomate of the American Board of Pathology; first black fellow of the College of American Pathologists; National Medical Association; member, Editorial Board, *Punjab Medical Journal*, a publication of Public Health, Medical News, Indian and Foreign, published in Banga, Punjab, India; AAAS.

Ref: *Educating Black Doctors*, p. 70.
The History of the Negro in Medicine, p. 92.
They Set the Pace, p. 1.
American Men of Science, 8th ed., p. 2004.
National Medical Association, *Journal*, v. 33, Mar. 1941, p. 89.
National Medical Association, *Journal*, v. 45, July 1953, p. 298–300. [p] obit
Dictionary of American Medical Biography, p. 618–619.
Leaders in American Science, 1953–54, p. 541. [p]
Crisis, Dec. 1919, p. 64–65. [p]
Crisis, Nov. 1938, p. 370. [p]

R

Rabb, Maurice F., Jr.   (1932– ——, M)

Physician. Surgeon. Ophthalmologist. Born in Kentucky, Aug. 7, 1932. B.S., University of Louisville, 1954; M.D., University of Louisville, 1958. Director, Illinois Eye Bank and Research Laboratory; Associate Professor, Ophthalmology, Illinois Medical School; Director, Fluorescein Angiography Laboratory, Michael Reese Hospital, Chicago; Co-Director, Sickle Cell Center, University of Illinois Medical Center. Chief, Ophthalmology, Mercy Hospital, Chicago.

Memberships and awards: President, John A. Andrew Clinical Society; American Board of Ophthalmology; Awards for his photographs of the inside of the eye, 1962 and 1964; President, Chicago Ophthalmology Society; Honorary Degree, University of Louisville, 1983.

Pub: *Clinico-Pathologic Correlation of Ocular Disease.* Mosby, 1974. (co-author)
Macular Disease, Boston, Little, Brown, 1981. (editor)
Ocular Pathology: Clinical Application and Self-Assessment. St. Louis, Mosby, 1985. (co-author)

Ref: *Jet*, Sept. 2, 1954, p. 38.
National Medical Association, *Journal*, v. 48, July 1956, p. 301. [p]
Blacks in Science: Astrophysicist to Zoologist, p. 48 [p] after p. 48.
Ebony, July 1974, p. 60. [p]
Ebony, Sept. 1975, p. 55–56, 58, 60, 62. [p]
Biographical Membership Directory and Resource Manual of the American Academy of Ophthalmology, p. 349.
Black Enterprise, Oct. 1988, p. 78. [p]

Rainbow-Earhart, Kathryn A.   (1921– ——, F)

Physician. Psychiatrist. Born in Wheeling, WV, Mar. 21, 1921. B.S., Fort Valley State College, 1942; M.D., Meharry Medical College, 1948; Menninger School of Psychiatry, 1965. Private Pediatric Practice, 1952–54; Staff Physician, Lakin State Hospital, 1954–59; Clinical Director, 1959–60; Superintendent, 1960–62; Staff Psychiatrist, Topeka State Hospital, 1956–79; Staff Psychiatrist, Shawnee Community Mental Health Center, Inc., 1979–81.

Memberships and awards: Alpha Kappa Alpha; Black Psychiatrists of America; American Medical Association; Medical Women's Association; National Medical Association; several fellowships; Delta Kappa Gamma.

Ref: *Jet*, Dec. 1, 1960, p. 45. [p]
Who's Who Among Black Americans, 1985, p. 691.

Raines, Eugene D.   (1900s, M)

Chemist (physical). B.S., Howard University; M.A., Fisk University, TN; M.S., Indiana University; Ph.D., Indiana University, 1938. Professor of Chemistry, Kentucky State College.

Dissertation title: Nickel, Cadmium, and Lead Sulfides as Catalysts in the Vapor Phase Reduction of Nitrobenzene.

Ref: *Holders of Doctorates Among American Negroes*, p. 156.

Ramey, Melvin Richard   (1938,– ——, M)

Engineer (civil). Born in Pittsburgh, PA, Sept. 13, 1938. B.S., (civil engineering), Pennsylvania State University, 1960; M.S., (civil engineering), Carnegie-Mellon University, 1965; Ph.D. (civil engineering), 1967. Bridge Design Engineer, Pennsylvania Department of Highways, 1960–63; Research Assistant, Carnegie-Mellon University, 1963–67; from Assistant Professor to Associate Professor, 1967–73; Professor of Civil Engineering, University of California, Davis, 1973–; Consultant in various architectural design firms, 1970–.

Memberships and awards: American Society of Civil Engineers; American Concrete Institute; International Society of Biomechanics in Sports.

Dissertation title: The Flexural Behavior of Fiber Reinforced Concrete Beams.

Ref: *Black Engineers in the United States,* p. 164.
American Men and Women of Science, 16th ed., p. 38.

Randolph, Lynwood Parker   (1938- ——, M)

Physicist. Engineer (aerospace). Born in Richmond, VA, May 21, 1938. B.S., Virginia State University, 1959; M.S., Howard, 1964; Ph.D. (physics), 1972; Harvard University Business School, 1982; Physicist Harry Diamond Laboratories, 1964–70; Research Physicist, 1970–75; Manager, Aerospace and Space Technology, NASA, 1975–82; Deputy Director of Productivity, 1982–; University of the District of Columbia, 1973–; Howard University, 1980–; Research in solar energy; lasers.

Memberships and awards: AIAA; American Physical Society; Sigma Pi Sigma; Beta Kappa Chi; Harvard Program for Management and Development; Alpha Phi Alpha Scholarship Award; AAAS; National Society of Black Physicists.

Dissertation title: Radiation-Induced changes in the Photoluminiscence Spectrum of Cadmium Sulfide.

Ref: *American Men and Women of Science,* 15th ed., p. 45
Who's Who in Aviation and Aerospace, 1983, p. 797.
Who's Who in Frontiers of Science and Technology, 2nd ed., p. 415

Rann, Emery Louvelle   (1914- ——, M)

Physician. Born in Keyestone, WV, Mar. 9, 1914. B.S. (cum laude), Johnson C. Smith University, 1934; M.S., University of Michigan, 1963; M.D., Meharry Medical College, 1948.

Memberships and awards: President, National Medical Association, 1973–74; Chairman, 6th Imhotep Conference on Hospital Integration; Honorary D.Sci., Johnson C. Smith University, 1981; North Carolina Academy of Family Practice; President, Old North State Medical Society, 1959; Board of Trustees; Johnson C. Smith University, 1966–; Alpha Phi Alpha; first Black member, Mecklenburg County Medical Association; Johnson C. Smith Meritorious Award, 1954, 1968; Alpha Man of the Year, 1969; Sigma Pi Phi.

Ref: National Medical Association, *Journal,* v. 54, Jan. 1962, p. 116. [p]
Ebony, May 1974, p. 92. [p] only
Who's Who Among Black Americans, 1977, p. 739–40.

Ransom, Preston Lee   (1936- ——, M)

Engineer (electrical). Born in Peoria, IL, Jan. 2, 1936. B.S. (electrical engineering), University of Illinois, 1962; M.S., 1965; Ph.D. 1969. Electrical Engineer, Raytheon Company, 1962–63; Graduate Research Assistant, University of Illinois, 1963–67; Instructor, 1967–70; Assis-

tant Professor, Electrical Engineering, 1970–72; Associate Professor, Electrical Engineering, University of Illinois, 1972–.

Memberships and awards: Research fellow, University College of London, 1976; IEEE; Optical Society of America; American Society for Engineering Education, Sigma Xi.

Dissertation title: The Diffraction Transformation of Electromagnetic Fields between Two Parallel Planes.

Ref: *American Men and Women of Science,* 16th ed., p. 50.
Black Engineers in the United States, p. 165.
Who's Who Among Black Americans, 1985, p. 694.

Rawls, George   (1928- ——, M)

Physician. Surgeon. Born in Gainesville, FL, June 2, 1928. B.S., Florida A & M University, 1948; M.D., Howard University Medical School, 1952; Surgical Residency, V.A. Hospital, Dayton, OH, 1955–59; Clinical Instructor, Surgery, Ohio State University, 1957–59.

Memberships and awards: Alpha Phi Alpha, Board of Directors; fellow, American College of Surgeons; Guest Examiner, American Board of Surgeons; Diplomate, American Board of Surgery; President Marion County Medical Society; Citizen of the Year, Omega Psi Phi, 1971.

Pub: Articles in surgical journals.

Ref: *Who's Who Among Black Americans,* 1985, p. 695.

Rayfield, W. A.   (1873–19??, M)

Architect. Born in Macon, GA, May 10, 1873. B.S., Howard University, 1896; Certificate in Architecture, Pratt Institute, Brooklyn, NY, 1898; B.Arch., Columbia University, NY, 1899. Taught in Tuskegee Institute, AL, for 10 years, at the request of Booker T. Washington. Became Official Architect of the AME Zion Church; Architect for 16th Street Baptist Church, Birmingham, AL, costing $50,000; built doctor's residences at $35,000 and $10,000 respectively, Trinity Baptist Church, and many others.

Memberships and awards: General Supervising Architect of the Freedmen's Aid Society.

Ref: *Beacon Lights of the Race,* p. 457. [p] biog.

Read, Edward Parker   (1868–19??, M)

Physician. Born in Keysville, VA, 1868. Studied under private tutors. M.D., Baltimore University, 1889; received degree, Doctor of Refraction, Philadelphia Optical College, 1899; Ph.D., Princeton (IN) Normal & Industrial University, 1914.

Memberships and awards: Opened first drug store operated by a black person in Petersburg, VA, 1889. Physician specializing in women and children. Medical Examiner for Consolidated Benefit Association, Provident

Life Association, Galilean Fishermen, Good Templars and True Reformers, 1890. Opened a drug store in Philadelphia, 1891; established Eclectic Optical Institute and Eureka Sanitarium Association, Inc.; founded town of Readville, NJ.

Pub: *How, Where and When to Incorporate,* 1895.
Arranged Eureka Perpetual Calendar (copyright, 1904)

Ref: *Who's Who of the Colored Race,* 1915, p. 227–228.

Reddick, Mary Logan   (1914–1966, F)

Neuroembryologist. Born in Atlanta, GA, Dec. 31, 1914. B.A., Spelman College, 1935; M.S., Atlanta University, 1937; M.A., Radcliffe College, 1943; Ph.D., 1944. Instructor, Spelman College, 1937–39; Instructor to Professor, Morehouse College, 1939–52; Professor, Atlanta University, 1953–.

Memberships and awards: Phi Beta Kappa; Sigma Xi; Beta Kappa Chi; General Education Board fellow, Radcliffe; Ford Foundation fellow; Tissue Culture Association; Society of Zoologists; New York Academy of Sciences.

Dissertation title: The Differentiation of Embryonic Chick Medulla in Chorioallantoic Grafts.

Ref: *American Men of Science,* 11th ed., p. 4257.
Jet, Nov. 3, 1966, p. 17.
The Negro in Science, p. 180.
Who's Who of American Women, 1958, p. 1057.

Redmond, Sidney Dillon   (1871–1948, M)

Physician. Surgeon. Born in Ebenezer Holmes County, MS, Oct. 12, 1871. B.S., Rust College, 1894; M.A., 1904; M.D., Illinois Medical College, 1897. Passed Medical Exam State of Mississippi number one of 250 and one of the best in the history of the state, regardless of race. Chicago University. Postgraduate work at Harvard, Massachusetts General, and Mount Sinai Hospitals. Surgeon, owner of more than 100 houses in Mississippi, his wealth over six figures.

Ref: Wilson, Charles H. *God, Make Me a Man,* Boston, Meador, 1950. 61 p. (book about S. D. Redmond).
Mississippi Black History Makers, p. 355–360.
Beacon Lights of the Race, p. 133–138. [p] biog.

Reed, Cordell   (1938– ——, M)

Engineer (mechanical). Born in Chicago, IL, Mar. 26, 1938. B.S., M.E., University of Illinois, 1960. Design and construction operator, nuclear power generating station for 13 years; Vice-President, Commonwealth Edison Company of Chicago, which is in charge of nuclear licensing and environmental activities.

Memberships and awards: American Nuclear Society; Western Society of Engineers; National Technical Association.

Ref: *Black Contributors to Science and Energy Technology.*
Who's Who Among Black Americans, 1985, p. 699.

Reed, George W.   (1920– ——, M)

Chemist (nuclear). Geochemist. Born in Washington, DC. Sept. 25, 1920. B.S., Howard University, 1942; M.S., 1944; Ph.D. (chemistry), University of Chicago, 1952. S.A.M. Laboratories, 1944–45; Metallurgical Laboratories, University of Chicago, 1945–47; Associate Chemist. Argonne National Laboratories, 1952–68; Senior Scientist, Argonne National Laboratory, 1968–.

Memberships and awards: Sigma Xi; American Chemical Society; Rosenwald fellow, Chicago, 1948–49; American Physical Society.

Pub: *Radiation Dosimetry.* New York, Academic Press, 1964. (editor)

Ref: *American Men and Women of Science,* 14th ed., p. 4137.
In Black and White, p. 802.
The Negro in Science, p. 185.
Who's Who Among Black Americans, 1980–81, p. 663.
Ebony, Sept. 1970, p. 36.

Reed, James Whitfield   (1934– ——, M)

Physician. Endocrinologist. Born on Pahokee, FL, 1934. B.S., West Virginia State College; M.D., Howard University College of Medicine, 1963. Chairman, Department of Medicine, Morehouse School of Medicine; research in identification of lipid abnormalities in diabetes and similar diseases.

Memberships and awards: Fellowship, University of California Medical Center, San Francisco, 1977; American Endocrinology Society; American Diabetes Association.

Ref: *ABMS Compendium of Certified Medical Specialists,* v. 2, p. 1362.
Black Enterprise, Oct. 1988, p. 94.

Reid, Clarice D. Wills   (1931– ——, F)

Physician. Hematologist. Born in Birmingham, AL, Nov. 21, 1931. B.S., Talladega College, AL, 1952; Medical Technology, Meharry Medical College, 1954; M.D., University of Cincinnati School of Medicine, 1959. Deputy Director, Sickle Cell Program, Health Service Administration 1973–76; Chief, Sickle Cell Disease Branch and National Coordinator, Sickle Cell Disease Program, 1976; Director, Department of Pediatrics, Jewish Hospital, 1968–70; Acting Director, Division of Blood Diseases and Resources, National Heart, Lung and Blood Institutes.

Memberships and awards: National Medical Association; AAAS; American Academy of Pediatrics; American Public Health Association; American Society of Hematology; International Association for Sickle Cell Disease.

Pub: Co-author, Pediatric Chapter, in *Family Care*, Baltimore, Williams & Wilkins, 1973.

Ref: *Who's Who Among Black Americans*, 1985, p. 701.
Black Enterprise, Oct. 1988, p. 66. [p]

Reid, Edith C. (1934- ——, F)

Physician. Cardiologist. Born in Atlantic City, NJ, 1934. B.A., Hunter College; M.D., Meharry Medical College. Clinical Assistant and Assistant Physician, Flower and 5th Avenue Hospital; New York City Department of Health, Physician in the Chest Clinic; Chief of Medicine, Carter Community Health Center.

Memberships and awards: Queens Clinical Society; First Female and first black member of the State Board of Medicine; National Medical Association; New York Heart Association; American Geriatric Society; Achievement Award, Omega Psi Phi; Outstanding Service, Delta Sigma Theta.

Ref: *Profiles in Black*, p. 202-203. [p] p. 203.
Who's Who Among Black Americans, 1985, p. 701.

Remond, Sarah Parker (1826-1887?, F)

Physician. Born in Salem, MA, June 26, 1826. Academy of Salem, MA; Bedford College for Ladies (London), 1859-61; Medical study, Santa Maria Nuova Hospital, Florence, Italy, 1866-68. After 1868 practiced medicine in Italy (Florence and Rome). One of the first black women trained in a medical school and teaching hospital.

Memberships and awards: Participated regularly in the work of the Salem Female, Essex County, and Massachusetts Anti-Slavery Societies, Lectured throughout the North as an agent for American Anti-Slavery Society, 1856-58.

Ref: *Dictionary of American Medical Biography*, p. 631.
Porter, Dorothy B. Sarah Parker Remond, Abolitionist & Physician.
Journal of Negro History, v. 20, 1935, p. 287-293.
Notable American Women, 1607-1950, p. 136-137.

Renfroe, Earl Wiley (1907- ——, M)

Dentist. Orthodontist. Born in Chicago, IL, Jan. 9, 1907. D.D.S., University of Illinois, 1931; M.S., 1942. Professor Emeritis in Orthodontics, 1932-73; first black orthodontist in the United States.

Memberships and awards: Illinois and Chicago Dental Societies; American Dental Association; American Association of Orthodontists; Illinois State Society of Orthodontists; Chicago Council of Foreign Relations; Alpha Phi Alpha; President, Chicago Association of Orthodontists, 1963-64; Alumni Loyalty Award, University of Illinois, 1971; first Black Full Professor, University of Illinois; first Black Department Head, University of Illinois Medical Campus; first Black Colonel, U.S. Army, 1941-46.

Ref: *American Men and Women of Science*, 13th ed., p. 3654.
Who's Who Among Black Americans, 1985, p. 703.
Ebony, May 1954, p. 23. [p]

Reynolds, H. H. (1800s, M)

Inventor. Window ventilator for railroad cars, patent # 275,271, 1883; safety gate for bridges, patent #537,937, 1890, a barrier for bridges that could be opened or closed when the bridge was up.

Ref: *At Last Recognition in America*, v. 1, p. 36, 40.

Reynolds, James Richard (1870-19??, M)

Engineer. Mathematician. Born in Rockingham County, NC, Feb. 12, 1870. B.A., Bennett College, 1895; M.A., 1898; Engineering course, American School of Correspondence (Armour Institute), Chicago, IL; Ph.D. Wiley University, 1914. Teacher, Bennett College, 1895-98; Professor, Mathematics, Wiley University, 1909-11; led group of students who won prize for preparing college algebra key; as an electrical engineer, constructed light plant for Wiley University, installed lighting system, Boley, OK, largest black town in the United States.

Ref: *Who's Who of the Colored Race*, 1915, p. 229.

Rhaney, Mahlon Clifton (1916- ——, M)

Physiologist. Biologist. Born in Brunswick, GA, Oct. 31, 1916. B.A., Dillard University, 1939; M.S., University of Michigan, 1943; Ph.D., 1948. Assistant in Biology, Dillard University, 1939-40; Instructor, Physics, Florida A & M College, 1941; Instructor, Biology, Fort Valley State College, 1941-42; Instructor to Professor and Chairman of the Science Department. 1943-48; Professor and Head of the Biology Department, Florida A & M College, 1948-51 and Director of Division of Science, 1949-51; Dean of Instruction, 1951-53, and Dean of the College of Arts and Sciences, 1953-70; Vice-President for Academic Affair, 1970-.

Memberships and awards: AAAS; Sigma Xi; Florida Academy of Sciences; Beta Kappa Chi.

Dissertation title: Some Aspects of the Carbohydrate Metabolism of the Kingsnake (Lampropeltis Cetulus Floridana).

Ref: *American Men and Women of Science*, 12th ed., p. 5204.
Negro in Science, p. 180.

Rhodes, J. B. (1800s, M)

Inventor. Water closet, patent #639,290, 1899, similar to Latimer's of 1874 but used in homes, no more outhouses.

Ref: *At Last Recognition in America*, v. 1, p. 13.

Richard, Howard Mark Simon   (1934- —— , M)

Mathematician. Born in Baton Rouge, LA, June 16, 1934. B.S., Southern University; M.S. (mathematics), University of Notre Dame, 1963; Ph.D., Ohio State University, 1972. Instructor, Mathematics, West Livingston High School, Denham Springs, LA, 1955-57; Instructor, Mathematics, McKinley High School, Baton Rouge, LA, 1957-61; Assitant Professor, Mathematics, Southern University; Research Associate, Computer Center, Ohio State University, 1964-65; Teaching Associate, Department of Mathematics, Ohio State University, 1966-70; Assistant Professor, Mathematics, Ohio State University, 1970-72; Director, Computer Sciences and Professor, Mathematics, Norfolk State College, 1972-.

Memberships and awards: Pi Mu Epsilon, American Mathematical Society; Mathematical Association of America, National Association of Mathematicians.

Dissertation title: New Careers Mathematics: The Effect upon Achievement in Mathematics of Supplementing a Concept Centered Course for Adults with Experiences in Computer Utilization.

Ref: *Black Mathematicians and Their Works,* p. 293.
National Faculty Directory, 1988, p. 3158.

Richardson, A. C.   (1800s, M)

Inventor. Casket lowering device, patent #529,311, 1894, pulleys and strong straps lowering casket so they are not dropped or slipped, damaging the casket.

Ref: *At Last Recognition in America,* v. 1, p. 41.

Richardson, W. H.   (1800s, M)

Inventor. Patent #405,600, June 1889, for a leveler for a child's baby carriage to prevent it from tipping over.

Ref: Baker, *Inventions by Blacks, 1871-1900.*
Negro Almanac, p. 1069.

Richey, Charles U.   (1800s, M)

Inventor. Washington, DC, invented and patented several devices for registering calls and detecting the unauthorized use of the telephone.

Ref: *Negro in Our History,* 5th ed., p. 462.

Rickman, A. L.   (1800s, M)

Inventor. Rubberized shoe to act as covering to prevent feet from getting wet. Patent #598,816, 1898, forerunner of modern rubbers.

Ref: *At Last Recognition in America,* v. 1, p. 12.

Riddle, Estelle Massey   (1901-1981, F)

See: Osborn, Estelle Massey.

Rieras, Joseph Harrison   (1892-19??, M)

Architect. Engineer (architectural). Born in New Orleans, LA, Dec. 31, 1892. A & M College, 1908; Southern University, 1910; Professional Teachers College, Southern University, LA, 1922. Wilson Engineering Corporation; Professor, Physics and Chemistry, St. Joseph's College, Montgomery, AL, 1911-12; Junior Engineer, Kosky and Company, 1912-14; Professor, Mechanical Drafting, Houston Senior High School, 1914-; Architectural Engineer, 1920-.

Memberships and awards: American Technical Society; National Builder's Conference; Kappa Alpha Psi.

Ref: *Who's Who in Colored America,* 1941-44, p. 439.

Rillieux, Norbert   (1806-1894, M)

Inventor. Engineer. Born in New Orleans, LA, 1806. His father sent him to L'Ecole Central in Paris, 1830. He studied evaporating engineering. Invented a sugar refining pan in 1846, patent #4879. It was used later by sugar manufacturers in Cuba and Mexico. It was stated by Charles Brown, a chemist in the U.S. Department of Agriculture, that this was the greatest invention in the history of American Chemical Engineering. He died and was buried in Paris, France, 1894.

Ref: *At Last Recognition in America,* v. 1, p. 29.
Dictionary of American Negro Biography, p. 525-526.
Biographical History of Blacks in America Since 1528, p. 395-396.
Encyclopedia of Black America, 1981, p. 731-732.
Great Negroes Past and Present, p. 49-50, 62.
Negro Almanac, p. 640.
The Role of the American Negro in the Field of Science, p. 12-16.
Meade, George. Negro Scientist of Slavery Days. *Negro History Bulletin,* April 1957, p. 159-163. Reprinted from *Scientific Monthly,* 1946, p. 317-326.
Historical Afro-American Biographies, p. 117-118. [p]
Black Pioneers of Science and Invention, p. 13-23. [p] p. 14.
Ebony, May 1967, p. 48. [p]
Ebony, Oct. 1967, p. 45. [p]
The Black Book, p. 112-113.

Roberts, Carl Glennis   (1886-1950, M)

Physician. Surgeon. Gynecologist. Born in Hamilton County, IN, Dec. 15, 1886. Fairmont High School and Academy, 1905; M.D. Chicago College of Medicine and Surgery, Valparaiso University, 1911, he was the first black graduate of the Medical Department of Valparaiso University. First black gynecologist, Provident Hospital, 1916-30; Commandant of Sanitary Corps, Chicago Chapter of Red Cross, 1918-20; one of three physicians to appear before the American Medical Association requesting the removal of "Col." after the names of black physicians in the *AMA Directory;* they succeeded.

Memberships and awards: President, National Medical Association, 1927; Chicago Medical Society; Cook County Physicians Association; American Medical Association; Illinois Medical Association; Chicago Medical Society; Cook County Physicians Association; President, Chicago Physician, Dental, and Pharmaceutical Association; Kappa Alpha Psi; one of the first four blacks admitted to the American College of Surgeons.

Ref: Who's Who of the Colored Race, 1915, p. 232.
Who's Who in Colored America, 1927, p. 169–170. [p] opp. p. 170.
Who's Who in Colored America, 1928–29, p. 310.
Who's Who in Colored America, 1933–37, p. 444. [p] p. 441.
History of the Negro in Medicine, p. 77, 281. [p]
Dictionary of American Medical Biography, p. 641.
A Century of Black Surgeons, p. 273–276.
Drew, Charles R. Carl Glennis Roberts, M.D., 1886–1950. National Medical Association, Journal, v. 42, Mar. 1950, p. 109–110.
National Medical Association, Journal, v. 41, July 1949, p. 189–190.
Cobb, W. Montague. Carl Glennis Roberts, M.D., 1886–1950. National Medical Association, Journal, v. 52, Mar. 1960, p. 146–147.

Roberts, Erskine G.   (1919- —, M)

Engineer. Born in Cambridge, MA, Aug. 23, 1919. B.S.M.E., Northeastern University, 1932; B.S., MIT, 1932; M.S., 1933. Assistant to Director, Technical Division, Tuskegee Institute, 1933–35; Instructor, Electrical and Mechanical Engineering, Howard University, 1935–38; Associate Engineer Examiner, Power Division, Federal Works Agency, DC, 1938–40; Assistant Professor, Lincoln University, PA, 1940–42; Design and Development Engineer, P. R. Mallory Company, Inc., 1942–46; Chief Engineer, W. C. Grant Company, Inc., 1946–47; Consulting Engineer, 1947–54; Supervisory Project Engineer, Engineering Department of Public Works and Supply Division, 1954–56; Principal Engineer, Chicago, U.S. Public Housing Administration, 1956–60; Planning and Development Engineer, Argonne National Laboratories, 1960–69; Principal Engineer, P & W Engineers, Inc., 1969–71; Vice-President of W. U. Rouse Associates, Ltd.-Consultants, 1971–; research on power generation and systems—energy, magnet and nuclear coaling loops.

Memberships and awards: Army and Navy E Award, P. R. Mallory Company, Inc., 1944; Certificate of Merit, State of Indiana, 1956; National Society of Professional Engineers.

Ref: American Men and Women of Science, 12th ed., p. 5273.
Ebony, Mar. 1972, p. 7 [p]

Roberts, Eugene P.   (1868–1953, M)

Physician. Born in Louisburg, NC, Oct. 5, 1868. B.A., Lincoln University, 1891; M.A., Lincoln University;

M.D., New York Homeopathic Medical Association and Flower Hospital. 1894.

Memberships and awards: National Medical Society; New York Material Medica Society; Medico-Chirurgical Society; Academy of Pathological Science; Durham Medical Club; Board of Health, New York City, 1898–1912; Medical Society of Inspectors of Greater New York; Inspector of Department of Health and Lecturer on care of babies in Public School of New York City; Physician-in-charge, St. Cyprian's Baby Clinic; first Black member of the Board of Trustees of Lincoln University.

Ref: Who's Who in Colored America, 1928–29, p. 313.
Who's Who in Colored America, 1933–37, p. 444.
Who's Who in Colored America, 1941–44, p. 440.
History of the Negro in Medicine, p. 73. [p] p. 73.
Nine Black American Doctors, p. 84.
Crisis, May 1917, p. 231. [p]
New York State Journal of Medicine, April 1985, p. 143–144. [p]

Roberts, Louis W.   (1913- —, M)

Physicist. Born in Jamestown, NY, Sept. 1, 1913. B.A., Fisk University, 1935; M.S., University of Michigan, 1937. Research Assistant, Standard Oil of New Jersey, 1935–36; Graduate Assistant, University of Michigan, 1936–37; Instructor, Physics, St. Augustine's College, 1937–39; Professor, 1941–43; Associate Professor, Howard University, 1943–44; Director of Research, Microwave Associates, Inc., 1950–; Director of Energy and Environment, Transportation Systems Center, Department of Transportation, 1977–; research in microwave and optical techniques and components, plasma research and solid state component and circuit development; founded and ran his own microwave concern; NASA.

Memberships and awards: American Physical Society; American Mathematical Society.

Ref: American Men and Women of Science, 14th ed., p. 4237.
Black Contributions to Science Energy Technology, p. 110–111.
The Negro in Science, p. 190.

Roberts, Richard Samuel   (18??–1936, M)

Photographer. Self-taught. Operated a studio for 15 years, making individual and group portraits of the elite among blacks.

Ref: A True Likeness: The Black South of Richard Samuel Roberts, 1920–1936. [p] p. 83.
Fraser, C. Gerald. Blacks Before the Camera, New York Times Book Review, Mar. 19, 1987. p. 22.

Roberts, Shearley Olimer   (1910–19??, M)

Psychologist. Born in Alexandria, VA, 1910. B.A., Brown University, 1932; M.A., 1933 (both with honors); Ph.D. (psychology), University of Minnesota, 1944. Instructor,

Atlanta University, 1933–36; Teacher and Dean of Students, Arkansas A M & N College, 1939–42; Acting Dean, Dunbar Junior College, 1942–43; A M & N, 1944–45; Established and chaired the Psychology Department, Fisk University, 1951–52.

Memberships and awards: Fellow, Society for Research in Child Development; Division of Developmental Psychology, American Psychological Association; Sigma Xi; Psi Chi.

Dissertation title: The Measurement of Adjustment of Negro College Youth: Personality Scales for Whites Versus Criteria Intrinsic to Negro Groups.

Ref: *Even the Rat Was White,* p.168 [p] p. 169.

Robeson, Eslanda Goode   (1896–1965, F)

Anthropologist. Chemist. Born in Washington, DC, Dec. 15, 1896. B.S., Columbia University, 1918; one year, Columbia University Medical School. Chemist and Surgical Technician in charge of Surgical Pathological Laboratory of Presbyterian Hospital, NY, 1918–25; first black on the staff of the Presbyterian Hospital, resigned in 1925 to follow her husband, Paul Robeson, as his manager.

Pub: *African Journey,* 1945.

Ref: *Jet,* Dec. 30, 1965, p. 26–27. [p] p. 27.
Who's Who in Colored America, 1927, p. 171.
Selected Black American Authors.
Current Biography, 1945, p. 505–506. [p]

Robinson, Bernard Whitfield   (1918–1972, M)

Physician. Radiologist. Boston College; M.D., Harvard University. In 1942, while a student in Harvard Medical School, was made an ensign in the U.S. Naval Reserve; was first black to win a commission, U.S. Navy, June 18; Chief of Radiology at V.A. West Side Hospital in Chicago; first black Chief-of-Service in Chicago area V.A. Hospitals; Chief-of-staff, V.A. Hospital, New Haven, CT, 1965.

Ref: *Jet,* June 24, 1965, p. 11. [p]
Blacks in America, 1492–1976, p. 33.
Ebony, Mar. 1963, p. 73. [p]

Robinson, Elbert R.   (1800s, M)

Inventor. Chicago. Electric railway trolley, patent # 505,370, 1893, using electricity in overhead wires to propel a passenger carrying vehicle. Patents infringed upon by two large corporations, American Car & Foundry Company and Chicago City Railway Company. Instituted proceedings up to Supreme Court but was unable to have his patent protected. Won $31 million Supreme Court decision on invention of the grooved railway wheel.

Ref: *At Last Recognition in America,* v. 1, p. 24.
Negro Makers of History, 5th ed., p. 466–467.
Afro-American Encyclopedia, v. 5, p. 1275.
Blacks in Science: Astrophysicist to Zoologist, p. 36.

Robinson, Emory Irving   (1889–1961, M)

Physician. Born in 1889. B.A., Seldon Institute; M.D., Meharry Medical College, 1919. Anatomy Instructor, Meharry Medical College, 1919–21; House Physician, Hubbard Hospital, 1920–21; practiced medicine in Atlanta, GA, 1922–34; Courtesy Staff, California Hospital; Examining Physician, State Athletic Commission; Relations Committee, Social Agencies of Los Angeles.

Memberships and awards: Los Angeles County Medical Association; California State Medical Association; Southern California Medical, Dental, and Pharmaceutical Association; National Advisory Council of Colored Graduate Nurses Association; Vice-Speaker, House of Delegates, National Medical Association, four years, President, 1944-45.

Ref: *History of the Negro in Medicine,* p. 142. [p]
National Medical Association, Journal, v. 36, Nov. 1944, p. 200.
National Medical Association, Journal, v. 49, Nov. 1957, p. 422.
National Medical Association, Journal, v. 54, Nov. 1962. p. 724, 731. obit. [p] only

Robinson, Hilyard R.   (1899–1986, M)

Architect. Born in 1899. University of Pennsylvania; B.A., Columbia University School of Architecture, 1924 and University of Berlin. Designed public housing. Designed Henry Hudson Hotel in Troy, NY, 1926. Professor and Chairman, Department of Architecture, Howard University, 13 years.

Memberships and awards: Along with McKissack & McKissack Construction Company, was awarded contract for design and construction of Army AF Base, Tuskegee.

Ref: *In Black and White,* p. 825.
Negro Almanac, 1983, p. 1063–1064.
Jet, June 9, 1960, p. 9. [p]
Washington Post, Oct. 16, 1986, p. DC2.
Historical Afro-American Biographies, p. 243–244. [p]

Robinson, Lawrence Baylor   (1919– ——, M)

Physicist. Born in Tappahannock, VA, Sept. 14, 1919. B.S., Virginia Union University, 1939; M.A., Harvard, 1941; Ph.D. 1946. Instructor, Mathematics and Physics, Virginia Union, 1941–42; Instructor, Physics and Chemistry, 1944; Assistant Professor, Physics, Howard University, 1946–47; Instructor, Physical Sciences, University of Chicago, 1947–48; Associate Professor, Howard University, 1948–51; Research Physicist, Atomic Energy Research Division, U.S. Naval Research Laboratory, 1953–54; Assistant Professor, Brooklyn College, 1954–56; Member, Technical Staff, Space Technology Laboratories, Inc., Division of Thompson Ramo Wooldridge, Inc., 1956–60; Lecturer to Associate Professor to Professor of Engineering to Assistant Dean of the School of Engineering and Applied Sciences, University of California at Los Angeles, 1957–86.

Memberships and awards: John Thornton Kirkwood fellow, Harvard, 1945–46; American Physical Society; Sigma Xi; Beta Kappa Chi; Sigma Pi Sigma; New York Academy of Sciences.

Dissertation title: The Electric Potential at the Interface between Vitreous Silica and Aqueous Solutions of Electrolytes.

Ref: *The Negro in Science,* p. 191.
American Men and Women of Science, 13th ed., p. 3728.
Who's Who Among Black Americans, 1985, p. 720.
National Faculty Directory, 1986, p. 2863.
Crisis, Aug. 1946, p. 238. [p] only

Robinson, Lula Belle Stewart   (1920–1965, F)

Physician. First black specialist in children's heart cases and a staff physician in three hospitals.

Robinson, Paul Timothy   (1898–1966, M)

Physician. Surgeon. Pathologist. Born in Lewisville, AR, June 23, 1898. B.A., Bishop College, 1921; M.D., Meharry Medical College, 1931. Founded the Robinson Infirmary and Clinic, a 40-bed private hospital in New Orleans; Member, Surgical Staff and Senior Associate in Pathology, Flint Goodridge Hospital, New Orleans, 1937–; Re-established his surgical practice in Richmond, CA, 1953; Very active in civil rights.

Memberships and awards: Diplomate, National Board of Medical Examiners, 1936; American Medical Association; California Medical Association; Alameda Contra Costa Medical Association; National Medical Association .

Ref: Cobb, W. Montague. Paul Timothy Robinson, M.D., 1898–1966. National Medical Association, *Journal,* v. 58, July 1966, p. 321–323.
Medico-Chirurgical Society of the District of Columbia, Inc., *Bulletin,* Feb. 1949, p. 12.

Robinson, Roscoe, Jr.   (1928– ——, M)

Military (Army). General. Engineer. Born in St. Louis, MO, Oct. 11, 1928. B.S. (military engineering), U.S. Military Academy; M.P.I.A., University of Pittsburgh. Commanding General, Army, A.U.S. Garrison, Okinawa; Base Commander, 1975–78; Seventh Army, 1978–; NATO Military Command, U.S. Representative, 1982–.

Memberships and awards: First black four-star general in U.S. Army, Aug. 1982; second black to become a four-star general; Master Parachutist Badge; Silver Star with oak leaf cluster; Legion of Merit with two oak leaf clusters; Distinguished Flying Cross; Bronze Star; Air Medal (10 awards).

Ref: *In Black and White,* p. 829.
Who's Who Among Black Americans, 1985, p. 722.

Ebony, Nov. 1985, p. 342. [p]
Ebony, May 1978, p. 42. [p]
Black Americans in Defense of Our Nation, p. 120. [p]

Robinson, William Henry   (1900–19??, M)

Physicist (mathematical). Mathematician. Born in Louisville, KY, Mar. 3, 1900. B.S., University of Pittsburgh, 1922; M.A., Boston University, 1932; Ph.D. (physics), 1937. Chief Draftsman, Beckham Company, 1918; Power Plant Operator, Westinghouse, 1922; Assistant Director, Mechanics, Prairie View College, 1922–24; Chief Draftsman, L. A. S. Bellinger Company, 1924–25; Head, Department of Mathematics and Physics, Brick Junior College, 1925–33; Tillotson College, 1933–36; Head, Department of Physics and Chairman, Science Division, North Carolina College, 1938–; Director ESMWT Program, 1942–45; research in the measurement of elastic constants of crystals by determining the velocity of sound in the crystal.

Memberships and awards: National Institute of Science; American Association of Physics Teachers; Beta Kappa Chi; Mathematical Association of America.

Dissertation title: The Use of a Lummer Plate as an Auxiliary Spectrograph in the Study of H-Alpha of Hydrogen.

Ref: *Holders of Doctorates Among American Negroes,* p. 156.
American Men of Science, 10th ed., p. 3414.
The Negro in Science, p. 191.
Crisis, Aug. 1937, p. 230. [p]

Rock, John Sweat   (1825–1866, M)

Physician. Dentist. Lawyer. Born in Salem, NJ, Oct. 13, 1825. He studied medicine under Dr. Shaw and Dr. Gibbon and studied dentistry under Dr. Hubbard, opening an office in 1850. He was not admitted to medical school due to his color. Years later, he was admitted to the American Medical College, and upon completion, practiced both Medicine and Dentistry. In 1861 passed the bar in Massachusetts and was appointed justice of the peace. One of the first blacks to earn a medical degree in the United States, 1852 or 1853.

Memberships and awards: Appears to have been a member of Massachusetts Medical Science, but the Society records do not show it; first black to be sworn in to argue cases before the Supreme Court, 1865.

Ref: Brown, W. W. *The Black Man: His Antecedents, His Genius, and His Achievement.* p. 266–270, 1969.
Dictionary of American Negro Biography, p. 529–531.
History of the Negro in Medicine, p. 26–27. [p]
National Medical Association, *Journal,* v. 73, Suppl. Dec. 1981, p. 1209.
Dictionary of American Medical Biography, p. 645.
Contee, Clarence G. John Sweat Rock, M.D., Esq., 1825–66. National Medical Association, *Journal,* v. 68, May 1976, p. 237–242. [p] cover

Roddy, Leon (1922-——, M)

Entomologist. Born in 1922. B.S., Texas College; Ph.D., Ohio State University. Spider classification.

Dissertation title: A Morphological study of the Respiratory Horns Associated with the Puparia of some Diptera, Especially Ophyra Anescens (WIED.).

Ref: *Ebony,* Mar. 1962, p. 65-70. [p]

Rodgers, Moses (18??-1890, M)

Engineer (mining). Born in Missouri. Owned and managed several mines in California.

Ref: *Historical Afro-American Biographies,* p. 118.

Rogers, Charles Calvin (1929-——, M)

Military (Army). Major General. Retired. Born in Claremont, WV, Sept. 6, 1929. B.S. (general mathematics), West Virginia State College; M.S., Shippenburg College; Field Artillery School; Artillery and Missile School. Over 24 years of active command service. Major General, Sept. 1975.

Memberships and awards: Distinguished Flying Cross; Bronze Star with V Device and three Oak Leaf Clusters; Air Medal; Army Commendation Medal with three Oak Leaf Clusters; Joint Service Commendation Medal; Purple Heart; Parachutist Badge.

Ref: *Black Americans in Defense of Our Nation,* p. 123. [p]
    Ebony, May 1978, p. 42. [p]
    Who's Who Among Black Americans, 1985, p. 724.

Rolfe, Daniel Thomas (1902-1968, M)

Physician. Physiologist. Born in Tampa, FL, Mar. 1, 1902. B.S., Florida A & M College, 1925; M.D., Meharry Medical College, 1927. Instructor in Anatomy, Meharry Medical College, 1927-28; Professor, Meharry Medical College, 1930-38; Chairman, Department of Physiology and Pharmacology, 1938-; Dean, School of Medicine, Meharry Medical College, 1952-66.

Memberships and awards: Rockefeller Foundation fellow, Medical School, Cornell University, 1944; General Education Board fellow, 1928-30; Distinguished Service Medal, National Medical Association, 1956; National Association of Biology Teachers; Executive Secretary, Meharry Alumni Association, 1939-59.

Ref: National Medical Association, *Journal,* v. 44, Sept. 1952, p. 395. [p]
    National Medical Association, *Journal,* v. 60, Nov. 1968, p. 528, 530-531. obit, eulogy, biog

Roman, Charles Lightfoot (1889-19??, M)

Physician. Born in Port Elgin, Ont., Canada, May 19, 1889. B.S., Fisk University, 1910; M.D., McGill University, 1919. Soldier in Canadian Army Medical Corps in France, 1914-17; House Surgeon, Senior Resident, Admitting Officer and Acting Medical Superintendent, The Montreal General Hospital, 1917-21.

Memberships and awards: Canadian Medical Association; Imperial Register, Great Britain and Ireland.

Pub: Severe Industrial Injuries to the Fingers and Their Treatment. *Canadian Medical Journal,* Sept. 1923.
    Sacrifice & Burnt Incense. *Social Welfare Journal,* Aug. 1924.

Ref: *Who's Who in Colored America,* 1927, p. 174. [p] opp. p. 174.
    Who's Who in Colored America, 1933-37, p. 449.
    Who's Who in Colored America, 1938-40. [p]

Roman, Charles Victor (1864-1934, M)

Physician. Otolaryngologist. Born in Williamsport, PA, July 4, 1864. M.A., Fisk University; M.D., Meharry Medical College, 1890. Royal Ophthalmic Hospital and Central Nose, Throat, and Ear Hospital, London, 1904. Director of Health, Fisk University, 1919-33; established and headed the Department of Eye, Ear, Nose and Throat, Meharry Medical College, 27 years, becoming Emeritus Professor, 1931.

Memberships and awards: Fifth President, National Medical Association, 1904-05; first editor of *Journal* of the National Medical Association, 1909-19; Official Medical Lecturer, U.S. Army, 1918-19.

Pub: *American Civilization and the Negro,* Philadelphia, Davis, 1916. 434 p.
    Meharry Medical College, A History. Freeport, N.Y., Books for Libraries Press, 1972, 224 p.
    Numerous articles in the National Medical Association, *Journal.*
    A Knowledge of History is Conducive to Racial Solidarity, Nashville TN, Sunday School Union Print. 1911, 54 p.

Ref: *Dictionary of American Negro Biography,* p. 532.
    Encyclopedia of Black America, p. 735-736.
    Who's Who of the Colored Race, 1915, p. 233.
    Who's Who in Colored America, 1927, p. 174. [p] opp. p. 174.
    Who's Who in Colored America, 1928-29, p. 316. [p] opp. p. 316.
    Who's Who in Colored America, 1933-37, p. 450.
    Educating Black Doctors, p. 33-34.
    Dictionary of American Medical Biography, p. 646-647.
    History of the Negro in Medicine, p. 68-70. [p] p. 69.
    Cobb, W. Montague. Charles Victor Roman. National Medical Association, *Journal,* v. 45, July 1953, p. 301-305.
    Crisis, Nov. 1918, p. 30. [p] only

Romm, Harry Josef (1899-19??, M)

Biologist. Plant Morphologist. Born in Navasota, TX, Sept. 3, 1899. B.S., Iowa State College, 1930; M.S., 1934;

Ph.D. (plant morphology), 1946. Instructor, Biology, Tuskegee Institute, 1926–28; Associate Professor, Prairie View College, 1928–29; Professor and Head of the Department, Tuskegee Institute, 1930–.

Memberships and awards: Sigma Xi; Botanical Society; National Institute of Science.

Dissertation title: the Development and Structure of the Vegetative and Reproductive Organs of Kudzu, Pueraria Thunbergiana (Sieb. and Zucc.) Benth.

Ref: *American Men of Science,* 8th ed., p. 2106.
National Register, 1952, p. 218.
Crisis, Aug. 1946, p. 243. [p]

Rose, Raymond Edward   (1926– ——, M)

Engineer (aerospace). Born in Canton, OH, July 17, 1926. B.S. (aerospace engineering), University of Kansas, 1951; M.S., University of Minnesota, 1956; Ph.D. 1966. From Junior Engineer to Scientist in Aerodynamics, Rosemont Aero Laboratories, University of Minnesota, 1951–59; Scientist, 1959–62; Principal Research Scientist to Project Staff Engineer/Supervisor, Aerodynamics, Fluid Mechanics and Control Science Section, Research Department, Systems and Research Center, Honeywell, Inc., Minneapolis, MN, 1966–76; Program Manager, Aerodynamics and Active Controls, Aircraft Energy Efficiency Program Officer, 1976–79; Program Manager, General Aviation, Subsonic Aircraft Technology Officer, 1979–84; Manager, General Aviation/Commuter Aerodynamics and Coordinator, Technology Transfer Control, Washington, DC, 1984–.

Memberships and awards: American Helicopter Society; AIAA; Tau Beta Pi; Sigma Gamma Tau; Sigma Tau.

Dissertation title: Experimental Investigations of Instability of Supersonic Flow about Cup-Shaped Bodies.

Ref: *Profiles in Excellence (NASA),* p. 66. [p]
Who's Who Among Black Americans, 1985, p. 727.

Ross, Julian Waldo   (1884–1961, M)

Physician. Obstetrician. Born in Albany, GA, July 10, 1884. B.A., Lincoln University, 1907; M.D., Howard University, 1911; Postgraduate work, Gynecology, Women's Hospital and Harlem Hospital, 1923. Staff, Freedmen's Hospital, 1914–; Head of Department of Obstetrics and Gynecology, Howard University College of Medicine; taught 44 years known as "Mr. Chips."

Memberships and awards: Kappa Alpha Psi.

Ref: *Who's Who in Colored America,* 1928–29, p. 316.
Who's Who in Colored America, 1927, p. 175.
Jet, April 20, 1961, p. 50. [p]
Who's Who in Colored America, 1933–37, p. 450.
Dictionary of American Medical Biography, p. 650.
Cobb, W. Montague. Julian Waldo Ross, M.D., 1884–. National Medical Association, *Journal,* v. 48, Nov. 1956, p. 430.

Cobb, W. Montague. Julian Waldo Ross, M.D., 1884–. National Medical Association, *Journal,* v. 52, May 1960, p. 220–222. List of his publications included on cover. [p]

Ross, Marshall E.   (1892–19??, M)

Physician. Surgeon. Gynecologist. Born in Newport, RI, Nov. 3, 1893. B.S., Howard University, 1918; M.D., 1922; New York Post Graduate Medical College, 1923. Outpatient Department, Medical Clinic, Harlem Hospital, 1923–24; Out-patient Department, Gynecological Clinic, 1923–24; Chief Gynecological Clinic, Harlem Hospital, 1927–.

Memberships and awards: American Medical Association; New York County Medical Society; North Harlem Medical Society; Chi Delta Mu Medical Fraternity; second black to be appointed Adjunct Gynecologist of Harlem Hospital, 1927.

Ref: *Who's Who in Colored America,* 1928–29, p. 316. [p] opp. p. 320.
Who's Who in Colored America, 1941-44, p. 446.

Ross, William A.   (1937– ——, M)

Physician. Orthopedist. Surgeon. Born in Detroit, MI, Nov. 26, 1937. B.S., Wayne State University, 1960; M.D., Meharry Medical College, 1964, Orthopedic Consultant, West Oak Health Center; Teacher, Children's Hospital, 1964–65; in the Navy's 66-year history of Submarine Service, he was the first black Submarine Doctor on the George C. Marshall commissioned in Newport News, 1966–69.

Memberships and awards: Arlington Medical Group; American Medical Association; National Medical Association; Alpha Phi Alpha.

Ref: *Ebony,* Nov. 1966, p. 112–114, 116, 118. [p]
Who's Who Among Black Americans, 1985, p. 729.

Rouse, Carl Albert   (1926– ——, M)

Physicist. Astrophysicist. Born in Youngstown, OH, July 14, 1926. B.S., Case Western Reserve, 1951; M.S., California Institute of Technology, 1953; Ph.D. (physics), 1956. Senior Research Engineer, North American Aviation, Inc., 1956–57; Theoretical Physicist, Lawrence Radiation Laboratory, CA, 1957–65; Research Associate in Theoretical Physics, Space Science Laboratories, CA, 1965–68; Staff Physicist, Gulf Radiation Technologies, 1968–74; Staff Scientist, General Atomic Company, 1974–.

Memberships and awards: AAAS; fellow, American Physical Society; American Astronomical Society; International Astronomical Union.

Dissertation title: Proportional-Counter Selection of Cloud Chamber events.

Ref: *American Men and Women of Science*, 15th ed., p. 313.

Routen, Louie (188?–1986, M)

Physician. B.S.; M.D. One of the first black physicians in Arkansas. He practiced medicine in Little Rock and North Little Rock from 1921 to the mid-seventies and founded Routen Nursing Home in 1961. Died in Los Angeles.

Ref: *Jet*, Sept. 8, 1986, p. 18.

Royal, Frank Spencer (1939– ——, M)

Physician. Born in Lynchburg, VA, Sept. 15, 1939. B.S. (chemistry) (cum laude), Virginia Union University, 1961; M.D., Meharry Medical College, 1968. Private practice, family medicine, 1969–; Assistant Clinical Professor, Family Practice, Medical College of Virginia.

Memberships and awards: Advisory Board of Trustees, Richmond Memorial Hospital; President, National Medical Association, 1980–81; American Academy of Family Physicians; Richmond Academy of Family Practice; American Medical Association; Medical Society of Virginia; Richmond Academy of Medicine; Governor's Advisory Committee on Medicare and Medicaid for the commonwealth of Virginia.

Ref: National Medical Association, *Journal*, v. 73, Nov. 1981, p. 1093. [p]
National Medical Association, *Journal*, v. 74, June 1982. [p] cover

Ruggles, David (1810–1849, M)

Hydropathic Practitioner. Born in Norwich, CT, Mar. 15, 1810. Free-born black who, although blind, built the first building in the United States for hydrotherapeutic purposes. Northampton Water Cure Establishment, Florence, MA.

Ref: *History of the Negro in Medicine*, p. 23–24. [p]
National Medical Association, *Journal*, v. 73, 1981, p. 1208.
Porter, Dorothy B. David Ruggles, 1810–1849, Part I, Hydropathic Practitioner. National Medical Association, *Journal*, v. 49, Jan. 1957, p. 67–72.
Porter, Dorothy B. David Ruggles, Part II. National Medical Association, *Journal*, v. 49, Mar. 1957, p. 130–134. (extensive bibliography)

Russell, Alfred Pierpont, Jr. (1881–19??, M)

Dentist. Born in South Norfolk, VA, Sept. 18, 1881. St. Paul's College, 1896–1901; B.S., Howard University, 1905; D.M.D., Harvard University Dental School, 1908. Gave clinic on treatment of cleft palate cases on invitation from Massachusetts Dental Society, Boston, MA,

May 8, 1914. First black appointed on visiting staff of Forsyth Dental Infirmary for Children, 1915–23.

Memberships and awards: University Dental Alumni Association; Massachusetts Dental Society; American Dental Society; Bay State Medical and Dental Society; Omega Psi Phi.

Ref: *Who's Who in Colored America*, 1927, p. 176. [p]
Who's Who in Colored America, 1928–29.
Who's Who of the Colored Race, 1915, p. 235.
Who's Who in Colored America, 1933–37, 452. [p]
Who's Who in Colored America, 1938–40, p. [p]
Who's Who in Colored America, 1941–44, p. 450. [p]

Russell, Edwin Roberts (1913– ——, M)

Chemist. Inventor. Born in Columbia, SC, June 19, 1913. B.A., Benedict College, 1935; M.S., Howard University, 1937; Assistant and Instructor, Chemistry, Howard University, 1936–42; Assistant, Metallurgical Laboratories, University of Chicago, 1942–47; Consultant in Chemistry, 1947–49; Chairman, Division of Science, Allen University, 1947–53; Research Chemist, E. I. DuPont de Nemours & Company, Inc., 1953–; conducted research in bio-assay, radioactive tracer, gas absorption and ion exchange absorption, monomolecular films, radioactive waste treatment.

Memberships and awards: AAAS; American Chemical Society; Honorary Dr. of Science, Benedict College, 1974; eleven patents on atomic energy processes.

Ref: *Who's Who Among Black Americans*, 1985, p. 733.
American Men and Women of Science, 13th ed., p. 3823.
The Negro in Science, p. 185.

Russell, L. A. (1800s, M)

Inventor. Guard attachment for beds, preventing invalids and infants from falling out. Patent #544,381, 1895.

Ref: *At Last Recognition in America*, v. 1, p. 11.

Ruth, William Chester (1880–19??, M)

Inventor. Inventor of baler feeder, cinder spreader, automatic tie for hay baler, and war time bombsight.

Ref: *Ebony*, Oct. 1950, p. 87–92. [p]

Ryder, Earl T. (1900s, M)

Engineer. At one time, Chief Engineer, Champion Company, Springfield.

Ref: Drew. Negro Scholars in Scientific Research. *Journal of Negro History*, v. 35, 1950: p. 142.

S

Sampson, Calvin Coolidge (1928- ——, M)

Physician. Pathologist. Born in Cambridge, MD, Feb. 1, 1928. B.S. (chemistry), Hampton Institute, 1947; M.D., Meharry Medical College, 1951. Assistant Director of Laboratory, Episcopal Hospital, Philadelphia, PA, 1956-58; Director of Laboratories, Freedmen's Hospital, Howard University, 1958-75; Assistant Professor and Professor of Pathology, Howard University School of Medicine, 1958-.

Memberships and Awards: Editor, *Journal of the National Medical Association*, 1978-80; Vice-President, Board of Trustees, Hospital for Sick Children, Washington, D.C., 1979-.

Pub: Eighty scientific articles in medical journals.

Ref: National Medical Association, *Journal*, v. 73, Dec. 1981, p. 1235.
Who's Who Among Black Americans, 1985, p. 736.
ABMS Compendium of Certified Medical Specialists, v. 4, p. 508.

Sampson, G. T. (1800s,-M)

Inventor. Born in Dayton, OH. Clothes dryer, patent # 476, 416, 1892, a heating device operated by a motor extracting moisture from clothing. Forerunner of present day gas and electric dryers.

Ref: *At Last Recognition in America*, v. 1, p. 10.
The Black Book, p. 110.

Sampson, Henry Thomas (1934- ——, M)

Engineer (nuclear). Inventor. Born in Jackson, MS, April 22, 1934. B.S. (chemical engineering), Purdue University, 1956; M.S. (engineering), University of California, L.A., 1961; Ph.D. (nuclear engineering), University of Illinois, 1967. Research Engineer, U.S., Naval Weapons Center, 1956-62; Member of the Technical Staff, 1967-81; Director of Planning and Operations, Space Text Program, Aerospace Corporation, 1981-; Several patents for propellants.

Memberships and Awards: AAAS; American Nuclear Society; American Institute of Aeronautics and Astronautics; AEC fellowship, 1962-67; Omega Psi Phi; Advisory Commission on Nuclear Engineering.

Dissertation title: A theoretical and Experimental Analysis of the Gamma-Electric Cell.

Pub: Journal articles in Nuclear Society publications.

Ref: *Black Engineers in the United States*, p. 174-175.
American Men and Women of Science, 16th ed., p. 415.
Who's Who Among Black Americans, 1985, p. 736

Samuels, John Clifton (1924- ——, M)

Engineer (electrical). Born in Bishopville, NC, June 26, 1924. B.S. (electrical engineering), Polytech Institute of Brooklyn, 1948; M.S. (applied mathematics), New York University, 1950; Ph.D. (engineering science), Purdue University, 1957. Aeronautical Research Scientist, NASA Lewis Flight Propulsion Laboratory, 1948-52; Electronics Research Engineer, Farnsworth Electronics Laboratory, 1952-54; Assistant in Engineering Science, Purdue University, 1954-57; Associate, 1957-65; Professor of Mechanical Engineering and Head of the Department, 1965-66; Professor of Electrical Engineering and Chairman of the Department, Howard University, 1966-.

Memberships and awards: American Society of Engineering Education; Institute of Electrical and Electronics Engineers; Acoustical Society of America; Society of Engineering Science; New York Academy of Science; Beta Kappa Nu; Tau Beta Pi.

Dissertation title: On Stochastic Linear Systems.

Ref: *Black Engineers in the United States*, p. 175.
American Men and Women of Science, 14th ed., p. 4398.

Sanders, Robert (1900s,- M)

Engineer (electrical). Inventor. B.S. (electrical engineering), Pacific State University; M.S., West Coast University. He holds eight patents in antenna microwave technology. Manager of Antenna/Microwave Section, ITT Gilfillan, Van Nuys, CA.

Ref: *Ebony*, Jan. 1987, p. 6. [p]

Sanders, Robert B. (1938- ——, M)

Biochemist. Born in Augusta, GA, Dec. 9, 1938. B.S., Paine College, 1959; M.S., University of Michigan, 1961; Ph.D., 1964; Post-Doctoral, 1965. Visiting Scientist, Batelle Memorial Institute, 1970-71; Visiting Associate Professor, University of Texas Medical School, 1974-75; Program Director, National Science Foundation, 1978-79; Associate Professor, University of Kansas, 1966; Consultant, National Research Council, 1973-77; Intery Research Corporation, 1972-80; Department of Education, 1983; National Science Foundation, 1983-84.

Memberships and awards: Board of Higher Education of the United Methodist Church; Board of Directors of the Child Development Center, 1968-; Post-Doctoral fellowship, NIH, 1974-75; American Cancer Society, 1964-66; Sigma Xi; American Society of Biological Chemists.

Dissertation title: The Effect of Insulin on 1-Aminocyclopentane-Carboxylic Acid Distribution in the Rat.

Pub: 45 scientific articles.

Ref: *Who's Who Among Black Americans,* 1985,p. 738.
American Men and Women of Science, 16th ed., p. 423.

Santomee, Lucas (1600s–M)

Physician. Born in the 1600s. Received a medical degree in Holland and practiced in the Colony of New York under the Dutch and the British. Also received a grant of land for his services to the Colony in 1667. First black physician in the United States.

Ref: *Ebony Handbook,* 1974, p.361.
Encyclopedia of Black America, p. 670.
Great Negroes Past and Present, p. 49.
Nine Black American Doctors, p. 6.

Sarreals, E. Don (1931– ——, M)

Meteorologist. Born in Winston Salem, NC, Sept. 22, 1931. B.S. (meteorology), 1957; M.S., New York University, 1961. National Weather Service, Forecast Office, New York, NY, Supervisor, Radar Meteorologist, 1961–69; WRCTV Meteorologist, 1969–75; President/Consultant, Storm Finders, Inc., 1969–76; Dissemination Meteorologist, National Weather Service Headquarters, 1976–80; TV Meteorologist, Maryland Center for Public Broadcasting, 1976–81; Chief Operator NEXRAD Project, NOAA/ NWS.

Memberships and awards: National Academy of Sciences; Common Disasters and Media, 1977–75; National Telecommunications Information Agency's Teletext Committee,1978–80; American Meteorological Society, 1955–; National Weather Association, 1980–; Ward Medal in Meteorology, City College of New York,1957.

Pub: National Weather Service Forecasting Handbook #2, 1978.

Ref: *Who's Who Among Black Americans,* 1985, p. 739.

Satcher, David (1941– ——, M)

Physician. Certified Family Practice. College President. Born in Anniston, AL, Mar. 2, 1941. B.S., Morehouse College, 1963; M.D., Case Western Reserve; Ph.D., 1970. Director, King-Drew Medical Center, 1972–75; Associate Director, King-Drew Sickle Cell Center, 1973–75; Assistant Professor, UCLA School of Medicine, 1974–76; Professor and Chairman, Department of Family Medicine, Morehouse College School of Medicine; President, Meharry Medical College, 1982–.

Memberships and awards: American Academy of Family Physicians; American Society of Human Genetics; Board of Directors, Society of Teachers of Family Medicine; Phi Beta Kappa; Outstanding Morehouse Alumnus Award, 1973; Award for Medical Education for Sickle Cell Disease, 1973; Macy Foundation Faculty fellow in Community Medicine, 1972–73; Dudley Seaton Memorial Award; Outstanding Alumnus, Case Western Reserve University, 1980.

Dissertation title: The Effects of Iodine-131 and X-Radiation on the Chromosomes of Peripheral Blood Leukacytes.

Ref: *Jet,* Mar. 17, 1986, p.23.
Who's Who Among Black Americans, 1985, p. 739.
Jet, June 16, 1986, p.37.
Ebony, Mar. 1986, p.42, 44, 46, 48, 50. [p] p.44.
National Medical Association, *Journal,* v. 75, Feb. 1983, p. 210, 213.[p] Inauguration

Saulsberry, Guy O. (1909–19??, M)

Physician. Born in Greenville, KY, July 15, 1909. M.D., Howard University Medical School, 1927. Founder and Medical Director, Kirwood General Hospital, 1943—two buildings with 84 beds, it was the largest black-owned hospital in Detroit.

Memberships and awards: Omega Psi Phi; Seminar Society; National Medical Associations; Detroit Medical Association; Wolverline Medical Association; Honorary Dr. of Humane Letters, Shaw College of Detroit, 1972; Flight for Freedom Award; Physician of the Year, Detroit Medical Society, 1968; General Practitioner of the Year Award, National Medical Association, 1972.

Ref: *Who's Who Among Black Americans,* 1985, p. 740.
Ebony, Oct. 1950, p. 38. [p]
National Medical Association, *Journal,* v. 61, Sept. 1969, p. 446–448. [p]

Saunders, Elijah (1934– ——, M)

Physician. Surgeon (cardiac). Born in Baltimore, MD, Dec. 9, 1934. B.S., Morgan State College, 1956; M.D., University of Maryland School of Medicine, 1960. Intern, Residency, University of Maryland Hospital, 1960–63. Chief, Cardiology, Provident Hospital, 1966–.

Memberships and awards: American Medical Association: Maryland Society of Cardiology; American College of Physicians; American College of Cardiology; Bronze Service Medal; Founder, Heart House.

Ref: *Who's Who Among Black Americans,* 1985, p. 740.
Black Enterprise, Oct. 1988, p. 94.

Saunders, Griffin Augustus (188?–1955, M)

Physician. Born in Newark, DE, Sept. 13, 18??. M.D., Medical Chirurgical College, 1914. Douglas Staff Physician, Philadelphia's Mercy Hospital, 25 Years.

Memberships and awards: National Medical Association; Philadelphia County Medical Association; American Medical Association; Alpha Phi Alpha.

Ref: *Jet,* July 14, 1955, p. 49.
Who's Who in Colored America, 1941–44, p. 454.

Sayles, James H.   (1919– ——, M)

Chemist. Born in San Antonio, TX, Oct. 17, 1919. B.A., Arkansas State College, 1941; M.S., Michigan State College, 1947. Chairman of the Science Division, Bennett College, 1948–; specialized in boron chemistry.

Memberships and awards: National Institute of Science; Beta Kappa Chi.

Ref: *The Negro in Science,* p. 185.
National Faculty Directory, 1987, p. 2986.

Scott, Benjamin Franklin   (1922– ——, M)

Radiochemist. Chemist (inorganic). Born in Columbia, SC, Oct. 19, 1922. B.A., Morehouse College, 1942; M.S., University of Chicago, 1950, Junior Chemist, Metallurgical Laboratory, University of Chicago, 1943–46; Subcontractor, manufacturer of Geiger counters, 1946–50; Radio-chemist, Nuclear Instrument and Chemical Company, 1950; Chemist to Chief Chemist, Nuclear-Chicago Corporation, 1949–63; Technical Director, NEN Assay Corporation, 1963–.

Memberships and awards: American Chemical Society; member of Subcommittee on quantitative measurement of radioactive particles, the evaluation of counting errors, and counter efficiency.

Ref: *The Negro in Science,* p. 186.
American Mean of Science, 11th ed., p. 4779.

Scott, David Jr.   (1936– ——, M)

Engineer (civil). Chemist. Born in Campbell, OH, July 13, 1936. B.S. (chemistry), Central State College, 1957; M.S. (civil engineering), Oklahoma State University, 1971; Ph.D., 1973. Chemist, Bowser Morner Testing Laboratory, 1957–58; Research Chemist, University of Oklahoma Medical School, 1960–63; Industrial Waste Chemist, U.S. Air Force, Tinker Air Force Base, OK, 1963–65; Sanitary Chemist, Oklahoma State Department of Health, 1965–70; Traineeship, Oklahoma State University, Stillwater.

Memberships and awards: American Society of Civil Engineers; American Chemical Society; Chi Epsilon.

Dissertation title: Studies on the Performance of the "Hydrolytically Assisted" Extended Aeration Process as a Means of Treating Soluble Organic Waste Materials.

Ref: *Black Engineers in the United States,* p. 176.

Scott, Douglas Grant   (1868–19??, M)

Physician. Born in Melvale, MD, Sept. 6, 1868. Morgan College, Baltimore, 1885; M.D., Howard University Medical College, 1895.

Ref: *Who's Who in Colored America,* 1941–44, p. 455.
Howard University Medical Department, p. 213.
A Century of Black Surgeons, p. 449.

Scott, Evelyn Patterson   (19??– ——, F)

Mathematician. Born in Birmingham, AL. B.S., Alabama A & M University, Normal, AL; M.S. (mathematics), Atlanta University; Ph.D. (mathematics), Wayne State University, 1974. Operations Research Analyst, Center of Naval Analysis; Operations Research Analysts, General Services Administration.

Dissertation title: An Alternative Bayesian Model.

Ref: *Kenschaft, Patricia C. Black Women in Mathematics in the United States, American Mathematical Monthly,* v. 88, Oct. 1981, p. 600.

Scott, Roland Boyd   (1909– ——, M)

Physician. Pediatrician. Born in Houston, TX, April 18, 1909. B.S., Howard University, 1931; M.D., 1934. First black pediatrician, American Board of Pediatrics, 1939. Professor of Pediatrics, Howard University Medical College, 1947–73; Director, Center for Sickle Cell Disease, 1971–; Chief Pediatrician, Freedmen's Hospital (now Howard University Hospital); delivered first scientific paper ever by a black before the District of Columbia Medical Society.

Memberships and awards: Distinguished Service Medal, National Medical Association, 1966; Board of Directors, Health Foundation of DC, 1965–72; Visiting Professor, Children's Medical Center and Department of Pediatrics, Harvard Medical School, 1970; Advisory Committee, National Sickle Cell Disease Program, National Institutes of Health, 1982–86; Jacobi Award, American Academy of Pediatrics, 1985; American Medical Association; AAAS; American Society of Pediatric Hematology and Oncology; American Pediatric Society; Vice-President, American Academy of Allergy, 1966–67; 1987 recipient of $100,000 Award of Excellence from Ronald McDonald's Childrens Charities for his work with sickle cell disease to be used by the Center at Howard University for research; first black physician certified in Pediatrics.

Ref: *ABMS Compendium of Certified Medical Specialist,* v. 4, p. 1221.
American Men and Women of Science, 16th ed., p. 588.
Encyclopedia of Black America, p. 748–749.
Who's Who Among Black Americans, 1985, p. 746.
Jet, May 29, 1952, p. 15. [p]
Jet, Mar. 20, 1958, p. 11.
Ebony, Dec. 1949, p. 85. [p]
Ebony Success Library, v. 1, p. 276. [p]
Medico-Chirurgical Society of the District of Columbia, Inc., *Bulletin,* May/Sept. 1949, p. 3. [p]
Leaders in American Science, 5th ed., p. 625.

Scrottron, S. R.   (1800s, M)

Inventor. Curtain rod, long metal tube open at each end to attach curtains to a supporting wall structure, patent

#481,720, 1892, no further need to nail curtains over windows.

Ref: At Last Recognition in America, v. 1, p. 10.

Scurlock, Addison M.   (1883–1964, M)

Photographer. Born in Fayetteville, NC, 1883. Silver prints. His photographs are in Moore and Spingarn Research Center, Howard University, Schomberg Center, Library of Congress, and the Corcoran Gallery of Art. Studio in Washington, DC for many years.

Ref: Black Photographers 1840–1940 a Bio-Bibliography, p. 15. [p] p. 61.
Crisis, June 1932, p. 186.

Scurlock, Herbert Clay   (1875–1952, M)

Physician. Chemist. Born in Fayetteville, NC, 1875. B.A., Livingstone College, NC, 1895; M.D., Howard University Medical School, 1900; M.A., Columbia University, 1915. Assistant in Chemistry and Lecturer in x-Ray and Electrotherapy, Howard University Medical School; in charge of Chemistry and Physics in the School of Liberal Arts, 1905; Full Professor and Head of the Department of Physiological Chemistry.

Memberships and awards: President, Medico-Chirurgical Society of the District of Columbia, 1916; American Chemical Society; AAAS; National Geographic Society; National Medical Society.

Ref: National Medical Association, Journal, v. 45, Jan. 1953, p. 78. [p]

Seacole, Mary Grant   (1805–1881, F)

Nurse. Born of Jamaican parents in 1805. With no formal training she nursed in Panama and Cuba during cholera and yellow fever epidemics; performed a post mortem on an infant who had died of cholera in order to learn more about the disease. She was denied her request to join Florence Nightingale in the Crimea. She purchased supplies and on her own opened a lodging house in the Crimea to nurse the sick. She also volunteered in the hospital working with Florence Nightingale and thus saved thousands of lives.

Memberships and awards: Long after the war, the British government gave her a medal for her services. Mary Seacole Hall is on the Campus of the University of the West Indies.

Ref: The Path We tread, p. 2–4. [p]

Seaton, Alberta Jones   (1924– ——, F)

Embryologist. Born in Houston, TX, Dec. 31, 1924. B.A., Howard University, 1946; M.S., 1947; Sc.D., University of Brussels, Belgium, 1949. Chairman, Department of Biology, Wiley College, Marshal, TX, 1950–51; Visiting Professor of Biology and Embryology, Makerere College, Uganda, 1952–53; Assistant Professor of Biology, Spelman College, 1953–54; Associate Professor, Texas Souther University, 1954–61; Professor, 1961–; Director of Freshman Studies, 1970.

Memberships and awards: National Science Foundation science faculty research fellow, Brussels, 1965–66; AAAS; American Society of Zoologists.

Ref: The Negro in Science, p. 180.
American Men of Science, 12th ed., p. 5666.
Who's Who of American Women, 1974, p. 862.

Sebastian, Simon Powell   (1879–19??, M)

Physician. Surgeon. Born in Antigua, B.W.I., June 10, 1879. M.D., Shaw University, Raleigh, NC, 1912. Founder of L. Richardson Memorial Hospital which had 60 beds and opened May 18, 1927, fully approved by the American Medical Association and the American College of Surgeons, with school for nurses connected with it.

Ref: Who's Who in Colored America, 1933–37, p. 465. [p] p. 469.
Who's Who of the Colored Race, 1915, p. 239–240.

Sellers, Phillip A.   (1919– ——, M)

Chemist (nuclear). Born in Scottsville, VA, April 12, 1919. B.S., St. Augustine's College, 1942; M.S., Northwestern University, 1950. Instructor in public schools in Baltimore, MD, 1942–44; U.S. Navy, 1944–45; Associate Research Chemist, Argonne National Laboratories, 1945–.

Memberships and awards: Sigma Xi; American Chemical Society.

Ref: The Negro in Science, p. 186.
Ebony, Sept. 1949, p. 26. [p]

Shabazz, Lonnie   (1927– ——, M)

Mathematician. Born in Bessemer, AL, May 22, 1927. B.S. (chemistry and mathematics), Lincoln University; M.S., Massachusetts Institute of Technology, 1951; Ph.D., Cornell University, 1955. Assistant Mathematician, Cornell Aeronautical Laboratory, Buffalo, 1952–53; Graduate student and Teaching Assistant, Cornell University, 1953–55; Research Mathematician, Metals Research Laboratory of the Electron Metallurgical Company, Niagara Falls, 1955; Assistant Professor of Mathematics, Tuskegee Institute, 1956–57; Associate Professor of Mathematics and Chairman of the Department of Mathematics, Atlanta University, 1957–63; Director, Muhammad University of Islam No. 4.

Memberships and awards: Graduated with honors, Lincoln University, 1949; Sigma Xi; American Mathematical Society; American Society of Engineering Education;

National Institute of Science; Mathematical Association of America.

Ref: Black Mathematicians and Their Works, p. 294. [p]

Shadd, Furmann Jeremiah   (1852–1908, M)

Physician. Surgeon. Born in Washington, DC, Oct. 23, 1852. He was one of the first students at Howard University, completing the preparatory course, B.S., 1875; M.S., 1878; M.D., 1881, class valedictorian. Appointed Assistant Surgeon and Resident Physician at the Freedmen-'pris Hospital until 1895 when he went into private practice.

Memberships and awards: Secretary and Treasurer of the faculty, Howard University Medical Department; Trustee, District of Columbia Public Schools; applied to join the white Medical Society of the District of Columbia in 1891, but was turned down although he received the majority, but not the required two-thirds votes.

Ref: Howard University Medical Department, p. 126–127. [p]
Dictionary of American Medical Biography, p. 673–674.
Robinson, Henry S. Furman Jeremiah Shadd, M.D., 1852–1908. National Medical Association, *Journal,* v. 72, Feb. 1980, p. 151–153. [p]

Shaw, Earl   (1937– ——, M)

Physicist. Inventor. Born in Clarksdale, MS, 1937. B.S. (physics), University of Illinois, 1960; M.A., Dartmouth College, 1964– Ph.D. (physics), University of California, 1969. Research Scientist, Bell Laboratories, Murray Hill, NJ; Co-inventor of the spin-flip tunable laser.

Memberships and awards: National Society of Blacks Physicists.

Dissertation title: Nuclear Relaxation in Ferromagnetic Cobalt.

Ref: Blacks in Science: Astrophysicist to Zoologist, p. 42. [p]
after p. 48

Sheffey, Fred C.   (1928– ——, M)

Military (Army). Major General. Retired. Born in McKeesport, PA, Aug. 27, 1928. B.S., Central State College, 1950; M.B.A., Ohio State University, 1962; M.S., George Washington University, 1969; Command and General Staff College, 1965; National War College, 1969.

Memberships and awards: Purple Heart; Bronze Star Medal; Legion of Merit with two Oak Leaf Clusters; Army of Occupation Medal; United States Service Medal; Legion of Merit with two Oak Leaf Clusters; Army of Occupation Medal; United States Service Medal; Korean Service Medal.

Ref: Who' Who Among Black Americans, 1985, p. 754.
Black American in Defense of Our Nation, p. 123. [p]
Ebony, May 1978, p. 42. [p]

Shepard, C. H.   (18??–19, M)

Physician. Surgeon. B.S.; M.D. Chief Surgeon, Lincoln Hospital, Durham, NC.

Ref: National Medical Association, Journal, v. 3, April–June 1911. Back of contents page.

Sherard, George W.   (1918– ——, M)

Physicist. Born in Fitzgerald, GA, Mar. 15, 1918. B.A., Cincinnati University, 1940; M.S., 1942. Physicist, U.S. Signal Corps, Fort Monmouth, NJ, 1942–45; Instructor in Physics, Clark College, 1945; Howard University, 1945–48; Electronics Engineer, U.S. Signal Corps, 1950–.

Memberships and awards: special Scholar in Physics, Cincinnati, 1940–41; Hanna fellow, 1941–42; A.E.C. fellow, Pennsylvania, 1948–50; Sigma Xi; Beta Kappa Chi; American Physical Society.

Ref: The Negro in Science, p. 191.

Sherrod, Daniel Webster   (1867–1931, M)

Physician. Surgeon. Born in Macon, MS, Mar. 10, 1867. B.A., Fisk University, 1892; M.D., Meharry Medical College, 1896. Conducted Macon Drug Store, proprietor of Sherrod Drug Company.

Memberships and awards: Board of U.S. Examining Physicians for Meridian, MS; Secretary of U.S. Board of Examining Surgeons for four years; President, Mississippi Colored Anti-Tuberculosis League and Mississippi Medical, Dental, and Pharmaceutical Association; National Medical Association.

Ref: Who's Who in Colored America, 1927, p. 183. [p]
Who's Who of the Colored Race, 1915, p. 243.
Who's Who in Colored America, 1928–29, p. 333. [p]
Crisis, May 1928, p. 164. [p]
Crisis, April 1931. [p]

Sherrod, Theodore Roosevelt   (1915– ——, M)

Pharmacologist. Born in AL, July 29, 1915. B.A., Talladega College, 1938; M.S., University of Chicago, 1941; Ph.D. (pharmacology), University of Illinois, 1945; M.D., 1949. Instructor to Professor of Pharmacology, University of Illinois College of Medicine, 1945–58; Professor of Pharmacology, University of Illinois College of Medicine, 1958–; research in cardiovascular and renal pharmacology.

Memberships and awards: National Institutes of Health Research Grant Advisory Group; American Society of Pharmacology and Experimental Therapeutics; Society for Experimental Biology and Medicine; Award "Golden Apple" presented to him in 1953 by the Sophomore class as outstanding teacher in the Medical School, University of Illinois.

Dissertation title: A Study of the Effects of Digitalis on the Electrolytes of Heart Muscle.

Ref: *American Men and Women of Science,* 16th ed., p. 691.
Encyclopedia of Black America, p.745.
National Faculty Directory, 1988, p. 3472.

Shockley, Dolores Cooper   (1930– ——, F)

Pharmacologist. Born in Clarksdale, MS, April 21, 1930. B.S., Louisiana State University, 1951; M.S., Purdue University, 1953; Ph.D. (pharmacology), 1955. Assistant in Pharmacology, Purdue University, 1951–53; Assistant Professor, Pharmacology, Meharry Medical College, 1955–67; Associate Professor of Pharmacology, Meharry Medical College, 1967–; research in measurement of non-marcotic analgesics; effect of drugs on stress conditions; effect of hormones on connective tissue.

Memberships and awards: Fulbright fellow, Copenhagen University, 1955–56; Visiting Professor, Einstein College of Medicine, 1959–62; Lederle faculty awards, 1963–66; AAAS; American Pharmaceutical Association; first black female Ph.D. from Purdue and first black female Ph.D. in Pharmacology.

Ref: *American Men and Women of Science,* 14th ed., p. 4641.
In Black and White, p. 873.
Ebony, Aug. 1977, p. 116.
National Medical Association, *Journal,* v. 55, may 1963, p. 246–247. [p]
Crisis, Mar. 1955, p. 184.

Shorter, D. W.   (1800s, M)

Inventor. Livestock feed rack which permitted livestock to be fed without the farmer physically having to do so.

Ref: *At Last Recoginition in America,* v. 1, p. 4.

Shurney, Robert E.   (19??– ——, M)

Engineer (aeronautical). B.S. (physics), A & I State University, TN. Research Engineer, Marshall Space Flight Center, since early 1960s. Designed the refuse disposal units aboard Skylab. He had over 400 hours of weightlessness aboard the KC-135 weightless condition testing his designs.

Ref: *Blacks in Science, Ancient and Modern,* p. 249–251. [p]

Simms, Nathan Frank, Jr.   (1932– ——, M)

Mathematician. Born in Winston-Salem, NC, Oct. 20, 1932. B.S. (mathematics), North Carolina Central University, 1954; M.S., 1960; Ph.D. (pure mathematics), Lehigh University, 1970. Associate Professor, Professor, and Chairman, Mathematics Department, Winston-Salem State University, 1970–; Department of Mathematics and Computer Sciences, North Carolina State University, Greensboro; research in category theory and homological algebra.

Memberships and awards: American Mathematical Society; National Association of Mathematicians; Sigma Xi.

Dissertation title: Stable Homotopy in Frobenius Categories.

Ref: *Black Mathematicians and Their Works,* p. 294.
American Men and Women of Science, 16th ed., p. 758.

Sinclair, William Albert   (1858–1926, M)

Physician. Born in Georgetown, SC, Mar. 25, 1858. Attended the South Carolina College at Columbia until 1877, when it was closed to blacks. B.A., Howard University, 1881; M.A., 1887; M.D., Meharry Medical College, 1887. Became Financial Agent of Howard University, traveling all over the country for the university. He also spent time in England, Scotland and Wales.

Ref: *Howard University medical Department,* p. 92. [p]
Crisis, Dec. 1926, p. 83–84. [p]

Singleton, Elizabeth   (1800s, F)

Midwife. Born in Wayne County, GA. Delivered over 1,000 babies and died at the age of 104 in Tennessee.

Ref: *Contributions of Black Women to America,* p. 359.

Sinkford, Jeanne Frances Craig   (1933– ——, F)

Dentist. Physiologist. Born in Washington, DC, Jan. 30, 1933. B.S., Howard University, 1953; D.D.S., 1958 (valedictorian); M.S., Northwestern University, 1962; Ph.D. (physiology), 1963. Instructor, Howard University College of Dentistry, 1958–60; Dean, Howard University Dental School, 1975–; first Black woman to become head of a university department of Dentistry.

Memberships and awards: American Dental Association; International Association of Dental Research.

Dissertation title: Counter Irritation: The Effects of Endocrine Ablations on Experimentally Induced Counter-Irritation.

Ref: *American Men and Women of Science,* 14th ed., p. 4700.
Encyclopedia of Black America, p. 755.
In Black and White, p. 883.
Profiles in Black, p. 154–155. [p]
Jet, v. 14, July 10, 1958, p. 49. [p]
Scientists in the Black Perspective.
Ebony, July 1986, p. 134. [p]

Sinkler, William H.   (1906–1960, M)

Physician. Surgeon. Born in Summerville, SC, Dec. 24, 1906. B.A., Lincoln University, PA, 1928; M.D., Howard University, 1932. Internship and Residency in Surgery, St. Louis General Hospital. Medical Director, Homer G. Phillips Hospital in St. Louis, 1941–60; member of the Faculty, Department of Surgery, Washington University School of Medicine and Homer G. Phillips Nursing

School; Associate Director of Surgery, Homer G. Phillips Hospital; Visiting Surgeon, St. Mary's Infirmary.

Memberships and awards: Honorary D.Sci., Lincoln University, 1954; Distinguished Service Alumni Award, Howard University, 1959; Diplomate, American Board of Surgery, 1947; fellow, American College of Surgeons, 1948; International College of Surgeons, 1949; Kappa Pi Medical Honorary Society; Vice-Chairman, Surgical Section, National Medical Association, 1941–49, Chairman, 1950; American Medical Association; St. Louis Medical Society; Missouri Medical Society; Mound City Medical Forum; Alpha Phi Alpha; Chi Delta Mu; first black surgeon to operate at the Cardinal Glennon Children's Hospital, St. Louis and the first black surgeon on Surgical Service and the Faculty of the Washington University Medical School.

Ref: National Medical Association, Journal, v. 52, Nov. 1960, p. 455. [p] obit
    A Century of Black Surgeons, p. 252–264. [p] (list of publications, p. 261–262.

Skinner, Elliott   (1924– ——, M)

Anthropologist. Born in Trinidad-Tobago, June 20, 1924. B.A., University College, New York University; M.A., Columbia University, 1952; Ph.D., Columbia University, 1955. Frank Boaz Professor, Columbia University, 1969–; Chairman, Columbia University Department of Anthropology, 1972–75; Associate Professor, 1963–66; Assistant Professor, New York University, 1959–63.

Memberships and awards: Board of Directors, American Foundation for Development of Health Education in Africa, 1965–68; Board of American Association of Social Psychiatry, 1972–75; Board of Directors, American Anthropological Association, 1973–76; Chairman, Subcommittee for International Exchange of Scholars, 1971–; Board of Directors of the African-American Scholars Council, 1971–; Guggenheim fellow, 1971–72.

Dissertation title: Ethnic Interaction in a British Guiana Rural Community: a Study in Secondary Acculturation and Group Dynamics.

Ref: Jet, June 30, 1955, p. 22.
    Who's Who Among Black Americans, 1980–81, p. 731.

Slaton, William H.   (1910–19??, M)

Chemist. Atomic Energy Project, University of California, Los Angeles, (3 years); Chemist for Product Development and Research Department, Rexall Drug Co.

Ref: Ebony, Jan. 1957, p. 5.
    Who's Who in America, 1974, p. 2854.

Slaughter, John Brooks   (1934– ——, M)

Physicist. Engineer (electrical). Born in Topeka, KS, Mar. 16, 1934. B.S. (electrical engineering), Kansas State University, 1956; M.S. (engineering), University of California, 1961; Ph.D. (engineering science), 1971. Electronics Engineer, General Dynamics, 1956–60; Physical Science Administrator, Information Systems, Naval Electronics Laboratory Center, 1960–75; Director, Applied Physics Laboratory, University of Washington, 1957–77; Assistant Director, National Science Foundation, 1977–; Academic Vice-President and Provost, Washington State University, 1979–80; Presidential appointment to Director, National Science Foundation (first black), 1980–82; Chancellor of the University of Maryland, College Park, 1982–. Editor, International Journal of Computers and Electrical Engineering, 1977.

Memberships and awards: Ten honorary Doctoral Degrees; Scientist of the year, 1965.

Dissertation title: The Solution of a Class of Optimal Control Problems by Linear and Piecewise Linear Programming Techniques.

Ref: American Men and Women of Science, 16th ed., p. 805.
    Black Engineers in the United States, p. 181.
    Who's Who in Engineering, p. 612.
    Who's Who Among Black Americans, 1985, p. 767.
    Black Collegian, Feb./Mar. 1981, p. 158, 160, 162, 164, 166. [p]

Sleet, Jessie C. (Scales)   (18??–19??, F)

Nurse. Born in Stratford, Ontario, Canada. Graduated from Provident Hospital School of Nursing, Chicago, 1895. Went to Freedmen's Hospital in Wash., D.C., where she studied under Dr. Daniel Williams. In 1900 she became the first black public health nurse.

Ref: The Path We Tread, p. 146–148. [p] p. 147.
    Pathfinders, p. 15–17. [p] after p. 96.
    History of the Negro in Medicine, p. 71.

Sleet, Moneta J., Jr.   (1926– ——, M)

Photographer. Born in Owensboro, KY, Feb. 14, 1926. B.A., Kentucky State College, 1947; M.A., New York University, 1950. Photographer, Johnson Publishing Company, 1955–.

Memberships and awards: Won $12,900 gift from anonymous donor and certificate of recognition signed by Edward Steichen, famed photographer, and Urban League officials for picture in Jet, April 27, 1961, p. 25, Pulitzer Prize, first black photographer, for portrait of Mrs. King with daughter Bernice at Martin Luther King, Jr.'s funeral; citation for excellence, Overseas Press Club of America, 1957; first black artist to have one man show at museum, 1970.

Ref: *Ebony*, Nov. 1985, p. 320. [p]
         Jet, April 27, 1961, p. 24.
         Ebony, Jan. 1987, p. 66–68, 70–72, 74. [p]
         Who's Who Among Black Americans, 1985, p. 768.
         Ebony Success Library, v. 1, p. 283. [p]
         Crises, May, 1970, p. 187–188. [p]
         Ebony, April 1968, p. 103–104, 106–108. [p]

Smart, Brinay   (1800s, M)

Inventor. Born in Tennessee. Invented a number of reverse valve gears.

Ref: Negro in Our History, 5th ed., p. 469.

Smith, Alonzo De Grate   (1890–1970, M)

Physician. Pediatrician. Born in East Orange, NJ, July 29, 1890. B.S., Howard University, 1913; M.D., Long Island College Hospital, 1919; B.S.S., College of the City of New York, 1923. Clinical Assistant, Vanderbilt Clinic, 1922–26; Bellevue O.P.D., 1927–28; Assistant Attending Physician, Vanderbilt Clinic, 1926–27; Assistant, Department of Diseases of Children, Columbia University, 1925–28; Assistant O.P.D., Children's Dispensary, Mt. Sinai Hospital, 1923–25; Physician, Children's Dispensary, Harlem Hospital, 1926–32; Faculty, Howard University Medical School, 1932–56; Pediatrician, Freedmen's Hospital, 1932–45; Emeritus Associate Professor of Pediatrics, Howard University College of Medicine, 1956–70; began the Pediatrics Residency Program at Howard.

Ref: *National Cyclopedia of American Biography*, v. 56. p. 182–183. [p]
         Crisis, April 1925, p. 263–264. [p]
         Who's Who in Colored America, 19, p. 352. [p] p. 346
         National Medical Association, *Journal*, v. 61, July, 1969, p. 358–360. [p] on cover

Smith, Barnett Frissell   (1909–19??, M)

Parasitologist. Born in Montgomery, AL, Jan. 17, 1909. B.S., Morehouse College, 1932; M.S., Atlanta University, 1934; Ph.D. (zoology), University of Wisconsin, 1944. Teacher of General Science and Biology, Washington High School, Atlanta, GA, 1933–36; Associate Professor of Biology, Alabama State Teachers College, 1937–45; Professor of Biology, Spelman College, 1945–.

Memberships and awards: AAAS; American Society of Zoologists; American Society of Parasitologists; Society of Protozoologists; American Microscopical Society; New York Academy of Sciences; National Institute of Science; Ford Foundation fellow in Zoology, University of California at Los Angeles, 1945–55.

Dissertation title: The Respiration of the Protozoan Parasite Eimeria Tenella.

Ref: *The Negro in Science*, p. 180.
         American Men and Women of Science, 14th ed., p. 4734.
         Who's Who in the South & Southeast, 1978, p. 678.

Smith, Calvin L.   (1907–1968, M)

Pharmacist. Former Deputy Coroner of Cook County and Chief Pharmacist at Cook County Jail.

Memberships and awards: President, Chicago Pharmaceutical Association.

Ref: *Jet*, July 18, 1968, p. 53. [p]

Smith, Carter Charles   (1926– ——, M)

Physicist. Born in Kansas City, KS, Feb. 21, 1926. B.A., North Carolina College, Durham, 1947; M.S., Howard University, 1952. Junior Engineer, Baird Associates, Inc.; Junior Engineer, Raytheon Manufacturing Company; Staff Associate, Howard University; Physicist, National Bureau of Standards.

Memberships and awards: Beta Kappa Chi; Sigma Pi Sigma.

Ref: *The Negro in Science*, p. 191.

Smith, Eunice Lewis   (19??–1984, F)

Nurse. B.S., Florida A & M University; M.S., Catholic University of America, Washington, DC. Thirty-one years (1951–82) at St. Elizabeth's Hospital, the first black headnurse, first black supervisor, and first black Director of Nursing, St. Elizabeth's Hospital.

Ref: *The Path We Tread*, p. 187. [p]

Smith, Georgia Caldwell   (1909–1960, F)

Mathematician. Born in Atchison, KS, Aug. 28, 1909. B.A., University of Kansas, 1928; M.A., 1929. Mathematics teacher, Spelman College, 1929–38; Head, Mathematics Department, 1945–; Ph.D., University of Pittsburgh, 1960, died before conferring of degree in early 1961.

Memberships and awards: American Mathematical Society; Mathematical Association of America; Phi Beta Kappa; Pi Mu Epsilon.

Dissertation title: Some Results on the Anticenter of a Group.

Ref: Kenschaft, Patricia C. Black Women in Mathematics in the United States. *American Mathematical Monthly*, v. 88, Oct. 1981, p. 593, 597.
         The Negro in Science, p. 189.

Smith, James McCune   (1811–1865, M)

Physician. Born in New York, NY, April 18, 1811. B.A., 1835; M.A., 1836; M.D., Glasgow University, Scotland, 1837. First black American to receive a medical degree. He practiced in New York. Studied at Paris Hospital. Medical Practice, 1838–63. Showed data on high incidence of black lunacy to be false. Attacked argument on weight of the black brain with information based on his knowledge of medicine. First black to operate a pharmacy in the

United States. Served on the Medical Staff of Free Negro Orphan Asylum, New York, NY, for 20 years.

Pub: *The Anatomy and Physiology of the Races.*
         The Colored American. (editor).

Ref: Miller, Kelly. Historic Background of the Negro Physician. *Journal of Negro History,* v. 1, Fro-, p. 104.
         Ebony Handbook, 1974, p. 361.
         Encyclopedia of Black American, p. 797–798.
         History of the Negro in Medicine, p. 31–35. [p] p. 31.
         In Black and White, p. 892–893.
         Weadon, *The Negro from 1863–1963.*
         National Medical Association, *Journal,* v. 73, Dec. 1981, p. 1205.
         Dictionary of American Medical Biography, p. 693.
         Cobb, W. Montague. Jame McCune Smith. *Negro History Bulletin,* v. 9, 1945, p. 41–42.
         Historical Afro-American Biographies, p. 125. [p]
         Dictionary of American Biography, p. 288.

Smith, James Webster   (18??–1876, M)

Military. First black appointed to the U.S. Military Academy, West Point, July 1, 1870. Did not graduate due to dismissal in 1874 for deficiency in natural and experimental philosophy after several court-martials for conduct unbecoming a gentleman. He was discriminated against and mistreated by his fellow cadets and was never really accepted.

Ref: *Black Americans in Defense of Our Nation,* p. 141.

Smith, Martha Lee Gladys   (1901–19??, F)

Mathematician. Born in Richmond, VA, Jan. 2, 1901. B.A., Hartshorn Memorial College, 1922; B.A., Virginia Union University, 1924; M.S., University of Chicago, 1930. Mathematics teacher, Academy, Virginia Union University, 1920–27; Acting and Principal, Academy, Virginia Union University, 1926–29; Professor of Mathematics, Virginia Union University, 1929–.

Ref: *Who's Who in Colored America,* 1933–37, p. 480.

Smith, P. D.   (1800s, M)

Inventor. Potato digger which scooped the potatoes from the soil and left them exposed to be picked up. Patent # 455, 206, 1891.

Ref: *At last Recognition in America,* v. 1, p.4.

Smith, Perry   (1926- —— , M)

Engineer (electrical). Advanced solid state amplifier design.

Ref: *In Black and White,* p. 896.

Smith, Phillip M., Sr.   (19??- —— , M)

Physician. Obstetrician. Gynecologist. B.S. (zoology), State University of Iowa; M.D., Meharry Medical College, 1956. Medical Director, Martin Luther King, Jr. Hospital, Los Angeles, which he helped to develop; Police Advisory Committee; Member, Joint Commission for Accreditation of Hospitals.

Memberships and awards: President, National Medical Association, 1985; President, Charles R. Drew Medical Society of Los Angeles; Golden State Medical Association of California; Hospital Commission of Los Angeles County.

Ref: *Black Family International Journal,* 1985, p. 21. [p]
         Ebony, Oct. 1976, p. 37. [p] only
         National Medical Association, *Journal,* v. 77, June 1985. [p] on cover.

Smith, Relliford Stillman   (1889–1965, M)

Physician. Obstetrician. Gynecologist. Born in Americus, GA, Nov. 30, 1889. B.S., Shaw University, 1910; Leonard Medical College, 1910–14; M.D., University of West Tennessee Medical College, 1914; M.D., Meharry Medical College, 1916; Postgraduate Courses, Medical College of Georgia; Grady Hospital, 1931–32; Gynecology and Venereal Disease Courses, University of Georgia, 1935–41. Passed State Medical exams in Georgia, South Carolina, Maryland, and the District of Columbia.

Memberships and awards: President, National Medical Association, 1957–58; Chair, Budget Committee, House of Delegates, 24 years; President, Macon Academy of Medicine, Dentistry, and Pharmacy; Georgia State Medical Association of Physicians and Pharmacists; Bibb County Medical Society.

Ref: Cobb, W. Montague. Relliford Stillman Smith, M.D., 1889–1965. National Medical Association, *Journal,* v. 58, Mar. 1966, p. 145–147.
         National Medical Association, *Journal,* v. 49, Nov. 57, p. 419–420. [p]

Smith, Robert Tecumseh   (1900–1958, M)

Physician. Born in Goliad, TX, Jan. 4, 1900. B.S., Wiley College, 1922; M.D., Meharry Medical College, 1931. Medical Director of Hubbard Hospital; Director of Outpatient Clinic and Assistant Professor of Medicine at Meharry Medical College, 1936–. Died of heart ailment at Hubbard in Nashville.

Memberships and awards; Certificate of award, National Medical Association, 1957; American Medical Association, National Medical Association; R.F. Boyd Medical Society; Nashville Academy of Medicine; Phi Beta Sigma.

Ref: *Jet*, 58?

National Medical Association, *Journal*, v. 50, Sept. 1958, p. 400. obit.

National Cyclopedia of America, Biography. v. 46, p. 363. [p]

Smith, Robert Wilson, Jr.   (1918– ——, M)

Mathematician. Born in Philadelphia, PA, April 2, 1918; B.A., Temple University, 1941; M.A., University of Pennsylvania, 1948; Postgraduate work, University of Pittsburgh; Chief, Special Design and Superintendent, ADP Systems Branch, Pittsburgh Energy Technology Center; Regional Director, Authorization Systems, Inc., 1981–.

Memberships and awards: American Association of Computing Machinery; AAAS; American Society of Public Administration; Kappa Alpha Psi; Pittsburgh Man of the Year, 1966; Outstanding Achievement in Science, *Pittsburgh Courier* newspaper, 1962; Service Award, Pittsburgh Board of Public Education, 1965.

Ref: Who's Who Among Black Americans, 1985, p. 780.

Smith, Thomas Manuel   (1891– ——, M)

Physician. Cardiologist. Born in Sedalia, MO Sept. 7, 1891. B.S., George R. Smith College, Sedalia, MO, 1909; M.D., Meharry Medical College, 1915. Chief, Division of Cardiology, Provident Hospital.

Memberships and awards: President, National Medical Association, 1942–43; Distinguished Service Medal, National Medical Association, 1961; American Heart Association; Cook County Physicians Association; American Medical Association; Meharry Alumini Association; John A. Andrew Clinical Society; Chairman for seven years, Medical Section, National Medical Association.

Ref: National Medical Association, *Journal*, v. 34, Sept. 1942, p. 177. [p]

Who's Who in Colored America, 1941-44, p. 475.

Smith, Victor Claude   (1899–19??, M)

Engineer (chemical). Born in Beaufort, SC, May 16, 1899. B.S., MIT, 1924; Sc.D., 1930. Research Associate, MIT, 1929–35; research in fuels for General Motors Corporation, 1935; research in fuels and their combustion.

Memberships and awards: Chemical Society.

Dissertation title: A Study of Homogeneous Combustion in Gases.

Ref: American Men of Science, 7th ed., p. 1660.

Holders of Doctorates Among American Negroes, p. 134.

Snead, Jonathan L.   (1921– ——, M)

Chemist (organic). Born in Farmville, VA, Aug. 29, 1921. B.S., Virginia Union University, 1942; M.S., Howard University, 1944. Junior Chemist, Frankford Arsenal, Philadelphia, 1944–47; Instructor in Chemistry, Fisk Univer-

sity, 1947–49; Lincoln University, PA, 1949–50; Chemist, Pitman-Dunn Laboratories, Frankford Arsenal, Philadelphia, 1950–.

Memberships and awards: American Chemical Society; Scientific Research Society of America; Beta Kappa Chi.

Ref: *The Negro in Science*, p. 186.

Somerville, Veda Watson   (18??–19??, F)

Dentist. D.D.S., University of Southern California Dental School, 1918, only woman and only black in her class. First Black female dentist in California, scoring among the highest in the state dental examination.

Memberships and awards: National Dental Association; Los Angeles Chamber of Commerce.

Ref: *Black Women Makers of History: A Portrait*, 1977, p. 91–93. [p] p. 92.

Crises, June, 1923, p. 73 [p] only

Contributions of Black Women to America, p. 395.

Songonuga, Oluwole Oladapo   (1939– ——, M)

Engineer (civil). Born in Aiyepe, Nigeria, Nov. 6, 1939. B.S. (civil engineering), University of Nigeria, 1965; M.S., McGill University, Canada, 1967; Ph.D. (civil engineering), West Virginia University, 1969. Assistant Professor of Civil Engineering, Newark College of Engineering, Newark, NJ.

Memberships and awards: American Society of Civil Engineers; Sigma Xi; Chi Epsilon.

Dissertation title: Acid, Gas and Microbial Dynamics in Sanitary Landfills.

Ref: *Black Engineers in the United State*, p. 185.

American Men and Women of Science, 12th ed., p. 5983.

Spaulding, Dean Major Franklin   (1900–1946, M)

Agronomist. Born in Clarkston, NC, Sept. 18, 1900. B.S.A., North Carolina State College, 1925; B.S., Cornell, 1927; M.S., 1928; Ph.D., Massachusetts State College, 1935. Professor of Agronomy, North Carolina State College, 1928–37; Director of Agronomy, 1928–37; Professor of Agronomy and Plant Physiology, Prairie View State College, 1937–38; Research Professor, Tuskegee Institute, 1938–40; Professor of Agronomy, 1942–45; Professor and Director of Agronomy, Langston University, 1940–42; Professor and Head of the Department, Tennessee A & I State College, 1946–58; Dean of the School of Agronomy and Home Economics, 1958–.

Memberships and awards: Society of Agronomy; Soil Science Society; International Society of Soil Science.

Dissertation title: Factors Influencing the Rate of Decomposition of Different Types of Plant Tissue and the Influence of the Products on Plant Growth.

Ref: *American Men of Science,* 10th ed., p. 3846.
Holders of Doctorates Among American Negroes, p. 134.

Spaulding, George H. (1908–19??, M)

Chemist. Born in Whitesboro, NJ, Sept. 11, 1908. B.S., Morgan State College, 1930; M.S., University of Pennsylvania, 1936; Ph.D. (chemistry), 1942. Instructor to Professor of Chemistry and Head of the Department, Morgan State College, 1945–; research in organic analysis, behavior of mercuric sulfide in solutions of mercuric nitrite.

Memberships and awards: Chemical society; fellow, National Institute of Science.

Ref: *American Men of Science,* 10th ed., p. 3846.
Holders of Doctorates Among American Negroes, p. 156.
Crisis, Aug. 1942, p. 251. [p] only

Speller, John Finton (1910– ——, M)

Physician. Urologist. Surgeon. Born in Philadelphia, PA, April 13, 1910. B.A., Lincoln University, 1932; M.D., Howard University, 1940; Postgraduate, University of Pennsylvania, 1945–46. Secretary of Health, Commonwealth of Pennsylvania, 1971–75.

Memberships and awards: Medical Advisory Board, Philadelphia Planned Parenthood Association; Delegate to the White House Conference on Aging; Pennsylvania Medical Society; American Medical Association; American College of Surgeons; Diplomate, American Board of Urology.

Ref: *Ebony Success Library,* v. 1, p. 289. [p]
Who's Who Among Black Americans, 1985, p. 788.

Spellman, Mitchell Wright (1919– ——, M)

Physician. Surgeon. Born in Alexandria, LA, Dec. 1, 1919. B.A., Dillard, 1940; M.D., Howard University, 1944; Ph.D. (surgery), University of Minnesota, 1955; Professor of Surgery and Assistant Dean of Postgraduate Medical School of the University of California, 1969–78; Professor of Surgery and Dean of Medical Service, Harvard Medical School, 1978–; Executive Vice-President, Harvard Medical Center; research in radiation biology, cardiovascular physiology.

Memberships and awards: American Board of Surgery Diplomate, 1953. District of Columbia Board of Examiners, Medicine and Osteopathy, 1955–68; Executive Vice-President and member of the Board of Regents, Georgetown University, 1972–78; Sinkler Award in Surgery, National Medical Association, 1968; Warfield Award, Freedmen's Hospital, 1969; Institute of Medicine, National Academy of Sciences; American Association of University Professors; Society of University Surgeons; American Medical Association; American Surgical Association; National Medical Association; fellow, American College of Surgeons.

Dissertation title: A Study of the Pathogenic Mechanisms which Underlie the Production of Bacterial Endocarditis in Dog with Large, Chronic Arteriovenous Fistulae.

Ref: *American men and Women of Science,* 16th ed., p. 930.
Encyclopedia of Black America, p. 806–807.
National Medical Association, *Journal,* v. 53, July 1961, p. 429. [p]
ABMS Compendium of Certified Medical Specialists, v. 6, p. 631.
Who's Who in America, 1978, p. 3070–3071.
Who's Who in the West, 1978, p. 684.
National Medical Association, *Journal,* v. 70, Aug. 1978, p. 606. [p]
A Century of Black Surgeons, p. 633–636. [p] p. 634.

Spencer, Michael G. (195?– ——, M)

Engineer. B.S.; M.S.; Ph.D., Cornell, 1980. Rockwell Solid State Laboratory of Howard University.

Dissertation title: Electrical Characterization of Grain Boundaries in Gullium-Arsenide and Their Relationship to Solar Cell Performance.

Ref: *Ebony,* Aug. 1985, p. 64. [p]

Spikes, Dolores (19??– ——, F)

Mathematician. Born in Baton Rouge, LA. B.S., Southern University, Baton Rouge; M.S., University of Illinois, 1958; Ph.D. (mathematics), Louisiana Southern University, 1971. Taught at Southern University for two years; Mossville High School in Westlake, LA for four years; Professor of Mathematics, Southern University.

Memberships and awards: USF Science Faculty fellowships; Ford Foundation fellowship.

Dissertation title: Semi-Valuations and Groups of Divisibility.

Ref: Kenschaft, Patricia C. Black Women in Mathematics in the United States. *American Mathematical Monthly,* v. 88, Oct. 1981. p. 600.

Spikes, Richard B. (18??–1962, M)

Inventor. Invented automatic car wash and auto directional signals in 1913. (Pierce Arrow). the automatic gear shift, Patent #1,889,814, Dec. 6, 1932 and the transmission and shifting thereof, Patent #1,936,996, Nov. 28, 1933. Shortly before his death he patented a brake system combining hydraulic and electrical approaches, Patent #3,015,522.

Ref: *Black Inventors of America,* p. 40–47.

Spratlin, Paul Edward (1861–19??, M)

Physician. Born in Wetumpka, AL, Oct. 9, 1861. B.A., Atlanta University, 1881; M.A., 1896; M.D., Denver University, 1892. Medical Inspector and Chief Quarantine Officer, Denver Health Department, 1895–27;

Memberships and awards: Trustee, Lincoln-Douglas Consumptive Sanitarium.

Ref: *Who's Who of the Colored Race,* 1915, p. 251.
Who's Who in Colored America, 1927, p. 190. [p]

Spratling, Willis   (1924- ——, M)

Engineer (mechanical). Born in Chicago, IL, June 11, 1924. B.S., Bradley University, 1974; M.S. (mechanical engineering), University of Illinois, Urbana, 1949. Rocket Test Manager, Bell Aircraft Company, 1949-55; Design Specialist, Boeing Company, 1955-56; Manager, Solid Rocket Plant Test Division, Aerojet General, supervising over 500 engineers, mechanics and technicians, 1956-; Vice-President, Design Support Department, Xerox Corporation, 1971-80; Vice-President for Community Affairs, 1980-.

Ref: *Who's Who Among Black Americans,* 1985, p. 789.
Ebony, 1964, p. 46-48, 50, 52, 54-55. [p]

Springer, George   (1924- ——, M)

Mathematician. Born in Cleveland, OH, Sept. 3, 1924. B.S., Case Institute, 1945; M.S., Brown University, 1946; Ph.D. (mathematics), Harvard University, 1949. Moore Instructor in Mathematics, M.I.T, 1949-51; Assistant Professor, Northwestern University, 1951-54; from Associate Professor to Professor, University of Kansas, 1955-64; Professor and Chairman of the Mathematics Department, Indiana University, 1969. Research in the theory of functions of one and several complex variables.

Memberships and awards: Consulting Editor, McGraw Hill Book Company, 1971-; American Mathematical Society; Mathematical Association of America; AAAS.

Dissertation title: The Coefficient Problem for Univalent Mappings of the Exterior of the Unit Circle.

Ref: American Men and Women of Science. 16th ed., p. 953.

Springs, Andrew Wilton   (1869-19??, M)

Physician. Surgeon. Born in Charlotte, NC, May 22, 1869. B.S., Fisk University, 1901; M.D., National Medical University, Chicago, IL, 1906; Graduate, Illinois Mine Rescue and First Aid Commission Station, Benton, IL, 1914; studied helmet work at American Mine and Safety Association, Pittsburgh, PA, 1914. Physician and Surgeon to Madison Coal Corporation, Dewmaine, IL, 1912-; Physician in charge of the Corporation Hospital.

Memberships and awards: First physician, black or white, to pass examination in helmet work as prescribed by Illinois Mine Rescue Commission. Married to Dr. Birdie Springs. On Oct. 27, 1914, he descended into a mine following an explosion and fire at Roylton, IL. He was the one of 50 doctors called who had a pulmotor and knew how to use it. He aided 52 miners who were trapped and was awarded the Carnegie Medal for his bravery.

Ref: *Who's Who of the Colored Race,* 1915, p. 251.
Jet, Oct. 28, 1971, p. 10.

Springs, Birdie E. McLain   (1886-19??, F)

Physician. Born in Carthagene, OH, Dec. 4, 1886. M.D., Bennett Medical College, 1912; Graduate, Illinois Mine Rescue Commission Station, Benton, IL, 1914; Chataugua School of Nursing, 1914. Superintendent, Madison Coal Corporation Hospital, Dewmaine, IL.

Memberships and awards: Service Member, American Mine Safety Associations.

Ref: *Who's Who of the Colored Race,* 1915, p. 251-252.

Spurlock, Jeanne   (1921- ——, F)

Physician. Psychiatrist. Born in Sandusky, OH, 1921. M.D., Howard University, 1947; Postgraduate study, Chicago Institute for Psychoanalysis. Professor and Chairman, Department of Psychiatry, Meharry Medical College.

Memberships and awards: First black and first woman to receive Strecker award of the Institute of Pennsylvania for outstanding contributions in psychiatric care and treatment, 1971; American Psychiatric Association; National Medical Association; American Academy of Child Psychiatry.

Ref: *Black American Reference Book,* P. 375.
Encyclopedia of Black America, p. 752-753.
Jet, May 27, 1971, p. 49. [p]
Who's Who Among Black Americans, 1985, p. 790.
Ebony Success Library, v. 1, p. 291. [p]
ABMS Compendium of Medical Specialists, v. 5, 747.

St. Mary, Donald Frank   (1940- ——, M)

Mathematician. Born in Lake Charles, LA, July 22, 1940. B.S., McNeese State College, 1962; M.A., University of Kansas, 1964; Ph.D. (mathematics), University of Nebraska, 1968. Instructor, Mathematics, University of Nebraska, 1969-67; Instructor, Mathematics, Iowa State University, 1967-68; Assistant Professor, Mathematics, University of Massachusetts, 1968-75; Associate Professor, 1975-.

Membership and awards: Sigma Xi; American Mathematical Society (papers presented 1968, 1969, 1971); Mathematical Association of America; Participant, Symposium on Ordinary Differential Equations, University of Colorado, June-July 1967.

Dissertation title: Oscillation and Comparison Theorems for Second Order Linear Differential Equations.

Pub: Some Oscillations and Comparison Theorems for $(r(t)y')'$ $+ p(t)y + 0$.
Journal of Differential Equations, v. 5, 1969.

(With S. B. Eliason) Upper Bound of Tp(t) and the Differential Equation (X;2pri = P9t)x = O. *Journal of Differential Equations*, v. 5, 1969.

(With A. M. Fink) On an Inequality of Nehari, American Mathematical Society, *Proceedings*, V. 21, no. 1, 1969.

(With A. M. Fink) A Generalized Sturm Comparison Theorem and Oscillation Coefficients. *Monatsh. Math.*, v. 73, 1969.

On Oscillation of Complex Linear Differential Systems. American Mathematical Society, *Proceedings*, v. 36, 1972.

Ref: *American Men and Women of Science*, 15th ed., p. 384.
Black Mathematicians and Their Works, p. 293.

Staley, Frank Marcellus   (1890–19??, M)

Agriculturist. Born in Americus, GA, Dec. 11, 1890. B.A., Morehouse College, Atlanta, GA, 1912; B.S., Cornell, 1915; M.S. (chemistry, dairying), 1928. Teacher of Dairying, Agriculture and Chemistry in South Carolina, 1914–17; Teacher, Tuskegee Institute, 1917–19; Itinerant Teacher-Trainer, Agriculture, 1919–25; Director of Agriculture, A & T College, Greensboro, NC, 1925–.

Memberships and awards: Omega Psi Phi.

Ref: *Who's Who in Colored America*, 1928–29, p. 346. [p]
Who's Who in Colored America, 1933–37, p. 489. [p]

Stamps, Herman Franklin   (1924– ——, M)

Dentist. Born in Washington, DC, Jan. 20, 1924. B.S., Howard University, 1945; D.D.S., 1948; M.Sci, University of Michigan, 1953. Director of Clinics, College of Dentistry, 1967–70; Professor, 1969–; Faculty member, Howard University, 1948–.

Memberships and awards: Robert T. Freeman Dental Society, President, 1959–61; National Dental Association; American Dental Association; D.C. Dental Society; American Society for the History of Dentistry (charter); American Association of Endodontics; Omicron Kappa Upsilon.

Pub: *Modern Prescription Writing*, 1959.

Ref: *Who's Who Among Black Americans*, 1985, p. 791.

Stancell, Arnold Francis   (1936– ——, M)

Engineer (chemical). Born in New York, NY, Nov. 16, 1936. B.S. (chemical engineering), College, City of New York, 1958; Ph.D. (chemical engineering), MIT, 1962. research management in petrochemicals and plastics, 1962–70– Chemical Business Planning, 1972–76; Vice-President and General Manager of Plastics Packaging Film Business, Mobil Corporation, 1977–79; Manager Planning of Mobil Corporation, 1980–81; Executive Vice-President, Mobil Europe Marketing and Refining Business, 1982–84; Vice-President, Worldwide Marketing and Refining, 1984–. Research in Polymer structure and properties.

Memberships and awards: Tau Beta Pi; Phi Lambda Upsilon; Sigma Xi; American Institute of Chemical Engineers.

Dissertation title: Effect of Chromatographic Transport of Reverse-Wetting Agents on Oil Displacement from Porous Media.

Pub: Diffusion Through Polymers. In: *Polymer Science and Materials*, Mark & Tobolsky.

Ref: *Black Engineers in the United States*, p. 187.
Who's Who in Engineering, 6th ed., p. 630.
American Men and Women of Science, 14th ed., p. 4854.

Standard, J.   (1800s, M)

Inventor. Refrigerator, Patent #455,891, 1891. Refrigerator invented, 1834, but Standar's refrigerator used compressed air and ether as a coolant. Oil Stove, patent # 413,869k, 1889.

Ref: *At Last Recognition in America*, v. 1, p. 9, 23.

Stanford, John Thomas   (1861–19??, M)

Physician. Born in Caroline County, MD, Aug. 19, 1861. B.A., Lincoln University, PA, 1891; M.A., Howard University Medical College, 1895. Taught Latin, Greek, and Mathematics, Eastern Branch, Maryland Agricultural College, Princess Anne, MD, before going to medical school. After graduation, he passed the state medical examination in Pennsylvania.

Memberships and awards: Miller Award for excellence in the physical sciences, Lincoln University.

Ref: *Howard University Medical Department*, p. 218–219. [p]

Staupers, Mabel Keaton   (1890–19??, F)

Nurse. Born in Barbados, B.W.I., 1890. Freedmen's Hospital School of Nursing, 1917. In 1934 began campaign to increase opportunities in nursing.

Memberships and awards: Winner of 1951 Spingarn Medal for her contribution to Negro nursing; Executive Secretary and President, National Association of Colored Graduate Nurses.

Pub: *No Time for Prejudice.*

Ref: *Black Leaders of the 20th Century*, p. 241–257. [p] opp. p. 241.
Smithsonian Black Women Achievers Against Odds, p. 31.
AFRO USA, 1971 (update of *Negro Almanac*), p. 212.
History of the Negro in Medicine, p. 102. [p] p. 102.
National Medical Association, *Journal*, v. 43, Sept. 1951, p. 344. [p]
Who's Who of American Women, 1968. p. 1156.

Stent, Theodore Robert   (1924– ——, M)

Physician. Radiologist. Born in Charleston, SC, Jan. 7, 1924. B.A., Talladega College, 1944; M.D., Meharry Medical College, 1948. Associate Professor of Radiology, Columbia University, 1966–73; Director, School for Nuclear Medical Technology, 1971; Associate Professor of Radiology, Columbia University, Harlem Hospital Center, New York, 1973–; Medical Director, Ebony Medex, 1974.

Memberships and awards: National Medical Association; New York Roent. Society; American College of Radiology; Radiological Society; American Institute of Ultrasound Medicine; American College of Nuclear Medicine; Society of Nuclear Medicine; Omega Psi Phi; fellow, Radiation Therapy; American Medical Association.

Ref: *Who's Who Among Black Americans,* 1985, p. 794.
    ABMS Compendium of Medical Specialists, v. 3, p. 361.

Stephens, Clarence Francis   (1917– ——, M)

Mathematician. Born in Gaffney, SC, July 24, 1917. B.A., Johnson C. Smith University, 1938. M.S., University of Michigan, 1939; Ph.D. (mathematics), 1943. Instructor in Mathematics, Prairie View A & M College, 1940–42; Professor, 1946–47; Professor and Head of the Department, Morgan State College, 1947–62; Professor, State University of New York, 1962–69; Professor of Mathematics and Chairman of the Department, State University of New York College, Potsdam, 1969–.

Memberships and awards: Honorary D.Sc., Johnson C. Smith University, 1954; American Mathematical Society; Mathematical Association of America.

Ref: *Black Mathematicians and Their Works,* p. 294.
    American Men and Women of Science, 14th; ed., p. 4892.
    The Negro in Science, p. 189.
    Who's Who in America, 1978, p. 3112.

Stepto, Robert Charles   (1920– ——, M)

Physician. Obstetrician. Gynecologist. Pathologist. Surgeon. Born in Chicago, IL, Oct. 6, 1920. B.S., Northwestern University, 1941; M.D., Howard University Medical College, 1944; Ph.D. (pathology), University of Chicago, 1948. Chairman, Department of Obstetrics, Mount Sinai Hospital, 1970–75; Professor of Obstetrics and Gynecology, Rush Medical College, 1957–79; Chief of Gynecology, University of Chicago, 1979–; research in endocrine pathology.

Memberships and awards: Fellow, American College of Obstetricians and Gynecologists; American College of Surgeons; International College of Surgeons; Chicago Board of Health; President, Association of Gynecological Oncologists, 1983; President, National Medical Fellowship Board; fellow, USPHS, 1948–50; National Medical Association.

Dissertation title: Studies of the Metabolic Effects of Testosterone Propionate in Tissue Synthesis.

Ref: *American Men and Women of Science,* 15th ed., p. 988.
    Who's Who Among Black Americans, 1985, p. 795.
    Jet, April 30, 1970, p. 45. [p]
    Jet, Feb. 9, 1978, p. 28. [p]
    Ebony Success Library, v.1, p. 292. [p]
    ABMS Compendium of Medical Specialists, v. 3, p. 820.

Sterrs, Willis Edward   (1868–19??, M)

Physician. Born in Montgomery, AL, Oct. 18, 1868. B.S., Lincoln University, Marion, AL, 1885; M.D., University of Michigan, Ann Arbor, 1888; Professor of Bacteriology, Meharry Medical College, 1891; Pension Surgeon for the United States, 1892–1914; conducted Cottage House Infirmary and Nurses Training School since 1908.

Memberships and awards: National Medical Association, Secretary four years and President nine years.

Ref: *Who's Who of Colored Race,* 1915, p. 252–253.

Stevens, George D.   (1860–1940, M)

Inventor. Paper company chief engineer. Director of 1st Barberton Fire Department, Chief. Invented paper company machines now standard in paper mills industry.

Ref: *Ebony,* May 1958, p. 101–110. [p]

Steward, Susan Maria Smith McKinney   (1847–1918, F)

Physician. Born in Brooklyn, NY, 1847. M.D., New York Medical College and Hospital for Women, 1870 (valedictorian); Posgraduate courses, Long Island Medical College Hospital, 1888, only woman in the entire college. First black female physician in New York State, third in the nation. In 1881 co-founded Women's Hospital and Dispensary at Myrtle and Grand Avenues in Brooklyn and was a member of the staff until 1896. (Memorial Hospital for Women and Children). From 1892–1896, she was manager and one of two female members of the medical staff of the Brooklyn Home for Aged Colored People.

Memberships and awards: King's County Homeopathic Society; New York State Medical Society; Junior High School in Brooklyn named for her (Susan Smith McKinney.

Ref: *Dictionary of American Negro Biography,* p. 569–570.
    Homespun Heroines and Other Women of Distinction, p. 160–164. [p]
    Noted Negro Women, p. 269–270.
    Profiles of Negro Womanhood, v. 1, 312–313.
    Medico-Chirurgical Society of the District of Columbia, Inc., *Bulletin,* Jan. 1949, p.3.
    Crisis, v. 8, Jan. 1980, p. 21–23.
    National Medical Association, *Journal,* v. 67, Mar. 1975, p. 173–175. [p] on cover.

Stewart, Aileen Cole   (1900–19??, F)

Nurse. 1918 Among a small group of professional nurses allowed to serve in the Army Nurse Corp in World War I when the number of white nurses was reduced by a flu epidemic.

Ref: *Smithsonian. Black Women Achievers Against Odds,* p. 28.

Stewart, Albert Clifton   (1919– ——, M)

Chemist (inorganic). Chemist (radiation). Born in Detroit, MI, Nov. 25, 1919. B.S., University of Chicago, 1942; M.S., 1948; Ph.D. (chemistry), St. Louis University, 1951. First black Director of Sales, Chemical and Plastics Division, Union Carbide, 1977–; research in physical, inorganic, and radiation chemistry.

Memberships and awards: First black with a Ph.D. to serve on the Atomic Energy Commission staff at Oak Ridge. American Chemical Society; AAAS; Sigma Xi; St. Louis University Alumni Merit Award, 1958; Radiation Research Society; American Nuclear Society; Alpha Phi Alpha.

Dissertation title: Reactions of Sodium Borohydride, Lithium-Aluminum-Hydride, and Lithium-Borohydride with Metal Ions.

Ref: *American Men and Women of Science,* 14th ed., p. 4900.
In Black and White, p. 918.
Who's Who Among Black Americans, 1985, p. 797.
The Negro in Science, p. 186.
Jet, Sept. 9, 1965, p. 11. [p]
Ebony, July 1959, p. 7. [p]
Leaders in American Sci, 1962–63, p. 674. [p]

Stewart, Ella Nora Phillips   (1893–19??, F)

Pharmacist. In 1948 elected President of the National Association of Colored Women.

Ref: *Smithsonian Black Women Achievements Against All Odds,* p. 35.
Who's Who of American Women, 1974.
Who's Who in America, 1976, p.
Contribution of Black Women to America, p. 398.

Stewart, Ferdinand Augustus   (1862–19??, M)

Physician. Surgeon. Born in Mobile, AL, Aug. 6, 1862. B.A., Fisk University, 1885; M.A., 1890; M.D., Harvard Medical School, 1888. Physician and Surgeon, Fisk University, 1889–; Professor of Pathology, 1889–1908; Professor of Surgery, Meharry Medical College, 1908.

Memberships and awards: President, Tennessee State Medical Association; President, National Medical Association, 1903. First honors in his class of over one hundred at Harvard University Medical School.

Ref: *Who's Who of the Colored Race,* 1915, p. 253–254.
Progress of a Race or the Remarkable Advancement of the Negro, p. 594.

Still, Donald Eric   (1946– ——, M)

Engineer (mechanical). Born in Camden, NJ, July 14, 1946. B.S. (mechanical engineering), Northeastern University, 1969; M.S., MIT, 1971. Bell Telephone Laboratories, Indianapolis, IN, specialist in heat transfer and acoustics.

Memberships and awards: American Society of Mechanical Engineers; Pi Tau Sigma; Sigma Xi; Phi Kappa Phi.

Ref: Black Engineers in the United States, p. 188.

Still, James   (1812–1885, M)

Physician. Practitioner. Self-taught. Born in Indian Mill, NJ, April 9, 1812. In 1843 he began to make his own medicines, selling them to buy medical books. Known in New Jersey as the "Black Doctor." Practiced for 40 years, well respected, treating both white and black patients. He was the uncle of Dr. Caroline Virginia Still Anderson.

Pub: Early Recollections and Life of Dr. James Still. Philadelphia, Lippincott, 1877. 274 p. (autobiography).

Ref: Early Recollections and Life of James Still. (Reprint 1971)
Encyclopedia of Black America, p. 809.
History of the Negro in Medicine, p. 21–23. [p]
National Medical Association, *Journal,* v. 83, Suppl., Dec. 1981, p. 1208–1209.
Dictionary of American Medical Biography, p. 720.
Cobb, W. Montague. Dr. James Still—New Jersey Pioneer. National Medical Association, *Journal,* v. 55, Mar. 1963, p. 196–199. [p] on cover

Stokes, Rufus   *(1924– ——, M)*

Inventor. Patent, 1968, for an air purification service to reduce to a safe level the gases and ash from furnace and powerplant smoke.

Ref: Black Contributors to Science and Energy Technology, p. 15.
In Black and White, p. 923.

Stubblefield, Beauregard   (1923– ——, M)

Mathematician. Born in Navasota, TX, July 31, 1923. B.S., Prairie View College, 1943; M.A., Prairie View College, 1945; M.S., University of Michigan, 1951; Ph.D. (mathematics), University of Michigan, 1959. Professor and Head, Department of Mathematics, University of Liberia, Monrovia, Liberia, West Africa, 1952–56 (serving as U.S. Department of State exchange professor); Research Mathematician, Detroit Arsenal, 1957–60; Lecturer and National Science Foundation Post-doctoral fellow, University of Michigan, 1959–60; Assistant Professor, Stevens Institute of Technology, 1960–61; Associate Professor of Mathematics, Oakland University, Rochester, MI, 1961–67 (on leave 1967–70); Senior National Teaching Fellow, Prairie View College, 1967–68; Visiting Professor and Visiting Scholar, Texas Southern University, 1968–69; Director, Mathematics, the Thirteen-College Curriculum Program, 1969–71; Professor, Mathematics, Appalachian State University, 1971–75; Mathematician, National Oceanic and Atmospheric Administration, Environmental Research laboratory, 1976–.

Memberships and awards: Sigma Xi; Alpha Kappa Mu; Outstanding Educator of America for 1972; Writing team of the National Committee on the Undergraduate Program in Mathematics (CUPM) which prepared the outlines for the Level I Training of elementary school teachers; Vice-Chairman of the Michigan Section of the Mathematical Association of America, 1966–67; Chairman, Michigan Section of the Mathematical Association of America, 1967–68.

Dissertation title: Some Compact Product Spaces Which Cannot be Imbedded in Euclidean n-Space.

Pub: Some Compact Product Spaces Which Cannot Be Imbedded in Euclidean n-Space, University of Michigan Press.
Informal Geometry. The Shebarb Co., 1967.
An Intuitive Approach to Elementary Geometry. Cole Co., The Books, 1969.
Structures of Numbers Systems, Shebarb Co., 1969.
Base Numeration Systems and Introduction to Computer Programming I, Newton, Mass, Curriculum Resources Groups, 1969.
Similarity and Theory of Trigonometry of Triangle. Newton, Mass, Resources Group, 1969.
Number Systems and Elements of Geometry. Belmont, Calif., Wadsworth, 1971.

Ref: Black Mathematicians and Their Works, p. 210–222, 294–295. [p] (List of publications)
American Men and Women of Science, 15th ed., p. 1069.

Stubbs, Frederick Douglas   (1906–1947, M)

Physician. Surgeon. Born in Wilmington, DE. B.S., Dartmouth College (magna cum laude), 1927; M.D., Harvard Medical School (cum laude), 1931. First black admitted to American College of Surgeons. First black formally trained in thoracic surgery. First black appointed to the staff of Philadelphia General Hospital. Administrator of the Philadelphia Health Center; Chief, Division of Surgery, Douglas and Mercy Hospitals; Acting Chief, Division of Tuberculosis, Philadelphia General Hospital.

Memberships and awards; First black elected to the Harvard Chapter of the honorary medical fraternity, Alpha Omega Alpha; Philadelphia County Medical Society; American Medical Association; National Medical Association; Laeneec Society of Philadelphia; American Trudeau Society; National Tuberculosis Association; Pennsylvania Tuberculosis Society; American Public Health Association; University of Pennsylvania Public Health Association; American Board of Surgery, 1941.

Ref: History of the Negro in Medicine, p. 135–136, 281. [p]
Cobb, W. Montague. Frederick Douglas Stubbs, 1906–1947. National Medical Association, *Journal,* v. 40, Jan. 1948, p. 24–26. [p]
Dictionary of American Medical Biography, p. 724–725.
A Century of Black Surgeons, p. 529–557. [p]

Stubbs, Ulysses Simpson, Jr.   (1911–19??, M)

Chemist. Born in Kingstree, SC, Dec. 11, 1911. B.S., Claflin College, 1935; M.S., Columbia University, 1939; Ph.D. (chemistry), New York University, 1958. Instructor, Chemistry, Hampton Institute, 1939–41; Acting Head, Physics Department, 1943–46; Assistant Professor, Chemistry, 1946–47; Assistant Professor, Chemistry, Morgan State College, 1947–68; Professor, Chemistry, Morgan State College, 1968–; research in heterocyclic compounds (nicotine).

Memberships and awards: Phi Delta Kappa; Kappa Delta Phi; American Chemical Society; AAAS.

Dissertation title: A Comparison of Two Methods of Teaching Certain Quantitative Principles of General Chemistry at the College Level.

Ref: American Men and Women of Science, 14th ed., p. 4963.
The Negro in Science, p. 186.

Suggs, Daniel Cato   (18??–19??, M)

Mathematician. B.A., Lincoln University, PA, 1884; studied at Cornell, Harvard and the University of Chicago. Professor of Mathematics and Physical Science, Livingston College, Salisbury, NC, 1888–1891; Director, Department of Natural Science and Vice-President, Georgia State Industrial College, Savannah, 1891–.

Memberships and awards: Honorary M.A. and Ph.D.

Ref: Who's Who of the Colored Race, 1915, p. 256.

Sullivan, Frances   (19??– ——, F)

Mathematician. Born in Orangeburg, SC. B.A., Orangeburg State College, 1965; M.S. (mathematics), University of South Carolina, 1968; Ph.D., CUNY, 1980. Faculty of City College of New York; Mathematics Faculty, Jackson State University, Mississippi, 1980–.

Dissertation title: Wreath Products of Lie Algebras.

Ref: Kenschaft, Patricia C. Black Women in Mathematics in the United States. *American Mathematical Monthly,* v. 88, Oct. 1951, p. 602.

Sullivan, Louis W. (1933- ——, M)

Physician. Hematologist. Born in Atlanta, GA, Nov. 3, 1933. B.S., Morehouse College, 1954; M.D. (Cum Laude), Boston University, 1958. Instructor in Medicine, Harvard Medical School; Assistant Professor of Medicine, New Jersey College of Medicine; Professor of Medicine, Boston University School of Dentistry and Medicine, 1974-75. Dean, Morehouse School of Medicine 1975-; First President Morehouse School of Medicine, 1981-. Presidential Cabinet Member: Secretary of Health and Human Services, 1989-.

Memberships and awards: Phi Beta Kappa; Institute of Medicine (National Academy of Science) Fellow, American College of Physicians, 1980. Founding President of the Association of Minority Health Professions Schools; Joint Committee on Policy of the Association of American Universities; National Association of Land Grant Colleges and Universities. One of three black leaders in the United States to serve as a member of George Bush's twelve member team to seven African Countries in 1982.

Pub: The Education of Black Health Professionals, 1977.
Over fifty articles in numerous medical journals.

Ref: Black Family International Journal '85. p. 70-71. [p]
Who's Who Among Black American, 1985, p. 804.
American Men and Women of Science, 16th ed., p. 1127.

Sumner, Francis Cecil (1895-1954, M)

Psychologist. Born in Pine Bluff, AR, Dec. 7, 1895. B.A., Lincoln University, PA; B.A., Clark University, MA; M.A., Lincoln University; Ph.D., Clark University, 1920. Professor and Head, Department of Psychology, Howard University, 1930-54; First black Ph.D. in Psychology.

Memberships and awards: University fellow and University Scholar, Clark University. Psychological Association of the East; Southern Society of Philosophy and Psychology; Psychological Association of DC; fellow, American Psychological Association; AAAS; American Educational Research Association; Kappa Alpha Psi.

Dissertation title: Psychoanalysis of Freud and Adler.

Pub: Hygiene of the Mind (translation from the German). New York, MacMillan, 1933. 150 p.
The Nature of Emotion. *Howard Review,* v. 1, June 1924.

Ref: Holders of Doctorates Among American Negroes, p. 210-211.
Even the Rat Was White, p. 175-189. [p]
Washington Afro American, Jan. 16, 1954, p. 5. Funeral at Howard for Dr. F. Sumner.
Crisis, July, 1920, p. 127. [p] only

Sutton, Louise Nixon (1925- ——, F)

Mathematician. Born in Hertford, NC, Nov. 4, 1925. B.S., Agricultural and Technical State University of North Carolina, 1946; M.A., New York University, 1951; Ph.D., New York University, 1962. Instructor, Mathematics, James B. Dudley High School, Greensboro, NC, 1946-47; Instructor, Assistant Professor, Agricultural and Technical State University, 1947-54; Assistant Professor, Delaware State College, 1957-62; Professor, Mathematics and Chairman, Department of Mathematics, Elizabeth City State University, 1962-.

Memberships and awards: Board of Directors, Perquimons County Industrial Development Corps, 1967-72; Co-Director, National Science Foundation Institute, 1971-72, 1973-74; Chairman, 1977-78; National Association of University Women; Alpha Kappa Mu; Beta Kappa Chi Scientific Society; Mathematical Association of America; North Carolina Council of Teachers of Mathematics; National Council of Teachers of Mathematics; *National Register of Prominent Americans, Outstanding Mathematicians.*

Dissertation title: Concept Learning in Trigonometry and Analytic Geometry at the College Level: A Comparative Study of Two Methods of Teaching.

Ref: American Men and Women of Science, 16th ed., p. 1146.
Black Mathematicians and Their Works, p. 295. [p]
Who's Who of American Women, 1972.
Trigonometry and Analytic Geometry at the College Level.

Svager, Thyrsa Frazier (19??- ——, F)

Mathematician. B.S., Antioch College; M.A., Ohio State University, Ph.D. (mathematics), 1965. Statistical analyst, Wright-Patterson Air Force Base for one year; faculty member, Central State University, 1954-.

Dissertation title: On the Product of Absolutely Continuous Transformations of Measure Spaces.

Pub: On Strong Differentiability. Abstract. *American Mathematical Monthly,* 1967.
Modern Elementary Algebra Workbook. Wm. C. Brown, 1969.
Essential Mathematics for College Freshmen, Kendall-Hunt, 1976.

Ref: Kenschaft, Patricia C. Black Women in Mathematics in the United States. *American Mathematical Monthly,* v. 88, Oct. 1981, p. 598.
National Faculty Directory, 1988, p. 3725.

Swan, Lionel Fitzroy (1909–19??, M)

Physician. Born in Trinidad, W.I., April 1, 1909. B.S., Howard University, 1932; M.D., 1939. Physician and President, Detroit Medical and Surgical Center.

Memberships and awards: President, National Medical Association, 1966–67; Founder, National Medical Association Foundation; Detroit Medical Society; American Medical Association; Michigan State Medical Society; Wayne County Medical Society; Michigan Health Council; Michigan Health Maintenance Organization; Phi Beta Sigma; District Service Award; Michigan Health Council, 1968; fellow, American Family Practice.

Ref: Who's Who Among Black Americans, 1985, p. 806.
National Medical Association, *Journal,* v. 58, Nov. 1966. p. 470–471. [p]

Sweres, Mary Agnes (1890–19??, F)

Bacteriologist. Nurse. Born in Appleton, WI, Jan. 27, 1890. Nurse, St. Joseph's Hospital, Milwaukee, 1912–23; Marquette Medical School, 1917–18; B.S., University of Chicago, 1923. Senior Bacteriologist for the United States with an office in Chicago.

Ref: Who's Who in Colored America, 1928–29, p. 352. [p]

Syphax, Burke (1910– ——, M)

Physician. Surgeon. Born in Washington, DC, Dec. 18, 1910. B.S., Howard University, 1932; M.D., Howard University medical School, 1936. Assistant in Surgery, Howard University Medical School, 1940–41; Instructor, Surgery, 1942–44; Assistant Professor, Surgery, 1944–50; Associate Professor, 1950–58; Acting Chief, Division of General Surgery, 1951–52; Chief, 1958–70; Senior Professor, Surgery, 1970–; research in oncology, gastroenterology.

Memberships and awards: Alpha Phi Alpha; Kappa Pi; Alpha Omega Alpha; Outstanding Alumnus Award, New York Alumni Association; First Distinguished Professor Award, 1974; Rockefeller fellow in surgery, Strong Memorial Hospital, University of Rochester, 1941–42; Diplomate, American Board of Surgeons; American Medical Association; fellow, American College of Surgeons; National Medical Association.

Ref: Who's Who Among Black Americans, 1985, p. 808.
American Men and Women of Science, 14th ed., p. 5015.
National Medical Association, *Journal,* v. 66, Nov. 1974, p. 528. [p]
National Medical Association, *Journal,* v. 70, Aug. 1978, p. 605. [p]
A Century of Black Surgeons, p. 636–639. [p]

T

Tackett, J. S. (1873–19??, M)

Physician. Born in Pickens, Holmes Co., MS, Jan. 18, 1873. B.A., New Orleans University, LA, 1891. Became Schoolmaster, 1896, in Madison Co., MS; M.D. Illinois Medical College, 1904. Practiced in Edmondson, AR.

Memberships and awards: President, People's Telephone Company and a stockholder in Edmondson Home and Improvement Company.

Ref: *Beacon Lights of the Race,* p. 303–309. [p]

Talbot, Walter Richard (1909–1977, M)

Mathematician. Born in Pittsburgh, PA, 1909. B.A. (mathematics and physics), University of Pittsburgh, 1931; Ph.D. (mathematics), University of Pittsburgh, 1934. Assistant Professor, Associate Professor, and Chairman, Department of Mathematics, Lincoln University, 1934–63; Lecturer, National Science Foundation Summer Institute, North Carolina College, Durham, NC, 1957–59; Director, Academic Year Institute in Mathematics, 1965–71; Director, Ford Mathematics Curriculum Conference, Morgan State College, Apr. 1969; Director, Conference on Mathematics at Developing Colleges, Laramie, WY, Aug. 1970; Professor and Chairman, Department of Mathematics, Morgan State College, 1963–77.

Dissertation title: Fundamentals of Regions in Six-Space for the Simple Quarternary Group of Order Sixty.

Pub: *Several articles in mathematics journals.*

Ref: *American Men and Women of Science,* 13th ed., p. 4415.
Black Mathematicians and Their Works, p. 296, 224–239.
Holders of Doctorates Among American Negroes, p. 157.

Talley, Thomas Washington (18??–19??, M)

Chemist (inorganic). Born in Shelbyville, TN. B.A., Fisk University, 1890; M.A., 1892; Sc.D., Walden University, TN, 1896; M.S. (chemistry), University of Chicago, 1931. Instructor in Science, Alcorn, MS, A & M College, 1899–1900; Professor of Sciences and Vice-President, Florida A & M College, Tallahassee, FL, 1900–02; Instructor, Analytical and Applied Chemistry, Tuskegee Institute, 1902–03; Professor, Chemistry and Biology, Fisk University, 1903–.

Memberships and awards: Society of Chemical Industry, London; American Chemical Society.

Ref: *Who's Who of the Colored Race,* 1915, p. 258.
American Men of Science, 8th ed., p. 2456.
Crisis, Jan. 1932, p. 463, 466. [p]

Tardy, Walter James, Jr.   (1941- ——, M)

Physician. Psychiatrist. psychoanalyst. Born in Verona, MS, May 19, 1941. B.A., Tennessee State University, 1962; M.D., University of Wisconsin Medical School, 1967; M.P.H., Harvard School of Public Health, 1969; College of Physicians and Surgeons, Columbia University; Director of Psychiatry, State University of New York at Stony Brook; Assistant Professor of Psychiatry, Department of Behavioral Science; Medical Director, Addition Research and Treatment Corporation, 1972; Chief Epidemiologist, 1st Medical Service, Clark Air Force Base, Phillipines, 1971; Psychoanalyst, Columbia Center for Psychoanalytic Research, 1957–83; Director of Psychiatry, Long Island Jewish Hillside Medical Center, Queens Hospital Center, 1978–.

Memberships and awards: American Medical Association; American Public Health Association; Association of Psychiatrists in Africa; American Psychiatric Association; Royal Society of Harvard School of Public Health Alumni Association; Harvard Club of New York; Association for Academic Psychiatry; AAAS; President, International Psychoanalytical Students Organization; Black Psychiatrists of America; Physicians Recognition Award, American Medical Association, 1972; National Psychiatric Endowment Fund Award, 1975.

Ref: Who's Who Among Black Americans, 1985, p. 809.
ABMS Compendium of Medical Specialists, v. 5, p. 764.
Biographical Directory of the American Psychiatric Association, 1983, p. 1199.

Taylor, Daniel Bernette   (1900–19??, M)

Chemist. Physician. Surgeon. Born in Philadelphia, PA, Mar. 18, 1900. B.S., Pennsylvania State College, 1922; M.D., Howard University, 1930. Professor, Agricultural Chemistry, Tuskegee Institute, 1922–24; Professor, Chemistry and Physics, A & T College, Greensboro, NC, 1924; Surgeon-on-staff, Mercy Hospital, 1931–.

Memberships and awards: Omega Psi Phi; American Chemical Society; Liebig Chemical Society (Pennsylvania); participated in Intercollegiate track championship competition, 1920, University of Pennsylvania and Harvard University, 1922.

Pub: "Chemistry in its Relation to Agriculture." King's Agricultural Digest, Tuskegee, 1923 (pointing out the necessity of a knowledge of chemistry in agricultural practice).

Ref: Who's Who in Colored American, 1928–29, p. 355–356.
Who's Who in Colored America, 1933–37, p. 502, 505. [p] p. 507.
Jet, Mar. 3, 1955, p. 15. [p]?
Who's Who Among Black Americans, 1977, p. 870.

Taylor, Edward Walter   (1926 ——, M)

Architect. Born in Baltimore, MD, July 17, 1926. B.S., Hampton Institute, 1950. Chief Drafter, U.S. Government, 1950–59; Architectural Manager, Henry L. Lines, Baltimore, 1958–63; Mechanical Designer, Westinghouse Electric, 1960–73; Architect, Edward Q Rogers, Baltimore, 1964–67; Architectural Manager, Sultor Campbell Architects, 1968–73; Owner, Atti Consulting, Ltd., 1973–.

Memberships and awards: National Technical Association; American Institute of Architects; Director, Model Cities Housing Corporation; Technical Consultant, E. Baltimore Community Corporation; Samuel Cheevers Award; Tribute Award, National Technical Association.

Ref: Who's Who Among Black Americans, 1985, p. 812.
Who's Who in the East, 1977, p. 759.

Taylor, Eugene Donaldson   (1922 ——, M)

Physician. Obstetrician. Gynecologist. Surgeon. Born in St. Louis, MO, Oct. 10, 1922. B.S., Virginia State College, 1947; Wilberforce University, 1948; M.D., Howard University Medical School, 1954. Associate Director, Obstetrics and Gynecology, Homer G. Phillips Hospital, 1967.

Memberships and awards: FACOB-GYN, 1962; American Board of Obstetrics and Gynecology, 1962; American College of Obstetrics and Gynecology; St. Louis Medical Society; Missouri Medical Society; American Medical Association; Missouri Pan American Medical Association; Medical Advisory Committee, Planned Parenthood Association, 1973; American College of Surgeons.

Ref: Who's Who Among Black Americans, 1985, p. 812.
ABMS Compendium of Medical Specialists, v. 3, p. 832.

Taylor, Harold Leon   (1946 ——, M)

Dentist. Oral Surgeon. Born in Memphis, TN, Mar. 7, 1946. B.S., Morehouse College, 1968; D.D.S., Howard University, 1972; Certificate in Oral Surgery, 1975; Dentist, Oral Maxilofacial Surgery, 1975–. Assistant Professor, Tennessee College of Dentistry, 1975–.

Memberships and awards: National Dental Association; Memphis Society of Oral Surgeons; Alpha Phi Alpha; Chi Delta Mu; President, Shelby County Dental Society, 1979; American Association of Oral and Maxillofacial Surgeons; American Dental Association; Editorial Board, Dental Students Magazine, 1972; fellowship, Memorial Hospital of Cancer, 1971; Dean's award, Howard University, 1972; Omicron Kappa Upsilon National Honor Society.

Ref: Who's Who Among Black Americans, 1985, p. 812.

Taylor, Jerome   (1940 ——, M)

Psychologist. Born in Waukegan, IL, Jan. 26, 1940. B.A., University of Denver, 1961; Ph.D., Indiana University,

1965. Director of Mental Health Unit, Topeka, 1968–69; Director, University of Pittsburgh Clinical Psychology Center, 1969–71; Associate Professor of Education and Psychology.

Memberships and awards: Menninger Foundation Postdoctoral fellow, 1965–67; American Psychological Association; Association of Black Psychologists; Omicron Delta Kappa; Sigma Xi.

Dissertation tile: The Effects of Population Density upon Correlates of Emotionality.

Ref: *Who's Who Among Black Americans,* 1985, p. 813.

Taylor, Julius Henry (1914 ——, M)

Physicist (solid state). Born in Cape May, NJ, Feb., 15, 1914. B.A., Lincoln University, PA, 1939; M.S., University of Pennsylvania, 1941; Ph.D. (physics), 1950. Research Assistant, Pennsylvania, 1941–45; Associate Professor, Physics, West Virginia State College, 1945–46; Research Physicist, University of Pennsylvania, 1947–49; Associate Professor, Physics, Morgan State College, 1949–50; Professor of Physics and Head of the Department, Morgan State College, 1950–.

Memberships and awards: Rosenwald fellow; Pennsylvania, 1943–44; American Physical Society; American Institute of Physics; Beta Kappa Chi; National Institute Science; Sigma Xi; National Science Foundation; National Committee of Physics in Secondary Education of the American Association of Physics Teachers; Research Award, Office of Ordinance Research, U.S. Army, each year from 1953 to 1957.

Dissertation title: The Pressure Dependence of Resistance of Germanium.

Pub: *The Negro in Science,* Baltimore, Morgan State University Press, 1955. 192 p.

Ref: *American Men and Women of Science,* 14th ed., p. 5055.
In Black and White, p. 940.
The Negro in Science, p. 101.
Who's Who Among Black Americans, 1985, p. 813.
Encyclopedia of Black Americans, 1984, p. 814.

Taylor, Lawnie (1902–19??, M)

Physicist. Born in 1902. B.S., Columbia University; M.S.; Ph.D, University of Southern California. Chief of Market Development and Training Department of Energy's Solar Office.

Ref: *Contributors to Science and Energy Technology,* p. 24–25.

Taylor, Moddie Daniel (1912–1976, M)

Chemist (inorganic). Chemist (physical). Born in Nymph, AL, Mar. 3, 1912. B.S., Lincoln University, MO, 1935;

M.S., University of Chicago, 1938; Ph.D., 1943. University of Chicago's Manhattan Project during World War II. Professor of Chemistry, 1959–69; Chairman, Chemistry Department, Howard University, 1969–1976.

Memberships and awards: Certificate of Merit, 1945, from Secretary of War for his work on the Manhattan Project, 1943–45; 1960, Annual Manufacturing Chemists' Award, one of six best Chemistry Teachers in the United States; Ford Foundation fellow, 1953; AAAS; American Chemical Society; Washington Academy of Science; Beta Kappa Chi; Sigma Xi; National Institute of Science.

Dissertation title: Acid-base Studies in Gaseous Systems; The Dissociation of the Addition Compounds of Trimethylboron with Aliphatic Amines.

Pub: *First Principles of Chemistry.* New York, Van Nostrand, 1960. 688 p.

Ref: *American Men and Women of Science,* 13th ed., p. 4440.
Encyclopedia of Black America, p. 814.
Jet, May 26, 1960, p. 19. [p]
The Negro in Science, p. 186.
Holders of Doctorates Among American Negroes, p. 57.
World Who's Who in Science, p. 1653–1654.
National Cyclopedia of American Biography, v. 59, p. 193. [p]

Taylor, Robert B., Sr. (1900s, M)

Dentist. Meharry Medical School.

Memberships and awards: Dentist of the Year, National Dental Association, 1958. Thirty-one years in practice.

Taylor, Susie King (1848–1912, F)

Nurse. Born into slavery on the Isle of Wight in Liberty County, GA. Working as a laundress for Company E of the First South Carolina Volunteers, she offered her nursing services to the wounded troops. In 1863 she met Clara Barton and worked with her. She later worked as a volunteer nurse on the battlefront for four years. She received no pay and because she was not under contract she received no pension.

Pub: *Reminiscences of My Life in Camp.* New York, Arno Press, 1968, 82 p.

Ref: *The Path We Tread,* p. 9–11. [p]
Her Way, 1984, p. 238.
Booker, Simeon. *Susie King Taylor, civil War Nurse,* McGraw-Hill, 1969. (Grades 4–9)
McGraw-Hill Encyclopedia of World Biography, v. 10, p. 372. (with bibliography)

Taylor, Welton Ivan (1919 ——, M)

Bacteriologist. Microbiologist. Born in Birmingham, AL, Nov. 12, 1919. B.A., University of Illinois, 1941; M.S., 1947; Ph.D. (bacteriology), 1948. From Instructor to Assistant Professor of Bacteriology, University of Illinois

College of Medicine, 1948-54; Research Bacteriologist, Swift & Co., 1954-59; Supervisor of Clinical Microbiology, Children's Memorial Hospital, 1959-64; Bacteriologist-in-Chief, West Suburban Hospital, Oak Park, IL, 1964-69; Associate Professor of Microbiology, University of Illinois Medical Center, 1969-.

Memberships and awards: Special Research fellow, National Institute of Allergy and Infectious Diseases, Institut Pasteur, France, and Central Public Health Laboratory, England, 1961-62; Consultant, Armour & Co., 1966-68; National Communicable Disease Center Research Grant, 1966-68; American Society of Microbiology; fellow, American Academy of Microbiology; New species of bacterium *Enterobacter taylorae* named for him in 1985; Board of Directors, American Board of Bioanalysis, 1973-; Vice-President, Chicago Mycological Society; consultant microbiologist, several hospitals.

Dissertation title: The Growth and Toxin Production of Clostridium Botrelinum in Cottage Cheese.

Ref: *Who's Who Among Black Americans,* 1985, p. 816.
American Men and Women of Science, 15th ed., p. 47.
Ebony, May 1954, p. 24. [p]

Taylor, William Charles (1929 ——, M)

Chemist (inorganic). Engineer. Born in Sanford, NC, Mar. 29, 1929. B.S. (chemistry), North Carolina A & T State University, 1953; M.S. (chemistry), Stevens Institute of Technology, 1960; Ph.D. (chemistry), University of Connecticut, 1963. Supervisor of Chemical Research, Combustion Engineering, Inc., 1957-59, Windsor, CT; Assistant Instructor and Research Assistant, University of Connecticut, 1959-63; Supervisor, Analytical Chemistry, Nuclear Division, Combustion Engineering, Inc., 1963-68; Senior Professional Project Engineer, Utility Division, Kreisinger Development Laboratory, 1968-71; Supervisor, Chemical Research, Air Pollution Control Section, 1971-.

Memberships and awards: American Chemical Society; New York Academy of Science; Sigma Xi; Phi Lambda Upsilon; Beta Kappa Xi; Alpha Kappa Mu; AAAS; Scientific Research Society of America.

Dissertation title: The Photochemistry of Some Tris-Diamine Cobalt (III) Complexes in Aqueous Solution.

Ref: *Black Engineers in the United States,* p. 192.
American Men and Women of Science, 12th ed., p. 6316.

Tazewell, Joseph H. (1932 ——, M)

Chemist (plastic). Born in Portsmouth, VA, June 1, 1932. B.S., Hampton Institute, 1953; M.S., University of Akron.

Memberships and awards: Army citation for excellence in teaching chemical warfare; American Chemical Society.

Ref: *Ebony,* Nov. 1961, p. 7. [p]
Ebony Success Library, v. 3, p. 170-171. [p]

Tearney, Russell James (1938 ——, M)

Physiologist. Born in Syracuse, NY, Aug. 10, 1938. B.S., Virginia Union University, 1961; M.S., Howard University, 1969; Ph.D., 1973. Assistant Professor of Physiology and Biophysics, Howard University, 1973-.

Memberships and awards: AAAS; Sigma Xi; Porter fellowship, 1969-72; American Physiological Society, 1977; Graduate Assistant Professor, Graduate School of Arts and Sciences, Howard University; American Heart Association; Black Scientists of America.

Dissertation title: Left Ventricular Function in Conscious Instrumented Dogs with Experimental Renal Hypertension.

Ref: *Who's Who Among Black Americans,* 1985, p. 816.

Temple, Lewis (1800-1854, M)

Inventor. Born in Richmond, VA, never learned to write his name. A Blacksmith with a whalecraft shop on Coffins Wharf in New Bedford, he invented the toggle harpoon in 1848 which became a boon to the whaling industry, the "Temple Toggle-Iron."

Ref: *At Last Recognition in America,* v. 1, p. 29.
Dictionary of American Negro Biography, p. 582-583.
Encyclopedia of Black America, p. 814.
Negro Almanac, p. 640.
Kaplan, Sidney, Lewis Temple and the Hunting of the Whale. *Negro History Bulletin,* Oct. 1953, p. 7-10. Biography with bibliography.
Eight Black American Inventors.

Temple, Ruth J. (1900s, F)

Physician. M.D., Loma Linda University, 1918. First black female physician in California; Director, Public Health Programs, Los Angeles, holding seminars on health, smoking, diet, etc., in the Biltmore Hotel.

Ref: *Women Makers of History: A Portrait.* p. 94, 96. [p]
Contributions of Black Women to America, p. 384.

Terrell, Francis (1944 ——, M)

Psychologist. B.S., Wilmington College, OH, 1968; M.S., University of Pittsburgh, 1972; Ph.D. (clinical psychology), 1975. Assistant Professor, Texas Christian University, 1976-80; Associate Professor and Director of Clinical Training, North Texas State University, 1980-; Director, Clinical Training, 1981.

Memberships and awards: American Psychological Association; Black Psychological Association, 1976-80; Sigma Xi; Regional Mental Health Consultant, U.S. Labor Department, 1978-; fellow, Society for the Study of Personality, 1984; University of Pittsburgh Post Doctoral fellow, 1975–76.

Dissertation title: The Development of an Inventory to Measure Aspects of Black Nationalism Ideology.

Pub: Self Concept of Juveniles Who Commit Black on Black Crimes. *In* Corrective and Social Psychiatry, 1980.
Effects of Race on Examiner and Type of Reinforcement on the Intelligence Test of Black Children. *Psychology in the Schools,* 1980.
Over 30 other journal articles.

Ref: Who's Who Among Black Americans, 1985, p. 817.
Directory of the American Psychological Association, p. 1035.

Terrell, Wendell Phillips   (1884–19??, M)

Engineer (mechanical). Born in Fort Worth, TX, Mar. 1, 1884. Kansas State Agricultural College, 1904; B.S., Massachusetts Institute of Technology, 1906. Superintendent of Mechanics and Mechanical Engineer, Prairie View State Normal and Industrial College, TX.

Ref: Who's Who of the Colored Race, 1915, p. 260.

Terrence, August Caswell   (1901– ——, M)

Physician. Born in New Orleans, LA. B.S., Howard University, 1924; M.D., 1928; Private practice, Opelousas, LA, 1931–74.

Memberships and awards: President, National Medical Association, 1955–56; President, Howard University Medical Alumni Association; President, Temco Development Corporation of Opelousas, LA; Distinguished Alumni Award, Howard University, 1955.

Ref: Who's Who Among Black Americans, 1985, p. 818.
National Medical Association, *Journal,* v. 67, Jan. 1975, p. 84–85. [p]
National Medical Association, *Journal,* v. 79, Apr. 1987, p. 353–355. (his letter to the editor, of historic value)

Terry, Robert James   (1922 ——, M)

Zoologist. Born in Crockett, TX, May 1, 1922. B.S., Texas Southern University, 1946; M.S., Atlanta University, 1949; Ph.D., University of Iowa, 1954. Instructor to Professor of Biology, Texas Southern University, 1948–50; Professor, 1954–69; Dean and Professor, 1969–71; Dean, 1971–73; Vice-President for Academic Affairs, 1973–; Associate Director, National Science Foundation, 1966–67; Science Consultant, Government of India, 1967.

Memberships and awards: National President, Beta Kappa Chi Science Honor Society, 1964–67; National Institutes of Health Research Grant Advisory Group.

Dissertation title: Studies on Midbrain Regeneration in Embryos and Larvae of Rana Pipiens.

Ref: American Men and Women of Science, 15th ed., p. 66.
Who's Who Among Black Americans, 1985, p. 818.
World Who's Who in Science, p. 1659.

Thatcher, Harold W.   (1908–19??, M)

Physician. Dermatologist. Born in Kansas City, KS, 1908. B.S., University of Minnesota, 1929; M.B., 1931; M.D., 1932. Associate of Dr. Theodore Lawless, Dermatologist. Chief, Medical Service for Regional and Station Hospitals during World War II, Fort Huachuca, AZ.

Memberships and awards: Legion of Merit for meritorious conduct, U.S. Department of War; Board of Trustees, Cook County Hospital Nursing School; Chicago Metropolitan Dermatological Society.

Ref: Ebony Success Library, v. 1, p. 301. [p]
Who's Who Among Black Americans, 1985, p. 818.

Thaxton, Hubert Mach   (1912–1974, M)

Physicist (mathematical). Physicist (theoretical). B.S., Howard University, 1931; M.S., 1933; M.A., Wisconsin University, 1936; Ph.D., 1939. Professor of Physics and Head of Department, North Carolina A & T College, 1939–; Solar Manufacturing Company; International Electronics; Tube Deutschmann Corp.; Sperry Gyroscope Co.; Sylvania Electronic Co.; Walter Henry Junior College; Lecturer, Project Engineer, College of the City of New York; worked with five Nobel Prize winners.

Memberships and awards: American Mathematical Society; American Physical Society.

Dissertation title: Scattering of Protons.

Pub: Over 200 articles in 14 languages.

Ref: American Men of Science, 7th ed., p. 1771.
Holders of Doctorates Among American Negroes, p. 157.
Blacks in Science: Astrophysicist to Zoologist, p. 61.

Theus, Lucius   (1922 ——, M)

Military (Air Force). Major General. Born in Bell, TN, Oct. 11, 1922. B.S., University of Maryland, 1956; M.B.A., George Washington University, 1957; Harvard Business School Graduate, Advanced Management Program, 1969; Distinguished Graduate, Armed Forces Staff College, 1960; retired.

Memberships and awards: National Association of Accountants; National Association of Black Accountants; Vice-President and Member of the Board of Directors, Harvard Business School Club of Washington, DC, 1972–74; Distinguished Service Medal with Oak Leaf Cluster; Legion of Merit Bronze Star Medal.

Ref: Black Americans in Defense of Our Nation, p. 130. [p]
Ebony, May 1978, p. 42. [p]

Who's Who Among Black Americans, 1985, p. 818.
One Thousand Successful Blacks, p. 301. [p]
Crisis, Dec. 1973, p. 346. [p]

Thomas, Alfred E. (Alf) (1909-1968, M)

Physician. Son of Dr. Alf E. Thomas. Founded three hospitals, Bethesda Hospital, Detroit, 1931; Edyth K. Thomas Hospital, 1937, and Linda L. Convalescent Home, 1953.

Ref: *Jet*, Nov. 26, 1956, p. 48. [p]
      Jet, July 18, 1968, p. 48. [p]
      Ebony, Oct. 1950, p. 40.
      Ebony, Nov. 1953, p. 71. [p] p. 72, 77-78, 80.

Thomas, Gerald Eustis (1929 ——, M)

Military (Navy). Rear Admiral. Biochemist. Born in Natick, MA, June 23, 1929. B.A. (biochemistry), Harvard University, 1951; M.S. (international affairs), George Washington University, 1966; Ph.D., Yale University, 1973. U.S. Naval War College (Russian). Main Battery Officer and Radio Officer, USS Worcester, 1954; Executive Officer, USS Lowe, 1960; First Command, USS Impervious, 1962; Commander, Destroyer Squadron Nine, U.S. Navy; retired, 1981; Ambassador, Guyana, 1981-83; Ambassador, Kenya, 1983-.

Memberships and awards: Navy Commendation Medal; Vietnam Service Medal; Board of Overseers, Harvard University; Organization of American Historians; Rear Admiral for 30 years.

Dissertation title: William D. Leahy and America's Imperial Years, 1893-1917.

Ref: *Black American in Defense of Our Nation*, p. 127. [p] only.
      Ebony, May 1978, p. 46. [p] only.
      Who's Who Among Black Americans, 1985, p. 820.
      Living Legends in Black, p. 23. [p]

Thomas, Hyram S. (1800s, M)

Inventor. Invented potato chips, known as Saratogo chips, while working as a chef in Saratoga Springs, NY.

Ref: *Ebony Handbook*, p. 371.

Thomas, Joseph Turner (1874-19??, M)

Physician. Born in Greenville, AL, Dec. 25, 1874. B.S., Alabama A & M, 1896; M.D., Meharry Medical College, 1905. Physician, 1905-28. Founder, Lincoln Hospital, Cleveland, OH. Wrote several songs.

Ref: *Who's Who in Colored America*, 1928-29, p. 361.
      Who's Who in Colored America, 1933-37, p. 513.

Thomas, Maceo A. (1897-19??, M)

Agriculturist. Born in Baltimore, MD, May 22, 1897. Lincoln University, 1817-18; B.S., Cornell University, 1922; Advanced work in Physics, Columbia University, 1924. Teacher in charge of vocational agriculture, Lane College, summer, 1922. Teacher, Tuskegee Institute, 1922-23; Teacher of Physics and Chemistry, Douglas High School, Baltimore, MD, 1923-25; Salesman and Executive Manager, Dobbins Coal Co., New York, NY, 1925-. While teaching at Tuskegee, he started the college course of agriculture under Director Benjamin Hubert, taught Biology and Bacteriology and had charge of dairy herd and creamery, with special instruction in poultry.

Memberships and awards: Alpha Phi Alpha.

Ref: *Who's Who in Colored America*, 1933-37, p. 514.

Thomas, Marguerite (19?? ——, F)

See: Williams, Marguerite Thomas.

Thomas, William McKinley (1903-1958, M)

Physician. Surgeon. Born in Bryan, TX, May 5, 1903. B.A., Wiley College, Marshall, TX, 1926; M.D., Meharry Medical College, 1930; Postgraduate Study, Harvard School of Public Health, 1941-42; Army Medical Inspectors School, 1943. Medical practice, Leavenworth, KS, 1931-41; U.S. Army Medical Corps, 1942-45; Surgeon, San Francisco, 1945-58; first black physician named to a standing External Advisory Group of Public Health Service, 1954, for five years.

Memberships and awards: Board of Trustees, National Medical Association, 1934-41; Chairman, NMA-AMA Liaison Committee, 1953; Chair, Committee of Distinguished Service Award.

Ref: *Who's Who in Colored America*, 1950, p. 504.
      Dictionary of American Medical Biography, p. 739.
      Cobb, W. Montague. William McKinley Thomas, M.D., 1903-1958. National Medical Association, *Journal*, v. 50, May 1958, p. 221.

Thompson, Emanuel B. (1928 ——, M)

Pharmacologist. B.S., Rockhurst College, 1955; B.S., University of Missouri, Kansas City, 1959; M.S., University of Kansas, 1963; Ph.D., University of Washington, 1966. Associate Professor of Pharmacology, University of Illinois, Medical Center, 1973-; research in cardiovascular pharmacology.

Dissertation title: The Action of a Beta-Receptor Antagonist on the Positive Chronotropic Response to Nerve Stimulation and Applied Catecholamine in Isolated Rabbit Atria.

Ref: *American Men and Women of Science*, 14th ed., p. 5102.

Thompson, Floyd, Sr.   (1914 —— , M)

Dentist. Born in Houston, TX, Aug. 5, 1914. B.A., Wiley College, 1937; D.D.S., Howard University Dental School, 1942. Postgraduate, University of Southern California Dental School, 1964. Private practice to 1985.

Memberships and awards: Arizona State Dental Society; National Dental Association; American Dental Association; Alumni Award for Outstanding Contributions to Civic and Community Activities, 1971.

Ref: *Who's Who Among Black Americans*, 1985, p. 826.

Thompson, Solomon Henry   (1870–1950, M)

Physician. Surgeon. Born in Charlestown, WV, Aug. 10, 1870. B.S., Storer College, Harpers Ferry, WV, 1886; M.D., Howard University, 1892. Surgeon-in-Chief and Founder, Douglas Hospital, Kansas City, KS, first black hospital west of the Mississippi River and training school for nurses; Surgeon-in-Chief, Douglas Hospital, 1892–1946 (Douglas Hospital merged with Mercy Hospital in 1946); Lecturer in Physiology, Western University, KS, and Assistant Surgeon, St. Mary's Hospital, Kansas City, KS.

Ref: *Who's Who in Colored America*, 1927, p. 201–202.
    Who's Who in Colored America, 1928–29, p. 365.
    Who's Who in Colored America, 1933–37.
    Howard University Medical Department, p. 222.
    Dictionary of American Medical Biography, p. 740.
    Cobb, W. Montague. Solomon Henry Thompson, M.D., 1870–1950. National Medical Association, *Journal*, v. 49, July 1957, p. 274–278. [p]

Thompson, Vertis Raymond   (1925 —— , M)

Physician. Obstetrician. Gynecologist. Born in Muskogee, OK, Nov. 1, 1925. B.S., Howard University, 1948; M.D., Howard University Medical College, 1952. Gynecological Staff, Agnew State Hospital, CA, 1957–59; Private Practice, Oakland, CA, 1959–; Lecturer, UCLA, Berkeley, School of Public Health, 1976–78.

Memberships and awards: President, National Medical Association, 1979–80; American Medical Association; Diplomate, National Board of Medical Examiners; American Board of Obstetrics and Gynecology; San Francisco Gynecological Society; California Association for Maternal and Child Health; Northern California Medical, Dental, and Pharmaceutical Association; Golden State Medical Association; Kappa Alpha Psi.

Ref: *Jet*, July 31, 1980, p. 38. [p]
    ABMS Compendium of Medical Specialists, v. 3, p. 836.
    National Medical Association, *Journal*, v. 72, Jan. 1980, p. 66. [p]
    National Medical Association, *Journal,*, v. 73, June 1981. [p] cover

Thompson, William   (19??–1950, M)

Military (Army). PFC. Congressional Medal of Honor Posthumously. First black since the Spanish-American War. Killed in Korea when he refused to withdraw, and though wounded, fought while his buddies retreated to safety.

Ref: *Jet*, Aug. 8, 1963, p. 11.
    Black Americans in Defense of Our Nation, p. 66.

Thoms, Adah B.   (1863–1943, F)

Nurse. Born in Richmond, VA, 1863. Only black in a class of 30 from the Women's Infirmary and School of Therapeutic Massage, 1900; School of Nursing, Lincoln Hospital, New York, NY, 1905. Operating Room Nurse, Lincoln Hospital, 1905–06; Assistant-Director of Nursing, Lincoln Hospital, 1906–23; during World War I, she led a successful fight for the acceptance of black nurses into the American Red Cross and the Army Nurse Corps.

Memberships and awards: President, National Association of Colored Graduate Nurses, 1916–23; Represented Lincoln Hospital at the International Congress of Nurses, Cologne, 1912; National Negro Health Circle; League of Nursing Education; New York State Nurses Association; President, Lincoln Hospital Colored Graduate Nurses; Lincoln Hospital Alumnae Association; first recipient of the Mary Mahoney Award, 1936.

Pub: *Pathfinders, The Progress of Colored Graduate Nurses.* New York, Kay Printing House, 1929, 240 p. Reprinted, New York, Garland, 1985, 240 p.

Ref: *History of the Negro in Medicine*, p. 73–74.
    Makers of Nursing History, p. 31–32.
    Who's Who in Colored America, 1933–37, p. 477 under Smith, Adah B.
    The Path We Tread, p. 97. [p]
    No Time for Prejudice, p. 10–11.

Thornton, Robert Ambrose   (1902–1982, M)

Physicist. Born in Houston, TX, 1902. B.S., Howard University 1922; M.S., Ohio State, 1925; Ph.D. (philosophy of science), University of Minnesota, 1946. Rockefeller fellow, University of Chicago, 1928–29; Instructor in Physics and Mathematics, Shaw University, 1922–25; Physics and Mathematics, Talladega College, AL, 1929–44; Director, Basic Studies and Professor of Physics, U.P.R., 1944–47; Associate Professor, Physical Sciences, University of Chicago, 1947–50; Postgraduate, Harvard University, summers, 1949 and 1951; Associate Professor, Physics, Brandeis University, 1950–53; Dean, Dillard University, 1953–55; Dean, Basic College, Fisk University, 1955–56; Professor, Physics, San Francisco State University, 1956–63; Dean, School of Natural Sciences, San Francisco State University, 1963–67; Professor, Physics, University of San Francisco, 1967–.

Memberships and awards: Advanced Panel for Natural and Physical Sciences, Accreditation Committee, California Board of Education, 1965–; Statewide Liaison Committee for Natural Science, 1965–69; American Physics Society; NAACP; Phi Beta Sigma; Phi Delta Kappa; Recipient of Association of Students Faculty Awards, San Francisco State College, 1959; Distinguished Teaching Award, California; State College, 1968. In April 1982 dedication services were held at San Francisco State University in California for Robert A. Thornton Hall named for him as the first Dean of the School of Science there (served on faculty of eight other colleges). From 1980 until his death, he was a Visiting Professor of Physical Science at the University of the District of Columbia, Washington, DC. The $6.1 million facility in San Francisco is considered one of the finest in the country.

Dissertation title: Measurement, Concept Formation and Principles of Simplicity: A Study in the Logic and Methodology of Physics.

Pub: (Co-author) *Introduction to the Physical Sciences,* 1937.
Problems in Physics, 1949.
Courses in the Physical Sciences, 3 vols., 1949.

Ref: *American Men of Science,* 8th ed., p. 2501.
Who's Who Among Black Americans, 1980–81, p. 791.

Thwealt, Delhi Elmore, Jr.   (1947 ——, M)

Engineer (electrical). Engineer (biomedical). Born in Baltimore, MD, Mar. 16, 1947. B.S. (electrical engineering), Howard University, 1970; Ph.D. (biomedical engineering), University of North Carolina, 1972. Specializes in design of medical instrumentation for patient monitoring, operating and related research procedures.

Ref: *Black Engineers in the United States,* p. 194.

Tignor, Charles A.   (1875–19??, M)

Physician. Born in Washington, DC, Aug. 11, 1875. Phar. D., Howard University, 1898; M.D., 1901. Clinician, Freedmen's Hospital, 1903–23; Medical Inspector, Public Schools, Washington, DC.

Memberships and awards: National Medical Association; Medico-Chirurgical Society; Director, Tuberculosis Association.

Ref: *Who's Who in Colored America,* 1933–37, p. 521.

Tildon, James Tyson   (1931 ——, M)

Biochemist. Born in Baltimore, MD, Aug. 7, 1931. B.S., Morgan State College, 1954; Ph.D. (biochemistry), Johns Hopkins University, 1965. Research Assistant, Sinai Hospital, Baltimore, 1954–59; Assistant Professor, Goucher College, 1967–68; Research Assistant and Professor of Biochemistry and Pediatrics, 1968–71; Director, Pediatric Research, 1970–83; Professor, Pediatrics, School of Medicine, University of Maryland, Baltimore, 1974–; Professor, Biochemistry, 1982–.

Memberships and awards: Fulbright scholar, University of Paris, 1959–60; AAAS; American Society of Biological Chemists; American Society of Neurochemists; American Chemical Society; Tissue Culture Association; credited in 1972 with the discovery of a new disease in children called COA transverse deficiency, relating to ketone bodies as an energy source for the nervous system in infants; research in developmental biochemistry and metabolic control processes.

Dissertation title: I. The Reaction of Thiols with Para-Nitrophenyl Acetate. II. The Reaction of Bovine Serum Mercaptalbumin with Para-Nitrophenyl Acetate.

Ref: *Encyclopedia of Black America,* p. 817.
American Men and Women of Science, 16th ed., p. 132.

Tildon, Toussaint Tourgee   (1893–1964, M)

Physician. Psychiatrist. Born in Waxahachie, TX, Apr. 5, 1893. B.A., Lincoln University, PA, 1912; Pre-Law, Harvard University, 1912–13; Medical School, Meharry Medical College; M.D., Harvard University, 1923; Special training in Psychiatry and Neurology, Boston University for Veterans Bureau Hospital, Tuskegee, AL, 1923; Veterans Administration Hospital, Tuskegee, 1923–58, Director, 1946.

Ref: Younge, Samuel L. Toussaint Tourgee Tildon, Sr., M.D., 1893–1964. National Medical Association, *Journal,* v. 56, Nov. 1964, p. 565–567.
Dictionary of American Medical Biography, p. 743.

Tilmon, James Alphonso   (1934 ——, M)

Pilot. Meteorologist. Born in Guthrie, OK, July 31, 1934. B.A. (music), Lincoln University, took engineering courses also. Worked eight years with the Army Corps of Engineers, accepted for pilot training, took advanced flight training at Fort Rucker, AL, 1959. In 1965 he became a pilot for American Airlines; Captain, 1956–; Weatherman, WMAQ-TV, 1974–.

Memberships and awards: Army Commendation Medal; third black pilot hired by American Airlines; Trustee, Kendall College; Board of Governors, Chicago Heart Association; Captain Chair Award, American Airlines, 1969; Emmy, National Academy TV Arts and Science, 1974.

Ref: *Profiles in Black,* p. 30–31. [p]
Who's Who Among Black Americans, 1985, p. 832.

Tinch, Robert J.   (1917 ——, M)

Biochemist. Born in Moreland, GA, May 5, 1917. B.A., Fisk University, 1935; M.S., Tufts College, 1949. U.S. Army Air Force, 1943–46; Staff member, Division of Industrial Cooperation, MIT, 1949–50; Operations Engineer, Blood Preservation and Characterization Laboratory, Harvard University, 1950–; research in protein and plasma fractionation, ion-exchange resins, mild fractionation; separation and concentration of formed elements of blood, new bio-mechanical apparatus for blood work and blood preservation, and silicones and plastics used in blood work.

Ref: *The Negro in Science*, p. 186.

Tolbert, Margaret Ellen Mayo   (1943 ——, F)

Biochemist. Born in Suffolk, VA, Nov. 24, 1943. B.S., Tuskegee Institute, 1967; M.S., Wayne State, 1968; Ph.D. (biochemistry), 1974. Instructor, Opportunities Industrialization Center, 1971–72; Instructor, Mathematics, Tuskegee Institute, 1969–70; Assistant Professor, Chemistry, 1973–76; Associate Professor, Pharmaceutical Chemistry and Associate Dean, School of Pharmacy, FLorida A & M University, 1977–78; Professor, Chemistry and Director, Carver Research Foundation, Tuskegee Institute, 1979–; research in metabolic studies involving isolated rat hepatic cells.

Memberships and awards: Sigma Xi; American Chemical Society; Organization of Black Scientists; American Association of Colleges of Pharmacy; AAAS.

Dissertation title: Studies on the Regulation of Gluconeogenesis in Isolated Rat Hepatic Parenchymal Cells.

Ref: *American Men and Women of Science*, 16th ed., p. 151.
  Who's Who Among Black Americans, 1985, p. 151.
  Essence, Aug. 1980, p. 37–38.

Tomes, Evelyn Kennedy   (19?? ——, F)

Nurse. Ph.D., Union for Experimental Colleges & Universities, 1978. In 1982 a masters program was introduced in the School of Graduate Studies and Research at Meharry Medical College School of Nursing, Nashville, under the direction of Dr. Tomes. She was at that time Professor and Chairman of the Department of Nursing Education, Meharry Medical College.

Memberships and awards: In 1976 she was awarded one of six grants from the American Nurses Foundation to collect information on black Nurses entitled *Black Nurses—An investigation of Their Contribution to Health Services and Health Education.*

Ref: *The Path We Tread*, p. 40–41, 90, 243. [p] p. 41.
  Directory of Nurses with Doctoral Degrees, 1984, p. 73.

Tompkins, George Ricks   (1881–19??, M)

Engineer (mechanical). Born in Rochester, NY, Oct. 23, 1881. M.E., Cornell University, 1907. Assistant Foreman, Pierce-Arrow Automobile House, George N. Pierce Co., 1900–1901; Machinest, Buffalo Division, Erie Railroad, 1903–07; Engineer of road tests, 1907–08; Director, Me-

chanical Department, Agricultural and Mechanical College, Greensboro, NC, 1908–10; Mechanical Engineer, Wilberforce, OH, 1910–.

Ref: *Who's Who of the Colored Race*, 1915, p. 265–266.

Townes, Charles Henry   (1915 ——, M)

Physician. Physicist. Born in Petersburg, VA, May 30, 1915. B.S., Virginia State College, 1935; M.S., Pennsylvania State College, 1938; Ph.D. (physics), 1942; M.D., Howard University, 1947. Physics Teacher, Virginia State College, 1936–37; Instructor, Chemistry and Physics, 1938–44; Lecturer, Howard University, 1944–47; Intern Freedmen's Hospital, Washington, DC, 1947–48; Physician, Chief Health Service and Medical Director, Memorial Hospital, Virginia State College, 1948–68; College Physician and Medical Director, Memorial Hospital, Virginia State College, 1968–74; Chief of Staff, 1974–76; member of the staff, Petersburg General Hospital and Private Practice, 1976–.

Memberships and awards: Board member, Chesterfield Red Cross; American Medical Association; National Medical Association.

Dissertation title: An X-Ray Study of the Time Rate Precipitation from a Solid Solution of Cu in Al.

Ref: *American Men of Science*, 8th ed., p. 2522.
  Holders of Doctorates Among American Negroes, p. 158.

Towns, Myron Bumstead   (1910–19??, M)

Chemist (physical). Born in Atlanta, GA, Oct. 4, 1910. B.A., Atlanta University, 1930; M.A., Michigan University, 1933; Ph.D. (electrochemistry), 1942. Chemistry Professor, North Carolina A & T, Greensboro, NC, 1935–45; Tennessee A & I, 1945–57; Lincoln University, PA, 1947–52; Fisk University, 1960–; research in kinetics of electrode reactions.

Memberships and awards: Phi Beta Kappa; American Chemical Society; AAAS; Electrochemical Society; National Institute of Science; Sigma Xi; Phi Lambda Upsilon; Phi Kappa Phi.

Dissertation title: A Study of Phenomena Occuring in the Neighborhood of the Potential of the Riversible Hydrogen Electrode.

Ref: *American Men of Science*, 11th ed., p. 5450.
  The Negro in Science, p. 186.
  Holders of Doctorates Among American Negroes, p. 158.

Townsend, Arthur Melvin, Sr.   (1875–1959, M)

Physician. Born in Winchester, TN, Oct. 26, 1875. B.A., Roger Williams University, 1898; M.D., Meharry Medical College, 1902. Professor, Pathology, Meharry Medical College, 1902–13; President, Roger Williams University, 1913–; Chairman, Pellagra Commission; Physician in

Nashville, TN, where he recognized the first case of pellagra in Nashville.

Memberships and awards: Boyd Medical Society, 1906–08; President, Volunteer State Medical Association, 1910–13; National Medical Association; Rock City Academy of Medicine and Surgery.

Ref: *History of the Negro in Medicine*, p. 87, 281. [p] p. 87.
   National Medical Association, *Journal*, v. 51, July 1959, p. 323–324.
   Who's Who of the Colored Race, 1915, p. 266.

Tresville, Walter M. S., Jr. (1930 ——, M)

Engineer (civil). Born in Philadelphia, PA, Mar. 11, 1930. B.S. (chemistry), Pennsylvania State University, 1952; B.S., (civil engineering), Carnegie-Mellon University, 1963; M.S. (environmental engineering), University of Pittsburgh, 1966. Facilities Sanitary Engineer, Pennsylvania Department of Health, 1955–56; Project Engineer, Calgon Corporation, 1966–68; Development Engineer, Dravo Corporation, 1968; Director, City of Cleveland Southerly Wastewater Treatment, 1968–70; Assistant Commissioner, City of Cleveland, Water Pollution Control Division, 1971; Vice-President Engineer, Madison-Madison International Architectural Engineering Planners, 1972–. First black engineer to direct and operate a large water pollution control facility, $200 million, Cleveland, OH, in programming technology for large plant in Ohio, saving millions in operating expenses.

Memberships and awards: American Society of Civil Engineers; Alpha Phi Alpha; National Society of Professional Engineers.

Ref: *Black Engineers in the United States*, p. 195.
   Who's Who Among Black Americans, 1985, p. 838.

Trice, Virgil Garnett, Jr. (1926 ——, M)

Engineer (chemical). Born in Indianapolis, IN, Feb. 3, 1926. B.S., M.S., Purdue University, 1945; M.S. (industrial engineering), Illinois Institute of Technology, 1970. Chemical Engineer, Argonne National Laboratory, 1947–71; Nuclear Waste Management Engineer, Energy Research and Development Administration, 1971–77; Senior Program Analyst, 1977–81; Program Manager, U.S. Department of Energy, 1981–; research and work in radioactive waste management.

Memberships and awards: Sigma Xi; American Nuclear Society.

Ref: *American Men and Women of Science*, 16th ed., p. 190.
   Black Contributors to Science and Energy Technology, p. 17.
   Blacks in Science: Astrophysicist to Zoologist, p. 66.

Trotman, James Augustus (1876–19??, M)

Physician. Surgeon. Gynecologist. Obstetrician. Born in Georgetown, British Guiana (now Guyana), Mar. 11,

1876. University of Vermont, 1904–07; M.D., Temple University, 1908; Postgraduate work, 1920–22; fellowship courses in Surgery, Royal College of Surgeons, Royal Pathological Museum, Royal Infirmary, Edinburgh, Scotland; Postgraduate courses, Faculte de Med., Universite de Paris. Surgery (gynecology, urology) and obstetrics.

Memberships and awards: Philadelphia County Medical Society; American Medical Association; National Medical Association; Kappa Alpha Psi.

Ref: *Who's Who in Colored America*, 1928–29, p. 370. [p] opp. p. 370.
   Who's Who in Colored America, 1933–37, p. 526. [p] p. 527.

Truth, Sojourner (1797–1883, F)

(Isabella Van Wagener) Nurse. Born in Ulster County, NY, 1797, changed her name from Isabella Van Wagener to Sojourner Truth to reveal the nature of her mission. Worked as a nurse for the Freedmen's Relief Association during Reconstruction in the Washington, DC area. Cared for wounded soldiers and emancipated slaves during the Civil War. She visited Abraham Lincoln in 1864. Organized a corps of women to clean Freedmen's Hospital because the sick could not get well in dirty surroundings.

Ref: *Jet*, Dec. 2, 1971, p. 10. [p]
   Black Collegian, v. 5, May/June 1978, p. 14, 16, 82. [p] p. 14.
   Negro History Bulletin, v. 36, Mar. 1973, p. 63–65.
   The Path We Tread, p. 6–8. [p]
   Her Way, 1984, p. 244–245.
   Ebony, 1964, p. 62–64, 66, 68–70. [p] biog
   Historical Negro Biographies, 1967, p. 130–131. [p]
   Pioneer Women Orators, p. 45, 88–89, 180, 194, 202, 221, 224.
   Dictionary of American Negro Biography, p. 605–606.

Tubman, Harriet Ross (1820–1913, F)

Nurse. Born in Bucktown, Dorchester County, MD, 1820. Although best known for her "Underground Railroad" during the Civil War, she served as a nurse in the Sea Islands off the coast of South Carolina caring for the sick and wounded regardless of color.

Memberships and awards: Acting Assistant Surgeon General Henry K. Durrant sent her a note commending her for "kindness and attention to the sick and suffering"; the U.S. Government honored her with a commemorative postage stamp.

Ref: *The Path We Tread*, p. 8–10. [p]
   Her Way, 1984, p. 246–248.

Tucker, Alpheus W. (18??–19??, M)

Physician. One of the first three black doctors presented to the District Medical Society for membership in 1869. The membership was refused.

Ref: Cobb, F. Montague. *The First Negro Medical Society.* Washington, DC, 1939, 159 p.
      History of the Negro in Medicine, p. 52–57.

Tulane, Victor Julius   (1895–19??, M)

Chemist. Born in Montgomery, AL, Apr. 18, 1895. B.S., Howard University, 1924; M.S., University of Michigan, 1929; Ph.D., 1933. Assistant Chemist, Howard University, 1924–25; Instructor, 1925–36; Assistant Professor, 1936–46; Associate Professor, 1946–59; Professor, Chemistry, Livingstone College, 1959–; President's Assistant, 1959–; Dean, College of Liberal Arts, 1956–65; research in methionine in human skin.

Memberships and awards: AAAS; Chemical Society; New York Academy of Sciences; Sigma Xi.

Dissertation title: Hippuric Acid Synthesis in Hydrazine Poisoning.

Ref: *American Men of Science,* 11th ed., p. 5488.
      Holders of Doctorates Among American Negroes, p. 158.
      Crisis, Oct. 1933, p. 233. [p]

Turner, Alberta Banner   (1909–19??, F)

Psychologist. Born in Chicago, IL, in 1909. B.S. (home economics), Ohio State University, 1929; M.A. (education), 1931; Ph.D. (psychology), 1935. Head, Home Economics Departments, Winston-Salem College, Lincoln University (MO), and Southern University (LA), 1935–39; Professor and Head of the Department of Home Economics, Bennett College, 1939–42; Clinician, Ohio Bureau of Juvenile Research, 1944–63; Director of Research, Ohio Youth Commission, 1963–71; retired; Administrative Assistant to Weight Watchers of Ohio, using her background in the psychology of obesity.

Memberships and awards: Citation from the State of Ohio and the Ohio Youth Commission; Ohio Psychological Association; Diplomate in Clinical Psychology.

Dissertation title: The Effects of Practice Upon the Perception and Memorization of Digits Presented in Single Exposures.

Ref: *Holders of Doctorates Among American Negroes,* p. 211.
      Even the Rat Was White, p. 146–148. [p]

Turner, Charles Henry   (1867–1923, M)

Zoologist. Born in Cincinnati, OH, Feb. 3, 1867. B.S., University of Cincinnati, 1891; M.S., University of Cincinnati, 1892; Ph.D., University of Chicago, 1907. Biology Professor, Clark College, 1893–95; high school Biology Teacher, 1908–23, during which time he carried out his insect research; first to prove that insects can hear and distinguish pitch and that roaches learn by trial and error; an authority on behavioral patterns of ants and spiders.

Dissertation title: The Homing of Ants: An Experimental Study of Ant Behavior.

Pub: Forty-nine papers on invertebrates.

Ref: *Holders of Doctorates Among American Negroes,* p., 194–95.
      American Men of Science, 3d ed., p. 695.
      Dictionary of American Negro Biography, p. 608.
      Encyclopedia of Black America, p. 820.
      Negro History Bulletin, May 1939, p. 68.
      Who's Who of the Colored Race, 1915, p. 267–268.
      Crisis, June 1923, p. 71–72. [p]
      Blacks in Science: Astrophysicist to Zoologist, p. 24–25.
      Seven Black American Scientists.
      Scientists in the Black Perspective.
      Negroes in Science: Natural Science Doctorates, 1876–1969, p. 41.
      Famous Firsts of Black Americans, p. 58–60. [p]

Turner, Ethel Marie   (1900s, F)

Mathematician. B.S., Trenton State; M.A., Columbia University; D.Ed., Columbia University. Chairman, Department of Mathematics, Cheyney State College.

Pub: *Teaching Aides for Elementary Mathematics.* New York, Holt Rinehart and Winston, 1966. 149 p.

Ref: Kenschaft, Patricia C. Black Women in Mathematics in the United States.
      American Mathematical Monthly, v. 88, Oct. 1981, p. 60.
      Black Mathematicians and Their Works, p. 296.

Turner, John Patrick   (1885–1958, M)

Physician. Surgeon. Born in Raleigh, NC, Nov. 1, 1885. City College of New York, 1903; M.D., Shaw University Medical School, 1906. Medical Examiner. Public Schools of Philadelphia for many years; Philadelphia Police Surgeon (first black) for many years; Board of Public Education, Douglas Hospital, 1906–48.

Memberships and awards: Founded Pennsylvania State Medical, Dental, and Pharmaceutical Association; American Medical Association; President, National Medical Association, 1921–22; Philadelphia Academy of Medical and Allied Sciences; Distinguished Service Medal, National Medical Association, 1946; Kappa Alpha Psi; Editorial Board, National Medical Association, *Journal.*

Pub: *The Physician and the Church.*
      Ringworm, F. A. Davis Co., 1921. 62 p.

Ref: *Who's Who of the Colored Race,* 1915, p. 268–269.
      Who's Who in Colored America, 1927, p. 206.
      Who's Who in Colored America, 1933–37, p. 529.
      Ebony, Nov. 1947, p. 19–22. [p]
      Cobb, W. Montague. John Patrick Turner, M.D., 1885–1958. National Medical Association, *Journal,* v. 51, Mar. 1959, p. 160–161.
      National Medical Association, *Journal,* v. 41, May 1949, p. 134–135.
      Dictionary of American Medical Biography, p. 755.
      Crisis, Dec. 1931, p. 426–427. [p]

Turner, Thomas Wyatt   (1877–1978, M)

Botanist. Born in Hughsville, MD, Mar. 16, 1877. B.A., Howard University, 1901; M.A., 1905; Ph.D., Cornell University, 1921. Professor of Botany, Howard University, 1914–24; Biology Professor and Head of the Department, Hampton Institute, 1924–45; Emeritus, 1945–78.

Memberships and awards: AAAS; Virginia Academy of Science; Botanical Society of America; American Phytopathological Society; American Society of Horticultural Science.

Dissertation title: Studies of the Mechanism of the Physiological Effects of Certain Mineral Salts in Altering the Ratio of Top Growth to Root Growth in Seed Plants.

Pub: Mineral Nutrition of Plants. American Journal of Botany, 1922.
Ideals of Biological Laboratory. Education, 1927.
Mineral Nutrition of Plants. Soil Science, 1926.

Ref: American Men of Science, 10th ed., p. 4161.
The Negro in Science, p. 180.
Holders of Doctorates Among American Negroes, p. 194–195.
Who's Who of the Colored Race, 1915, p. 269.
Who's Who in Colored America, 1927, p. 206.
Scientists in the Black Perspective.
New York Times Biographical Service, 1978.

Turner, Valdo D.   (1866–19??, M)

Physician. Surgeon, Born in Dixon Spring, TN, Dec. 10, 1866. Graduated Literary School, Knoxville, TN, 1890; M.D., Meharry Medical College, 1894; Postgraduate course, University of Minnesota, 1913; attended Mayo Clinic for five years.

Memberships and awards: National Medical Association.

Ref: Who's Who of the Colored Race, 1915, p. 269.
Who's Who in Colored America, 1927, p. 207.

Tyler, Sylvanus A.   (1914 ——, M)

Mathematician. Born in Chicago, IL, Aug. 21, 1914. B.A., Fisk University, 1936; M.S. University of Chicago, 1938. Associate, Mathematics, Argonne National Laboratory, 1946–; worked on cosmic ray analyses with Arthur Compton.

Memberships and awards: Fellow, AAAS.

Ref: American Men of Science, 11th ed., p. 5508–5509.
Ebony, Nov. 1949, p. 27. [p]

Tzomes, Chancellor A.   (1944 ——, M)

Military (Navy). Commander. B.S., U.S. Naval Academy, 1967. First black to command a nuclear submarine, commander of the USS Houston based in San Diego.

Ref: Ebony, Dec. 1985, p. 45–46, 50. [p].

U

Underwood, Edward Ellsworth   (1864–19??, M)

Physician. Surgeon. Born in Mt. Pleasant, OH, June 7, 1864. Mt. Pleasant High School (first black to attend), OH, 1881; M.D., Western Reserve University, 1891. Assistant City Physician, 1897; Secretary, Board of Pension Examining Surgeons, 1900–14; Secretary Anti-Tuberculosis League; first black Trustee, Kentucky State Normal School; Visiting Physician and Lecturer on Anatomy, Physiology, and Hygiene, Kentucky Normal and Industrial Institute

Memberships and awards: National Medical Association; National Association of Pension Examining Surgeons; President, Kentucky State Medical Society

Ref: Who's Who of the Colored Race, 1915, p. 271
Who's Who in Colored America, 1927, p. 207–208. [p] opp. p. 208
Who's Who in Colored America, 1928–29, p. 374–375
Who's Who in Colored America, 1933–37, 530, 533. [p] p. 531

Urdy, Charles Eugene   (1933– ——, M)

Chemist (inorganic). X-Ray crystallographer. Born in Georgetown, TX, Dec. 27, 1933. B.S. (chemistry), Huston-Tillotson College, 1954; Ph.D. (chemistry), University of Texas, 1962. Professor of Chemistry, Huston-Tillotson College, 1961–62; Associate Professor, North Carolina College, Durham, 1962–63; Professor, Prairie View A & M College, 1963–72; Professor of Chemistry, Huston-Tillotson College, 1972–

Memberships and awards: Robert A. Welch Foundation fellow, University of Texas, Austin, 1962; American Institute of Chemistry fellow; American Crystallography Association; American Chemical Society; Sigma Xi

Dissertation title The Crystal Structure of Palladium (II) 2-(Ortho-Hydroxyphenyl) Benzoxazale

Ref: American Men and Women of Science, 16th ed., p. 258
Who's Who Among Black Americans, 1985, p. 847.

V

Valentine, Anthony James   (1941– ——, M)

Engineer (electronic). Born in New York, NY, Nov. 1, 1941. B.S., New York Institute of Technology, 1963; National Aeronautics and Space Administration Certificate, 1964; M.B.A., Columbia University, 1973; Engineering Consultant, Lewis Turner Partnership Engineering; Engineering Consultant, Pacific Missile Range, Department of Defense; Test Director, Grumman Aerospace Corporation Apollo Spacecraft.

Memberships and awards: Omega Psi Phi; National Association of Black MBAs; Grumman Aerospace Management Fellowship, 1971–73; Cogme Management fellowship, 1971–73; IEEE.

Ref: *Black Engineers in the United States,* p. 196–197.
   Who's Who Among Black Americans, 1985, p. 847.

Van Der Zee, James Augustus Joseph   (1886–1983, M)

Photographer. Born in Lenox, MA, June 29, 1886. Photographer, 1918–69. Dark Room Assistant, 1915.

Memberships and awards: Honorary Ph.D. Seton Hall University, 1976; Pierre Touissant Award, Cardinal Cook, St. Patrick Cathedral, 1978; Living Legacy Award, U.S. President Jimmy Carter, White House, 1979; Honorary Degree, Haverford College; fellow for life, Metropolitan Museum of Art.

Pub: The World of James Van Der Zee: a visual record of Black Americans. New York, Grove Press, 1969, 165 p.
   Van Der Zee, James, *The Harlem Book of the Dead.* Dobbs Ferry, NY, Morgan and Morgan, 1978. 85 p.

Ref: *Who's Who Among Black Americans,* 1985, p. 848.
   James Van Der Zee. Edited by Lillian De Cook and Reginald McGhee. Dobbs Ferry, NY, Morgan and Morgan, 1974. 159 p.
   Haskins, James. *James Van Der Zee, The Picture-Takin Man.* New York, Dodd, Mead, 1979. 256 p.
   Ebony, Oct. 1970, p. 85–88, 90–91, 94. [p]
   Black Photographers 1840–1940: A Bio-Bibliography, p. 15–16. (contains bibliography of works about him)

Van Dyke, Henry Lewis   (1903–19??, M)

Chemist (organic). Physicist. Born in Vandalia, MI, June 7, 1903. B.A., Western Michigan College, 1927; M.S., University of Michigan, 1934; Ph.D., Michigan State College, 1944. Director of Academic Department, Southern Normal and Industrial Institute, Brewton, AL, 1927–34; Professor of Chemistry and Chairman of the Department of Science, Alabama State College, 1934–; Dean, College of Arts and Sciences, 1959–; research in preparation and identification of alkyl benzenes.

Memberships and awards: American Chemical Society; National Institute of Science; American Philosophical Society; Sigma Xi; AAAS; President, Beta Kappa Chi, 1948–50; Alpha Kappa Mu.

Dissertation title: A Study of the Fragmentation of Some Tertiary Carbinols When Condensed With Benzene in the Presence of Aluminum-Chloride.

Ref: *The Negro in Science,* p. 186.
   American Men of Science, 11th ed, p. 4194.
   Crisis, Aug. 1985, p. 225. [p]

Vance, Irvin Elmer   (1928– —, M)

Mathematician. Born in Mexico, MO, April 8, 1928. B.S., Wayne State University, 1957; M.A., Washington University, 1959; D.Ed. (mathematics), University of Michigan, 1967. Instructor, Mathematics Northeastern and Southeastern High School, Detroit, 1956–62; Instructor, Mathematics, University of Michigan, Dearborn Campus, 1964–65; Associate Director, Grand Rapids Middle School Laboratory Project, National Science Foundation, 1967–68; Staff member, In-Service Institute, Michigan State University, 1968–71; Assistant Professor, Mathematics, Michigan State University, 1966–70; Associate Professor, 1970–71; Director, Michigan State University Inner City Mathematics Project, 1968–71; Coordinator, Ethnic Studies and Associate Professor, Mathematics, New Mexico State University, 1971–71; Professor, 1982–.

Memberships and awards: Teaching fellow, University of Michigan, 1967; AAAS; National Council of Teachers of Mathematics, American Mathematical Association of America; Alpha Kappa Mu; Phi Delta Kappa; National Advisory Board for Individual Mathematics Program of Regional Education Laboratory for Carolinas and Virginias, 1970–.

Dissertation title: Geometries of the Erlanger Program.

Pub: Several articles in mathematical journals.

Ref: *National Faculty Directory,* 1987, p. 3814.
   American Men and Women of Science, 16th ed., p. 273.
   Black Mathematicians and Their Works, p. 296–297.
   Who's Who Among Black Americans, 1985, p. 848.

Vanderpool, Eustace Arthur   (1934– —, M)

Microbiologist. Virologist. Born in Nassau, Bahamas, Dec. 11, 1934. B.S., Howard University, 1964; M.S., 1967; Ph.D., 1971. Associate Professor, Howard University College of Medicine, 1973; Virologist, Department of Microbiology, Howard University College of Medicine, 1973; Electron Microscopist-Virologist, Microbiological Society of Maryland, 1969; Guest Scientist, Naval Medical Research Institute 1974; Associate Professor, Graduate School of Arts and Sciences, Howard University, 1979–.

Memberships and awards: American Society of Microbiology; Tissue Culture Association; National Institute of Science; Research Grant, American Cancer Society.

Dissertation title: Effect of Anti-Lymphocyte Serum on Lymphocytes and Lymphoid Cells in Vitro and in Vivo: An Electron-Microscopy Study.

Ref: *Who's Who Among Black Americans,* 1985, p. 849.

Vaughn, Arthur N.   (18??–19??, M)

Physician. Surgeon. Born in Kentucky. B.A., Lane College, 1913; M.D., Meharry Medical College, 1917. Practiced in St. Louis for 21 years; Chairman of a committee that established a postgraduate course given each summer at St. Louis University Medical School; Chief of Staff, St. Mary's Infirmary; Visiting Surgeon, Peoples Hospital and Homer G. Phillips Hospital.

Memberships and awards: President, National Medical Association, 1940–41; President, Mound City Medical Forum; President, Missouri Pan Medical Association; Special Liaison on a National Medical Association Committee dealing with problems of interest to both the National Medical Association and the American Medical Association.

Ref: National Medical Association, Journal, v. 31, Nov. 1939,
            p. 262. [p]
        National Medical Association, Journal, v. 32, Sept. 1940,
            p. 185. [p]
        A Century of Black Surgeons, p. 217. [p]

Vaughn, Clarence Benjamin   (1928–   , M)

Physician. Oncologist. Surgeon. Chemist (physiological). Born in Philadelphia, PA, Dec. 14, 1928. B.S., Benedict College, 1951; M.S., Howard University, 1955; M.D., 1957; Ph.D. (chemistry), Wayne State University, 1965. Research Physician, 1964–70; Clinical Director, Milton A. Darling Memorial Center, 1970–72; Principle Investigator, S.S. Oncology Study Group, 1978–; Associate Clinical Professor, Wayne State University, 1978–; Director of Oncology, Providence Hospital, 1973–. Research in estrogen metabolism; organic acid metabolism.

Memberships and awards: Board of Directors, American College of Physicians; American Association of University Professors; American Medical Association, National Chairman, Aerospace and Military Section of National Medical Association; American Society of Clinical Oncology; Wayne City Medical Society; Oakland City Medical Association; U.S. Association of Military Reserve Aerospace Medical Physician Award, 1974; AFRES Command Flight Surgeon of the Year, 1974; Coop Breast Cancer Study Group.

Dissertation title: The Pattern of Urinary Organic Acids in
            Porphyria.

Ref: Who's Who Among Black Americans, 1985, p. 849.
        American Men and Women of Science, 16th ed., 307.

Vaughn, Norval Cobb   (1800s, M)

Physician. Inventor. Born in Farmville, VA, in the 1800s. Educated, Richmond Institute; B.A., Virginia Normal and Collegiate Institute, Petersburg, VA; M.D., Howard University Medical College, 1897. Invented and patented a bullet proof shield. Practiced medicine in Cincinnati, OH.

Memberships and awards: Academy of Medicine, Cincinnati, OH.

Ref: Afro-American Encyclopedia, v. 5, p. 1280.

Velez-Rodriguez, Argelia   (1936–   , F)

Mathematician. Born in Havana, Cuba, Nov. 23, 1936. B.S., Marcanao Institute, Cuba, 1955; Sc.D., University of Havana, 1960. Did most of her work in differential equations and astronomy. Taught in several American schools; Chairman of Department of Mathematical Science, Bishop College, 1975–78; Associate Director, Cooperative Doctoral Program in Mathematics Education between University of Houston and Bishop College, 1973–75; Program Manager of Minority Institutions Science Improvement Program in Washington, D.C., Department of Education, Program Director for the preceding program, 1980–.

Memberships and awards: AAAS; American Mathematical Society; National Council of Teachers of Mathematics; Mathematics Association of America.

Ref: American Men and Women of Science, 15th ed., p. 236.
        Kenschoft, Patricia C. Black Women in Mathematics in
            the United States. American Mathematical Monthly,
            v. 88, Oct. 1981, p. 597–598. (under Rodriguez)

Venable, Howard Phillip   (1913–   , M)

Physician. Surgeon. Ophthalmologist. Born in Windsor, Ont., Jan. 27, 1913. B.S., B.M., M.D., Wayne State University, 1935–39. Director, Department of Ophthalmology, Homer G. Phillips Hospital; Examiner, American Board of Ophthalmology, since 1959, first black named to the Examining Board.

Memberships and awards: American College of Surgeons, 1952–; Mound City Medical Forum; St. Louis Medical Society; fellow, American Academy of Ophthalmology; Distinguished Merit Award, Homer G. Phillips Hospital; Interne Alumni Association; 1967–77; Teacher of the Year, St. Louis University, 1963; Honored by Washington University Medical School for 25 years of dedicated service to students, faculty and community, 1983; Diplomate, American Board of Ophthalmology, made one of the highest grades ever on the examination.

Pub: Glaucoma in the Negro, 1944.

Ref: Encyclopedia of Black America, p. 826.
        Who's Who Among Black Americans, 1985, p. 850.
        Jet, Dec. 3, 1959, p. 54. [p]
        National Medical Association, Journal, v. 51, Nov. 1959,
            p. 479. [p]
        National Medical Association, Journal, v. 53, Nov. 1961,
            p. 551. [p]
        National Medical Association, Journal, v. 58, May 1966,
            p. 220. [p]
        Ebony, Jan. 1963, p. 40. [p]

Vincent, Ubert Conrad   (1892–1938, M)

Physician. Surgeon. Urologist. Born in Raleigh, NC, Jan. 5, 1892. B.A., Shaw University, 1914; Leonard Medical

College, 1914–15; M.D., University of Pennsylvania, 1918. Interned Bellvue Hospital, N.Y. after pressure was applied, owing to racial prejudice. Private Practice, 1920–38. Director, Vincent Sanitorium which he established for Harlem residents. It failed due to his illness and the crash of the stock market.

Ref: Cobb, W. Montague. Ubert Conrad Vincent, B.S., M.D., 1892–1938. National Medical Association, *Journal*, v. 67, Jan. 1975, p. 73–80. [p] cover

Vincent, Walter   (1900s, M)

Architect. Teacher of Architectural Engineering at Tennessee State University School of Engineering and Technology.

Ref: *Ebony*, May, 1986, p. 96. [p]

W

Wagner, John A.   (1923– ——, M)

Biologist. Born in Sipsey, AL, Jan. 7, 1923. B.S., Southern University, 1948; M.S., Duquesne University, 1951; Ph.D., Michigan State University, 1962. Biologist, U.S. Public Health Service, Tokyo, 1948–50; Assistant Professor, Biology, Benedict College, 1951–53; Associate Professor, South Carolina State College, 1953–56; Head, Department of Biology, Bay City Junior College, 1956–63; Chairman and Biology Professor, Southern University, 1963–64.

Memberships and awards: Omega Psi Phi; Beta Kappa Chi; American Society of Cell Biology; American Society of Zoologists; National Institute of Science.

Dissertation title: Gross and Microscopic Anatomy of the Digestive and Urinary Systems and Histology of the Reproductive System of the Nutria, Myocastor Coypus Bonariensis (Geoffroy).

Ref: *Ebony Success Library*, v. 1, p. 315. [p]
Who's Who Among Black Americans, 1977, p. 916.
American Men and Women of Science, 12th ed., p. 6645.

Walden, Emerson Coleman   (1923– ——, M)

Physician. Surgeon. Born in Cambridge, MD, Oct. 7, 1923. M.D., Howard University Medical School, 1947. Chief of Surgery Service, USAF Hospital, Mitchell Air Force Base, 1951–53; Chief of Surgery, Provident Hospital, Baltimore, 1964–68; Part-time School Physician, Baltimore City Health Department.

Memberships and awards: President, National Medical Association, 1970–71; President, Maryland Medical Association; Vice-President, Monumental City Medical Society; Board of Regents, University of Maryland; Baltimore City Medical Society; One of the Physicians who toured the Peoples Republic of China in 1972.

Ref: *Who's Who Among Black Americans*, 1985, p. 853.
Ebony Success Library, v. 1, p. 315 [p]
National Medical Association, *Journal*, v. 62, Nov. 1970, p. 457. [p]
National Medical Association, *Journal*, v. 65, Jan. 1973, p. 1. [p]

Walker, Henry Harvey   (1888–19??, M)

Physician. Surgeon. Born in Davison County, TN, June 13, 1988. B.A., Walden University; M.D. Meharry Medical College, 1913. Surgical Assistant to John H. Hale at Hale Hospital, 1913–1917; Professor, Clinical Surgery, Meharry Medical College.

Memberships and awards: President, National Medical Association, 1949–50; Chairman, Hospital Homes Association; President, Meharry Alumni Association.

Ref: National Medical Association, *Journal*, v. 41, Nov. 1949, p. 266. [p]

Walker, Joseph F.   (1900–, M)

Engineer (civil). Liberian Undersecretary of Public Works. MIT graduate. Constructed many bridges on Liberia's main roads.

Ref: *Jet*, Dec. 5, 1957, p. 46.

Walker, M. Lucius, Jr.   (1936– ——, M)

Engineer (mechanical). Born in Washington, DC, Dec. 16, 1936. B.S., Howard University, 1957; M.S., Carnegie Institute of Technology, 1958; Ph.D. (mechanical engineering), 1966. Assistant Dean, School of Engineering, Howard University, 1965–66; Acting Chairman, Department of Mechanical Engineering, 1968–73; Associate Dean, 1973–74; Acting Dean, 1977–78; Dean, 1978–.

Memberships and awards: Consultant, Biomedical Cardiovascular Renal Research Team, Howard University, 1966–; Consultant, Ford Motor Co., 1971–; Engineering Manpower Commission of Engineers Council of Professional Development, 1972–; American Society of Engineering Education; American Society of Mechanical Engineers; Tau Beta Pi; Board of Trustees, Carnegie Mellon University, Biotechnology Resources Review Committee, National Institutes of Health, 1980–84; Sigma Xi; Ford Foundation fellowship; Ralph R. Tutor Award.

Dissertation title: Laminar Compressible Flow in the Entrance Region of a Tube.

Ref: *Who's Who in Engineering*, 1985, p. 687.
Who's Who Among Black Americans, 1985, p. 857.
American Men and Women of Science, 16th ed., p. 390.
Washington Post, June 2, 1988. [p]

Walker, Matthew   (1906–1978, M)

Physician. Surgeon. Gynecologist. Born in Waterproof, LA, Dec. 7, 1906. B.A., Louisiana State University (now

Dillard), 1929; M.D., Meharry Medical College, 1934. Chairman, Department of Surgery and Gynecology, Meharry Medical College, 1944–; Cancer Coordinator; research in experimental peretonitis and penicillin, anticancer drugs in treatment of cancer.

Memberships and awards: President, National Medical Association, 1954–55; Distinguished Service Medal, National Medical Association, 1959. Health Center, Meharry Medical College named for him; General Education Board fellow, Howard University, 1938–39.

Ref: *American Men and Women of Science*, 14th ed., p. 5336.
      Ebony, Aug. 1955, p. 82. [p]
      National Medical Association, *Journal*, v. 62, 1970, p. 306, 309 [p]
      Ebony, Oct. 1976, p. 38. [p]
      National Medical Association, *Journal*, v. 65, July 1973, p. 309. [p] (article by him)
      National Medical Association, *Journal*, v. 66, Nov. 1974, p. 528–529. [p]
      National Medical Association, *Journal*, v. 71, May 1979, p. 433, 505–512. (tributes)
      A Century of Black Surgeons, v. 1, p. 116–133, 138–140.

Walker, Sarah Breedlove McWilliams   (1869–1919, F)

(Madame C. J.) Inventor. Business Executive. Invented a metal heating comb and conditioner for straightening hair in 1905. Door-to-door selling of her cosmetics, she amassed a fortune. In 1910 she built a factory in Indianapolis to manufacture her cosmetics. Before her death she was a millionaire, one of the most successful businesswomen of the early 20th century.

Ref: *Great Negroes, Past and Present*, p. 84.
      Biographical History of Blacks in America Since 1528, p. 435–437.
      Dictionary of American Negro Biography, p. 621.
      Encyclopedia of Black America, p. 830.
      Great Negroes Past and Present, p. 68.
      Historical Afro-American Biographies, p. 138. [p]
      In Black and White, p. 998.
      Ebony, Jan. 1949, p. 162–164. [p]

Walker, Thaddeus Addison   (1866–19??, M)

Physician, Gynecologist. Obstetrician. Born in New Orleans, LA, July 1, 1866. B.A., Leland University, 1881; M.A., 1889; M.D., Meharry Medical College, 1885. Excelled in Gynecology while at Meharry.

Memberships and awards: Historian, National Medical Association for 10 years.

Ref: *Who's Who in Colored America*, 1927, p. 211. [p] opp. 212.
      Who's Who in Colored America, 1928–29, p. 380.

Walker, William McAlpine   (19??–1976, M)

Physician. Surgeon. Born in Selma, AL. B.S. (chemistry, biology), Morehouse College, 1941; M.D., University of Illinois Medical School, 1945. Residency, Cook County Hospital, Chicago, 1949–53. Chief, Breast Service Clinic, Northwestern Memorial Hospital, Chicago; Surgical faculty, Northwestern University; Noted Cancer Surgeon specializing in breast cancer; developed several procedures for the treatment of breast cancer; lectured in Austria and Japan; Joined Columbus Hospital Surgery Department in 1962; Senior attending Surgeon, Provident Hospital.

Memberships and awards: Founder-Director, Midwest Medical Center in Chicago; Diplomat, American Board of Surgeons, 1955; American Medical Association; National Medical Association; fellow, American College of Surgeons; International College of Surgeons; Alpha Phi Alpha; Assistant Medical Director, Supreme Life Insurance Co., 1964.

Ref: *Jet*, April 23, 1964, p. 44. [p]
      Jet, April 5, 1966, v. 21, no. 24. p. 27.
      Jet, Nov. 14, 1957, v. 13, p. 29. [p]
      Ebony Success Library, v. 1, p. 316. [p]
      National Medical Association, *Journal*, v. 69, Sept. 1977, p. 679. obit

Wall, Arthur Albert   (1914–, M)

Chemist. Born in Rankin, PA, Jan. 4, 1914. B.S. University of Pittsburgh, 1937; M.S., 1940. Assistant, Howard University, 1937–41; Assistant Custodian, University of Pittsburgh, 1941–42; Instructor, Chemistry, Virginia Union University, 1942–43; Assistant of the Manhatten Project, 1944; Assistant Professor, 1944–.

Memberships and awards: Chemical Society; National Institute of Science.

Ref: *American Men of Science*, 8th ed., p. 2607.

Wall, Limas Dunlap   (1902–19??, M)

Parasitologist. Born in Rockingham, NC, Mar. 27, 1902. B.S., Virginia Union University, 1928; M.S., University of Michigan, 1933; Ph.D., 1940. Associate Professor of Biology, Virginia Union University, 1927–1941; Professor, 1941–. Research at Meharry Medical College, 1947–. Researched the life history and development of the spirorchis elephantis.

Memberships and awards: Sigma Xi.

Dissertation title: Spirorchis Parvum (Stunkard 1932), Its Life History and the Development of Its Excretory System (Tremotoda: Spirorchiidae).

Ref: *American Men of Science*, 8th ed., p. 2607
      Holders of Doctorates Among American Negroes, p. 195–196.
      Crisis, Aug. 1940, p. 237. [p] only

Wallace, James C., Jr. (1922–1969, M)

Dentist. Born in Beaumont, TX, 1922. M.D., Meharry Medical College, 1944. Dental Director, Chicago's Martin Luther King Comprehensive Health Center; Chairman, Chicago Halfway House Committee for Unfortunate Young Girls.

Memberships and awards: President, Meharry Medical Alumni Association; honorary membership, American Dental Society; fellow, American College of Dentists; President, National Dental Association, 1969.

Ref: *Jet,* p. 29, Nov. 6, 1969. [p]

Wallace, John Howard (1925–, M)

Bacteriologist. Microbiologist. Immunologist. Born in Cincinnati, Oh, Mar. 8, 1925. B.S., Howard University, 1947; M.S., Ohio State University, 1949; Ph.D., 1953. Assistant in Virology, Children's Hospital Research Foundation, Cincinnati, 1947 and 1949–51; Assistant Bacteriologist, Ohio State University, 1951–53; Assistant Bacteriologist, Leonard Wood Memorial Laboratory; Research Associate in Bacteriology and Immunology, Harvard University Medical School, 1955–59; Assistant Professor to Professor, Meharry Medical College, 1959–66; from Associate Professor to Professor, School of Medicine, Tulane University, 1966–70; Professor, Ohio State University, 1970–72; Professor of Microbiology and Immunology and Chairman of the Department of Microbiology, University of Louisville School of Medicine, 1971–79; Associate Dean for Academic Affairs, 1971–79.

Memberships and awards: NIH postdoctoral fellowship, 1979–80; USPHS Senior Research fellow, 1959–61; NIH Career Research Development Awards, 1961–66: National Institute of Allergy and Infectious Diseases, 1982–; American Association of Immunology; Transportation Society; fellow, American Academy of Microbiology; American Association of Cancer Research; Society of Experimental Biology and Medicine; Sigma Xi.

Dissertation title: A Serologic Study of Virus Modified Erythrocytes.

Ref: *American Men and Women of Science,* 16th ed., p. 397–398.
Encyclopedia of Black America, p. 745.
Who's Who Among Black Americans, 1985, p. 859.

Wallace, Leon M. (1900s, M)

Physician. Director, Veterans Administration 945 bed Hospital, Pittsburgh, PA, which is affiliated with the University of Pittsburgh's Medical School.

Ref: *Jet,* Sept. 2, 1971, p. 29. [p]

Wallace, William James Lord (1908– ——, M)

Chemist (physical). Born in Salisburgy, NC, Jan. 13, 1908. B.S., University of Pittsburgh, 1927; M.A. (without examination due to the quality of his work in chemistry), Columbia University, 1931; Ph.D. (physical chemistry), Cornell University, 1937. Instructor, Science, Livingstone College, 1927–28; Instructor, Chemistry, 1928–32; Instructor, West Virginia State College, 1933–34; Assistant Professor, 1934–37; Associate Professor, 1937–43; Professor, 1943–; Administrative Assistant to the President, 1944–50; Acting President, 1952–53; President, 1953–73; retired; Emeritis Professor of Chemistry and Emeritus President, West Virginia State College, 1975–; research in freezing points of aqueous solutions of alpha amino acids.

Memberships and awards: General Education Board fellow, 1930–31; Sage fellow in Chemistry, Cornell University, 1936–37; Sigma Xi; American Chemical Society; Beta Kappa Chi; National Institute of Science; West Virginia Academy of Science; American Association of State Colleges and Universities; Social Action Achievement Award; Phi Beta Sigma, 1955; Alpha Phi Alpha; Numerous other organizations.

Dissertation title: The Freezing Points of Aqueous Solutions of Alpha Amino Acids.

Pub: *Chemistry in Negro College.* Institute, WV, 1940. 34 p.

Ref: *American Men and Women of Science,* 13th ed., p. 4690.
Holders of Doctorates Among American Negroes, p. 158–159.
Who's Who Among Black Americans, 1985, p. 860.
The Negro in Science, p. 187.
Crisis, May 1931, p. 164.

Walton, Adolphus (1891–198?, M)

Dentist. Born in Jamaica, B.W.I., June 3, 1891. D.D.S., Howard University, 1918; Summer courses, University of Toronto, Canada, 1924. Associate Professor (propatic dentistry), Howard Dental College.

Memberships and awards: Honorary member, Odonto Chirurgical Society of Philadelphia; Honorary member of Old State Medical Association of North Carolina; Dental Clinician for Old North State; Lone Star State Dental Association, TX; Robert T. Freeman Dental Society of the District of Columbia; National Medical Association; Inter-State Dental Association; Phi Lambda Kappa.

Ref: *Who's Who Among Colored Americans,* 1928–29, p. 383.
Who's Who Among Colored Americans, 1933–37, p. 545.
Ebony, Jan. 1960, p. 22. [p]
Who's Who Among Black Americans, 1977.

Ward, Joseph H. (1870–1956, M)

Physician. Born in Indianapolis, IN, 1870. M.D., Indiana Medical College. Established Ward Sanitarium in Indianapolis; Head, Veterans Administration Hospital, Indianapolis, 12 years.

Memberships and awards: First black to be appointed to head a V.A. Hospital; Chief Medical Officer, Tuskegee Veterans Administration Hospital, 12 years; Air Corps, Lt. Colonel, World War II.

Ref: *History of the Negro in Medicine*, p. 115. [p], p. 115
        Jet, Dec. 27, 1956, p. 50.
        Jet, Dec. 17, 197?, p. 15. [p]
        National Medical Association, *Journal*, v. 16, July–Sept. 1924, p. 203–204.
        Crisis, Sept. 1924, p. 214. [p]

Ware, Ethan Earl (1900–19??, M)

Zoologist. Anatomist. Born in Easley, SC, Nov. 29, 1900. B.S., Bates College, 1924; M.S., Cornell University, 1933. Instructor, Biology and Head of the Department, Bishop College, 1924–27; Instructor, Florida A & M College, 1927–28; Assistant Professor, 1928–30; Associate Professor, Biology and Head of the Department of Science, 1931–47; Associate Professor, Zoology, Fort Valley State College, 1947–49; Associate Professor, Developmental Anatomy, Florida A & M University; 1949–62; Professor, 1962–70; retired, 1970.

Memberships and awards: General Education Board fellow, University of Chicago, 1930–31; Research Grant-in-Aid, Carnegie Research Fund, 1949; AAAS; National Institute of Science.

Ref: *American Men and Women of Science*, 12th ed., p. 6707.

Warfield, William Alonza (1866–1951, M)

Physician. Surgeon. Born in Hyattstown, MD, Nov. 17, 1866. B.S., Morgan College, Baltimore, MD; M.D., Howard University School of Medicine, 1894. Surgeon-in-Chief, Freedmen's Hospital, 1901–1936; Professor, Abdominal Surgery, Howard University Medical School, 1928–38; Emeritus Status, 1936–1951.

Memberships and awards: Developed Freedmen's Hospital's residency program to one of stature, set the tone for nurse training; took office when Freedmen's Hospital and Howard University Medical School were in the same building; when he retired, Freedmen's Hospital had a 322-bed capacity, with six wings and covered four city blocks.

Ref: Cobb, W. Montague, William Alonza Warfield, J.D., 1866–1951. National Medical Association, *Journal*, v. 44, May 1952, p. 207–219. [p]
        Howard University Medical Department, p. 139. [p]
        History of the Negro in Medicine, p. 79. [p]

Who's Who of the Colored Race, 1915, p. 276.
Who's Who in Colored America, 1927, p. 213.
Who's Who in Colored America, 1928–29, p. 384.
Who's Who in Colored America, 1933–37, p. 546.
Jet, Nov. 18, 1965, p. 11.
Dictionary of American Medical Biography, p. 774.
Medico-Chirurgical Society of the District of Columbia, Inc., *Bulletin*, Dec. 1951, p. 8. [p]

Waring, Mary Fitzbutler (18??–19??, F)

Physician. Born in Louisville, KY. Graduate, National Medical College, Louisville, KY; M.D., Chicago Medical College, Chicago, IL, 1923. Chairman of Health and Hygiene for the National Association of Colored Women, 1911–1936.

Memberships and awards: President, National Association of Colored Women; Medical Examiner for the Elks and Odd Fellows, 1928–; National Medical Association; Delta Sigma Theta.

Ref: *Who's Who in Colored America*, 1933–37, p. 549.

Warlick, Lula G. (18??–19??, F)

Nurse. Born in the 1800s. Educated at Scotia Seminary, NC, 1907; Lincoln School for Nurses, NY, 1910. Head Nurse, Gynecology Department and Operating Room, Lincoln Hospital; Assistant Superintendent of Nurses, Provident Hospital, Chicago, 1911; Superintendent of Nurses, General Hospital no. 2, Kansas City, MO, a 300-bed hospital, Superintendent of Nurses, Mercy Hospital, Philadelphia, PA, 1920, where she developed the nursing school to Class A. She took courses at the University of Iowa to keep herself and her students informed of the latest developments in nursing.

Memberships and awards: The Mary Mahoney Award, 1940.

Ref: *The Path We Tread*, p. 153–154. [p] p. 153.
        Crisis, Feb. 1927, p. 208 [p]

Washington, Edward L. (1900s, M)

Physical education. B.A., University of Illinois; M.A., Columbia University; Ed.D., New York University, 1935.

Dissertation title: An Evaluation of the New York City Junior High School Physical Fitness Tests.

Ref: *Holders of Doctorates Among American Negroes*, p. 109.

Washington, G. Kenneth (1900s, M)

Physician. B.S., University of Chicago; M.D., Indiana University Medical School.

Memberships and awards: Gary, Indiana Board of Health for two years, became first black to head the Board.

Ref: *Jet,* v. 12, June 13, 1957, p. 29.
         Ebony, Jan, 1958, p. 86. [p]

Washington, Lawrence C.   (1900s, M)

Military (Army). Nurse. Diploma, Freedmen's Hospital School of Nursing, DC; B.S., University of Maryland; M.S., Catholic University of America. Assistant Chief, Department of Nursing, William Beaumont Army Medical Center, TX; first black male to receive a regular commission in the Army Nurse Corps, 1967.

Ref: *The Path We Tread,* 173-174. [p]

Washington, Warren Morton   (1936- ——, M)

Meteorologist. Born in Portland, OR, Aug. 28, 1936. B.S. (physics), Oregon State University, 1958; M.S. (meteorology), 1960; Ph.D., Pennsylvania State University, 1964. Research Assistant, Meteorology, Pennsylvania State University, 1961-63; Scientist, National Center for Atmospheric Research, 1963-; Adjunct Professor, Meteorology and Oceanography, University of Michigan, 1969-71.

Memberships and awards: National Academy of Sciences; National Science Foundation; Government Science Advisory Committee, State of Colorado, 1975-78; Presidential appointment to National Advisory Committee, Oceans and Atmospheres, 1978-; AAAS; American Meteorological Society; Minorities in Science.

Dissertation title: Initialization of Primitive-Equation Models for Numerical Weather Prediction.

Ref: *Ebony,* Jan. 1974, p. 7. [p]
         American Men and Women of Science, 16th ed., p. 446.
         Who's Who Among Black Americans, 1977, p. 932.

Washington, William J.   (1924- ——, M)

Physician. Internist. Born in Bessemer, AL, July 5, 1924. B.A., Talladega College, 1944; M.D., Howard University Medical College, 1947; Air Force School of Aviation Medicine, Randolph Air Force Base, TX; Chief Resident in chronic chest disease, Freedmen's Hospital, 1955-56; Supervising Medical Officer, Glenn Dale Hospital, 1958-; Clinical Instructor, Medicine, Georgetown University, 1958-; Clinical Assistant Professor, 1964-; Temporary Special Assistant, to the District of Columbia's Mayor Washington to coordinate activities between the Mayor's Office and the Health Department of DC General Hospital; Associate Director of Hospitals, DC Department of Public Health.

Memberships and awards: American Thoracic Society; Vice-President, District of Columbia Thoracic Society, 1962-63, President, 1966; Headed the team of investigators to survey private hospitals in the District of Columbia for licensure requirements; Board of Appeals and Reviews, 1958-61.

Ref: National Medical Association, *Journal,* v. 62, Jan. 1970, p. 68. [p] biog.
         Who's Who in Government, 1977.

Watkins, Levi, Jr.   (1945- ——, M)

Physician. Surgeon (cardiac). Born in Parsons, KS, June 13, 1945. B.S., Tennessee State University, 1966; M.D., Vanderbilt University School of Medicine, 1970; Residency, Johns Hopkins University Hospital. Professor, Surgery, Johns Hopkins University Hospital, 1970-78; implants automatic implantable defibrillators first one in 1980; recruits black students for Johns Hopkins.

Memberships and awards: First black graduate of Vanderbilt University School of Medicine; first black resident, Johns Hopkins; panel for coronary artery bypass surgery; Alpha Kappa Mu; Alpha Omega Alpha; American Board of Surgery; American Board of Thoracic Surgery.

Ref: *A Century of Black Surgeons,* p. 932-933. [p]
         Ebony, Jan, 1982, p. 96-98, 100. [p]
         Black Enterprise, Oct. 1988, p. 58.

Watson, Veda

See: Somerville, Veda Watson.

Wattleton, Alyce Faye   (1943- ——, F)

Nurse. Public Health Executive. Born in St. Louis, MO, July 8, 1943. B.S. (nursing), Ohio State University, 1964; M.S. (maternal and infant health care), Columbia University, 1967. Instructor, Miami Valley School of Nursing, Dayton, Ohio, 1964-66; Assistant Director of Nursing, Dayton Public Health Nursing Association, 1967-70; Executive Director, Planned Parenthood Association of Miami Valley, Dayton, Ohio, 1970-78; first black woman and first black to be President of Planned Parenthood Federation of America, Inc., 1978-.

Memberships and awards: American Public Health Association; American College of Nurse-Midwives; citations for Outstanding Achievement, State of Ohio House of Representatives, 1978; citation for Outstanding Achievement, *Ms* magazine.

Ref: *Ebony,* Aug. 82, p. 53. [p]
         Who's Who Among Black Americans, 1985. p. 873.
         The Path We Tread, p. 141-142. [p] p. 142.
         Ebony, Nov. 1985, p. 42. [p]
         Ebony, Sept. 1978, p. 85-86, 88, 90. [p]

Watts, Fred J.   (1930, M)

Engineer. Detroit City.

Ref: *In Black and White,* p. 1018.

Watts, Frederick Payne   (1904–19??, M)

Psychologist. Born in Staunton, VA, 1904. B.A., Howard University, 1926; M.A.; Ph.D. (psychology), University of Pennsylvania, 1941. First black to receive this degree from the University of Pennsylvania; Assistant Chief Clinical Psychologist, Veterans Administration Regional Office, Philadelphia; Director, Howard University Counseling Service, 1948–70; retired.

Memberships and awards: Diplomate, Clinical Psychology (ABEPP).

Dissertation title: A Comparative and Clinical Study of Delinquent and Non-Delinquent Negro Boys.

Ref: *Holders of Doctorates Among American Negroes*, p. 211.
Even the Rat Was White, p. 158–160. [p]

Watts, George R., Sr.   (19??–1977, M)

Physician. Sickle cell researcher. M.D., Howard University Medical College, 1955. Chief, Hematology and Director, Sickle Cell Screening and Counseling, V.A. Hospital, Tuskegee, AL.

Ref: *Jet*, Jan. 5, 1978, p. 53.
National Medical Association, *Journal*, v. 70, May 1978, p. 372. obit

Watts, Johnnie Hines   (1922– ——, F)

Chemist. Nutritionist. Born in Atlanta, GA., Feb. 26, 1922. B.S., Spelman College, 1941; M.S., Columbia University, 1946; Ph.D., University of Chicago, 1952. Instructor, Foods, Washington High School, Atlanta, GA, 1941–45; Instructor, Chemistry, Southern University, 1947–48; Research, Associate, Carver Foundation, 1952–; research in amino acid nutrition problems.

Memberships and awards: Special fellow, National Institute of Health, California, Los Angeles, 1958–59; Dietetic Association; Institute of Nutrition; Institute of Food Technology; Sigma Xi; Beta Kappa Chi; Sigma Delta Epsilon.

Dissertation title: The Relation of the Rates of Inactivation of Peroxidase, Catecholase, and Ascorbase to the Oxidation of Ascorbic Acid in Vegetables.

Ref: *American Men of Science*, 10th ed., p. 4308.
The Negro in Science, p. 186.
Ebony, Oct. 1960, p. 7. [p]
Blacks in Science: Astrophysicists to Zoologists, p. 28.
Who's Who of American Women, 1964, p. 1069.

Weatherless, Nelson Ellismere   (18??–19??, M)

Science teacher. Born in Bedford County, VA. Knoxville, College, TN, 1884; B.A., Howard University, 1893; LL.B., 1896; LL.M., 1898; Certificate, Rochester Athenaeum and Mechanics Institute, Rochester, NY, 1900; M.S., Columbia University, 1911. Teacher, High School, Washington, DC, 1900–; Head, Science Department, Public Schools, Washington, DC, 1906–.

Memberships and awards: Secretary, Board of Examiners, Public School, Washington, DC; while at Howard University, he won the Kelly Miller Gold Medal for the highest average for four years in Mathematics; Robert B. Warder Prize for highest average in Physics; Kanaston Prize for excellence in Greek.

Ref: *Who's Who in Colored America*, 1928–29, p. 386. [p] opp. 386.
Who's Who in Colored America, 1933–37, p. 55. [p] p. 551.

Weaver, Rufus J.   (1900s, M)

Inventor. Born in New London, CT. Invented stair climbing wheelchair.

Ref: *Jet*, May 1, 1969, p. 51.

Webb, Arthur Harper   (1915– ——, M)

Biologist. Bacteriologist. Born in Washington, DC, Dec. 28, 1915. B.A., University of Illinois, 1939; M.S., 1940, Ph.D. (bacteriology), 1944. Assistant Animal Pathologist, University of Illinois, 1942–43; from Instructor to Associate Professor, Bacteriology, College of Medicine, Howard University, 1944–60; Professor, Biology, Maryland State College, Princess Anne, 1960–61; Professor, Biology and Chairman, Division of Science, Southern University, 1961–68; Professor, Biology, University of the District of Columbia, 1968–.

Memberships and awards: AAAS; American Society of Microbiology.

Dissertation title: Effect of Spices and Essential Oils on Growth of Yeasts.

Ref: *American Men and Women of Science*, 15th ed., p. 460.

Webb, Mary C.   (1900, F)

Nurse. Graduate of Davis Maternity Sanitarium specializing in Obstetrics and Pediatrics; Superintendent of Nurses, Davis Maternity Sanitarium, 1923–24; Kansas City, KS.

Ref: *Who's Who in Colored America*, 1927, p. 216.

Weddington, Wayne   (1936– ——, M)

Physician. Otolaryngologist. Born in McGee, AK, 1936. B.A., University of Arkansas A M & N College; M.D., Howard University College of Medicine, 1963. Chairman, Department of Otolaryngology, Germantown Hospital and Medical Center, Philadelphia, 1974–.

Ref: *Black Enterprise*, Oct. 1988, p. 95.

Weekes, Leroy Randolph (1913- ——, M)

Physician. Obstetrician. Gynecologist. Born in Atlantic City, NJ, Jan. 17, 1913. B.S., Howard University, 1935; M.D., Howard University, 1939. California Board of Medical Examiners, 1964–; President and Chairman of the Board, Julina W. Ross Medical Center, Los Angeles; Clinical Professor, Obstetrics and Gynecology, University of Southern California School of Medicine.

Memberships and awards: Distinguished Service Medal, National Medical Association, 1968; Diplomate, American Board of Obstetrics and Gynecology; Kappa Alpha Psi; National Medical Association; Los Angeles County Medical Society; Charles Drew Medical Society; California State Board of Medical Examiners; Alpha Omega Alpha; Kappa Alpha Psi; American College of Surgeons; Certificate of Merit, Los Angeles County Cancer Society; William Alonzo Warfield Award, 1967; Alumnus of the Year, Howard University, 1978; Chairman, Board of Trustees, Charles R. Drew Postgraduate Medical School.

Ref: *History of the Negro in Medicine,* 187. [p] p. 187.
Current Black Man Decade 70, p. 153. [p]
Who's Who Among Black Americans, 1977, p. 940–941.
National Medical Association, *Journal,* v. 66, Nov. 1974, p. 536. [p]

Weir, Charles Edward (1911- ——, M)

Physicist. Chemist. Born in Washington, DC, Sept. 29, 1911. B.S., University of Chicago, 1932; M.S., Howard University, 1934. Assistant in Chemistry, Howard University, 1934–38; Physicist, National Bureau of Standards, 1944–.

Memberships and awards: American Physical Society; Washington Academy of Science; American Leather Chemistry Association; Beta Kappa Chi; Phi Beta Kappa; Sigma Xi.

Ref: *The Negro in Science,* p. 191.

Welsing, Frances Cress (1935- ——, F)

Physician. Psychiatrist. Born in Chicago, IL, Mar. 18, 1935. B.S., Antioch College, 1957; M.D., Howard University School of Medicine, 1962. Research in General Psychiatry, St. Elizabeth's Hospital, 1963–68; Assistant Professor, Howard University College of Medicine, 1968–75; Clinical Director, Hillcrest Children's Center, 1975–76; Private Practice.

Memberships and awards: Fellowship, Child Psychiatry, Cook County Hospital, 1966–68; National Medical Association; American Medical Association; American Psychiatric Association.

Pub: *The Cress Theory of Color Confrontation and Racism.*

Ref: *Ebony Success Library,* 1 v. 1, p. 324. [p]
Who's Who Among Black Americans, 1985, p. 878.

Welters, Edward A. (18??–1964, M)

Dentist. B.S., Florida A & M; D.D.S., Meharry Medical College. Owner of Welters Products Company, manufacturer of dental products; spent two years in Illinois Legislature; graduate of Meharry Medical College.

Memberships and awards: 1960, Award for 50 years of outstanding service to mankind and is included in Florida A & M University Hall of Fame.

Ref: *Jet,* Sept. 3, 1964, p. 51. [p]

Wesley, Allen Alexander (1856–19??, M)

Physician. Surgeon. Born in Dublin, IN, Sept. 1856. B.A. Fisk University, 1884; M.D., Northwestern University Medical School, 1887. Teacher of Mathematics and Latin, Fisk University, 1878–83; one of the founders of Provident Hospital, Chicago, IL, Surgeon-in-charge, 1894; Vice-president, 1900–; Lecturer on Surgical Emergencies, Provident Nurse Training School; District Physician for Cook County.

Memberships and awards: American Medical Association; Illinois State Medical Society; Chicago Medical Society.

Pub: *The Spanish-American War As Seen By the Military Surgeon.*

Ref: *Who's Who of the Colored Race,* 1915, p. 280.
National Cyclopedia of American Biography, v. 18. p. 372.

West, Abel E. (1876–19??, M)

Physician. Otolaryngologist. Born in Accomac County, VA, April 11, 1876. Virginia Normal and Industrial Institute, 1900–04; Shaw University, 1904–08; M.D., 1908. Chief, Department of Ophthalmology, Douglass Memorial Hospital; Associate Otolaryngologist, Douglass Memorial Hospital.

Memberships and awards: National Medical Association; Philadelphia and State Medical Societies; Alpha Phi Alpha.

Ref: *Who's Who in Colored America,* 1933–37, p. 561.

West, Charles Ignatius (1869–1936, M)

Physician. Surgeon. Born in Washington, DC, Oct. 23, 1869. M.D., Howard University Medical School, 1895. Professor, Topographical and Clinical Anatomy, Howard University; Head, Anatomy Department, Howard University.

Memberships and awards: National Medical Association; Association of American Anatomists; won the Seaman Prize in Microscopy and Chemistry, 1st Prizes in Anatomy and History, while in Medical School.

Pub: *Anatomy of the American Negro,* Medico-Chirurgical Society, 1895.

Ref: *Who's Who in Colored America,* 1927, p. 217.
Who's Who in Colored America, 1928–29, p. 389–390.
Who's Who in Colored America, 1933–37, p. 561.

West, Frank G., Jr.   (1924–1987, M)

Architect. Born in St. Louis, MO, 1924.

Ref: *Washington Post,* obituary, May 29, 1987.
Afro-American Artists.

West, Harold Dadford   (1904–1974, M)

Biochemist. Chemist. Born in Flemington, NJ, July 16, 1904. B.A., University of Illinois, 1925; M.S., Julius Rosenwald Fund fellow, 1930; Ph.D., Rockefeller Foundation fellow, 1937. Professor, Chemistry, Head of Department of Science, Morris Brown College, 1925–27; Associate Professor, Physiological Chemistry, Meharry Medical College, 1927–38; Professor, Biochemistry, 1939–52; President, Meharry Medical College, 1952–66 (first black president); Professor, Biochemistry, 1966–73; Trustee, retired.

Memberships and awards: Alpha Phi Alpha; Alpha Omega Alpha; Omicron Kappa Upsilon; Honorary L.L.D., Morris Brown College, 1955; Honorary D.Sc., Meharry Medical College, 1970; Society of Experimental Biology and Medicine; Sigma Xi; Kappa Pi; Pinter Society of Biological Chemists; first Honorary member, National Medical Association; Rosenwald fellow; General Education Board fellow; Science Center at Meharry named for him.

Dissertation title: The Chemistry and Nutritive Value of Essential Amino Acids.

Ref: *Educating Black Doctors: A History of Meharry Medical College,* p. 108–111. [p] (see also index)
Holders of Doctorates Among American Negroes, p. 135–136.
Jet, June 10, 1965, p. 24–25. [p]
The Negro in Science, p. 187.
Who's Who Among Black Americans, 1985, p. 880.
American Men and Women of Science, 13th ed., p. 4798.
Dictionary of American Medical Biography, p. 792–793.
National Medical Association, *Journal,* v. 68, July 1976, p. 328–331. (list of publications)
National Medical Association, *Journal,* v. 66, Sept. 1974, p. 448–449. [p] cover

West, Lightfoot Allen   (18??–1942, M)

Physician. B.A., Rust College; M.D., Meharry Medical College. Founder of Mercy Hospital, Memphis, TN, 1917.

Memberships and awards: President, National Medical Association, 1929–30; one of the founders of the National Hospital Association.

Ref: National Medical Association, *Journal,* Oct.–Dec., v. 21, 1929, p. 160. [p]
National Medical Association, *Journal,* Oct.–Dec., v. 20, 1928, p. 194.

National Medical Association, *Journal,* v. 33, Mar. 1943, p. 65.

Weston, Anthony (Slave)   (1800s, M)

Inventor. Slave. Born in Charleston, SC. In 1831 he improved the threshing machine invented by W. T. Catto. The improvement so increased the efficiency that Weston's master, Benjamin Hunt, made a fortune from the patent.

Ref: *Afro-American Encyclopedia,* v. 5, p.1 275.

Wethers, Doris Louise   (1900s, F)

Physician. Pediatrician. B.S., Queens College, New York, NY; M.D., Yale University Medical School. Sickle Cell Specialist; Director of Pediatrics, Knickerbocker Hospital, NY, 1965–73; Sydenham Hospital, 1969–74; organized three clinics for sickle cell anemia; counseled both government and private organizations in the United States and the Bahamas as well as setting up parent groups of children with the disease; Pediatric faculty, Columbia University College of Physicians and Surgeons, 1957–; Director, Pediatrics Department, St. Luke's Hospital Center, 1974–.

Ref: *Profiles in Black,* p. 148–149. [p]

Wheatland, Marcus Fitzherbert   (1868–1934, M)

Physician. Born in Bridgetown, Barbados, B.W.I., Feb. 17, 1868. M.D., Howard University Medical College, 1895. Practiced medicine in Newport, RI.

Memberships and awards: President, National Medical Association, 1910.

Ref: *Howard University Medical Department,* p. 228. [p]
History of the Negro in Medicine, p. 228. [p] p. 87.
Who's Who of the Colored Race, 1915, p. 281.

Wheeler, Albert Harold   (1915– ——, M)

Public Health Specialist. Bacteriologist. Born in St. Louis, MO, Dec. 11, 1915. B.A., Lincoln University, 1936; M.S., Iowa State College, 1937; M.S.P.H., University of Michigan, 1938; Ph.D., 1944. Clinical Technician, Howard University College of Medicine, 1938–40; Assistant, 1941–44; Research Associate, University Hospital, 1944–52; Assistant Professor, Bacteriology, 1952–58 (first full-time black professor); Associate Professor, Bacteriology, Michigan University Medical School, Ann Arbor, 1959–; Associate Professor, Microbiology, 1974–; Mayor, Ann Arbor, MI, 1975–78; Consultant, Serology Laboratory, University of Michigan.

Memberships and awards: American Association of Immunology; first President, National Commission for Campaign for Human Development, 1970–74; Commission to Study the Problems of Aging; Commission to

Study the Problems of Youth; first black Mayor of Ann Arbor.

Dissertation title: A Study of Certain Factors in Attempts to Alter Resistance of Animals to Virus Infections of the Respiratory Tract.

Ref: *American Men and Women of Science*, 14th ed., p. 5479.
Who's Who Among Black Americans, 1977, p. 946.
Who's Who in America, 1978, p. 3444.
Who's Who Among Black Americans, 1985, p. 882.

Wheeler, Emma R.   (1882–19??, F)

Physician. Born in Gainesville, FL, Feb. 8, 1882. Attended Cookman Institute; Walden University; M.D., Meharry Medical College. Owner and Superintendent of Walden Hospital, founded in 1915.

Memberships and awards: Alpha Kappa Alpha; Mountain City Medical Society; Volunteer State Medical Association.

Ref: *National Register*, 1952, p. 624.

Whipper, Iona Rollins   (1872–1953, F)

Physician. Obstetrician. Born in Beaufort, SC, 1872. M.D., Howard University Medical School, 1903. One of first women graduates of Howard University Medical School in Washington, DC. Served as resident; 40 years of medical service to Washington, DC; opened Iona Whipper Home for Unwed Mothers, 1931; Licensed in 1911; died in New York, NY, April 23, 1953.

Ref: *Dictionary of American Negro Biography*, p. 642–643.
Send Us a Lady Physician, p. 114.

White, Augustus A., III   (1936– ——, M)

Physician. Surgeon (orthopedic). Engineer (biomedical). Born in Memphis, TN, June 4, 1936. B.A. (cum laude), Brown University, 1957; M.D., Stanford University, 1961; D.Med.Sci., Karolinska Institute, Sweden, 1969. Assistant Professor, Othopedic Surgery, Yale University, 1969–72; Associate Professor, 1972–76; Professor, 1977–; Professor, Orthopedic Surgery, Harvard Medical School, 1978–; Orthopedic Surgeon-in-Chief, Beth Israel Hospital, 1978–.

Memberships and awards: Advisory Council, National Institute of Arthritis, Metabolism and Digestive Disease, NIH, 1979–82; Admissions Committee, Yale Medical School, 1970–72; one of ten Outstanding Young Men, United States; Junior Scientist of the Year, CIBA-GEIGY Corp., 1982; Martin Luther King, Jr. Medical Achievement Award. 1972; Kappa Delta award, National Prize for Outstanding Research in Orthopedics Field, 1975; American Orthopedic Association; fellow, American Academy of Orthopedic Surgeons; Scoliosis Research Society; Orthopedic Research Society; Sigma Xi; National Medical Association.

Pub: *Clinical Biomechanics of the Spine*, (with M. Punjabi), Lippincott, 1978.

Ref: *American Men and Women of Science*, 14th ed., p. 5486.
Ebony, June 1979, p. 44–52. [p]
Who's Who Among Black Americans, 1985, p. 883.
Who's Who in America, 1986–87, p. 2958.
Ebony, June 1964, p. 215. [p]
Ebony, Feb. 1980, p. 84.

White, Booker Taliafero W.   (1907–19??, M)

Chemist. Biochemist. Born in Tryon, NC, Sept. 3, 1907. B.S., West Virginia State College, 1929; M.S., Ohio State University, 1937; Ph.D. 1945. Instructor in Chemistry, Kittrell College, 1930–32; Principal, High School, 1932–36; Instructor, Junior College, SC, 1937–38; Halifax County Training School, 1938–40; Morristown Junior College, 1940–41; Alabama A & M College, 1945–47; Professor, Chemistry and Chairman of the Department, North Carolina A & I College, 1947–67; Director of Research, 1953–67; Chairman, Department of Natural Science, Alabama A & M University, 1967–70; Professor of Chemistry, 1967–75.

Memberships and awards: American Chemical Society; National Institute of Science.

Dissertation title: A Study of the Chemical Composition of the Seeds of the Ohio Buckeye (Aesculus Glabra, Wild) with Special Reference to Their Saponin Content.

Ref: *American Men and Women of Science*, 13th ed., p. 4817.
Who's Who Among Black Americans, 1985, p. 883.

White, Clarence Reed   (1907–1969, M)

Mathematician (applied). Born in McKamie, AR, Nov. 6, 1907. B.A., Amerst, 1928; M.A., Howard University, 1930. Instructor, Mathematics, Howard University, 1930–31; Teacher and Dean of Men, Bethune Cookman Junior College, 1939–40; Teacher, Washington, District of Columbia School System, 1940–41; Associate Physicist, Evans Signal Laboratories, U.S. Army Signal Corps, 1942–46; Associate Professor, Mathematics, Hampton Institute, 1946–51; Physicist, Missile Test Center, Holloman A.F. Base, NM, 1951–52; Professor, Mathematics, South Carolina State College, 1952–55; Mathematician, Aberdeen Proving Ground, 1955–63; Professor, Mathematics and Physics, Fort Valley State College, 1963–.

Memberships and awards: General Education Board fellow, 1933–34; Mathematical Society; Mathematical Association.

Ref: *American Men and Women of Science*, 11th ed. p. 5811.
In Black and White, p. 1031.

White, Jack E.   (1921–1988, M)

Physician. Surgeon. Oncologist. Born in Stuart, FL, July 24, 1921. B.A., Florida A & M University, 1941: M.D., Howard University School of Medicine, 1944. Assistant

Resident Surgeon, U.S. Marine Hospital, Boston, 1946–47; Assistant Professor, Associate Professor, 1951–; Director, Howard University Cancer Center, 1972–.

Memberships and awards: Fellow, American College of Surgeons; Society of Surgical Oncology, Institute of Medicine, National Academy of Sciences, 1977–; American Medical Association; National Medical Association; AAAS; Medico-Chirurgical Society of the District of Columbia; American Cancer Society; International Union Against Cancer; Washington Academy of Surgery; Society of Head and Neck Surgeons; Alpha Omega Alpha; Capital Press Club Pioneer Award, 1978.

Ref: Who's Who Among Black Americans, 1985, p. 885.
        Ebony, Feb. 1974, p. 94. [p] only
        Ebony, April 1978, p. 129. [p]
        American Men and Women of Science, 16th ed., p. 580.
        National Medical Association, Journal, v. 73, Jan. 1981,
            p. 67–69. [p] (article on the cancer center)

White, James Randall   (1870–19??, M)

Physician. Gynecologist. Born in Nashville, TN, Dec. 24, 1870. B.A., Fisk University, TN, 1894; M.D., Meharry Medical College, 1897. Chief, Gynecology Staff, Provident Hospital, Chicago, IL, 1929–. Major in the Medical Corps, U.S. Army.

Memberships and awards: Croix de Guerre for Meritorious Service in France during World War I; National Medical Association; Cook County Physician's Association.

Ref: Who's Who in Colored America, 1933–37, p. 565.
        Who's Who in Colored America, 1941–44, p. 554.

White, John H.   (1945– ——, M)

Photographer. Born in Levington, NC, Mar. 18, 1945. A.A.S., Central Piedmont College, Photographer, U.S. Marine Corps, Quantico, VA., 1966–68; Tom Walters Photography, Charlotte, NC., 1968–69; Photojournalist, Chicago Daily News, 1969–78; Chicago Sun Times, 1978–; Lecturer.

Memberships and awards: Over 200 Photography in Journalism Awards; Pulitzer Prize for feature photography, 1982 (Chicago Sun Times); National Press Photographers Association; Illinois Press Photographers Association (Photographer of the Year, 1971, 1979 and 1982); President, Chicago Press Photographer Association, 1977–78; Chicago Association of Black Journalists.

Ref: Who's Who in America, 1986–87, p. 2961.
        Jet, Nov. 17, 1986, p. 35.
        Jet, May 20, 1971, p. 4. [p]
        Who's Who in the Midwest, 1978, p. 752.

White, Thomas J.   (1800s, M)

Physician. Born in Brooklyn, NY. M.D., Bowdoin College, Maine, 1849. Second black to finish a medical school along with John V. DeGrasse. They were preceded only by David Peck of Rush Medical College in 1847.

Whitehead, John L., Jr.   (1924– ——, M)

Military (Air Force). Lt. Colonel. Engineer (industrial). Born in Lawrenceville, VA, May, 14, 1924. Pilot training, Tuskegee Institute, 1943; B.S. (industrial engineering), West Virginia State College, 1948; USAF Test Pilot School, Edwards AF Base, 1958; Chief, USAF Flight Test Center, Edwards AF Base, 1968–70; Group Commander, Maintenance and Supply Group, Edwards AF Base, 1971–72; Associate Management Analyst, City of Sacramento, 1972–.

Memberships and awards: Much decorated ace from World War II's 332nd Fighter Group; Board of Directors, Tuskegee Airmen, Inc., 1978–80; Reserve Officers Association, 1979–80; Military Medal Air Medal with seven Oak Leaf Clusters, USAF, 1952; Army Commendation Medal, 1953; Distinguished Unit Citation Cluster, USAF, 1963; Military Order of World Wars, USAF, 1970; European Ribbon with three Battle Stars, USAF; Korean Ribbon with three Battle Stars, USAF; Lt. Colonel, USAF, 29 years service.

Ref: Ebony, Aug. 1985, p. 174. [p]
        Who's Who Among Black Americans, 1985, p. 888.

Whiteman, Neville C.   (1899–19??, M)

Physician. Hematologist. Born in St. Georges, Grenada, B.W.I., Mar. 10, 1899. B.S., College of the City of New York, 1921; M.D., New York University, 1925. Assistant Physician, Out Patient Department, Harlem Hospital, New York, NY, 1926–30; Chief, Medical Clinic, Harlem Hospital, 1930–.

Memberships and awards: Fellow, American Medical Association; New York County Medical Society; North Harlem Medical Society; Manhattan Medical Society; Cosmopolitan Medical Society.

Ref: Who's Who in Colored America, 1933–37, p. 566. [p]

Whitlock, Lula   (1900s, F)

Nurse. B.S., Tuskegee Institute School of Nursing; M.S.N., Catholic University of America, Washington, D.C. Director, Nursing Department, St. Elizabeth's Hospital, Washington, DC, 1982–.

Ref: The Path We Tread, p. 187.

Whitten, Charles F.   (1922– ——, M)

Physician. Pediatrician. Hematologist. Born in Wilmington, DE, Feb. 2, 1922. B.A., University of Pennsylvania, 1942; M.D., Meharry Medical College, 1945; University of Pennsylvania Graduate School, 1954. Appointed Chief of Pediatrics, Detroit Receiving Home, first black to head a department in a city hospital; Instructor to Professor, Pediatrics, Wayne State University, 1962–70; Director of Clinical Research, Sickle Cell Center, 1962–73; Director, Sickle Cell Center, 1973–; Associate Dean of Current Affairs, Wayne State University, 1976–; Sickle Cell Disease Specialist; Professor of Pediatrics, Wayne State University School of Medicine; Program Director, Comprehensive Sickle Cell Center, Wayne State University.

Memberships and awards: Named "Physician-Scientist of the Year" by the Detroit Medical Society in 1965; received research grants totaling $105,000 between 1959 and 1965; American Academy of Pediatrics; American Federation of Clinical Research; American Pediatric Society; American Society of Clinical Nutrition; American Society of Hematology; Society of Pediatric Research; National Academy of Science; President, National Association for Sickle Cell Disease, Inc.; *Ad Hoc* Committee, Hemaglobinopathies of the National Academy of Science; Alpha Omega Alpha; Sigma Xi.

Ref: *Jet,* July 1, 1967, p. 19.
Jet, Dec. 27, 1956, p. 49.
Who's Who Among Black Americans, 1985, p. 889.
Profiles in Black, p. 104–105. [p]
Ebony, Oct. 1965, p. 93–94, 96, 98, 100.

Whittico, James Malachi, Sr.   (1893–1975, M)

Physician. Surgeon. Born in Ridgeway, WV, Sept. 23, 1893. B.S., Walden University, Nashville, TN; M.D., Meharry Medical College, 1912. Served blacks and whites in Williamson, WV, for over 60 years; aided other blacks in medical careers.

Memberships and awards: National Medical Association; Sargeant-at-Arms, House of Delegates and Chairman, Surgical Section.

Ref: *Dictionary of American Medical Biography,* p. 801–802.
History of the American Negro, v. 7, 1923, p. 268–271.
Cobb, W. Montague. James Malachi Whittico, Sr., M.D., 1893–1975. National Medical Association, *Journal,* v. 68, Sept. 1976, p. 441–443. [p] cover
National Medical Association, *Journal,* v. 56, May 1964, p. 299. [p] only

Whittico, James Malachi, Jr.   (1916– ——, M)

Physician. Surgeon. Born in Williamson, WV, Nov. 18, 1916. B.A., Lincoln University, 1936; M.D., Meharry Medical College, 1940. Director, Surgical Tumor Clinic, Homer G. Phillips Hospital, St. Louis, 1960; Surgeon, St. Louis Police Department, 1966; Commissioner, Board of Health of St. Louis, 1967.

Memberships and awards: Distinguished Service Medal, National Medical Association, 1976; President, National Medical Association, 1967–68; Consultant, Missouri Department of Health, Education, and Welfare; Consultant, Missouri Department of Vocational Rehabili-

tation; Diplomate, American Board of Surgery; fellow, American College of Surgeons; American Medical Association; Missouri Medical Association; Chi Delta Mu; Alpha Phi Alpha.

Ref: *Encyclopedia of Black America,* p. 855.
National Medical Association, *Journal,* v. 53, Nov. 1961, p. 534. [p] p. 533.
National Medical Association, *Journal,* v. 60, Jan. 1969, p. 50–51. [p] biog.
A Century of Black Surgeons, p. 236. [p]

Whittier, Charles Austin   (18??–1969, M)

Physician. B.S., Wiley College, Wiley TX; M.D., Meharry Medical College, 1917. Established Whittier Clinic, 1927.

Memberships and awards: President, National Medical Association, 1947–48; President, Lone Star State Medical Association; Board of Trustees, National Medical Association.

Ref: National Medical Association, *Journal,* v. 40, Nov. 1948, p. 261. [p]
National Medical Association, *Journal,* v. 61, May 1969, p. 291. obit

Wiggins, Joseph C.   (1909–19??, M)

Physician. Born in Petersburg, VA, Sept. 19, 1909. B.A., Fisk University, 1932; M.D., Meharry Medical College, 1940; postgraduate research, Ohio State University and Case Western Reserve. Chief, Department of General Medicine, Forest City Hospital, Cleveland, OH.

Memberships and awards: Cleveland Academy of General Medicine; American Medical Association; National Medical Association; Omega Psi Phi.

Ref: *Ebony Success Library,* v. 1, p. 328. [p]
Who's Who Among Black Americans, 1985, p. 891.

Wigington, Clarence W.   (188?–1967, M)

Architect. Born in Lawrence, KS. Architectural Designer, St. Paul, MN, 30 years.

Ref: *Jet,* Aug. 3, 1967.

Wilbrun, Frank E.   (1935– ——, M)

Engineer (automotive). Born in Detroit, MI, Sept. 12, 1935. B.S. (electrical engineering), MSU, 1957, M.S.E.E., University of Michigan, 1965; Ph.D. (electrical engineering), 1968.

Ref: *Who's Who Among Black Americans,* 1977, p. 956.
Who's Who Among Black Americans, 1985, p. 891.

Wiley, William Rodney   (1931– ——, M)

Bacteriologist. Microbiologist. Born in Oxford, MS, Sept. 3, 1931. B.S. (chemistry), Tougaloo College, 1954; M.S. (microbiology), University of Illinois, 1960; Ph.D. (bacteriology), Washington State University, 1965. Research Scientist, Battelle Pacific Northwest Laboratories, 1965–69; Manager, Cellular and Molecular Biology Section, 1969–72; Coordinator, Life Sciences Program, 1972–74; Manager, Biology Department, 1974–79; Director of Research, 1979–84. Director, Pacific Northwest Division, Battelle Memorial Institute, 1984–.

Memberships and awards: Board of Regents, Gonzaga University, 1968–81; Advisory Committee for Advanced Studies in Biomedical Sciences, University of Washington, 1976–79; American Society of Biological Chemists; American Society for Microbiology; fellow, Rockefeller Foundation, University of Illinois, 1959.

Dissertation title: Function of PH and Amonium Ion in the Metabolism of Bacillus Pasteurii.

Ref: *Who's Who Among Black Americans*, 1985, p. 892.
Black Collegian, v. 11, Feb./Mar. 1981, p. 110–120. [p]
American Men and Women of Science, 16th ed., p. 625.

Wilkerson, Vernon Alexander   (1901–1968, M)

Physician. Surgeon. Biochemist (agricultural). Born in Kansas City, MO, Aug. 21, 1901. B.A., University of Kansas, 1921; M.D., University of Iowa, 1925; Ph.D. (biochemistry), University of Minnesota, 1932. House Surgeon, Wheatly Provident Hospital, 1926–27; Assistant Surgeon, City Hospital, 1927–28; Associate Professor, Biochemistry, Howard University College of Medicine, 1932–37; Professor, 1937–48; Head of the Department, 1934–48; Lecturer, 1953–66.

Memberships and awards: General Education Board fellow; AAAS; American Society of Biological Chemists; American Medical Association; New York Academy of Sciences; President, International Society of Biological Chemists, 1944; National Medical Association; Daniel Hale Williams Reading Club; first black Ph.D., University of Minnesota.

Pub: Contributions to journals.

Dissertation title: A Biochemical Study of Embryonic (Pig) Growth with Special Reference to Nitrogenous Compounds.

Ref: *Dictionary of American Medical Biography*, p. 805–806.
American Men of Science, 11th ed., p. 5859.
Holders of Doctorates Among American Negroes, p. 136.
National Medical Association, *Journal*, v. 60, July 1968, p. 344–345. [p] biog & obit (list of publications)
Crisis, May 1932, p. 163.

Wilkins, J. Ernest, Jr.   (1923– ——, M)

Physicist. Mathematician. Engineer (mechanical). Engineer (nuclear). Born in Chicago, IL, Nov. 27, 1923. B.S., University of Chicago, 1941; M.S., 1941; Ph.D. (mathematics), 1942; B.M.E., New York University, 1957; M.M.E., 1960. Instructor, Mathematics, Tuskegee Institute, 1943–44; Associate Physicist to Physicist, Manhat-

tan Project, Metall Laboratory, University of Chicago, 1944–46; Mathematician, American Optical Company, 1946–50; Senior Mathematician, Nuclear Development Corporation of America, 1950–55; Manager of Physics and Mathematics Department, 1955–57; Assistant Manager, Research and Development, 1958–59; Manager, 1959–60; Assistant Chairman, Theoretical Physics Department, General Atomic Division, General Dynamics Corporation, 1960–65; Assistant Director of the laboratory, 1965–70; Distinguished Professor, Howard University, 1970–.

Memberships and awards: Phi Beta Kappa at 16 years of age.

Dissertation title: Multiple Integral Problems in Parametric Form in the Calculus of Variations.

Pub: Over 40 research articles.

Ref: *American Men and Women of Science*, 16th ed., p. 630.
Encyclopedia of Black America, p. 745, 856.
Ebony, Sept. 1950, p. 20. [p]
In Black and White, p. 1040.
Jet, April 28, 1955, p. 21.
Black Mathematicians and Their Works, p. 297–299. [p] p. 240.
Blacks in Science: Astrophysicist to Zoologist, p. 44–45.
Crisis, Sept. 1940, p. 288. [p]

Wilkins, Jay W.   (1883–19??, M)

Engineer (highway construction). Born in Houston, TX, Dec. 31, 1883. New York Evening High School, Morrison Sanitarium; Meharry Medical College. Appointed by Governor Donahey as the first black foreman in the Texas State Highway Department.

Ref: *Who's Who in Colored America*, 1928–29, p. 397.
Who's Who in Colored America, 1933–37, p. 567–568. [p] p. 562.

Wilkins, Raymond Leslie   (1925– ——, M)

Chemist (organic). Inventor. B.A., University of Chicago, 1951; M.S., 1954; Ph.D. (chemistry), 1957. Senior Scientist, 1956–68; Head, Instrument Technology Laboratory, 1968–73; Manager, Chemical Process Research Department, 1974–78; Manager, Process Control Analysis Department, 1971–81; Manager, Special Projects, Rohm & Hass Co., 1982–; Helped develop electron microscope; research in mechanism of polymer formation.

Memberships and awards: Electron Microscopy Society of America; New York Academy of Sciences; fellow, Royal Microscopy Society; American Chemical Society.

Dissertation title: I. The Reactions of Grignard Reagents and Ethyl-Bromide in the Presence of Metal-Halides. II. The Reaction of Aliphatic Hydrocarbons with Maleic Anhydride.

Ref: *American Men and Women of Science*, 16th ed. p. 630.
In Black and White, p. 1040.
Ebony, Oct. 1967, p. 6. [p]

Wilkins, Roger L.   (1928-　——, M)

Physicist (chemical). Born in Newport News, VA, Dec. 14, 1928. B.S., Hampton Institute, 1951; M.S., Howard University, 1952; Ph.D. (chemical physics), 1967. Aeronautical Scientist, NASA, OH, 1952–55; Senior Technical Specialist, Rocketdyne Division, North American Aviation, Inc., 1955–60; Senior Staff Scientist, Aerophysics Department, Aerodynamics and Propulsion Research Laboratory, 1960–80; Senior Staff Scientist, Chemical Kinetics Department, Aerophysics Laboratory, Aerospace Corporation, 1980–.

Memberships and awards: Combustion Institute; AIAA; President, Southern California National Hampton Alumni Association, 1972–74.

Dissertation title: A Self-Consistent Field For Molecular Hydrogen and Its Applications.

Ref: *American Men and Women of Science*, 16th ed., p. 630.
Who's Who Among Black Americans, 1985, p. 894.

Wilkinson, Robert Shaw, Sr.   (1899–1984, M)

Physician. Surgeon. Born in Orangeburg, SC, Nov. 11, 1899. B.A., Dartmouth College, 1924; M.D., Harvard Medical School, 1927. Assistant to Associate Visiting Surgeon, Harlem Hospital, 1930–52; Instructor, Surgery, Harlem Hospital Nurses School, 1930–; Full Visiting College, 1952–; First Director of Surgery, Mount Morris Park Hospital, 1948–52; Chief of Surgery, Upper Manhattan Medical Group, Health Insurance Plan of New York. Acting Chief of Surgery, Tuskegee Veterans Administration Hospital, 1962–63, 1964–66.

Memberships and awards: Diplomate, National Board of Medical Examiners; American Medical Association; New York State Medical Society; New York County Medical Society; Secretary, Manhattan Medical Society; Omega Psi Phi; Phi Delta Kappa (Darthmouth); fellow, American College of Surgeons; National Medical Association.

Ref: *Who's Who Among Colored Americans*, 1933–37, p. 568.
National Medical Association, Journal, v. 54, Jan. 1962, p. 126. [p]
National Medical Association, Journal, v. 77, Feb. 1985, p. 149–150. [p]
Crisis, June 1932, p. 202. [p]
A Century of Black Surgeons, p. 357, 352. [p]

Williams, Albert Wilberforce   (1863–19??, M)

Physician. Surgeon. Born in Monro, LA, Jan, 31, 1863. Graduate, Normal School, Jefferson City, MO: M.D., Northwestern University Medical School, 1894. Special-

ized in the treatment of tuberculosis and heart disease. Editor of Health Column in the *Chicago Defender.*

Memberships and Awards: Treasurer, National Medical Association for seven years; American Medical Association; Mississippi Valley Tuberculosis Conference; Executive Board, Robert Koch Society for the Prevention and Study of Tuberculosis; National Medical Association; President, Physicians, Dentists, and Pharmacists Association of Chicago.

Pub: Tuberculosis and the Negro, *Journal of Outdoor Life*, Feb. 1915.

Ref: *Who's Who of the Colored Race*, 1915, p. 284.
Who's Who in Colored America, 1928–29, p. 397–398.
Who's Who in Colored America, 1933–37, p. 568.
History of the Negro in Medicine, p. 87.

Williams, Charles Lee   (1900s, M)

Physician. Born in El Paso, TX. M.D., Howard University. Chairman, Department of Medicine, Provident Hospital, Chicago; Appointed Clinical Instructor, University of Illinois Medical School and attending physician at Illinois Research Hospital.

Memberships and Awards: American Board of Internal Medicine.

Ref: *Jet*, May 16, 1963, p. 55. [p]
National Medical Association, *Journal*, v. 66, Nov. 1974, p. 520. [p]

Williams, Daniel Adolph, Jr.   (1924-　——, M)

Chemist (physical). Born in Kansas City, MO, Mar. 25, 1924. B.A., State University of Iowa, 1944; M.S., 1947. Research Chemist, Argonne National Laboratory, 1947; Assistant Professor of Analytical Chemistry, Fisk University, 1948–50; Head, Division of Natural Sciences, Morris College, 1950–53; Allen University, 1953; Analytical Chemist, Cardinal Manufacturing Co., 1953–.

Memberships and awards: American Chemical Society.

Ref: *The Negro in Science*, p. 187.

Williams, Daniel Hale   (1856–1931, M)

Physician. Surgeon. Born in Hollidaysburg, PA, Jan. 18, 1856. Hare's Classical Academy, 1877; M.D., Chicago Medical College (Northwestern Medical School), 1883. Helped found Provident Hospital and Training School for Nurses; performed first heart surgery in 1893 by removing a knife from the heart of a stab victim and sewing up the pericardium—the victim recovered and lived several years afterwards. Established a training school for nurses and first divided Freedmen's Hospital, Washington, DC, into departments (Medical, Surgical, Gynecological, Obstetrical, Dermatological, Genito-urinary, and Throat and Chest), where he was Surgeon in Chief;

founded Provident Hospital and Medical Center in Chicago, 1891—it is the oldest free-standing black-owned hospital in America.

Memberships and awards: In 1913 he was the only black among a group of 100 charter members of the American College of Surgeons. Founded and became the first vice president of the National Medical Association; bill introduced in Congress, 1970, for a commemorative stamp in his honor.

Ref: National Medical Association, *Journal*, v. 34, May 1942, p. 118–119.
National Medical Association, *Journal*, v. 62, Sept. 1970, p. 372.
Daniel Hale Williams: Negro Surgeon, 1954.
Daniel Hale Williams: Open Heart Doctor, 1971.
History of the Negro in Medicine, p. 74–75, 77–78. [p]
Nine Black American Doctors, p. 9–11.
Cobb, W. Montague. Dr. Daniel Hale Williams. National Medical Association, *Journal*, v. 45, Sept. 1953, p. 379–384.
Black Pioneers of Science & Invention, p. 122–138. [p]
Dictionary of American Medical Biography, p. 806–807.
Dictionary of American Negro Biography, p. 654–655.
National Medical Association, *Journal*, v. 36, 1944, p. 158–159.
Encyclopedia of Black America, p. 857.
Historical Afro-American Biographies, p. 262. [p]
Lonesome Road, J. S. Redding, p. 154–178.
Negro Digest, Feb. 1944, p. 73–77.
Who's Who in Colored America, 1927, p. 221–222. [p]
Negro History Bulletin, Jan. 1954, p. 92. [p]
Famous American Negroes, p. 57–60. [p] p. 56.
Ireland's *Index to Scientists of the World*, p. 644.
World Who's Who in Science: Antiquity to the Present, p. 1801.
In Spite of Handicaps, p. 51–57. [p]
Howard University Medical Department, p. 132. [p]
Ebony, Feb. 1955, p. 67–72. [p]
Ebony, April 1967, p. 93. [p]
Ebony, Sept. 1968, p. 10–11. [p]
Blacks in Science: Astrophysicist to Zoologist, p. 57–58.
Crisis, Jan. 1932, p. 461. [p] biog
A Century of Black Surgeons, p. 268–271, 311–334. [p] p. 312.

Williams, David George   (1939-   , M)

Nurse. Physician. Born in Chicago, IL, Jan. 5, 1939. R.N., Provident Hospital, Chicago, 1961; B.A., Trenton State College, 1972; M.D., Hahnemann Medical College, Philadelphia, 1976. President, Bell-Williams Medical Association, Pennsylvania, 1979–; Director of Medicine, New Jersey Prison System, 1977–.

Memberships and awards: American Medical Association; National Defense Service Medal; Vietnam Service Medal, 1965; Republic of Vietnam Campaign Medal with Device.

Ref: *Who's Who Among Black Americans*, 1985, p. 898.

Williams, Eddie Robert   (1945-   , M)

Mathematician. Born Jan. 6, 1945. B.A., Ottawa University, 1966; Ph.D. (mathematics), Columbia University, 1970. Instructor, Mathematics, Intensive Summer Studies Program, Columbia University, 1970; Assistant Professor, Mathematics, Northern Illinois University, 1970–.

Memberships and awards: New York Academy of Sciences; American Mathematical Society; Sigma Xi.

Dissertation title: The Poincare Lemma with Estimates.

Ref: *American Men and Women of Science*, 16th ed., p. 640.
Black Mathematicians and Their Works, p. 299. [p]

Williams, Ernest Young   (1899-19??, M)

Physician. Neuro-Psychiatrist. Born in Nevis, B.W.I. B.S., Howard University, 1927; M.D., 1930. Interned Freedmen's Hospital; Chief, Division of Neuro-Psychiatry, Freedmen's Hospital, 1940, where he had established a 24-bed psychiatric service; Head, Department of Neurology and Psychiatry, Howard University College of Medicine, 1957–.

Memberships and awards: General Education Board fellow in Neuro-Psychiatry, Columbia University College of Physicians and Surgeons; Association of Research in Nervous and Mental Diseases; American Psychiatric Association; American Group Therapy Association; American Academy of Neurology; Medico-Chirurgical Society of the District of Columbia; National Medical Association; AAAS.

Pub: Over 20 papers on neuro-psychiatric subjects.

Ref: National Medical Association, *Journal*, v. 49, Mar. 1957, p. 120. [p]
American Men and Women of Science, ed., p.
Who's Who Among Black Americans, 1977.
Biographical Directory of the American Psychiatric Association, 1977.

Williams, Henry Roger   (1869-1929, M)

Physician. Pharmacist. Born in 1869.

Ref: *Who's Who in Colored America*, 1928-29, p. 399.
Black American Writers, Past and Present.

Williams, J. Milton   (18??-19??, M)

Physician. Surgeon. Born in New York, NY. B.S., City College of New York; M.D., Long Island College Hospital, 1883. First black physician to be identified with New York City Health Department, 1896–1902.

Ref: *Who's Who in Colored America*, 1928-29, p. 400.

Williams, James B.   (1900s, M)

Physician. Surgeon. Born in El Paso, TX. M.D., Creighton University Medical School; M.Sc., Creighton University,

1954. Providence Hospital Staff; Surgery Teaching Staff, Stritch Medical School, Loyola University; Chairman, Division of General Surgery, Creighton Hospital, 1956.

Memberships and awards: Diplomate, American Board of Surgery, 1957.

Ref: Jet, May 16, 1963, p. 55.

Williams, Jasper F.   (1918- ——, M)

Physician. Obstetrician. Gynecologist. Surgeon. Born in El Paso, TX, Feb. 8, 1918. B.S., Tuskegee Institute, AL, 1940; licensed driller after World War II; M.D., Creighton University Medical School, 1953. With his two brothers, James and Charles, operates Williams Clinic in Chicago, opened in 1960.

Memberships and awards: President, National Medical Association, 1974-75; Diplomate, American Board of Obstetrics and Gynecology, 1961; fellow, American College of Surgeons; International College of Surgeons; American Geriatric Society; American Medical Association; President, Cook County Physicians Association; Phi Delta Pi.

Ref: Jet, May 16, 1963, p. 55.
  Ebony, May 1976, p. 68. [p] only
  Ebony, Oct. 1976, p. 37. [p] only
  Who's Who Among Black Americans, 1977, p. 970.
  National Medical Association, *Journal*, v. 66, Nov. 1974, p. 519-521. [p]

Williams, Joseph Leroy   (1906-1965, M)

Zoologist. Born in Portsmouth, VA, Feb. 4, 1906. B.A., Lincoln University, Pennsylvania, 1929; M.A., University of Pennsylvania, 1937; Ph.D. (zoology), 1941; M.D., Howard University, 1948. Dover Instructor in Medicine, Hahnemann Medical College, 1953-59; Associate Professor, 1959; Instructor, Biology and Chemistry, Lincoln University, Pennsylvania, 1929-37; Assistant Professor, 1937-41; Associate Professor, 1941-45; Professor, 1945-46; Interne, Mercy Douglas Hospital, 1948-49; Assistant Pathologist, House Physician, and Professor of Biology, Training School for Nurses, 1949-; Chemist, Douglass Hospital, 1935-44; research on internal genitalia of *Lepiodoptera* and *Coleoptera*.

Memberships and awards: Director, Eastern Division, National Institute of Science; Entomological Society of America; Association of Scientific Workers; Genetic Association; New York Zoological Society; Royal Entomological Society.

Dissertation title: The Anatomy of the Internal Genitalia and Mating Behavior of Some Lasiocompid Moths.

Ref: American Men of Science, 10th ed., p. 4435.
  Holders of Doctorates Among American Negroes, p. 196.
  Jet, July 22, 1965, p . 24. [p]

Williams, Lloyd Kenneth   (1925- ——, M)

Mathematician. Born in Bennington, OK, Oct. 6, 1925. B.A., University of California, Berkeley, 1948; M.A., 1949; Ph.D. (mathematics), 1956. Professor and Chairman, Department of Mathematics, Atlanta University, 1964-; Texas Southern University.

Dissertation title: On Separating Transcendency Bases.

Ref: American Men and Women of Science, 12th ed., p. 6931.
  Black Mathematicians and Their Works, p. 299. [p] p. 254.

Williams, Marguerite Thomas   (1895-19??, F)

Geologist. Geographer. Born in Washington, DC, Dec. 24, 1895. B.A., Howard University, 1923; M.A., Columbia University, 1930; Ph.D. (geology), Catholic University, 1942. Teacher, Miner Teachers College (now part of the University of the District of Columbia), 1923-29; Chairman, Division of Geography, 1923-33; Assistant Professor to Professor, Social Sciences, Miner Teachers College, 1943-55; Instructor, Evening School, Howard University, 1944.

Memberships and awards: Association of American Geographers; Academy of Political and Social Science; first black female Ph.D. in Geology.

Dissertation title: A Study of the History of Erosion in the Anacostia Drainage Basin.

Ref: Holders of Doctorates Among American Negroes, p. 159-160.
  American Men of Science, 10th ed., p. 1173.

Williams, Minnie C.   (19??-1977, F)

Pharmacist. Mississippi's first black pharmacist.

Ref: Jet, Jan. 5. 1978, p. 15.

Williams, O. S.   (1921- ——, M)

Engineer (aeronautical). Inventor. B.S.; M.S. (aeronautical engineering). Developed first airborne radar beacon for locating lost aircraft; chief developer of lunar lander's guidance rocket engines; first black to be hired as a design engineer by Republic Aviation—within four years he was Senior Aerodynamicist; Greer Hydraulics, 1956-62; Specialist in small rocket engine design, Reaction Motors Division, Thiokol Chemical Corporation, 1962-; Rocket Propulsion Engineer, Grumman Aerospace Corporation, 1961-; Task Force Leader in activating students in black colleges to prepare for Business and Technology; Market Survey Mission to West Africa to establish Grumman African headquarters, 1973; Vice-President, Grumman International.

*Ref: Department of Energy Poster on Black Contributors in Science and Technology.

Black Contributors to Science and Technology, 1979, p. 12–13.
In Black and White, p. 84–85.
Ebony, Sept. 1970, p. 36. [p]

Williams, Paul R.   (1894–19??, M)

Architect. Born in Los Angeles, CA, Feb. 18, 1894. Educated at University of Southern California; designed Julie London's home among several others including Lon Chaney's and one for Frank Sinatra, 1950s; designed colored YMCA, Los Angeles; designed and erected sorority and fraternity houses, UCLA.

Memberships and awards: Beaux Arts Institute of Design, Arts Medal; Spingarn Medal for contributions as a designer and architect, 1953; won three national and four western competitions; certified architect, 1915; American Institute of Architects; The City Planning Commission; Omega Psi Phi.

Ref: *Who's Who in Colored America,* 1928–29, p. 400.
Who's Who in Colored America, 1933–37, p. 576.
Jet, Dec. 10, 1957, p. 28. [p]
Jet, Mar. 26, 1959, p. 20. [p]
Historical Afro-American Biographies, p. 262–263. [p]
Ebony, July 1953, p. 44. [p] only
Ebony, Jan. 1957, p. 81–82, 84–86. [p]
Ebony Success Library, v. 1, p. 333. [p]
Ebony, Sept. 1950, p. 78.
Ebony, Sept. 1963, p. 232. [p] only
Who's Who Among Black Americans, 1977.
Crisis, June 1917, p. 82–83. [p] (as a young man)
Crisis, July 1941, p. 213. [p] only

Williams, Richard Arnett   (1878–19??, M)

Physician. Born in Forrest City, AR, Sept. 13, 1878. B.A., Arkansas Baptist College, Little Rock, 1896; M.D., 1902. School teacher at age 14; grocer from 1896 to 1898 when he went to Meharry Medical College; opened practice in Helena, AR, 1905; founded Royal Circle of Friends of the World in 1909. By 1911 there were 9,000 members, with 300 lodges—this organization acts as an insurance company paying beneficiaries of its members $300 upon proof of member's death.

Ref: *Who's Who in Colored America,* 1933–37, p. 576.
Beacon Lights of the Race, p. 287–296. [p]

Williams, Roger Kenton   (1914– ——, M)

Psychologist. Born in Harrisburg, PA, Feb. 18, 1914. B.A., Caflin College, 1936; M.S., 1940; Ph.D. (psychology), Pennsylvania State University, 1946, Associate Professor, Education and Psychology, North Carolina A & T, 1941–; served in World War II and then returned to Pennsylvania State University for his Ph.D.; Professor, Psychology and Director, Veterans Administration Guidance Center, 1946–48; Professor, Education and Director, Student Personnel, Morgan State College, 1948–68; Acting

Dean, Graduate School, 1968–69; Vice-President for Academic Affairs, 1972–73; Vice-President for Planning and Operations Analysis, Morgan State University, 1973–76; retired.

Memberships and awards: Chairman, Maryland State Board of Examiners of Psychologists, Omega Psi Phi; Distinguished Teacher of the Year, Morgan State University, 1966–67.

Dissertation title: A Comparison of College Students Classified by a Psychological Clinic as Personality Maladjustment Cases and as Vocational Guidance Cases.

Ref: *Even the Rat Was White,* p. 170–171. [p]
Who's Who Among Black Americans, 1985, p. 910.

Williams, Scott Warner   (1943– ——, M)

Mathematician. Born in Staten Island, NY, April 22, 1943. B.S., Morgan State College, 1964; M.S., Lehigh University, 1967; Ph.D. (mathematics), Lehigh University, 1969. Research Associate, Department of Mathematics, Pennsylvania State University, 1968–71; Assistant Professor, Mathematics, State University of New York at Buffalo, 1971–85; Professor, 1985–.

Memberships and awards: Ford Foundation Senior Research fellow, 1980–81; National Science Foundation research grant, 1983–87; American Mathematical Society.

Dissertation title: The Transfinite Cardinal Covering Dimension.

Ref: *Black Mathematicians and Their Works,* p. 300. [p]
American Men and Women of Science, 16th ed., p. 653.
Who's Who Among Black Americans, 1985, p. 910.

Williams, Theodore Shields   (1911–19??, M)

Veterinarian. Born in Kansas City, KS, June 2, 1911. D.V.M., Kansas State, 1935; M.S., Iowa State University, 1946. College Veterinarian, Prairie View State College, 1936; Veterinarian Inspector, Meat Inspection Division, U.S.D.A., 1936–45; Head of Department, Tuskegee Institute, 1945–51; Dean, 1947–72; Professor of Pathology and Parasitology, School of Veterinary Medicine, Tuskegee, 1945–81; retired; research in pathological lesions associated with tissue invading migratory parasites in animals.

Memberships and awards: President, American Association of Veterinary Medical Colleges, 1969–70; American Veterinary Medicine Association.

Ref: *American Men and Women of Science,* 16th ed., p. 653.
Who's Who in America, 1978, p. 3492.

Williams, Vernon   (1926– ——, M)

Mathematician. Born in Baton Rouge, LA, Nov. 10, 1926. B.A., Paine College, 1949; M.A., University of Michigan, 1953; D.Ed., Oklahoma State University, 1969. Instructor, Mathematics, Paine College, 1949–54; Instructor, Mathematics, Florida A & M University; 1954–56; Assistant, Professor, Southern University, 1956–60; Teaching Associate, Wayne State University, 1960–61; Professor, Mathematics, Southern University, 1962–.

Memberships and awards: Alpha Kappa Mu; Phi Delta Kappa; Pi Mu Epsilon; Louisiana Academy of Sciences; Mathematical Association of America; National Council of Teachers of Mathematics.

Dissertation title: A Multi-Predictive Measure to Predict Success at Two Levels in Freshman College Mathematics.

Ref: *Black Mathematicians and Their Works*, p. 300. [p]
American Men and Women of Science, 16th ed., p. 654.

Willis, Floyd Williams   (1885–1951, M)

Physician. Radiologist. Born in Crestwood, KY, April 6, 1885. M.D., Meharry Medical College, 1913; postgraduate courses in X-ray, Howard University and Freedmen's Hospital, Washington, DC, 1919; X-ray work, Cook County Hospital, Chicago, IL, 1920; Electro-Physio-Therapy, Fischer School of Electro-Therapy, 1921–22; Visiting Lecturer, in X-ray to Roentgenologist, Meharry Medical College Clinics, 1920–21.

Memberships and awards; National Medical Association; Central Society of Physical Therapists; Chicago Medical Society; Cook County Physicians Association; American Medical Association.

Ref: National Medical Association, *Journal*, v. 44, Jan. 1952, p. 73. obit
Who's Who in Colored America, 1927, p. 224.
Who's Who in Colored America, 1928–29, p. 403.
Who's Who in Colored America, 1933–37, p. 579.

Williston, Edward Davis   (1865–1928, M)

Physician. Born in Fayetteville, NC, Dec. 24, 1865. Graduated from Fayetteville Normal School, 1881; B.A., Howard University, 1890; M.D., Howard University Medical School, 1894. Interned at Freedmen's Hospital as its first interne. First black physician to pass the Medical Examining Board of Washington, DC.

Memberships and awards: National Medical Association.

Ref: National Medical Association, *Journal*, v. 20, Oct.–Dec., 1928, p. 193–194.

Wills, Frances   (1900s, F)

Military (Navy). In 1944, with Harriet Pickens, became first black woman in the WAVES.

Ref: Smithsonian. *Black Women Achieve Against All Odds*, p. 32.

Wilson, C. Leon   (1895–19??, M)

Physician. Surgeon. Obstetrician. Born in Cario, IL, June 5, 1895. B.S., University of Illinois, 1918; M.D., College of Medicine, 1920. Medical Examiner, Victory Life Insurance Co., Health Officer, Chicago Health Department; Chief Obstetrician, John T. Wilson Medical Foundation; Attending Obstetrician, Provident Hospital, Chicago; Lecturer in Obstetrics, John A. Andrews Clinical Society, Tuskegee, AL.

Memberships and awards: Fellow in Obstetrics, University of Chicago, for research in obstretrics at the Chicago Lying-in Hospital and Michael Reese Hospital, 1931–; Fellow, American Medical Association; National Medical Association; Illinois Medical Society; Cook County Physicians Association.

Ref: *Who's Who in Colored America*, 1933–37, p. 580.

Wilson, Donella   (1952– ——, F)

Biologist (molecular). Born in 1952. Harvard. Ph.D. (molecular biology). Princeton.

Dissertation title: An Analysis of the Hisu Regulatory Mutation in Salmonella Typhimurium; Altered Stable RNA Synthesis and the Pleiotropic Effects on ILV Regulation.

Ref: *Ebony*, Aug. 1985, p. 66. [p]

Wilson, Henry Spence   (1902–19??, M)

Chemist (inorganic). Born in 1902. B.A., Indiana University, 1923; M.S., 1927; Ph.D. 1938. Professor, Physics, Johnson C. Smith University, 1923–24; Professor, Chemistry, 1924–26; Professor, Chemistry and Chairman, Division of Natural Science, Louisville Municipal College, 1931–; research in qualitative method of testing calcium in the presence of barium and calcium. Removal of sulphur from laboratory glassware.

Dissertation title: A Study of the Plasticities of Lime.

Ref: *American Men of Science*, 8th ed., p. 2729.
In Black and White, p. 1062.
Holders of Doctorates Among American Negroes, p. 160.

Wilson, John Louis   (1900s, M)

Architect. Born in New Orleans, LA. B.A., Columbia University, 1928. Registered Architect and Staff Member, Design Division, New York City Board of Transportation.
Memberships and awards: Alpha Phi Alpha.

Ref: *Who's Who in Colored America*, 1933–37, p. 583.

Wilson, John Thomas   (1867–19??, M)

Physician. Born in Atlanta, GA, Mar. 27, 1867. Walden University, 1889; M.D., Meharry Medical College, 1895; LL.B., Turner University. Donated $50,000 in 1929 and made possible the purchase of the buildings and equipment at 34th and Rhodes in Chicago, IL, for the Wilson Hospital which contained six operating rooms, 100 beds, X-ray equipment, pharmacy and laboratory. Organized Wilson Sanitarium, Nashville, TN, 1897 and the Wilson Hospital, Memphis, TN, 1916.

Ref: *Who's Who in Colored America,* 1928-29, p. 404. [p]

Wilson, Julien Harmon   (1892-19??, M)

Physician. Surgeon. Born in Chattanooga, TN, May 5, 1892. B.S., Ohio State University; M.D., 1922. Exchange Scholar, University of Lyons, France, 1922.

Memberships and awards: Phi Beta Kappa; Ohio State Medical Association; fellow, American Medical Association; Kappa Alpha Psi.

Ref: *Who's Who in Colored America,* 1933-37, p. 583.

Wiltshire, Courtenay   (1900s, M)

Optometrist. Born in Barbados, B.W.I. Pennsylvania College of Optics and Ophthalmology, Philadelphia, PA; American Institute of Optometry, NY; Opt.D., Pennsylvania College of Optics and Ophthalmology, 1933. Optometrist, Georgetown, Demerara, S.A., 1922. Optometrist, Brooklyn, NY, 1925-.

Memberships and awards: Phi Beta Sigma.

Ref: *Who's Who in Colored America,* 1928-29, p. 405.
        Who's Who in Colored America, 1933-37, p. 583-584. [p]

Winstead, George Lee   (1878-1962, M)

Physician. Born in Nash County, NC, Sept. 30, 1878. B.A., Johnson C. Smith University, 1903; M.D., Shaw University, Leonard Medical College, Raleigh, 1908. Director, Livingstone Memorial Hospital, Pittsburgh, PA, 1923-.

Memberships and awards: President, Allied Medical Society of Western Pennsylvania, 1927; National Medical Association; Pennsylvania State Medical, Dental and Pharmaceutical Association; Allied Medical Society of Western Pennsylvania; Board of Trustees, Johnson C. Smith University.

Ref: *Who's Who in Colored America,* 1933-37, p. 587.
        National Medical Association, *Journal,* v. 54, Nov. 1962, p. 724. obit

Winston, Hubert Melvin   (1948- ——, M)

Engineer (chemical). Born in Washington, DC, May 29, 1948. B.S., North Carolina State University, 1970; M.S., 1973; Ph.D. (chemical engineering), 1975. Assistant Professor, Department of Chemical Engineering, North Car-

olina State University, 1975-77; Research Specialist, Exxon Production Research Co., 1977-83; Associate Professor, Undergraduate Administrative Department of Chemical Engineering, North Carolina State University, 1983-.

Memberships and awards: American Institute of Chemical Engineers; National Organization for the Professional Advancement of Black Chemists and Chemical Engineers; Instrument Society of America.

Dissertation title: An Examination of the Mechanism for Heat Transfer in the Evaporator Zone of the Heat Pipe.

Ref: *Who's Who Among Black Americans,* 1985, p. 922.
        Black Engineers in the United States, p. 211.

Woode, Charles Henri   (1865-19??, M)

Physician. Surgeon. Born in Rodney, MS, Oct. 31, 1865. B.S., Alcorn A & M College, 1884; M.D., Howard University Medical College, 1892. Passed Mississippi medical examination, Oct. 1892 and practiced medicine in Vicksburg, MS.

Memberships and awards: Secretary, Board of U.S. Examining Surgeons.

Ref: *Howard University Medical Department,* p. 230. [p]

Woods, Geraldine Pittman   (1921- ——, F)

Neuroembryologist. Born in West Palm Beach, FL, 1921. Talladega College, 1938-40; B.S., Howard University, 1942; M.A., Radcliffe College, 1943; Ph.D. Harvard University, 1945. Instructor, Biology, Howard University, 1945-46; Special Consultant, National Institute of General Medical Science, National Institutes of Health, 1969-; Assisted in the development of minority access to research careers and biomedical research support.

Memberships and awards: Board of Trustees, Howard University, 1975-; Chairman, Defense Advisory Commission on Women in Services, 1968; AAAS; Federation of American Scientists; National Institute of Science; "Scroll of Merit," National Medical Association; National President, Delta Sigma Theta, 1963-67; selected as one of 20 famous American Black Scientists; Board of Directors, Robert Wood Johnson Health Policy Fellowship, Institute of Medicine Academy of Sciences, 1973-78; Phi Beta Kappa; Consultant to National Institutes of Health to develop research training and fellowship programs in predominately black colleges and universities, 1969; Honorary D.Sc., Benedict College, 1977; Talladega College, 1980.

Dissertation title: The Development of the Spinal Cord of the Chick Embryo in Chorio-Allantoic Grafts.

Ref: *Who's Who Among Black Americans,* 1985, p. 928.
        Smithsonian. *Black Women Achieve Against All Odds.*
        American Men and Women of Science, 16th ed., p. 752.
        Who's Who Among American Women, 1978, p. 957.

Who's Who in the West, 1978, p. 792.

Woods, Granville T.   (1856–1910, M)

Inventor. Born in Australia, April 23, 1856. First patent on steam boiler furnace, #299,894, 1884; patented the Synchronous Multiplex Railway telegraph; railways communications specialty, Woods Electric Company, Cincinnati; air brakes in 1902, 1903, and 1905; invented overhead conducting system for electrical railways in 1888 which led to the development of elevated railway systems in metropolitan areas; more than 60 patents, including an incubator, forerunner of present machine capable of hatching 50,000 eggs at a time; was victorious in court twice against Thomas A. Edison contesting the rights to electrical inventions; sold many of his patents to General Electrical and Bell Telephone.

Ref: *At Last Recognition in America*, v. 1, p. 18–22.
Biographical History of Blacks in America Since 1528, p. 470–472.
Dictionary of American Negro Biography, p. 663–665.
Encyclopedia of Black America, p. 867.
Great Negroes Past and Present, p. 52.
Historical Afro-American Biographies, p. 145. [p]
Negro in Our History, 5th ed., p. 464–465.
Men of Mark, 1968, p. 107–112. [p]
Jet, April 23, 1964, p. 11. [p]
Black Pioneers of Science and Invention, p. 41–48. [p] p. 42.
Black Inventors of America, p. 24–39. [p] p. 24.
Jet, April 26, 1982, p. 24.
Jet, April 29, 1971, p. 10.
Ebony, Feb. 1967, p. 10. [p]
Ebony, Mar. 1972, p. 121.
Blacks in Science: Astrophysicist to Zoologist, p. 35.

Woods, Lloyd Lander   (1908–19??, M)

Chemist (organic). Born in Iola, KS, Mar. 2, 1908. B.A., Friends University, 1930; M.S., Kansas State College, 1933; Ph.D., 1944. Head, Department of Chemistry, St. Augustine's College, 1931–47; Professor, Chemistry and Head of the Department, Texas Southern, 1948–68; Distinguished Professor, 1968–; Chairman, Division of Natural and Physical Sciences, 1957–68.

Memberships and awards: Kansas Academy of Science; Texas Academy of Science; American Chemical Society; Phi Lambda Upsilon; Beta Kappa Chi; fellow, American Institute of Chemistry; New York Academy of Sciences.

Dissertation title: The Chemical Composition of Kaffir Bran.

Ref: *American Men and Women of Science*, 12th ed., p. 7041.
The Negro in Science, p. 187.

Woodson, George Frederick, Jr.   (1901– ——, M)

Mathematician. Born in Wilberforce, OH, Nov. 2, 1901. B.S., Wilberforce, 1923; M.A., Ohio State University, 1927. High School Principal, Pineville, KY, 1923; Head, Department of Mathematics, Paul Quinn College, 1924–25; Johnson C. Smith University, 1927–47; Central State College, 1947–.

Memberships and awards: General Education Board fellow, 1937; Beta Kappa Chi; Mathematical Association of America; Chairman, Mathematics Section, National Institute of Sciences, 1953.

Ref: *The Negro in Science*, p. 189.

Woodward, Dudley Welson   (1900s, M)

Mathematician. B.S. (with honors), Wilberforce University, 1903; B.S., University of Chicago, 1906; Ph.D. University of Pennsylvania, 1928. Practical Arithematic, Tuskegee Institute 1935.

Dissertation title: On 2-Dimensional Analysis Situs with Spherical Reference to the Jordan Curve Theorem.

Ref: *Black Mathematicians and Their Works*, p. 300.
Holders of Doctorates Among American Negroes, p. 160.

Woolfolk, E. Oscar   (1921– ——, M)

Chemist (organic). Born in Tupelo, MS, Mar. 9, 1912. B.A., Talladega College, AL, 1934; M.S., Ohio State University, 1939; Ph.D., University of Pittsburgh, 1949. Research Assistant, Ohio State University, 1938–40; Instructor, Chemistry, Claflin College, 1940–42; Director, Chemistry Laboratory, Scioto Ordance Plant, 1942–43; Research Chemist, U.S. Bureau of Mines, 1943–49; Professor of Chemistry and Chairman of the Department, Central State College, 1949–68; Dean, College of Arts and Sciences, Central State University, 1967–68; Vice-President for Academic Affairs, 1968–71; Visiting Lecturer, Urbana College, 1967–68; Dean, Fisk University, 1973–78; research in identification of amines; retired.

Memberships and awards: American Chemical Society; AAAS; Vice-President, Central Region, Beta Kappa Chi; Director, Midwest Region, National Institute of Science; American Association of University Professors; Sigma Xi; Phi Lambda Upsilon.

Dissertation title: A Study of Some Oxygenated Compounds Produced in Cool Hydrogenation.

Pub: *Journal of Organic Chemistry*, v. 21, 1956.

Ref: *The Negro in Science*, p. 187.
Who's Who Among Black Americans, 1985, p. 929.
Crisis, Oct. 1956, p. 504.

Wormly, Roscoe Conklin   (1882–19??, M)

Dentist. Born in Washington, DC, July 22, 1882, D.D.S., Howard University School of Medicine, 1905. Demonstrator in the Dental Department Howard University, 1909–12. Dental Inspector in DC public Schools, 1912.

Memberships and awards: Robert Freeman Dental Association; North Jersey Medical Society.

Ref: *Who's Who of the Colored Race*, 1915, p. 293.

Wright, Barbara P.   (1900s, F)

Physician. B.A., Mt. Holyoke College; M.D., Columbia University College of Physicians and Surgeons. Specialist in Industrial Medicine; Medical Staff, Metropolitan Life Insurance Company; sister of Jane Cooke Wright; daughter of Louis Tompkins Wright.

Ref: *Ebony*, May, 1964, p. 76. [p]

Wright, Charles H.   (1918– ——, M)

Physician. Born in Dothan, AL, Sept. 20, 1918. B.S., Alabama State College, 1939; M.D., Meharry Medical College, 1943. Assistant Clinical Professor, Obstetrics and Gynecology, Wayne State University Medical School.

Memberships and awards: Founder and President, African Medical Education Fund; Chairman of the Board, Afro-American Museum of Detroit; Physician of the Year, Detroit Medical Society, 1965; Physician of the Year, Michigan State Medical Society, 1968; served as Staff Obstetrician-Gynecologist aboard the hospital ship Hope during its third tour of duty, June–Aug. 1967.

Ref: *Who's Who Among Black Americans*, 1985, p. 931.
          Black Family International Journal, 1985, p. 27.
          National Medical Association, *Journal*, v. 60, July 1968, p. 343. [p]

Wright, Clarence William   (1912–1968, M)

Anatomist. Endocrinologist. Born in Thomasville, GA, July 5, 1912. B.S., Wilberforce University, 1932; M.S., Ohio State, 1936; Ph.D. (anatomy), Ohio State University. 1965. First black and 15th from Ohio State University. Only six other blacks had that degree in 1965. Professor, Anatomy, Meharry Medical College, 1946–68.

Memberships and awards: One of the founders of the National Institute of Science.

Pub: Co-author, *Human Anatomy, A Guide to the Study of Gross Structures.*

Dissertation title: A Study of The Development, Gross, and Microscopic Anatomy of the Human Prenatal and Postnatal Veriform Appendix.

Ref: *Jet*, Jan. 14, 1965, p. 27. [p]
          The Negro in Science, p. 180.
          National Medical Association, *Journal*, v. 63, Jan. 1961, p. 74–75. obit

Wright, Howard Emery   (1908–1988, M)

Psychologist. Born in Philadelphia, PA, 1908. B.A., Lincoln University, 1932; M.A., Ohio State University, 1933; Ph.D. (psychology), 1946. School Principal, several different schools, 1933–45; Chairman, Psychology Department, North Carolina College, Durham, 1945–48; Chairman, Division of Education and Psychology, Texas Southern University, 1948–53; Chairman, Psychology Department, North Carolina State, 1953–61; President, Allen University, SC, 1961–65; Regional Director, Community Action Programs, Office of Economic Opportunity, 1966–67; Branch Chief, Division of College Support, U.S., Office of Education, 1967; Academic Dean, Maryland State College, Princess Anne, 1967–70; Acting Chancellor, University of Maryland, 1970–72; Director, Division of Social Sciences, Hampton Institute, 1972–74; Professor, Psychology, Salisbury State College, 1974–.

Memberships and awards: Omega Psi Phi; American Association of University Professors; American Psychological Association.

Dissertation title: Racial Humor, A Value Analysis.

Ref: *Even the Rat Was White*, p. 172–173. [p]
          Jet, Feb. 1988, p. 19. obit

Wright, Jane Cooke   (1919– ——, F)

Physician. Surgeon. Cancer Research Specialist. Born in New York City, NY, Nov. 17, 1919. B.A., Smith College, 1942; M.D., New York Medical College, 1945. Cancer Research Foundation of Harlem Hospital, 1946–; Professor, Surgery, New York Medical College, 1967–; research in cancer chemotherapy, 1950–. Daughter of Dr. Louis Tompkins Wright.

Memberships and awards: President's Commission on Heart Disease, Cancer and Stroke, 1963–; "Finer Womanhood Award," 1975 given by the Black Women's International Conference on Priorities and Directions.

Ref: *American Men and Women of Science*, 14th ed., p. 5647.
          Black Women Makers of History, p. 269.
          In Black and White, p. 1078.
          Nine Black American Doctors, p. 108–117. [p]
          Who's Who Among Black Americans, 1985, p. 932.
          Women Pioneers of Science, p. 117–127. [p]
          Current Biography, 1968, p. 443–445. [p]
          Ebony, Nov. 1949, p. 43. [p] (Jane Wright Jones)
          Ebony Success Library, v. 1, p. 338. [p]
          Ebony, May 1964, p. 69. [p]
          Ebony, May 1968, p. 72–74. [p]

Ref.   *Crisis*, Aug. 1942. [p] cover
        Crisis, May 1965, p. 328. [p]

Wright, Louis Tompkins   (1891–1952, M)

Physician. Surgeon. Born in La Grange, GA, July 23, 1891. B.A., Clark College, Atlanta, GA, 1911; M.D. (cum laude), Harvard University Medical School, 1915; D.Sc., Clark University, 1938. One of the first black graduates of Harvard Medical School (fourth in his class); first black doctor appointed to a municipal hospital position in New York City; first black police surgeon, 1929–; headed the team which was the first to use aueromycin, the "wonder drug"; Founder, Cancer Research Center, Harlem Hospital; President, Medical Board of Harlem Hospitals, 1948; originated intradermal method of vaccination against smallpox.

Memberships and awards: American Medical Association; National Medical Association; Harlem Hospital Clinical Society; New York Surgical Society; American Board of Surgery; voted the man in his class, at his 25th class reunion, who had devoted the most to medical knowledge; winner of 25th Spingarn medal in 1940 for his contribution to medicine; second black member, American College of Surgeons.

Pub: Chapter XXII Head Injuries. In *The Treatment of Fractures*, by Charles L. Scudder.
        Author of many articles in medical journals.

Ref.   The Negro Physician. *Crisis*, Sept. 1929, p. 305–306.
        Cobb, W. Montague. Louis Tompkins Wright, 1891–1952. National Medical Association, *Journal*, v. 45,1 1953, p. 130–148.
        Crisis, Nov. 1952, p. 548–550. [p] obit
        Blacks in Science: Astrophysicist to Zoologist, p. 58.
        National Cyclopedia of American Biography, v. 43, p. 390–391.
        A Century of Black Surgeons, p. 160–171. [p]
        Nine Black American Doctors, p. 46–63. [p] p. 46.
        Crisis, Feb. 1933, p. 45.
        Kingdom, Frank. Patriot and Physician. *Crisis*, Jan. 1940, p. 14–15, 27. [p]

Wright, Phillip   (1900s, M)

Physician. Surgeon (cardiac). Set up practice in 1977 and had five heart patients. By 1980 he had 600 patients.

Ref.   *Jet*, May 8, 1980, p. 30.

Wright, Thomas   (1880–19??, M)

Physician. Surgeon. Born in Alexandria, VA, Sept. 25, 1880. M.D., Medical Department, New Orleans University, 1901. Established the Wright Sanitarium and Maternity Home where patients could be cared for by their own physicians. First institution of its kind for blacks in New Jersey.

Ref.   *Who's Who in Colored America*, 1928–29, p. 414.

Y

Yancey, Asa G., Sr.   (19??– ——, M)

Physician. Surgeon. Born in Atlanta, GA. B.S., Morehouse College, 1937; M.D., University of Michigan, 1941. Chief of Surgery, Hughes Spalding Hospital, 1958–72; Medical Director, Grady Memorial Hospital, 1972–; Associate Dean, Emory University School of Medicine, 1972–.

Memberships and awards: Board of Trustees, Georgia Division, American Cancer Society; fellow, American College of Surgeons; Diplomate, American Board of Surgery; American Surgical Association; Distinguished Service Award, Morehouse College.

Ref: *Ebony*, Feb. 1974, p. 94. [p] only
        Ebony, Sept. 1963, p. 166.
        Who's Who Among Black Americans, 1985, p. 935.
        A Century of Black Surgeons, p. 883–914, 934–936. [p]

Yates, Josephine A. Silone   (1852–1912, F)

Professor. Rhode Island State Normal School, 1879. Taught Lincoln University, Jefferson City, MO, 1880–1889; Head, Department of Natural Sciences and first woman elected to full Professorship at Lincoln University. Began writing as a child under pen name of R. K. Potter.

Ref: *Noted Negro Women*, p. 44–50.
        Profiles of Negro Womanhood, v. 1, p. 332–333.
        Index of Women, p. 568.

Yerby, Alonzo Smythe   (1921– ——, M)

Physician. Born in 1921. B.S., University of Chicago, 1941; M.D., Meharry Medical College, 1946; M.P.H., Harvard, 1948. Executive Director, Medical Care Services, City Department of Health and Coordinator of Welfare Services for the Hospitals Department, 1960–65; Professor and Chairman of Health Service Administration, School of Public Health, Harvard University, 1966; research in health; Director, Arthur D. Little, Inc., one of the largest scientific consulting firms in the world, 1971; Administration Public Health Practice.

Ref: *American Men and Women of Science*, 14th ed., p. 5681.
        History of the Negro in Medicine, p. 200. [p]
        In Black and White, 1083.
        Jet, p. 21, Jan. 21, 1971. [p]
        Who's Who Among Black Americans, 1980–81, p. 892.
        Historical Afro-American Biographies, p. 266–267. [p]

Young, Archie R., II   (1928– ——, M)

Chemist (physical). Born in 1928. B.A., (chemistry), Lincoln University, 1949; M.S., University of Pennsylvania, 1950; Ph.D. (physical chemistry), University of Pennsylvania, 1955. Senior Research Chemist, Exxon Research and Engineering Company; research in aluminum hydride and inorganic flourine chemistry.

Dissertation title: Alkali Metal Studies III. The Conductance of Concentrated Solutions of Lithium in Methylomine at -23 Degrees C.

Ref: *American Men and Women of Science,* 15th ed., p. 808.
Who's Who Among Black Americans, 1980–81, p. 893.

Young, Charles A.   (1864–1922, M)

Military (Army). Lt. Colonel. Born in Mayslick, KY, 1864. B.S., U.S. Military Academy, West Point, 1889, third black to graduate, first to achieve distinction; appointed Lt. Colonel in 1916, highest ranking black officer in World War I; Instructor, Military Science and Tactics, French, and Trigonometry, Wilberforce University, Ohio, 1894–98; U.S. Military Attache to Haiti, 1904–11; Attache to Liberia, 1915; retired by the War Department rather than promoted to Colonel, claiming he had various disabilities; recalled to active duty, 1919, but given no command; Military Attache to Liberia until his death, 1922.

Memberships and awards: Buried in Arlington Cemetery; highest ranking black in the army at the time of his death; winner of the second Spingarn Medal.

Ref: *Biographical History of Blacks in America Since 1528,* p. 479–481.
Dictionary of American Negro Biography, p. 677.
Famous Heroes in America, p. 129–137.
Great Negroes Past and Present, p. 111.
Negro Builders and Heroes, p. 167–172.
Historical Afro-American Biographies, p. 268. [p]
Ebony, Sept. 1963, p. 110. [p of tombstone]
Ebony, Nov. 1974, p. 86–88, 90, 92, 94–96. [p]
Black Defenders of America, 1775–1973, p. 158–163. [p]
Crisis, Mar. 1916, p. 240–242. [p]
Black Americans in Defense of Our Nation, p. 143–144. [p]
Crisis, Feb. 1922, p. 155. (tribute)
Crisis, July 1923, p. 105–106. (opinion)

Young, James Edward   (1926– —— , M)

Physicist. Born in Wheeling, WV, Jan. 18, 1926. B.A., Howard University, 1946; M.S., 1949; M.S., MIT, 1951; Ph.D., 1953. Instructor, Physics, Hampton Institute, 1946–49; Research Assistant, Physics, MIT, 1949–53; Research Staff, Acoustics Laboratory, 1953–55; Staff Member, Los Alamos Science Laboratory, 1956–69; Physics Professor, MIT, 1970–.

Memberships and awards: Acoustical Society of America; Sigma Xi; Beta Kappa Chi; American Physical Society; Postdoctoral fellow, MIT, 1953–55; fellow, Aeronautics Department, Southampton, England, 1956; National Academy of Sciences/National Research Council fellow, Neils Bohr Institute, Copenhagen, 1961–62.

Ref: *The Negro in Science,* p. 191–192.
American Men and Women of Science, 14th ed., p. 5694.
Who's Who Among Black Americans, 1985, p. 939.

Young, Moses Wharton   (1904–19??, M)

Neuroanatomist. Anatomist. Born in Spartanburg, SC, Oct. 24, 1904. B.S., Howard University, 1926; M.D., 1930, Ph.D., University of Michigan, 1934. Assistant Professor, Anatomy, Howard University, 1934–41; Associate Professor, 1941–47; Professor, 1947–70; Emeritus Professor, Neuroanatomy, Howard University Medical School, 1973–; Professor, Anatomy, College of Medicine, University of Maryland, Baltimore, 1973–; research in hypertensive deafness and the structure of the inner ear.

Memberships and awards: Rockefeller fellow in Anatomy, Michigan University, 1932–34; Visiting Professor, Anatomy, Meharry Medical College, 1940; Visiting Fulbright Professor, Anatomy, Chiba Medical College, Japan, 1952–53; American Association of Anatomists; AAAS; National Medical Association; Japanese Anatomical Society; Kappa Pi.

Dissertation title: the Nuclear Pattern and Fiber Connections of the Non-Cortical Centers of the Telencephalon of the Rabbit (Lepus Cuniculus).

Ref: *American Men and Women of Science,* 13th ed., p. 4999.
The Negro in Science, p. 180–181.
Holders of Doctorates Among American Negroes, p. 136.
Crisis, Aug. 1930, p. 266. [p] only

Young, Roger Arliner   (1900s, F)

Biologist. Zoologist. B.S., Howard University; M.S., University of Chicago; Ph.D., University of Pennsylvania, 1940.

Dissertation title: The Indirect Effects of Roentgen Rays on Certain Marine Eggs.

Ref: *Holders of Doctorates Among American Negroes,* p. 197.
Negroes in Science: Natural Science Doctorates, 1876–1969, p. 60.

AAAS ELECTIONS PAMPHLET A pamphlet sent to all members of the American Association for the Advancement of Science announcing the list of members who are running for offices within the AAAS, their qualifications, pictures, and a short biography.

ABMS COMPENDIUM OF CERTIFIED MEDICAL SPECIALISTS American Board of Medical Specialists. *American Board of Medical Specialists Compendium of Certified Medical Specialists.* 7 vols. Chicago: ABMS, 1986. Published in 1987 as a merger of the previously published individual lists of board certified medical specialists.

AFRO AMERICAN ENCYCLOPEDIA Rywell, Martin (chief compiler), and Wesley, Charles H. et al. (consulting editors); 10 vols. *Afro American Encyclopedia.* North Miami, FL: Educational Book Publishers, 1974.

AFRO AMERICANS IN DENTISTRY: SEQUENCE AND CONSEQUENCE OF EVENTS Dummett, Clifton, and Dummett, Lois. *Afro Americans in Dentistry: Sequence and Consequence of Events.* 1st ed. Los Angeles: C. Dummett, 1978. 144 p.

AFRO AMERICANS IN SCIENCE AND INVENTION Hayden, Robert C. Afro Americans in Science and Invention. *Journal of African Civilizations* (November 1959): 59–72.

AFRO USA Ploski, Harry A. *Afro USA: A Reference Work on the Black Experience.* Compiled and edited by Harry A. Ploski and Ernest Kaiser. New York: Bellwether Publishing Company; distributed by Afro American Press, 1971. 1110 p.

AMERICAN JOURNAL OF NURSING The American Journal of Nursing. Philadelphia, PA: J. B. Lippincott Co., for the American Journal of Nursing Co.

AMERICAN LIBRARIES American Libraries. Chicago: American Library Association, 1970–.

AMERICAN MATHEMATICAL MONTHLY American Mathematical Monthly: The official journal of the Mathematical Association of America. 1894–.

AMERICAN MEN AND WOMEN OF SCIENCE American Men and Women of Science: The Physical and Biological Sciences. New York: Bowker, 1971–. A continuation of *American Men and Women of Science, 1906–1968.* This begins with the 12th edition.

AMERICAN MEN OF SCIENCE American Men of Science: A Biographical Directory. New York: Bowker, 1906–1968. 1st–11th editions. 1st through 8th, published by the Science Press; 9th edition by Bowker; 10th edition by Jaques Cattell Press. Contained Black scientists from the beginning, but did not identify as such.

AMERICAN NEGRO REFERENCE BOOK Saythe, Mabel M., ed. *The Black American Reference Book.* Englewood Cliffs, NJ: Prentice-Hall. Sponsored by the Phelps-Stokes Fund. Previously published as *American Negro Reference Book.*

AMERICAN PSYCHIATRIC ASSOCIATION, DIRECTORY Biographical Directory of the Fellows and Members of the American Psychiatric Association. Washington, DC: American Psychiatric Association, c1983.

AMERICAN PSYCHOLOGICAL ASSOCIATION, DIRECTORY Directory of the American Psychological Association. Washington, DC: APA, 1978–.

AMERICAN WOMEN OF NURSING Yost, Edna. *American Women of Nursing.* Rev. ed. Philadelphia, PA: Lippincott, 1955.

AMSTERDAM NEWS New York. *Amsterdam News,* 1919–.

ASIMOV'S BIOGRAPHICAL ENCYCLOPEDIA OF SCIENCE AND TECHNOLOGY Asimov, Isaac. *Asimov's Biographical Encyclopedia of Science and Technology.* Garden City, NY: Doubleday, 1982. 941 p.

AT LAST RECOGNITION IN AMERICA Williams, James C., (compiler). *At Last Recognition in America: A Reference Handbook of Unknown Black Inventors and Their Contributions to America.* Chicago: B.C.A. Publishing Corp., c1978. 48 p.

BEFORE THE MAYFLOWER Bennett, Lerone, Jr. *Before the Mayflower: A History of Black America.* Chicago: Johnson Publishing Co., 1982. 681 p.

BEST DOCTORS IN THE UNITED STATES Pekkanen, John. *The Best Doctors in the U. S.* Rev. ed. New York: Seaview Books, c1981.

BIOGRAPHICAL DICTIONARY OF AMERICAN SCIENCE Elliott, Clark A. *Biographical Dictionary of American Science: The Seventeenth Through Nineteenth Centuries.* Sally Gregory Kohlstedt et al., Consulting editors. Westport, CT: Greenwood Press, 1979. 360 p.

BIOGRAPHICAL DICTIONARY OF AMERICAN PSYCHIATRIC ASSOCIATION Biographical Dictionary of the American Psychiatric Association. Washington, D.C.: American Psychiatric Association, c1983. Also known as Biographical Directory of the Fellows and Members of the American Psychiatric Association.

BIOGRAPHICAL HISTORY OF BLACKS IN AMERICA SINCE 1528 Toppin, Edgar Allen. *A Biographical History of Blacks in America Since 1528.* New York: McKay, 1971. 499 p.

BIOGRAPHICAL MEMBERSHIP DIRECTORY AND RESOURCE MANUAL OF THE AMERICAN ACADEMY OF OPHTHALMOLOGY American Academy of Ophthalmology. *Biographical Membership Directory & Resource Manual.* San Francisco, CA: The Academy, c1985

BLACK AMERICAN WRITERS PAST AND PRESENT Rush, Theressa Gunnels, Myers, Carol Fairbanks, and Arata, Esther Spring, *Black American Writers Past and Present: A Biographical and Bibliographic Dictionary.* 2 vols. Metuchen, NJ: Scarecrow Press, 1975. 875 p.

BLACK AMERICANS IN AUTOBIOGRAPHY Brignano, Russell Carl. *Black Americans in Autobiography: An Annotated Bibliography of Autobiographies and Autobiographical Books Written Since the Civil War.* Durham, NC: Duke University Press, 1974. 118 p.

BLACK AMERICANS IN DEFENSE OF OUR NATION *Black Americans in Defense of Our Nation.* Washington, DC: Office of the Deputy Assistant Secretary of Defense for Equal Opportunity and Safety Policy, Department of Defense, 1987. 189 p. Available from the U. S. Government Printing Office, Washington, DC.

BLACK APOLLO OF SCIENCE Manning, Kenneth R. *Black Apollo of Science: The Life of Ernest Everett Just.* New York: Oxford University Press. 1983. 416 p.

BLACK BOOK The Black Book. Compiled by Middleton Harris, New York: Random House, 1974. 198 p.

BLACK COLLEGIAN The Black Collegian. New Orleans, LA: Black Collegiate Services, 1969/1970–.

BLACK CONTRIBUTIONS TO SCIENCE AND ENERGY TECHNOLOGY A Pamphlet by the Federal Government containing biographical sketches of 24 Black inventors who made contributions in the area of energy.

BLACK ENGINEERS IN THE UNITED STATES Ho, James K. *Black Engineers in the United States—A Directory.* Washington, DC: Howard University Press, 1974. 281 p.

BLACK ENTERPRISE Black Enterprise. New York: Earl G. Graves Publishing Co., 1970–.

BLACK FAMILY INTERNATIONAL JOURNAL Black Family International Journal. Chicago, IL: Black Family International Journal, Inc., c1985–.

BLACK INVENTORS OF AMERICA Burt, McKinley, Jr. *Black Inventors of America.* Portland, OR: National Book Co., c1969.

BLACK LEADERS OF THE 20TH CENTURY Franklin, John Hope, and Meier, August, eds. *Black Leaders of the 20th Century.* Urbana: University of Illinois Press, c1982. 400 p.

BLACK MAN: HIS ANTECEDENTS, HIS GENIUS AND HIS ACHIEVEMENTS Brown, William Wells. *The Black Man: His Antecedents, His Genius and His Achievements.* Boston: J. Redpath, 1863. Reprint. New York: Kraus Reprint Co., 1969. 312 p.

BLACK MAN IN VETERINARY MEDICINE Waddell, William H. *The Black Man in Veterinary Medicine: Afro-American, Negro-Colored.* Rev. Ed. Honolulu, HI: W. H. Waddell, 1982. 176 p.

BLACK MATHEMATICIANS AND THEIR WORKS Newell, Virginia K., et al., eds. *Black Mathematicians and their Works.* Ardmore, PA: Dorrance, c1980. 127 p.

BLACK PHOTOGRAPHERS, 1840–1940: A BIO-BIBLIOGRAPHY Willis-Thomas, Deborah. *Black Photographers, 1840–1940: A Bio-Bibliography.* New York: Garland, 1985. 159 p.

BLACK PIONEERS OF SCIENCE AND INVENTION Haber, Louis. *Black Pioneers of Science and Invention.* New York: Harcourt, Brace & World, 1970. 181 p.

BLACK SWALLOW OF DEATH Carisella, P. J., and Ryan, James W. *The Black Swallow of Death: The Incredible Story of Eugene Jacques Bullard, the World's First Black Combat Aviator.* Boston: Marlborough House, 1972. (Distributed by Van Nostrand Reinhold, New York) 271 p.

BLACK WINNERS Douglass, Melvin I. *Black Winners: A History of Spingarn Medalists, 1915–1983.* Illustrated by James Brown, foreword by William H. Booth. Brooklyn, NY: T. Gaus, c1984. (Distributed by D. A. Reid Enterprises) 160 p.

BLACK WOMEN ACHIEVEMENTS AGAINST THE ODDS *Black Women Achievements Against the Odds.* Washington, DC: Smithsonian Institution Traveling Exhibition Service, 1984. Pamphlet listing the achievements of Black Women since Slavery. Suggestions for Exhibitions and Sources of Materials.

BLACK WOMEN IN MATHEMATICS IN THE UNITED STATES Kenschaft, Patricia C. "Black Women in Mathematics in the United States." *American Mathematical Monthly* 88 (October 1981): 599–600.

BLACK WOMEN MAKERS OF HISTORY Jackson, George F. *Black Women Makers of History: A Portrait.* Rev. Ed. Sacramento, CA: Fong and Fong, c1977. 289 p.

BLACKS IN AMERICA, 1492–1970 Sloan, Irving J. *Blacks in America, 1492–1970: A Chronology & Fact Book.* 3rd Edition. Dobbs Ferry, NY: Oceana Publications, 1970. Fourth edition has title, *The Blacks in America, 1492–1977.* Dobbs Ferry, NY: Oceana Publications, 1977.

BLACKS IN SCIENCE: ANCIENT AND MODERN Journal of African Civilizations 5, no. 1 (April 1983) and no. 2 (November 1983). New Brunswick: Transition Books, 1984. A series of essays by experts in various aspects of Africa and Afro American Scientific History. Edited by Irvan Van Sertima. Part I, African Science, Part II, Afro American Science.

BLACKS IN SCIENCE: ASTROPHYSICIST TO ZOOLOGIST Carwell, Harrie. *Blacks in Science: Astrophysicist to Zoologist.* Hicksville, NY: Exposition Press, c1977. 95 p.

BLOOD BROTHERS Sterne, Emma Gelders. *Blood Brothers: Four Men of Science.* 1st ed. Illustrated by Oscar Liebman. New York: Knopf, 1959. 174 p.

BOOK OF PRESIDENTS: LEADERS OF ORGANIZED DENTISTRY Webb, Harvey, Jr., and Lloyd, Cecil Rhodes. *The Book of Presidents: Leaders of Organized Dentistry.* Charlottesville, VA: National Dental Association, 1977. 63 p.

CENTURY OF BLACK SURGEONS Organ, Claude H., Jr., and Kosiba, Margaret M., eds. *A Century of Black Surgeons: The U.S.A. Experience.* 1st ed. 2 vols. Norman, OK: Transcript Press, c1987. 1010 p.

CHARLES RICHARD DREW Hardwick, Richard. *Charles Richard Drew, Pioneer in Blood Research.* New York: Scribner, 1967. 144 p.

CHICAGO BLACK DENTAL PROFESSIONALS Driskell, Claude Evans. *History of Chicago Black Dental Professionals, 1850–1983.* Chicago, IL: C. E. Driskell, c1982.

CHICAGO DEFENDER Chicago Defender. Black Newspaper. Chicago: R. S. Abott, 1966–1973.

CLEVELAND CALL AND POST Cleveland Call and Post. Newspaper. Cleveland, OH.

THE COLORED INVENTOR Baker, Henry Edwin. *The Colored Inventor: A Record of Fifty Years.* New York: Crisis Publishing Co., 1913. 12 p.

COMPLETE GUIDE TO SELECTED HEALTH AND HEALTH-RELATED CAREERS Lynch, L. Riddick. *The Complete Guide to Selected Health and Health-Related Careers.* Riddick Lynch, in collaboration with Urella Chatman, Phoebe Slade, and Joyce C. Truesdale. Teaneck, NJ: Ros Bernard Publications, 1980. 163 p.

CONTEMPORARY BLACK AMERICA Contemporary Black America. Prepared by Edit, Inc., with Onnie Kirk et al. Nashville, TN: Southwestern Co., c1980. 530 p.

CONTRIBUTIONS OF BLACK WOMEN TO AMERICA Davis, Marianna W., ed. 2 vols. *Contributions of Black Women to America.* Columbia, SC: Kenday Press, 1982, c1981.

CRISIS The Crisis. Baltimore, MD: Crisis Publishing Co., 1910–. Official Organ of the National Association for the Advancement of Colored People.

CURRENT BIOGRAPHY Current Biography Yearbook. 15 vols. New York: H. W. Wilson Co., 1940–. Annual.

CURRENT BLACK MAN: DECADE 70 Goodson, James A. *The Current Black Man: Decade 70.* 1st ed. Los Angeles: Record Publishing Co., 1971–.

DAWN MAGAZINE Dawn Magazine. Baltimore, MD: Afro American Newspapers, 1974–. Monthly.

DICTIONARY OF AMERICAN MEDICAL BIOGRAPHY Kaufman, Martin, Galishoff, Stuart, and Savitt, Todd L. ed. 2 vols. *Dictionary of American Medical Biography.* Westport, CT: Greenwood Press, 1984. 1027 p.

DICTIONARY OF AMERICAN NEGRO BIOGRAPHY Logan, Rayford W., and Winston, Michael R., eds. *Dictionary of American Negro Biography.* 1st edition. New York: Norton, c1983. 680 p.

DICTIONARY OF INTERNATIONAL BIOGRAPHY Dictionary of International Biography. Cambridge, England: International Biographical Centre, 1963–. Annual, 1971–1981, Biennial, 1982–1986.

DICTIONARY OF NURSES WITH DOCTORAL DEGREES Directory of Nurses with Doctoral Degrees. Kansas City, MO: American Nurses Association. 1980.

DIRECTORY OF THE AMERICAN PSYCHOLOGICAL ASSOCIATION. SEE AMERICAN PSYCHOLOGICAL ASSOCIATION, DIRECTORY

EARLY RECOLLECTIONS AND LIFE OF DR. JAMES STILL, 1812–1885 Still, James. *Early Recollections and Life of Dr. James Still, 1812–1885.* Facsimile ed. Medford, NJ: Medford Historical Society, 1970, c1877. 274 p.

EBONY Ebony. Chicago: Johnson Publishing Co., 1945–.

EBONY HANDBOOK Saunders, Doris E., ed. *The Ebony Handbook by the Editors of Ebony.* Chicago: Johnson Publishing Co., 1974. 553 p.

EBONY PICTORIAL HISTORY OF BLACK AMERICA Ebony Pictorial History of Black America. Vol. 1. Introduction by Lerone Bennett. Chicago: Johnson Publishing Co., 1971.

EBONY SUCCESS LIBRARY Ebony Success Library. 1,000 Successful Blacks, vol. 1, 341 p. Famous Blacks Give Secrets of Success, vol. 2, 309 p. Career Guide: Opportunities and Resources For You, vol. 3, 278 p. Chicago: Johnson Publishing Co., 1973.

EDUCATING BLACK DOCTORS Summerville, James. *Educating Black Doctors: A History of Meharry Medical College*. Foreword by Lloyd E. Elam. University, AL: University of Alabama Press, c1983. 288 p.

EIGHT BLACK AMERICAN INVENTORS Hayden, Robert C. *Eight Black American Inventors*. Reading, MA: Addison-Wesley, 1972. 142 p.

ENCYCLOPEDIA OF BLACK AMERICA Low, Augustus, and Clift, Virgil A., eds. *Encyclopedia of Black America*. New York: McGraw Hill, c1984. 941 p.

ESSENCE Essence. New York: Essence Communications, 1970–.

EVEN THE RAT WAS WHITE Guthrie, Robert V. *Even the Rat was White: A Historical View of Psychology*. New York: Harper & Row, c1976. 224 p.

FIRST NEGRO MEDICAL SOCIETY Cobb, William Montague. *The First Negro Medical Society*. Washington, DC: The Associated Publishers, 1939. 159 p.

GREAT NEGROES, PAST AND PRESENT Adams, Russell L. *Great Negroes, Past and Present*. 3rd ed. Illustrated by Eugene Winslow. Edited by David P. Ross, Jr. Chicago: Afro American Publishing Co., 1984. 212 p.

HER WAY Siegel, Mary-Ellen. *Her Way: A Guide to Biographies of Women for Young People*. 2nd ed. Chicago: American Library Association, 1984. 418 p.

HIDDEN CONTRIBUTORS Klein, Aaron E. *The Hidden Contributors: Black Scientists and Inventors in America*. Garden City, NY: Doubleday, 1971. 203 p.

HISTORICAL NEGRO BIOGRAPHIES Robinson, Wilhelmena S. *Historical Negro Biographies*. 2nd ed. New York: Publishers Co., 1968. 291 p.

HISTORY OF BLACK AMERICANS: FROM AFRICA TO THE EMERGENCE OF THE COTTON KINGDOM Foner, Philip S. *History of Black Americans: From Africa to the Emergence of the Cotton Kingdom*. Westport, CT: Greenwood Press, 1975–1983.

HISTORY OF NURSING Goodnow's History of Nursing. 1st ed., Philadelphia: W. B. Saunders Co., 1916–

HISTORY OF THE NEGRO IN MEDICINE Morais, Herbert Montfort. *The History of the Negro in Medicine*. New York: Publishers Co., 1967. 317 p.

HISTORY OF THE NEGRO RACE IN AMERICA FROM 1619–1880 Williams, George Washington. *History of the Negro Race in America from 1619–1880*. 2 vols. New York: Bergman Publishers, 1968.

HOLDERS OF DOCTORATES AMONG AMERICAN NEGROES Greene, Harry Washington. *Holders of Doctorates Among American Negroes: An Educational and Social Study of Negroes Who Have Earned Doctoral Degrees in Course, 1876–1943*. Boston: Meador Publishing Co., 1946. 275 p.

HOMESPUN HEROINES AND OTHER WOMEN OF DISTINCTION Homespun Heroines and Other Women of Distinction. Compiled by Hallie Q. Brown, with an introduction by Randall K. Burkett. New York: Oxford University Press, 1988. 284 p.

HOWARD UNIVERSITY: THE FIRST HUNDRED YEARS Logan, Rayford Whittingham. *Howard University: The First Hundred Years, 1867–1967*. New York: New York University Press, 1969. 658 p.

HOWARD UNIVERSITY MEDICAL DEPARTMENT Howard University Medical Department, Washington, DC: A Historical Biographical and Statistical Souvenir. Compiled and edited for and by Authority of the Medical Faculty of Howard University by Daniel Smith Lamb. Freeport, NY: Books for Libraries Press, 1971. 301 p. Reprint of the 1900 edition.

IN BLACK AND WHITE Spradling, Mary Mace, ed. *In Black and White: A Guide to Magazine Articles, Newspaper Articles and Books Concerning More than 15,000 Black Individuals and Groups*. 3rd ed. 2 vols. Detroit, MI: Gale Research Co., c1980. 1312 p.

IN SPITE OF HANDICAPS Bullock, Ralph W. *In Spite of Handicaps: Brief Biographical Sketches with Discussion Outlines of Outstanding Negroes Now Living Who are Achieving Distinction in Various Lines of Endeavor*. With a foreword by Channing Tobias. Freeport, NY: Books for Libraries Press, 1968. 140 p.

INDEX TO SCIENTISTS OF THE WORLD Ireland, Norma Olin. *Index to Scientists of the World from Ancient to Modern Times: Biographies and Portraits*. Boston: F. W. Faxon Co., 1962. 662 p.

INDEX TO WOMEN Ireland, Norma Olin. *Index to Women of the World from Ancient to Modern Times: Biographies and Portraits*. Westwood, MA: F. W. Faxon Co., 1970. 573 p.

INTERNATIONAL DIRECTORY OF NURSES WITH DOCTORAL DEGREES International Directory of Nurses With Doctoral Degrees. New York: American Nurses' Foundation, 1973–.

JET Jet. Chicago: Johnson Publishing Co., 1951–.

JOURNAL OF AFRICAN CIVILIZATIONS Journal of African Civilizations. New Brunswick, NJ: Douglas College, Rutgers University, 1979–. Semiannual.

JOURNAL OF COLLEGE SCIENCE TEACHING Journal of College Science Teaching. Washington, DC: National Science Teachers Association, 1971–

JOURNAL OF NEGRO HISTORY *The Journal of Negro History.* New York: United Publishing Corp., 1969–. Reprint of the Quarterly Periodical, founded and for many years edited by Carter G. Woodson. Issued in Washington by the Association for the Study of Negro Life and History.

LADIES' HOME JOURNAL *Ladies' Home Journal.* New York, 1889–.

LEADERS IN AMERICAN SCIENCE *Leaders in American Science.* 8 vols. Nashville, TN: Who's Who in American Education, 1953–1968.

LIVING BLACK AMERICAN AUTHORS *Living Black American Authors: A Biographical Directory.* Ann Ellen Shockley and Sue P. Chandler. New York: R. R. Bowker Co., 1973. 220 p.

LIVING LEGENDS IN BLACK Bailey, J. Edward. *Living Legends in Black.* Detroit, MI: Bailey Publishing Co., 1976. 173 p.

LONESOME ROAD Redding, J. Saunders. *The Lonesome Road: The Story of the Negro's Part in America.* 1st ed. New York: Doubleday, 1958. 355 p.

MAKERS OF NURSING HISTORY Pennock, Meta Rutter, ed. *Makers of Nursing History.* New York: Lakeside Publishing Co., 1940. 142 p.

MAN WITH A MILLION IDEAS Ott, Virginia, and Swanson, Gloria. *Man With a Million Ideas: Fred Jones, Genius Inventor.* Minneapolis: Lerner Publications Co., c1976. 109 p.

MARYLAND STATE MEDICAL JOURNAL *Maryland State Medical Journal.* Baltimore, MD: Medical and Chirurgical Faculty of the State of Maryland, c1985–.

MCGRAW-HILL ENCYCLOPEDIA OF WORLD BIOGRAPHY *The McGraw-Hill Encyclopedia of World Biography: An International Reference Work.* 12 vols. New York: McGraw-Hill, 1975.

MEDICINE, MOTHERHOOD AND MERCY Scally, M. Anthony. *Medicine, Motherhood and Mercy: The Story of a Black Woman Doctor.* Washington, DC: Associated Publishers, c1979. 121 p.

MEDICO-CHIRURGICAL SOCIETY OF DC, INC., BULLETIN Washington, DC: *Medico-Chirurgical Society of the District of Columbia Bulletin.*

MEMOIRS OF THE LATE BESSIE COLEMAN, AVIATRIX Patterson, Elois Coleman. *Memoirs of the Late Bessie Coleman, Aviatrix, Pioneer of the Negro People in Aviation.* 1 vol. No Publisher, 1969. (unpaginated).

MEN OF MARK Simmons, William J. *Men of Mark: Eminent, Progressive and Rising.* Cleveland, OH: The Rewell Publishing Co., 1891. 736 p. Reprint. New York: Arno Press, 1968. 1141 p. Reprint of 1887 edition.

MINORITIES IN SCIENCE: THE CHALLENGE FOR CHANGE IN BIOMEDICINE Melnick Viiaya L., and Hamilton, Franklin D., eds. *Minorities in Science: The Challenge for Change in Biomedicine.* New York: Plenum Press, c1977. 296 p.

MISSISSIPPI BLACK HISTORY MAKERS Sewell, George A., and Dwight, Margaret L. *Mississippi Black History Makers.* Revised and enlarged edition. Jackson: University Press of Mississippi, c1984. 486 p.

NATIONAL CYCLOPEDIA OF AMERICAN BIOGRAPHY *The National Cyclopedia of American Biography.* New York: J. T. White, 1898–1984.

NATIONAL FACULTY DIRECTORY *The National Faculty Directory.* Detroit, MI: Gale Research Co., 1970–.

NATIONAL MEDICAL ASSOCIATION JOURNAL *Journal of the National Medical Association.* East Norwalk, CT: Appleton-Century Crofts, 1909–.

NATIONAL REGISTER *The National Register: Pertinent Facts about Colored Americans.* Louisville, KY: Register Publications, 1952–.

NEEDLES' HISTORICAL MEMOIR OF THE PENNSYLVANIA SOCIETY FOR PROMOTING THE ABOLITION OF SLAVERY Needles, Edward. *The Pennsylvania Society for Promoting the Abolition of Slavery.* New York: Arno Press, 1969. 116 p. Reprint of the 1848 edition published under the title, *An Historical Memoir of the Pennsylvania Society for Promoting the Abolition of Slavery.*

NEGRO ALMANAC *The Negro Almanac: A Reference Work on the Afro American.* Compiled and edited by Harry A. Ploski and James Williams, 4th ed. New York: Wiley, c1983. 1550 p. Previous editions under Ploski, Harry. First edition titled *AFRO USA.*

NEGRO BUILDERS AND HEROES Brawley, Benjamin Griffith. *Negro Builders and Heroes.* Chapel Hill: The University of North Carolina Press, 1937. 315 p.

NEGRO FROM 1863–1963 Wheadon, Augusta Austin. *The Negro from 1863 to 1963.* 1st ed. New York: Vantage Press, 1964, c1963. 91 p.

NEGRO HISTORY BULLETIN *Negro History Bulletin.* Washington, DC: Association of the Study of Negro Life and History, 1937–.

NEGRO IMPACT ON WESTERN CIVILIZATION Roucek, Joseph Slabey, and Kiernan, Thomas. *The Negro Impact on Western Civilization.* New York: Philosophical Library, 1970. 506 p.

NEGRO IN OUR HISTORY Woodson, Carter Godwin. *The Negro in our History.* 5th ed. Washington, DC: The Associated Publishers, Inc., c1928. 628 p.

THE NEGRO IN SCIENCE Taylor, Julius, ed. *The Negro in Science.* Baltimore, MD: Morgan State College Press, 1955. 192 p.

NEGRO MAKERS OF HISTORY Woodson, Carter G. *Negro Makers of History.* Washington, DC: The Associated Publishers, Inc., 1938. 362 p.

NEGRO MEDAL OF HONOR MEN Lee, Irvin H. *Negro Medal of Honor Men.* New York: Dodd, Mead, 1967. 139 p.

NEGRO, TOO, IN AMERICAN HISTORY Eppse, Merl Raymond. *The Negro, too, in American History.* Nashville, TN: National Publication Co., 1949. 644 p.

NEGROES AND MEDICINE Reitzes, Dietrich C. *Negroes and Medicine.* Cambridge: Harvard University Press, 1958. Published on the behalf of the Commonwealth Fund. 400 p.

NEGROES IN SCIENCE: NATURAL SCIENCE DOCTORATES 1876–1969 Jay, James Monroe. *Negroes in Science: Natural Science Doctorates, 1876–1969.* Detroit, MI: Balamp Publishing Co., 1971. 87 p.

NEW YORK STATE JOURNAL OF MEDICINE New York State Journal of Medicine. Lake Success, NY: Medical Society of the State of New York, 1901–.

NEW YORK TIMES BIOGRAPHICAL SERVICE The New York Times Biographical Service. Ann Arbor, MI: University Microfilms International, vol. 5, 1974–.

NINE BLACK AMERICAN DOCTORS Hayden, Robert C., and Harris, Jacqueline. *Nine Black American Doctors.* Reading, MA: Addison-Wesley, c1976. 144 p.

NO TIME FOR PREJUDICE Staupers, Mabel Keaton. *No Time for Prejudice: A Story of the Integration of Negroes in Nursing in the United States.* New York: Macmillan, 1961. 206 p.

NOTABLE AMERICAN WOMEN Notable American Women. Cambridge, MA: Belknap Press of Harvard University Press, 1980. 773 p.

NOTED NEGRO WOMEN Majors, Monroe Alphus. *Noted Negro Women, Their Triumphs and Activities.* Freeport, NY: Books for Libraries Press, 1971, c1893. 365 p.

THE PATH WE TREAD Carnegie, Mary Elizabeth. *The Path We Tread: Blacks in Nursing, 1854–1984.* Foreword by Josephine Dolan. Philadelphia: Lippincott, c1988. 254 p.

PATHFINDERS Thoms, Adah H. *Pathfinders: A History of the Progress of Colored Graduate Nurses.* New York: Garland, 1984. Reprint of 1929 edition, published in New York by Kay Printing House.

PIONEER WOMEN ORATORS O'Conner, Lillian. *Pioneer Women Orators: Rhetoric in the Ante-Bellum Reform Movement.* New York: Columbia University Press, 1954. 264 p.

PROFILES IN BLACK Innis, Doris Funnye, and Wu, Juliana, eds. *Profiles in Black: Biographical Sketches of 100 Living Black Unsung Heroes.* Consulting editor, Joyce Duren. 1st ed. New York: CORE Publications, 1976. 240 p.

PROFILES IN EXCELLENCE

PROFILES OF NEGRO WOMANHOOD Dannett, Sylvia G. L. *Profiles of Negro Womanhood.* 1st ed. 2 vols. Yonkers, NY: Educational Heritage, 1964–66.

PROGRESS OF A RACE, OR, THE REMARKABLE ADVANCEMENT OF THE AMERICAN NEGRO Kletzing, Henry F. and Crogman, William H. *Progress of a Race; or, The Remarkable Advancement of the Afro-American Negro from the Bondage of Slavery, Ignorance and Poverty, to the Freedom of Citizenship, Intelligence, Affluence, Honor and Trust.* Atlanta, GA, and Naperville, IL: J. L. Nichols & Co., 1898. 23–663.

REACHING FOR FREEDOM Harbison, David. *Reaching for Freedom: Paul Cuffe, Norbert Rillieux, Ira Aldridge, James McCune Smith.* New York: Scholastic Book Service, 1972. 128 p.

ROLE OF THE AMERICAN NEGRO IN THE FIELDS OF SCIENCE Haber, Louis. *The Role of the American Negro in the Fields of Science.* New York, 1966. 70 p.

SCIENCE Science. Washington, DC: American Association for the Advancement of Science, 1883–.

SCIENTISTS IN THE BLACK PERSPECTIVE Young, Herman A., and Young, Barbara H. *Scientists in the Black Perspective.* Sponsored by the Lincoln Foundation, 1974. 185 p.

SELECTED BLACK AMERICAN, AFRICAN AND CARIBBEAN AUTHORS Page, James A. and Roh, Jae M. *Selected Black American, African and Caribbean Authors: A Bio-Bibliography.* Boston: G. K. Hall, c1977. 398 p.

SEND US A LADY PHYSICIAN Abram, Ruth J., ed. *Send Us a Lady Physician: Women Doctors in America, 1835–1920.* 1st ed. New York: Norton, 1986. 255 p.

SEVEN BLACK AMERICAN SCIENTISTS Hayden, Robert C. *Seven Black American Scientists.* Reading, MA: Addison-Wesley c1970. 172 p.

SIGNIFICANT AMERICAN BLACKS Significant American Blacks. Chicago: Childrens Press, c1975. 78 p.

SMITHSONIAN. BLACK WOMEN ACHIEVEMENTS AGAINST THE ODDS, SEE: BLACK WOMEN . . .

SPACE CHALLENGER: THE STORY OF GUION BLUFORD Haskins, James, and Benson, Kathleen. *Space Challenger: The Story of Guion Bluford: An Authorized Biography.* Minneapolis: Carolrhoda Books, c1984. 86 p.

STRENGTH FOR THE FIGHT Nalty, Bernard C. *Strength for the Fight: A History of Black Americans in the Military.* New York: Free Press. London: Collier MacMillan, c1986. 424 p.

THEY CAME BEFORE COLUMBUS Van Sertima, Irvan. *They Came Before Columbus: The African Presence in Ancient America.* New York: Random House, 1977

THEY SHOWED THE WAY Rollins, Charlemae Hill. *They Showed the Way: Forty American Negro Leaders.* New York: Crowell, 1964. 165 p.

TRAILBLAZER: NEGRO NURSES IN THE AMERICAN RED CROSS Pitrone, Jean Maddern. *Trailblazer: Negro Nurses in the American Red Cross.* 1st ed. New York: Harcourt, Brace & World, 1969. 191 p.

A TRUE LIKENESS Roberts, Richard Samuel. *A True Likeness: The Black South of Richard Samuel Roberts, 1920-1936.* Phillip C. Dunn and Thomas L. Johnson, eds. Chapel Hill, NC: Algonquin Books of Chapel Hill, c1986. 188 p.

VIEWFINDERS: BLACK WOMEN PHOTOGRAPHERS Moutoussamy-Ashe, Jeanne. *Viewfinders: Black Women Photographers, 1839-1985.* 1st ed. New York: Dodd, Mead, c1986. 224 p.

WASHINGTON POST The *Washington Post.* Washington, DC: The Washington Post Co., 1974–

WE ARE YOUR SISTERS Sterling, Dorothy, ed. *We Are Your Sisters: Black Women in the 19th Century.* 1st ed. New York: W. W. Norton, c1985. 560 p.

WHO WAS WHO IN AMERICAN HISTORY–SCIENCE AND TECHNOLOGY Who Was Who in American History–Science and Technology: A Component of Who's Who in American History. 1976 Bicentennial edition. Chicago: Marquis Who's Who. c1976. 688 p.

WHO'S WHO AMONG BLACK AMERICANS Who's Who Among Black Americans. Northbrook, IL: Who's Who Among Black Americans, Inc., Publishing Co., 1975/1976–.

WHO'S WHO IN AMERICA Who's Who in America. Chicago: Marquis Who's Who, 1899/1900–.

WHO'S WHO IN AMERICAN NURSING Who's Who in American Nursing. Washington, DC: Society of Nursing Professionals, 1984–.

WHO'S WHO IN COLORED AMERICA Who's Who in Colored America: A Biographical Dictionary of Notable Living Persons of Negro Descent in America. New York: Who's Who in Colored America Corp., 1927–.

WHO'S WHO IN ENGINEERING Who's Who in Engineering. New York: American Association of Engineering Societies, 1977–.

WHO'S WHO IN GOVERNMENT Who's Who in Government. Chicago: Marquis Who's Who, 1971/73-1977.

WHO'S WHO IN THE EAST Who's Who in the East. Boston: Larkin, Roosevelt and Larkin, 1943–.

WHO'S WHO IN THE MIDWEST Who's Who in the Midwest. Chicago: Marquis Who's Who, 1949–.

WHO'S WHO IN THE SOUTH AND SOUTHWEST Who's Who in the South and Southwest. Chicago: Marquis Who's Who, 1947–.

WHO'S WHO OF AMERICAN WOMEN Who's Who of American Women. 6th ed. Chicago: Marquis Who's Who, Inc., 1970/71–.

WHO'S WHO OF THE COLORED RACE Mather, Frank Lincoln, ed. *Who's Who of the Colored Race: A General Biographical Dictionary of Men and Women of African Descent,* vol. 1. Detroit, MI: Gale Research Co., 1976, c1915. 296 p.

WISE WOMEN Rayner, William P. *Wise Women: Singular Lives that Helped Shape Our Century.* Foreword by Francine du Plessix Gray. 1st ed. New York: St. Martin's Press, c1983. 242 p.

WOMEN IN AERONAUTICS May, Charles Paul. *Women in Aeronautics.* New York: Nelson, 1962. 260 p.

WOMEN IN AVIATION Pecham, Betty. *Women in Aviation.* New York: Nelson & Sons, 1945. 164 p.

WOMEN PIONEERS OF SCIENCE Haber, Louis. *Women Pioneers of Science.* Rev. ed. New York: Harcourt Brace Jovanovich, c1979. 171 p.

WOMEN SCIENTISTS FROM ANTIQUITY TO THE PRESENT Herzenberg, Caroline L. *Women Scientists from Antiquity to the Present: An Index. An International Reference Listing and Biographical Directory of Some Notable Women Scientists from Ancient to Modern Times.* West Cornwall, CT: Locust Hill Press, 1986. 200 p.

WOMEN SCIENTISTS IN AMERICA Rossiter, Margaret. *Women Scientists in America: Struggles and Strategies to 1940.* Baltimore, MD: Johns Hopkins University Press, c1984. 439 p.

WORLD WHO'S WHO IN SCIENCE Debus, Allen G. ed. *World Who's Who in Science: Biographical Dictionary of Notable Scientists from Antiquity to the Present.* 1st ed. Chicago: Marquis Who's Who, Inc., 1968. 1855 p.

WORLD'S GREAT MEN OF COLOR Rogers, J. A. *World's Great Men of Color.* 2 vols. New York: Macmillan, 1972, c1946–47.

YALE JOURNAL OF BIOLOGY AND MEDICINE *Yale Journal of Biology and Medicine.* New Haven, CT: Yale Journal of Biology and Medicine, Inc., 1928–.

INDEX HEADINGS

AGRICULTURISTS

Atwood, Rufus Ballard
Bassett, Emmett
Carver, George Washington
Coruthers, John Milton
Davis, Walter Strother
Grant, Ernest A.
Hill, Walter Andrew
Hoffman, John Wessley
Hubert, Benjamin F.
Kennedy, Wadaran Latimore
Lowery, Samuel R.
Norris, Ernest M.
Spaulding, Dean Major Franklin
Staley, Frank Marcellus
Thomas, Maceo A.

ANATOMISTS

Bush, Gow Max
Cobb, William Montague
Hubert, Charles Edward
Lloyd, Ruth Smith
McKinney, Roscoe Lewis
Ware, Ethan Earl
Wright, Clarence William
Young, Moses Wharton

ANTHROPOLOGISTS

Cobb, William Montague
Davis, William Allison
Gwaltney, John Langston
Robeson, Eslanda Goode
Skinner, Elliott

ARCHEOLOGIST

Gilbert, John Wesley

ARCHITECTS

Anderson, Carey Laine
Bailey, Walter Thomas
Brown, Leroy J. H.
Campbell, Wendell Jerome
Cassell, Albert I.
Doman, James Richard, Jr.
Dozier, Richard K.
Edwards, Gaston Alonzo
Jones, George Maceo
Jones, W. Fontaine
Lankford, John Anderson
Mackey, Howard Hamilton, Sr.
Madison, Robert Prince
O'Neal, Kenneth
Pittman, William Sidney

Rayfield, W. A.
Rieras, Joseph Harrison
Robinson, Hilyard R.
Taylor, Edward Walter
Vincent, Walter
West, Frank G., Jr.
Wigington, Clarence W.
Williams, Paul R.
Wilson, John Louis

ASTRONAUTS

Bluford, Guion Stewart, Jr.
Bolden, Charles F.
Dwight, Edward J.
Gregory, Frederick Drew
Jemison, Mae C.
Lawrence, Robert Henry, Jr.
McNair, Ronald Erwin

AUDIOLOGISTS

Hurst, Charles G.
Lewis, H. Donell

BACTERIOLOGISTS

Amos, Harold
Brown, Russell Wilfred

BACTERIOLOGISTS
(Continued)

Buggs, Charles Wesley
Campbell, Haywood
Clarke, Richard Claybourne
Ford, Charles Marion
Hammond, Benjamin Franklin
Hinton, William Augustus
Jay, James M.
Johnson, Charles William
Jones, Woodrow Harold
Lee, James Sumner
Moore, Ruth Ella
Poindexter, Hildrus A.
Price, Jessie Isabelle
Quinland, William Samuel
Sweres, Mary Agnes
Taylor, Welton Ivan
Wallace, John Howard
Webb, Arthur Harper
Wheeler, Albert Harold
Wiley, William Rodney

BIOCHEMISTS

Campbell, Haywood
Chappelle, Emmet W.
Daly, Marie Maynard
Deese, Dawson Charles
Dyce, Barbara Jeanne
High, Edward Garfield
Kountz, Samuel Lee, Jr.
Lewis, Roscoe Warfield
Marshall, Lawrence Marcellus
Maxwell, Ucecil Seymour
Sanders, Robert B.
Thomas, Gerald Eustis
Tildon, James Tyson
Tinch, Robert J.
Tolbert, Margaret Ellen Mayo
West, Harold Dadford
White, Booker Taliafero W.
Wilkerson, Vernon Alexander

BIOLOGISTS

Abram, James Baker, Jr.
Alexander, Lloyd Ephraim
Anderson, Everett
Anderson, Russell Lloyd
Birnie, James Hope
Booker, Walter Monroe
Bradley, Walter Oswald
Bright, William Michael

Buggs, Charles Wesley
Chase, Hyman Yates
Christian, Eugenia D.
Cobb, Jewel Plummer
Coffin, Alfred O.
Crooks, Kenneth Bronstorph M.
Dowdy, William Wallace
Ferguson, Edward, Jr.
Foreman, Madeline Clark
Frederick, Lafayette
Gibson, Walter William
Greene, Lionel Oliver, Jr.
Griffith, Booker Taliaferro
Hamblin, Adolf Putnam
Hansborough, Louis Armstead
Harris, Mary Styles
Holland, James Philip
Howard, Roscoe Conkling
Hunter, Jehu Callis
Jay, James M.
Just, Ernest Everett
King, John Wesley
Monroe, Clarence Lee Edward
Parnell, John Vaze, Jr.
Peele, Amanda E.
Reddick, Mary Logan
Rhaney, Mahlon Clifton
Romm, Harry Josef
Wagner, John A.
Webb, Arthur Harper
Wilson, Donella
Woods, Geraldine Pittman
Young, Roger Arliner

BOTANISTS

Henderson, James Henry
    Meriwether
King, John Wesley
Lislet, Geoffrey Jean Baptiste
Mark, Jessie Jarue
Myles, Marion Antionette Richards
Parker, Charles Stewart
Turner, Thomas Wyatt

CHEMISTS

Abron-Robinson, Lillia Ann
Acker, Daniel R.
Alexander, Benjamin Harold
Anderson, Gloria Long
Antoine, Albert Cornelius
Ashley, William Ford
Atkins, Cyril Fitzgerald
Baker, Thomas Nelson, Jr.

Barnes, Robert Percy
Bate, Langston Fairchild
Baulknight, Charles Wesley, Jr.
Beal, Robert S.
Beck, James T.
Belton, William Edward
Bembry, Thomas Henry
Bluford, John Henry
Brady, St. Elmo
Branson, Herman Russell
Brookes, E. Luther
Browne, Frederick
Calloway, Nathaniel Oglesby
Carter, Thomas J.
Cason, Louis Forrester
Chandler, Edward Marion Augustus
Christian, John B.
Clarke, Richard Claybourne
Clarke, Wilbur Bancroft
Cole, Thomas Winston, Jr.
Cooke, Lloyd Miller
Cooper, John R.
Cooper, Stewart Rochester
Cotton, Donald
Dacons, Joseph Carl
Daly, Marie Maynard
Dent, Samuel George
Derbigny, Irvin Anthony
Diuguid, Lincoln I.
Dorman, Linnaeus Cuthbert
Dove, Ray Allen
Duvalle, Sylvester Howard
Elliott, Irvin Wesley, Jr.
Evans, Harold Bethuel
Ferguson, Lloyd Noel
Fields, Victor Hugo
Forbes, Dennis Arthur
Ford, Leonard A.
Fort, Marron William
Foster, William Clarence
Franks, Cleveland James
Gainer, Frank Edward
Gibbs, James Albert
Green, Harry James, Jr.
Greene, Bettye Washington
Hall, Lloyd Augustus
Harris, Edward Lee
Harris, James Andrew
Harris, Robert McCants
Harvey, Burwell Towns, Jr.
Hawkins, Walter Lincoln
Henry, Warren Elliott
Hill, Carl McClellan
Hill, Henry Aaron
Hill, Mary Elliot
Hodge, John Edward

Holly, William G.
Howard, Ralph
Huggins, Kimuel Alonzo
Hunter, John McNeile
Imes, Elmer Samuel
Jeffries, Louis Freeman
Johnson, Bernard Henry, Jr.
Johnson, William Thomas Mitchell
Jones, John Leslie
Julian, Percy Lavon
King, James, Jr.
Knox, Lawrence Howland
Knox, William Jacob, Jr.
Lawson, Katheryn Emanuel
Lester, William Alexander, Jr.
Lewis, Richard Hanna
Lloyd, Birtill Arthur
Lomax, Eddie, Jr.
Lu Valle, James Ellis
Lynk, Beebe Steven
Maloney, Kenneth Morgan
Mason, Clarence Tyler
Massie, Samuel Proctor, Jr.
Maxwell, Ucecil Seymour
McBay, Henry Cecil Ransom
McBay, Shirley Mathis
McMillan, Julius Augustus
Milligan, Dolphus Edward
Millington, James E.
Mitchell, James Winfield
Moore, Paul Joaquin
Morris, Kelso Bronson
Neal, Xenophon Lamar
Neblett, Richard Flemon
Perry, Rufus Patterson
Prince, Frank Roger
Quaterman, Lloyd Albert
Raines, Eugene D.
Reed, George W.
Robeson, Eslanda Goode
Russell, Edwin Roberts
Sayles, James H.
Scott, Benjamin Franklin
Scott, David, Jr.
Scurlock, Herbert Clay
Sellers, Phillip A.
Slaton, William H.
Snead, Jonathan L.
Spaulding, George H .
Stewart, Albert Clifton
Stubbs, Ulysses Simpson, Jr.
Talley, Thomas Washington
Taylor, Daniel Bernette
Taylor, Moddie Daniel
Taylor, William Charles

Tazewell, Joseph H.
Towns, Myron Bumstead
Tulane, Victor Julius
Urdy, Charles Eugene
Van Dyke, Henry Lewis
Vaughn, Clarence Benjamin
Wall, Arthur Albert
Wallace, William James Lord
Watts, Johnnie Hines
Weir, Charles Edward
West, Harold Dadford
White, Booker Taliafero W.
Wilkins, Raymond Leslie
Williams, Daniel Adolph, Jr.
Wilson, Henry Spence
Woods, Lloyd Lander
Woolfolk, E. Oscar
Young, Archie R., II

DENTISTS

Alexander, Walter Gilbert, II
Allen, Elbert E.
Altemus, Leonard A.
Anderson, Arnett Artis
Anderson, Subbeal Stewart
Badger, Robert
Badger, Roderick
Beamon, Reginald Emmett
Beekman, Walter Nathaniel
Belsaw, E. T.
Bently, Charles E.
Beshears, Rufas P.
Bolden, Theodore Edward
Boyd, Robert Fulton
Brown, Roscoe Conklin
Catchings, James A. A.
Colleymore, Errold Duncan
Collins, Daniel A.
Cox, Wendell
Davis, Jackson Lee
Dixon, Russell Alexander
Dummett, Clifton Orin
Ferguson, David Arthur
Francis, John Richard
Freeman, C. V.
Freeman, Robert Tanner
Gans, Louis H.
Garrott, Alva Curtis
Garvin, Walter B.
Grant, George F. (or George F. Grand)
Greene, Clarence Sumner
Griffiths, Norman Henry Campbell
Hammond, Benjamin Franklin

Horne, Woody Lemuel
James, Thomas Leslie
Jamison, Francis Trevanian
Johnson, Gladys L.
Jones, Yvonne
Langston, Theophilus Steward
Lassiter, Norman
Lee, Roseau Franklin
Lewis, Stephen J.
Maddox, Elton Preston, Jr.
Marshall, Vereen Marion
McLinn, Harry Marvin
McPherson, Gertrude Elizabeth Curtis
Meaddough, Ray James
Mitchell, Matthew
Nelson, Ida Gray
Owens, Hugo, Sr.
Porter, James Reynolds
Primas, H. Raymond
Renfroe, Earl Wiley
Rock, John Sweat
Russell, Alfred Pierpont, Jr.
Sinkford, Jeanne Frances Craig
Somerville, Veda Watson
Stamps, Herman Franklin
Taylor, Harold Leon
Taylor, Robert B., Sr.
Thompson, Floyd, Sr.
Wallace, James C., Jr.
Walton, Adolphus
Welters, Edward A.
Wormly, Roscoe Conklin

DESIGNERS

12th Street WMCA, Washington DC: Pittman, William Sidney
Alternate Landing Gear System, Boeing 747: Jackson, Richard H.
AME Zion Churches (Official Architect): Rayfield, W. A.
Founders Library, Howard University: Cassell, Albert I.
Jet-Propelled Plane, P-59, (co-designer): Blanton, John W.
Julie London's Home: Williams, Paul R.
K Street Freeway, Washington, DC: Alexander, Archie Alphonso
Lon Chaney's Home: Washington, DC: Williams, Paul R.
Mother AME Zion Church, NY: Jones, W. Fontaine
Postage Stamp: Olden, Georg

DESIGNERS (*Continued*)

Radio City Music Hall Heating
System: Crosthwait, David
Nelson, Jr.
Refuse Disposal Units For Skylab:
Shurney, Robert E.
Submarine Tracking Systems:
McCoy, Caldwell
Tidal Basin Bridge, Washington, DC:
Alexander, Archie Alphonso

DEVELOPERS

Cancer Treatment: Walker, William
McAlpine
Electron Microscope (Assisted In
Development): Wilkins,
Raymond Leslie
Lunar Lander's Guidance Rocket
Engines: Williams, O. S.
Mercy Hospital To Class A: Warlick,
Lula G.

DISCOVERERS

Chloraseptic With Dr. Bookhardt:
Giles, Julian Wheatley
David-Hinton Blood Test: Hinton,
William Augustus
Dimethoxy Reserpine For
Hypertension: Calloway,
Nathanial Oglesby
Rattlesnake Bite Cure: Cesar
(Slave)

ELECTRICAL CONTRACTOR

Jones, William H., Sr.

EMBRYOLOGISTS

Alexander, Lloyd Ephraim
Graves, Artis P.
Hansborough, Louis Armstead
Nabrit, Samuel Milton
Parnell, John Vaze, Jr.
Seaton, Alberta Jones

ENGINEERS

Abron-Robinson, Lillia Ann
Agbanobi, Raymond Omavuobe

Alexander, Archie Alphonso
Alexander, Walter Gilbert, II
Alexander, Winser Edward
Allen, John Henry, Jr.
Amory, Reginald L.
Anderson, Giovonnae
Apea, Joseph Bennet Kyeremateny
Baltimore, Jeremiah Daniel
Bates, Clayton Wilson, Jr.
Berry, Jesse Frank
Bianchi, La Bonnie
Bishop, Alfred A.
Blakney, Eustis Joel
Blanton, John W.
Bliss, Norman Randolph
Bragg, Robert Henry
Branch, Melvyn Clinton
Brandford, Paul
Branner, George Richard
Brooks, Robert Roosevelt
Brown, Delores Elaine Robinson
Burrell, Montrust Q.
Callender, Leroy Nathaniel
Campbell, Robert Lee
Cannon, Joseph Nevel
Carruthers, George R.
Carter, Willie James
Cassell, Albert I.
Clark, Yvonne Young
Conliffe, Calvin Hughes
Cooper, Lois Louise
Craig, Arthur
Craig, George
Crawford, Charles Linwood
Crossley, Frank Alphonso
Crosthwait, David Nelson, Jr.
Crummie, John H.
Curby, Norma
Daniel, Walter Thomas
Darden, Christine Mann
Davis, Charles Alexander
Davis, Stephen Smith
Dennar, Ezenwa A.
Dent, Anthony L.
Douglas, Aurelius William, Jr.
Douglas, Joseph Francis
Downing, Lewis King
Duke, Charles Sumner
Dukes, Lamar
Dutton, Benson Leroy
Earls, Julian Manley
Early, Benjamin Nathaniel
Edwards, Robert Valentino
Ellis, James Riley, Jr.
Esogbue, Augustine Onwuyalim
Eubanks, Robert Alonzo

Evans, James Carmichal
Evans, Wilson Lovett
Ferguson, George Alonzo
Finney, Essex Eugene, Jr.
Fletcher, Douglas Wellington
Florant, Leroy Frederic
Ford, Denise Annette
Fort, Marron William
Frank, Rudolph Joseph
Franklin, Benjamin
Gay, Edward Charles
Gier, Joseph Thomas
Gourdine, Meredith C.
Govan, Charles
Green, Harry James, Jr.
Greene, Frank S., Jr.
Grooms, Henry Randall
Hampton, Delon
Harris, Gary L.
Harris, Wesley Leroy, Sr.
Harwell, William
Hawkins, Walter Lincoln
Henderson, Henry Fairfax, Jr.
Hope, Edward Swain, Jr.
Hubbard, Philip Gamalieh
Isibor, Edward Iroguehi
Jackson, Larry Eugene
Jackson, Richard H.
Jones, George Maceo
Jones, Howard St. Claire, Jr.
Jones, Irving Wendell
Keyser, George Ficklin
King, Wendell
Lankford, John Anderson
Latimer, Lewis Howard
Levert, Francis Edward
Lewis, Harold Ralph
Lewis, James Earl
Ligon, Claude Matthew
Liston, Hardy, Jr.
Madison, Shannon L.
Malone, Huey Perry
Mann, Frank
Marsh, Alphonso Howard
McAfee, Leo Cecil, Jr.
McCoy, Caldwell
McCoy, Elijah
McSwain, Berah Davis
Mills, William Louis
Montez, Billy V.
Morris, Joel M.
Moss, Leon Wilson
Ndefo, Ejike D.
Nelson, Edward O.
Nwude, Joseph Kanayo
Oseni, Hakeem O.

ENTOMOLOGISTS

EXPLORERS

FIRST BLACK

FIRST BLACK (*Continued*)

Diplomate, American Board of Urology: Jones, Richard Francis (Frank)

Diplomate, American Board of Radiologists: Allen, William Edward, Jr.

Director of Nursing, St. Elizabeth's Hospital: Smith, Eunice Lewis

Drugstore, KY: Ballard, William Henry

Drugstore in Philadelphia: Minton, Henry McKee

Drugstore, Petersburg, VA: Read, Edward Parker

Electrical Engineer Graduate in US: Craig, Arthur

Engineer Operating a 200-Million Dollar Facility, Cleveland: Tresville, Walter M. S., Jr.

Engineer, Beech Aircraft: Jackson, Richard H.

Faculty Member Medical School, University of IL: Brooks, Roosevelt

Female Army Lt. Colonel: Bowen, Clotilde Marian Dent

Female Astronaut: Jemison, Mae C.

Female Chief, NASA's Human Resource Branch, Biomedical Office: Long, Irene

Female Dentist: Nelson, Ida Gray

Female Dentist in California: Somerville, Veda Watson

Female Dentist in NY: McPherson, Gertrude Elizabeth Curtis

Female Diplomate, American Board of Medical Examiners: Clark, Lillian Atkins

Female Fellow, American College of Surgeons: Logan, Myra Adele

Female, Gastroenterology Dept. Head: Palmer, Doreen Pamela

Female General in Army: Johnson-Brown, Hazel Winifred

Female Graduate, Bellevue Hospital Medical College: Chinn, May Edward

Female Graduate, Meharry Medical School: Gregg, Anna D.

Female Graduate of Women's Medical College of PA: Cole, Rebecca J.

Female Graduate, Wayne State Medical School: Peebles-Meyers, Helen Majorie

Female Graduate, First Institute of Podiatry: Charlton, Emily C.

Female Graduate, Stritch School of Medicine: Jefferson, Milfred Fay

Female Head of Cook County Hospital: Lattimer, Agnes

Female Head of University Dental Department (Howard): Sinkford, Jeanne Frances Craig

Female in American College of Surgeons: Dickens, Helen Octavia

Female Intern, Detroit Receiving Hospital: Peebles-Meyers, Helen Majorie

Female Intern, Harlem Hospital: Chinn, May Edward

Female MD: Lee, Rebecca

Female MD on Visiting Staff, Grady Hospital: Mannings, Gwendolyn Cooper

Female MD, Nassau County, NY: Jones, Verina Morton

Female Member State Board of Medicine, NY: Reid, Edith C.

Female Navigator, USAF: Payne, Betty J.

Female Omicron Kappa Upsilon Dental Society: Jones, Yvonne

Female Oral & Maxillofacial Surgeon: Johnson, Gladys L.

Female Pharmacist in Mississippi: Williams, Minnie C.

Female PhD Anatomy: Lloyd, Ruth Smith

Female PhD Bacteriology: Moore, Ruth Ella

Female PhD Chemistry: Daly, Marie Maynard

Female PhD from Purdue: Shockley, Dolores Cooper

Female PhD Geology: Williams, Marguerite Thomas

Female PhD in Pharmacology: Shockley, Dolores Cooper

Female PhD in Pure Math: Granville, Evelyn Boyd Collins

Female PhD Library Science: Gleason, Eliza Veleria Atkins

Female PhD Mathematics (one of the first): Browne, Marjorie Lee

Female PhD Nutrition: Kittrell, Flemmie Pansy

Female PhD Physics, MIT: Jackson, Shirley Ann

Female PhD Psychology: Beckham, Ruth Winifred Howard

Female PhD, University of Texas: Bradley, Lillian Katie

Female Physician & Surgeon in TN: Patton-Washington, Georgia Esther Lee

Female Physician in AL: Johnson, Hallie Tanner Dillon

Female Physician in CA: Temple, Ruth J.

Female Physician in Columbia, SC: Evans, Matilda Arabella

Female Physician in KY: Gilbert, Artishia Garcia

Female Physician in US: Cole, Rebecca J.

Female Physician, Charleston, SC: Brown, Lucy Hughes

Female Physician in NY State (3rd in Nation): Steward, Susan Maria Smith McKinney

Female Pilot: Coleman, Bessie

Female PhD in Chemical Engineering: Patrick, Jennie R.

Female to pass VA Medical Board: Jones, Sarah Garland Boyd

Female to read a paper before the VA Academy of Science: Peele, Amanda E.

Female trained in Medical School & Teaching Hospital (one of): Remond, Sarah Parker

Forensic Pathologist: Burton, John Frederick

Forsythe Dental Infirmary Staff: Russell, Alfred Pierpont, Jr.

Franklin Institute Member: Baltimore, Jeremiah Daniel

General (4-Star): James, Daniel (Chappie)

General in Air Force: Davis, Benjamin O., Jr.

General in Army: Davis, Benjamin O., Sr.

Geological Engineering Graduate, University of Missouri: Ford, Denise Annette

Graduate of American Medical School: Peck, David John

Graduate, Medical College of VA: Harris, Jean Louise

Graduate, New England Female Medical College: Crumpler, Rebecca

Gynecologist, Provident Hospital Chicago: Roberts, Carl Glennis

Harvard Chapter, Alpha Omega Alpha: Stubbs, Frederick Douglas

Harvard College Graduate: Greener, Richard Theodore

Harvard Instructor, Dental School: Grant, George F. (or George F. Grand)

Harvard Professor, Medical School: Hinton, William Augustus

Harvard University Medical School Graduate: Howard, Edwin Clarence Joseph Turpin

Harvard Dental School Graduate: Grant, George F.

Head Board of Health, Indiana: Washington, G. Kenneth

Head of V.A. Hospital: Ward, Joseph H.

Head Physician, Freedmen's Hospital: Augusta, Alexander Thomas

Head, Obstetrics & Gynecology, Akron General Medical Center: Ivy, Mark, III

Heart Surgery: Williams, Daniel Hale

House of Delegates Member AMA: Murray, Peter Marshall

Hubbard Hospital Intern: Francis, Grossi Hamilton

Implantation Automatic Defibrillator: Watkins, Levi, Jr.

In Mississippi State Medical Examination: Redmond, Sidney Dillon

International Brotherhood of Electrical Workers: Nelson, Edward O.

International College of Surgeons: Dailey, Ulysses Grant

Intern, Major American Hospital, Bellevue: Vincent, Ubert Conrad

Leader Army Division: Davison, Frederic Ellis

Louisville Hospital Staff: James, Grace Marilyn

MD, Iowa State University: Carter, Edward Albert

Major in Army: Delaney, Martin Robinson

Male PhD Nurse: Hatcher, Warren

Marine Corps General: Peterson, Frank E., Jr.

Marine Corps Major, 1 of 2: Berthoud, Kenneth H., Jr.

Mayor of Ann Arbor, MI: Wheeler, Albert Harold

MD (1 of 2): White, Thomas J.

MD Degree in US: Rock, John Sweat

MD in NY City Health Department: Williams, J. Milton

MD in US, Degree in Holland: Santomee, Lucas

MD Medical Department, Valpariso University: Roberts, Carl Glennis

MD Presented to DC Medical Society for Membership (1 of 3): Tucker, Alpheus W.

MD to pass DC Medical Exam: Williston, Edward Davis

MD to pass Examination in Helmet Work (Black or White): Springs, Andrew Wilton

MD University of Arkansas: Jones, Edith Mae Irby

MD, Louisville, KY: Fitzbutler, William Henry

MD, University of Michigan Medical School: Fitzbutler, William Henry

Med School, University of PA: Mossell, Nathan Francis

Medal of Honor, Marine, Viet Nam: Anderson, James, Jr.

Medical Association Member: De Grasse, John Van Surley

Medical Commission (Major, 1863): Augusta, Alexander Thomas

Medical Director, Detroit Board of Health: Ames, James Webb

Medical Director, Greystone Hospital: Lathen, John William

Medical Journal Publisher: Lynk, Miles Vandahurst

Medical School Faculty Member: Augusta, Alexander Thomas

Medical Textbook Published: Hinton, William Augustus

Member, American College of Surgeons: Stubbs, Frederick Douglas

Member, Edison Pioneers: Latimer, Lewis Howard

Member, Examining Board of Ophthalmology: Venable, Howard Phillip

Mental Health Director, WV: Bateman, Mildred Mitchell

Military Academy Appointee: Smith, James Webster

National Academy of Sciences Mathematician: Blackwell, David Harold

National Science Director: Slaughter, John Brooks

Naval Academy Graduate: Brown, Wesley A.

Naval Officer to die in an American War: Brown, Jesse

Navy Admiral: Gravely, Samuel Lee, Jr.

Navy Photographer of the Year: Griffin, Clarence W.

Newark City Hospital Staff: McCarroll, E. Mae

Nurse Integrated in Regular Army Nurse Corps: Leftenant, Nancy C.

Nurse Midwife Graduate in MS: Holmes, Beatrice Josephine

Nurse on Board of Directors, American Nurses Association: Osborne, Estelle Massey Riddle

Nurse, American Red Cross: Elliott, Frances Reed

Nurse, Lt. Colonel: Bailey, Margaret E.

Nurse, Medical Inspection Team Chief: Boyd, Marie Rozina

Nurse, Professional: Mahoney, Mary Elizabeth

Nursing Department Chief, Walter Reed Army Medical Center: Adams-Ender, Clara I.

Nursing Department Head, Walter Reed: Abram, James Baker, Jr.

NY State Pediatric Society 1896: Emanuel, Jonah

Officer Commissioned in Regular Army: Brown, Arthur McKimmon

One-Man Show at Museum: Sleet, Moneta J., Jr.

Optometrist: Lawson, William Hiram

Optometrist, Southeastern U.S., 1945: Kelly, Anguis D.

Oral Surgeon: Lee, Roseau Franklin

Orthodontist: Renfroe, Earl Wiley

FIRST BLACK (*Continued*)

Otolaryngologist: Mabrie, Herman James, III

Otolaryngologist in Baltimore: Montague, William Henry

Paine Institute Faculty Member: Gilbert, John Wesley

Patentee, 1834: Blair, Henry

Pediatric Heart Disease Specialist: Robinson, Lula Belle Stewart

Pharmacy Operator: Smith, James McCune

PhD Physics: Bouchet, Edward Alexander

PhD Anatomy: McKinney, Roscoe Lewis

PhD Anatomy: Wright, Clarence William

PhD Astronomy: Banks, Harvey Washington

PhD Bioscience: Coffin, Alfred O.

PhD Botany: Mark, Jessie Jarue

PhD Chemistry: Brady, St. Elmo

PhD Dairy Technology: Bassett, Emmett

PhD Dentistry: Freeman, Robert Tanner

PhD Engineering: Daniel, Walter Thomas

PhD in Physics since Bouchet (1876): Imes, Elmer Samuel

PhD in Pure Mathematics (4th): Talbot, Walter Richard

PhD Mathematics: Cox, Elbert Frank

PhD Metallurgical Engineering, IIT: Crossley, Frank Alphonso

PhD Nurse: Kent, Elizabeth Lipford

PhD Pathology: Jason, Robert Stewart

PhD Pharmacy: Darlington, Ray Clifford

PhD Physiology: Lewis, Julian Herman

PhD Psychology: Sumner, Francis Cecil

PhD Psychology, University of PA: Watts, Frederick Payne

PhD Public Health: Cornely, Paul Bertau

PhD University of MN: Wilkerson, Vernon Alexander

PhD Meteorology: Anderson, Charles Edward

Phi Beta Kappa: Bouchet, Edward Alexander

Photographer: Farley, James

Physician certified in Pediatrics: Scott, Roland Boyd

Physician in Durham, NC: Moore, Aaron McDuffie

Physician in Montgomery, AL: Adair, Roman T.

Physician in US: Derham, (Durham) James

Physician on DC Board of Medical Examiners: Purvis, Charles Burleigh

Physician to Pass Medical Boards in CA: Majors, Monroe Alpheus

Physician to Receive Reciprocity License from MS: Hedrick, Robert Milton

Physician, Nashville, TN: Noel, H. T.

Pilot License, Commercial: Anderson, Charles A.

Pilot, Transatlantic: Hutcherson, Fred, Jr.

Pilot, United Airlines: Norwood, William R.

Police Surgeon: Wright, Louis Thompkins

Police Surgeon, Philadelphia: Turner, John Patrick

Postage Stamp Designer: Olden, Georg

Practitioner in AL: Dorsette, Cornelius Nathaniel

Presbyterian Hospital Staff, NY: Robeson, Eslanda Goode

President National Tuberculosis Association: Payne, Howard Marshall

President of Planned Parenthood: Wattleton, Alyce Faye

President, American Cancer Society: Leffall, La Salle Doheney, Jr.

President, GA Academy of Family Surgeons: Jones, Ernest J.

President, Meharry Medical College: West, Harold Dadford

President, NY County Medical Society: Murray, Peter Marshall

President, American Nursing Association: Nichols, Barbara Lauraine

Professor of Pharmacology in US: Maloney, Arnold Hamilton

Professor, University of Illinois: Renfroe, Earl Wiley

Psychiatrist: Fuller, Solomon Carter

Psychiatrist, Head, Provident Hospital Narcotic Addict Clinic: Adams, Walter Anderson

Public Health Nurse: Sleet, Jessie C.

Public Health Service External Advisory Group Member: Thomas, William McKinley

Pulitzer Prize for Photography Winner: Sleet, Moneta J., Jr.

Regular Commissioned Officer, US Navy: James, Thomas Leslie

Roentgenologist in NY: Powell, Clilan Bethany

Rosenwald Fellow: Quinland, William Samuel

SC Hall of Science and Technology Inductee: Fraser, Thomas Petigru

Secretary-Treasurer Jefferson County Medical Society, AR: Lawlah, Clyde Avery

Signal Corps Officer Promoted to General: Paige, Emmett, Jr.

Space Shuttle Commander: Gregory, Frederick Drew

St. Louis Medical Society: Morman, William Daniel

Staff Member Municipal Tuberculosis Sanitarium, Chicago: Payne, Clarence H.

State Medical Board in PA, Passed: Pastles, David Wilbert

Submarine Doctor, 1966: Ross, William Alexander Jackson

Surgeon and Faculty, Washington University Medical School: Sinkler, William H.

Surgeon in Charge of a Hospital (Freedmen's): Purvis, Charles Burleigh

Surgeon to Operate Children's Hospital, St. Louis: Sinkler, William H.

TN State Medical Board of Examiners Monitor: Phillips, Jasper Tappan

Thoracic Surgeon: Stubbs, Frederick Douglas

Thoracic Surgeon in MI: Maben, Hayward C., Jr.

Urologist: Francis, Milton A.

Urologist, Lakeland Hospital: Garvin, Charles Herbert

US Military Academy Graduate, West Point: Flipper, Henry Ossian

Vanderbilt University Medical School Graduate, 1970: Watkins, Levi, Jr.

Veterinarian Graduate: Lushington, Augusta Nathaniel

Veterinarian in Alabama: Allen, Raleigh H.

Virginia Board of Dental Examiners: Ferguson, David Arthur

Visiting Nurse, Henry Street: Barringer, Elizabeth Tyler

WAVE (1 of 2): Wills, Frances

WAVE (1 of 2): Pickens, Harriet F.

West Point Graduate to Attain Distinction (3rd Graduate): Young, Charles A.

Woman in WAAC: Jarrett, Bessie

WV State Board of Health: Higginbotham, Peyton Randolph

X-Ray Specialist in Baltimore: Cargill, William Harrison

Yale MD: Penn, William

FIRSTS (BLACK OR WHITE)

Dental Examinations for School Children: Bently, Charles E.

Female Administrator, Medical Department, Howard University: Franklin, Eleanor

Female Engineering Graduate, Tuskegee: Brown, Delores Elaine Robinson

Female Full Professor, Lincoln, NE: Yates, Josephine A. Silone

Female MD in MS: Jones, Verina Morton

Female Physician, Santo Domingo: Fraser, Sarah Logan

Female President of D.C. Podiatry Society: Osborne, Muriel

Female to Operate on the Heart: Logan, Myra Adele

Female to Receive Strecker Award for Psychiatric Care: Spurlock, Jeanne

Hydrotherapeutic Facility: Ruggles, David

Mahoney Award Recipient: Thoms, Adah H.

Male Commission, Army Nurse Corps: Washington, Lawrence C.

Man at North Pole: Henson, Matthew Alexander

Member State Board of Medicine, NY: Reid, Edith C.

National Medical Association President, 1895: Boyd, Robert Fulton

National Monument to a Black: Carver, George Washington

President, Morehouse Medical School: Sullivan, Louis W.

Sickle Cell Anemia Pioneer: Cardoza, William Warrick

Vice-President National Medical Association: Williams, Daniel Hale

FOUNDERS

African Medical Education Fund: Wright, Charles H.

Alpha Delta Alpha Scientific Society, Clark University: Brookes, E. Luther

Alpha Hospital, OH: Method, William Arthur

Alpha Omega Alpha (Co-Founder): Cardoza, William Warrick

Alpha Phi Alpha (Co-Founder): Callis, Henry Arthur

American College of Surgeons, Memphis: Ish, George William Stanley, Jr.

American Health Care Plan (Co-Founder): Coleman, Arthur H.

Andrew Clinical Society, Tuskegee: Hunter, John Edward

Arthur B. Lee Hospital: Alston, John Henry

Association for Advancement of Negro Country Life: Hubert, Benjamin F.

Barnett Hospital, WV: Barnett, Constantine Clinton

Bedford Stuyvesant Alcoholism Treatment Center: Abrahams, Andrew Wordsworth

Bethesda Hospital, MI: Thomas, Alfred E. (Alf)

Black Psychiatrists of America (Co-Founder): Comer, James Pierpont

Blood Bank: Drew, Charles Richard

Boyd Infirmary, TN: Boyd, Robert Fulton

Breast Examination Center of Harlem: Freeman, Harold P.

Brookhaven Hospital: Brooks, Adrian D.

Cancer Research Center, Harlem Hospital: Wright, Louis Thompkins

Carson's Hospital, DC: Carson, Simeon Lewis

Charleston Hospital & Nurse Training School: Brown, Lucy Hughes

Cincinnati Medical Association: Beamon, Reginald Emmett

Clement Atkinson Memorial Hospital, PA: Atkinson, Whittier Cinclair

College of Women of Jersey City: Edwards, Lena Frances

Cook County Physician Association: Hall, George Cleveland

Davis Maternity Sanitarium: Davis, Albert Porter

Doman & Associates Architectural Firm: Doman, James Richard, Jr.

Douglas Hospital, Kansas City: Thompson, Solomon Henry

Edyth K. Thomas Hospital: Thomas, Alfred E. (Alf)

Fair Haven Infirmary, GA: Butler, Henry Rutherford

First Black owned Hospital in MS: Miller, Lloyd

First Private Sanitarium in Greensboro, NC: Cordice, John Walter Vincent

First Venereal Disease Clinic: Byrd, David Wellington

Flying School: Brown, Willa B.

Forest City Hospital Association: Lambright, Middleton Hughes, Sr.

Frederick Douglas Memorial Hospital, PA: Mossell, Nathan Francis

Georgia Medical, Dental, & Pharmaceutical Association: Butler, Henry Rutherford

Good Samaritan Hospital: McKenzie, Bertha B.

Hale Infirmary: Dorsette, Cornelius Nathaniel

Hedrick Hospital: Hedrick, Robert Milton

FOUNDERS (Continued)

Wilson Hospital: Hargrave, Frank Settle

Wilson Hospital & Sanitarium: Wilson, John Thomas

Women's Institute: Ferebee, Dorothy Boulding

GENETICISTS

Bowman, James E., Jr.
Dooley, Thomas Price
Harris, Mary Styles
Munday, Reuban A.
Murray, Robert F.

GEOGRAPHERS

Williams, Marguerite Thomas

GEOLOGISTS

Gipson, Mack, Jr.
Hall, Raymond E.
Lislet, Geoffrey Jean Baptiste
Williams, Marguerite Thomas

HEALTH WORKERS

Cesar (Slave)
Collins, Daniel A.
Comer, James Pierpont
Cornely, Paul Bertau
Darity, William Alexander
Douglas, William R.
Evans, Therman Eugene
Haughton, James G.
Holloman, John Lawrence Sullivan, Jr.
Moore, James A.
Papan (Slave)
Wattleton, Alyce Faye
Wheeler, Albert Harold

HYDROPATHIC PRACTITIONER

Ruggles, David

INVENTIONS

Adjustable Sides for Trucks, Express Baggage, etc.: Butteese, Shearman

Agricultural Implements: Murray, George W.

Airborne Radar Beacon: Williams, O. S.

Almanac, 1792: Banneker, Benjamin

Anemometer to Measure Fluid Turbulence: Hubbard, Philip Gamalieh

Animal Trap: Lee, H.

Animal Trap, Automatic Resetting: Campbell, W. S.

Antenna Feed for Tracking Radars: Lewis, James Earl

Artificial Heart Stimulator (pacemaker): Boykin, Otis

Assisted Bell by Drawing Plans for Telephone: Latimer, Lewis Howard

Assisted Morse with Code: Brown, Solomon G.

Assisted McCormick with Reaper: Anderson, Jo (Slave)

Austenitic Alloy Steels: Parsons, James A.

Automatic Car Wash: Spikes, Richard B.

Automatic Serving System: Doyle, James

Automobile Directional Signal: Spikes, Richard B.

Baby Carriage Leveler: Richardson, W. H.

Baler Feeder: Ruth, William Chester
Bombsight: Ruth, William Chester
Bridge Safety Gate: Reynolds, H. H.
Broom Moistner: Benjamin, L. W.
Bulletproof Shield: Vaughn, Norval Cobb

Casket Lowering Device: Richardson, A. C.

Chemical Patents: Julian, Percy Lavon

Chemical Patents for Dow Chemical: Dorman, Linnaeus Cuthbert

Cinder Spreader: Ruth, William Chester

Clothes Dryer: Sampson, G. T.
Clothes Line Support: Allen, J. B.
Conditioner for Straightening Hair: Walker, Sarah Breedlove McWilliams

Corn Planting Machine: Blair, Henry
Corn Shelling Device: Blue, L.
Cosmetics: Carver, George Washington

Cotton Picking Machine: Albert, A. P.

Curtain Rod: Scrottron, S. R.
Cuspidor, Sanitary: Baker, David
Dirigible With Electric Motor: Pickering, J. F.

Derrick: Benton, J. W.
Device for Overcoming Dead Center for Compound Engine: Johnson, William H.

Device Detecting Unauthorized Use of Telephone: Richey, Charles U.

Dispenser to Prevent Tuberculosis: Campbell, David Newton Emanuel

Doppler Operation Test Set: Allen, John Henry, Jr.

Dough Kneading Machine: Lee, Joseph

Dyes: Carver, George Washington
Eggbeater: Johnson, W.
Electric Railway Trolley with Overhead Wires: Robinson, Elbert R.

Electrical Insulating Paper: Millington, James E.

Electrolysers, Furnace: Jackson, Benjamin F.

Elevator Scales: Baker, David
Eleven Atomic Energy Processes: Russell, Edwin Roberts

Engineering Patents (31): Jones, Howard St. Claire, Jr.

Fire Escape, Portable: McCree, D.
Flag Making Method: Bowman, Henry A.

Fog Disperser: Gourdine, Meredith C.

Furniture Caster: Fisher, D. A.
Gas Mask: Morgan, Garrett Augustus

Gear Shift: Spikes, Richard B.
Golf Tee: Grant, George F.
Gong and Signal Chair: Benjamin, Miriam E.

Grain Binder: Marshall, W.
Grease Composition for Vacuum Apparatus: Christian, John B.

Grooved Railway Wheels: Robinson, Elbert R.

Guard Attachment for Children & Invalid Beds: Russell, L. A.

Guided Missile Device: Boykin, Otis
Hair Straightener: Morgan, Garrett Augustus

INVENTIONS (Continued)

HAME Attachment: Abrams, W. B.
Hand Stamp: Purvis, William B.
Hatrack and Table: Ballow, W. J.
Hot-Air Register Attachments: Hilyer, Andrew F.
Hydrocarbon Burner System: Jackson, Benjamin F.
Ice Cream: Jackson, Augustus
Improved the Thrashing Machine: Weston, Anthony (Slave)
Incineraid: Gourdine, Meredith C.
Intradermal Smallpox Vaccination: Wright, Louis Tompkins
Ironing Board: Boone, Sarah
"Jenny" Coupler: Beard, Andrew Jackson
Jet Engine, Small, Low-Fuel for Missiles & Helicopters: Logan, Joseph G., Jr.
Key Fastener: Lowden, Fred J.
Ladder Scaffold-Support: Bailes, William
Lawn Sprinkler: McCoy, Elijah
Letter Box: Becket, G. E.
Livestock Feed Rack: Shorter, D. W.
Lock, Forerunner of Modern Lock: Martin, W. A.
Locomotive Smoke Stack: Bell, L.
Lunar Surface Ultraviolet Camera: Carruthers, George R.
Mechanical Tabulator: Davidson, Shelby J.
Metal Heated Comb: Walker, Sarah Breedlove McWilliams
Nuclear Core Flow Distributor: Bishop, Alfred A.
Occustat: Elder, Clarence L.
Oil Stove: Standard, J.
Paper Bag Making Machine: Purvis, William B.
Paper Company Machine: Stevens, George D.
Paper Process for Corrugated Shipping Containers: Atkins, Cyril Fitzgerald
Pasting Machine: Pelham, Robert A., Jr.
Pituitary Gland Instrument: Barnes, William Harry
Player Piano Appliances: Dickenson, J. H.
Portable X-Ray Machine: Jones, Frederick McKinley

Potato Chips: Thomas, Hyram S.
Potato Digger: Smith, P. D.
Propellants: Sampson, Henry Thomas
Pullman Upper Berth Folding Bed: Bailey, L. C.
Pyrometer: Baltimore, Jeremiah Daniel
Radioactive Tracer: Russell, Edwin Roberts
Railroad Signal for Engineers: Blackburn, A. B.
Railway Bridge Signal: Baker, David
Refrigerated Trucks for Long Distance Travel: Jones, Frederick McKinley
Refrigerating Apparatus: Elkins, T.
Refrigerator (Compressed Air): Standard, J.
Reverse Valve Gears: Smart, Brinay
Rotary Engine: Beard, Andrew Jackson
Rubber Scraping Knife: Booker, L. F.
Sail Handling Device: Forten, James, Sr.
Scales, Portable as seen in Post Offices: Hunter, J. H.
Self-Binding Harvesting Machinery: Douglas, William
Self-Feed Rifle: Johnson, Frederick, M.
Self-Leveling Table: Allen, C. W.
Shampoo Headrest: Bailliff, C. O.
Shoe Covers for Rain: Rickman, A. L.
Shoe Lasting Machine: Matzeliger, Jan Earnst
Speed Boat Torpedo for Long-Range Bombing: Blair, Joseph N.
Spin-Flip Tunable Laser (Co-Inventor): Shaw, Earl
Spring Seat for Chairs: Blackburn, A. B.
Stairclimbing Wheelchair: Weaver, Rufus J.
Steam Boiler Furnace: Woods, Granville T.
Steam Engine Lubricator (the real McCoy): McCoy, Elijah
Street Sprinkler: Binga, M. W.
Street Sweeper: Brooks, C. B.
Sugar Refining Pan: Rillieux, Norbert
Supersonic & Hypersonic Wind Tunnel Nozzles: Davis, Stephen Smith

Synchroncous Multiflex Railway Telegraph: Woods, Granville T.
Tabulating Machine for Census of Manufacturing: Pelham, Robert A., Jr.
Tarsal Arch Support: Hillery, John Richard
Thermal Photograph Detail Enhancer: Alexander, Winser Edward
Ticket-Dispensing Machine for Movie Theatre: Jones, Frederick McKinley
Tobacco Press Screw: Parker, John P.
Toggle Harpoon for Whaling: Temple, Lewis
Traffic Signal (three-way): Morgan, Garrett Augustus
Trocar & Canula: Dumas, Albert W., Sr.
Truss and Bandage: Bailey, L. C.
Valve for Steam Engines: Campbell, Robert Lee
Valves for Steam Engines: Ferrell, Frank J.
Varicocele Procedure in Surgery: Vincent, Ubert Conrad
Water Closet for Homes: Rhodes, J. B.
Water Closet for Railroad Cars: Latimer, Lewis Howard
Window Ventilator for Railroad Cars: Reynolds, H. H.
Wooden Striking Clock, 1761: Banneker, Benjamin

INVENTORS

Abrams, W. B.
Albert, A. P.
Alexander, Winser Edward
Allen, C. W.
Allen, J. B.
Allen, John Henry, Jr.
Anderson, Jo (Slave)
Atkins, Cyril Fitzgerald
Bailes, William
Bailey, L. C.
Bailliff, C. O.
Baker, David
Ballow, W. J.
Baltimore, Jeremiah Daniel
Banneker, Benjamin
Barnes, G. A. E.
Barnes, William Harry

Beard, Andrew Jackson
Becket, G. E.
Bell, L.
Benjamin, L. W.
Benjamin, Miriam E.
Benton, J. W.
Binga, M. W.
Bishop, Alfred A.
Blackburn, A. B.
Blair, Henry
Blair, Joseph N.
Blue, L.
Booker, L. F.
Boone, Sarah
Bowman, Henry A.
Boykin, Otis
Brooks, C. B.
Butteese, Shearman
Campbell, David Newton
   Emanuel
Campbell, Robert Lee
Campbell, W. S.
Carruthers, George R.
Carter, Thomas J.
Carver, George Washington
Christian, John B.
Cooper, John R.
Crosthwait, David Nelson, Jr.
Crummie, John H.
Davidson, Shelby J.
Davis, Stephen Smith
Dickenson, J. H.
Dorman, Linnaeus Cuthbert
Douglas, William
Doyle, James
Dumas, Albert, W., Sr.
Elder, Clarence L.
Elkins, T.
Ferrell, Frank J.
Fisher, D. A.
Forbes, Dennis Arthur
Forten, James, Sr.
Gier, Joseph Thomas
Grant, George F. (or George F.
   Grand)
Hall, Lloyd Augustus
Hillery, John Richard
Hilyer, Andrew F.
Hubbard, Philip Gamalieh
Hunter, J. H.
Jackson, Augustus
Jackson, Benjamin F.
Johnson, Frederick M.
Johnson, W.
Johnson, William H.
Jones, Frederick McKinley

Jones, Howard St. Claire, Jr.
Jones, John Leslie
Julian, Percy Lavon
Kreamer, Henry
Latimer, Lewis Howard
Lee, H.
Lee, Joseph
Lewis, James Earl
Logan, Joseph G., Jr.
Lowden, Fred J.
Marshall, W.
Martin, W. A.
Matzeliger, Jan Earnst
McCoy, Elijah
McCree, D.
Millington, James E.
Montez, Billy V.
Morgan, Garrett Augustus
Murray, George W.
Parker, John P.
Parsons, James A.
Pelham, Robert A., Jr.
Pickering, J. F.
Purvis, William B.
Reynolds, H. H.
Rhodes, J. B.
Richardson, A. C.
Richardson, W. H.
Richey, Charles U.
Rickman, A. L.
Rillieux, Norbert
Robinson, Elbert R.
Russell, Edwin Roberts
Russell, L. A.
Ruth, William Chester
Sampson, G. T.
Sampson, Henry Thomas
Sanders, Robert
Scrottron, S. R.
Shaw, Earl
Shorter, D. W.
Smart, Brinay
Smith, P. D.
Spikes, Richard B.
Standard, J.
Stevens, George D.
Stokes, Rufus
Temple, Lewis
Thomas, Hyram S.
Vaughn, Norval Cobb
Walker, Sarah Breedlove McWilliams
Weaver, Rufus J.
Weston, Anthony (Slave)
Wilkins, Raymond Leslie
Williams, O. S.
Woods, Granville T.

MATHEMATICIANS

Aheart, Andrew Norwood
Armstrong, Prince Winston
Arrington-Idowu, Elayne
Banneker, Benjamin
Battle, Joseph
Bennett, John Henry
Bharucha-Reid, Albert Turner
Blackwell, David Harold
Blakney, Simmie Samuel
Bradley, Lillian Katie
Brothers, Warren Hill
Browne, Marjorie Lee
Butcher, George Hench, Jr.
Cansler, Charles W.
Carroll, Edward Major
Certaine, Jeremiah
Clarkson, Llayron L.
Claytor, William Waldron Shiefflin
Cooper, Lois Louise
Cox, Elbert Frank
Craig, Suzanne
Darden, Geraldine Claudette
Deconge, Sister Mary Sylvester
Dennis, Joseph J., Jr.
Donaldson, James Ashley
Dougles, Samuel Horace
Drew, James William
Easley, Annie
Eldridge, Henry Madison
Ellis, James R.
Ellis, Wade
Embree, Earl Owen
Ewell, John Albert, III
Falconer, Etta Zuber
Fletcher, William Thomas
Fuller, Joseph Everett
Fuller, Thomas
Gasaway, Sadie Catherine
Gee, Fannie
Gillam, Isaac Thomas, IV
Gipson, Joella Hardeman
Glover, Israel Everett
Granville, Evelyn Boyd Collins
Hall, Japheth, Jr.
Hargrave, Charles William
Haskins, Ethelbert William
Hewitt, Gloria Conyers
Hunt, Fern
Hytche, William Percy
Jeffries, Jasper Brown
Johnson, Elgy Sibley
Johnson, Katherine G.
Jones, Eleanor Green Dawley
Jones, Major Boyd

MATHEMATICIANS
(Continued)

King, Calvin Elijah
King, John Quill Taylor
Knight, Genevieve Madeline
Love, Theodore Arceola
Madison, Eugene W.
Manuey, Nan Phelps
Martin, Benjamin Joseph
Mayes, Vivienne Lucille Malone
McBay, Shirley Mathis
McCreadie, Rada Higgins
McDaniel, Reuben Roosevelt
McNeil, Phillip Eugene
Means, Curtis S.
Means, James Horatio
Miller, Kelly
Mishoe, Luna Isaac
Murray, Diane P.
Nelms, Ann T.
Newman, Rogers
Pierce, Joseph Alphonso
Pitts, Raymond Jackson
Pollard, Nathaniel, Jr.
Reynolds, James Richard
Richard, Howard Mark Simon
Robinson, William Henry
Scott, Evelyn Patterson
Shabazz, Lonnie
Simms, Nathan Frank, Jr.
Smith, Georgia Caldwell
Smith, Martha Lee Gladys
Smith, Robert Wilson, Jr.
Spikes, Dolores
Springer, George
St. Mary, Donald Frank
Stephens, Clarence Francis
Stubblefield, Beauregard
Suggs, Daniel Cato
Sullivan, Frances
Sutton, Louise Nixon
Svager, Thyrsa Frazier
Talbot, Walter Richard
Turner, Ethel Marie
Tyler, Sylvanus A.
Vance, Irvin Elmer
Velez-Rodriguez, Argelia
White, Clarence Reed
Wilkins, J. Ernest, Jr.
Williams, Eddie Robert
Williams, Lloyd Kenneth
Williams, Scott Warner
Williams, Vernon
Woodson, George Frederick, Jr.
Woodward, Dudley Welson

METEOROLOGISTS

Anderson, Charles Edward
Bacon-Berey, June
Sarreals, E. Don
Tilmon, James Alphonso
Washington, Warren Morton

MICROBIOLOGISTS

Brown, Russell Wilfred
Campbell, Haywood
Hammond, Benjamin Franklin
Johnson, Charles E.
Johnson, Charles William
Lockett, John L.
Pickrum, Harvey
Price, Jessie Isabelle
Taylor, Welton Ivan
Vanderpool, Eustace Arthur
Wallace, John Howard
Wiley, William Rodney

MIDWIVES

Blackburn, Laura
Brewer, Mattie D.
Carter, Ellen Woods
Francis, Marie Jones
Singleton, Elizabeth

MILITARY

Adams-Ender, Clara I.
Allinsworth, Allen
Anderson, Charles A.
Anderson, James, Jr.
Bailey, Margaret E.
Barnes, Julia O.
Beck, James
Becton, Julius Wesley, Jr.
Berthoud, Kenneth H., Jr.
Beverly, Clara E.
Billups, Rufus
Bluford, Guion Stewart, Jr.
Bousfield, Midian Othello
Bowen, Clotilde Marian Dent
Boyd, Marie Rozina
Bradley, James T.
Brooks, Harry Williams, Jr.
Brown, Jesse
Brown, Wesley A.
Cadoria, Sherian Grace
Campbell, Robert Lee
Carney, William H.

Cartwright, Roscoe Conklin
Chambers, Andrew P.
Chambers, Lawrence C.
Charlton, Cornelius H.
Clifford, Thomas E.
Cromartie, Eugene R.
Crummie, John H.
Davidson, Frederick Ellis
Davis, Benjamin O., Jr.
Davis, Benjamin O., Sr.
Davis, Rodney Maxwell
Davison, Frederic Ellis
Dickerson, Spencer Cornelius
Dillard, Oliver William
Flipper, Henry Ossian
Gravely, Samuel Lee, Jr.
Greer, Edward
Gregg, Arthur James
Gregory, Frederick Drew
Hamlet, James Frank
Hope, Edward Swain, Jr.
James, Thomas Leslie
Jarrett, Bessie
Joel, Lawrence
Johnson-Brown, Hazel Winifred
Lawrence, Robert Henry, Jr.
Lawson, John
Leftenant, Nancy C.
Mann, Marion
Miller, Dorie
Olive, Milton Lee
Overton, Norris Webster
Paige, Emmett, Jr.
Pease, Joachim
Petersen, Frank E., Jr.
Pickens, Harriet F.
Powell, Colin
Robinson, Roscoe, Jr.
Rogers, Charles Calvin
Sheffey, Fred C.
Smith, James Webster
Theus, Lucius
Thomas, Gerald Eustis
Thompson, William
Tzomes, Chancellor A.
Washington, Lawrence C.
Whitehead, John L., Jr.
Wills, Frances
Young, Charles A.

MISCELLANEOUS

Marriage License Bill, NJ:
    Alexander, Walter Gilbert
Mathematician: Fuller, Thomas

NEUROSURGEONS

Barber, Jesse Belmary, Jr.
Canady, Alexa I.
Carson, Benjamin S.
Greene, Clarence Sumner
Hyde-Rowan, Maxine Deborah
Joyner, John Erwin

NURSES

Adams-Ender, Clara I.
Anderson, Edgar L., Jr.
Andrews, Ludie A.
Bailey, Margaret E.
Barnes, Julia O.
Barringer, Elizabeth Tyler
Bellamy, Verdelle B.
Benoit, Edith B.
Bessent, Hattie
Beverly, Clara E.
Blackburn, Laura
Bourgeois, Marie
Boyd, Marie Rozina
Bullock, Carrie E.
Carnegie, Mary Elizabeth
Carter, Ellen Woods
Clark, Mary Frances
Coles, Anna Louise Bailey
Curtis, Namahyoke Sockum
Dumas, Rhetaugh
Elliott, Frances Reed
Franklin, Martha
Harper, Mary Starke
Hatcher, Warren
Hernandez, Marion Pettiford
Holmes, Beatrice Josephine
Humphrey, Betty Jean
Johnson, Christine Hedgley
Johnson-Brown, Hazel Winifred
Kemp, Nancy Lois
Kent, Elizabeth Lipford
Laney, Lucey Craft
Ledbetter, Ruth Pope
Leftenant, Nancy C.
Mahoney, Mary Eliza
McArthur, Barbara Martin
McKenzie, Bertha B.
Murray, Beatrice L.
Nichols, Barbara Lauraine
Osborne, Estelle Massey Riddle
Passon, Myrtle Ashe
Patterson, Annie Elizabeth
Pinn, Petra Fitzalieu
Seacole, Mary Grant
Sleet, Jessie C. (Scales)

Smith, Eunice Lewis
Staupers, Mabel Keaton
Stewart, Aileen Cole
Sweres, Mary Agnes
Taylor, Susie King
Thoms, Adah H.
Tomes, Evelyn Kennedy
Truth, Sojourner (Isabella Van Wagener)
Tubman, Harriet Ross
Warlick, Lula G.
Washington, Lawrence C.
Wattleton, Alyce Faye
Webb, Mary C.
Whitlock, Lula
Williams, David George

NUTRITIONISTS

Edwards, Cecile Hoover
High, Edward Garfield
Kittrell, Flemmie Pansy
Leevy, Carroll Moton
Lewis, Roscoe Warfield
Moore, John E.
Moragne, Lenora
Watts, Johnnie Hines

OPTOMETRISTS

Kelly, Anguis D.
Lawson, William Hiram
Mitchell, Dolphus Burl
Powell, C. Clayton
Wiltshire, Courtenay

ORGANIZERS

Aesculapian Medical Society: Moten, Edwin Donerson
Dental Unit, Arkansas Colored Medical Association: Meaddough, Ray James
Fall City Medical Society: Lattimore, John Aaron Cicero
Fraternal Hospital Training School for Nurses: Potter, May Etta
Hoosier State Medical Society (Co-Organizer): Moten, Edwin Donerson
Indiana State Medical, Dental, & Pharmaceutical Society: Moten, Edwin Donerson

Kentucky Medical Society of Negro Physicians & Dentists: Porter, Otho Dandrith
National Association of Colored Graduate Nurses: Franklin, Martha
Oral Surgery Dept., Freedmen's Hospital: Lee, Roseau Franklin
Pediatric Residency Program, Howard University: Smith, Alonzo De Grate
Sickle Cell Clinics: Wethers, Doris Louise
State Society of Registered Nurses: Potter, Mary Etta
WVA State Medical Society: Gamble, Henry Floyd

PARASITOLOGISTS

Abram, James Baker, Jr.
Briscoe, Madison Spencer
Crooks, Kenneth Bronstorph M.
Davis, Toye George
Finley, Harold Eugene
Smith, Barnett Frissell
Wall, Limas Dunlap

PATHOLOGISTS

Adams, George Williams
Berry, Leonidas Harris
Blache, Julian Owen
Bolden, Theodore Edward
Bowman, James E., Jr.
Burton, John Frederick
Collins, Daniel A.
Collins, Elmer Ernest
Fuller, Solomon Carter
Grant, William H.
Hinton, William Augustus
Jason, Robert Stewart
Johnson, Frank Bacchus
Lewis, H. Donell
Lewis, Julian Herman
Mann, Marion
Payne, Howard Marshall
Phillips, Mildred E.
Pinn-Wiggins, Vivian Winona
Quinland, William Samuel
Robinson, Paul Timothy
Sampson, Calvin Coolidge

PHARMACISTS

Ashley, Harry E.
Ballard, William Henry
Bell, Alexander F.
Boutte, Matthew Virgile
Boyd, Robert Fulton
Burwell, Alphonso Colfax
Cooper, Chauncy Ira
Dabney, Maurice B.
Darlington, Ray Clifford
Elfe, Wilcie (Slave)
Harris, Robert McCants
Hughes, Julia Pearl
Ivy, Mark, III
Landry, Eldridge Percival
Lynk, Beebe Steven
Marble, Harriett Beecher Stowe
Miller, Theodore L.
Moore, Paul Joaquin
Oliver, Edwin E.
Peters, Henry R.
Smith, Calvin L.
Stewart, Ella Nora Phillips
Williams, Henry Roger
Williams, Minnie C.

PHARMACOLOGISTS

Booker, Walter Monroe
Gant, Virgil Arnett
Hudson, Roy Davage
Maloney, Arnold Hamilton
Proctor, Charles D.
Sherrod, Theodore Roosevelt
Shockley, Dolores Cooper
Thompson, Emanuel B.

PHOTOGRAPHERS

Andrews, Bert
Cille, Michel Du
Farley, James
Franklin, Hal Addison, II
Griffin, Clarence W.
Hansen, Austin
Jackson, Ann Elizabeth
Lewis, Matthew, Jr.
Lion, Jules
Morgan, Don
Parks, Gordon Alexander Buchanan
Roberts, Richard Samuel
Scurlock, Addison M.
Sleet, Moneta J., Jr.

Van Der Zee, James Augustus
  Joseph
White, John H.

PHYSICAL EDUCATORS

Hawkins, Charles Clinton
Washington, Edward L.

PHYSICIANS

Abbott, Anderson Ruffin
Abraham, Guy Emmanuel
Abrahams, Andrew Wordsworth
Adair, Robert A.
Adair, Roman T.
Adams, Billie Morris Wright
Adams, George Williams
Adams, Numa Pompilius Garfield
Adams, Walter Anderson
Adamson, Garland Norman
Adom, Edwin
Agee, Robert Edward
Aldrich, James Thomas
Alexander, Ernest Raymond
Alexander, Joseph Lee
Alexander, Leslie Luther
Alexander, Walter Gilbert
Alexis, Carlton Peter
Alfred, Dewitt Clinton, Jr.
Allen, Aris T.
Allen, Browning E., Jr.
Allen, Farrow Robert
Allen, Gloria Marie
Allen, William Edward, Jr.
Allison, James M., Jr.
Allman, Marian Isabel
Alston, John Henry
Alsup, Frederick Werthly
Ames, James Webb
Anderson, Albert Douglas
Anderson, Carolyn Virginia Still
Anderson, John Alexander
Anderson, John Thomas
Anderson, John Wesley
Anderson, Peyton Fortine
Anderson, Robert Spencer
Anderson, Russell Lloyd
Anthony, Benjamin William
Arbulu, Augustin
Archer, Juanita Almetta
Armstrong, Wiley T.
Atkins, Leland L.
Atkinson, Whittier Cinclair
Augusta, Alexander Thomas

Barabin, Joseph Hercules
Barber, Jessie Belmary, Jr.
Barker, Prince Patanilla
Barnes, William Harry
Barnett, Constantine Clinton
Bateman, Mildred Mitchell
Beckford, Samuel McDonald
Bell, Carl Compton
Bell, James Milton
Berry, Joseph A.
Berry, Leonidas Harris
Blache, Julian Owen
Blackman, Edson Ervin
Boddie, William Fisher
Bookert, Charles C.
Bookhardt, A. L.
Boswell, Paul P.
Bouchet, Edward Alexander
Bousfield, Midian Othello
Bowen, Clotilde Marian Dent
Bowles, George William
Boyd, Robert Fulton
Bradshaw, Walter H., Jr.
Braithwaite, John Alexander
Brooks, Adrian D.
Brooks, Edward B.
Brooks, Roosevelt
Brown, Arthur McKimmon
Brown, Dorothy Lavinia
Brown, E. P.
Brown, John Ollis
Brown, Lucy Hughes
Brown, Randolph Kelly
Brown, W. Roderick, Jr.
Brown, William Wells
Browne, Hugh A.
Burt, Robert Tecumseh
Burton, Aldrich Robert
Burton, John Frederick
Burwell, T. Spotuos
Busch, Oliver Roy
Butler, Henry Rutherford
Byas, A. D.
Byas, James Spencer, Sr.
Byer, Erroll
Byrd, David Wellington
Cabaniss, George Williamson
Cabiniss, Charles
Callender, Clive Orville
Callis, Henry Arthur
Calloway, Nathaniel Oglesby
Campbell, David Newton Emanuel
Canady, Alexa I.
Cann, John William
Cannon, George Dows
Cannon, George E.

PHYSICIANS (*Continued*)

Jackson, Robert L.
Jackson, Rudolph Ellsworth
James, Grace Marilyn
Jason, Robert Stewart
Jefferson, Mildred Fay
Jemison, Mae C.
Jenkins, Charles M.
Jenkins, Melvin E.
Jenkins, N. A.
Johnson, Charles William
Johnson, Frank Bacchus
Johnson, Hallie Tanner Dillon
Johnson, Halvern H.
Johnson, John Beauregard, Jr.
Johnson, John Hayden
Johnson, Joseph Lealand
Johnson, Peter A.
Jones, Edith Mae Irby
Jones, Ernest J.
Jones, Frank
Jones, Herbert C.
Jones, Joseph H. N.
Jones, Leroy
Jones, Richard Francis (Frank)
Jones, Robert E.
Jones, Sarah Garland Boyd
Jones, Thomas Adolphus
Jones, Thomas Edward
Jones, Verina Morton
Jones, William Moses
Joyner, John Erwin
Kenney, John Andrew, Jr.
Kenney, John Andrew, Sr.
Kenniebrew, Alonzo H.
Kountz, Samuel Lee, Jr.
Lambright, Middleton Hughes, Jr.
Lambright, Middleton Hughes, Sr.
Landry, Lord Beaconsfield
Lane, Willard Mercer
Lathen, John William
Lattimer, Agnes
Lattimore, John Aaron Cicero
Laurey, James Richard
Lawlah, Clyde Avery
Lawlah, John Wesley
Lawless, Theodore Kenneth
Lawrence, Margaret Morgan
Lawrence, Montague Schiels
Lee, Henry Eugene
Lee, Rebecca
Leevy, Carroll Moton
Leffall, La Salle Doheney, Jr.
Lester, John Angelo
Levy, James R.

Lewis, Julian Herman
Linder, J. W. E.
LittleJohn, Clarence G.
Lloyd, Frank P.
Lofton, William Garvin
Logan, Arthur C.
Logan, Myra Adele
Lomax, Eugene W.
Long, Irene
Lowery, John Edward
Lucas, Wendell M.
Lynk, Miles Vandahurst
Maben, Hayward C., Jr.
Mabrie, Herman James, III
Majors, Monroe Alpheus
Maloney, Arnold Hamilton
Malveaux, Floyd
Mann, Marion
Mannings, Gwendolyn Cooper
Marchbanks, Vance Hunter
Marshall, Charles Herbert
Martin, Hamilton St. Clair
Martin, James L.
Mason, Ulysses Grant
Mason, Vaughn Carrington
Mason, William Alfred Madison
Matory, William Earle
Maynard, Aubre De L.
Mazique, Douglas Wilkerson
Mazique, Edward C.
McArthur, Rutherford Benjamin
McBroom, Fletcher Pearl Riley
McCarroll, E. Mae
McCauley, Lewyn Eugene
McClellan, Alonzo C.
McCoo, Mary Holloway
McCown, Ira
McDonough, David K. (Slave)
McKane, Alyce Woodby
McKinney, Thomas Theodore
McMillan, Julius Augustus
McNeill, William Clarence
Method, William Arthur
Miller, Dublin B.
Miller, Lloyd
Miller, Russell L., Jr.
Mills, Joseph Napoleon
Minton, Henry McKee
Mitchell, Chauncey Depew Haillee
Mitchell, Eric Ignatius
Montague, William Henry
Moore, Aaron McDuffie
Moore, George Sheppard
Morgan, Charles L.
Morman, William Daniel
Mossell, Nathan Francis

Moten, Edwin Donerson
Murray, Peter Marshall
Murray, Robert F.
Nelson, William Thomas
Nichols, Victoria
Noel, H. T.
Norman, John C.
Northcross, Daisy Hill
Organ, Claude H., Jr.
Owens, O'Dell M.
Oxley, Lucy Orintha
Palmer, Doreen Pamela
Palmer, Edward
Patterson, Raymond Frederick
Patton-Washington, Georgia Esther
   Lee
Payne, Clarence H.
Payne, Fitz-Melvin Carrington
Payne, Howard Marshall
Peck, David John
Peebles-Meyers, Helen Marjorie
Penn, Irvine Garland
Penn, William
Perdue, Omer Felix
Perry, John Edward
Perry, John Sinclair
Peyton, Thomas R.
Phillips, Charles Henry, Jr.
Phillips, Clyde W.
Phillips, Jasper Tappan
Phillips, Joseph R., Sr.
Phillips, Mildred E.
Pinderhughes, Charles Alfred
Pinn-Wiggins, Vivian Winona
Plummer, John Owens
Poindexter, Hildrus A.
Porter, E. S.
Porter, Otho Dandrith
Potter, Mary Etta
Poussaint, Alvin Francis
Powell, Charles William
Powell, Clilan Bethany
Presnell, J. H.
Primus (Slave)
Purvis, Charles Burleigh
Quinland, William Samuel
Rabb, Maurice F., Jr.
Rainbow-Earhart, Kathryn A.
Rann, Emery Louvelle
Rawls, George
Read, Edward Parker
Redmond, Sidney Dillon
Reed, James Whitfield
Reid, Clarice D. Wills
Reid, Edith C.
Remond, Sarah Parker

Roberts, Carl Glennis
Roberts, Eugene P.
Robinson, Bernard Whitfield
Robinson, Emory Irving
Robinson, Lula Belle Stewart
Robinson, Paul Timothy
Rock, John Sweat
Rolfe, Daniel Thomas
Roman, Charles Lightfoot
Roman, Charles Victor
Ross, Julian Waldo
Ross, Marshall E.
Ross, William Alexander Jackson
Routen, Louie
Royal, Frank Spencer
Sampson, Calvin Coolidge
Santomee, Lucas
Satcher, David
Saulsberry, Guy O.
Saunders, Elijah
Saunders, Griffin Augustus
Scott, Douglas Grant
Scott, Roland Boyd
Scurlock, Herbert Clay
Sebastian, Simon Powell
Shadd, Furmann Jeremiah
Shepard, C. H.
Sherrod, Daniel Webster
Sinclair, William Albert
Sinkler, William H.
Smith, Alonzo De Grate
Smith, James McCune
Smith, Phillip M., Sr.
Smith, Rellifold Stillman
Smith, Robert Tecumseh
Smith, Thomas Manuel
Speller, John Finton
Spellman, Mitchell Wright
Spratlin, Paul Edward
Springs, Andrew Wilton
Springs, Birdie E. McLain
Spurlock, Jeanne
Stanford, John Thomas
Stent, Theodore Robert
Stepto, Robert Charles
Sterrs, Willis Edward
Steward, Susan Maria Smith
    McKinney
Stewart, Ferdinand Augustus
Still, James
Stubbs, Frederick Douglas
Sullivan, Louis W.
Swan, Lionel Fitzroy
Syphax, Burke
Tackett, J. S.
Tardy, Walter James, Jr.

Taylor, Daniel Bernette
Taylor, Eugene Donaldson
Temple, Ruth J.
Terrence, August Caswell
Thatcher, Harold W.
Thomas, Alfred E. (Alf)
Thomas, Joseph Turner
Thomas, William McKinley
Thompson, Solomon Henry
Thompson, Vertis Raymond
Tignor, Charles A.
Tildon, Toussaint Tourgee
Townes, Charles Henry
Townsend, Arthur Melvin, Sr.
Trotman, James Augustus
Tucker, Alpheus W.
Turner, John Patrick
Turner, Valdo D.
Underwood, Edward Ellsworth
Vaughn, Arthur N.
Vaughn, Clarence Benjamin
Vaughn, Norval Cobb
Venable, Howard Phillip
Vincent, Ubert Conrad
Walden, Emerson Coleman
Walker, Henry Harvey
Walker, Matthew
Walker, Thaddeus Addison
Walker, William McAlpine
Wallace, Leon M.
Ward, Joseph H.
Warfield, William Alonza
Waring, Mary Fitzbutler
Washington, G. Kenneth
Washington, William J.
Watkins, Levi, Jr.
Watts, George R., Sr.
Weddinton, Wayne
Weekes, Leroy Randolph
Welsing, Frances Cress
Wesley, Allen Alexander
West, Abel E.
West, Charles Ignatius
West, Lightfoot Allen
Wethers, Doris Louise
Wheatland, Marcus Fitzherbert
Wheeler, Emma R.
Whipper, Iona Rollins
White, Augustus A., III
White, Jack E.
White, James Randall
White, Thomas J.
Whiteman, Neville C.
Whitten, Charles F.
Whittico, James Malachi, Jr.
Whittico, James Malachi, Sr.

Whittier, Charles Austin
Wiggins, Joseph C.
Wilkerson, Vernon Alexander
Wilkinson, Robert Shaw, Sr.
Williams, Albert Wilberforce
Williams, Charles Lee
Williams, Daniel Hale
Williams, David George
Williams, Ernest Young
Williams, Henry Roger
Williams, J. Milton
Williams, James B.
Williams, Jasper F.
Williams, Richard Arnett
Willis, Floyd Williams
Williston, Edward Davis
Wilson, C. Leon
Wilson, John Thomas
Wilson, Julien Harmon
Winstead, George Lee
Woode, Charles Henri
Wright, Barbara P.
Wright, Charles H.
Wright, Jane Cooke
Wright, Louis Tompkins
Wright, Phillip
Wright, Thomas
Yancey, Asa G., Sr.
Yerby, Alonzo Smythe

PHYSICISTS

Banks, Floyd Regan, Jr.
Banks, Harvey Washington
Basri, Gibor Broitman
Bates, Clayton Wilson, Jr.
Bouchet, Edward Alexander
Bragg, Robert Henry
Branson, Herman Russell
Carruthers, George R.
Coleman, John William
Eagleson, Halson Vashon
Edwards, Donald Anderson
Gourdine, Meredith C.
Hargrave, Charles William
Henry, Warren Elliott
Higgs, Roland Wellington
Hunter, John McNeile
Imes, Elmer Samuel
Jackson, Shirley Ann
Jeffries, Jasper Brown
Johnson, Katherine G.
Jones, Major Boyd
Kildare, Albert Alexander

PHYSICISTS (*Continued*)

King, James, Jr.
Koontz, Roscoe L.
Lawson, James Raymond
Lewis, Harold Ralph
Logan, Joseph G., Jr.
Martin, Alfred E.
Mason, William Alfred Madison
Massey, Walter Eugene
McAfee, Walter Samuel
McCane, Charles Anthony
McNair, Ronald Erwin
Mickens, Ronald Elbert
Mishoe, Luna Isaac
Morrison, Harry L.
Mtingwa, Sekazi
Neal, Homer Alfred
Nelms, Ann T.
Peery, Benjamin Franklin, Jr.
Person, Waverly
Posey, Leroy Raadell, Jr.
Powell, Robert Lee
Quaterman, Lloyd Albert
Randolph, Lynwood Parker
Roberts, Louis W.
Robinson, Lawrence Baylor
Robinson, William Henry
Rouse, Carl Albert
Shaw, Earl
Sherard, George W.
Slaughter, John Brooks
Smith, Carter Charles
Taylor, Julius Henry
Taylor, Lawnie
Thaxton, Hubert Mach
Thornton, Robert Ambrose
Townes, Charles Henry
Van Dyke, Henry Lewis
Weir, Charles Edward
Wilkins, J. Ernest, Jr.
Wilkins, Roger L.
Young, James Edward

PHYSIOLOGISTS

Birnie, James Hope
Booker, Walter Monroe
Bowie, Walter C.
Bryant, J. Edmond
Burgess, Landry Edward
Cobb, Jewel Plummer
Dupre, Ernest Frank
Hawthorne, Edward William
Henderson, James Henry
    Meriwether

Inge, Frederick Douglas
Johnson, Joseph Lealand
Just, Ernest Everett
Mark, Jessie Jarue
Myles, Marion Antoinette Richards
Nabrit, Samuel Milton
O'Hara, Leon P.
Proctor, Nathaniel Kipling
Rhaney, Mahlon Clifton
Rolfe, Daniel Thomas
Sinkford, Jeanne Frances Craig
Tearney, Russell James

PILOTS

Brown, Willa B.
Bullard, Eugene Jacques
Coleman, Bessie
Hutcherson, Fred, Jr.
Norwood, William R.
Payne, Betty J.
Tilmon, James Alphonso

PODIATRISTS

Charlton, Emily C.
Emanuel, Jonah
Haskins, Alma Mary
Hillery, John Richard
Osborne, Muriel

PROTOZOOLOGISTS

Finley, Harold Eugene
Hunter, Norvell Witherspoon
Lee, James Warren
McArthur, William Henry

PSYCHIATRISTS

Adams, Walter Anderson
Adom, Edwin
Alfred, Dewitt Clinton, Jr.
Barker, Prince Patanilla
Bateman, Mildred Mitchell
Bell, Carl Compton
Bell, James Milton
Bowen, Clotilde Marian Dent
Bradshaw, Walter H., Jr.
Cobbs, Price Mashaw
Comer, James Pierpont
Davis, Elizabeth Bishop
Elam, Lloyd Charles
Francis, Richard Louis

Fuller, Solomon Carter
Harrison-Ross, Phyllis Ann
Hastings, Alicia Elizabeth
Henry, E. Pentoka
James, Grace Marilyn
Lathen, John William
Lawrence, Margaret Morgan
Patterson, Raymond Frederick
Perry, John Sinclair
Phillips, Joseph R., Sr.
Pinderhughes, Charles Alfred
Poussaint, Alvin Francis
Rainbow-Earhart, Kathryn A.
Spurlock, Jeanne
Tardy, Walter James, Jr.
Tildon, Toussaint Tourgee
Welsing, Frances Cress
Williams, Ernest Young

PSYCHOLOGISTS

Bayton, James Arthur
Beckham, Ruth Winifred Howard
Canady, Herman George
Chisum, Gloria Twine
Clark, Kenneth Bancroft
Clark, Mamie Phipps
Cotton, Carol Blanche
Cowings, Patricia
Davis, Alonzo Joseph
Eagleson, Oran Wendle
Fairchild, Halford H.
Goodlett, Carlton B.
Harper, Mary Starke
Kyle, George Thomas
Morton, James Thomas, Jr.
Phillips, Frederick Brian
Presnell, Walter Madison
Pugh, Roderich Wellington
Roberts, Shearley Olimer
Sumner, Francis Cecil
Taylor, Jerome
Terrell, Francis
Turner, Alberta Banner
Watts, Frederick Payne
Williams, Roger Kenton
Wright, Howard Emery

RESEARCH

Abelian Group Theory: Darden,
    Geraldine Claudette
Abelian P-Groups: Jones, Eleanor
    Green Dawley

RESEARCH (*Continued*)

High Polymer Stabilzation: Hawkins, Walter Lincoln
Hodgkins Disease: Hicks, William J.
Hormones: Collins, Daniel A.
Hydrogen Secondary Spectrum Lines: Kildare, Albert Alexander
Hydrogen-2: Gibbs, James Albert
Hyperbolic Differential Equations: Brothers, Warren Hill
Immunity: Lewis, Julian Herman
Infrared Spectroscopy: Posey, Leroy Raadell, Jr.
Infrared Spectroscopy: Lawson, James Raymond
Infrared Spectroscopy of Blood Vessel Intima: Johnson, William Thomas Mitchell
Inorganic Fluorine Chemistry: Young, Archie, R., II
Insulin: Archer, Juanita Almetta
Ion Exchange Chromatography: Dove, Ray Allen
Ion Exchange Absorption: Russell, Edwin Roberts
Ketenes, Monomeric & Dimetric: Hill, Mary Elliot
Kidney Transplantation: Kountz, Samuel Lee, Jr.
Kinetics of Gaseous Reactions: Ashley, William Ford
Landau Theories: Jackson, Shirley Ann
Landing Radar for Apollo Lunar Landings: Dukes, Lamar
Laser Therapy: Palmer, Edward
Lasers & Bypass Surgery: Watkins, Levi, Jr.
Lead Poisoning: Lattimer, Agnes
Legumes: Lockett, John L.
Lepiodoptera: Williams, Joseph Leroy
Leukemia: Hicks, William J.
Lignin: Cooke, Lloyd Miller
Lipid Abnormalities: Reed, James Whitfield
Liver Cirrhosis: Burgess, Landry Edward
Liver Cirrhosis: Leevy, Carroll Moton
LSD-25: Presnell, Walter Madison
Luminescence of Inorganic Phosphors: Martin, Alfred E.

Lunar Radar Contact, 1940s: McAfee, Walter Samuel
Magnet & Nuclear Rolling Loops: Roberts, Erskine G.
Magnet & Nuclear Rolling Loops: Spikes, Richard B.
Magnetic Resonance: Lu Valle, James Ellis
Manhattan Project: Florant, Leroy Frederic
Manhattan Project: Jeffries, Jasper Brown
Manhattan Project: Knox, William Jacob, Jr.
Manhattan Project: Quaterman, Lloyd Albert
Manhattan Project: Taylor, Moddie Daniel
Manhattan Project: Wall, Arthur Albert
Manhattan Project: Wilkins, J. Ernest, Jr.
Many-Body Problems: Massey, Walter Eugene
Mathematical Biology: Branson, Herman Russell
Mathematical Statistics: Pierce, Joseph Alphonso
Mecuric Sulfide in Mercuric Nitrite Solution: Spaulding, George H.
Metabolism: Elders, Minnie Joycelyn
Microwave & Optical Techniques & Components: Roberts, Louis W.
Mortality & Morbidity in Black Population: Donnell, Clyde
Neisseria: Monroe, Clarence Lee Edward
Nematodes: Crouch, Hubert Branch
Neuroanatomy: Hubert, Charles Edward
Neurochemistry: Proctor, Charles D.
Neuroembryology: Hubert, Charles Edward
Nicotine Effects: Hudson, Roy Davage
Nuclear Medicine: Allen, William Edward, Jr.
Nucleic Acids: Daly, Marie Maynard
Obstetrics: Wilson, C. Leon
Oncology: Syphax, Burke
Oncology: Cobb, Jewel Plummer
Oncology: Leffall, La Salle Doheney, Jr.
Oncology: White, Jack E.

Oral Microbiology: Hammond, Benjamin Franklin
Organic Chemistry: Hill, Carl McClellan
Organic Microanalyis: Huggins, Kimuel Alonzo
Organometallic Compounds: Cason, Louis Forrester
Organophosphorus Compounds: Alexander, Benjamin Harold
Osteogenesis Electrically Induced: Mitchell, Eric Ignatius
Palatine Tonsil Histopathology: Jason, Robert Stewart
Parasitic Protozoa: Crouch, Hubert Branch
Peanuts: Carver, George Washington
Pekin Duck Infections: Price, Jessie Isabelle
Pellagra: Townsend, Arthur Melvin
Peritonitis & Penicillin: Walker, Matthew
Perturbation Theory: Donaldson, James Ashley
Pesticide Chemicals: Alexander, Benjamin Harold
Photochemistry: Lu Valle, James Ellis
Physics of Electrons: Coleman, John William
Physostigmine: Julian, Percy Lavon
Picrotoxin: Maloney, Arnold Hamilton
Pigmentation: Kenny, John Andrew, Jr.
Plant Genus Carex: Parker, Charles Stewart
Plant Vascular Diseases: Frederick, Lafayette
Plant Virus Diseases: King, John Wesley
Plastics: Mason, Clarence Tyler
Plastics: Jones, John Leslie
Plastics for Telecommunications: Hawkins, Walter Lincoln
Polio: Givens, John Talmadge
Polymer Formation: Wilkins, Raymond Leslie
Polymer Structure: Stancell, Arnold Francis
Power Generation: Roberts, Erskine G.
Protein Requirements in Adults: Kittrell, Flemmie Pansy
Protein Structure: Branson, Herman Russell

Protozoa Motor Activities: Lee, James Warren

Psychological Aspects of Obesity: Turner, Alberta Banner

Public Health: Yerby, Alonzo Smythe

Quantitative Television Microscopy: Lawson, Katheryn Emanuel

Quasigroups: Falconer, Etta Zuber

Radiation Biology: Spellman, Mitchell Wright

Radiation Detection: Koontz, Roscoe L.

Radioactive Iodine in Hyperthyroidism: Johnson, John Beauregard, Jr.

Radiology: Alexander, Leslie Luther

Radiometry: Martin, Alfred E.

Random Stratified Sampling Formulae: Pierce, Joseph Alphonso

Respiratory Mechanism (Hiebs Cycle): Marshall, Lawrence Marcellus

Rheumatism: Jackson, Algernon Brashear

Somatomedin in Leukemia: Elders, Minnie Joycelyn

Salmon Points in Projective Geometry: Drew, James William

Seed Germination: Inge, Frederick Douglas

Semiconductors: Powell, Robert Lee

Sickle Cell Anemia: Epps, Roselyn P.

Sickle Cell Anemia: Cardoza, William Warrick

Sickle Cell Anemia: Ferguson, Angela Dorothea

Sickle Cell Disease: Reid, Clarice D. Wills

Sickle Cell Disease: Whitten, Charles F.

Sickle Cell Disease: Adams, Billie Morris Wright

Sickle Cell Disease: Watts, George R., Sr.

Silkworm Culture: Lowery, Samuel R.

Solid State Circuit Development: Roberts, Louis W.

Spectrum Analysis Thermionics: McCane, Charles Anthony

Spirorchis Elephantis: Wall, Limas Dunlap

Stapendectomy: Mazique, Douglas Wilkerson

Sterols: Julian, Percy Lavon

Stroke Prevention: Cooper, Edward Sawyer

Sweet Potatoes: Carver, George Washington

Synthesis of Anesthetics & Analgesics: Perry, Rufus Patterson

Synthesis of Isotopically Labeled Compound: Gibbs, James Albert

Synthetic Organic Chemistry: Knox, Lawrence Howland

Termites: Collins, Margaret Strickland

Theoretical Nuclear Physics: McAfee, Walter Samuel

Theoretical Physics: Jackson, Shirley Ann

Theoretical Physics: Rouse, Carl Albert

Theory of Function of Complex Variable: Springer, George

Thermionics: Hunter, John McNeile

Thin Film Application to Dialysis: Green, Harry James, Jr.

Toxicity of Oil Field Waste: Jones, Woodrow Harold

Tranquilizers: Proctor, Charles D.

Transonic Flow: Harris, Wesley Leroy, Sr.

Transplutonium Elements: Harris, James Andrew

Tropical Medicine: Grigsby, Margaret E.

Tuberculosis: Monroe, Clarence Lee Edward

Tuberculosis: Minton, Henry McKee

Tuberculosis: Brown, W. Roderick, Jr.

Tuberculosis: Browne, Hugh A.

Tumor Metabolism: Hunter, Jehu Callis

Venus Fly Trap: Bias, John Henry

Vitamins: Derbigny, Irvin Anthony

SCIENCE EDUCATORS

Atkins, Cyril Fitzgerald
Bias, John Henry
Blanchet, Waldo Willie Emerson
Brookes, E. Luther
Brown, Solomon G.
Cansler, Charles W.
Clark, Julia V.
Collins, Daniel A.
Fraser, Thomas Petigru

Goins, William Fauntleroy, Jr.
Lacey, Archie L.
Weatherless, Nelson Ellismere

SHIP CAPTAINS

Cuffee, Paul
Mulzac, Hugh Nathaniel

SURGEONS

Abbott, Anderson Ruffin
Adair, Roman T.
Adamson, Garland Norman
Alexander, Joseph Lee
Alexander, Walter Gilbert
Allen, Browning E., Jr.
Allen, Farrow Robert
Allison, James M., Jr.
Anderson, John Thomas
Arbulu, Augustin
Atkins, Leland L.
Augusta, Alexander Thomas
Barber, Jesse Belmary, Jr.
Beckford, Samuel McDonald
Berry, Joseph A.
Blackman, Edson Ervin
Boyd, Robert Fulton
Brown, Dorothy Lavinia
Burt, Robert Tecumseh
Busch, Oliver Roy
Butler, Henry Rutherford
Byas, James Spencer, Sr.
Cabiniss, Charles
Callender, Clive Orville
Carson, Simeon Lewis
Carter, Edward Albert
Clement, Kenneth Witcher
Cobb, William Montague
Comer, James Pierpont
Cowan, James Rankin
Curtis, Austin Maurice, Jr.
Curtis, Austin Maurice, Sr.
Dailey, Ulysses Grant
Davis, Albert Porter
Dawson, Robert Edward
De Grasse, John Van Surley
Dibble, Eugene Heriot
Dibble, Joseph Edgar
Dickens, Helen Octavia
Downing, Lylburn Clinton
Drew, Charles Richard
Dyer, W. H.
Epps, Charles Harry, Jr.
Falls, Arthur Grand Pre

SURGEONS (*Continued*)

Forney, Claudius Langdon
Frederick, Rivers
Freeman, Harold P.
Funderburk, William Watson
Gamble, Henry Floyd
Garland, Cornelius N.
Garvin, Charles Herbert
Gibbs, William Walden
Giles, Roscoe Conkling
Gladden, James Robert
Goin, Logwood Ulysses
Green, Henry M.
Griffin, Joseph Howard
Hale, John Henry
Hall, George Cleveland
Hargrave, Frank Settle
Hedrick, Robert Milton
Hill, Julius Wanser
Hilliard, Robert Lee Moore
Hinson, Eugene Theodore
Holley, Alonzo Potter Burgess
Holliday, Alfonso David
Howard, Theodore Roosevelt Mason
Hunter, John Edward
Hutchinson, John E., III
Ish, George William Stanley, Jr.
Ish, George William Stanley, Sr.
Jackson, Algernon Brashear
Jackson, Robert L.
Jenkins, N. A.
Johnson, Gladys L.
Johnson, Halvern H.
Jones, Herbert C.
Jones, Leroy
Jones, Richard Francis (Frank)
Jones, Thomas Adolphus
Jones, Thomas Edward
Kenniebrew, Alonzo H.
Kountz, Samuel Lee, Jr.
Lambright, Middleton Hughes, Jr.
Lane, Willard Mercer
Laurey, James Richard
Lawlah, John Wesley
Lawrence, Montague Schiels
Leffall, La Salle Doheney, Jr.
Lester, John Angelo
Lloyd, Frank P.
Logan, Arthur C.
Logan, Myra Adele
Long, Irene
Lucas, Wendell M.
Maben, Hayward C., Jr.
Mabrie, Herman James, III
Majors, Monroe Alpheus

Mason, Ulysses Grant
Mason, Vaughn Carrington
Matory, William Earle
Maynard, Aubre De L.
Mazique, Douglas Wilkerson
McArthur, Rutherford Benjamin
McCauley, Lewyn Eugene
McCellan, Alonzo C.
McKinney, Thomas Theodore
McMillan, Julius Augustus
McNeill, William Clarence
Method, William Arthur
Miller, Lloyd
Mitchell, Eric Ignatius
Morman, William Daniel
Murray, Peter Marshall
Murray, Robert F.
Norman, John C.
Organ, Claude H., Jr.
Palmer, Edward
Patton-Washington, Georgia Esther
  Lee
Payne, Clarence H.
Payne, Fitz-Melvin Carrington
Penn, William
Perdue, Omer Felix
Perry, John Edward
Phillips, Charles Henry, Jr.
Phillips, Clyde W.
Powell, Charles William
Presnell, J. H.
Purvis, Charles Burleigh
Rabb, Maurice F., Jr.
Rawls, George
Redmond, Sidney Dillon
Roberts, Carl Glennis
Robinson, Paul Timothy
Ross, Marshall E.
Ross, William Alexander Jackson
Saunders, Elijah
Sebastian, Simon Powell
Shadd, Furmann Jeremiah
Shepard, C. H.
Sherrod, Daniel Webster
Sinkler, William H.
Speller, John Finton
Spellman, Mitchell Wright
Springs, Andrew Wilton
Stepto, Robert Charles
Stewart, Ferdinand Augustus
Stubbs, Frederick Douglas
Syphax, Burke
Taylor, Daniel Bernette
Taylor, Eugene Donaldson
Taylor, Harold Leon
Thomas, William McKinley

Thompson, Solomon Henry
Trotman, James Augustus
Turner, John Patrick
Turner, Valdo D.
Underwood, Edward Ellsworth
Vaughn, Arthur N.
Vaughn, Clarence Benjamin
Vernable, Howard Phillip
Vincent, Ubert Conrad
Walden, Emerson Coleman
Walker, Henry Harvey
Walker, Matthew
Walker, William McAlpine
Warfield, William Alonza
Watkins, Levi, Jr.
Wesley, Allen Alexander
West, Charles Ignatius
White, Augustus A., III
White, Jack E.
Whittico, James Malachi, Jr.
Whittico, James Malachi, Sr.
Wilkerson, Vernon Alexander
Wilkinson, Robert Shaw, Sr.
Williams, Albert Wilberforce
Williams, Daniel Hale
Williams, J. Milton
Williams, James B.
Williams, Jasper F.
Wilson, C. Leon
Wilson, Julien Harmon
Woode, Charles Henri
Wright, Jane Cooke
Wright, Louis Tompkins
Wright, Phillip
Wright, Thomas
Yancey, Asa G., Sr.

VETERINARIANS

Allen, Raleigh H.
Estep, Roger D.
Lushington, Augusta Nathaniel
Patterson, Frederick Douglas
Perry, Thomas Gilbert
Williams, Theodore Shields

ZOOLOGISTS

Abram, James Baker, Jr.
Alsup, Frederick Werthly
Arrington, Richard, Jr.
Baker, Percy Hayes
Bradley, Walter Osward
Bright, William Michael
Chase, Hyman Yates